DEFINING ISSUES IN
INTERNATIONAL ARBITRATION

FOREWORD

When the Institute of Arbitrators (as it was then known) opened its first office at 32 Old Jewry Street in the City of London in 1915, one may reasonably suppose that nobody would have foreseen the issues and concerns that would exercise the authors of its celebration volume, one hundred years later.

In 1915, and indeed for many years thereafter, the Institute operated in a different arbitral universe. Somewhat in contrast to the flamboyance of its first president, Rowland George Allanson Allanson-Winn, the 5th Baron Headley—also known as Shaikh Rahmatullah al-Farooq, an Irish peer, Muslim convert, keen boxer, leading civil engineer, expert on the protection of intertidal zones and co-author of the still authoritative work *Broadsword and Singlestick* (with chapters on quarter-staff, bayonet, cudgel, shillalah, walking-stick, umbrella, the 'leg of an old chair', and other increasingly unlikely everyday articles deployable in self-defence), whose many claims to fame included the distinction of having been offered the throne of Albania together with a healthy stipend, and the even more notable distinction of having declined it—the practice of arbitration was relatively limited in scope and lacking in diversity. In its early years, the Institute was groundbreaking in its mandate and made strides in professional education and training. But the landscape in which it operated, for several decades, was largely domestic (i.e. English) and homogeneous; primarily focused upon local construction disputes; and with limited involvement of lawyers and, indeed, law.

Viewed now, from the 100-year milestone, this landscape is almost unrecognizable. In the intervening years the rapid expansion of international trade has been matched by an explosion in the activity and reach of arbitration. Bolstered by landmark developments such as the New York Convention in 1958, the Washington Convention in 1965, the first edition of the UNCITRAL Rules in 1976, and the UNCITRAL Model Law in 1985, arbitration has become the most common form of international dispute resolution, accepted, practised, and trumpeted throughout all trading nations and serving the needs of an increasingly broad spectrum of economic activity. Modern and comprehensive arbitration laws have been passed in numerous countries and have spawned increasing numbers of reliable arbitral seats worldwide. Arbitration institutions have multiplied, as have international arbitration bodies and committees with enduring enthusiasm for the promulgation of rules, regulations, protocols, guidelines, and notes (in colourful A5 booklets) to regulate the field. This in turn has allowed for a universal arbitral language of acronyms, and sentences such as 'UNCITRAL arbitration under SIAC using IBA rules'. Third-party and other forms of funding have arrived, allowing the arbitral process in and of itself to become a vehicle for investment. And with the relatively recent emergence of investor-state arbitration, all of this activity has been afforded a wholly new course, with arbitration expanding into a new and very public environment. And here, no doubt to what would have been a collective gasp of amazement in 1915, previously commercial arbitration practitioners have reinvented themselves as public international lawyers and now routinely rule upon increasingly sensitive aspects of sovereign discretion.

Alongside all this—again perhaps inconceivable in 1915—arbitration has evolved into a legal and academic discipline in its own right. Most large law firms now advertise arbitration departments. There is now an international arbitration conference circuit, with near daily offerings in ever-more exotic locations worldwide, where (frequently the same) people address each other on aspects of the process, by way of interlude between vital networking coffee breaks. The law and practice of arbitration in its various forms is now the subject of university courses throughout the world; countless journals and textbooks; and many now esteemed academic careers. And all this has permitted a new and intriguing sister discipline, namely 'Backlash Studies', itself the subject of treatises and courses and no doubt future professorial chairs, focusing upon the evils and inadequacies of the arbitral process, in particular when utilized to resolve issues of wider public concern.

But while this is a new world of arbitration, it is a singular testament to the Chartered Institute of Arbitrators that it remains not only alive and well, but the only body internationally of its kind. It has itself transformed over the years, now with 13,000 members, in thirty-seven branches, in 125 countries, and around 60 per cent of its membership based outside the United Kingdom. And the extraordinary collection of articles in this *liber amicorum* is the most fitting celebration of its longevity, its continued standing in this field, and the nature of the changes brought by the last 100 years.

Under the masterful editorial steerage of Julio César Betancourt, this volume brings together both scholarly, technical analyses of key aspects of the law of arbitration and very personal and invaluable insights on its practice from some of the most respected individuals in the field—individuals who have themselves shaped the practice that now prevails. Contributions have come from the leading arbitral practitioners and thinkers (and celebrities) of our time, and their combined wisdom and scholarship will no doubt be a major resource for years to come.

But if one pervading theme emerges from this collection, it is that for all the expansion and increasing complexity of arbitration, one must never lose sight of its fundamental origins, and the basic goals that motivated the Institute's establishment back in 1915: that this must be a flexible, efficient, and cost-effective alternative to national court litigation, and a service for its users. Much of the analysis over the following pages describes the manifold ways in which arbitration has proven untrue to these principles, and the pressures that bear upon it. At the core, there is a repeated call for arbitral creativity: for tribunals to utilize all the tools available to them to ensure the process remains tailored to the particular needs of the particular dispute. A call that has been made for many years, whether in treatises, conferences, legislation, rules, or other guidelines, and a call which the Chartered Institute of Arbitrators must continue to champion, as it heads towards its bicentennial celebration.

Toby T Landau QC
5 February 2016

CONTENTS

Table of Cases — xi
Table of Arbitral Decisions and Awards — xxi
Table of European and International Court Decisions — xxv
Table of Legislation — xxvii
Notes on the Contributors — xxxvii
List of Abbreviations — xlvii

The Chartered Institute of Arbitrators (1915–2015) — 1
Julio César Betancourt

I INTERNATIONAL ARBITRATION LAW, ARBITRAL JURISDICTION, AND ARBITRAL INSTITUTIONS

1. Explaining Arbitration Law — 7
   William W Park
2. Experiences and Suggestions Regarding the Functioning of International Arbitration Institutions — 20
   Karl-Heinz Böckstiegel
3. The New 2014 LCIA Rules: An Introductory Explanation — 27
   V V Veeder

II UNDERSTANDING THE USERS OF INTERNATIONAL ARBITRATION

4. Putting the Client First — 45
   Peter J Rees
5. How Easy Is It Not to Take Adequate Care of the Proper Expectations of the Parties? — 56
   Mauro Rubino-Sammartano

III INTERNATIONAL ARBITRATION AGREEMENTS: ISSUES AND PERSPECTIVES

6. Some Reflections on the Making of International Arbitration Agreements for the Resolution of Commercial Disputes — 61
   Lord Saville
7. Arbitrability Decisions Before, During, and After Arbitration — 67
   John J Barceló III

8. The Dangers of Neglect: Governing Law of Arbitration Agreements 81
   Neil Kaplan and Olga Boltenko
9. The Law Governing the Arbitration Agreement: A Transnational Solution? 93
   Renato Nazzini
10. Silent Talk: Identifying the Language of an Arbitration When the Arbitration Clause Is Silent 105
    Michael Young

IV ARBITRAL PROCEDURE AND PROCEDURAL MISDEMEANOUR

11. Is International Arbitration Becoming Too Confrontational and Counter-Intuitive? And Some Guidelines as to How Not to Irritate a Tribunal! 115
    Hilary Heilbron
12. Procedural Efficiency in International Commercial Arbitration: Building It into the Process 126
    Elizabeth Snodgrass
13. Ethics in Arbitration: Party and Arbitral Misconduct 138
    Lord Hacking and Sophia Berry

V EMERGENCY ARBITRATORS AND INTERIM RELIEF

14. Emergency Arbitrators and Court-Ordered Interim Measures: Is the Choice Important? 149
    Doug Jones
15. Legal Standards Applicable to Deciding Applications for Interim Relief 158
    Grant Hanessian

VI DISCOVERY AND DOCUMENT PRODUCTION

16. Discovery in Arbitration: Can Parties Use 28 USC § 1782 to Circumvent the Process Ordered by the Arbitral Tribunal? 169
    Alexander A Yanos
17. Meeting the Requirements of Article 3(3) of the IBA Rules: Recommendations for Successful Requests for Document Production 174
    Mark McNeill and Margaret Clare Ryan

VII WITNESSES AND PERJURY

18. Cross-Examination of Fact Witness Statements in International Arbitration 187
    Lawrence W Newman

19. The Expert Witness in International Arbitration — 192
Bernardo M Cremades

20. Oaths and Perjury — 197
Audley Sheppard

VIII ARBITRATORS' DECISION-MAKING POWER AND ARBITRAL TRIBUNALS' CESSATION OF FUNCTIONS

21. Inherent and Implied Powers of Arbitrators — 209
Margaret L Moses

22. Good (and Bad) Initiatives of Arbitrators: Where to Draw the Line between Activism and Passivity? — 222
Sébastien Besson

23. The Law Is What the Arbitrator Had for Breakfast: How Income, Reputation, Justice, and Reprimand Act as Determinants of Arbitrator Behaviour — 239
Thomas Schultz and Robert Kovacs

24. Functus Officio? — 257
Greg Fullelove

IX COSTS, FUNDING, AND IDEAS FOR OPTIMIZATION

25. The Harmonization of Costs Practices in International Arbitration: The Search for the Holy Grail — 271
Michael O'Reilly

26. The Costs and Funding of International Arbitration — 285
Joe Tirado, Daniel R Meagher, and Arpan Gupta

27. 'Other Costs' in International Arbitration: A Review of the Recoverability of Internal and Third-Party Funding Costs — 293
Marie Berard

28. Optimizing the Use of Mediation in International Arbitration: A Cost–Benefit Analysis of 'Two Hat' Versus 'Two People' Models — 305
Jeffrey Waincymer

X JUDICIAL REVIEW, JUDICIAL PERFORMANCE, AND ENFORCEMENT

29. Judicial Review of the Merits of Arbitration Awards under English Law — 319
Sir Bernard Rix

30. Improving Judicial Performance in Matters Involving
    International Arbitration — 334
    S I Strong
31. The Principled English Ambivalence to Law and Dispute Resolution
    beyond the State — 341
    Alex Mills

XI PUBLIC POLICY AND ABUSE OF PROCESS

32. Public Policy Rules in English Arbitration Law — 353
    Stavros Brekoulakis
33. The Role of Abuse of Process in Protecting the Integrity
    of Arbitration Awards — 370
    David J Sandy

XII INTERNATIONAL ARBITRATION: MYTHS AND PERSPECTIVES

34. Arbitration in the UAE: Demystifying the Myths — 381
    Gordon Blanke

XIII DISPUTE RESOLUTION IN THE CONSTRUCTION INDUSTRY

35. Managing Construction Conflict: Unfinished Revolution,
    Continuing Evolution — 399
    Thomas J Stipanowich
36. Shifting the Burden of Proof: Revisiting Adjudication Decisions — 428
    Andrew Tweeddale and Keren Tweeddale

XIV FINAL REFLECTIONS AND LOOKING AHEAD

37. Recollections of Past Events and Reflections on Future Trends — 443
    Martin Hunter

Index — 449

TABLE OF CASES

Aastha Broadcasting Network Ltd v Thaicom Public Co Ltd [2011] FAO(OS) 411/2011 (High Court, New Delhi) 9.16
Abouloff v Oppenheimer & Co (1882) 10 QBD 295 .... 32.53, 32.55
Abrath v North Eastern Railway Co (1886) 11 App Cas 247 .... 36.09
Abuja International Hotels Ltd v Meridien SAS [2012] EWHC 87 (Comm) 9.16
Actival International SA v Conservas El Pilas SA, Tribunal Supremo, 16 April 1996, YCA XXVII (2002) 528 .... 7.49
Aerospace Publishing Ltd v Thames Water Utilities Ltd [2007] EWCA Civ 3 .... 27.32
AG of Belize v Belize Telecom Ltd [2009] UKPC 10 .... 36.30
Aguiar v Ford Motor Co, 683 So 2d 1158 (Fla Dist Ct App 1996) 36.20
Airmec Dubai, LLC v Maxtel International, LLC, Case No 132/2012 Commercial, Ruling of the Dubai Court of Cassation of 18 October 2012 .... 20.43, 34.27, 34.37
Alcatel Australia Ltd v Scarcella (1998) 44 NSWLR 349 .... 8.20
American Express Co v Italian Colors Rest, 133 S Ct 2304 (2013) 1.40
Amin Rasheed Shipping Corp v Kuwait Insurance Co [1984] AC 50 .... 31.07
Amos v Hughes (1835) 174 ER 160, 1 Mood & R 464 .... 36.09, 36.27
Antaios, The, Antaios Cia Naviera SA v Salen Rederierna AB [1985] AC 191 .... 29.46
Application of Consorcio Ecuatoriano de Telecomunicaciones SA, 747 F 3d 1262, 1770 n 4 (11th Cir Fla 2014) 16.07
Application of Euromepa SA, Re 51 F 3d 1095 (2d Cir 1995) 16.09
Application of Hallmark Capital Corp, Re, 534 F Supp 2d 951 (D Minn 2007) 16.07
Application of Oxus Gold Plc, Re, No 06-82, 2006 WL 2927615 (DNJ 11 October 2006) 16.07
Applied Industrial Materials Corp (AIMCOR) v Ovalar Makine Ticaret Ve Sanayi, 492 F 3d 132 (2d Cir 2007) 1.11
Arbitration In London, England Between Norfolk Southern Corp, Norfolk Southern Railway Co, and General Security Insurance Co and ACE Bermuda Ltd, Re, 626 F Supp 2d 882 (ND Ill 2009) 16.07
Arsanovia Ltd v Cruz City 1 Mauritius Holdings [2012] EWHC 3702 (Comm), [2013] 2 All ER (Comm) 8.25, 9.22
Arts & Antiques v Richards [2013] EWHC 3361 (Comm) 33.11, 33.24
Asia Maritime Pacific Ltd, Re, No 15-CV-2760 (VEC), 2015 WL 5037129, at *3 and n 6 (SDNY 26 August 2015) 16.08
Aspect Contracts (Asbestos) Ltd v Higgins Construction Plc [2015] UKSC 38; [2013] EWCA Civ 1541, [2013] EWHC 1322 (TCC), [2013] WLR (D) 211 ...... 36.17, 36.23, 36.27, 36.28, 36.30, 36.32
AT&T Mobility LLC v Concepcion, 131 S Ct 1740, 1753 (US 2011) 1.08, 1.42
Atwood v Welton, 7 Conn 66 (1828) 20.06
Avista Management v Wausau Underwriters Insurance, US Dist Court Mid Dist Fla (6 June 2006) 11.30
Avitzur v Avitzur, 58 NY 2d 108 (1983) 1.05

Babcock Borsig AG, Re, 583 F Supp 2d 233 (D Mass 2008) 16.09
Baiti Real Estate Development v Dynasty Zarooni Inc, Case No 14/2012, Ruling of the Dubai Court of Cassation (16 September 2012) 34.43
Baker v Fales, 16 Mass 488 (1820) 1.05
Banyan Tree Corporate PTE Ltd v Meydan Group LLC, Case No ARB 003/2013, DIFC Court of First Instance (27 May 2014) 34.41
Bauer v Bauer (No 507082/2013, NY Sup Ct 2014) 1.28
Beaufort Developments (NI) Ltd v Gilbert-Ash (NI) Ltd [1999] 1 AC 266, [1998] 2 All ER 778, [1998] 2 WLR 860 .... 36.19, 36.35, 36.38, 36.40

Bechtel Co Ltd v Department of Civil Aviation of the Government of Dubai, 300 F Supp 2d
    112 (DDC 2004) 20.42, 20.43, 20.44
Bellway Homes Ltd v Seymour (Civil Engineering Contractors) Ltd [2013] EWHC 1890
    (TCC), [2013] All ER (D) 82 (Jul) 36.17
Beximco Pharmaceuticals Ltd v Shamil Bank of Bahrain EC [2004] EWCA Civ 19 ....31.05
BG Group Plc v Argentina, 134 S Ct 1198 (2014) 1.29, 1.31, 7.10, 7.13, 7.23, 7.24
Bidermann Industries Licensing, Inc v Avmar NV, 570 NYS 2d 33 (1st Dept 1991) 21.30
Bouygues UK Ltd v Dahl-Jensen UK Ltd [2000] EWCA Civ 507, [2001] 1 All ER (Comm)
    1041 .... 36.42
BP Refinery (Westernport) Pty Ltd v The President, Councillors and Ratepayers of the Shire of
    Hastings (1978) 52 ALJR 20 .... 36.30
BTP Tioxide Ltd v Pioneer Shipping Ltd (Leave to Appeal) (No 1) [1980] 1 Lloyd's Rep 519
    ....29.32, 29.37
BTP Tioxide Ltd v Pioneer Shipping Ltd and Armada Marine SA (The Nema) (No 2) [1980]
    2 Lloyd's Rep 83 ....29.31–29.43
Bulgarian Foreign Trade Bank Ltd v AI Trade Finance Inc, Swedish Supreme Court,
    T 1881-99 (27 October 2000)..9.29
Bundesgerichtshof (BGE) (1984) Neue Juristische Wochenschrift, Heft 12 ....7.29
Bundesgerichtsof (BGE) (1999) Neue Juristische Wochenschrift, Heft 9 ....7.29
Burger King Corp v Hungry Jack's Pty Ltd (2001) 69 NSWLR 558 ....8.20

C v D [2007] EWCA Civ 1282 ....9.16
Cable & Wireless v IBM [2002] EWHC 2059 (Comm) 8.19
Cablevision Systems Development Co v Shoupe (1986) 39 WIR 1...................... 32.26
Cape Flattery Ltd v Titan Maritime, 647 F 3d 914 (9th Cir 2011) 1.37
Caratube Int'l Oil Co LLP, Re, 730 F Supp 2d 101 (DDC 2010) 16.12
Carr & Brookside Farm Trust Ltd v Gallaway Cook Allan [2014] NZSC 75 (Sup Ct New
    Zealand 2014).. 1.14, 1.15
Case No 321/Judicial Year 19, Abu Dhabi Court of Cassation (25 April 1999) 34.21
Case No 22/Judicial Year 22, Abu Dhabi Court of Cassation (3 March 2002) 34.19
Case No 186/Judicial Year 2, Abu Dhabi Court of Cassation (8 June 2008) 34.24
Case No 170/Judicial Year 4, Abu Dhabi Court of Cassation (28 April 2010)................34.18
Case No 447/Judicial Year 4, Abu Dhabi Court of Cassation (30 September 2010) 34.33
Case No 795/Judicial Year 4, Abu Dhabi Court of Cassation (9 December 2010) 34.18
Case No 955/Judicial Year 4, Abu Dhabi Court of Cassation (29 December 2010) 34.20
Case No 834/2010, Abu Dhabi Court of Cassation (30 December 2010) 34.16
Case No 679/2010, Abu Dhabi Court of Cassation (16 June 2011)....................... 34.37
Case No 1283/2010, Abu Dhabi Court of Cassation (11 October 2011) 34.18
Case No 519/2013, Abu Dhabi Court of Cassation (2 October 2013) 34.35
Case No 176/Judicial Year 17, Federal Supreme Court (Abu Dhabi)
    (21 November 1995) 34.05, 34.39
Case No 263/Judicial Year 18, Federal Supreme Court (Abu Dhabi) (8 December 1996) 34.39
Case No 449/Judicial Year 21, Federal Supreme Court (Abu Dhabi) (11 April 2001).......... 34.16,
    34.39, 34.40
Case No 84/Judicial Year 22, Federal Supreme Court (Abu Dhabi) (22 January 2002)........ 34.25
Case No 640/Judicial Year 22, Federal Supreme Court (19 November 2002) 34.33
Case No 304/Judicial Year 23, Federal Supreme Court (Abu Dhabi) (25 March 2003)........ 34.08
Case No 92/Judicial Year 25, Federal Supreme Court (Abu Dhabi) (8 June 2003) 34.19
Case No 16/Judicial Year 23, Federal Supreme Court (Abu Dhabi) (29 April 2003) 34.30
Case No 32/Judicial Year 23, Federal Supreme Court (Abu Dhabi) (8 June 2003) 34.19, 34.39
Case No 118/Judicial Year 23, Federal Supreme Court (Abu Dhabi)
    (21 January 2004) 34.31, 34.39
Case No 491/Judicial Year 24, Federal Supreme Court (Abu Dhabi) (28 November 2004) 34.19
Case No 764/Judicial Year 24, Federal Supreme Court (Abu Dhabi) (7 June 2005)............34.38
Case No 56/Judicial Year 27, Federal Supreme Court (Abu Dhabi) (21 May 2006) 34.39
Case No 924/Judicial Year 3, Federal Court of Cassation (17 December 2009) 34.22

Case Nos 267 and 297/Judicial Year 20, Federal Supreme Court (14 May 2000) 34.23
Case No 531/2011, Dubai Court of Appeal (6 October 2011) 34.37
Case No 1/2013, Dubai Court of Appeal (9 July 2013) 34.37
Case No 294/1994, Dubai Court of Cassation (26 November 1994) 34.31
Case No 178/1996, Dubai Court of Cassation (25 January 1997) 34.33
Case No 186/1996, Dubai Court of Cassation (5 January 1997) 34.31
Case No 403/2003, Dubai Court of Cassation (13 March 2004) 34.39
Case No 503/2003, Dubai Court of Cassation (15 May 2005) 34.27
Case No 100/2004, Dubai Court of Cassation (9 January 2005) 34.20
Case No 322/2004, Dubai Court of Cassation (11 April 2005) 34.27
Case No 64/2005, Dubai Court of Cassation (18 April 2005) 34.20, 34.25
Case No 174/2005, Dubai Court of Cassation (19 December 2005) 34.20
Case No 225/2005, Dubai Court of Cassation (12 December 2005) 34.30, 34.40
Case No 141/2006, Dubai Court of Cassation (10 October 2006)........................34.33
Case No 273/2006, Dubai Court of Cassation (4 February 2007).......................34.39
Case No 72/2007, Dubai Court of Cassation (10 June 2007) 34.39, 34.40
Case No 140/2007, Dubai Court of Cassation (7 October 2007)........................34.25
Case No 233/2007, Dubai Court of Cassation (13 January 2008) 34.30
Case No 146/2008, Dubai Court of Cassation (9 November 2008)......................34.16
Case No 148/2008, Dubai Court of Cassation (16 September 2008)....................34.19
Case No 164/2008, Dubai Court of Cassation (10 October 2008).......................34.20
Case No 204/2008, Dubai Court of Cassation (12 October 2008) 34.20, 34.25
Case No 32/2009, Dubai Court of Cassation (29 March 2009) 34.16, 34.27
Case No 38/2009, Dubai Court of Cassation (4 April 2010)............................34.18
Case No 67/2009, Dubai Court of Cassation (24 May 2009) 34.22, 34.30
Case No 156/2009, Dubai Court of Cassation (27 October 2009).......................34.30
Case No 157/2009, Dubai Court of Cassation (27 September 2009)....................34.33
Case No 191/2009, Dubai Court of Cassation (13 September 2009)....................34.21
Case No 207/2009, Dubai Court of Cassation (19 April 2010).........................34.31
Case No 181/2011, Dubai Court of Cassation (12 February 2012)......................34.43
Case No 282/2012, Real Estate Cassation, Dubai Court of Cassation
  (3 February 2013)...34.05, 34.12, 34.32
Case No 156/2013, Dubai Court of Cassation (18 August 2013) 34.37
Case No 35/2010, Ruling of the Fujairah Federal Court of First Instance (27 April 2010) 34.37
Castle Inns (Stirling) Ltd v Clark Contracts Ltd [2005] ScotCS CSOH 178 (29 December
  2005)..36.29
CE International Resources Holdings LLC v SA Mineral Ltd Partnership, 2012 US Dist
  LEXIS 176158, Case No 12 Civ 8087(CM) (SDNY 2012) 15.11
CFW Architects (A Firm) v Cowlin Construction Ltd [2006] EWHC 6 (TCC) 36.17
Channel Tunnel Group Ltd v Balfour Beatty Construction Ltd [1993] 1 All ER 664, [1993]
  AC 334..9.05, 9.16, 31.17
Chantiers de l'Atlantique SA v Gaztransport & Technigaz SAS [2011]
  EWHC 3383 (Comm)..20.31
Chartered Institute of Arbitrators v John D Campbell QC, Decision of the Disciplinary
  Tribunal of CIArb (5 May 2011) 13.29
Chevron Corp, Re, 633 F 3d 153 (3d Cir NJ 2011)......................................16.09
Chevron Corp, Re, 749 F Supp 2d 141 (SDNY 2010)...................................16.05
Chevron Corp, Re, 762 F Supp 2d 242 (D Mass 2010) 16.09, 16.10
Chevron Corp, No 7:10-MC-00067-JCT, 2010 WL 4883111, at *3 (WD Va
  24 Nov 2010) 16.12
Chin Yoke Choong Bobby v Hong Lam Marine Pte Ltd [2000] 1 SLR 137..................25.20
China Nanhai Oil Joint Service Corp, Shenzhen Branch v Gee Tai Holdings Co [1994] 3
  HKC 375 (Hong Kong Court of First Instance)..................................28.49
Chromalloy v Arab Republic of Egypt, 939 F Supp 907, DDC 1996 ....1.27
City Inn Ltd v Shepherd Construction Ltd [2002] SLT 781 ....36.12, 36.13, 36.14, 36.15, 36.17,
                                                                              36.23, 36.26

CJ O'Shea Construction Ltd v Bassi [1998] ICR 1130 .... 4.53
CMA CGM SA v Beteiligungs-KG MS 'Northern Pioneer' Schiffahrtsgesellschaft-mbH &
    Co [2002] EWCA Civ 1878, [2003] 1 WLR 1015, [2003] 3 All ER 330, [2003] 1 All ER
    (Comm) 204, [2003] 1 Lloyd's Rep 212 .... 29.46, 29.52
Coal Cliff Collieries Pty Ltd v Sijehama Pty Ltd (1991) 24 NSWLR 1 .... 8.20
Comision Ejecutiva v Nejapa Power Co, LLC, No 08-135-GMS, 2008 WL 4809035 (D Del,
    14 October 2008) 16.07
Commissions Imp Exp SA v Republic of Congo, 2014 WL 3377337 (DC Cir 2014) 1.24
Con Kallergis Pty Ltd (t/as Sunlighting Australia) v Calshonie Pty Ltd (formerly C W Norris
    Pty Ltd) (1998) 14 BCL 201 .... 8.20
Consorcio Ecuatoriano de Telecomunicaciones SA v JAS Forwarding (USA), Inc, 685 F 3d
    987 (11th Cir Fla 2012) 16.07
Consortium member A v Consortium member B (Switzerland), Polimeles Protodikio (Court
    of First Instance, Multi-Judge Panel), Rodopi, Decision No 84 of 2005 .... 9.13
Construction Centre Group Ltd, The v The Highland Council [2002] ScotCS
    CSOH 354 .... 36.18, 36.38
Corneforth v Geer (1715) 23 ER 1038 .... 29.04
Corporacion Mexicana de Mantenimiento Integral, S de RL de CV v Pemex-Exploracion y
    Produccion, 962 F Supp 2d 642 (SDNY 2013) 1.27
Coxe v Phillips (1736) 95 ER 152 .... 3.38
Cross v Kirkby, The Times, 5 April 2000 (CA) 32.20
Czarnikow v Roth, Schmidt & Co [1922] 2 KB 478 .... 1.08, 29.01, 29.09, 29.10–29.15, 29.26,
                                                                                29.35, 29.56

Daimler Co Ltd v Continental Tyre and Rubber Co Ltd [1916] 2 AC 307 .... 32.70
Dallah Real Estate & Tourism Holding Co v Ministry of Religious Affairs, Government of
    Pakistan [2010] UKSC 46, [2010] 3 WLR 1472 .... 1.24, 7.49, 8.37, 31.17, 31.24
Decision 4A_108/2009, Swiss Federal Tribunal (9 June 2009), (2010) 3 ASA Bull 511 .... 22.46
Decision 4A_14/2012, Swiss Federal Supreme Court (2 May 2012), (2013)
    2 ASA Bull 322 .... 24.17, 24.21
Decision 4A_46/2011, Swiss Federal Tribunal (16 May 2011), (2011) 3 ASA Bull 643 .... 22.54
Decision 4P 100/2003, Swiss Federal Tribunal (30 September 2003) DTF 130 III 35, (2004)
    3 ASA Bull 574 .... 22.43, 22.46, 22.54
Decision of the Swiss Federal Tribunal (18 August 1992) ATF 118 II 359 .... 22.18
Della Sanara Kustvaart-Bevrachting & Overslagbedrijf BV v Fallimento Cap Giovanni
    Coppola srl (in liquidation), Genoa Court of Appeal (3 February 1990) 9.13
Deutsche Bank AG v Sebastian Holdings Inc and Alexander Vik [2014] EWHC
    2073 (Comm) 33.05
Deutsche Schachtbau- und Tiefbohrgesellschaft mbH v The Government of the State of R'as
    Al Khaimah and The R'as Al Khaimah Oil Co (The Rakoil Case) [1987] 2 All ER 769 ..... 31.17
Deutsche Schachtbau- und Tiefbohrgesellschaft mbH v The Government of the State of R'as
    Al Khaimah and The R'as Al Khaimah Oil Co (The Rakoil Case) [1990] 1 AC 295 .... 31.17
Dollar Land (Cumbernauld) Ltd v CIN Properties Ltd, 1998 SC (HL) 90 .... 36.29
Doshion Ltd v Sembawang Engineers and Constructors Pte Ltd [2011] SGHC 46 ...... 24.35, 24.40
Duke Group Ltd, The (in liquidation) v Alamain Investments Ltd [2003] SASC 272 .... 28.34

Earl of Chesterfield, The v Sir Abraham Janssen (1750) 1 Atk 301 .... 32.08, 32.12
Egerton v Brownlow (1853) 4 HL Cas 1, 22 ER 961 .... 32.14, 32.22
Eitzen Bulk A/S v Ashapura Minechem Ltd, AIR 2011 Guj 13 .... 9.16
El Paso Corp v La Comision Ejecutiva Hidroelectrica Del Rio Lempa, 341 Fed Appx 31 (5th
    Cir Tex 2009) 16.06
Elektrim SA v Vivendi Universal SA [2007] EWHC 11 (Comm) 20.31
Elliman v Carrington [1901] 2 Ch 275 .... 32.17
Emirates Trading Agency LLC v Prime Mineral Exports Private Ltd [2014] EWHC 2104
    (Comm), [2014] WLR (D) 293 .... 8.19, 8.21

Table of Cases

Emirates Trading Agency LLC v Sociedade de Fomento Industrial Private Ltd [2015] EWHC 1452 (Comm) 24.02
Enercon India v Enercon GMBH, Civ App 2086/7, Supreme Court of India (14 February 2014) 9.16
Erich Schroeder, The [1974] 1 Lloyd's Rep 192 . . . . 25.19

First Options of Chicago, Inc v Kaplan, 514 US 938 (1995) 7.19, 7.50
FirstLink Investments Corp Ltd v GT Payment Pte Ltd [2014] SGHCR 12 . . . . 8.26, 9.27, 9.29, 9.39
Foster v Driscoll [1929] 1 KB 470 . . . . 32.27
Freaner v Valle, 966 F Supp 2d 1068, 1075 (SD Cal 2013) 30.21

Gao Haiyan v Keeneye Holdings Ltd [2011] HKCA 459, [2011] 3 HKC 157, [2011] HKEC 514 . . . . 13.07, 28.34, 28.49
Glass, Molders, Pottery, Plastics and Allied Workers Int'l Union AFI-CIO, CLC, Local 182B v Excelsior Foundry Co, 56 F3d 884 (7th Cir 1995) 24.07, 24.41
Glencot Development & Design Ltd v Ben Barrett & Son (Contractors) Ltd [2001] EWHC Technology 15 (13 February 2001) 28.34
Golden Strait Corp v Nippon Yusen Kubishika Kaisha (The Golden Victory) [2007] UKHL 12, [2007] 2 AC 353, [2007] 2 WLR 691, [2007] 3 All ER 1, [2007] 2 All ER (Comm) 97, [2007] 2 Lloyd's Rep 164 . . . . 29.50
Government of Ghana v ProEnergy Services, LLC, No 11-9002-MC-SOW, 2011 WL 2652755 (WD Mo 6 June 2011) 16.09
Government of the Republic of the Philippines v Philippine International Air Terminals Co [2007] 1 SLR 278 (Singapore) 9.29
Granvias Oceanicas Armadora SA v Jibsen Trading Co (The Kavo Peiratis) [1977] 2 Lloyd's Rep 344 . . . . 29.21
Gray v Thames Trains Ltd [2009] 1 AC 1339 . . . . 32.20

Habas Sinai Ve Tibbi Gazlar Istihsal Endustrisi AS v VSC Steel Co Ltd [2013] EWHC 4071 (Comm) 8.25, 9.25
Halfdan Grieg & Co A/S v Sterling Coal & Navigation Corp (The Lysland) [1973] 1 QB 843 . . . . 29.18–29.21
Hall Street Associates v Mattel, Inc, 552 US 576 (2008) 1.16
Halpern v Halpern [2007] EWCA Civ 291, [2007] 3 All ER 478 . . . . 31.05
Hampshire County Council v Pendragon (unreported 2003) 20.12
Harbour Victoria Inv Holdings Ltd Section 1782 Petitions, Re, No 15-MC-127 (AJN), 2015 WL4040420, at *5 (SDNY 29 June 2015) 16.08
Henderson v Henderson (1843) 3 Hare 100 . . . . 33.06, 33.18, 33.19
Holloway v Chancery Mead Ltd [2007] EWHC 2495 (TCC), [2008] 1 All ER (Comm) 653 . . . . 8.19
Holman v Johnson (1775) 1 Cowp 341 . . . . 32.20
Howard v Duke of Norfolk (1681–5) 3 Ch Cas 1 . . . . 32.08
Hussman (Europe) Ltd v Al Almeen Development and Trade Co [2000] 2 Lloyd's Rep 83 . . . . . . 9.10
Hussmann (Europe) Ltd v Ahmed Pharaon [2003] EWCA Civ 266, [2003] 1 All ER (Comm) 879 . . . . 24.29–24.34, 33.18
Hutchins v Hutchins (1738) 95 ER 406 . . . . 29.04

Imanagement Servs, Ltd, Re, 2005 US Dist LEXIS 17025, 2005 WL 1959702 (EDNY 2005) 16.09
Infineon Techs AG v Green Power Techs Ltd, 247 FRD 1 (DDC 2005) 16.09
Injazat Technology Capital Ltd v Dr Hamid Najafi [2012] EWHC 4171 (Comm) 33.16, 33.21
Insurance Co v Reinsurance Co, Tribunal Fédéral (Swiss Federal Supreme Court) (21 March 1995) 9.13
Int'l Tank and Pipe SAK v Kuwait Aviation Fuelling Co KSC [1975] QB 224 . . . . 3.29
Int'l Bechtel v Dep't of Civil Aviation of the Gov't of Dubai, Case No 503/2003, Dubai Court of Cassation (15 May 2005) 34.27
Intel Corp v Advanced Micro Devices Inc, 542 US 241 (2004) 16.06, 16.07, 16.08, 16.10

Interdesco SA v Nullfire Ltd [1992] 1 Lloyd's Rep 180 . . . . .32.55
International Paper Co v Schwabedissen Maschinen & Anlagen GmbH, 206 F 3d 411 (4th Cir
    2000) 9.35
Island Territory of Curacao v Solitron Devices, Inc, 489 F 2d 1313 (2d Cir 1973) 1.24

Janson v Driefontein Consolidated Mines [1902] AC 484 . . . . .32.17
Jiangsu Steamship Co v Success Superior Ltd, No 14-CV-9997 (CM), 2015 WL 3439220, at
    *5 (SDNY 6 January 2015) 16.08
Jivraj v Hashwani [2009] EWHC 1364 (Comm) 3.12, 3.45
Jivraj v Hashwani [2010] EWCA Civ 712, [2010] ICR 1435 (CA) 3.12, 3.46
Jivraj v Hashwani [2011] UKSC 40, [2011] 1 WLR 1872. . . . . 1.05, 3.12, 3.45–3.47
Johnson v Gore Wood & Co [2002] 2 AC 1. . . . . 33.05, 33.18, 33.28
Jones v Randall (1774) I Cowp 37. . . . . .32.10
Joseph Constantine Steamship Line Ltd v Imperial Smelting Corp Ltd [1942] AC 154. . . . . .35.06

K/S A/S Bani v Korea Shipbuilding and Engineering Corp [1987] 2 Lloyd's Rep 445 . . . . .25.18
Kahn Lucas Lancaster v Lark Int'l Ltd, 186 F 3d 210 (2d Cir 1999). 1.09
Karapschinsky v Rothbaum, 163 SW 290 (Mo Ct App 1914) 1.28
Kelantan Government v Duff Development Co [1923] AC 395 (HL) 29.17
Kensington Int'l Ltd v Republic of Congo, Slip Copy, 2007 WL 2456993 (SDNY 24 August
    2007) 21.27
Kent v Elstob (1802) 102 ER 502 . . . . .29.04
Kill v Hollister (1746) 1 Wils KB 129. . . . . .29.04
Kin Shing (Leung's) General Contractors Ltd v Chinese University of Hong Kong [2011]
    HKEC 284 . . . . .25.20
KIS France SA v SA Société Générale (France), Paris Court of Appeal, 31 October 1989, 1992
    Rev arb 90 . . . . .9.33
Kuwait Airways Corp v Iraqi Airways Co [2002] UKHL 19 . . . . 32.36
Kyocera Corp v Prudential-Bache Trade Services, 341 F 3d 987 (9th Cir 2003) 1.17

Ledee v Ceramiche Ragno, 684 F 2d 184 (1st Cir 1982) 9.36
Lemenda Trading Co Ltd v African Middle East Petroleum Co Ltd [1988] QB 448 . . . . 32.28, 32.38
Lesotho Highlands Development Authority v Impregilo SpA [2006] 1 AC 221, [2005]
    UKHL 43 . . . . 1.20, 29.01, 29.04, 29.53

M/S Bremen v Zapata Off-Shore Co, 407 US 1 (US 1972) 1.08
M&C Corp v Erwin Behr GmbH & Co KG, 326 F 3d 772 (6th Cir 2003). 24.25, 24.27
M&C Corp v Erwin Behr GmbH & Co KG, No 06-2344 (6th Cir 2008) 24.25, 24.26, 24.27
Malev Hungarian Airlines, Re, 964 F 2d 97, 100 (2d Cir 1992) 16.09
Martin Dawes v Treasure and Son Ltd [2010] EWHC 3218 (TCC). 24.03, 24.09, 24.35, 24.36,
                                                                                                        24.37, 24.38
Mason v Porsche Cars of North America, 621 So 2d 719 (Fla 5th DCA1993). 36.20
Matermaco SA v PPM Cranes Inc, Legris Industries SA, Tribunal de Commerce, Court of
    First Instance (20 September 1999) 9.29
Maxtel International FZE v Airmec Dubai LLC, Case No 132/2012, Dubai Court of
    Cassation (18 October 2012). 20.43, 34.27, 34.37
Maxtel International FZE v Airmec Dubai LLC, Commercial Action No 268/2010, Court of
    First Instance (12 January 2011) 20.43
Merchant International Co Ltd v Natsionalna Aktsionerna Kompaniya Naftogaz Ukrayiny
    [2012] EWCA Civ 196, [2012] 1 WLR 3036 . . . . .31.28
Mesa Power Group, LLC, Re, 2013 WL 1890222 (DNJ 19 April 2013) 16.05, 16.12
Mesa Power Group, LLC, Re, 878 F Supp 2d 1296 (SD Fla 2012) 16.09
Michael Wilson and Partners v Sinclair [2012] EWHC 2560 (Comm) 33.11, 33.14, 33.24, 33.43
Michel v Reynolds (1711) 1 P Wms 181 . . . . 32.08
Microsoft, Re, 428 F Supp 2d 188 (SDNY 2006) 16.11

Middle East Foundations LLC v Meydan Group LLC (formerly Meydan LLC), Case
  No 249 of 2013, Commercial Appeal, Ruling of the Dubai Court of Appeal
  (15 January 2014) 34.33
Minatec Fin SARL v SI Group Inc, No 1:08-CV-269 (LEK/RFT), 2008 WL 3884374, at *8
  (NDNY 18 August 2008) 16.12
Miss Universe LP v Monnin, 952 F Supp 2d 591 (SDNY 2013) 1.40
Mitsubishi Motors v Soler Chrysler-Plymouth, 473 US 614 (1985) 7.50
Moses H Cone v Mercury Construction Corp, 460 US 1 (1983) 7.50
Municipalité de Khoms El Mergeb v Société Dalico, Cass 1e civ, 20 December 1993, 1994 Rev
  arb 116 ....9.31
Musawi v RE International (UK) Ltd [2007] EWHC 2981 (Ch) 31.05, 31.17

National Thermal Power Corp v The Singer Co, Civ App No 1978, Supreme Court of India
  (7 May 1992), YCA VIII (1993) 403 ....9.16
NBC v Bear Stearns & Co, 165 F 3d 184 (2d Cir 1999) 16.04
Nomihold Securities Inc v Mobile TeleSystems Finance SA (No 2) [2012] EWHC 130
  (Comm) 33.19, 33.21
Nordenfelt v Maxim Nordenfelt Guns and Ammunition [1894] C 535 ....32.19
North Shore Ventures Ltd v Anstead Holdings Inc [2012] EWCA Civ 11 ....17.30
Northern Regional Health Authority v Derek Crouch Construction Co Ltd [1984] QB 644,
  [1984] 2 WLR 676, [1984] 2 All ER 175 (CA) 36.34, 36.35
Northwestern Nat'l Ins Co v Insco, Ltd, 2011 WL 4552997 (SDNY 2011) 21.30
NYK Bulkship (Atlantic) NV v Cargill International SA [2014] EWCA Civ 403 ....24.22

Occidental Exploration & Production Co v Republic of Ecuador [2005] EWCA
  Civ 1116 ....31.09
OMV Petrom SA v Glencore International AG [2014] EWHC 242 (Comm), [2014] All ER
  (D) 78 ....33.14, 33.24
Owerri Commercial Inc v Dielle srl, Gerechtshof, Court of Appeal, The Hague
  (4 August 1993) 9.29

Partington & Son v Thameside (1985) 33 BLR 150 ....36.35
Penelope, The [1928] P 180 ....29.34
Peterson Farms Inc v C&M Farming Ltd [2004] EWHC 121 (Comm), [2004] 1 Lloyd's Rep
  603 ....8.18, 9.33
Petrasol BV v Stolt Spur Inc, Arrondissementsrechtbank, Court of First Instance, Rotterdam
  (28 September 1995), YCA XXII (1997) 762 ....9.29
Pioneer Shipping Ltd v BTP Tioxide Ltd (The Nema) (No 2) [1980] QB 547 ....29.33
Pioneer Shipping Ltd v BTP Tioxide Ltd (The Nema) (No 2) [1982] AC 724 ....29.34
Poiré v Tripier, Cass mixte, 14 February 2003, 2003 Rev arb 403 ....7.29
Prima Paint Corp v Flood & Conklin Mfg Co, 388 US 395 (1967) 1.08
PT First Media TBK v Astro Nusantara International BV [2013] SGCA 57 ....8.37
PT Putrabali Adyamulia v Rena Holding Ltd, Cass 1e civ, 29 June 2007, 2007 Rev arb 507 .....1.23

R v Archer (Jeffrey) [2002] EWCA Crim 1996 ....20.24, 20.26
R v Chapman [1980] Crim LR 42 ....20.12
R v Hamid and Hamid [1979] 69 Cr App R 324 ....20.19
R v Hayes (Geoffrey) [1977] 1 WLR 234 ....20.07
R v Healey (1990) 12 Cr App R (S) 297 ....20.21
R v Kemble [1990] 1 WLR 1111 ....20.12
R v Mehrban [2001] EWCA Crim 2627 ....20.12
R v Millward [1985] QB 519, 80 Cr App R 280 ....20.16
R v Pendragon (unreported 1997) 20.12
R v Simmonds (George Lewis James) (1969) 53 Cr App R 488 ....20.21
R v Visitors to the Inns of Court, Ex parte Calder [1994] QB 1 ....3.38

R v Warne (1980) 2 Cr App R (S) 42 .... 20.21
Rechtbank Groningen (Groningen Court of First Instance), Case No 49632/HA ZA 00-915
  (24 January 2002) 20.39
Regina v Emanuel Tew (1855) 169 ER 766, (1855) Dears 429 .... 20.06
ReliaStar v EMC National Life Co, 564 F 3rd 81 (2d Cir 2009) 21.35
Renault v V2000, Cass 1e civ, 21 May 1997, 1997 Rev arb 537 .... 9.31
Republic of Ecuador v Chevron Corp, 638 F 3d 384 (2d Cir 2011) 7.24, 21.17
Republic of Ecuador v Bjorkam (Chevron), 801 F Supp 2d 1121 (D Colo 2011) 16.05
Republic of Ecuador, Re, No C-10-80225 Misc CRB (EMC), 2010 WL 3702427 (ND Cal,
  15 September 2010) 16.05
Republic of Kazakhstan v Biedermann International, 168 F 3d 880 (5th Cir 1999) 16.04, 16.06
Republic of Kazakhstan, No 15 Misc 0081 (SHS), 2015 WL 3855113, at *5 (SDNY 22 June
  2015) 16.09
Rex v Threlfall [1914] 10 Cr App R 112 .... 20.19
Richardson v Mellish (1824) 2 Bing 229 .... 32.02, 32.13
Rocky Mountain Biologicals, Inc v Microbix Biosystems, Inc, 2013 WL (D Mont, 30 October
  2013) 15.12
Rodriguez v Speyer Bros [1919] AC 59 .... 32.23, 32.70
Royal Brompton Hospital NHS Trust v Hammond [2002] EWHC 2037 .... 36.33
Royal Brompton Hospital NHS Trust v Hammond (No 3) [2002] UKHL 14, [2002] 1 WLR
  1397; [2002] App LR 04/25 .... 36.33, 36.36, 36.37
Roz Trading Ltd, Re, 469 F Supp 2d 1221 (ND Ga 2006) 16.07
Roz Trading Ltd, Re, 2007 US Dist LEXIS 2112, 2007 WL 120844 (ND Ga
  11 January 2007) 16.09
Russell v Pellegrini, 6 E&B 1020 (KB 1856) 29.07

SA Burkinabe des ciments et matériaux v Société des ciments d'Abidjan, Paris Court of
  Appeal, 25 November 1999, 2001 Rev arb 165 .... 9.31
Sandvik AB v Advent International Corp, 220 F 3d 99 (3rd Cir 2000) 1.21
SCA Packaging Ltd v Boyle (Northern Ireland) [2009] UKHL 37 .... 4.53
Scherk v Alberto-Culver, 417 US 506 (1974) 1.43
Schwartzman v Harlap, 377 Fed Appx 108 (2d Cir NY 2010) 1.28
Scott v Avery, 10 ER 1121, (1856) 5 HL Cas 811 .... 29.07
Secretary of State for Trade and Industry v Bairstow [2003] EWCA Civ 321,
  [2004] Ch 1 .... 33.09, 33.10, 33.12, 33.28, 33.42
Seller v Buyer, Oberlandesgericht Celle, 4 September 2003, YCA XXX (2005) 536 ...... 7.49
Serbian Orthodox Diocese v Milivojevich, 426 US 696 (1976) 1.05
SGL Carbon Fibres Ltd v RBG Ltd [2012] CSOH 19 (27 January 2012) 36.37
Société d'études et représentations navales et industrielles v Société Air Sea Broker Ltd, Cass 1e
  civ, 8 July 2009, 2009 Rev arb 529 .... 9.31
Société Hilmarton Ltd v Société OTV, Cass 1e civ, 23 March 1994, 1994 Rev arb 327 .. 1.23
Société Korsnas Marma v Société Durand-Auzias, Paris Court of Appeal, 30 November 1988,
  1989 Rev arb 691 .... 9.33
Société Nihon Plast Co v Société Takata-Petri Aktiengesellschaft, Paris Court of Appeal,
  4 March 2004, 2005 Rev arb 143 .... 7.29
Société Ofer Bros v The Tokyo Marine and Fire Insurance Co Ltd, Paris Court of Appeal,
  14 February 1989, 1989 Rev arb 691 .... 9.33
Société Uni-Kod v Société Ouralkali, Cass 1e civ, 30 March 2004, 2005 Rev arb 959 .. 9.31
Soinco SACI v Novokuznetsk Aluminium Plant, The Times, 29 December 1997 .... 32.27, 32.40
Soleimany v Soleimany [1998] EWCA Civ 285, [1999] QB 785 ..... 1.05, 32.35, 32.36, 32.43, 32.49
Sonatrach Petroleum Corp v Ferrell International Ltd [2002] 1 All ER (Comm) 627 ... 9.16
Sonatrach v Distrigas Corp, 80 BR 606 (Bankr D Mass 1987) 1.43
Sphere Drake Ins v Marine Towing, 16 F 3d 666 (5th Cir 1994) 1.09
Spivey v Teen Challenge of Florida, 122 So 3d 986 (Fla Dist Ct App 2013) 1.05
Stolt-Nielsen SA v Animal Feeds Int'l Corp, 559 US 662 (2010) 1.20

Table of Cases

SulAmérica Cia Nacional de Seguros SA v Enesa Engenharia SA [2012] EWCA
  Civ 638 ....1.34, 8.24–8.27, 9.16, 9.21, 9.22, 9.23, 9.25, 9.26, 9.27, 9.36, 9.37, 9.39, 9.40
Sumitomo Heavy Industries v Oil and Natural Gas Commission [1994] 1 Lloyd's Rep 45.......9.16

T Co Metals LLC v Dempsey Pipe & Supply, Inc, No 07-civ-7747 (SDNY 8 July 2008) 24.15
T Co Metals LLC v Dempsey Pipe & Supply, Inc, 592 F3d 329 (2d Cir 2010) 24.13, 24.14, 24.16
Telecordia Tech v Telkom SA, 458 F 3d 172 (3d Cir 2006)...................................1.25
Termorio SA ESP v Electranta SP, 487 F 3d 928 (DC Cir 2007) 1.27
Thai-Lao Lignite (Thail) Co, Re, 821 F Supp 2d 289, 297 (DDC 2011)...................16.12
Three Valleys Municipal Water District v EF Hutton, 925 F 2d 1136 (9th Cir 1991)............1.21
Tinsley v Milligan [1994] 1 AC 340 (HL) 32.20
Torch Offshore LLC v Cable Shipping Inc [2004] EWHC 787 (Comm) 24.10
Transfield Shipping Inc v Mercator Shipping Inc (The Achilleas) [2009] AC 61 (HL)..........29.50
Tubular Holdings (Pty) Ltd v DBT Technologies (Pty) Ltd (2013) Case No 06757/13
  (South Gauteng High Court, South Africa) 36.39, 36.44

Union of India v Cairn India Ltd, CS(OS) No 2445/2015..........................24.04, 24.12
United Group Rail Services Ltd v Rail Corp of New South Wales [2009]
  74 NSWLR 618 ....8.20, 8.21
United States Anti-Doping Agency v Lance Armstrong, Reasoned Decision of the United
  States Anti-Doping Agency on Disqualification and Ineligibility (10 October 2010) 13.06
Ust-Kamenogorsk Hydropower Plant JSC v AES Ust-Kamenogorsk Hydropower Plant LLP
  [2013] UKSC 35..31.02

Veiga, Re, 746 F Supp 2d 8 (DDC 2010) 16.09
Vervaeke v Smith [1983] 1 AC 145 ....32.26
VV v VW [2008] 2 SLR 929 ....25.20
Vynior v Wilde (1609) 8 Coke Rep 81b, 77 ER 595 (KB)................................29.03

Walford v Miles [1992] 2 AC 128 ....8.21
Walker Construction (UK) Ltd v Quayside Homes Ltd [2014] EWCA Civ 93......... 36.11, 36.21,
                                                                             36.26, 36.31
Westacre Investments Inc v Jugoimport SDPR Holding Co Ltd [2000] 1 QB 288...... 32.27, 32.35,
                                                   32.38, 32.44, 32.45, 32.49, 32.50, 32.51, 32.58, 32.59

X1, X2 v Y1, Y2, Case No ARB 002/2013, DIFC Court of First Instance (2014)..............34.41
XL Insurance Ltd v Owens Corning [2001] 1 All ER (Comm) 530 ....9.16

Yukos Capital SARL v OAO Rosneft, Court of Appeal of Amsterdam (Enterprise Division),
  28 April 2009 ....1.26, 31.26
Yukos Capital SARL v OAO Samaraneftegaz, 963 F Supp 2d 289 (SDNY 2013) 30.21
Yukos Capital SARL v OJSC Rosneft Oil Co [2012] EWCA Civ 855, [2013]
  1 All ER 223 ....1.26, 31.25–31.27

Yukos Capital SARL v OJSC Rosneft Oil Co [2014] EWHC 2188 (Comm) 1.26, 31.27

TABLE OF ARBITRAL DECISIONS AND AWARDS

Abaclat v Argentine Republic, ICSID Case No ARB/07/5, Decision on Jurisdiction and
  Admissibility (4 August 2011)..21.15
Adem Dogan v Turkmenistan, ICSID Case No ARB/09/9..................................13.10
Aguas Argentina SA, Suez, Sociedad General de Aguas de Barcelona SA and Vivendi Universal
  SA v The Argentine Republic, ICSID Case No ARB/03/19, Amicus Curiae Order
  (12 February 2007) 21.35
Al Reyami Group LLC v BTI Befestigungstechnik GmbH & Co KG, Case No 434/2014,
  Dubai Court of Cassation (23 November 2014)..................................... 34.37
Andersen Consulting Business Unit Member Firms v Arthur Andersen Business Unit Member
  Firms and Andersen Worldwide Société Coopérative, ICC Case No 9797, Final Award
  (2000), (2000) 15(8) Mealey's IAR Doc A1 ....27.29
ATA Construction, Industrial and Trading Co v The Hashemite Kingdom of Jordan, ICSID
  Case No ARB/08/2, Order Taking Note of the Discontinuance of the Proceedings (11
  July 2011) 25.17
Behring Int'l Inc v Islamic Rep Iranian Air Force, Iran Aircraft Indus, and Gov't of Iran,
  Award No ITM/ITL 52-382-3 (21 June 1985), 8 Iran-US Claims Tribunal
  Reports 238...15.16
Biwater Gauff (Tanzania) Ltd v United Republic of Tanzania, ICSID Case No ARB/05/22,
  Procedural Order No 1 (31 March 2006) 15.19
Burlington Resources Inc v Republic of Ecuador, ICSID Case No ARB/08/5, Procedural
  Order No 1 (29 June 2009)...15.19
Chevron Co and Texaco Petroleum Co v Republic of Ecuador, PCA Case No 2009-23, Second
  Interim Award on Interim Measures (16 February 2012) 15.15, 15.22
Churchill Mining Plc v Republic of Indonesia, ICSID Case No ARB/12/14, Procedural Order
  No 3 (4 March 2013) 15.27
City Oriente Ltd v Republic of Ecuador and Petroecuador, ICSID Case No ARB/06/21,
  Decision on Provisional Measures (19 November 2007) 15.19
Clayton and Bilcon of Delaware Inc v Government of Canada, UNCITRAL/NAFTA,
  Procedural Order No 8 (25 November 2009) 17.33
CME Czech Republic BV (The Netherlands) v The Czech Republic, UNCITRAL, Final
  Award (14 March 2003)...17.32
Company A (Italy) v 6 Respondents (Italy), ICC Case No 14046, Final Award (2010) YCA V
  (2010) 241 ....25.16, 27.07
ConocoPhillips Petrozuata BV v Bolivarian Republic of Venezuela, ICSID Case No ARB/07/
  30, Decision on Respondent's Request for Reconsideration (10 March 2014) 21.24
Consultant (France) v Egyptian Local Authority, ICC Case No 6162, Award (1990) YCA
  XVII (1992) 153...7.37
Corn Products International v Mexico, ICSID Case No ARB(AF)/04/01, Decision on
  Responsibility (15 January 2008)..31.09
Distrib A v Mfg B, ICC Case No 1596, Interlocutory Award (2000) 15.16, 15.26
Dow Chemical Co v ISOVER Saint Gobain, ICC Case No 4131, Interim Award (23
  September 1982) YCA IX (1984) 131...9.33
El Paso Energy International Co v The Argentine Republic, ICSID Case No ARB/03/15,
  Procedural Order No 1 (28 July 2005) 17.23, 17.25
El Paso Energy International Co v The Argentine Republic, ICSID Case No ARB/03/15,
  Decision on Jurisdiction (27 April 2006) 17.23, 17.25
Emmis Int'l Holding BV v Republic of Hungary, ICSID Case No ARB/12/2, Decision on
  Respondent's Objection under ICSID Arbitration Rule 41(5) (11 March 2013)..........12.41
Global Trading Resource Corp and Globex International, Inc v Ukraine, ICSID Case No
  ARB/09/11, Award (1 December 2010)..................................4.38, 4.39, 12.41

Table of Arbitral Decisions and Awards

Gold Reserve Inc v Venezuela, ICSID Case No ARB(AF)/09/1 ....24.10
Guaracachi America Inc and Rurelec Plc v Bolivia, PCA Case No 2011-17, Procedural Order
    No 14 (11 March 2013) 15.20
Himpurna California Energy Ltd v Republic of Indonesia, Final Award (16 October 1999),
    YCA XXV (2000) 109...13.06
Hrvatska Elektroprivreda dd v The Republic of Slovenia, ICSID Case No ARB/05/24,
    Tribunal's Ruling regarding the Participation of David Mildon QC in Further Stages of
    the Proceedings (6 May 2008) 3.12, 3.34–3.36, 13.11, 13.13, 21.14, 21.20, 21.33
ICC Case No 10982, Award (2001) JDI 2005, 1256 .... 36.08
ICC Case No 11413, First Interim Award (2001), (2010) 21 ICC Int'l Ct Arb Bull 34...........4.36
ICC Case No 12297, Procedural Order No 1 (22 August 2003), ICC Int'l Ct Arb Bull, Special
    Supplement (2011) 47 ....4.36
ICC Case No 12745, Final Award (2010) YCA V (2010) 40 .... 25.16, 25.31
ICC Case No 13507, Final Award (2010) YCA V (2010) 158.....................................25.34
ICC Case No 13676, Final Award (2010) YCA V (2010) 168 ....25.26
ICC Case No 14020, Final Award (2011) YCA VI (2011) 126....................................25.34
ICC Case No 14108, Final Award (2011) YCA VI (2011) 135..........................25.16, 25.34
ICC Case No 16879 (2013)..27.20, 27.29
ICC Case No 17333 (2011)..27.19
ICC Case No 2626 (1977), Sigvard Jarvin and Yves Derains (eds), Collection of ICC Arbitral
    Awards 1974–1985, vol I (Kluwer Law International 1994) 316.........................9.16
ICC Case No 5029, Award (1991), (1993) 4 ICC Int'l Ct Arb Bull......................................27.29
ICC Case No 5103, Award (1988) Sigvard Jarvin, Yves Derains and Jean-Jacques Arnaldez
    (eds), Collection of ICC Arbitral Awards 1986–1990, vol II (Kluwer Law International
    1995) 361..9.33
ICC Case No 5759, Final Award (1989) YCA XVIII (1993) 34......................................27.29
ICC Case No 6293, Final Award (1990), (1993) 4(1) ICC Int'l Ct Arb Bull 43................27.29
ICC Case No 6379, Final Award (1990) YCA XVII ((1992) 212..................................9.16
ICC Case No 6564, Final Award (1993), (1993) 4 ICC Int'l Ct Arb Bull 46 ...... 27.20, 27.26, 27.33
ICC Case No 6752, Final Award (1991) YCA XVIII (1993) 54....................................9.16
ICC Case No 6959, Final Award (1992), (1993) 4 ICC Int'l Ct Arb Bull 49 ....27.33
ICC Case No 8786, Final Award (1997), (2002) ASA Bull 68.......................................27.20
International Thunderbird Gaming Corp (United States of America) v United Mexican States,
    NAFTA/UNCITRAL, Procedural Order No 2 (31 July 2003).........................17.09
Ioannis Kardassopoulos & Ron Fuchs v Georgia, ICSID Case Nos ARB/05/18 and ARB/07/
    15, Award (3 March 2010)..27.46
Libananco Holdings Co Ltd v Republic of Turkey, ICSID Case No ARB/06/8, Decision on
    Preliminary Issues (23 June 2008) 13.06
Libananco Holdings Co Ltd v Republic of Turkey, ICSID Case No ARB/06/8, Award (2
    September 2011)...13.06
Metal-Tech v Republic of Uzbekistan, ICSID Case No ARB/10/3, Award (4 October 2013) 22.76
Mobil Cerro Negro v PDVSA and PDVSA-CN, ICC Case No 15416/JRF/CA (2011) 20.37
Oxus Gold Plc v Republic of Uzbekistan, the State Committee of Uzbekistan for Geology &
    Mineral Resources, and Navoi Mining & Metallurgical Kombinat, UNCITRAL Case,
    Award (1 January 2012).. 26.37
Pabalk Ticaret Sirketi SA (Turkey) v Norsolor SA, ICC Case No 3131, Award (26 October
    1979) YCA IX (1984) 109 ....9.33
Perenco Ecuador Ltd v Republic of Ecuador, ICSID Case No ARB/08/6, Decision on
    Provisional Measures (8 May 2009)..15.19
Quasar de Valores SICAV SA v The Russian Federation, SCC Arbitration No 24/2007, Award
    (20 July 2012)..27.47
Rachel S Grynberg, Stephen M Grynberg, Miriam Z Grynberg and RSM Production Co v
    Grenada, ICSID Case No ARB/10/6, Award (10 December 2010) 4.38, 4.39
Reinhard Hans Unglaube and Marion Unglaube v Republic of Costa Rica, ICSID Case Nos
    ARB/09/20 and ARB/08/1, Award (16 May 2012) 25.19

Rio Grande Irrigation and Land Co, Ltd (Great Britain) v United States, Award of the United
   States-United Kingdom Mixed Claims Commission (28 November 1923), 1990 (IV)
   RIAA 131 ....21.20
Rompetrol Group NV v Romania, ICSID Case No ARB/06/3, Decision on Respondent's
   Preliminary Objections on Jurisdiction and Admissibility (18 April 2008) 3.36
Rompetrol Group NV v Romania, ICSID Case No ARB/06/3, Decision of the Tribunal on
   the Participation of a Counsel (14 January 2010) 13.11, 13.13, 21.31, 21.32, 21.33
RSM Production Corp v Grenada, ICSID Case No ARB/05/14, Order of the Committee
   Discontinuing the Proceeding and Decision on Costs (28 April 2011) 12.41, 27.46
S&T Oil Equipment and Machinery Ltd v Romania, ICSID Case No ARB/07/13, Order
   Taking Note of Discontinuance of the Proceeding (16 July 2010) 27.40
Seller D v Buyer S, ICC Case No 10329 (2000) YCA XXIX (2004) 108 ....27.33
Sergei Paushok, CJSC Golden East Co, and CJSC Vostokneftegaz Co v The Government of
   Mongolia, UNCITRAL, Order on Interim Measures (2 September 2008) 15.16, 15.25
Supplier v First distributor, Second distributor, ICC Case No 7006, Final Award (1992),
   (1993) 4(1) ICC Int'l Ct Arb Bull 49 ....27.45
Swisslion DOO Skopje v The Former Yugoslav Republic of Macedonia, ICSID Case No ARB/
   09/16, Award (6 July 2012) 25.16
Tethyan Copper Co v Pakistan, ICSID Case No ARB/12/1, Decision on Provisional Measures
   (13 December 2012)... 15.25, 15.27
Tokios Tokelés v Ukraine, ICSID Case No ARB/02/18, Procedural Order No 1
   (1 July 2003) 15.19
Toto Costruzioni Generali SpA v Republic of Lebanon, ICSID Case No ARB/07/12, Award
   (7 June 2012)..25.16
Trust C (Isle of Sark), US Corp (US) and Others v Latvian Group (Latvia), Latvian
   Finance Co (Latvia) and Others, ICC Case No 10973, Interim Award (2001), YCA
   XXX (2005) 77 .... 15.26, 15.28
Victor Pey Casado and President Allende Foundation v Republic of Chile, ICSID Case No
   ARB/98/2, Decision on Revision (18 November 2009).........................24.10, 24.12
Vito G Gallo v The Government of Canada, NAFTA/UNCITRAL, Award (15 September
   2011) 17.15, 17.32
Vito G Gallo v The Government of Canada, NAFTA/UNCITRAL, Procedural Order No 2
   (10 February 2009)... 17.15
Vito G Gallo v The Government of Canada, NAFTA/UNCITRAL, Procedural Order No 1
   (4 June 2008) 17.16
Waste Management Inc v Mexico, ICSID Case No ARB(AF)/00/3, Decision on Mexico's
   Preliminary Objection Concerning the Previous Proceedings (26 June 2002)............13.13

TABLE OF EUROPEAN AND INTERNATIONAL COURT DECISIONS

Allianz Spa & Generali Ass Gen Spa v West Tankers Inc (C-185/07) [2009]
  ECR I-663 (ECJ) 3.12, 3.48–3.50, 31.02
Case Concerning the Delimitation of the Continental Shelf between the United Kingdom
  of Great Britain and Northern Ireland and the French Republic, Decision (14 March
  1978) XVIII RIAA 271 . . . . 24.10
Case Concerning the Payment in Gold of the Brazilian Federal Loans Issued in France (French
  Republic v Kingdom of the Serbs, Croats and Slovenes), Judgments 14 and 15 (12 July
  1929) PCIJ Series A Nos 20/21 . . . . 31.08
E-Systems Inc v Iran, Iran-United States Claims Tribunal, Interim Award No ITM 13-388-
  FT (4 February 1983), [1983] 2 Iran-US Claims Tribunal Reports 51 . . . . 13.11, 13.13
Gazprom OAO (C-536/13) EU:C:2015:316; [2015] 1 Lloyd's Rep 610 (ECJ) 3.49
Iran v United States, Iran-United States Claims Tribunal, Decision No DEC 134-A3/A8/A9/
  A14/B61-FT, Decision Ruling on Request for Revision by Iran (1 July 2011). 13.11
Maritime Delimitation and Territorial Questions between Qatar and Bahrain (Qatar v
  Bahrain) (16 March 2001), ICJ Rep 40 . . . . 13.06
Military and Paramilitary Activities in and against Nicaragua (Nicaragua v USA), Provisional
  Measures (Order of 10 May 1984), 1984 ICJ Rep 169 . . . . 15.27
Passage through the Great Belt (Finland v Denmark), Provisional Measures (29 July 1991),
  1991 ICJ Rep 12 . . . . 15.21, 15.25, 15.27
Pulp Mills on the River Uruguay (Argentina v Uruguay), Provisional Measures (13 July 2006),
  2006 ICJ Rep 113. . . . . 15.18, 15.22, 15.25
STL (Appeal Chamber) Case No CH/AC/2010/2, Decision on Appeal of Pre-Trial Judge's
  Order Regarding Jurisdiction and Standing (10 November 2010) 13.11
Turner v Grovit (C-159/02) [2004] ECR I-3565 (ECJ). 31.02
WTO, Mexico: Tax Measures on Soft Drinks and Other Beverages, Appellate Body Report
  No WT/DS308/AB/R (24 March 2006). 13.11

TABLE OF LEGISLATION

AAA Code of Ethics for Arbitrators in Commercial Disputes (1 March 2004) 1.11, 13.26
AAA Commercial Arbitration Rules (1 October 2013) 15.05
   r 9 .... 35.61
   r 21 .... 35.61
   r 22 .... 35.61
   r 23 .... 35.61
   r 33 .... 35.61
   r 38 .... 35.61
   r 58 .... 35.61
AAA Construction Industry Arbitration Rules (1 October 2009) 35.20, 35.22
AAA Optional Appellate Rules (1 November 2013) 35.58
ABA/AAA Revised Code of Ethics for Arbitrators in Commercial Disputes (9 February 2009) 13.04
ACICA Arbitration Rules incorporating the Emergency Arbitrator Provisions (1 August 2011) 3.23, 14.06, 14.11, 14.19, 14.20
   Sch 2, r 1.3 .... 14.16, 14.17, 14.18
   Sch 2, r 3.5 .... 14.15
   Sch 2, r 4.2 .... 14.32
   Sch 2, r 5.2 .... 14.28
   Sch 2, r 7.1 .... 14.12
   Art 39(e) 27.14
   Art 41.1 .... 25.23
Agreement on Legal and Judicial Cooperation with Egypt (2000) 34.38
Agreement on Legal and Judicial Cooperation with Jordan (1999) 34.38
Agreement on Legal and Judicial Cooperation with Libya (1999) 34.38
Agreement on Legal and Judicial Cooperation with Somalia (1972) 34.38
Agreement on Legal and Judicial Cooperation with Syria (2002) 34.38
ALI Restatement (Third) of the US Law of International Commercial Arbitration (September 2010) 1.25, 7.49, 30.25, 31.31
ALI/UNIDROIT Principles of Transnational Civil Procedure 2004 ...25.38
   Principle 25 .... 25.38, 25.39
Appellate Jurisdiction Act 1876 .... 32.16
Arbitration Law of the People's Republic of China 1995 .... 28.08
ARIAS Arbitration Rules (2nd edn 1987) 9.16
ARIAS Arbitration Rules (3rd edn 2014) 9.16
Australian International Arbitration Act 2010
   s 27(1) 25.16
Austrian ZPO (Code of Civil Procedure)
   Art 204 .... 28.08, 28.38
   Art 609 .... 25.21
BAC Arbitration Rules 2007 .... 13.07
Bar Standard Boards, 2015 Entity Regulation 3.36
Belgian Judicial Code 2013
   Art 1700(4) 20.40
British Columbia International Arbitration Act 1996
   s 38(1) 25.16
Brussels Convention on Jurisdiction and the Enforcement of Judgments in Civil and Commercial Matters (signed 27 September 1968, entered into force 1 February 1973) 32.56
CANACO Arbitration Rules 2008 .... 15.04
CEPANI Arbitration Rules (1 January 2013) 3.23
Chief Coroner Guidance No 3 Oaths and Robes (16 July 2013) 20.10
CIArb Arbitration Rules 2000 .... 33.34, 33.36
   Art 7.8 .... 15.06
CIArb Arbitration Rules 2015
   Art 26 .... 15.06
   Art 34(2) 33.34, 33.36
CIArb Code of Professional and Ethical Conduct for Members (October 2009) 13.04, 13.28
CIArb Guideline for Arbitrators on Making Orders Relating to the Costs of the Arbitration (Practice Guideline 9) 27.08, 27.23, 27.31
CIArb Royal Charter (as amended in 1998)
   Art 4(1) 36.01
CIETAC Arbitration Rules (1 May 2012) 15.07
CIETAC Arbitration Rules (1 January 2015) 13.07, 14.06, 15.07
   Ch IV 12.27
   Art 23 .... 15.04
   Art 23(3) 15.05

Art 35(2) 12.38	s 1.2 . . . . .12.30
Art 43(1) 22.36	s 3.1. . . . . .12.29
Art 52(2) 25.23	s 4.3 . . . . .12.29
Art 56(1) 12.28	s 5.2 . . . . .12.29
Art 58. . . . . .12.29	s 6.2 . . . . .12.30
Art 59 . . . . .12.29	s 7 . . . . .12.29
Art 60. . . . . .12.29	District of Columbia Money Judgments
Art 62(1). 12.30	Recognition Act 2011 . . . . 1.24
Art 62(2) 12.31	Dubai Government Decree establishing
Common Law Procedure Act 1854. . . . . . .29.06	a special judicial committee to
s 5 . . . . .29.08	settle disputes related to Zabeel
Convention on Choice of Court	Investments LLC (9 February
Agreements (The Hague Choice	2011) 34.13
of Court Convention) (concluded	Dubai Government Decree No 57 of
30 June 2005, entered into force 1	2009, establishing a tribunal to
October 2015). 1.08	decide the disputes related to the
Convention on Judicial Cooperation and	settlement of the financial position
the Recognition and Enforcement of	of Dubai World and its subsidiaries
Judgments in Civil and Commercial	(14 December 2009) 34.13
Matters between the UAE and the	Dubai Government Decree No 61 of
Republic of France 34.38	2009, forming a special judicial
Convention on the Law Applicable to	committee to settle the disputes
Contractual Obligations (Rome	related to Amlak Finance PJSC and
Convention) (opened for signature	Tamweel PJSC (27 December
19 June 1980, entered into force 1	2009). 34.13
April 1991)	Dubai Instruction Order (6 February
Art 3 . . . . .31.05	1998) 34.25
Council of Ministers Decision No 406/2	Dubai Law No 6, 1997 . . . . .34.25
of 2003. . . . . .34.25	Dubai Law No 12, 2004 (as amended by
CPS Prosecution Policy and Guidance. . . .20.20	Dubai Law No 16, 2011) 34.41
CRCICA Arbitration Rules (1 March	Dubai Law No 13, 2008. . . . . .34.12
2011) 15.07	Dubai Law No 32, 2008
Art 26(3) 15.08	Art 8 . . . . .34.25
Art 26(4) 15.09	Art 9 . . . . .34.25
Art 42.2(g) 27.14	Egyptian Civil Code. 34.03
DIAC Arbitration Rules (7 May	Energy Charter Treaty (opened for
2007). . . .27.14, 34.06, 34.22, 34.30, 34.33	signature 17 December 1994,
Art 22. . . . . .34.28	entered into force 16 April 1998) 1.26
Art 28.5 . . . . .34.26	England and Wales Rules of Civil
Art 31.5 . . . . 15.05	Procedure 1998. . . . . 19.04
Art 39 . . . . .34.31	English Arbitration Act 1889 . . . . 3.01, 3.02
Appendix on Costs 34.26, 34.32	s 7 . . . . 29.08, 29.11, 29.12, 29.15
DIFC Arbitration Law No 1, 2008 . . . . . . 34.02,	s 19 . . . . 29.08, 29.09, 29.11, 29.12, 29.15
34.03, 34.04	English Arbitration Act 1934 . . . . .3.10, 29.15
Art 42(1) 34.38	s 9(1) 29.15
DIFC-LCIA Arbitration Rules	English Arbitration Act 1950
(17 February 2008). 34.07	s 12(3) 20.28
Art 28.3 . . . . 27.14	s 21 . . . . 29.15, 29.27
DIS Arbitration Rules (1 July	English Arbitration Act 1979 . . . . . 29.16–29.30,
1998) 2.26, 2.27	29.40, 29.43, 29.45, 29.46, 29.49
s 27 . . . . .22.33	s 1 . . . . 29.35
s 27.1. . . . . .22.35	s 1(5) 29.27
s 32.1 . . . . .28.08	s 1(6) 29.27
DIS Supplementary Rules for Expedited	s 1(7) 29.27
Proceedings (April 2008) 12.27	s 1(7)(b) 29.32
s 1.1. . . . . .12.28	s 2 . . . . 29.28

English Arbitration Act 1996............1.19,
    1.37, 2.27, 3.05, 3.06, 3.27, 3.29, 3.31,
    3.48, 3.49, 6.04, 6.14, 6.16, 6.21, 6.27,
    9.16, 20.28–20.31, 24.09, 25.12,
    29.40, 29.48, 32.61, 37.11, 37.20
  s 3 .... 6.15
  s 15(3)............................. 12.16
  s 30................................ 24.36
  s 33 .... 3.43, 6.26, 12.06, 22.09
  s 33(1)............................. 22.09
  s 33(1)(b) 3.51
  s 34(2)(f) 37.12
  s 34(2)(g) 22.07, 22.11, 22.22, 22.44
  s 35 .... 3.31
  s 38................................ 15.06
  s 38(5)...................... 20.01, 20.28
  s 40(1)............................. 12.06
  s 44................................ 31.02
  s 46 .... 31.13, 31.17, 31.18
  s 48(5)(b) 3.10
  s 50................................ 12.26
  s 51(2)............................. 24.37
  s 57(3)(b) 24.10
  s 57(4)............................. 24.11
  s 57(6)............................. 24.11
  s 58(1)............................. 33.37
  s 61(1) 27.41
  s 61(2)...................... 25.22, 27.42
  s 63................................ 27.10
  s 63(4)............................. 27.10
  s 67 .... 9.22, 9.33, 24.31
  s 67(1)............................. 24.31
  s 68................................ 24.21
  s 68(2)(b) 29.53, 29.55
  s 68(2)(g) 20.31, 32.60
  s 68(3)............................. 24.21
  s 69 .... 24.21, 29.44–29.52
  s 69(3)............................. 29.45
  s 69(7) 24.21
  s 103 .... 31.24
  s 103(2)(b) 9.13
  s 103(3)............................ 32.33
English Civil Procedure Act 1698 .... 29.04
English Civil Procedure Rules (CPR)
    1998............................. 19.04
  Pt 22............................... 20.14
  r 31.8 .... 17.30
  r 31.8(1) 17.29, 17.30
  r 31.8(2) 17.29, 17.30
  Pt 32............................... 20.14
  Pt 32, PD 9.1 .... 20.13
English Criminal Justice Act 2003 .... 20.24
English Criminal Procedure Rules 2015
  Pt 16.2 .... 20.14
English Evidence Act 1851
  s 16 .... 20.13
English Evidence Act 1869...............20.06
English Oaths Act 1775 ....20.08
English Oaths Act 1978 ....20.08–20.14, 20.29
  s 1 ....20.12
  s 1(3)...............................20.09
English Oaths of Minors Act 1681 ....20.08
English Perjury Act 1911 ....20.15–20.27, 20.29
  s 1 ....20.15
  s 1(2)...............................20.29
  s 1(6)...............................20.16
  s 2 ....20.15
  s 4 ....20.15
  s 5 ....20.15
  s 6 ....20.15
  s 9 ....20.20
  s 13 ....20.18
English Prosecution of Offences
    Act 1985
  s 28 ....20.20
European Convention on International
    Commercial Arbitration (opened for
    signature 31 April 1961, entered into
    force 7 January 1964)
  Art VII 31.14
European Court of Arbitration (ECA)
    Rules 1997........................ 5.11
Finnish Arbitration Act 1992............25.21
Finnish Code of Judicial Procedure
  Ch 21, s 1 ....25.21
Florida Lemon Law (Ch 88-95, Laws of
    Florida) 36.20
French Code of Civil Procedure (CPC)
  Art 10..............................22.11
  Art 21..............................28.38
  Art 1448.....................1.21, 7.25
  Art 1464(2) 22.11
  Art 1467............................22.10
  Art 1506.................... 1.21, 22.11
  Art 1506(3) 22.10
  Art 1520(1) 7.40
GCC Convention for the Execution of
    Judgments, Delegations and Judicial
    Notifications (opened for signature
    1987, entered into force 1995).......34.38
General Guidelines for the Parties' Legal
    Representatives (Annex to the LCIA
    Rules 2014) 3.42, 13.03, 13.22
Geneva Convention on the Execution
    of Foreign Arbitral Awards (The
    Geneva Convention) (enacted 26
    September 1927, entered into force
    25 July 1929)
  Art 1(a)............................. 8.42
German Civil Procedure Code (ZPO) 33.37
  s 278 ....28.08, 28.38
  s 1042..............................22.13

s 1042(4) 22.12, 22.13, 22.14
s 1057(1). 25.21, 27.10
Hague Convention on the Civil Aspects
  of International Child Abduction
  (concluded 25 October 1980,
  entered into force 1 December
  1983) 30.20
HKIAC Administered Arbitration Rules
  (1 November 2013). 8.08, 14.06, 26.08
  Art 16. . . . . 10.16
  Art 23.1 . . . . 15.04
  Art 24.2 . . . . 33.33
  Art 33.1 . . . . 27.14
  Art 34.3 . . . . 33.35
  Art 41. . . . . 14.11
  Sch 4. . . . . 15.04
  Sch 4, Art 16 . . . . 14.32
  Sch 4, Art 18 . . . . 14.28
  Sch 4, Art 22 . . . . 14.12
Hong Kong Arbitration Ordinance (Cap
  609) (1 June 2011) 20.39
  s 22B. 14.30
  s 33 . . . . .28.08, 28.34, 28.43
Housing Grants, Construction and
  Regeneration Act 1996
  (HGCRA). 36.42
  s 108. . . . . 35.14
  s 108(3). 36.15, 36.16, 36.41
IBA Guidelines on Conflicts of Interest in
  International Arbitration (22 May
  2004, 23 October 2014) 1.11, 13.04
  GS 4(d). 28.08
  GS 7(a) 3.36
IBA Guidelines on Party Representation
  in International Arbitration (25 May
  2013) 3.39, 11.22, 13.03,
    13.15–13.19, 13.20, 13.23, 13.31
  Guideline 4 . . . . 13.19
  Guideline 6 . . . . 13.16
  Guidelines 7–8 . . . . 13.07
  Guidelines 9–25 . . . . 13.16
  Guideline 25 . . . . 26.15
  Guideline 26 . . . . 13.17
  Guideline 26(c) 13.21
IBA Rules of Ethics for International
  Arbitrators 1987 . . . . 6.23, 13.04
IBA Rules on the Taking of Evidence in
  International Arbitration (1 June
  1999) 17.01, 37.14
  Art 8(3) 20.36
IBA Rules on the Taking of Evidence in
  International Arbitration (29 May
  2010) 4.30, 6.23, 11.34, 13.08, 17.01,
    17.02, 35.97, 37.14, 37.15, 37.19
  Preamble 17.33, 25.29
  Art 3. . . . . 17.01, 17.02, 17.16

Art 3.1 . . . . 17.06
Art 3.3 . . . . 17.02, 17.03, 17.05, 17.11,
    17.13, 17.35
Art 3.3(a) 17.04, 17.05, 17.10, 17.11,
    17.14, 17.16
Art 3.3(a)(i) 17.02
Art 3.3(a)(ii). 17.02, 17.09
Art 3.3(b) 17.02, 17.18, 17.22, 17.23
Art 3.3(c) 17.26, 17.27, 17.31
Art 3.3(c)(i) 17.02
Art 3.3(c)(ii) 17.02
Art 3.4 . . . . 17.07
Art 3.5 . . . . 17.07, 17.11
Art 3.7 .17.12, 17.13
Art 3.10 . . . . 17.16, 22.37
Art 4.2 . . . . .34.29
Art 4.10 . . . . 22.37, 22.38
Art 6.1 . . . . .22.37
Art 8.4 . . . . .20.36
Art 9.2 . . . . 17.11, 17.12
Art 9.2(c) 17.33
Art 9.2(a) 17.11
Art 9.7 . . . . .25.30
ICC Arbitration Rules 1931 . . . . 3.23
ICC Arbitration Rules 1955
  Art 29.2 . . . . 29.41
ICC Arbitration Rules 1998. . . . . 25.31
  Art 20. .22.23, 22.25
  Art 20(1) 22.28
  Art 31. . . . . 27.29
  Art 31.1 . . . . 27.14
  Art 34.6 . . . . 33.35
  Art 35 . . . . .24.27
ICC Arbitration Rules (1 January
  2012) 1.33, 2.12, 3.23, 3.24,
    3.26, 3.27, 8.03, 11.07, 12.07, 12.19,
    13.26, 14.06, 14.19, 14.20, 16.07,
    20.34, 21.16, 22.26, 22.27, 25.32,
    27.43, 32.45, 34.06, 34.08
  Art 12(2) 12.16
  Art 17. . . . . 31.14
  Art 20. . . . . 10.14
  Art 21(1). 21.20
  Art 22(1) 12.06
  Art 22(2) 12.39, 21.09
  Art 22(4) 4.34
  Art 24(1) 4.21
  Art 25. . . . . 22.23, 22.25, 22.31
  Art 25(1). 17.14, 22.23, 22.28
  Art 25(2) 12.38, 22.23
  Art 25(5) 22.23
  Art 28(1) 15.05
  Art 29(1) 15.04, 15.23
  Art 29(2) 14.32
  Art 29(3) 14.28
  Art 29(7) 14.12

Art 34.6 . . . . 29.50, 33.33
Art 35 . . . . 24.10
Art 35(4) 24.27
Art 37(1) 25.11, 27.11, 27.13, 27.14
Art 37(5) 27.24, 27.43
Art 38(1) 12.24
Art 40(5) 25.32
Art 41 . . . . 21.03, 31.16
Art 51(1) 24.12
App V 15.04
App V, Art 1.6 . . . . 14.08
App V, Art 3 . . . . 14.18
ICDR Arbitration Rules (1999) 3.23
ICDR Arbitration Rules (2006) 3.23
ICDR Arbitration Rules (2009) 24.13
   Art 19 . . . . 36.07
   Arts 30(1)–(2) 24.13
   Art 30(1) 24.13, 24.14, 24.15, 24.16
ICDR Arbitration Rules (1 June 2014, Fee
   Schedule Amended and Effective
   1 November 2014) 15.11, 20.34
   Art 19 . . . . 21.17
   Art 20(2) 21.19
   Art 21(1) 15.05
   Art 20(6) 21.26
   Art 30.1 . . . . 33.33, 33.35
   Art 31(1) 21.09
   Art 37(1) 15.04
   Art 34 . . . . 27.15
   Art 44 . . . . 25.19
ICSID Convention (Convention on the
   Settlement of Investment Disputes
   between States and Nationals of
   Other States) (opened for signature
   18 March 1965, entered into force
   14 October 1966) 2.13, 34.38
   Art 25(1) 15.27
   Art 26 . . . . 15.07
   Art 44 . . . . 21.14
   Art 47 . . . . 15.04
   Art 52 . . . . 1.18, 1.30, 1.31
   Art 52(1)(b) 1.20
   Art 53 . . . . 1.18
   Art 54 . . . . 1.30
   Art 61(2) 27.10, 27.41
ICSID Rules of Procedure for Arbitration
   Proceedings (ICSID Arbitration
   Rules) (April 2006) 1.30, 4.38
   r 1(4) 28.08
   r 19 . . . . 21.14
   r 35(2) 20.35
   r 35(3) 20.35
   r 39(1) 15.04
   r 41(5) 4.37, 12.41, 12.43
   rr 49–55 . . . . 24.10
   r 51(1) 24.10
ICSID Additional Facility Rules (2006)
   Arts 55–7 . . . . 24.10
ILA Recommendations on Lis Pendens
   and Res Judicata in International
   Commercial Arbitration (2007)
   rec II.5 . . . . 33.30, 33.31
Indian Arbitration and Conciliation Act
   1996 . . . . 9.22
   s 30(1) 28.08
Indian Oaths Act 1969 . . . . 20.39
Inter-American Convention on
   International Commercial
   Arbitration (Panama Convention)
   (opened for signature 30 January
   1975, entered into force 16 June
   1976) 1.25
Irish Arbitration Act 2010 . . . . 27.10
JAMS Comprehensive Arbitration Rules
   (1 July 2014)
   Art 26.1 . . . . 15.05
   r 29 . . . . 21.26
Japanese Arbitration Law 2003
   Art 38(4) 28.08, 28.38
JCAA Arbitration Rules (1 February
   2014) 14.06
   Ch V 12.27
   Ch VI 14.11
   r 47 . . . . 28.38
   r 66.8 . . . . 14.32
   r 70.1 . . . . 14.32
   r 70.7 . . . . 14.08
JCAA International Commercial
   Mediation Rules (1 January 2009)
   r 8 . . . . 28.38
   r 11 . . . . 28.38
JCT/CIMAR Arbitration Rules 2005 . . . . 24.36
   r 3.3 . . . . 24.39
Judicial Authority Law of 2008 . . . . 34.41
KLRCA Arbitration Rules (24 October
   2013) 15.07
   r 7(2) 15.04
   r 26(3) 15.08
   r 26(4) 15.09
   r 40(2)(e) 27.14
   Sch 2 . . . . 15.04
LCIA Arbitration Rules 1978 . . . . 3.02, 12.37
   Art 19 . . . . 29.41
LCIA Arbitration Rules 1981 . . . . 3.02, 3.05, 3.06
LCIA Arbitration Rules 1985 . . . . 3.02, 3.05,
                          3.06, 3.07, 3.11, 3.33, 3.47
   Art 16.8 . . . . 29.42
LCIA Arbitration Rules (1 January
   1998) 3.02, 3.05, 3.06, 3.07, 3.11, 3.19,
               3.23, 3.33, 22.22, 33.25, 34.07
   Art 5.5 . . . . 3.47
   Art 6.1 . . . . 3.47

Art 6.2 . . . . 3.47
Art 9 . . . . 3.13, 3.20, 3.22, 14.11
Art 20.3 . . . . 20.32
Art 27 . . . . 24.10
LCIA Arbitration Rules (1 October
    2014) 3.01–3.53, 8.04, 12.19,
        12.24, 12.37, 13.20–13.23, 13.26,
        13.31, 14.06, 16.07, 21.16, 25.33,
        27.43, 33.29, 34.07
Art 1 . . . . 3.17
Art 1.1(i) 3.34
Art 1.2 . . . . 3.14
Art 1.3 . . . . 3.18
Art 2 . . . . 3.17
Art 2.1(i) 3.34
Art 2.2 . . . . 3.14
Art 2.3 . . . . 3.18
Art 5.8 . . . . 12.16
Art 6.3 . . . . 3.11
Art 9 . . . . 3.19
Art 9A 3.19–3.22, 3.28, 14.11
Art 9B 3.22, 3.23–3.28, 15.04
Art 9.11 . . . . 14.28
Art 9.12 . . . . 14.12
Art 14.1 . . . . 3.52
Art 14.2 . . . . 12.39
Art 14.4 . . . . 12.06
Art 14.5 . . . . 12.06
Art 14.4(i) 3.42, 4.34
Art 14.4(ii) 3.42, 3.51
Art 15 . . . . 3.52
Art 15.2 . . . . 3.17
Art 15.3 . . . . 3.17
Art 16.2 . . . . 3.30
Art 17 . . . . 10.15
Art 18 . . . . 21.33
Art 18.2 . . . . 3.34
Art 18.3 . . . . 3.35, 21.33
Art 18.4 . . . . 3.35, 3.36, 21.33
Art 18.5 . . . . 3.42, 13.22
Art 18.6 . . . . 3.37, 3.42, 3.43, 13.20,
        21.16, 21.26
Art 19.1 . . . . 12.38
Art 20.2 . . . . 20.32
Art 22.1(iii) 17.14, 22.22
Art 22.1(v) 22.22
Art 22.1(vii) 3.10, 3.49
Art 22.1(viii) 3.33
Art 22.1(ix) 3.31, 3.33, 21.16
Art 22.1(x) 21.16
Art 22.1(c) 22.44
Art 22.3 . . . . 21.20
Art 22.6 . . . . 3.33
Arts 23.1–23.5 . . . . 3.49
Art 23.1 . . . . 21.17
Art 25.1 . . . . 15.06

Art 26.7 . . . . 12.38
Art 26.8 . . . . 29.50, 33.33, 33.35
Art 28.3 . . . . 25.46, 27.10, 27.14
Art 28.4 . . . . 13.21, 25.23, 25.46, 27.24, 27.42
Art 32.2 . . . . 21.03, 31.16
Art 32.3 . . . . 3.47
Annex 1.11
Memorandum of Guidance as to
    Enforcement between the DIFC
    Courts and the Commercial Court,
    Queen's Bench Division, England
    and Wales (23 January 2013) 34.05
Memorandum of Guidance between
    the DIFC Courts and the Supreme
    Court of New South Wales (9
    December 2013) 34.05
Mexican Commercial Code
    Art 1455 . . . . 25.22
    Art 1465 . . . . 7.28
NAI Arbitration Rules (1 January 2010)
    Art 42a 15.04
    Art 42b 15.04
Netherlands Arbitration Act 1986 . . . . 3.32
Netherlands Code of Civil Procedure
    Art 1043 . . . . 28.08, 28.38
New York Civil Practice Law and
    Rules 2015
    Art 7505 . . . . 20.39
New York Convention (United Nations
    Convention on the Recognition and
    Enforcement of Foreign Arbitral
    Awards) (signed 10 June 1958,
    entered into force 7 June 1959) 1.08,
        1.25, 1.43, 2.06, 3.23, 3.27, 3.49,
        6.02–6.05, 6.13, 7.03, 7.37, 7.50, 8.32,
        11.12, 12.09, 12.46, 14.28, 14.31,
        21.15, 24.05, 24.27, 29.42, 30.22,
        31.10, 32.01, 32.02, 32.39, 32.42,
        32.59, 32.60, 33.39–33.40, 33.44,
        34.27, 34.37, 34.38, 34.46
New York Judiciary Law
    s 5 . . . . 1.28
New Zealand Arbitration Act 1996
    Sch 2, Art 5(10) 1.15
North American Free Trade Agreement
    (NAFTA) (signed 17 December
    1992, entered into force 1 January
    1994) 17.15
Paris Arbitration Rules (15 April 2013)
    Art 7(6) 27.28
PCA Arbitration Rules (17 December
    2012)
    Art 40.2(e) 27.14
Practice Direction No 1 of 2010 issued by
    the Dubai World Special Tribunal,
    30 March 2010 . . . . 34.13

Table of Legislation

Practice Direction No 2 of 2012 DIFC
    Courts' Jurisdiction 34.46
Practice Direction No 2 of 2015 DIFC
    Courts' Jurisdiction 34.46
Practice Direction No 61 of 2009
    Concerning Formation of Special
    Judicial Committee to decide in the
    Disputes Relating to Amlak Finance
    PJSC and Tamweel PJSC issued by
    the Dubai Government (27 January
    2010) 34.13
Practice Direction No X of 2014,
    amending Practice Direction No 2 of
    2012 DIFC Courts' Jurisdiction 34.46
Principle No XII.1 Distribution of
    Burden of Proof 36.06
Principles on Choice of Law in
    International Commercial Contracts
    (approved on 19 March 2015)
    Art 3 . . . . 31.08
Protocol of Enforcement between
    Dubai Courts and DIFC
    Courts 2009 . . . . 34.04, 34.05
Protocol on Arbitration Clauses (Geneva
    Protocol) 24 September 1923
Regulation (EC) No 593/2008 of the
    European Parliament and of the
    Council of 17 June 2008 on the law
    applicable to contractual obligations
    (Rome I Regulation) 31.18
    Recital 13 . . . . 31.06
    Art 3 . . . . 31.05
Regulation (EU) No 1215/2012 of the
    European Parliament and of the
    Council of 12 December 2012 on
    jurisdiction and the recognition and
    enforcement of judgments in civil and
    commercial matters 3.23, 3.48, 32.56
Regulations of the Chartered Institute of
    Arbitrators (2014)
    Art 10 . . . . 13.28
Resolution on Transnational Rules
    adopted at the 65th International
    Law Association Conference (Cairo,
    26 April 1992) 31.14
Revised Brussels I Regulation No 1215/
    2012 on jurisdiction and the
    recognition and enforcement of
    judgments in civil and commercial
    matters (Brussels I Regulation
    Recast) (12 December 2012)
    (revising Regulation No 44/2001
    of 22 December 2000) 3.23, 3.48
    Recital 26 . . . . 32.56
Riyadh Convention on Judicial
    Cooperation between States of the
    Arab League (opened for signature
    1983, entered into force 1999) 34.38
Rules of Arbitration of the CAM
    (1 July 2009)
    Art 30(1) 15.05
Rules of International Arbitration of the
    Korean Commercial Arbitration
    Board (KCAB) (1 September 2011)
    Art 28(1) 15.05
SCC Arbitration Rules (1 January
    2010) 3.23, 3.24, 3.26, 3.27
    Art 19.1 . . . . 12.39
    Art 21 . . . . 10.15
    Art 22(1) 21.20
    Art 32(1) 15.05
    Art 38 . . . . 12.37
    Art 44 . . . . 25.23
    App II 15.04
SCC Rules for Expedited Arbitration
    (1 January 2010) 12.27, 12.31, 12.32
    Art 12 . . . . 12.29
    Art 36 . . . . 12.30
Scheme for Construction Contracts
    (England and Wales) Regulations 1998
    s 23(2) 36.41
Senior Courts Act 1981
    s 37 . . . . 31.02
SFO Guidance on Perjury 20.20, 20.21
SIAC Arbitration Rules (1 July 2010) 14.06
    r 26.2 . . . . 3.23
    Sch 1 . . . . 3.23
SIAC Arbitration Rules (1 April 2013) 3.24,
        3.26, 3.27, 12.32, 14.06, 14.24
    r 5 . . . . 14.11
    r 5.1(a) 12.28
    r 5.2(b) 12.29
    r 5.2(c) 12.30
    r 5.2(d) 12.30, 12.31
    r 5.3(e) 12.30
    r 16.1 . . . . 12.39
    r 16.4 . . . . 12.40
    r 19(1) 10.16
    r 21.1 . . . . 12.38
    r 26(1) 15.05
    r 26(2) 15.04
    r 26.3 . . . . 14.12
    r 28.9 . . . . 33.33, 33.35
    r 33 . . . . 27.14
    Sch 1, r 1 . . . . 14.19
    Sch 1, r 7 . . . . 14.28
    Sch 1, r 9 . . . . 14.32
Singapore International Arbitration Act
    1994 . . . . 14.29
Singapore International Arbitration Act
    2002 . . . . 14.29
    s 12(2) 20.39

s 17 . . . . .28.08, 28.34
  s 17(3) 28.43
Spanish Civil Procedure Law 2000 . . . . 19.04
State Immunity Act 1978
  s 20 . . . . .20.42
Statute of the International Court of
  Justice (ICJ) (26 June 1945) 15.19
  Art 41(1) 15.18
  Art 41(2) 15.21
Statute of Westminster 1275 (3 Edw
  1 c 29) 3.38
Swedish Arbitration Act 1999
  s 25(1) 22.20
  s 25(3) 20.40
  s 26(1) 20.40
Swiss Code of Obligations
  Art 124(1) 22.72
  Art 142 . . . . .22.72
Swiss Criminal Code 2014
  Art 307 . . . . .20.41
  Art 309 . . . . .20.41
Swiss Private International Law (PIL) 1987
  Art 177(2) 7.36
  Art 178(2) 8.10, 9.11, 9.37
  Art 184(1) 22.16
  Art 190.1 . . . . .33.37
  Art 190(2)(b) 7.40
Swiss Rules of International Arbitration
  (Swiss Rules) (1 June 2012) 3.21,
                      3.23, 3.24, 3.26, 3.27
  Art 24(3) 22.32
  Art 40(1) 25.23
  Art 40(2) 25.23
  Arts 42–3 . . . . 15.04
Taft-Hartley Labor-Management
  Relations Act, § 301, 29 USC § 185
  (2003) 1.40
TOMAC Arbitration Rules (1 November
  2014)
  Art 44(2) 25.23
Treaty on Judicial Cooperation in
  Criminal Matters, Extradition of
  Offenders, Cooperation in Civil,
  Commercial and Personal Matters
  with Morocco (2006) 34.38
Treaty on Judicial Cooperation,
  Recognition and Enforcement of
  Judgments in Civil and Commercial
  Matters with France (1992) 34.38
Treaty on Mutual Legal assistance in
  Criminal Matters, Extradition of
  Offenders, Cooperation in Civil,
  Commercial and Personal Matters,
  Service of Judicial and Extra-Judicial
  Documents, Obtaining Evidence,
  Commissions and the Recognition
  and Enforcement of Foreign
  Judgments and Arbitral Awards with
  Sudan (2005) .34.38
UAE Civil Procedure Code 1992
  Art 58(2) 34.19, 34.21
  Arts 203–218 . . . . .34.04
  Art 203(1) 34.05, 34.18, 34.22
  Art 204(1) 34.36
  Art 205 . . . . .34.31
  Art 208(1) 34.28
  Art 208(2) 34.26
  Art 208(3) 34.27
  Art 209(2)(b) 34.35
  Art 210(1) 34.33
  Art 211 . . . . 20.42, 20.43, 34.27
  Art 212(1) 34.29
  Art 212(5) 34.30
  Art 213(3) 34.34
  Art 216 . . . . .34.16
  Art 216(1)(a) 34.23
  Art 217 . . . . 34.04, 34.39
  Art 218 . . . . .34.32
  Art 236 . . . . .34.04
  Art 238 . . . . 34.04, 34.37
UAE Civil Transactions Code
  Art 3 . . . . 34.01, 34.42, 34.43
  Art 733 . . . . .34.12
  Art 1028(d) 34.20
UAE Federal Decree No 43 of 2006 . . . . . .34.37
UAE Federal Law No 11, 1973 on Judicial
  Relationships Amongst Emirates 34.41
UAE Federal Law No 8, 1980 on Labour
  Art 6 . . . . .34.13
  Art 7 . . . . .34.13
UAE Federal Law No 18, 1981 on
  Commercial Agencies (as amended
  by Federal Law No 14, 1988)
  Art 6 . . . . .34.13
UAE Federal Law No 10, 2005
  Amending Certain Provisions of
  Government Lawsuit Law No 3 of
  1996 . . . . .34.34
UAE Federal Law No 4, 2012 Concerning
  Regulating Competition 2013 . . . . . .34.13
UAE Federal Law No 8, 1984
  Concerning Commercial Companies
  Art 103 (Art 154, new law) 34.20
  Art 216 (Art 265, new law) 34.20
  Art 237 . . . . .34.20
UAE Law of Evidence
  Art 41 . . . . .34.29
  Art 41(2) 34.27
UK–Argentina Bilateral Investment
  Treaty 1990 . . . . .7.10, 7.23

Table of Legislation

UNCITRAL Arbitration Rules (1976)
  Art 4 . . . . 3.34
  Art 24(3) 22.32
UNCITRAL Arbitration Rules (as
  revised in 2010) 2.05, 2.07, 2.08,
    2.14, 2.19, 3.06, 3.07, 3.21, 7.24, 15.08,
    16.07, 27.43, 34.07, 36.08, 37.22
  Art 6(7) 3.47
  Art 7(1) 12.16
  Art 17 . . . . 21.09
  Art 17.1 . . . . 4.34
  Art 17.3 . . . . 4.34
  Art 19 . . . . 10.16
  Art 23 . . . . 21.17
  Art 26.3 . . . . 14.15
  Art 26(3)(a) 15.20
  Art 26(4) 15.09
  Art 27 . . . . 36.07
  Art 27(3) 22.32
  Art 33 . . . . 31.14
  Art 34.1 . . . . 12.37
  Art 34.2 . . . . 33.33, 33.35
  Art 36 . . . . 24.12
  Arts 37–8 . . . . 24.10
  Art 37 . . . . 24.12
  Art 40 . . . . 27.13
  Art 40(1) 25.12
  Art 40.2(e) 27.14
  Art 42.1 . . . . 25.23
UNCITRAL Arbitration Rules (with new
  article 1, paragraph 4, as adopted in
  2013) 20.34, 34.07
UNCITRAL Conciliation Rules
  1980 . . . . 28.29
  Art 19 . . . . 28.08
UNCITRAL Model Law on
  International Commercial
  Arbitration 1985 . . . . 1.18, 3.05, 9.12,
    9.13, 37.11
  Art 28 . . . . 31.14
  Art 34 . . . . 29.42
UNCITRAL Model Law on
  International Commercial
  Arbitration 1985 (as amended in
  2006) 2.27, 6.04, 6.05, 6.14,
    6.16–6.17, 7.46, 15.20, 21.16, 24.05,
    24.18, 24.42, 25.20, 34.01, 34.03,
    34.30, 34.45
  Art 10(1) 11.06
  Art 11(2) 11.06
  Art 13(1) 11.06
  Art 16 . . . . 24.40
  Art 16(3) 7.40
  Art 17 . . . . 21.16
  Art 17(1) 11.06
  Art 17A 15.08
  Art 17H 14.29
  Art 24(1) 15.07
  Art 32 . . . . 24.08, 24.12
  Art 32(2) 24.08
  Art 32(3) 24.09, 24.10
  Art 33 . . . . 24.08, 24.12, 24.20
  Art 34 . . . . 24.20, 29.42
  Art 34(2)(a)(i) 9.28
  Art 34(3) 24.20
  Art 34(4) 24.08, 24.20, 24.24
  Art 35(1) 33.37
  Art 36(1)(a)(i) 9.28
UNIDROIT Principles of International
  Commercial Contracts 2010 . . . . 1.11, 31.14
  Art II 1.09, 3.50, 7.45, 7.46, 9.11, 11.04
  Arts II(1)–II(3) 8.42
  Art II(1)(2) 9.11
  Art III 1.08, 33.39
  Art IV 7.45, 7.49
  Art V 1.18, 8.42, 21.22, 31.24,
    33.39, 34.44
  Art V(1) 7.47
  Art V(1)(a) 7.33, 7.47, 7.48, 7.49, 8.42,
    8.43, 9.11, 9.12, 9.13, 9.14, 9.28
  Art V(1)(b) 7.47, 21.34
  Art V(1)(c) 7.47, 7.50, 21.03
  Art V(1)(d) 7.47, 11.05
  Art V(1)(e) 7.31, 7.39, 7.47, 7.48
  Art V(2)(a) 7.44, 7.47
  Art V(2)(b) 21.29, 32.33
  Art VII 7.46
United States Bankruptcy Code 1.43
United States Code (USC), Title
  28: Judiciary and Judicial
  Procedure 16.01
US Federal Arbitration Act (FAA) 1.08,
    9.35, 9.36
  s 15(b) 4.41
US Federal Rules of Civil
  Procedure 12.34, 12.35, 16.01, 16.03
US Foreign Sovereign Immunities Act
  1976 . . . . 30.20
VIAC Rules (Vienna Rules) (1 July 2013)
  Art 44.1.3 . . . . 27.14
Vienna Convention on the Law of
  Treaties (concluded 23 May 1969,
  entered into force 27 January
  1980) 7.23
WIPO Arbitration Rules (1 October
  2002) 3.23
WIPO Arbitration Rules (1 June 2014)
  Art 46(a) 15.05
  Art 54(d) 20.33
  Art 73(c) 25.23

NOTES ON THE CONTRIBUTORS

John J Barceló III is the W N Cromwell Professor of International and Comparative Law at Cornell Law School in Ithaca, New York. He holds an SJD (doctorate) from Harvard Law School. He is admitted to practise law in New York, Washington, DC, and Louisiana. He teaches International Commercial Arbitration, WTO Law, and EU Law (formerly also International Business Transactions, Public International Law, Conflict of Laws, and Admiralty). He is author and co-author of many publications on arbitration, trade, international business transactions, and EU law, including *International Commercial Arbitration* (5th edn 2012). He has been an arbitrator and a visiting lecturer at many law schools throughout Europe, Latin America, and China.

Marie Berard is a partner at Clifford Chance LLP in London. For more than 14 years, she has acted as counsel and advocate for multinational corporations, governments, and individuals on a wide range of international arbitrations proceedings. Marie also sits as arbitrator. She is a member of the ICC UK Task Force on Arbitration and Financial Institutions. She is also a guest lecturer at several universities and speaks regularly on international arbitration at conferences and seminars. Marie has published a number of articles in the field of international arbitration and litigation, most recently 'The Limits to the Parties' Free Choice of Jurisdiction', Dossier XII of the ICC Institute of World Business Law (2015). Marie holds law degrees from King's College London and Université Paris I—Sorbonne.

Sophia Berry is a Barrister-at-Law practising at Littleton Chambers, London. She read law at Cambridge University and has a Master's in Law from King's College London. She was awarded the Dickson Poon School of Law prize for attaining the highest scores of any Master's student, including her international arbitration paper. She practised as a solicitor at Linklaters LLP before being called to the Bar in 2012. She has represented clients in international commercial arbitrations and acted as an administrative secretary to a commodities arbitration.

Sébastien Besson is a partner in the Geneva law firm of Lévy Kaufmann-Kohler. His practice focuses on international arbitration and sports-related disputes. He has acted as counsel and arbitrator in numerous disputes related to commercial contracts and has represented parties on numerous occasions in court proceedings related to arbitration, including setting aside proceedings against arbitral awards. Besson is a member of the Arbitration Court of the Swiss Chambers' Arbitration Institution. He is also a part-time professor at the University of Neuchâtel. He has authored many publications in the field of international arbitration and sport disputes.

Julio César Betancourt was admitted to the practice of law in 2001. He holds a Bachelor's degree in Law and postgraduate law degrees in the areas of Damages, Procedural Law, International Business Law, Constitutional Law, and Contract and Damages. Julio César obtained his Master's in Law from University College London, specializing in Alternative Dispute Resolution (ADR), Dispute Resolution and Conflict Management, and International Arbitration. He is currently a Visiting Research Fellow at King's College

London, a PhD Candidate at the University of Salamanca, and Head of Research and Academic Affairs at the Chartered Institute of Arbitrators' Headquarters in London.

Gordon Blanke, LLM, PhD, MCIArb, is a partner and heads the International Commercial Arbitration Group of DWF (Middle East) LLP in the DIFC, Dubai. He has acted as advising counsel and arbitrator under numerous arbitration rules, including ICC, LCIA, DIFC-LCIA, ADCCAC, DIAC, JAMS, GCC, SCC, as well as *ad hoc* arbitrations seated in the United States, Europe, and the Middle East across a wide range of sectors. Gordon is a regular commentator and presenter on UAE and international arbitration across Europe, the United States, and the Middle East. He has over 100 publications, including the *Annotated Guide to Arbitration in the UAE*, vol I: *The UAE Arbitration Chapter* (Thomson Reuters 2014).

Karl-Heinz Böckstiegel, Dr jur, Prof Emeritus, University of Cologne, has been independent arbitrator, sole arbitrator, and president of numerous arbitration tribunals in many national and international arbitrations under ICSID, ECT, ICC, LCIA, NAFTA, CAFTA, UNCITRAL, PCA, DIS, AAA, SCC, Swiss Rules, VIAC, and disputes between states, among others. Patron of the Chartered Institute of Arbitrators (CIArb, 2007–10); President of the International Law Association (ILA, 2004–06); President of the London Court of International Arbitration (LCIA, 1993–97); President of the Iran–United States Claims Tribunal, The Hague (1984–88); and Chairman of the Board, German Institution of Arbitration (DIS, 1996–2012). He has authored 12 books and over 350 articles, and edited 35 books.

Olga Boltenko is a senior associate with the investment arbitration practice of Clifford Chance. She is based in Singapore. Before moving to Singapore, she was an arbitral clerk to Neil Kaplan, CBE, QC, SBS, in Hong Kong, a legal counsel at the Permanent Court of Arbitration in The Hague, and an associate with the international arbitration practice of White & Case LLP in Paris. She is part of the editorial team of the *Investor-State Law Guide* and is on the advisory board of the ICCA Publications Committee.

Stavros Brekoulakis is a Professor in International Arbitration and Commercial Law at Queen Mary University of London, as well as an attorney-at-law. He teaches courses in international commercial arbitration, international construction contracts and arbitration, international commercial litigation and conflict of laws, and international commercial law. His academic work includes the leading monograph *Third Parties in International Commercial Arbitration* (OUP 2010), the book *Arbitrability: International and Comparative Perspectives* (Kluwer Law International 2009), and numerous publications in leading legal journals and reviews. Brekoulakis has been involved in international arbitration for more than 15 years as counsel, expert, and arbitrator.

Bernardo M Cremades, PhD, FCIArb, is founding partner of the firm B Cremades y Asociados in Madrid and a pioneer in the field of international arbitration. His experience centres on international commercial arbitration and investment disputes. Dr Cremades has participated in some of Spain's most important M&A transactions. He also acts as an arbitrator in domestic and international disputes, including both commercial arbitration and investment protection. He is a member of many professional and international arbitration institutions and is a frequent speaker at international arbitration conferences around the world.

Greg Fullelove is a partner in the International Arbitration Group at Osborne Clarke. He acts as arbitration counsel in international arbitrations worldwide and has also been appointed arbitrator. Greg writes and lectures regularly on international arbitration and, together with Professor Julian D M Lew QC and others, is an editor of the practitioner text on arbitration law and practice *Arbitration in England: With Chapters on Scotland and Ireland* (Kluwer Law International 2013). Greg studied Classics at the University of Cambridge and International Law at Leiden University in the Netherlands.

Arpan Gupta is a foreign associate in the London office of Winston & Strawn and focuses his practice on international arbitration and general litigation. He has advised in a number of international arbitrations under the rules of major arbitral institutions such as International Chamber of Commerce (ICC), London Court of International Arbitration (LCIA), and American Arbitration Association (AAA). He is also the co-author of *International Commercial Arbitration and Its Indian Perspective* (Universal Law Publishing 2011).

Lord (David) Hacking is an arbitrator and mediator at Littleton Chambers, London. He was educated at Cambridge University and the Inns of Court Law School. He is a Fellow of the Chartered Institute of Arbitrators in London and of the Singapore and Malaysian Institutes of Arbitrators. He has 50 years of experience practising as a Barrister-at-Law and a Solicitor of the Supreme Court and undertaking appointments as an arbitrator in international commercial arbitrations. Since January 2000, he has issued more than 200 arbitration awards.

Grant Hanessian is a partner in the New York office of Baker & McKenzie and Global Co-Chair of its International Arbitration Group. He maintains an active practice as counsel and arbitrator in international commercial and investment arbitrations. He has edited five books, authored more than 50 articles and book chapters, and spoken on international arbitration matters at conferences and universities throughout the world. He is recommended by Chambers Global and USA, Legal 500, PLC Which Lawyer, The International Who's Who of Commercial Arbitration, and Expert Guide to Leading Practitioners ('Best of the Best' in international commercial arbitration).

Hilary Heilbron QC is an English barrister. She has extensive experience as counsel acting for a wide range of national and international clients in very substantial disputes in international arbitration, court-related arbitration cases, and commercial litigation. She also sits regularly as an arbitrator, with more than 80 appointments (as chair, sole, and party or institution appointed), and is a member of several institutional panels. She is a member of the LCIA Court. She is the author of *A Practical Guide to International Arbitration in London* (2008) and has written and spoken extensively on international arbitration.

Martin Hunter is a Professor of International Dispute Resolution and teaches at several of the world's leading universities. He was a partner at Freshfields Bruckhaus Deringer for 27 years and, after retiring from the firm in 1994, has continued to practise in the field as a barrister from Essex Court Chambers. He has been a member of ICCA since 1989; was deputy chairman of the UK Government's Committee that created the English Arbitration Act 1996; and has participated in the work of the AAA, CIArb, DIAC, IBA, ICC, LCIA, and UNCITRAL. He has been a co-author of *Redfern and Hunter on International Arbitration*, now in its 6th edition, since it was first published in 1986.

Doug Jones AO graduated from the University of Queensland with a combined Bachelor of Arts and Laws degree in 1974, followed by a Master of Laws in 1977. Doug holds appointments to professional bodies, including: Past President of the Australian Centre for International Commercial Arbitration (2008–14) and Fellow, Chartered Arbitrator, and Past President of the Chartered Institute of Arbitrators, London (2011). He holds professorial appointments at Queen Mary University of London and the University of Melbourne. He was appointed an Officer of the Order of Australia in 2012 for his contributions to alternative dispute resolution. He practises as an international arbitrator based in London, Sydney, and Toronto.

Neil Kaplan, CBE, QC, SBS, was called to the Bar of England and Wales in 1965. In 1982, he moved to Hong Kong to serve as Principal Crown Counsel, a practising QC, and later a Judge of the Supreme Court. Since 1995, he has been involved in hundreds of arbitrations as co-arbitrator, sole arbitrator, or chairman. These arbitrations have included commercial, infrastructural, and investment treaty disputes under numerous procedural rules. He was Chair of HKIAC for 13 years and President of the Chartered Institute of Arbitrators (1999–2000). He is an arbitrator at Arbitration Chambers in Hong Kong.

Robert Kovacs is an associate in the International Arbitration Group at Linklaters in London. He co-chairs the Asia–Pacific Forum for International Arbitration and is a former Chair of the International Law Section of the Law Institute of Victoria. He holds BCom/LLB (Hons) degrees from Monash University and a PhD (*summa cum laude*) from the University of Geneva. Robert acts for clients across a wide range of industries, most recently representing clients in the energy and financial sectors. He has had numerous appointments as a tribunal secretary in international arbitration proceedings administered under the ICC, SIAC, HKIAC, ICSID, and UNCITRAL Rules.

Mark McNeill is a partner in Shearman & Sterling LLP's international arbitration practice and is based in London. He has over 15 years of experience representing companies and states in international arbitrations, both investor–state and commercial. Mark has handled significant matters involving issues of intellectual property, technology, nuclear construction, pharmaceuticals, aviation, mining, and reinsurance. He previously served as an Attorney-Advisor in the Office of the Legal Advisor of the US Department of State, where he represented the United States in investment arbitrations submitted under the North American Free Trade Agreement (NAFTA).

Daniel R Meagher is an associate in the London office of Winston & Strawn, with a practice focusing on international arbitration and cross-border disputes. He advises clients from a range of sectors (including energy, telecoms, mining, and financial services) and from regions including Russia/CIS, MENA, and Asia. He holds an undergraduate law degree and an LLM in International Legal Studies from Cambridge University and NYU School of Law respectively, and is dual-qualified in England and New York.

Alex Mills, LLM, PhD, is a Reader in Public and Private International Law at the Faculty of Laws, University College London (UCL). He has degrees in philosophy and law from the University of Sydney, and practised for three years as a solicitor in Sydney. He then completed an LLM and PhD (awarded the Yorke Prize) at the University of Cambridge, and subsequently taught at the University of Cambridge for five years, before joining UCL. He has published and lectured widely on issues of public and private international law and international investment law, and has been consulted by government departments, legal practitioners, and non-governmental organizations.

Notes on the Contributors

Margaret L Moses is Professor of Law and Director of International Programs at Loyola University Chicago. A scholar in the field of international commercial arbitration, she published the second edition of her treatise on international commercial arbitration in February 2012 with Cambridge University Press. She has participated as an arbitrator or advocate in arbitrations under the auspices of the ICC Court of Arbitration and the AAA's International Centre for Dispute Resolution, as well as in *ad hoc* arbitrations. Professor Moses heads Loyola's Vis Moot program, which sends law students to compete in both Vienna and Hong Kong.

Renato Nazzini is Professor of Law at the Dickson Poon School of Law and Director of Research at the Centre of Construction Law and Dispute Resolution at King's College London. Professor Nazzini is one of the leading experts in Commercial Arbitration, ADR, and Civil Procedure, as well as Transnational, EU, and UK Competition Law. He is regularly appointed as an arbitrator and advises clients in complex commercial disputes both in international arbitration and in court proceedings. Previously, he was a Professor of Competition Law and Arbitration at the University of Southampton.

Lawrence W Newman is Of Counsel at Baker & McKenzie in New York. His practice focuses on international arbitration and litigation. He is the author, co-author, and editor of numerous publications, including *The Leading Arbitrators' Guide to International Arbitration* (3rd edn 2014), *International Arbitration Checklists* (2nd edn 2009), *Take the Witness: Cross-Examination in International Arbitration* (2010), *Interim Measures in International Arbitration* (2014) and *Soft Law in International Arbitration* (2014). He has spoken on international arbitration all around the world and was an Adjunct Professor at Fordham Law School. He is the past Chairman of the Arbitration Committee of the International Institute for Conflict Prevention and Resolution (CPR).

Michael O'Reilly is a solicitor, specializing in commercial law. He has been the Legal Advisor to the Chartered Institute of Arbitrators, Professor of Law at Kingston University, and is editor of the Chartered Institute of Arbitrators' journal, *Arbitration: The International Journal of Arbitration, Mediation and Dispute Management* (Sweet & Maxwell). Michael is taking time out from international dispute resolution in frontline business where he is Senior Legal Counsel and Risk Management Director of one the United Kingdom's largest independent companies.

William W (Rusty) Park is Professor of Law at Boston University, President of the London Court of International Arbitration (LCIA), and general editor of *Arbitration International*. He has held visiting academic appointments at Cambridge, Dijon, Hong Kong, Auckland, and Geneva, and served on the Claims Resolution Tribunal for Dormant Swiss Bank Accounts and the International Commission on Holocaust Era Insurance Claims. He was appointed to the ICSID Panel of Arbitrators by the President of the United States. His books include *Arbitration of International Business Disputes* (OUP 2012), *International Forum Selection* (Kluwer Law International 1995), *Income Tax Treaty Arbitration* (2004), *Craig, Park, and Paulsson on ICC Arbitration* (Oceana 2000), and *International Commercial Arbitration* (2015) with Reisman, Craig, and Paulsson.

Peter J Rees QC is an arbitrator and counsel at 39 Essex Chambers. Prior to joining 39 Essex Chambers, Peter was Legal Director of Royal Dutch Shell Plc for just over three years, a partner at Debevoise & Plimpton for five years, and a partner at Norton Rose for 19 years, including eight years as Head of Global Dispute Resolution. He is a Chartered Arbitrator, a Member of the Board of Trustees of CIArb, a Member of the Court of the LCIA, and a former member of the Governing Body of the ICC Court of Arbitration.

Sir Bernard Rix recently retired from the Court of Appeal after 20 years as first a High Court Judge and then a Lord Justice of Appeal. He now practises as an arbitrator and accredited mediator at 20 Essex Street. Since his retirement, he has been appointed to positions as a member of the Cayman Islands Court of Appeal and a Professor of International Commercial Law at Queen Mary University of London. He was educated at New College, Oxford, of which he is an honorary fellow, and at Harvard Law School, where he was a Kennedy Scholar.

Mauro Rubino-Sammartano is a Chartered Arbitrator, President of the European Court of Arbitration (Strasbourg), and Immediate Past Chairman of the Mediation Committee of the International Bar Association. He has more than 30 years' experience practising as an international arbitrator. Mauro Rubino-Sammartano has been a visiting professor at the University of Padua and the University of Milan and now regularly lectures on international arbitration. He is the author of numerous publications, including *Arbitration International: Law and Practice* (Juris 2014), now in its 3rd edition. He continues to practise as an international arbitrator from Littleton Chambers in London and LawFed BRSA Studio Legale e Tributario in Milan.

Margaret Clare Ryan is an associate in Shearman & Sterling's International Arbitration Group and is based in London. Margaret has worked on international arbitrations conducted pursuant to the Rules of UNCITRAL, ICSID, SCC, ICC, LCIA, and CRCICA, with a focus on energy disputes and matters involving clients and interests in Africa. Margaret holds undergraduate and postgraduate law degrees from Cambridge and McGill Universities respectively. She won the Max Crestohl Prize at the McGill University Faculty of Law for her contribution to the McGill Law Journal entitled '*Glamis Gold v. The United States* and the Fair and Equitable Treatment Standard under NAFTA' and is a research assistant for the New York Convention Guide Project.

David J Sandy is a partner and Co-Head of International Arbitration at Simmons & Simmons LLP who practises in the area of international arbitration and commercial litigation, specializing in cross-border jurisdiction and conflict of laws issues. He was admitted as a Solicitor of the Supreme Court of England and Wales in 1981. He has an MA in History from Keble College, Oxford, and an LLM in Commercial Law from the University of London. He is a Solicitor-Advocate (All Higher Courts) and a Fellow of the Chartered Institute of Arbitrators.

Lord (Mark) Saville was educated at the University of Oxford. He was called to the Bar (Middle Temple) in 1962. Lord Saville was appointed as a Queen's Counsel in 1975, a Judge of the High Court in 1985, and a Judge of the Court of Appeal in 1994. He chaired the committee responsible for preparing and promoting new arbitration legislation, which resulted in the English Arbitration Act 1996. In 1997, he became a Law Lord. In 2009, the Law Lords became Justices of the new Supreme Court. He is an honorary fellow of Brasenose College, Oxford, and a Member of the LCIA. He continues to practise as an arbitrator from Essex Court Chambers, having retired from the Supreme Court in 2010.

Thomas Schultz is SNF Professor of International Law at the Graduate Institute of International and Development Studies, Geneva, Reader in Commercial Law in the Dickson Poon School of Law at King's College London, and editor-in-chief of the *Journal* of *International Dispute Settlement*. He has held visiting and other academic appointments at the University of Cambridge, the Thunderbird School of Global Management at Arizona State University, Essex University, the Catholic University of Lille, and the University of Geneva. His books include *Transnational Legality: Stateless Law and International Arbitration* (OUP 2014), *Information Technology & Arbitration* (Kluwer Law International 2006), *Réguler le commerce électronique par la résolution des litiges en ligne* (Bruylant 2005), and, with Gabrielle Kaufmann-Kohler, *Online Dispute Resolution: Challenges for Contemporary Justice* (Kluwer Law International 2004).

Audley Sheppard QC, FCIArb, is a partner of Clifford Chance LLP in London and co-global head of its International Arbitration Group. He is a Vice-President of the LCIA and a Visiting Professor at the School of International Arbitration at Queen Mary University of London. He is a former: Rapporteur of the International Arbitration Committee of the International Law Association (1996–2006); Co-Chair of the Arbitration Committee of the International Bar Association (2006–07); and Member of the ICC International Court of Arbitration (2008–12). He holds an LLB (Hons) and BCommerce from Victoria University of Wellington (New Zealand) and an LLM from the University of Cambridge (England).

Elizabeth Snodgrass is a London-based international arbitration specialist. She has been counsel in numerous investor-state and commercial arbitrations, including *ad hoc* arbitrations and international arbitrations under ICSID, UNCITRAL, ICC, and LCIA Rules, with seats in London, New York, Frankfurt, Geneva, Singapore, and Washington DC. She has an extensive advisory practice, focusing on the structuring of investments to optimize investment treaty protection, drafting complex dispute resolution agreements, and addressing the legal issues that arise in transactions involving states or state entities. For five years, Elizabeth taught the International Arbitration LLM Programme at University College London.

Thomas J Stipanowich, William H Webster Chair in Dispute Resolution; Professor of Law, Pepperdine University School of Law; Academic Director, Straus Institute for Dispute Resolution. Co-author, *Federal Arbitration Law* (Best New Legal Book, Association of American Publishers); *Commercial Arbitration at its Best* (2001); *Resolving Disputes: Theory, Practice, and Law* (2nd edn 2010). Recipient, D'Alemberte-Raven Award, ABA Dispute Resolution Section's highest honour (2008); twice received CPR Best Professional Article award and other honours. CEO of CPR (2001–06); Advisor, ALI's Restatement of American Law of International Arbitration; Academic Counsel, Institute for Transnational Arbitration; Founding Member, College of Commercial Arbitrators; Companion, Chartered Institute of Arbitrators.

S I Strong, FCIArb, is the Manley O Hudson Professor of Law at the University of Missouri and a dual-qualified lawyer (US attorney and English solicitor) with extensive practical experience in New York, London, and Chicago. She has taught at the Universities of Cambridge and Oxford in the United Kingdom, as well as the University of Georgetown and the University of Missouri in the United States, and has published over 100 books and articles. Professor Strong's work has won numerous accolades and has been translated into Spanish, French, Portuguese, Chinese, and Russian. Professor Strong, who holds a PhD in law from the University of Cambridge as well as a DPhil from the University of Oxford and a JD from Duke University, sits as an arbitrator on a variety of complex commercial matters.

Notes on the Contributors

Joe Tirado is Global Co-Chair of International Arbitration at Winston & Strawn and is based in London. He has more than 20 years of dispute resolution experience and has handled hundreds of cases as counsel, arbitrator, mediator, and expert determiner. He has been involved in a wide variety of contested matters in the United Kingdom and more than 40 other countries. Joe is ranked 'first class' for international arbitration and ADR (Chambers UK, 2011). He has extensive experience of both commercial and investment arbitration. Joe is fluent in Spanish and does a lot of work in Latin America, India, and the CIS.

Andrew Tweeddale is a Director at Corbett & Co International Construction Lawyers Ltd based in London. He is a Chartered Arbitrator and a qualified Solicitor-Advocate of the Senior Courts of England and Wales. Andrew represents clients in arbitrations, adjudications, and mediations worldwide, particularly under the FIDIC forms of contract. He specializes in complex road and rail disputes for both employers and contractors. He is co-author of *A Practical Approach to Arbitration Law* (Blackstone Press 1999) and *Arbitration of Commercial Disputes: International and English Law and Practice* (OUP 2007).

Keren Tweeddale is a barrister in London, having been called to the Bar (Lincoln's Inn) in 1991. Keren is also a Senior Lecturer at London South Bank University in the Department of the Built Environment, where she teaches modules in property law and dispute resolution to postgraduate students. Keren was admitted as a Fellow of the Chartered Institute of Arbitrators in 1995. She is co-author of *A Practical Approach to Arbitration Law* (Blackstone Press 1999) and *Arbitration of Commercial Disputes: International and English Law and Practice* (OUP 2007).

V V Veeder QC is an arbitrator specializing in commercial law and international investment disputes. He is a Fellow of the Chartered Institute of Arbitrators (CIArb), a Vice-President of the London Court of International Arbitration (LCIA), and a Visiting Professor on Investment Arbitration at the Dickson Poon School of Law, King's College London. He was a member of the Departmental Advisory Committee on Arbitration Law (DAC), which, among other things, drafted the bill that was later passed in the UK Parliament as the Arbitration Act 1996. Both as counsel and arbitrator, he has extensive experience in both *ad hoc* and institutional arbitrations under the rules of numerous institutions, including the ICC, LCIA, SCC, ICSID, NAFTA, and UNCITRAL.

Jeffrey Waincymer is an arbitrator and arbitration and mediation practitioner. He is also a professor at the Faculty of Law, Monash University. Jeff is an Australian Government Nominee as a panellist for the WTO, is a Fellow of ACICA, and is on the HKIAC, SIAC, KLRCA, and ICDR arbitration panels. He is the author or co-author of a number of books, including *Procedure and Evidence in International Arbitration* (Kluwer Law International 2012); *WTO Litigation: Procedural Aspects of Formal Dispute Settlement* (Cameron May 2002); *A Guide to the New UNCITRAL Arbitration Rules* (CUP 2013); and *A Practical Guide to International Commercial Arbitration* (Oceana 2000).

Alexander A Yanos is a partner of Hughes Hubbard in New York. He co-chairs the firm's Treaty Arbitration practice group. Mr Yanos's arbitration practice includes commercial, financial, and treaty-based disputes, particularly in the energy and mining sectors and in Latin America. He has acted in matters before nearly every international arbitration tribunal, including ICSID, ICC, LCIA, AAA, HKIAC, Inter-American Commercial

Arbitration Commission, ICJ, and the SCC. Mr Yanos also has considerable experience litigating multi-jurisdictional disputes involving the securities, banking, antitrust, and insurance industries. He is fluent in English, French, German, Greek, Russian, and Spanish.

Michael Young is a partner of Allen & Overy LLP based in Paris, and is Co-Head of the Firm's Global Arbitration Practice. He holds undergraduate and graduate law degrees from Cambridge and Oxford Universities, respectively. He is a Vice-President of the ICC Court of Arbitration. Michael represents clients in arbitrations worldwide, and sits frequently as an arbitrator himself. He has also written and spoken widely on arbitration, as well as teaching at Sciences Po and in the Faculty of the University of London LLM programme in Paris.

LIST OF ABBREVIATIONS

AAA	American Arbitration Association
ABA	American Bar Association
ACCL	American College of Construction Lawyers
ACCL J	Journal of the American College of Construction Lawyers
ACIArb	Associate of the Chartered Institute of Arbitrators
ACICA	Australian Centre for International Commercial Arbitration
ACResolution	ACResolution Magazine
ACTL	American College of Trial Lawyers
ADCCAC	Abu Dhabi Commercial Conciliation and Arbitration Centre
ADR	Alternative Dispute Resolution
AGC	Associated General Contractors of America
AIA	American Institute of Architects
AIDA	International Association of Insurance Law (Association Internationale de Droit des Assurances)
AJIL	American Journal of International Law
ALI	American Law Institute
Am Rev Int'l Arb	American Review of International Arbitration
Am U Int'l L Rev	American University International Law Review
Am UL Rev	American University Law Review
App	Appendix
Arb Int'l	Arbitration International
Arbitration	Arbitration: The International Journal of Arbitration, Mediation and Dispute Management
ARIAS	AIDA Reinsurance and Insurance Arbitration Society
Art/Arts	Article/Articles
ASA	Swiss Arbitration Association
ASA Bull	Swiss Arbitration Association Bulletin
Asia Pac L Rev	Asia Pacific Law Review
ATE insurance	after-the-event insurance
Aust YIL	Australian Yearbook of International Law
Austrian ZPO	Austrian Code of Civil Procedure (Zivilprozessordnung)
BAC	Beijing Arbitration Commission
BATNA	best alternative to a negotiated agreement
BCDR	Bahrain Chamber for Dispute Resolution
BCDR Int'l Arb Rev	BCDR International Arbitration Review
BCom	Bachelor of Commerce
Berkeley J Int'l L Publicist	Publicist (Online Publication of the Berkeley Journal of International Law)
BGH	Federal Court of Justice of Germany (Bundesgerichtshof)
BIM	Building Information Modelling
BIT	Bilateral Investment Treaty
BLR	Business Law Review, London
BMLA	British Maritime Law Association
Brooklyn L Rev	Brooklyn Law Review

Brussels Convention	Brussels Convention on Jurisdiction and the Enforcement of Judgments in Civil and Commercial Matters 1968
Brussels I Regulation Recast	Revised Brussels I Regulation No 1215/2012 on Jurisdiction and Enforcement of Judgments in Civil and Commercial Matters
BTE insurance	before-the-event insurance
Buff L Rev	Buffalo Law Review
BUL Rev	Boston University Law Review
Bus Law	The Business Lawyer
BYIL	British Yearbook of International Law
C Arb	Chartered Arbitrator
CAFTA	Central American Free Trade Agreement
Cahiers arb	Cahiers de l'arbitrage (Paris Journal of International Arbitration)
CAM	Arbitration Centre of Mexico
Cambridge LJ	Cambridge Law Journal
CANACO	Mexico City National Chamber of Commerce
CAP	Carolina Academic Press
CBE	Commander of the Most Excellent Order of the British Empire
CCA	College of Commercial Arbitrators
CCBE	Council of Bars and Law Societies of Europe
CCIAG	Corporate Counsel International Arbitration Group
CCIS	Chambers of Commerce and Industry of Switzerland
CEDR	Centre for Effective Dispute Resolution
CEO	chief executive officer
CEPANI	Belgian Centre for Arbitration and Mediation
CFA	conditional fee arrangement
ch/chs	chapter/chapters
CIArb	Chartered Institute of Arbitrators
CIETAC	China International Economic and Trade Arbitration Commission
CII	Construction Industry Institute
Cir	Circuit
CJ	Chief Justice
CJEU	Court of Justice of the European Union
CJICL	Cambridge Journal of International and Comparative Law
CLInt'l	Construction Law International
CLJ	Cambridge Law Journal
CLRC	Criminal Law Revision Committee
CMAA	Construction Management Association of America
COMESA	Common Market for Eastern and Southern Africa
Comp Lab L & Pol'y J	Comparative Labor Law & Policy Journal
Constr Law	The Construction Lawyer
Cornell L Rev	Cornell Law Review
CPR	Civil Procedure Rules (also Centre for Public Resources)
CPS	Crown Prosecution Service
CRCICA	Cairo Regional Centre for International Commercial Arbitration
Cr App R	Criminal Appeal Reports
Crim LR	Criminal Law Review
CUP	Cambridge University Press
CYArb	Czech (& Central European) Yearbook of Arbitration

List of Abbreviations

DAC	Departmental Advisory Committee on Arbitration
DAC Report	The Departmental Advisory Committee on Arbitration (DAC) Report on the Arbitration Bill (February 1996)
DAS	Dispute Appointment Service
DBA	damages-based agreement
Denver UL Rev	Denver University Law Review
DePaul Bus & Comm LJ	DePaul Business & Commercial Law Journal
DePaul L Rev	DePaul Law Review
DIAC	Dubai International Arbitration Centre
DIFC	Dubai International Financial Centre
DIS	German Institution of Arbitration (Deutsche Institution für Schiedsgerichtsbarkeit)
Disp Resol Int'l	Dispute Resolution International
Disp Resol Mag	Dispute Resolution Magazine
DPhil	Doctor Philosophiae (Doctor of Philosophy)
DPIC	Design Professionals Insurance Company
DRA	Dispute Resolution Advisor
DRB	Dispute Review Board
DRBF	Dispute Resolution Board Foundation
DRI	Dispute Resolution International
Duke LJ	Duke Law Journal
ECA	European Court of Arbitration
ECR	European Court Reports
ed/eds	editor/editors
edn	edition
eg	exempli gratia (for example)
EIC	European International Contractors
EJIL	European Journal of International Law
EJST	European Journal of Social Theory
ELF	European Legal Forum
English CPR	Civil Procedure Rules (81st Update)
English Law Commission	Law Commission of England and Wales
etc	et cetera (and so forth)
EU	European Union
EWCA Civ	England and Wales Court of Appeal Civil Division
EWCA Comm	England and Wales Court of Appeal Commercial Division
EWCA Crim	England and Wales Court of Appeal Criminal Division
EWHC	England and Wales High Court
FAA	Federal Arbitration Act
FCIArb	Fellow of the CIArb
FIDIC	International Federation of Consulting Engineers (Fédération Internationale des Ingénieurs-Conseils)
FINRA	Financial Industry Regulatory Authority
FJC	Federal Judicial Center
Fla St UL Rev	Florida State University Law Review
Fordham Int'l LJ	Fordham International Law Journal
Fordham Urb LJ	Fordham Urban Law Journal
French CPC	French Code of Civil Procedure (Code de procédure civile)
FTAC	Foreign Trade Arbitration Commission

List of Abbreviations

Ga J Int'l & Comp L	Georgia Journal of International and Comparative Law
German ZPO	German Code of Civil Procedure (Zivilprozessordnung)
Harv Int'l LJ	Harvard International Law Journal
Harv L Rev	Harvard Law Review
Harv Negot L Rev	Harvard Negotiation Law Review
HGCRA	Housing Grants, Construction and Regeneration Act 1996
HH	His/Her Honour
HKC	Hong Kong Cases
HKCA	Hong Kong Court of Appeal
HKEC	Hong Kong Electronic Citation
HKIAC	Hong Kong International Arbitration Centre
Hofstra L Rev	Hofstra Law Review
HUP	Harvard University Press
IAALS	Institute for the Advancement of the American Legal System
IAI	International Arbitration Institute
IAM	International Academy of Mediators
IBA	International Bar Association
IBA Arb News	International Bar Association Arbitration News
IBA Guidelines on Conflicts of Interest	IBA Guidelines on Conflicts of Interest in International Arbitration (23 October 2014)
IBA Guidelines on Party Representation	IBA Guidelines on Party Representation in International Arbitration (25 May 2013)
IBA Newsletter	Newsletter of the International Bar Association
IBA Rules of Ethics	IBA Rules of Ethics for International Arbitrators 1987
IBA Rules on the Taking of Evidence	IBA Rules on the Taking of Evidence in International Arbitration (29 May 2010)
ibid	ibidem (the same place)
ICAC	International Commercial Arbitration Court
ICC	International Chamber of Commerce
ICC Int'l Ct Arb Bull	ICC International Court of Arbitration Bulletin
ICCA	International Council for Commercial Arbitration
ICDR	International Centre for Dispute Resolution
ICJ	International Court of Justice
ICJ Rep	International Court of Justice Reports
ICLQ	International & Comparative Law Quarterly
ICSID	International Centre for Settlement of Investment Disputes
ICSID Convention	Convention on the Settlement of Investment Disputes between States and Nationals of Other States 1965
ICSID Rev	ICSID Review
ie	id est (that is)
IFCAI	International Federation of Commercial Arbitration Institutions
IJA	International Judicial Academy
IJAA	International Journal of Arab Arbitration
ILA	International Law Association
Ill L Rev	Illinois Law Review
Ind LJ	Indiana Law Journal
Int'l ALR	International Arbitration Law Review
Int'l Constr L Rev	International Construction Law Review

Int'l Law	International Lawyer
Int'l Org	International Organization
IPD	Integrated Project Delivery
J	Mr/Ms Justice
J Disp Resol	Journal of Dispute Resolution
J Econ Lit	Journal of Economic Literature
J Int'l Arb	Journal of International Arbitration
J Leg Stud	Journal of Legal Studies
J Legal Affairs & Disp Res in Eng'g and Constr	Journal of Legal Affairs and Dispute Resolution in Engineering and Construction
J Constr Eng'g & Mngmt	Journal of Construction Engineering and Management
J Manage Eng	Journal of Management in Engineering
J Priv Int'l L	Journal of Private International Law
JAMS	Judicial Arbitration and Mediation Services
JCAA	Japan Commercial Arbitration Association
JCAA Newsletter	Japan Commercial Arbitration Association Newsletter
JCT/CIMAR	Joint Contracts Tribunal Ltd/Construction Industry Model Arbitration Rules 2005
JDI	Journal du Droit International
JIDS	Journal of International Dispute Settlement
Kan JL & Pub Pol'y	Kansas Journal of Law and Public Policy
KCAB	Korean Commercial Arbitration Board
KLRCA	Kuala Lumpur Regional Centre for Arbitration
Ky LJ	Kentucky Law Journal
L Context	Law in Context
Law & Pol'y Int'l Bus	Law and Policy in International Business
LC	Lord Chancellor
LCIA	London Court of International Arbitration
LCJ	Lord Chief Justice
LGDJ	Librairie générale de droit et de jurisprudence
Liverpool L Rev	Liverpool Law Review
LJ	Lord Justice/Lady Justice
LJJ	Lord Justices/Lady Justices
LLB	Legum Baccalaureus (Bachelor of Laws)
LLM	Legum Magister (Master of Laws)
LMAA	London Maritime Arbitrators Association
LNG	liquefied natural gas
Lond Rev Int'l Law	London Review of International Law
LQR	Law Quarterly Review
LSLC	London Shipping Law Centre
MAC	Maritime Arbitration Commission
Marquette L Rev	Marquette Law Review
MCIArb	Member of the CIArb
MDB	Multilateral Development Bank
Mealey's IAR	Mealey's International Arbitration Report
MEDALOA	mediation followed by last-offer arbitration
MFN	most favoured nation

List of Abbreviations

Mich J Int'l L	Michigan Journal of International Law
Minn L Rev	Minnesota Law Review
MLR	Modern Law Review
Monash Uni LR	Monash University Law Review
MR	Master of the Rolls
mt	metric tonnes
n	note
NAFTA	North American Free Trade Agreement
NAI	Netherlands Arbitration Institute
NCL Rev	North Carolina Law Review
NEC	New Engineering Contract
New York Convention	UN Convention on the Recognition and Enforcement of Foreign Arbitral Awards 1958
NGO	non-governmental organization
No	Number (of a Report, etc)
Notre Dame L Rev	Notre Dame Law Review
NY Disp Res Law	New York Dispute Resolution Lawyer
NYIAC	New York International Arbitration Center
NYU J Int'l L & Pol	New York University Journal of International Law and Politics
NYU L Rev	New York University Law Review
NZLJ	New Zealand Law Journal
NZSC	Supreme Court of New Zealand
OAS	Organization of American States
ODR	online dispute resolution
Ohio St J Disp Resol	Ohio State Journal on Dispute Resolution
OUP	Oxford University Press
Panama Convention	Inter-American Convention on International Commercial Arbitration 1975
para/paras	paragraph/paragraphs
PACER	Public Access to Court Electronic Records
PCA	Permanent Court of Arbitration
PCIJ	Permanent Court of International Justice
Penn St L Rev	Pennsylvania State Law Review
Penn St YB Arb & Mediation	Pennsylvania State Yearbook on Arbitration and Mediation
Pepp Disp Resol LJ	Pepperdine Dispute Resolution Law Journal
PRC	The People's Republic of China
Publ Ch	Public Choice
QB	Queen's Bench Division
QC	Queen's Counsel
QMUL Survey	Queen Mary University of London's School of International Arbitration Surveys (2006–15) with Financial Support from PwC or White & Case
r/rr	rule/rules
RAIF	Regional Arbitral Institute Forum

List of Abbreviations

RERA	Dubai Real Estate Registration Agency
Rev arb	Revue de l'arbitrage
s/ss	section/sections
S Cal L Rev	Southern California Law Review
S Tex L Rev	South Texas Law Review
SAA	Swedish Arbitration Act
SC	Senior Counsel
SCC	Arbitration Institute of the Stockholm Chamber of Commerce
sch	schedule
SCL	Society of Construction Law
SDNY	Southern District of New York
SFO	Serious Fraud Office
SGHC	Singapore High Court
SIAC	Singapore International Arbitration Centre
SIArb	Singapore Institute of Arbitrators
Sing YIL	Singapore Yearbook of International Law
SLR	Singapore Law Reports
Stan J Int'l L	Stanford Journal of International Law
STL	Special Tribunal for Lebanon
Straus Institute	Straus Institute for Dispute Resolution
Sup Ct Econ Rev	Supreme Court Economic Review
Swiss Chambers	Swiss Chambers' Arbitration Institution
Swiss PIL Act	Swiss Private International Law Act 1987
Swiss Rules	Swiss Chambers' Arbitration Institution Rules
Syd LR	Sydney Law Review
tbl	Table
TCC	Technology and Construction Court
TDM	Transnational Dispute Management
TOMAC	Tokyo Maritime Arbitration Commission
Transnat'l Law	The Transnational Lawyer
U Ill L Rev	University of Illinois Law Review
U Kan L Rev	University of Kansas Law Review
U Pa J Int'l L	University of Pennsylvania Journal of International Law
U Pa L Rev	University of Pennsylvania Law Review
UAE	United Arab Emirates
UC Davis L Rev	University of California, Davis Law Review
UCLA Pac Basin LJ	UCLA Pacific Basin Law Journal
UK	United Kingdom of Great Britain and Northern Ireland
UKHL	House of Lords of the United Kingdom of Great Britain and Northern Ireland
UKPC	Privy Council of the United Kingdom of Great Britain and Northern Ireland
UKSC	Supreme Court of the United Kingdom of Great Britain and Northern Ireland
UN	United Nations
UNCITRAL	UN Commission on International Trade Law
UNCITRAL Model Law	UNCITRAL Model Law on International Commercial Arbitration 1985

List of Abbreviations

UNIDROIT	International Institute for the Unification of Private Law
Unif L Rev	Uniform Law Review
UNTS	UN Treaty Series
US	United States
USC	United States Code
Vand J Transnat'l L	Vanderbilt Journal of Transnational Law
VIAC	Vienna International Arbitration Centre
Wake Forest L Rev	Wake Forest Law Review
WATNA	worst alternative to a negotiated agreement
Windsor YB Access Just	Windsor Yearbook of Access to Justice
WIPO	World International Property Organization
Wis L Rev	Wisconsin Law Review
WTO	World Trade Organization
XAC	Xi'an Arbitration Commission
Yale J Int'l L	Yale Journal of International Law

THE CHARTERED INSTITUTE OF ARBITRATORS (1915–2015)

The year 2015 marked the 100th anniversary of the CIArb.[1] A hundred years is certainly not a long period of time in the history of an institution. The University of Oxford, for example, has more than 800 years of history. What is remarkable about the first 100 years of the Institute's lifespan is how much has been accomplished. The principal aim of the Institute was to raise the status of a professional arbitrator to a distinct and recognized position among the learned professions, specifically, by means of the study of the law and practice of arbitration.

Prior to the Institute's establishment, there was almost a complete absence of systematic study of this discipline, not only in England, but also in the United States, where arbitration had also found a ground. Notwithstanding the growing popularity of arbitration, and the existence of several different publications, numerous court decisions, and a rather favourable statutory response concerning the use of this mechanism, it is astonishing to find that, within the confines of the common-law arbitration 'renaissance' and, perhaps, long-awaited 'enlightenment' that took place in the second half of the nineteenth century, there were no training opportunities for arbitration enthusiasts.

In 1915, however, the 'Institute of Arbitrators' (as it was then called) assumed a leading role in the promotion of arbitration as a subject of academic and professional concern. The CIArb was the first ever learned society in the world to be devoted to the teaching of what we could describe as 'modern arbitration', the first institution to publish a journal dedicated exclusively to arbitration, the first institution to offer an arbitration-related membership programme, and, equally, the first institution entitled to confer a designated status in the form of post-nominal letters in the area of arbitration, ie ACIArb, MCIArb, FCIArb, and C Arb.

Over the last 100 years, the CIArb has witnessed quite a few changes, not only in the area of 'arbitration', but also in the field of 'international arbitration'. It has also become the alma mater of thousands of 'arbitration'—and 'international arbitration'—students from all around the world. The study of the law and practice of these disciplines has been fundamental to the professionalization of arbitrators and arbitration practitioners. Professionalism has brought about a better understanding of and a much clearer insight into the idea of arbitration, which may have assisted in the adaptation, modernization, and subsequent internationalization of this mechanism.

The most recent 'internationalization of arbitration', which came about with the rapid expansion of international commerce and the adoption of various legislative initiatives, such as the Geneva Protocol (1923), the Geneva Convention (1927), the New York Convention

---

[1] This section has been adapted from Julio César Betancourt, 'The Chartered Institute of Arbitrators (1915–2015): The First 100 Years' (2015) 81(4) Arbitration 375–80.

(1958), the Washington Convention (1965), the UNCITRAL Arbitration Rules (1976), and the UNCITRAL Model Law (1985), resulted in a new and much more sophisticated by-product of arbitration. This new form of arbitration was intended to be used as the primary means of dispute settlement in the international arena, and so a new era of 'international arbitration' was born.

During the last 50 years, the law and practice of international arbitration has grown at an exponential level. No doubt the arbitration profession has gained a foothold on an international scale. Publications on international arbitration abound, and the same can be said about the number of training programmes and international arbitration experts worldwide. This *liber amicorum*—or book of friends—has been written by some of them. These include both practitioners and academics and, indeed, some of the authors are so highly regarded by their peers that they have their own book of friends. These include Bernardo M Cremades, Karl-Heinz Böckstiegel, and Neil Kaplan.

The authors' level of expertise in the subject matter prompted me to enquire further into my job as an editor. In the 1960s, Chapline wrote:

> The function of an Editor is often confused with and limited to the skills of a copy editor, since this is what most journals and textbook publishers provide. The skills of a copy editor include knowledge of the grammatical rules of the language, punctuation conventions, and words and their meanings. But the function of an Editor is more than this: he represents the summation of all the potential readers of the text he is editing, with their diverse but potent faculties for misreading and misunderstanding. He serves his function by reading all copy with great care, seeking all those phrases or sentences which have the seemingly uncanny property of meaning something different from and often exactly opposite to that meant by the author. The perfect editor should be able to so channel the author's meaning as to make it almost impossible to be misinterpreted.[2]

Chapline went on to say: 'The editorial function, in general, is necessary for all kinds of writing; it is extremely difficult, if not impossible, for an author to edit his own work reliably.'[3] However, when you are fortunate enough to learn from and work with many of the most prominent individuals in the field of international arbitration, the task is not as challenging as it might appear. This *liber amicorum* is the product of a very distinguished, highly qualified, and, more importantly, well-published group of specialists in this burgeoning discipline.

Editorial changes were therefore kept to a minimum. Most of them were intended to achieve consistency in style and conform to the 'Oxford Standard for the Citation of Legal Authorities'. Headings and sub-headings were carefully placed throughout the whole publication so that the reader can easily ascertain the purpose of a given section within each chapter. Unnecessarily long paragraphs were broken up so as to improve readability. In this book, the masculine forms 'his' and 'he' are taken to include women too, mainly because, in some cases, it would have been rather difficult to use a singular pronoun to refer to someone without identifying that person as a male or female.

---

[2] J D Chapline, 'The Editorial Function in Scientific Organization' (1960) 3 Engineering Writing and Speech 48.
[3] ibid.

The book has been divided into 14 parts and contains 37 chapters relating to the field of international arbitration. The topics were selected by the authors in order to maximize their creative autonomy. Chapters were subsequently edited and organized in a systematic fashion. The result is an interesting and highly informative collection of topical and contemporary essays that address a broad spectrum of defining issues in the area of international arbitration, ranging from Professor William W Park's hands-on explanation of arbitration law to Professor Martin Hunter's recollection of past events and reflections on future trends.

This project would not have been possible without the participation of the individuals who contributed to this *liber amicorum*. I would like to thank each and every one of them for taking the time to write the relevant chapters. I would also like to thank my editorial team, ie Claudia Pharaon, Elina Zlatanska, Jason Crook, John Lee, and Sabina Adascalitei, for their tireless dedication to the project. Their editorial suggestions were crucial to the final manuscript's preparation. I am grateful to Professor Derek Roebuck, Michael Collett QC, John Tackaberry QC, Simon Nesbitt QC, Lucy Reed, and Alexis Mourre for taking the time to review the final manuscript. Last but not least, I wish to record my appreciation to Oxford University Press, most particularly Faye Mousley, Commissioning Editor, Jamie Berezin, Assistant Commissioning Editor, and the anonymous peer reviewers for their helpful comments.

This book is dedicated to H C Emery, F Malcolm Burr, I W Bullen, A Powells, and A Stevens, founders of the Institute of Arbitrators.

Julio César Betancourt
London, 14 March 2016

Part I

INTERNATIONAL ARBITRATION LAW, ARBITRAL JURISDICTION, AND ARBITRAL INSTITUTIONS

1

EXPLAINING ARBITRATION LAW

William W Park[*]

A. Introduction

(a) A framework for avoiding courts

Most fields of law provide guidance on how courts decide cases. In contrast, arbitration law tells judges when not to decide disputes, in deference to private decision-makers selected by the litigants. Agreements to avoid courts implicate an intricate interaction of treaties, statutes, and cases, which layer themselves like a Russian nested doll, with one carved figure opening to more diminutive figurines. Unlike a *matryoshka*, however, arbitration law often reveals exceptions as capacious as the rule from which they derogate.[1]   **1.01**

(b) Regretted decisions

People can change their minds, or differ in understanding what was agreed. If one side regrets a decision to arbitrate, or the parties diverge about what the arbitration clause covers, courts may be asked to assist in implementing the arbitration agreement or resulting award.   **1.02**

At such moments, arbitration law normally includes two limbs: first, to hold parties to their bargains to arbitrate; second, to monitor the basic integrity of the arbitral process, so the case will be heard by a fair tribunal that listens before deciding, stays within its mission, and respects the limits of relevant public policy. As we shall see, in applying these principles, the devil lurks in the details of each award, ruling, or contract.[2]   **1.03**

---

[*] © William W Park 2016. Adapted from William W Park, *The Role of Law in Arbitration* (OUP 2016), forthcoming.

[1] In a similar metaphor from the epic novel *Moby Dick*, the narrator explains his mental detours: 'Out of the trunk, the branches grow; out of them, the twigs. So in productive subjects grow the chapters'. Herman Melville, 'The Crotch' in *Moby Dick* (1851) ch 63, examining the organization of whaling boats.

[2] Identifying matters decided by arbitrators rather than courts remains distinct from articulating how arbitrators differ from judges in applying law in contract construction. The questions intersect in that legislators may be less inclined to enact arbitration-friendly legal regimes if they perceive arbitrators as prone to disregard law. Notwithstanding the oft-evoked image of 'split-the-baby' arbitrators, arbitrators in international matters may care more than judges about strict legal analysis. Particularly in the commercial realm, as creatures of contract arbitrators show special concern for party expectations evidenced by choice-of-law clauses, and will be less likely than judges to see their roles as advancing social or national policies. See William W Park, 'The Predictability Paradox: Arbitrators and Applicable Law' in Fabio Bortolotti and Pierre Mayer (eds), *The Application of Substantive Law by International Arbitrators* (Dossier XI of the ICC Institute of World Business Law, 2014). For a discussion of arbitrator motivations, see Thomas Schultz and Robert Kovacs, 'The Law is What the Arbitrator Had for Breakfast' in Julio César Betancourt (ed), *Defining Issues in International Arbitration: Celebrating 100 Years of the Chartered Institute of Arbitrators* (OUP 2016) ch 23.

1.04 Arbitration can exist without law, of course. Arbitration involves a dispute resolution process intended as binding by the parties themselves. Nothing stops merchants from making a deal to arbitrate even absent a legal mechanism to enforce the bargain. How courts address the arbitral process remains a question separate from the nature of the process itself, although the matters have understandably been joined, mingled, and blended, even by the best of minds.[3]

1.05 For relatively homogeneous communities, the sanction for breach of an arbitration agreement might lie in social pressures such as shunning or refusal to do business.[4] In a heterogeneous world, however, shame may not work. Moreover, even close-knit groups often seek judicial assistance in resolving property disputes.[5] Courts intervene in faith-based arbitration for Jewish,[6] Muslim,[7] and Christian[8] communities.

1.06 When one side ignores an asserted duty to arbitrate, judicial action may be sought to compel arbitration, to stay litigation, or to enforce awards against a loser's assets. In such instances, questions arise about what the parties agreed and whether proceedings went according to their expectations.[9]

1.07 Although contract principles provide a starting point for analysis, any suggestion that arbitration remains 'just' a matter of contract would seem excessive. Arbitration agreements pave the way for something unpredictable. Third parties called arbitrators—strangers to the agreement—make an award which replaces judicial decision-making. States giving effect to the process will want to monitor its legitimacy, to ensure that losers received due process and the arbitrator respected jurisdictional limits conferred by the litigants.

---

[3] See Wesley A Sturges, 'Arbitration—What Is It?' (1960) 35 NYU L Rev 1031, 1041–5, characterizing arbitration as a 'litigation substitute' so as to trigger Sunday hearing limitations.

[4] See Daniel Markovits, 'Arbitration's Arbitrage: Social Solidarity at the Nexus of Adjudication and Contract' (2010) 59 DePaul L Rev 431; Lisa Bernstein, 'Opting Out of the Legal System' (1992) 21 J Leg Stud 115; Jerold S Auerbach, *Justice without the Law?* (OUP 1983). See also Jan Paulsson, *The Idea of Arbitration* (OUP 2013) 1, speaking of 'binding resolution of disputes accepted with serenity by those who bear its consequences because of their special trust in chosen decision-makers'. For accounts of arbitration before any comprehensive legal framework on the matter, see Bruce Mann, *Neighbors and Strangers: Law and Community in Early Connecticut* (University of North Carolina Press 1987) and William W Park, 'The Cohasset Marshlands Arbitration' (Autumn 2014) ICCA Newsletter.

[5] In *Baker v Fales*, 16 Mass 488 (1820), the court set a framework for resolution of property disputes between Unitarian and Trinitarian elements in Massachusetts churches. For a more modern illustration, see *Serbian Orthodox Diocese v Milivojevich*, 426 US 696 (1976).

[6] See *Soleimany v Soleimany* [1998] EWCA Civ 285, [1999] QB 785. In a dispute between father and son arising from their carpet smuggling business, the English judiciary refused to enforce an award made by a Jewish court, or *Beth Din*, which violated public policy by reason of export control violations. See also *Avitzur v Avitzur*, 58 NY 2d 108 (1983), where a pre-nuptial agreement (*Ketubah*) contained provisions interpreted as analogous to an arbitration agreement, allowing the court to compel arbitration when the husband refused to grant a certificate (*get*) allowing his wife to remarry in the Jewish faith.

[7] In *Jivraj v Hashwani* [2011] UKSC 40, [2011] 1 WLR 1872, two Muslim businessmen agreed that disputes arising from their hotel venture would be decided by Muslim arbitrators who were 'respected members of the Ismaili community'. When one appointed a non-Muslim arbitrator, the other sought to invalidate the appointment. Faced with an argument that the religious requirement violated anti-discrimination law, the UK Supreme Court upheld the clause on the basis that arbitrators are not the parties' employees.

[8] *Spivey v Teen Challenge of Florida*, 122 So 3d 986 (Fla Dist Ct App 2013), involving a wrongful death action on behalf of a son who overdosed after treatment at a Christian rehabilitation programme. The son had signed an agreement for arbitration and mediation providing for prayer at the beginning of the hearings. The court enforced the clause, rejecting arguments that it violated a right to free exercise of religion.

[9] See Alan Scott Rau, 'Arbitral Jurisdiction and the Dimensions of "Consent"' (2008) 24 Arb Int'l 199.

Moreover, recognition of foreign awards can raise delicate questions of deference towards courts of other jurisdictions that may have vacated or confirmed the arbitrator's decision.

1.08 Arbitration statutes fill several functions. First, they send signals to curb judicial hostility towards any perceived 'ouster' of judicial jurisdiction.[10] Second, they enhance predictability in the prerequisites for valid arbitration agreements and awards,[11] without which practitioners would face a procedural morass much like the legal hodge-podge governing court selection and foreign judgments.[12] Finally, an arbitration act provides intellectual hooks on which to hang doctrines useful in addressing recurring problems. For example, the principle of 'separability' reduces prospects of arbitration being sabotaged by fraud allegations unrelated to the arbitration clause itself.[13]

1.09 Not all arbitration laws make arbitration easier than would be the case under general contract principles. Although oral contracts will often be enforced, arbitration law generally requires 'writing' of some sort, sometimes augmented by signature.[14] The requirement makes sense. It is no small matter to forego the proverbial day in court. A legal system that enforces waiver of recourse to judges will want to be sure that both sides really mean it. Of course, once a valid agreement to arbitrate has been found to exist, an arbitration-friendly framework reduces wiggle room for escape.[15]

(c) Hard law and soft law

1.10 Any attempt to explain the specific legal framework for arbitration requires at least a nod towards the question 'what is law', which by its vastness evokes the 'abandon all hope' warning at the door to Dante's 'Inferno'. The task implicates understanding not the law of gravity, the law of averages, or the law of God, but rather the authoritative dispute resolution

---

[10] In an early case involving an attempt at contractual circumvention of supervisory jurisdiction by the English courts, Scrutton J declared: 'There must be no Alsatia in England where the King's writ does not run'. *Czarnikow v Roth, Schmidt & Co* [1922] 2 KB 478, 488. Alsatia referred to a part of London near Fleet Street that had once been a sanctuary for criminals.

[11] For a most thoughtful excursion into how the text of a statute affects decisions on arbitration, see the concurrence by Thomas J in *AT&T Mobility LLC v Concepcion*, 131 S Ct 1740, 1753 (2011), addressing the interaction of ss 2 and 4 in the FAA.

[12] Although the New York Convention now gives international currency to arbitration awards in 156 countries, the Hague Choice of Court Convention 2005 gives similar effect to decisions of national courts. See New York Convention, Art III. See also *M/S Bremen v Zapata Off-Shore Co*, 407 US 1, 9-12 (US 1972), noting that court selection clauses 'have historically not been favored by American courts [and were often declined enforcement] on the ground that they were "contrary to public policy", or that their effect was to "oust the jurisdiction" of the court'.

[13] Separability permits arbitrators to do their job notwithstanding invalidity of the larger contractual framework, with arbitration clause remaining autonomous from the principal agreement. See William W Park, *Arbitration of International Business Disputes* (2nd edn, OUP 2012) 231–95; Alan Scott Rau, 'Everything You Really Need to Know about "Separability" in Seventeen Simple Propositions' (2003) 14 Am Rev Int'l Arb 1; *Prima Paint Corp v Flood & Conklin Mfg Co*, 388 US 395 (1967). Some defects in the contractual framework do affect the arbitration clause, of course, as with forgery or duress. However, if a buyer alleges that a company did not have the assets represented by the seller, that dispute would raise exactly the type of question expected to be resolved under the acquisition agreement's arbitration clause, notwithstanding allegations of misrepresentations which might ultimately lead to invalidation of the transaction.

[14] See, eg, New York Convention, Art II. cf *Kahn Lucas Lancaster v Lark Int'l Ltd*, 186 F 3d 210 (2d Cir 1999) (signature needed for contract with arbitration clause) and *Sphere Drake Ins v Marine Towing*, 16 F 3d 666, 669 (5th Cir 1994) (no signature needed).

[15] The notion of 'arbitration friendly' seems more apt than the oft-used term 'pro-arbitration' policy. The latter may be a misnomer, in that arbitration law relates to recognition of the parties' agreement, whatever that might be, rather than creating an obligation to arbitrate where none existed.

process elaborated through state-sponsored instruments that inform both substantive conduct and the way cases get decided.[16]

1.11 In arbitration, such authority will often be supplemented by the 'soft law' in guidelines of professional associations and the lore of practice, representing expectations of the commercial community. Particularly in cross-border disputes, such norms fill gaps in national standards on evidence and ethics, addressing matters such as document production, witness testimony, and conflicts of interest.[17]

1.12 Not all scholars feel comfortable with a porous membrane between government and non-government authorities. To count as law, some would argue, a decision-making system should clearly bear essential features such as public accessibility, normative coherence, and steadiness over time.[18] In reply to this concern, one might suggest that most human artefacts, including notions of law, vary depending on context. Tennis, squash, baseball, football, and basketball all involve robust physical activity applied to balls. All are called games. Chess involves less physical force and no balls, yet still qualifies as a game. Likewise, the contours of arbitration's legal framework, particularly for international transactions, may be different from the silhouettes of fiscal or banking regulations.[19]

1.13 General principles of arbitration law sometimes find simple application. Courts enforce arbitration agreements between sophisticated merchants covering the quality of grain, but decline to recognize awards procured by bribery or fraud. Although such clear-cut paradigms remain useful for analysis, they limp when applied to complex scenarios, where obvious answers remain elusive. In seeking equilibrium between enforcing bargains and monitoring fairness, arguments may be finely balanced concerning sensitive policies, ill-defined arbitral missions, nuanced facts, or parties with unequal bargaining power.

---

[16] Francophone jurists often distinguish between '*loi*' and '*droit*'. A tyrant's statute ('*loi*') might be law in the sense of an enactment, even if contrary to authoritative norms bearing deeper legitimacy ('*droit*'), not unlike the way American colonists once distinguished among laws and taxes imposed by Great Britain.

[17] For an example of soft law adopted in national court decisions, see *Applied Industrial Materials Corp (AIMCOR) v Ovalar Makine Ticaret Ve Sanayi*, 492 F 3d 132 (2d Cir 2007). Vacating an award for the arbitrator's failure to investigate business contacts with one party's affiliate, the district court made reference to the IBA Guidelines on Conflicts of Interest as well as the AAA Code of Ethics for Arbitrators. See generally William W Park, 'The Procedural Soft Law of International Arbitration' in Loukas Mistelis and Julian D M Lew (eds), *Pervasive Problems in International Arbitration* (Kluwer Law International 2006) 141. Sources of 'soft law' include not only the IBA and AAA pronouncements on ethics, but also guidelines from those bodies on evidence and information exchange, as well as UNIDROIT contract principles, and the LCIA Rules Annex on professional conduct.

[18] In particular, see Thomas Schultz, *Transnational Legality: Stateless Law and International Arbitration* (OUP 2014) 18–19 and Thomas Schultz, 'The Concept of Law in Transnational Arbitral Legal Orders' (2011) 2 JIDS 59, taking aim at the 'École de Dijon', which during the last century introduced into arbitration notions such as 'transnational law' and *lex mercatoria*.

[19] For a survey of law from a wider perspective, see Robert P George, 'What Is Law? A Century of Arguments' (2001) First Things 23, taking as a springboard the 'bad man theory' of Oliver Wendell Holmes presented in a lecture at Boston University, arguing that the best characterization of law would be prediction of what brings the sanction feared by a bad man. Oliver Wendell Holmes, Jr, 'The Path of the Law' (1897) 10 Harv L Rev 457. For an exploration of divisions between domestic and international law, see Jack Goldsmith and Daryl Levinson, 'Law for States: International Law, Constitutional Law, Public Law' (2009) 122 Harv L Rev 1792.

B. From General to Specific

(a) A New Zealand vignette

1.14 A recent decision of the New Zealand Supreme Court illustrates how challenges to arbitration agreements can trigger rival goals, each of which might be extended but for the existence of others.[20] After cancellation of an agreement for sale of farming and hotel assets, the disappointed party blamed its lawyers for mishandling the transaction. When the malpractice claims were arbitrated, both sides participated without complaint. The lawyers prevailed because of the client's inability to prove that attorney negligence caused the deal to fail. The losing side then moved to appeal, or alternatively to have the award set aside.

1.15 The arbitration agreement provided that the award might be challenged on 'questions of law and fact', a provision the court considered an impermissible expansion of relevant law. The New Zealand Arbitration Act permits appeal only for error of law, not mistake of fact.[21] The valid and invalid provisions were deemed incapable of being severed, and the award was set aside. All bets were off, since the parties did not get what they expected, which for the losing party included a chance to re-argue the facts of the case.[22]

1.16 This New Zealand case raised questions similar to those in a leading American decision, but with different results. The US Supreme Court held that federal law precludes appeal on the merits of an arbitrator's determination, no matter what the parties agreed.[23] In this respect, the American and New Zealand approaches converge. In the American case, however, the arbitrator's award was left standing, whereas the New Zealand award was annulled because valid and invalid elements of the agreement intertwined to thwart the parties' expectations.

1.17 The irony of the New Zealand decision will not escape thoughtful observers. Legislators sought to enhance arbitral finality by precluding appeal on questions of fact. In the end, however, the statute led to an award without consequences.

(b) The 'procedural fairness' model of arbitration

1.18 The New Zealand decision serves as a springboard from which to consider several themes in modern arbitration law. Most major business centres have abandoned hostility to arbitration, and have restricted appeal on the legal and factual merits of a case. Any rights of appeal can usually be waived by the parties. On the assumption that an arbitral award should be the end rather than beginning of litigation, the emerging trend grants deference to arbitrators' decisions,[24] while retaining mandatory judicial review only for defects

---

[20] *Carr & Brookside Farm Trust Ltd v Gallaway Cook Allan* [2014] NZSC 75 (Sup Ct New Zealand 2014). See note by John Walton, 'The Supreme Court in *Carr v Gallaway Cook Allan*' (2014) NZLJ 244, calling the case 'a disappointing outcome, but an object lesson all the same'.

[21] For domestic arbitration, appeal is allowed absent an agreement otherwise, while for international arbitration the parties must opt into an appellate regime. In either case appeal is allowed for 'incorrect interpretation of the applicable law', but not on whether the arbitrators drew correct inferences from relevant facts. New Zealand Arbitration Act 1996, sch 2, Art 5(10).

[22] The New Zealand Supreme Court found that the parties' agreed scope of appeal went 'to the heart of their agreement' to submit the dispute to arbitration. See *Carr* (n 20) [70] (McGrath J).

[23] *Hall Street Associates v Mattel, Inc*, 552 US 576 (2008). See also *Kyocera Corp v Prudential-Bache Trade Services*, 341 F 3d 987 (9th Cir 2003).

[24] Where appeal on points of law exists, it will usually derive from the parties' opting in (or failure to opt out) or through special regimes to protect consumers and employees against ill-informed choices.

related to jurisdiction, due process, and public policy.[25] This 'procedural fairness' model resonates with arbitration's treaty architecture, which gives awards an international currency subject to safeguards related to public policy and respect for the limits of arbitral authority.[26]

1.19 In some countries, notably England, the path to the 'procedural fairness' paradigm has been well documented. At one time, English law permitted de facto appeal through a procedure requiring arbitrators to 'state the case' for court determination. On the assumption that the commercial community had little interest in judges second-guessing arbitrators' decisions, the law in 1979 moved to a model in which courts no longer controlled the legal exactness of an award.[27] En route to the current statutory regime, amended again in 1996, the law flirted with a halfway house of merits appeal in maritime, insurance, and commodities cases, where arbitration was deemed of special value in fertilizing development of substantive legal principles.[28]

1.20 Even with arbitration-friendly paradigms, some grounds for challenge remain difficult to define with intellectual rigour.[29] In particular, no easy method exists to trace the line between excess of authority and an arbitrator's simple mistake, the latter normally being a risk assumed when parties agree to arbitrate.[30]

1.21 When law diverges from country to country, the disparity often derives not from discord on policy goals, but by reason of the relative weight given to rival risks. French courts generally delay judicial review of an arbitrator's jurisdiction until an award has been made, to reduce prospects for sabotage by dilatory challenges.[31] In comparison, American courts may assess the validity of an arbitration agreement at any moment, to avoid expensive proceedings that ultimately prove futile.[32]

---

[25] Notable jurisdictions include Belgium, England, France, Hong Kong, the Netherlands, Singapore, Sweden, Switzerland, and the United States, as well as countries that have adopted some form of the 1985 UNCITRAL Model Law such as Australia, Bermuda, Canada, and Germany. See William W Park, 'Jurisdiction to Determine Jurisdiction' in Albert Jan van den Berg (ed), *International Arbitration 2006: Back to Basics?* (ICCA Congress Series No 13, Kluwer Law International 2007) 55.

[26] New York Convention, Art V; ICSID Convention, Arts 52 and 53.

[27] William W Park, 'Judicial Supervision of Transnational Commercial Arbitration: The English Arbitration Act of 1979' (1980) 21 Harv Int'l LJ 87; William W Park, 'The Interaction of Courts and Arbitrators in England' (1998) 1 Int'l ALR 54. Julian D M Lew and others (eds), *Arbitration in England: With Chapters on Scotland and Ireland* (Kluwer Law International 2013).

[28] Appeal on questions of English law exists only if not 'otherwise agreed', with such opt-out allowed by reference to institutional rules. Challenge to awards as of right exists only for defects related to 'substantive jurisdiction' and 'serious irregularity'. English Arbitration Act 1996, ss 67–9.

[29] The English judge Lord Denning once suggested (albeit in an administrative context) that going wrong in law meant exceeding authority, since a tribunal was not authorized to decide in error. See Lord Denning, *The Discipline of the Law* (OUP 1979) 74. This position was rejected by the House of Lords in 2005 in the *Lesotho Highlands* decision. See *Lesotho Highlands Development Authority v Impregilo SpA* [2006] 1 AC 221.

[30] In some instances, challenge may be heard on hybrid grounds such as 'manifest disregard of the law', which falls shy of full appeal, albeit constituting something more than simple excess of authority. See *Stolt-Nielsen SA v AnimalFeeds Int'l Corp*, 559 US 662, 671 (2010). See also 'manifest excess of powers' in ICSID Convention, Art 52(1)(b).

[31] See French CPC, Arts 1448 and 1506.

[32] See *Three Valleys Municipal Water District v EF Hutton*, 925 F 2d 1136 (9th Cir 1991); *Sandvik AB v Advent International Corp*, 220 F 3d 99 (3rd Cir 2000).

(c) Annulled awards: convergence and conflict

1.22 The effect of award annulment remains an enduring source of divergence among legal systems in their assessment of optimum counterpoise among finality, efficiency, and fairness in arbitration. If a Swiss court sets aside an award made in Geneva, should the award be enforceable in Paris or London? To what extent does annulment at the seat of proceedings eliminate or restrict the award's effect in other countries? These questions overlap with, but remain distinct from, the debate on proper grounds for the setting aside at the arbitral seat.

1.23 French courts take a clear position, showing little difficulty giving effect to awards set aside where rendered. On receiving confirmation (*exequatur*), an award enters the French legal order with a *res iudicata* effect that trumps the effect of annulment by the curial courts at the seat of proceedings.[33]

1.24 Some scholars justify such recognition of annulled awards by reference to a free-floating international legal order.[34] Others remain sceptical.[35] Each side of the debate can invoke the rhetoric of regard for the parties' agreement. If litigants bargain to arbitrate, says one side, why defer to a judicial annulment? In reply, the other side can note that most arbitration clauses specify a geographical venue, thus implying expectation of judicial control at the arbitral seat.[36]

1.25 A middle position suggests that sound policy treats annulment decisions like other foreign country money judgments, respected unless reason exists to see the vacating judgment as lacking procedural integrity.[37] Initially suggested in an American law review article,[38] this intermediate view has gained traction in recent case law and scholarship.[39]

---

[33] *Société Hilmarton Ltd v Société OTV*, Cass 1e civ, 23 March 1994, 1994 Rev arb 327, note Charles Jarrosson; *PT Putrabali Adyamulia v Rena Holding Ltd*, Cass 1e civ, 29 June 2007, 2007 Rev arb 507, note Emmanuel Gaillard. See commentary by Philippe Pinsolle, 'The Status of Vacated Awards in France' (2008) 24 Arb Int'l 277; Richard Hulbert, 'When the Theory Doesn't Fit the Facts: A Further Comment on Putrabali' (2009) 25 Arb Int'l 157.

[34] Emmanuel Gaillard, *Aspects philosophiques du droit de l'arbitrage international* (Martinus Nijhoff Publishers 2008), adapted as *Legal Theory of International Arbitration* (Martinus Nijhoff Publishers 2010). cf Jan Paulsson, 'Enforcing Arbitral Awards Notwithstanding Local Standard Annulment' (1998) 9(1) ICC Int'l Ct Arb Bull 14.

[35] Albert Jan van den Berg, 'Enforcement of Arbitral Awards Annulled in Russia' (2010) 27(2) J Int'l Arb 189; and Albert Jan van den Berg, 'Should Setting Aside of the Arbitral Award Be Abolished?' (2014) ICSID Rev 1.

[36] Analogous issues arise for awards confirmed at the arbitral seat but challenged abroad. See *Commissions Imp Exp SA v Republic of Congo*, 2014 WL 3377337 (DC Cir 2014). A Paris award confirmed in England was subsequently presented for enforcement under the District of Columbia Money Judgments Recognition Act. Reversing the lower court, the Court of Appeals held that the FAA does not pre-empt the longer limitations period in the Judgments Act. See also *Island Territory of Curacao v Solitron Devices, Inc*, 489 F 2d 1313 (2d Cir 1973). cf *Dallah Real Estate & Tourism Holding Co v Ministry of Religious Affairs, Government of Pakistan* [2010] UKSC 46.

[37] For an illustration of questionable annulment, see *Telecordia Tech v Telkom SA*, 458 F 3d 172 (3d Cir 2006). An ICC award made in South Africa was vacated by a judge who, instead of letting the ICC name a new arbitrator, constituted a replacement tribunal composed of three retired South African judges nominated by the losing South African side.

[38] William W Park, 'Duty and Discretion in International Arbitration' (1999) 93 AJIL 805.

[39] See discussion below of the *Yukos* and *Pemex* decisions. See ALI, *Restatement (Third) US Law of International Commercial Arbitration, Tentative Draft No 2* (2012) ss 4–16, comment c: 'Though courts in the US ordinarily decline to recognize and enforce awards that have been set aside by a court having proper jurisdiction, the Restatement acknowledges that under the New York Convention and the Panama Convention, a court may in certain exceptional situations confirm, recognize, or enforce an award that has been set aside'.

1.26 Dutch and British courts have adopted this more nuanced view in recent cases arising from the much-publicized *Yukos* saga.[40] An Amsterdam court confirmed awards made in Moscow that had been vacated by Russian courts, reasoning that foreign annulments should be respected only if they meet minimal criteria for procedural due process.[41] Likewise, the English High Court ruled that annulment at the seat of arbitration does not automatically foreclose enforceability abroad under what the Court called an *ex nihilo nil fit* principle. It would be quite unsatisfactory to give effect to judgments that offended basic 'honesty, natural justice and domestic concepts of public policy'.[42]

1.27 American case law has evolved in a similar direction, respecting annulment except upon a showing of irregularity by the vacating court. In 2007, a federal court refused enforcement of an award made in Colombia that had been vacated because local law did not permit arbitration under the ICC Arbitration Rules.[43] Six years later, however, a federal court confirmed a Mexican award notwithstanding annulment in Mexico, reasoning that *ex post* application of Mexican procedural law violated basic notions of due process.[44]

C. Two Case Studies

1.28 The legitimacy of arbitration raises a range of questions touching everything from Sunday hearings[45] to waiver of arbitrator bias,[46] stopping along the way at two matters that persistently vex courts and commentators: (i) allocating tasks between judges and arbitrators; and (ii) determining what law applies to an arbitration clause. These questions were addressed recently in the well-publicized American and British cases discussed below.

---

[40] The Russian energy giant Yukos, once controlled by oligarch Mikhail Khodorkovsky, was declared bankrupt after a tax investigation resulting in its owner being eliminated as a political opponent of Vladimir Putin. In bankruptcy proceedings, Rosneft, an entity controlled by the Russian state, acquired the majority of Yukos' assets, giving rise to multiple arbitrations. The saga drew public attention in July 2014 when awards were issued in three Energy Charter Treaty arbitrations brought against the Russian Federation for which the PCA served as Registry. See Stanley Reed, 'Yukos Shareholders Awarded about $50 Billion in Court Ruling' *NY Times, Int'l Business* (28 July 2014).

[41] *Yukos Capital SARL v OAO Rosneft*, Court of Appeal of Amsterdam (Enterprise Division), 28 April 2009, LJN BI2451 s 3.10, refusing to recognize the Russian annulment. See Lisa Bench Nieuwveld, 'Yukos v Rosneft: The Dutch Courts find that Exceptional 27 Circumstances Exist' (*Kluwer Arbitration Blog*, 11 February 2010) <http://www.kluwerarbitrationblog.com>.

[42] *Yukos Capital SARL v OJSC Rosneft Oil Co* [2014] EWHC 2188 (Comm) (Simon J). An earlier English decision, *Yukos Capital SARL v OJSC Rosneft Oil Co* [2012] EWCA Civ 855 (Rix, Longmore, and Davis LJJ) held that Rosneft (the Russian-controlled entity) was not estopped from objecting to award enforcement in England since public policy issues (the fairness of the Russian annulments) might be decided differently from country to country.

[43] *Termorio SA ESP v Electranta SP*, 487 F 3d 928 (DC Cir 2007), which sounded the death knell of an earlier decision (*Chromalloy v Arab Republic of Egypt*, 939 F Supp 907, DDC 1996) enforcing an award made in Cairo but set aside by an Egyptian court.

[44] *Corporacion Mexicana de Mantenimiento Integral, S de RL de CV v Pemex-Exploracion y Produccion*, 962 F Supp 2d 642 (SDNY 2013), arising from an award made in Mexico in favour of a Mexican subsidiary of a US construction company against a state-owned Mexican petroleum entity.

[45] In *Bauer v Bauer* (No 507082/2013, NY Sup Ct 2014), an inheritance dispute was decided by a *Beth Din* after sitting on Sunday. At the request of the losing side, a Brooklyn judge annulled the award on the basis that arbitrators perform a judicial function and thus must respect s 5 of the New York Judiciary Law, which says that courts may not be open on Sunday. For a similar case decided earlier, but coming to a different result, see *Karapschinsky v Rothbaum*, 163 SW 290 (Mo Ct App 1914).

[46] *Schwartzman v Harlap*, 377 Fed Appx 108 (2d Cir NY 2010).

(a) **Who decides what?**

In *BG Group Plc v Argentina*, the US Supreme Court reviewed an award arising from gas distribution in Buenos Aires.[47] Argentine emergency measures had 'pesified' tariffs by converting dollar-denominated rates into pesos at a third of the original value. An UNCITRAL arbitral tribunal sitting in Washington awarded a British investor US$185 million for violation of the 'fair and equitable treatment' standard in the UK–Argentina investment treaty, which allowed arbitration by an investor, but only 18 months after submitting the dispute to host country courts. Notwithstanding failure to respect the 18-month rule, the arbitral tribunal took jurisdiction, reasoning that the emergency decrees restricted access to the judiciary so as to preclude a literal reading of that provision.

1.29

The award was challenged for excess of authority under the FAA.[48] A majority opinion by the US Supreme Court applied what it described as ordinary contract principles to require deference to the arbitrators' determination of the conditions at issue in the case. The 18-month rule was characterized as a purely procedural matter in the nature of a claims-processing rule governing when the arbitration may begin, not whether it may occur at all.

1.30

A dissent by Chief Justice Roberts reasoned that jurisdictional challenges bear an added layer of complexity for investment treaties and free trade agreements. Each state extends a standing offer to arbitrate, which the investor must accept on terms stipulated by the host country. Until acceptance of the offer, no agreement to arbitrate exists, since the investor was not party to the treaty.[49] It thus falls to courts to decide whether the offer was accepted, which in the instant case required consideration of whether a litigation attempt would have been futile.[50]

1.31

Arguments can certainly be made for an arbitrator's right to determine questions properly characterized as matters of ripeness, *recevabilité*, or admissibility, which may be cured during the arbitration. Much depends on the relevant arbitration provision. One treaty might say that arbitration claims may be filed 'only a year after a local court action has been commenced', while another might say arbitration can begin 'provided that if a court action has been filed the courts shall be given a year to resolve the matter'.

1.32

Whether pursuant to contract or treaty, some procedural steps remain essential to contract formation, and as such constitute preconditions to arbitral authority, while others do not.[51]

1.33

---

[47] 134 S Ct 1198 (2014). See Larry Shore and Amal Bouchenaki, 'Note' (2012) Cahiers arb 675; Brief for Professors and Practitioners as *Amici Curiae* Supporting Petitioner, *BG Group Plc v Argentina* (No 12-138).

[48] A different result might be obtained in arbitration conducted under the ICSID Rules, which enhance award finality by precluding challenge under the law of the arbitral seat, instead providing for consideration of the request for annulment by an *ad hoc* committee convened by ICSID. See ICSID Convention, Arts 52 and 54, the latter providing for award recognition in the same way as a judgment of the state where relied upon.

[49] For investment treaty arbitration, it might be possible that the contracting nations agree that alleged jurisdictional flaws be evaluated by some third body, whether a tribunal seized of the claim or an institution supervising the proceedings as happens in *ad hoc* review pursuant to Art 52 of the ICSID Convention. Whether such designation happens will depend on the facts of each case.

[50] In this connection, the concurring opinion of Sotomayor J urged that close attention be paid to expressions of intent as articulated by the treaty partners: 'if the local litigation requirement at issue here were labeled a condition on the treaty parties' consent to arbitrate, that would ... change the analysis as to whether the parties intended the requirement to be interpreted by a court or an arbitrator'. See *BG Group* (n 47) 1214.

[51] If a house-painting contract is offered on condition that the contractor post a bond, the painter cannot say that the contract's arbitration clause became effective although the bond was rejected. By contrast, if

Likewise, arbitrators possess discretion on some procedural matters, but not others.[52] Sound analysis requires attention to the facts of each case, along with the language and structure of the contract or treaty allegedly creating arbitral authority. Dispute resolution will be ill-served if judges and lawyers simply incant catchphrases about procedural conditions.

(b) What law applies?

1.34 On occasion, the law governing an agreement to arbitrate may differ from the legal principles applicable to other aspects of the parties' commercial relationship. *SulAmérica v Enesa Engenharia* involved claims under two insurance policies relating to construction of a hydroelectric plant in Brazil. English courts were asked to restrain litigation in Brazil.[53]

1.35 At first blush, applicability of English law seems odd. The contracts were concluded among Brazilian companies, with express choice of Brazilian law and exclusive jurisdiction given to Brazilian courts. Recourse to the law of England becomes more plausible, however, given the parties' agreement to arbitrate in London. The insurers commenced arbitration in order to contest liability, whereas the insured began a court action in Brazil. In considering whether to enjoin the Brazilian litigation, the English court had to decide what law governed the parties' agreement to arbitrate.[54]

1.36 The court reasoned that an arbitration clause might be subject to a law different from that of the substantive contract. The parties had not expressly chosen a law to govern the arbitration clause itself. Rejecting an implied choice of Brazilian law, the court found the law of England, as the seat of the arbitration, to have the most real connection with the question presented, and upheld the anti-suit injunction restraining the litigation.

1.37 Not all choice-of-law questions will be answered in favour of the arbitral seat. In one American case, a boat owner brought an action against a salvage company seeking indemnity or contribution for damages to a coral reef.[55] The court denied the salvage company's motion to compel arbitration, finding that US federal law, not English law as provided in the contract, applied to determine whether parties had agreed to arbitrate.

---

the contract provided for painting the second floor after payment for the first floor, a dispute about whether the first floor had been painted would fall to the arbitrator. See argument by counsel for Argentina, Oral Argument Transcript 2 December 2013, 51–2.

[52] If an adequate advance on cost must be deposited before proceedings begin, arbitrators would normally be the ones to decide what amount will be sufficient. By contrast, if the contract or treaty requires arbitration in Washington pursuant to the UNCITRAL, it would be a brave judge indeed who would defer to an arbitrator's decision to hear proceedings in Paris under the ICC Arbitration Rules, absent some special circumstance or further agreement by the parties.

[53] *SulAmérica Cia Nacional de Seguros SA v Enesa Engenharia SA* [2012] EWCA Civ 638.

[54] The notion of one proper law to govern an agreement's material validity, scope, and interpretation has deep roots in English legal thinking. With respect to arbitration agreements, the relevant principles have often been summarized through reference to r 57 of the Dicey, Morris, and Collins treatise on conflicts of law. For an exploration of the limits of this approach, see William W Park, 'Rules and Standards in Private International Law, Review Essay of Dicey, Morris and Collins on the Conflict of Laws (Sir Lawrence Collins, 14th edn)' (2007) 73(4) Arbitration 441.

[55] *Cape Flattery Ltd v Titan Maritime*, 647 F 3d 914 (9th Cir 2011). The contract provided that '[a]ny dispute arising under this Agreement shall be settled by arbitration in London, England, in accordance with the English Arbitration Act 1996 and any amendments thereto, English law'. The clause was interpreted to cover only disputes relating to interpretation and performance of the agreement itself.

D. Shifting Images of Arbitration

One challenge in explaining arbitration law lies in the dramatically divergent images evoked **1.38**
by arbitration. All may be correct, yet inadequate—in a way reminiscent of the Hindu parable
of blind men who experience an elephant differently depending on the parts being touched: a
wall (the side), a snake (the trunk), a tree (the knee), a fan (the ear), or a rope (the tail).[56]

Arbitrators determine billion dollar international investment claims. In some countries, **1.39**
they also hear claims related to student loans, credit card debt, consumer sales, and employment discrimination. Arbitrators address disputes arising from construction projects,
baseball salaries, biotech licences, uncompensated expropriation, automobile franchises,
liability insurance, and Internet domain names. Not surprisingly, the values that commend arbitration in transactions concluded by sophisticated business managers may seem
ill-placed when an arbitral clause sends poorly informed consumers to seek an uncertain
remedy in an inaccessible venue. In consequence, scholarly and judicial debate on arbitration often resemble the proverbial ships passing in the night, with different camps clinging
to contrasting notions of what remains at stake.

In a sense, arbitration has become a victim of its own success, with new frontiers creating new **1.40**
criticism.[57] Disputes decided by arbitration run far beyond traditional stomping grounds
of shipping, insurance, and merchant-to-merchant sales. Arbitrators address patent validity,
Olympic events,[58] and income tax allocations.[59] In the United States, with its distinctive legislative tradition,[60] arbitration can involve class actions,[61] sports doping,[62] beauty pageants,[63]
and trade unions grievances, the last being an outgrowth of labour's distrust of judges.[64]

---

[56] The poem by John Godfrey Saxe, 'The Blind Men and the Elephant', ends with the line, 'Though each was partly in the right, And all were in the wrong!'
[57] See William W Park, 'Arbitration's Discontents' in Louis D'Avout (ed), *Mélanges en l'honneur du Professeur Bernard Audit* (LGDJ 2014). One recent book carries a dedication page, 'For the Millions of Americans Unjustly Bound by an Arbitration Agreement'. See Imre Szalai, *Outsourcing Justice: The Rise of Modern Arbitration Laws in America* (CAP 2013), which started with a story about arbitration over rape in Baghdad. Compare a less sensationalized treatment of the subject in Ian R Macneil, *American Arbitration Law* (OUP 1992).
[58] Antonio Rigozzi, *L'arbitrage international en matière de sport* (Helbing & Lichtenhahn 2005); Gabrielle Kaufmann-Kohler, *Arbitration at the Olympics* (Kluwer Law International 2001).
[59] William W Park and David R Tillinghast, *Income Tax Treaty Arbitration* (Sdu Fiscale & Financiele Uitgevers 2004); William W Park, 'Arbitrability and Tax' in Loukas Mistelis and Stavros Brekoulakis (eds), *Arbitrability* (Kluwer Law International 2008) 179; Marcus Desax and Marc Veit, 'Arbitration of Tax Treaty Disputes: The OECD Proposal' (2007) 23 Arb Int'l 405.
[60] See Christopher Drahozal, 'In Defense of Southland: Reexamining the Legislative History of the Federal Arbitration Act' (2002) 78 Notre Dame L Rev 101.
[61] See, eg, *American Express Co v Italian Colors Rest*, 133 S Ct 2304, 2309 (2013); Laurence Tribe and Joshua Matz, *Uncertain Justice: The Roberts Court and the Constitution* (Henry Holt & Co 2014) 291–9; William W Park, 'La jurisprudence américaine en matière de "class arbitration": entre débat politique et technique juridique' (2012) 3 Rev arb 507.
[62] On 5 August 2013 Major League baseball announced the 211 game suspension of New York Yankees player Alex Rodriguez for use of steroids. The Uniform Player's Contract signed by major league players contains a grievance procedure which includes an agreement to arbitrate.
[63] *Miss Universe LP v Monnin*, 952 F Supp 2d 591 (SDNY 2013). A disappointed Miss Pennsylvania, failing to reach the finals and losing to Miss Rhode Island, charged the pageant was rigged.
[64] Concern about judicial hostility to trade unions led to arbitration of collective bargaining agreements in the United States, albeit on a statutory foundation separate from that of the FAA. See Taft-Hartley Labor-Management Relations Act, s 301, 29 USC s 185 (2003).

1.41 Notwithstanding its diversity and chameleon-like character, in all its forms the core of arbitration involves renunciation of otherwise competent courts in favour of a binding private adjudication. Such renunciation may be explained by a multitude of narratives.[65] In international disputes, arbitration enhances more level playing fields. In construction and insurance, the goal might be expertise. In the United States, arbitration removes disputes from the perceived vagaries of civil juries.

1.42 Inevitably, conclusions about why people arbitrate bear on how the law develops. In a case involving consumer cellphone contracts, the US Supreme Court struck down, as inconsistent with the purposes of arbitration, a California rule that had invalidated waivers of class arbitration. The rule was deemed to run afoul of the goals of arbitration, a conflict summarized as follows: 'class arbitration sacrifices the principal advantage of arbitration —its informality—and makes the process slower, more costly, and more likely to generate procedural morass than final judgment'.[66]

1.43 Careful thinkers may scratch their heads at the assertion that informality constitutes arbitration's 'principal advantage' in an era when arbitration routinely serves to decide complex international investment cases which often unfold like judicial proceedings. A more sensible summary might be taken from language in an earlier Supreme Court case, which spoke of arbitration as a process to avoid 'unseemly and mutually destructive jockeying by the parties to secure tactical litigation advantages'.[67]

E. Conclusion

1.44 One Nobel Prize winner suggested that understanding a subject means reducing it to a 'freshman level' of simplicity.[68] Such plain speaking will have obvious limits, of course. The best-chosen words connect themselves sequentially through human grammar, while the reality of legal doctrine implicates a multitude of caveats and exceptions that remain obstinately simultaneous in nature.

1.45 Hemmed by this caution, a tentative explanation of arbitration law suggests tension between two sets of expectations. First, courts should give effect to arbitration commitments obtained through informed consent. Second, judges must monitor arbitration's basic procedural integrity, which includes impartial arbitrators who hear before deciding and

---

[65] Even within a single field, such as investor-state arbitration, conflicting models present themselves. See Anthea Roberts, 'Clash of Paradigms: Actors and Analogies Shaping the Investment Treaty System' (2013) 107 AJIL 45; Joost Pauwelyn, 'At the Edge of Chaos: Foreign Investment Law as a Complex Adaptive System' (2014) 29 ICSID Rev 372; Charles N Brower, 'Investomercial Arbitration' (2014) 80(2) Arbitration 179. cf Gus van Harten, 'Investment Arbitrators' Evident Lack of Restraint' (2014) 5 JIDS 1.

[66] *AT&T Mobility LLC v Concepcion*, 131 S Ct 1740 (2011), 1751–3 (Scalia J).

[67] *Scherk v Alberto-Culver*, 417 US 506 (1974), echoed in a later case deciding that the New York Convention trumped the US Bankruptcy Code's automatic stay of arbitration. See *Sonatrach v Distrigas Corp*, 80 BR 606 (Bankr D Mass 1987), where Judge Young concluded: 'It is important and necessary for the United States to hold its domiciliaries to their bargains and not allow them to escape their commercial obligations by ducking into statutory safe harbors.'

[68] Attributed to Richard Feynman, winner of the 1965 Nobel Prize for Physics, who in his day combined academic recognition with an eccentric persona that created a wide public following.

respect both contractual limits of their authority and relevant public policy. The role of arbitration law thus aims to enhance the rule of law in its broadest sense, seeking balance between respect for parties' agreement and the correlative judicial duty to monitor fairness in the process. Thus conceived, arbitration law will serve to promote the type of economic cooperation enhanced by reliable vindication of *ex ante* expectations.

2

EXPERIENCES AND SUGGESTIONS REGARDING THE FUNCTIONING OF INTERNATIONAL ARBITRATION INSTITUTIONS

Karl-Heinz Böckstiegel

A. Introduction

2.01 It was with pleasure that I agreed to contribute to this *liber amicorum* celebrating 100 years of the CIArb. The Institute can proudly look back to not only a long, but also very impressive, period of accomplishments in the field of arbitration, first in the United Kingdom and also now for a long period at the international level. Others in this book are better informed to go into the details of these accomplishments and will do so in this book. My own personal close relationship with the CIArb was during my tenure as the Patron of the CIArb from 2007 to 2010. It was an experience I would not have wanted to miss.

2.02 If I compare the present role and activities of the CIArb and the environment of international arbitration in general to the situation at the time I contributed to the Millennium Edition of the Journal of CIArb dealing with 'Some Major Changes in International Arbitration: The Past, the Perspective', one is impressed by the many changes one has to note.[1]

2.03 As agreed with the editor, my contribution to this publication will focus on the role of institutions in international arbitration in general and on my own close experiences in this regard as an active arbitrator under the rules of many arbitral institutions throughout the world and also as President of the Iran–United States Claims Tribunal at The Hague, as President of the LCIA, and as President of the DIS.

B. General Aspects on the Role of Arbitral Institutions

(a) Institutional v *ad hoc* arbitration

2.04 Both in commercial and investment arbitration, the principal choice is between institutional and *ad hoc* arbitration. And in fact, both of these choices are frequently found in practice.

---

[1] Karl-Heinz Böckstiegel, 'Some Major Changes in International Arbitration: The Past, the Perspective' (1999) 65(4) Arbitration 244.

2.05 Commercial contracts, by their arbitration clauses, mostly express a choice for just one of these two options and, in practice, the large majority seems to choose institutional arbitration. In contrast, investment contracts between a state and a foreign investor, as well as bilateral investment treaties (BITs), often provide for a choice of several kinds of arbitration, for institutional arbitration under the rules of several arbitral institutions, and also for *ad hoc* arbitration, the latter mostly with a reference to the UNCITRAL Arbitration Rules.

2.06 The simple choice for *ad hoc* arbitration, sometimes found in domestic contracts, seems to be very rare in international contracts and state treaties. This is for obvious reasons: on the one hand, domestic arbitration clauses can rely on the domestic arbitration law of a particular state as a framework for the arbitral process and the parties will mostly be ready to do so. On the other hand, for international arbitrations, there is no such generally accepted and applicable framework—the New York Convention only deals with the recognition and enforcement of awards, and the parties from different national backgrounds will most often try to avoid the unwarranted interference of the national courts at the seat of arbitration.

2.07 Therefore, if for some reason the parties cannot agree on an arbitral institution, the compromise often found is the choice of the UNCITRAL Arbitration Rules, as they provide for *ad hoc* arbitration, but nevertheless a framework for the procedure. And in particular, they provide a default procedure in case a party does not appoint an arbitrator or an arbitrator is challenged, by authorizing an appointing authority selected by the parties or otherwise the PCA at The Hague to take decisions in this regard if the parties do not cooperate or cannot agree.

2.08 This shows already that, unless the parties are ready to accept the default provisions of the domestic law at the seat of arbitration which will normally authorize the domestic courts, they have to select institutional arbitration or at least the UNCITRAL Arbitration Rules, including their appointing authority.

(b) Different roles of arbitral institutions

2.09 If one turns to administered—or institutional—arbitration and to the arbitral institutions available, I will not enter into the very subjective discussion regarding which is 'the best' arbitral institution, one reason being that, as you will see, there is no general answer.

2.10 First of all, I think one can indeed distinguish between institutions which are well fit for international arbitration procedures and others which are not. Even if one neglects the many institutions that have been founded with ambitious claims, but are never chosen in practice, one could make a distinction among the well-known arbitral institutions. Over my many years in the field, I have gathered experience as an arbitrator in most of these institutions and, without mentioning names here, there are certainly some which did not seem to be well fit for or efficient in conducting international arbitral procedures. To some extent, this negative experience was due to the staff of the institution not being sufficiently trained or at least not being familiar with the specifics of international arbitration, and to some extent also due to organizational deficiencies such as limited lists of arbitrators or specific rules or formalities not fit for the practical demands of international arbitral procedures.

2.11 Conversely, international institutions such as the ICC, the LCIA, the PCA, or ICSID, as well as nationally based institutions also administering international arbitrations, such as the DIS, SCC, Swiss Chambers, and VIAC, have in my experience over many years displayed efficiency in the cases referred to them. Among these recommendable arbitral institutions, the choice must depend on the objective criteria which are most relevant to the parties. In this context, one should note first that the rules of these institutions are rather similar as they have been modernized and adapted to the development of international arbitral practice.

2.12 But there remain some important differences, particularly regarding the degree of involvement of the institution in their respective procedures. The greatest regulatory involvement is probably found in the ICC Arbitration Rules, including their latest version recently set in place, by the involvement of the ICC Court at the beginning of the procedure, by the terms of reference, and at the end of the procedure by the scrutiny of the draft award. But the ICC Secretariat, though informed on the progress of the procedure, will usually not get involved in the case management and the communications between the parties and the tribunal.

2.13 To the contrary, in ICSID cases, the Secretariat will be the continuing channel of communication between the parties and the tribunal, and, of course, the ICSID Convention provides for an annulment procedure after an award is issued.

2.14 The PCA, in its more recent development into a leading arbitral institution, though mostly active under the UNCITRAL Arbitration Rules and the wide discretion they give the arbitral tribunal, is not infrequently chosen to assist the tribunal in the administration of particularly large and complex cases. Similarly, the LCIA, as well as the nationally based arbitral institutions also regularly chosen for international disputes, provide probably the widest discretion of the parties and the tribunal regarding case management and shaping the procedure so it is made to measure to the respective particularities of the case.

2.15 And, of course, there are the different methods and scales for the remuneration of the arbitrators which may be considered relevant and may have varying impacts depending on the particularities of the case. Here, the major principle distinction is between the remuneration being based on the amount in dispute or on an hourly rate. Views on this can be a matter of subjective judgment and personal background. But, indeed, it may also make considerable practical differences depending on the case, the amount in dispute, and the volume of work and time required from the arbitrators.

2.16 In the context of continuing complaints over arbitration becoming too expensive, let me add that, as statistics show and as has been particularly well confirmed at the 2011 IFCAI Conference in Berlin, one should be aware that regularly more than 90 per cent of the arbitration costs are costs incurred and caused by the parties themselves for counsel, witnesses and experts, their battles of documents, etc, on which the influence of the arbitral institutions is rather limited. Any charges to cover the very small percentage going towards the administrative fee of the institution and the fees of the arbitrators, therefore, will have a relatively small impact on the general level of arbitration costs.[2] And, if one considers whether there may indeed be some influence exerted by the institution or the arbitrators to reduce the more than 90 per cent of the parties' costs, any effort for a slimmer procedure will

---

[2] For a discussion of the costs of international arbitration, see Joe Tirado and others, 'The Costs and Funding of International Arbitration' in Julio César Betancourt (ed), *Defining Issues in International Arbitration: Celebrating 100 Years of the Chartered Institute of Arbitrators* (OUP 2016) ch 26.

soon meet the limitation of the understandable desire and due process right of the parties and their counsel to fully present their case as they consider necessary.

In view of all these criteria and options, one obviously cannot generally say that, among the institutions available for efficient administration of cases, one is better than the other. It is up to the parties to decide which of the specific distinctions just indicated are most relevant to them for a particular contract, arbitration clause, and case. **2.17**

C. Personal Experiences in Some Institutions

While my above considerations reflect experiences of a more general kind as an active arbitrator, I can add a few experiences in administrative functions I have held in certain institutions. **2.18**

(a) The Iran–United States Claims Tribunal

The Iran–United States Claims Tribunal at The Hague is hardly comparable to the many other institutions of international arbitration. Though it works under an adapted version of the UNCITRAL Arbitration Rules, it was created after the Iranian Revolution by an international treaty between the two states as a permanent body to deal with the more than 4,000 cases which were excluded thereby from the jurisdiction of their domestic courts. In the present context, I cannot go into details of the functioning of the Tribunal, with its Full Tribunal and its three chambers of three judges each. **2.19**

From the very beginning, it was—and it still is—a highly politicized body between two states which still do not have diplomatic relations to this day. But it illustrates that even in such a hostile relationship, judicial functioning and a peaceful settlement of disputes is possible and that international arbitration can serve well in such an environment. **2.20**

There were drawbacks: when I was asked to become the President of the Tribunal in 1984, physical attacks by two Iranian judges against one of the three neutral judges had resulted in a breakdown of the functioning of the Tribunal and it took me three months to get the Tribunal working again on its heavy caseload. While this was achieved, the continuing tensions made almost every administrative decision difficult, and judicial decisions by procedural orders and awards could frequently only be taken by majority and were objected to by dissenting opinions from both Iranian and US judges. Nevertheless, most of the cases could be processed and decided and only very few public international law disputes between the two governments are presently still pending. **2.21**

(b) The LCIA

The LCIA is, of course, quite a different institution with a very long tradition, though it only became active again under the leadership and presidency of Sir Michael Kerr. When, after Sir Michael, I was asked to become the first non-English president, the LCIA had already established its name as an institution for international commercial arbitration. Since then, the caseload has increased continuously, and new activities such as the frequent, very popular international colloquia at Tylney Hall and in many venues throughout the world have provided for exchanges between practitioners of international arbitration. **2.22**

During my presidency, the LCIA was the first institution to organize a group of young arbitration practitioners and academics. This then became a general trend for most institutions and **2.23** today we have very effective networks of this kind throughout the world, which contribute to the promotion of international arbitration. Another notable development is that not only has the LCIA had non-English presidents after my resignation from that function, but also the LCIA Court and Board have fully international membership from many regions of the world. I was impressed, and—in my function as an active Honorary President of the Court—still am, by the readiness of so many extremely busy colleagues to devote time and work to the LCIA.

2.24 A specific experience as President was the function of coordinating the decisions of the LCIA Court on appointments of and challenges against arbitrators. These tasks were accomplished without delay with the very valuable help of members of the Court, and the considerations in these decisions have been made available to the public to provide information and guidance to the parties and their counsel. This is an approach different from that taken by the ICC and other institutions.

(c) The DIS

2.25 While the LCIA, though based in London, is an international institution, the DIS is of course a national one. Its membership is mostly from Germany—the Chambers of Commerce, other national organizations of the legal and business community, and a majority formed by lawyers, law firms, and academics. But there is also a considerable number of members from outside Germany.

2.26 Since the DIS Arbitration Rules are applicable to both domestic and international disputes, and are available in all major languages, proceedings can be held in any language and, in fact, a considerable portion of the DIS caseload involves non-German parties and counsel. My experiences during my 16 years as President of the DIS are to some extent comparable to those at the LCIA in so far as certain typical administrative functions are concerned, such as appointment of and challenges against arbitrators.

2.27 The legal basis is obviously different as Germany has adopted the UNCITRAL Model Law which contains a number of features different from the English Arbitration Act 1996. A specific difference is that, similarly to ICC arbitration, the administrative fee for the DIS and the fees of the arbitrators are based on the amount in dispute, though some flexibility is provided for. Another difference is that the DIS Rules, in the same way as German arbitration law, encourage the arbitrators to offer any help they can in amicable settlements of the dispute, even during the arbitral procedure, if the parties to the dispute so wish. This is an option which the parties frequently use in the practice of domestic procedures and to some extent also international procedures.

D. Some Suggestions to Improve Efficiency

2.28 Finally, let me add some suggestions as to how the work of arbitral institutions may be improved according to my personal experiences.

(a) Efficient staff at the institution

2.29 Only after I had several times experienced the kind of difficulties that can arise, if the tribunal is faced with incompetent staff, did I realize how much the efficient and speedy management of a procedure can be jeopardized. Obviously, this is even more so the more the institution is involved in the conduct of the procedure. But even at the start of the procedure, in the management and control of arbitration costs and respective timely deposits, and at the end of the procedure, much can go wrong. In this context, the particular problem seems to be that the institution's staff are not sufficiently qualified or at least not sufficiently familiar with the particular demands of international as compared to domestic arbitration.

(b) Flexibility of the procedure within the framework of the rules

2.30 Quite often, staff not sufficiently familiar with the particularities of international arbitration will stick to particular routines and formalities they have seen before at the domestic level and not understand or be ready to use the discretion provided by the rules of the institution to shape the procedure. Thereby, one of the great advantages of arbitration as compared to courts is lost, namely the ability to adapt the individual procedure to most efficiently deal with the specific demands of the case.

(c) Informal exchange with the institution

2.31 While, obviously, the rules of every arbitral institution provide a framework for what are the respective functions of the institution, the parties, and the arbitrators in the conduct of the procedure, in practice it may sometimes be easier, and cause fewer complications and delay, if an informal prior exchange can take place with regard to either the interpretation of certain provisions in the rules or regarding their practical application in similar earlier cases. But again, such an informal interaction can only be successful if experienced participants are on both sides of such an exchange. And, of course, the mandatory transparency must be maintained so as not to give one party an advantage over the other.

(d) Involve the parties beyond what is mandatory

2.32 Again, while respecting the fact that the rules of every arbitral institution provide a framework for what are the functions of the institution, of the parties, and of the arbitrators in the conduct of the procedure, I would suggest that both the institution and the arbitrators should make an effort to get prior comments from the parties, before major procedural decisions are taken and issued. For the institutional side, an example is that the ICC Court regularly indicates in advance to the parties if it has the intention to raise the deposit for arbitration costs, before indeed the decision is issued. As an example for the tribunal side, it may often be wise to send a draft of a procedural order No 1 ruling on the further procedure, or of the procedural order deciding the details of an upcoming hearing, to the parties asking for comments, and perhaps also to the institution, to make sure that no essential element or particularity of the case is overlooked.

E. Conclusion

2.33 Finally, permit me to convey a rather subjective recommendation: I suggest that all those involved in the interaction between the institution, the parties, and the tribunal suppress their egos as much as possible. Not infrequently have I experienced in disputes that the communication and a possible agreement were hindered, delayed, or even prevented by some participants considering it a personal offence that their views were not accepted. Sometimes, arbitrators of great reputation and experience, or who were in very high positions in their work outside of the arbitration field, considered it a lack of 'respect' if other participants in the exchange took a different view. And sometimes, a barrister or other high-level counsel for a party did not seem to be able to accept that the procedure was to proceed in a fashion he was not used to. And again sometimes, the representative of the arbitral institution seemed to be offended and unable to accept that a particular procedural decision was not following 'what had always been done'.

2.34 My suggestion to all involved in the interaction is, no matter how much experience you have, to listen, keep an open mind, and be ready for compromise, if it serves the smooth conduct of the procedure within the applicable rules.

3

THE NEW 2014 LCIA RULES
An Introductory Explanation

*V V Veeder**

A. Introduction

The LCIA is more than 120 years old. It was previously known by different names and sheltered for part of its long life in London under the protective wing of the CIArb. These two antiquarians, if not actual nestlings, share the same historical and geographical origins, providing arbitration services to domestic and international communities in England and around the world.[1]   **3.01**

B. The LCIA Rules

(a) A modest beginning

The LCIA's first arbitration rules were relatively modest. In olden days, under the English Arbitration Act 1889, it sufficed for an arbitration agreement under English law to so provide with the single word 'arbitration'; and, for an institutional arbitration serving a homogeneous business community, only a few additional provisions were necessary. The LCIA's later arbitration rules were equally succinct. The major changes began with the successive editions of the LCIA Rules in 1981, 1985,[2] 1998, and, most recently, 2014. The LCIA's 2014 Rules came into force on 1 October 2014.[3]   **3.02**

Each of these later editions set out in increasing detail the procedures for an LCIA arbitration, nonetheless retaining its traditional features. The LCIA's emphasis remains on referring   **3.03**

---

* All views regarding the LCIA Rules here expressed are personal to the author and should not be attributed to the LCIA. The author acknowledges with appreciation the work performed by the LCIA Court, the LCIA registry, and his fellow members of the LCIA Court's sub-committee responsible for drafting the LCIA's 2014 Rules, from which much has been gratefully borrowed for the purpose of this contribution.

[1] The LCIA was founded in 1891 by the Corporation of the City of London and the London Chamber of Commerce, after the failure of the Bramwell Arbitration Code culminating in the English Arbitration Act 1889. These sponsors were joined later (in 1975) by the CIArb. The LCIA became an independent arbitral institution in 1985/1986. See generally Edward Manson, 'The City of London Chamber of Arbitration' (1893) 9 LQR 86; and Michael Kerr, 'The London Court of International Arbitration 1892–1993' (1992) 8 Arb Int'l 317.

[2] Before 1985, the LCIA Rules were known as the London Court of Arbitration Rules.

[3] The LCIA's 2014 Rules are published on the LCIA website <http://www.lcia.org> accessed 25 September 2015.

the parties' dispute to the arbitral tribunal as soon as practicable, with the early formation of the tribunal, the immediate reference to that tribunal of questions of jurisdiction, and the fullest freedom of the parties to tailor their arbitration's procedure to the particular characteristics of their dispute. These features are intended to avoid many of the delays that can often follow the commencement of an international arbitration.

3.04 Thereafter, the conduct of an LCIA arbitration lies largely in the hands of the tribunal in consultation with the parties, with many of its arbitration rules operating as suggestions in default of agreement or order otherwise (such as Article 15). During the arbitration, the LCIA Court (with the LCIA registry) operates 'administration-lite' functions, save for the appointment (and removal) of arbitrators and the interim payment of arbitral fees. At the end of the arbitration, the LCIA Court fixes the costs of the arbitration (ie the tribunal's fees and the LCIA's own administrative charges); but the LCIA Court plays no part in reviewing the tribunal's award. From the beginning to the end of an LCIA arbitration, the parties are encouraged with the tribunal to settle their own procedures for what is their arbitration, with the LCIA Rules' default procedures operating only in the absence of such agreement (subject to mandatory minimum procedural safeguards).

3.05 The 1981 Rules were drafted by the CIArb's International Arbitration Committee (then chaired by Lord Steyn) under the guidance of Paul Sieghart, creating for the first time a regime for international users. The 1985 Rules were prepared by the LCIA Court (then chaired by Sir Michael Kerr) with Martin Hunter and Jan Paulsson, taking internationalism still further with the benefit of the 1985 UNCITRAL Model Law. The 1998 Rules were prepared by the LCIA Court (then chaired by Professor Karl-Heinz Böckstiegel) with Ken Rokison and the present author, primarily to take account of the English Arbitration Act 1996, itself much influenced by the 1985 UNCITRAL Model Law.

3.06 The 2014 LCIA Rules are the product of the LCIA Court (chaired by Professor William W Park) influenced by a mass of practical suggestions from numerous users, practitioners, and arbitrators based on the increased workload of the LCIA over the last 15 years and (as regards English law) English jurisprudence under the 1996 Act. The LCIA Court's drafting committee for this new edition was comprised of James Castello, Professor Boris Karabelnikov, and the present author, assisted by Amy Sander.[4] Mr Castello (an international arbitration specialist in Paris) has an unparalleled knowledge of drafting arbitration rules, having taken a leading part in the 2010 UNCITRAL Arbitration Rules; Professor Karabelnikov is a legal linguist and comparative lawyer (originally from Moscow), with a sixth sense for English ambiguities; and Ms Sander (of the English Bar) prepared several research papers on the LCIA's rules and procedures, identifying both red and amber flags.

---

[4] Mr Castello is a long-serving member of the US delegation to the UNCITRAL Working Group; and Professor Karabelnikov is a law professor (now in Latvia) who practises (*inter alia*) as an arbitrator in Moscow and London. Both were members of the LCIA Court. Ms Sander was the researcher for the Mance Committee's 2009 Report on s 69 of the 1996 Act; and for the 2014 LCIA Rules she produced a detailed schedule of historical changes from the 1981, 1985, and 1998 LCIA Rules with critical comments from available sources. The present author was a member of the UK delegation to the UNCITRAL Working Group, a member of the DAC responsible for the English Arbitration Act 1996, and the co-draftsman of the 1998 LCIA Rules.

(b) The 2014 Rules

3.07 In drafting the 2014 LCIA Rules, the LCIA sub-committee learnt much from the revisions made for the 2010 UNCITRAL Arbitration Rules and the work of the UNCITRAL Working Group on Arbitration generally. There was no attempt to assimilate the LCIA Rules to other institutional rules for international arbitration, or to the LCIA's other hyphenated arbitration rules in Dubai, India, and Mauritius (being site-specific). Account was taken of published criticisms made by commentators on the 1985 and 1998 LCIA Rules.[5]

3.08 In addition, many drafts were considered, line by line, with past and present members of the LCIA registry so as to ensure that the new 2014 LCIA Rules accorded with current LCIA practices. The LCIA Court devoted several private and public sessions to successive drafts, making important decisions of principle. Individual members of the LCIA Court also made their views known, particularly on the issue of the 'emergency arbitrator' (considered below). There were invaluable responses from the wider consultative processes conducted on several drafts. It was also the first time, since 1981, that an attempt was made as a matter of wording to 'scrub' the LCIA Arbitration Rules from beginning to end, so as to make them clearer, less London-centric, and more comprehensible to international users and practitioners.

3.09 These 2014 revisions fall into two basic groups: (i) necessary changes to correct earlier drafting inconsistencies (from 1981 to 1998), inaccurate reflections of actual LCIA practice, and excessively English legal language for an international arbitration; and (ii) new procedures decided by the LCIA Court. The first category lies outside the scope of this chapter: it would require a lengthy and tedious treatise. It may suffice here to give two brief examples.

3.10 First, for obscure historical reasons dating back to the English Arbitration Act 1934, section 48(5)(b) of the English Arbitration Act 1996 permits a tribunal to order specific performance of a contract, other than a contract relating to land unless otherwise agreed by the parties. At least one (non-English) commentator has mistakenly concluded from

---

[5] In particular, Peter Turner and Rez Mohtashami, *A Guide to the LCIA Arbitration Rules* (OUP 2009) and Robert Hunter and Sabine Konrad, 'LCIA Rules' in Rolfe A Schutze (ed), *Institutional Arbitration—Article by Article Commentary* (Beck–Hart Publishing 2013) ch VI, 413ff. See also Martin Hunter and Jan Paulsson, 'A Commentary on the 1985 Rules of the London Court of International Arbitration' in Pieter Sanders (ed), *Yearbook Commercial Arbitration*, vol X (Kluwer Law International 1985) 167; Marc Blessing, 'The LCIA Rules—Aus Sucht des Pratikers' (2003) SchiedsVZ 198; W Lawrence Craig, 'The LCIA and ICC Rules: the 1998 Revisions Compared' in Andrew Berkeley and Jacqueline Mimms (eds), *International Commercial Arbitration: Practical Perspectives* (Centre of Construction Law and Management 2001) 79; Ottoarndt Glossner and Jens Bredow, 'ICC, LCIA und DIS-Schiedsgerichtsordnng—Unterschiede und Gemeinsamkeiten' in Robert Briner and others (eds), *Law of International Business and Dispute Settlement in the 21st Century, Liber Amicorum Karl-Heinz Böckstiegel* (Carl Heymanns 2001) 219; Jonathan L Greenblatt and Peter Griffin, 'Towards the Harmonization of International Arbitration Rules: Comparative Analysis of the ICC, AAA, LCIA and CIETAC' (2001) 17 Arb Int'l 101; Sergei N Lebedev 'The LCIA Rules for International Commercial Arbitration' (1992) 8 Arb Int'l 321; Simon Nesbitt, 'LCIA Arbitration Rules' in Loukas Mistelis (ed), *Concise International Arbitration* (Kluwer Law International 2010) 412; Adam Samuel, 'Jurisdiction, Interim Relief and Awards under the LCIA Rules' in Andrew Berkeley and Jacqueline Mimms (eds), *International Commercial Arbitration: Practical Perspectives* (Centre of Construction Law and Management 2001) 35; V V Veeder, 'The New 1998 LCIA Rules' in Albert Jan van den Berg (ed), *Yearbook Commercial Arbitration*, vol XXIII (Kluwer Law International 1998) 366; Thomas W Walsh and Ruth Teitelbaum, 'The LCIA Court Decisions on Challenges to Arbitrators' (2011) 27 Arb Int'l 283; and Adrian Winstanley, 'The LCIA—History, Constitution and Rules' in Andrew Berkeley and Jacqueline Mimms (eds), *International Commercial Arbitration: Practical Perspectives* (Centre of Construction Law and Management 2001) 21.

this provision that, ordinarily, an English tribunal can never decide any contractual dispute relating to land (whether by ordering specific performance, damages, or at all). The solution to such misunderstandings lies in the new provision for such agreement 'otherwise' in Article 22.1(vii) of the LCIA Arbitration Rules, granting express power to the tribunal to order specific performance of any contract, including a contract relating to land.

3.11 Second, owing to the LCIA Court's broad interpretation of a corporation's nationality disqualifying the appointment of an arbitrator of the same 'nationality' when applied to Crown colonies or dependencies (such as Bermuda, the British Virgin Islands, and Gibraltar), many insurance and shareholder disputes from these jurisdictions were not referred to the LCIA under the 1985 and 1998 Rules. The solution lies in the new provision in Article 6.3 that provides that a legal person incorporated in a state's overseas territory shall be treated as a legal person incorporated in that overseas territory and not as a legal person incorporated in the state.

3.12 The latter category of revisions includes: the increased use of electronic communications by parties with the LCIA registry and LCIA tribunals, particularly for starting an LCIA arbitration; the procedure for an emergency arbitrator; the changes to the default arbitral seat of an LCIA arbitration; the consolidation, etc, of different arbitrations for multi-party disputes; a solution to the '*Slovenia*' problem regarding potential conflicts between an arbitrator and a party's legal representative; general guidelines for the conduct of the parties' legal representatives within the arbitration; the '*Jivraj*' problem regarding the selection of arbitrators based on nationality; the '*West Tankers*' problem regarding 'Italian Torpedoes' under the Brussels I Regulation; and further attempts to promote procedures to avoid unnecessary delay and expense. These revisions are briefly explained below, although much more could be said about each of them.

C. The Start of an LCIA Arbitration

(a) Commencing proceedings

3.13 The LCIA has hitherto enjoyed a relatively good record for the time taken from the LCIA's receipt of the claimant's request for arbitration to the formation of the LCIA tribunal. Excluding expedited formations of the tribunal under Article 9 introduced by the 1998 LCIA Rules (see below), the average time from the request to the tribunal's formation for 432 arbitrations commenced between January 2010 and May 2012 was 62 days (that is, 32 days from the end of the time for the respondent's response to the request); the longest time taken was 99 days (that is, 69 days from the end of the time for the response); and the shortest time was 32 days (that is, 2 days from the end of the time for the response). From the users' perspective (particularly claimants), there was, however, still room for improvement in the time ordinarily taken by the LCIA to form an LCIA tribunal from the LCIA registry's receipt of the request for arbitration. This cannot be dismissed as 'claimant's justice': it is a regrettable fact that starting any international arbitration is now much more laborious, expensive, bureaucratic, and slow than it used to be.

3.14 The LCIA Court decided that part of the solution was to encourage parties to move increasingly from paper to electronic communications from the outset of the arbitration in all communications between the parties, the LCIA registry, and the tribunal. In our own lifetimes, we have seen the rise and fall of the telex and fax machine; and international postal and courier services remain comparatively slow and expensive. It therefore makes good sense to encourage the electronic filing of requests for arbitration and responses (including all accompanying documentation), as now expressly provided in Articles 1.2 and 2.2 of the 2014 LCIA Rules.

Moreover, the paper tsunamis in large arbitrations have made it increasingly difficult for arbitral institutions and arbitrators to store paper files (particularly with long retention periods). In recent years, there has been a noticeable increase in electronic filings by parties to LCIA arbitrations (albeit usually followed with confirmatory paper filings): for requests, 14.8 per cent in 2010, 21.9 per cent in 2011, and 27.7 per cent in 2012 (to May 2012). It is significant that other arbitral institutions are also making increased use of electronic filings, websites, and even apps (eg SIAC and AAA). The lessons learnt from the current practice of electronic documentation at the LCIA show that it is best begun as early as possible in the life of an arbitration. It can waste significant time, money, storage, and effort to introduce electronic documentation later, particularly at the stage of an oral hearing. 3.15

Furthermore, the new systems for electronic documentation (such as Opus 2's Magnum) show how inefficient a mixed system can be, with hard and soft documentation running alongside each other for any significant period of time. This new form of electronic communication is not compulsory under the 2014 LCIA Rules; but it will be strongly encouraged by the LCIA Court. 3.16

The LCIA Court also determined that a significant number of parties, particularly those new to LCIA arbitration, often misunderstand what is required for a request or response at the beginning of an LCIA arbitration. Both documents can be relatively short, addressing in turn only the procedural requirements listed in Articles 1 and 2 of the 2014 LCIA Rules. It is not necessary in the vast majority of cases for a claimant or a respondent to set out there at length its substantive case on the merits, unless it has already decided that its request or response (as the case may be) should stand as its statement of case under Article 15.2 or 15.3 of the 2014 LCIA Rules. 3.17

The adverse reaction to Lord Woolf's reforms requiring a full pleading of a party's case at the outset of English civil litigation was a major factor in commercial parties switching from litigation to arbitration. It would therefore be unfortunate if parties unwittingly recreated the same difficulty for themselves in an LCIA arbitration. The start of an LCIA arbitration should be relatively easy and quick. Hence, it makes good sense to encourage parties to use the LCIA's standard electronic forms for both requests and responses under Articles 1.3 and 2.3 of the 2014 LCIA Rules, available online from the LCIA's website. Again, the use of these same forms is not compulsory under the 2014 LCIA Rules; but hopefully parties will make use of them, at least as a matter of guidance. 3.18

(b) Article 9A—expedited formation of tribunal

The LCIA's procedure under Article 9 of the 1998 LCIA Rules for the expedited formation of the tribunal worked well. It has been retained, with slight changes in wording, as Article 9A of the 2014 LCIA Rules. The 1998 draftsmen had originally considered a procedure for an emergency arbitrator; but the proposal had then been rejected by the LCIA Court. Article 9 of the 1998 Rules was to provide only for the expedited formation of the tribunal in appropriate cases of exceptional emergency, upon a reasoned application to the LCIA 3.19

Court by any party (whether claimant or respondent). Between 1998 and 2012, there were 111 applications for the expedited formation of tribunals, of which 46 were granted by the LCIA Court, 9 were agreed between the parties, 19 discontinued, and 37 rejected by the LCIA Court (ie about half of all applications were granted by the LCIA Court). Of those granted, the average time taken to appoint the tribunal expeditiously was 20 days from the date of the application under Article 9 and 14 days from the date of the LCIA Court's decision granting the application. These periods of time, of course, reflect the time abridged by the LCIA Court on different terms for each particular case; and, if necessary, the LCIA Court could appoint a tribunal under Article 9 within a day or even a few hours in a case of extreme urgency.

3.20 These and like statistics had been received with some scepticism in several quarters, it being felt that there may have been an increase in applications under Article 9 in recent times as a tactical manoeuvre by impatient claimants, particularly in default situations with a presumed absent respondent. Subject to this scepticism, there seemed to be no necessity to revise Article 9 of the 1998 Rules. There also seemed to be no need to introduce an entirely new procedure for an emergency arbitrator. On the face of it, the expedited formation of the actual tribunal within a short time period seemed preferable to the appointment of a (temporary) emergency arbitrator followed in turn by the appointment of the actual tribunal. This was so, even with the likely diminution or loss of the parties' rights (with Article 9's time constraints) to take part in the ordinary selection of the tribunal's members under the LCIA Rules.

3.21 In addition, urgent interim relief at the outbreak of a dispute can often be remedied more easily, quickly, and effectively by state courts of competent jurisdiction at the request of an aggrieved party before the commencement of any arbitration.[6] In such cases, both an emergency arbitrator and a tribunal are relative latecomers to the parties' dispute; and 'emergency' then bears a qualified meaning.[7] As was recognized in the drafting of the 2010 UNCITRAL Arbitration Rules, a private arbitrator (whether emergency or actual) is invariably no substitute for a state court, acting with *imperium*, in regard to urgent interim relief before, at, or shortly after the commencement of an arbitration.

3.22 Eventually, however, after a very lengthy debate, the LCIA Court decided both to keep the old procedure for the expedited formation of the tribunal under Article 9 of the 1998 LCIA Rules and to introduce a parallel new procedure for an emergency arbitrator. These provisions are now, respectively, Article 9A and Article 9B of the 2014 LCIA Rules. This subtle compromise may be regarded as an experiment. It is not known how the two procedures

---

[6] For discussion, Doug Jones, 'Emergency Arbitrators and Court-Ordered Interim Measures: Is the Choice Important?' in Julio César Betancourt (ed), *Defining Issues in International Arbitration: Celebrating 100 Years of the Chartered Institute of Arbitrators* (OUP 2016) ch 14.

[7] For example, a recently reported case under the Swiss Rules consisted of the following timetable: Day 1: request for emergency relief; Day 3: appointment of emergency arbitrator; Day 4: procedural meeting (by telephone conference call) followed by a procedural order and timetable; Days 8–12: written submissions filed by the parties; Day 15: oral hearing; and Day 17: decision of the emergency arbitrator—thereby meeting the deadline required by the Swiss Rules. This 17-day continuous time period, admirable for any arbitration tribunal, seems nonetheless slow for 'emergency' interim relief: a ship can sail in hours; a demand guarantee can be called in minutes; and monies can be transferred from a bank account in the mere twinkling of an email. This extended time period is not unusual for most procedures for emergency arbitrators, including the LCIA's new procedure under Article 9B of the 2014 LCIA Rules (see below).

will work in practice; but it makes good sense to offer to parties the choice of one or the other (or both).

(c) Article 9B—emergency arbitrator

As already described, the LCIA Court had considered introducing a procedure for an emergency arbitrator in the 1998 edition of the LCIA Rules. At that time, few arbitral institutions had done so, excepting the ICC (for a short time from 1931 onwards) and the international arbitration institutions in Moscow (MAC and FTAC, later the ICAC).[8] After 1998, several institutions introduced special procedures for an emergency arbitrator, most notably the SCC (2010), SIAC (2010), the ICC (2012), and the Revised Swiss Rules (2012), as to which there is now available a significant amount of public information.[9] There are other arbitration rules with broadly similar provisions, including ICDR (1999 and 2006), WIPO (2002), ACICA (2011), and CEPANI (2013), about which much less is publicly known of their practical application. It is clear, however, that many international users like the idea of an emergency arbitrator, although in practice there may remain unresolved problems regarding due process, arbitral challenges, high costs, and the cross-border enforcement of such emergency relief, particularly under the New York Convention and the Brussels I Regulation Recast.[10]

3.23

The published figures for emergency arbitrators before the SCC, SIAC, the ICC, and the Revised Swiss Rules are as follows: SCC (nine applications 2010–2013); SIAC (27 applications, including three arbitral challenges, 2010–2013); ICC (five applications 2012–2013); and the Revised Swiss Rules (one application 2012–2014). All these figures seem surprisingly low. (The ICC's procedure is only prospective, hence its significantly lower numbers given its overall higher caseload.) However, from anecdotal sources, it seems that applications are increasing before several of these institutions. Only time will tell whether any of these procedures will survive competition from state courts, particularly at the arbitral seat. It is perhaps ominous that the ICC once had an emergency procedure (administered by the ICC Court's President), but that the ICC later decided to abandon it.

3.24

Equally ominous is a frequent misunderstanding apparently shared by some parties and even certain practitioners. An emergency arbitrator does not conduct a fast-track arbitration or operate a summary procedure to decide finally the merits of the parties' dispute (as exists in some domestic arbitral jurisdictions, including the Netherlands).[11] It may be that an emergency arbitrator's decision can facilitate an early amicable settlement of the parties' dispute; but that arbitrator's decision, without more, is not a final adjudication of the parties' dispute. Arbitral institutions, including the LCIA, should be careful not to over-sell

3.25

---

[8] Under the 1931 ICC Rules, the ICC Court President could appoint an expert to take conservatory and other measures before the arbitration tribunal entered upon its duties: see Eric Schwartz, 'The Practices and Experience of the ICC Court' in *Conservatory and Provisional Measures in International Arbitration* (ICC Publishing 1993) 45, 46. The Moscow arbitral institutions were formed in 1930–1932 and may have been influenced by the ICC's example in Paris.

[9] See SCC Rules, Appx II; SIAC Rules, r 26.2 and sch 1; ICC Arbitration Rules, Art 29 and Appx V; and 2012 Swiss Rules, Art 43.

[10] For commentary see Andrew Dickinson and Eva Lein, *The Brussels I Regulation Recast* (OUP 2015).

[11] The '*kort geding*' procedure in the Netherlands, much misunderstood by foreigners, is in practice limited to summary orders for the immediate payment of indisputable monetary obligations.

the virtues of their procedures for an emergency arbitrator. An LCIA emergency arbitrator is not an LCIA tribunal.

3.26 Under Article 9B of the 2014 LCIA Rules, the LCIA is required, in principle, to appoint an emergency arbitrator within three days of the application (if granted by the LCIA Court); and the emergency arbitrator is then required to make his decision as soon as possible, but within 14 days of appointment. These deadlines are necessarily flexible in exceptional circumstances (subject to a decision by the LCIA Court), particularly the time required for the decision. As to that, the SCC Rules prescribe five days from appointment; and the ICC Arbitration Rules prescribe 15 days. The SIAC Rules appear to impose no time limit on the emergency arbitrator; but it is reported that two decisions were made within one day and seven days respectively. The Swiss Rules impose a 15-day time limit.

3.27 Article 9B of the 2014 LCIA Rules permits the arbitrator to make his decision as an order or an award, as likewise provided in the SCC, SIAC, and Swiss Rules. (The ICC Arbitration Rules limit the emergency arbitrator's decision to an 'order'.) Article 9B is intended to produce an order or an award enforceable in England under the English Arbitration Act 1996; but it is not clear whether an award would be enforceable in all countries under the New York Convention. For SIAC, Singapore enacted special legislation in 2012 to ensure enforcement within Singapore of orders and awards by an emergency arbitrator. The ICC suggested a like amendment to the 1996 Act (as regards the enforcement of an order in England); but its request was refused on the ground that such an order could already be enforced under the Act, without the need for any amending legislation.

3.28 Given the significant rule change in Article 9B for an LCIA arbitration, the LCIA Court decided that it should apply only to arbitration agreements made after the promulgation of the 2014 LCIA Rules, ie prospectively from 1 October 2014 onwards and not retrospectively. This was the approach taken in the ICC Arbitration Rules, for the same reason. The LCIA Court also decided to distinguish between different levels of urgency: Article 9A applies to a case of 'exceptional urgency', whereas Article 9B applies to a case of 'emergency'. For an applicant party, there may seem to be little difference. However, given that both procedures are subject to the decision of the LCIA Court, there may be a material difference in practice. There is, however, nothing to prevent an applicant party (claimant or respondent) from making simultaneous applications under both Article 9A and Article 9B of the 2014 LCIA Rules. (This issue does not arise under other arbitration rules with no like provision for a tribunal's expedited formation alongside a provision for an emergency arbitrator.)

(d) Arbitral seat

3.29 For any arbitration in England, there is a juridical need for an 'arbitral seat'. Most parties to LCIA arbitrations choose an arbitral seat, most often London. It is, of course, possible for parties to agree to any other arbitral seat. Difficulties have arisen in the past where no seat (English or foreign) was readily ascertainable at the outset of the arbitration, both under the English Arbitration Act 1996 and earlier English legislation. This seems to have affected ICC arbitrations where the parties left the choice of the arbitral seat to the ICC Court, ie to a decision necessarily after the ICC arbitration was to commence.[12] For the LCIA, the historical solution to this legal black hole was to designate London as a default seat under the LCIA Rules, in the absence of the parties' agreement otherwise.

3.30 This approach has hitherto worked well in practice, although it has invited criticism of a pro-London bias inapposite to an international arbitral institution. Under the new 2014 LCIA Rules, London as a default seat is necessarily maintained in Article 16.2. However, under Article 16.1, the parties can still agree upon any arbitral seat at any time before the formation of the tribunal by themselves and, after such formation, with the consent of the tribunal. In addition, under Article 16.2, in the absence of any agreement by the parties, the tribunal may itself choose the arbitral seat in consultation with the parties. Moreover, also by Article 16.2, the default seat of London must play no part in the selection and appointment of arbitrators by the LCIA Court.

(e) Multiparty, etc, disputes

3.31 About a third of all LCIA arbitrations are multi-party disputes. For 2010, 35.7 per cent of arbitrations were commenced with more than two parties (one with 39); for 2011, 33.5 per cent (one with 33); and for 2012, 33.5 per cent (one with 18). These are significant statistics. For the English Arbitration Act 1996, brave but forlorn attempts were made by the DAC to square the circle for the consolidation of multi-party disputes. The mouse-like result was section 35 of the 1996 Act that effectively leaves all to the agreement of the parties. This provision is mirrored in Article 22.1(ix) of the 2014 LCIA Rules, where the tribunal (with the approval of the LCIA Court) may order the consolidation of the LCIA arbitration with one or more other arbitrations into a single arbitration subject to the LCIA Rules where all parties so agree in writing.

3.32 There is, however, no problem where there is agreement: it arises only where there is no consent by the parties. It is significant that all previous attempts by legislation have been much criticized by users and arbitration practitioners, including, especially, the non-consensual powers under the Netherlands Arbitration Act 1986. In the absence of legislation, is it possible to impose a solution by arbitration rules taking the form of consent, at least as regards parties to one or more arbitration agreements incorporating the LCIA Rules? The answer is mixed, as appears from the LCIA Rules.

3.33 The 1985 and 1998 LCIA Rules contained a limited third-party procedure, now Article 22.1(viii) of the 2014 LCIA Rules. This provision permits the tribunal to join a third person to the arbitration with the consent of that third person and the party making the application. It does not require the consent of other parties to the arbitration (beyond their consent to the LCIA Rules). Article 22.1(ix) of the 2014 LCIA Rules seeks to go further, providing for the consolidation by the tribunal of arbitrations subject to the LCIA Rules commenced under the same or compatible arbitration agreements between the same disputing parties (with the approval of the LCIA Court), provided that no arbitral tribunal has yet been formed for such other arbitration(s), or if formed, provided that the other tribunal is composed of the same arbitrators. Under Article 22.6 of the 2014 LCIA Rules, the LCIA Court is given different powers to consolidate two or more arbitrations, before the formation of any tribunal, commenced subject to the LCIA Rules between the same disputing parties. It seems difficult

---

[12] For example, see *Int'l Tank and Pipe SAK v Kuwait Aviation Fuelling Co KSC* [1975] QB 224 (English Court of Appeal). Part 1 of the English Arbitration Act 1996 only applies to an arbitration with its seat in England, Wales, or Northern Ireland: see s 2(1).

(f) The *Slovenia* problem

3.34 Under Article 18.2 of the 2014 LCIA Rules, the LCIA registry and (when formed) the tribunal may require from the outset of the arbitration the names and addresses of the parties' legal representatives, if not supplied by the claimant with its request or the respondent with its response (as required by Articles 1.1(i) and 2.1(i) respectively). This is not a new idea: it derives from Article 4 of the 1976 UNCITRAL Arbitration Rules (albeit there extending beyond legal representation to legal 'assistance' also). If there is any risk of a '*Slovenia*-type' problem at the commencement of an arbitration preceding the LCIA tribunal's formation, it should be capable of resolution by the LCIA Court with no adverse effect on the arbitration's progress. The names of the parties' legal representatives would be ascertainable and taken into account by the LCIA Court in appointing the members of the tribunal; and indeed those names would be known to those members prior to accepting their appointment for the purpose of any conflict-check, like impediment, and disclosure.

3.35 At a later stage, problems can arise where a party changes or adds to its legal representation. Conflicts can then arise regarding the tribunal, leading to a challenge to an arbitrator (or even to the new legal representative) with the risk of disrupting the arbitral timetable, particularly at or shortly before an oral hearing. By Articles 18.3 and 18.4 of the 2014 LCIA Rules, any such intended change or addition must be notified promptly to all other parties, the tribunal, and the LCIA registry; it cannot be deliberately delayed to spring a tactical surprise on an opposing party; and it can only take effect with the prior approval of the tribunal. Such approval may not be given if the change or addition could compromise the composition of the tribunal or the finality of any award on the grounds of possible conflict or other like impediment.

3.36 Accordingly, mishaps, such as occurred in *Slovenia* (an ICSID case) shortly before the oral hearing, should not occur under the 2014 LCIA Rules.[13] Moreover, under Article 18.4 of the 2014 LCIA Rules, the tribunal has power to exclude any change to a party's legal representation in order to protect the arbitration from improper attempts to disrupt its procedures. Under English law, an arbitration tribunal probably enjoys this power already;[14] but it makes good sense to express an implied power in specific terms as an arbitration rule agreed by the parties.

(g) General guidelines

3.37 The 2014 LCIA Rules contain general guidelines for the conduct of the parties' legal representatives appearing in an LCIA arbitration, in a short one-page annex. The sanctions for

---

[13] *Hrvatska Elektroprivreda dd v The Republic of Slovenia*, ICSID Case No ARB/05/24, Tribunal's Ruling regarding the Participation of David Mildon QC in Further Stages of the Proceedings (6 May 2008); see also *The Rompetrol Group NV v Romania*, ICSID Case No ARB/06/3, Decision on Respondent's Preliminary Objections on Jurisdiction and Admissibility (18 April 2008). The former case concerned a barrister-arbitrator and a barrister-advocate from the same London barristers' chambers, foreshadowing further similar cases, unreported (particularly ICC arbitrations). Early disclosure (particularly by the barrister-advocate with better knowledge of a potential conflict) seems to be essential, as suggested by the IBA Guidelines on Conflicts of Interest (General Standard 7a). This is particularly so if, in the future, English barristers' chambers transform themselves into partnerships or professional corporations under the 2015 Entity Regulation.

[14] For a discussion, see Margaret L Moses, 'Inherent and Implied Powers of Arbitrators' in Julio César Betancourt (ed), *Defining Issues in International Arbitration: Celebrating 100 Years of the Chartered Institute of Arbitrators* (OUP 2016) ch 21.

deliberately infringing these guidelines, decided by the tribunal, are contained in Article 18.6 of the 2014 LCIA Rules. Of course, the annex is not essential to the conduct of an LCIA arbitration. The arguments against general guidelines and, still more, ethical codes for international arbitration practitioners are well known and hitherto persuasive. However, as the IBA initiative demonstrated (as also the earlier CCBE initiative within the EU), the battle against outside regulation is being lost in several jurisdictions. To the LCIA Court, it seemed wiser for the LCIA to attempt to influence the conduct of LCIA practitioners with its own internal guidelines, rather than have an ill-considered code thrust upon it by state regulators unsympathetic to international arbitration. Perhaps inevitably, these provisions generated much comment when put out in draft for public consultation, some enthusiastically supportive and others vociferously opposed.

The immediate origins of the annex may be found in the pioneering work of Professor Catherine Rogers,[15] to which much has since been added by other scholars and practitioners.[16] However, its roots lie in earlier professional concerns, particularly in England and the United States, over the effective regulation of international arbitration practitioners (not necessarily lawyers).[17] It should not be overlooked that sanctions for misconduct by English lawyers have even more ancient origins, namely the 'silencing' of advocates under the Statute of Westminster 1275 (3 Edw 1 c 29).[18] It is a rich field; and it is here only possible to give a brief account of the LCIA's relatively modest but innovative contribution.

3.38

It is first necessary to emphasize that the LCIA's general guidelines are limited to the relationship between the parties' named legal representatives, the LCIA Court, and the tribunal within the arbitration. They are accordingly more 'Sands-ILA' than 'Bishop-Stevens'. They also depart significantly from the more detailed approach to overall professional ethics taken by the IBA Guidelines on Party Representation and, to a much greater extent, from the CCBE's ambitious attempts to comprehensively regulate arbitration practitioners within the European Union.[19] Moreover, the LCIA's guidelines are by themselves hardly

3.39

---

[15] For example, see Catherine A Rogers, 'Context and Institutional Structure in Attorney Discipline: Developing an Enforcement Regime for Ethics in International Arbitration' (2002) 39 Stan J Int'l L 1; Catherine A Rogers, 'Fit and Function in Legal Ethics: Developing a Code of Attorney Conduct for International Arbitration' (2002) 23 Mich J Int'l L 341; and Catherine A Rogers, 'Lawyers without Borders' (2009) 30 U Pa J Int'l L 1035.

[16] For example, see William W Park, 'Arbitrator Integrity' (2009) 46 San Diego L R 629; William W Park, 'A Fair Fight: Professional Guidelines in International Arbitration' (2014) 30 Arb Int'l 409; and Edna Sussman and Solomon Ebere, 'All's Fair in Love and War—Or Is It? Reflections on Ethical Standards for Counsel in International Arbitration' (2011) 22 Am Rev Int'l Arb 611.

[17] Peter C Thomas, 'Disqualifying Lawyers in Arbitrations: Do the Arbitrators Play Any Proper Role?' (1990) 1 Am Rev Int'l Arb 562; John Toulmin, 'A Worldwide Common Code of Professional Ethics?' (1992) 15 Fordham Int'l LJ 673; Jan Paulsson, 'Standards of Conduct for Counsel in International Arbitration' (1992) 3 Am Rev Int'l Arb 214; John Uff, 'Duties at the Legal Fringe: Ethics in Construction Law' (Centre of Construction Law and Management, The Michael Brown Foundation King's College London, 19 June 2003) <http://www.scl.org.uk> accessed 25 September 2015; and Cyrus Benson, 'Can Professional Ethics Wait? The Need for Guidance in International Arbitration' (2009) 3 Disp Resol Int'l 78.

[18] The Statute of Westminster (repealed in 1948) was applied in *Coxe v Phillips* (1736) 95 ER 152 (Hardwicke LCJ) at 153: 'it is incumbent on Courts of Justice to keep the streams of justice clear, or they will be made use of as means of scandal'. See generally *R v Visitors to the Inns of Court, Ex p Calder* [1994] QB 1, 10 (CA). The penalties attaching to trial lawyers in the United States are described in Alex B Long, 'Attorney Deceit Statutes: Promoting Professionalism through Criminal Prosecutions and Treble Damages' (2010) 44 UC Davis L Rev 413.

[19] Doak Bishop and Margrete Stevens, 'International Code of Ethics for Lawyers Practising before International Arbitral Tribunals' in Albert Jan van den Berg (ed), *Arbitration Advocacy in Changing Times* (ICCA Congress Series No 15, Kluwer Law International 2011) 408; The ILA Hague Principles on Ethical

controversial: each targets deliberate misconduct within the arbitration that would be a criminal or, at least, a disciplinary offence under most legal and professional regimes.

3.40 Much of the criticism of the LCIA's new provisions may derive from the fact that international arbitration practitioners remain effectively unregulated and therefore fear any effective form of regulation. This approach might have had a certain charm a century or more ago; but today all professions are regulated around the world. There is no cause for international arbitration practitioners to be different. For such practitioners, the choice now lies only between regulation and self-regulation. If there is to be no self-regulation, outside regulators will inevitably seek to impose their own regulations, as has already happened to mediators. It is therefore necessary for arbitral institutions themselves to promote good professional conduct within their arbitrations and to discourage misconduct, with sanctions. There is still time to do so.

3.41 In an article written by the moral philosopher Lord Sacks, albeit addressing the recent banking and rate-fixing scandals in the City of London and not arbitration, the work of behavioural economists was much commended as a means of reinforcing the traditional virtues of self-restraint embedded in a culture and embraced by the majority of that culture's individuals:

> Dishonesty is contagious. Seeing colleagues cheat makes us more likely to do so. Most tempting of all, says Professor Ariely, is 'altruistic' cheating. If we can persuade ourselves that an act of dishonesty is for the good of our colleagues, even the best can go bad... How do you change a corporate culture? You need to go beyond codes of conduct, says Professor Ariely. He and his team tested students from two universities. The first were asked at the outset to sign an agreement that they would abide by their university code of honour. The second weren't. Predictably, the second group cheated, the first did not. The irony is that the first university didn't have a code of honour, while the second did. What matters, says Professor Ariely, is not the code but the constant reminder.[20]

3.42 The LCIA's annex is hardly a 'code'; but its necessary 'constant reminder' lies in Articles 18.5 and 18.6 of the 2014 LCIA Rules. The former requires each party to ensure that its legal representatives appearing by name in the arbitration have agreed to comply with the general guidelines in the annex, as a condition of such representation in the arbitration. The latter permits the tribunal to impose sanctions for a representative's deliberate violation of the general guidelines, such as a written reprimand, a written caution as to future conduct, or any other measure necessary for the tribunal to fulfil within the arbitration its general duties under Articles 14.4(i) and 14.4(ii) of the 2014 LCIA Rules.

3.43 These arbitral duties reflect, *inter alia*, the mandatory procedural requirements of section 33 of the English Arbitration Act 1996. Without these sanctions under Article 18.6, the general guidelines would be mere pious aspirations. That is not to say that sanctions are likely to be imposed by any tribunal: their very existence (or reminder) should ensure that they never will, or if so, only very rarely.

Standards (chaired by Professor Sands) <http://www.ucl.ac.uk> accessed 25 September 2015; and the IBA Guidelines on Party Representation <http://www.ibanet.org> accessed 25 September 2015.

[20] Jonathan Sacks, 'It is the End of a Dangerous Moral Experiment' *Daily Telegraph* (London, 7 July 2013). Lord Sacks (formerly the Chief Rabbi of the United Kingdom) was citing Professor D Ariely's work: Dan Ariely, *The (Honest) Truth about Dishonesty* (Harper Perennial 2013).

Given the concerns expressed by several commentators (but not the majority), the LCIA   **3.44**
Court decided to place the general guidelines in a separate annex to the 2014 LCIA Rules, susceptible to separate amendment under the preamble to the 2014 LCIA Rules. In the light of future experience and events, it may indeed be necessary to amend or even supplement the annex. This would be particularly so if further threats emerge from state regulators to regulate international arbitration practitioners, whether in the European Union or elsewhere.

(h) The *Jivraj* problem

While the immediate problem may have been successfully resolved with the UK Supreme   **3.45**
Court's innovative judgment in *Jivraj v Hashwani*,[21] there remain possible difficulties for the future in selecting arbitrators by reference to nationality under the laws of the European Union. This is not an isolated English problem or even particular to the LCIA. These possible difficulties would be EU-wide, affecting the great arbitral institutions located in Paris, The Hague, Brussels, Stockholm, Frankfurt, Vienna, and elsewhere. The losing party (Mr Hashwani) has filed a formal complaint before the European Commission against the United Kingdom for its Supreme Court's (alleged) disregard of mandatory rules of EU law.

That complaint is supported by the unprecedented law review article by Sir Richard Buxton   **3.46**
attacking the reasoning of the Supreme Court's judgment (the article's author, now retired, was a member of the Court of Appeal in *Jivraj* and party to its judgment, later overturned by the Supreme Court).[22] In December 2012, the European Commission admitted the complaint and required the United Kingdom formally to respond in writing, as the first step towards enforcement proceedings before the CJEU. If successful, these enforcement proceedings could require the Supreme Court to vacate its judgment and re-hear the case, arriving at a different result. There is no public information regarding the United Kingdom's response. Hence, possible difficulties remain until more is known of the Commission's eventual decision and, possibly, the judgment of the CJEU on any enforcement proceedings against the United Kingdom.

In these awkward circumstances, the options for the 2014 LCIA Rules were limited; namely   **3.47**
either retaining the wording of Articles 5.5, 6.1, and 6.2 of the 1998 LCIA Rules (first used in the 1985 Rules); or adopting the arguably different wording of Article 6(7) of the 2010 UNCITRAL Arbitration Rules; or drafting a completely new rule which, inevitably, would remove any reference to 'nationality' in the selection of arbitrators. The LCIA Court decided that the last of these three options would be unattractive to many users of LCIA arbitration, given the apparent effect of the UK Supreme Court's decision (at least for the time being) and the traditional use of an arbitrator's nationality as a badge of neutrality. The choice lay between the first and second options, neither of which was entirely satisfactory given the uncertain state of EU/UK law as regards discrimination on grounds of nationality and national origins. Eventually, the first option was chosen with slightly different wording,

---

[21] *Jivraj v Hashwani* [2011] UKSC 40, [2011] 1 WLR 1872, in Albert Jan van den Berg (ed), *Yearbook Commercial Arbitration*, vol XXXVI (Kluwer Law International 2001) 611 and (2011) 4 Rev arb 1007; reversing *Jivraj v Hashwani* [2010] EWCA Civ 712, [2010] ICR 1435 (CA); reversing *Jivraj v Hashwani* [2009] EWHC 1364 (Comm) (Steel J).
[22] The Rt Hon Sir Richard Buxton, 'Discrimination in Employment: The Supreme Court Draws a Line' (2012) 128 LQR 1. See also the response, R Davies (Mr Jivraj's Leading Counsel), 'A Line Drawn in the Right Place' (2013) 129 LQR 1.

together with the addition of a 'saving' provision for the arbitration agreement and award in Article 32.3 of the 2014 LCIA Rules in the case of nullity under EU law, as regards unlawful discrimination based on nationality.

(i) The *West Tankers* problem

3.48 The new 'arbitration exception' in the 12th Preamble to the Brussels I Regulation Recast looks like a 'Pyrrhic victory' for arbitration users in England, albeit far from the worst of the possible proposals made by the European Commission for revisions to the Brussels Regulation (with the Lugano Convention). There are likely to be continued representations by users (not limited to LCIA users) for a more secure solution to the problem of 'Italian Torpedoes' within the European Union (not, of course, limited to Italy). These are most unlikely to be met by UK legislation in the form of any amendment to the English Arbitration Act 1996; the Commission is unlikely to address the problem for several years; and, if anything could be done at all, it required new provisions to the 2014 LCIA Rules.[23]

3.49 Accordingly, after the tribunal is formed, Articles 23.1 to 23.5 of the 2014 LCIA Rules are designed to confer exclusive jurisdiction on the tribunal to decide upon its own jurisdiction, with the express power under Article 22.1(vii) to order specific performance of any arbitration agreement, not limited to the arbitration agreement founding the tribunal's jurisdiction. As regards the latter, albeit only as an arbitration rule, these provisions operate as both the positive and negative consequences of *kompetenz-kompetenz*. A remedy for the specific performance of an arbitration agreement was not thought previously available under English law, but by agreement it is now permitted by section 48(1) of the English Arbitration Act 1996. Any resulting award by the tribunal, including a first partial award on jurisdiction, could be enforced under the New York Convention in 'Italy', thereby avoiding several of the difficulties arising from the *West Tankers* problem (provided always that no final judgment on the merits has already been given by the 'Italian' state court).

3.50 It should be noted that the arbitral remedy is specific performance of the wrongdoer's promise to arbitrate, being the language of Article II of the New York Convention and of *pacta sunt servanda*. It is not an 'anti-suit injunction'. None of this can provide a complete solution to the problem of 'Italian Torpedoes', given also that 'Italian Torpedo' courts invariably do not act in good faith under EU law and circumvent the New York Convention, a regrettable fact of legal life in the European Union which appears to have gone unrecognized in the CJEU's judgment in *West Tankers*.[24]

(j) Avoiding unnecessary delay and expense

3.51 Under section 33(1)(b) of the English Arbitration Act 1996 (a mandatory provision), a tribunal is required to adopt procedures suitable to the circumstances of the particular case, avoiding unnecessary delay or expense. This general duty is re-stated in Article 14.4(ii) of the 2014 LCIA Rules; and by Article 14.5, the parties are required to do everything necessary in good faith for the efficient and expeditious conduct of the arbitration, including the tribunal's discharge of this general duty. This objective is usually supported by all users

---

[23] It was thought that the CJEU's Grand Chamber might review this aspect of *West Tankers* in the recent *Gazprom* case; however, the court did not address this particular question. See Case C-536/13 *Gazprom OAO* EU:C:2015:316; [2015] 1 Lloyd's Rep 610 (ECJ (Grand Chamber)).

[24] Case C-185/07 *Allianz Spa & Generali Ass Gen Spa v West Tankers Inc* [2009] ECR I-663.

of international arbitration, in principle. It is, however, sometimes difficult to apply in practice.

D. Conclusion

The LCIA Rules are designed to move the arbitration relatively quickly from the request, via the response, to the formation of the tribunal. Following the tribunal's formation, Article 14.1 of the 2014 LCIA Rules encourages the parties and the tribunal to make contact (whether by a procedural hearing in person or otherwise) as soon as practicable, but no later than 21 days from receipt of the notification of such formation. In the absence of agreement or order from the tribunal, the default procedure and timetable are set out in Article 15 of the 2014 LCIA Rules, with specific deadlines for the parties' written submissions (28 + 28 + 28 days). The tribunal with the parties must then address the need for an oral hearing, including its length, form, and content. Thereafter, the tribunal is encouraged to issue its award as soon as reasonable in accordance with a timetable notified to the parties and the LCIA registry (subject to revision and re-notification); and, in particular, the tribunal 'shall set aside adequate time for deliberations as soon as possible after the last submission from the parties and notify the parties of the time it has set aside'. While a set deadline for an award may have the attraction of simplicity, it would be unworkable for the vast range of different disputes decided by LCIA tribunals, where it would be either too short or too long.   **3.52**

In conclusion, the 2014 LCIA Rules will, it is hoped, remain in force for the next decade or so. There will be, of course, new challenges and fresh mishaps for LCIA arbitrations, in addition to further developments in international arbitral practice. It would greatly assist the LCIA Court for the next edition of the LCIA Rules for all users, practitioners, and arbitrators to send to the LCIA any record of their triumphs or disasters requiring changes to the 2014 LCIA Rules. Like Sisyphus, the work of revising arbitration rules is never finished, not even after 120 years.   **3.53**

Part II

UNDERSTANDING THE USERS OF INTERNATIONAL ARBITRATION

4

PUTTING THE CLIENT FIRST

Peter J Rees

A. Introduction

I was, understandably, excited when I made my first visit to the US Supreme Court. I would have been even more excited if the case hadn't been of such crucial importance to my company and to multinational corporations everywhere. I had read the briefs, including the legion of *amicus* briefs that had been filed in support of the respective parties and ISNP—'In Support of Neither Party'—an interesting concept in itself, and was looking forward to hearing the argument. **4.01**

My counsel had told me not to bring any electronic devices as they were forbidden, and so I had the liberating, but not entirely comfortable, feeling of being physically separated from my Blackberry for what turned out to be nearly six hours (we had a good lunch afterwards). I lost count of the number of times I instinctively reached into the inside pocket of my jacket only to find it was empty. My counsel had also told me that I wasn't allowed to bring any written material with me, no copies of the briefs, no folders, nothing. All I was allowed was a pad and a pencil. **4.02**

Finally, my counsel had also told me that on arrival (which she suggested should be about 9 am, an hour before the hearing was due to commence) I should report to the Marshal's office and from there I would be shown to my seat. While I was queuing to get to the Marshal's office, I was handed a small leaflet. It was entitled 'Supreme Court of the United States—Visitor's Guide to Oral Argument'. Inside, the opening words were: 'Welcome to the Supreme Court of the United States. This is your Supreme Court…' **4.03**

However, as I read further, and as I waited in the queue, and as, finally, I was shown to my seat, I began to wonder whose Supreme Court they meant it was. After the section explaining how the oral argument would run, there was another section entitled 'Participants in the Courtroom', which set out who does what and where they sit. **4.04**

They were listed as: **4.05**

'Justices'	who sit on the bench in order of seniority, with the Chief Justice in the middle;
'Clerk'	who sits to the left of the bench;
'Marshal'	who sits to the right of the bench;
'Marshal's Aides'	who are seated behind the Justices; and
'Attorneys'	those scheduled to argue the case are seated at tables facing the bench.

4.06 But it then went on to provide that attorneys who are admitted as members of the Supreme Court Bar may be seated in the chairs just beyond the bronze railing and that members of the Supreme Court bar may attend any argument, space permitting. Nowhere in the section headed 'Participants in the Courtroom' did I see where I, the client, should sit.

4.07 And then I noticed another section in the leaflet headed 'Others' and I thought—fair enough, I suppose I may be viewed as not being an actual participant (although I struggled to see how curious members of the Supreme Court Bar could be viewed as such) and so I looked at that section in anticipation of guidance as to where I should go.

4.08 First in the 'Others' section were 'Law Clerks'. Each Justice has the option of employing up to four law clerks, I read. They are seated in the chairs flanking the courtroom on the right. Next came 'Special Guests'. Aha, I thought, at last! But I was disappointed. It read: 'Guests of Justices are seated in the benches to the right of the Bench and are seated in order of the seniority of the Justice who invited them. The row of black chairs in front of the guest section is reserved for retired Justices and officers of the Court, such as the Reporter of Decisions or the Librarian.'

4.09 Finally in the 'Others' section came 'News Media', which read: 'Members of the Supreme Court press corps sit to the left of the Bench in the benches and chairs facing the guest section.' By this time it was 9.30 am and I had reached the front of the queue at the Marshal's office and I was shown to my seat—five rows back in the public seating area on the opposite side of the courtroom to my counsel.

4.10 'Welcome to the Supreme Court of the United States. This is your Supreme Court…' My conclusion was that it certainly wasn't the client's Supreme Court.

B. Client-Ccentred Processes

4.11 My US Supreme Court example is just one of a number of instances where, when you look at the processes that are adopted for resolving disputes between clients (and without clients there would be no disputes, no courts, and no arbitral tribunals), the interests of the client do not always seem to be at the forefront of the thinking of those responsible for formulating the way in which disputes are resolved.

4.12 Arbitration was created, and has evolved, as an alternative to the rigid formality of court proceedings. It is supposed to be a flexible, client-focused process, and in many respects it is. The client is usually involved in the selection process of the tribunal, the proceedings are often confidential to help protect client privacy, and the client has an expectation of a speedier, more cost-effective dispute resolution process.

4.13 However, as arbitration has continued to evolve in the modern era, it is valid to ask: has it retained that vital client focus? Perhaps the same question should be posed about arbitration as posed about the US Supreme Court. Whose arbitration is it anyway?

4.14 In pursuit of this question I intend to look at just two aspects of modern arbitration practice which may not be as client focused as they could, and should, be. Before doing so, however, I want to start with what sounds like a very basic and very obvious proposition, but which often gets forgotten when designing dispute resolution processes, namely that clients' interests are most likely to be aligned before there is a dispute. Once a dispute has arisen, even the most reasonable of clients can become unreasonable—at least unreasonable in the eyes of the client on the other side—which, of course, thinks it is being perfectly reasonable.

So, if anything is going to be done to address the expensive and time-consuming aspects of the dispute resolution process, it needs to be done before the dispute starts. It needs to be in the rules which will apply to the arbitration. **4.15**

Much of what I am about to say is not new. But I get the impression that, in the past, at least, although clients have said one thing, what has been heard by the rule-makers and those who apply the rules, namely arbitral institutions and arbitral tribunals, has been another thing. **4.16**

It rather reminds me of those apocryphal examples of 'squawks' from the US Air Force. Squawks are problems which are noted by US Air Force pilots and left for maintenance crews to fix before the next flight. The pilots leave a note with the problem described and the maintenance crews leave a note for the pilots with the solution. But what is reported as a problem, and what is done to address the problem, is not always what was expected. For example: **4.17**

(1) Problem: Left inside tyre almost needs replacement.
    Solution: Almost replaced left inside tyre.
(2) Problem: Something loose in cockpit.
    Solution: Something tightened in cockpit.
(3) Problem: Evidence of leak on right main landing gear.
    Solution: Evidence removed.

You get the idea. **4.18**

C. Reducing Time and Cost

Much is said in arbitration circles about the need to reduce the time and cost of arbitration, and that need is certainly there, but at the moment this is based on the flawed assumption that this is the only issue clients have with arbitration, and also the belief that with a little guidance and prodding, arbitral tribunals will magically become more proactive, more willing to take risks, more willing to impose efficient processes on parties even if it is against both parties' wishes, and, generally, will act a bit more like judges in the English court system. **4.19**

There is, sadly, no evidence that any of this is really happening. There is evidence that attempts are being made to address some of these issues, but the attempts are, to my mind, falling well short of what is needed. This is amply demonstrated by some of the latest rule changes that have been made in the cause of speed and efficiency. **4.20**

(a) Case management conferences

With much fanfare, the ICC included in its new 2012 Rules a provision that the arbitral tribunal must convene a case management conference. However, this is not a case management conference where the tribunal tells the parties what they should be doing, or restricts the parties' ability to play games with procedural issues. The lack of robustness in the approach is given away by the wording of Article 24(1), which says: 'the arbitral tribunal shall convene a case management conference to *consult the parties* on procedural measures that *may* be adopted'.[1] **4.21**

---

[1] Emphasis added.

4.22 I am afraid that I cannot see that provision giving an arbitral tribunal more teeth than it already has—and that is very few. Arbitral tribunals need to have their powers spelled out clearly and unambiguously and arbitral institutions need to be willing to give more power to arbitral tribunals, power that can be used even if the parties want to do something different.

4.23 As I said, clients' interests are most likely to be aligned before there is a dispute, and that is the time, therefore, to include provisions which will significantly speed up the dispute resolution process and, in so doing, reduce the cost.

(b) Historical advantages of arbitration

4.24 When I first started in the law in the late 1970s, I had drummed into me the six advantages of arbitration over litigation—speed, cost, flexibility, ability to choose your tribunal, confidentiality, and enforceability.

4.25 Speed and cost of arbitration have long since ceased to be advantages as litigation has got quicker and cheaper—at least as far as the vast majority of English Commercial and Technology and Construction Court cases are concerned. Confidentiality of arbitration in many jurisdictions is rapidly being eroded and, with the advent of the Brussels Regulation, arbitration only has the upper hand when it comes to enforcing outside Europe.

4.26 The ability to choose your tribunal remains, although increasingly that seems, to me, to be an illusory advantage and, as for flexibility, having been involved in arbitrations both as counsel and arbitrator for the last 30 years, I have concluded it was always a myth. I have seen very, very few flexible processes adopted by tribunals over the years and almost none when it was clear that the parties were not keen on departing from the well-trodden track.

4.27 But, wait a minute, why would a client argue for his wishes to be overridden by an overly assertive tribunal? Well, just as the most reasonable and sensible people can turn into aggressive maniacs once they get behind the wheel of a car, so can clients when they get into a dispute. All sense of reason, and reasonableness, goes, and the only imperative is to win, and to do whatever that takes, even when it is against your cultural and legal background.

4.28 By way of example, I chaired an arbitral tribunal a few years ago in a dispute between an Italian company and an English company. The arbitration clause in the contract provided for ICC arbitration with the seat to be in London. It said nothing about disclosure of documents.

4.29 If the parties had been asked at the time the contract was entered into how they wished disclosure to be dealt with, you might have expected them to respond in line with their legal and cultural backgrounds: the English party might have been in favour of fairly comprehensive disclosure and the Italian party may not have wanted any—or at least not much. Whether an agreement could have been reached at that stage as to how disclosure would be dealt with, who knows, but I wager it would have been easier than once the dispute started.

4.30 And what happened once the dispute started? At the procedural hearing, the Italian party pressed for full-blown English-court-style disclosure and the English party objected to such wide-ranging disclosure and looked to limit it as much as possible. My tribunal did what most arbitral tribunals usually do—and that was not to depart from the well-trodden track. We ordered disclosure in accordance with the IBA Rules on the Taking of Evidence. We felt, as I know many tribunals feel, that we didn't have the power at our disposal to be more flexible or radical.

4.31 Arbitral tribunals need to be invested with the power to be flexible; they need to be able to say to the parties: 'I am going to order this and you, as the parties, agreed that I have the power to do this because you gave it to me in your arbitration clause or in the institutional rules you agreed.' At present, however, arbitral tribunals cannot take that robust approach.

(c) A compromise approach

4.32 Redfern and Hunter write:

> Arbitral tribunals usually prefer to avoid making rulings on disputed procedural matters in the early stages of an arbitration. Where there is a disagreement between the parties, arbitrators often suggest compromise solutions. This appears to derive from the complexities of tribunal psychology, as a result of which individual members of arbitral tribunals (and particularly the presiding arbitrator) are reluctant to make rulings at the start of the arbitration that one of the parties may regard (however unjustifiably) as amounting to unfair treatment.[2]

4.33 This means that, absent party consent at the time of the dispute, arbitration is lacking certain procedural tools that are available to judges. Tools that can save a lot of time and cost. The two that I have particularly in mind are strike-outs and preliminary issues. Certainly, from the client's perspective, a tribunal which is not willing, or empowered, to strike out a clearly unmeritorious claim, or is not willing or empowered to order a preliminary issue to be dealt with, is one which is inevitably going to preside over proceedings which will take too long, cost too much, and not get the issue resolved as quickly as it should.

4.34 However, unless arbitral tribunals are specifically empowered to strike out cases which are without merit, they are not going to do so of their own accord, and, at the moment, the wording of many of the rules of the arbitration institutions make it clear that they cannot do so. The LCIA Rules (Article 14.4(i)) require the tribunal to 'act fairly and impartially as between all parties, giving each a reasonable opportunity of putting its case'. The ICC Arbitration Rules (Article 22(4)) require the arbitral tribunal to 'act fairly and impartially and ensure that each party has a reasonable opportunity to present its case'. The UNCITRAL Rules (Article 17.1) also require that 'at an appropriate stage of the proceedings each party is given a reasonable opportunity of presenting its case'. The UNCITRAL Rules (Article 17.3) go even further by providing that: 'If... any party so requests the arbitral tribunal shall hold hearings for the presentation of evidence by witnesses, including expert witnesses, or for oral argument.'

4.35 Although it is perfectly possible to argue that, if a party makes a strike-out application, the tribunal can say that this is the time for the other party to present its case as to why it shouldn't be struck out, it does not work like that. The vast majority of arbitrators take the view that, no matter how unmeritorious the case appears to be, it has to go through to the bitter end, including document disclosure, oral testimony, and legal submissions.

---

[2] Nigel Blackaby and others, *Redfern and Hunter on International Arbitration* (6th edn, OUP 2009) para 6.49.

4.36 As far as I can establish, there are only two published ICC cases[3] where summary motions were brought by respondents to the claim against them and, although the tribunals in question seemed to accept that they had power to consider the motions, both were dismissed on the basis that it wasn't crystal clear that the claims had no legal basis. It appears that a much higher threshold was adopted than the 'no reasonable grounds' we use in English court proceedings.

4.37 Interestingly, there is only one set of arbitration rules that provides for some form of summary judgment procedure and that is the ICSID Rules, Article 41(5) of which permits a strike-out application. It says: 'a party may ... file an objection that a claim is manifestly without legal merit. The party shall specify as precisely as possible the basis for the objection. The Tribunal, after giving the parties the opportunity to present their observations on the objection, shall, at its first session or promptly thereafter, notify the parties of its decision on the objection.'

4.38 The ICSID Rules also allow for other objections, including jurisdiction, to be raised and dealt with as preliminary issues. In 2009/2010, ICSID dismissed two cases following a preliminary hearing—*Global Trading Resource Corp and Global International, Inc v Ukraine*[4] and *RSM Production Co v Grenada*.[5] Neither was dismissed on the 'manifestly without legal merit' ground—one was on jurisdiction and the other on the basis that a previous case based on largely the same facts had decided the question brought—but, at least, they were got rid of at an early stage.

4.39 I say 'early stage'. The *Global Trading* case took 17 months to resolve and the *RSM* case 11 months, but if you contrast that with the average time for the other ICSID awards published around that time—42 months—it certainly speeded up resolution.

D. Challenges

4.40 Of course, the big fear that arbitral tribunals have, both generally and in the context of striking out applications, is that their awards will be open to challenge if they do not have clear powers or if they depart from the well-trodden track; and so, if we are to encourage the dismissal of unmeritorious cases at an early stage, arbitral tribunals need to be supported in every way possible.

4.41 This means both changing the rules of arbitration institutions to permit strike-outs and providing the necessary judicial support to uphold them. That support should be forthcoming in England and Wales given that summary judgment and strike-outs are part of our civil procedure, and, in the United States where the Revised Uniform Arbitration Act gives (in section 15(b)) specific power to arbitrators to deal with summary disposition of a claim. Even if other jurisdictions are less willing or able to give such support, a rule change implemented by the major institutions permitting strike-outs, and supported by English and US judiciary, would be a start.

---

[3] ICC Case No 11413, First Interim Award (December 2001) (2010) 21 ICC Int'l Ct Arb Bull 34 and ICC Case No 12297, Procedural Order No 1 (22 August 2003), 'Decisions on ICC Arbitration Procedure: A Selection of Procedural Orders Issued by Arbitral Tribunals Acting under the ICC Rules of Arbitration (2003–2004)' (2011) ICC Int'l Ct Arb Bull, 2010 Special Supplement, 47.

[4] ICSID Case No ARB/09/11, Award (1 December 2010).

[5] *Rachel S Grynberg, Stephen M Grynberg, Miriam Z Grynberg and RSM Production Co v Grenada*, ICSID Case No ARB/10/6, Award (10 December 2010).

4.42 The other area of focus for expediting arbitration proceedings should be preliminary issues. Arbitral tribunals need to be much more proactive in identifying preliminary issues at an early stage in the proceedings and then dealing with them. Even if the issue will not be dispositive of the case, much can be achieved by the parties knowing the answer to at least one, if not more, of the major issues between them, and this can often drive settlement.

4.43 Further, if a preliminary issue is identified early, and dealt with, the parties will not only have that part of their dispute resolved, but they will each have an insight into the approach the tribunal has taken to that issue, and that may, in turn, inform their thinking about how other issues in dispute may be handled.

4.44 Yes, on occasions, it may lead to a higher overall cost if the dispute is not settled and does proceed to a full-blown hearing, but the opportunity to try and cut things short should not be spurned too lightly, as it often is at present. It seems that, in this area, the innate conservatism of rule-makers and arbitrators has overridden what the clients would see as a straightforward risk issue.

4.45 Businesses work on risks. The risks involved in entering into a transaction, pursuing an exploration opportunity, working with a particular partner in a joint venture, or investing in the territory of a potentially unstable government are examined, calculated, and used by businesses in the decision-making process. Transactions are concluded and projects undertaken when the probability of success is well below 100 per cent (which it always is) and often when it is below 50 per cent.

4.46 So, when clients look at the risks involved in court and arbitration proceedings, they do so through an entirely different lens from their legal advisors. There can be certain upsides to having a particular issue dealt with early that may make the risk of increased costs worthwhile. The risk involved in having a tribunal or a court take a preliminary issue which may not be dispositive of the dispute, or make a significant overall saving in cost, is one which clients may, more often than not, be prepared to take.

4.47 The 2012 QMUL Survey included an examination of methods of expediting arbitral proceedings.[6] Practitioners were asked about the effectiveness of early identification by the tribunal of issues to be decided, and having those issues dealt with as soon as possible after constitution of the tribunal. Of those surveyed, 64 per cent said this was either most, or quite, effective at expediting arbitral proceedings. When you add to that figure the 13 per cent who said they had never seen it happen, then you arrive at the sorts of odds on which most commercial clients would happily take a risk.

4.48 The English courts already permit the hearing of preliminary issues, so can arbitrators—if armed with the ability in arbitration rules to use such tools—take lessons from the courts? The answer, to my mind, is a definite no. While it is clear that the courts have the ability to take preliminary issues, they seem to lack the necessary conviction. It is no good giving arbitral tribunals the tools if, like the courts, they are not prepared to use them, and use them imaginatively.

---

[6] 'Current and Preferred Practices in the Arbitral Process: International Arbitration Survey' <http://www.arbitration.qmul.ac.uk/research/index.html> accessed 25 September 2015.

4.49 The test adopted in the English court system for whether there should be a trial of preliminary issues falls way short, in my submission, of the flexibility that the arbitration system could apply if it only had the tools to do so, and it would be a serious mistake to seek to apply the English court test in an arbitration context. Nothing would be gained.

4.50 My view, as a former in-house counsel, and, I would hazard a guess, that of many other general counsel of large corporations, is that the test that should be adopted in deciding whether to have a trial of preliminary issues in arbitration proceedings is whether resolving the issue in question will help the parties involved to better understand their overall position or be better able to reach a settlement.

4.51 The approach used in the English courts is set out in the relevant Practice Direction,[7] which states that the test is whether 'it will be just and will save costs to order a split trial or the trial of one or more preliminary issues'.

4.52 At first glance this seems perfectly reasonable and not too far from what I have just suggested. The reality is, however, very different. The threshold applied in practice is much higher.

4.53 In *SCA Packaging Ltd v Boyle (Northern Ireland)*,[8] the House of Lords gave its guidance on the limited circumstances in which it would be appropriate to order the trial of preliminary issues. Lord Hope of Craighead observed that:

> The essential criterion for deciding whether or not to hold a pre-hearing is whether, as it was put by Lindsay J in CJ *O'Shea Construction Ltd v Bassi*,[9] there is a succinct, knockout point which is capable of being decided after only a relatively short hearing. This is unlikely to be the case where a preliminary issue cannot be entirely divorced from the merits of the case, or the issue will require a substantial body of evidence. In such a case it is preferable that there should be only one hearing to determine all the matters in dispute.

4.54 In addition, Lord Brown stated that unless there was a 'probability' that a preliminary issue would be 'determinative one way or another of the entire dispute', it was highly unlikely to be justifiable to set down the issue to be determined on a preliminary basis. What is clear from all this is that there is a fixation in the court system on there being a single hearing and that if a preliminary issue is to be tried it has to be a 'knockout point'.

4.55 Looked at from the perspective of ease of administration of the court system, I can see there are benefits to there being only a single, all-in hearing. However, looked at from the perspective of the parties, commercial parties at least, that is not necessarily what they want. It bears repeating that the determination of preliminary issues can be incredibly useful to clients even if the effect is not a knockout of the whole case. Decisions on certain issues can drive overall settlement and, even if it does not work out on every occasion and overall costs end up being more than they would if there had been a single hearing, commercial clients will often be prepared to take that risk.

4.56 Now, don't get me wrong, I am not advocating this adventurous approach only where both clients are in agreement. That would be too easy and would forget what I said earlier about

---

[7] Practice Direction 29, para 5.3(7).
[8] [2009] UKHL 37.
[9] [1998] ICR 1130, 1140.

the change in mindset of otherwise reasonable commercial organizations once a dispute has arisen. No, this is something an arbitral tribunal should be willing to do if there is a sound enough argument put forward by one of the parties because, inevitably, the other party, with an interest in prolonging proceedings, or waiting to see if something turns up, will almost certainly oppose it.

4.57 Let me use two examples of where a preliminary issue would, almost certainly, not be viewed in the courts as a knockout blow to the case, but which it would be nice to think an arbitral tribunal, armed with appropriate powers, would grasp with both (or all six) hands.

4.58 Suppose you have a dispute between a manufacturer and a customer. As is often the case in contracts for the manufacture of large engineering products (say air compressors) for inclusion in industrial projects, there is a limitation of liability provision limiting the manufacturer's liability for breach of contract to the contract price or a percentage of the contract price. Let's assume that limitation, in monetary terms, is £10 million. The customer is alleging breach of contract (the product failed), is claiming damages of £100 million, and is arguing that it is not bound by the limitation of liability. This can be for any number of reasons—battle of the forms, subsequent contractual variation, waiver, misrepresentation, and umpteen other possibilities. The manufacturer says it is not in breach of contract, but even if it is, its maximum liability is £10 million.

4.59 What is imperative for both clients to know is whether this is a £10 million case or potentially a £100 million case. The customer may not admit to that imperative because it thinks it may have a better chance of influencing the court its way if the court can see how egregious the manufacturer's contractual breach was, how much money it has actually lost as a result of the breach, or generally how poor in performance the manufacturer has been. Although prejudicial, none of this should impact on the legal consideration of the application of the limitation of liability.

4.60 What is clear, adopting the approach of the courts, is that a decision either way—confirming the cap applies and the maximum recovery would be £10 million or confirming the cap does not apply and damages could be much more—will not constitute a knockout blow and that to examine this issue as a preliminary point will not save costs overall if a settlement is not, subsequently, reached. There will, after all, still be the breach of contract issue to deal with as well as the actual damages to ascertain if the limitation on liability is broken.

4.61 However, from the parties' perspective, to know if this is a £10 million capped case or not is the sort of information on which a risk assessment can be performed as to whether to settle and at what amount. Depending on the result, you can see how the settlement dynamics will be driven for each party. This is just the sort of preliminary issue that arbitrators should feel comfortable they have the power to order be dealt with even against one party's wishes.

4.62 My second example involves a joint venture dispute as to the performance of each party under the joint venture agreement. One has purported to terminate the joint venture for the failure of the other to perform and has made a claim for the lost profits that would have been made by the venture but for the other party's default. The legal and factual issues surrounding the performance issues of the partners are complex and will involve a great deal of documentary and factual evidence. However, it is alleged by the respondent that, even if it was in default (which is denied), the venture would never have made any money anyway, and that this can be established quickly and simply.

4.63 How many arbitral tribunals, against the wishes of the claimant, would be willing to take, as a preliminary issue, the question of whether the venture would have made any money? In other words, dealt with quantum of damage first, before any finding on liability? I would doubt many would take that approach, but I can say that I am aware of one situation where precisely that was done by the tribunal, which found there were no damages. Not surprisingly, that proved to be the end of the matter.

4.64 Donald Rumsfeld memorably said: 'as we know, there are known knowns; there are things we know we know. We also know there are known unknowns; that is to say we know there are some things we do not know. But there are also unknown unknowns—the ones we don't know we don't know. And it is the latter category that tends to be the difficult one.'[10]

4.65 At present, the unknown unknowns in the arbitral process remain unknown for far too long, all in the interests of having a single, all-in hearing of even the most unmeritorious claims, or of claims involving issues which could be separated out and dealt with at an early stage. Allowing strike-outs and permitting the early hearing of preliminary issues would help turn those unknown unknowns into known knowns and enable commercial clients to have a better idea of the risks involved in proceeding with the case.

4.66 It needs the rule-makers to take the initiative and give clear powers to arbitral tribunals, which are not subject to party agreement, in their rules; it needs arbitral tribunals to exercise their powers robustly; and it needs courts to uphold decisions made robustly in the exercise of those powers. Finally, of course, it does require the clients to take the risk of including in their contracts arbitration clauses providing for such rules to apply. I am certain, however, that more clients will be willing to take the risk of doing so at the time of entering into the contract than after the dispute has arisen.

E. Conclusion

4.67 Unlike the feeling I was left with in the US Supreme Court, after reading the brochure which said 'this is your Supreme Court', of not being sure whose court it was, clients need to be clear and sure that the arbitral process is their process and not a process designed for the convenience or comfort of others, so that there is no longer a need to ask 'whose arbitration is it?'

4.68 And what happened at my Supreme Court hearing? Well, instead of getting a judgment on the issue that had been appealed from the Court of Appeals, we were asked by the Justices to submit briefs on another aspect of the case, which we duly did; and, six months later, I found myself back in the US Supreme Court for the first argument of the new judicial term. I knew the form this time, made my move quickly, and was able to get a seat only two rows from the front in the public seating area, and on the same side of the courtroom as my counsel.

---

[10] Donald H Rumsfeld, 'DoD News Briefing—Secretary Rumsfeld and Gen. Myers', US Department of Defense (12 February 2002) <http://archive.defense.gov> accessed 2 February 2016.

While I was waiting for the rest of the seating to fill up, and for the Justices to come in, I saw **4.69**
a gentleman approach one of the Marshal's Aides and say 'I am the petitioner in the case
immediately following this one. Where do I sit?' to which the reply was 'Wherever you can
find space, sir'.

You'll learn, I thought. **4.70**

5

HOW EASY IS IT NOT TO TAKE ADEQUATE CARE OF THE PROPER EXPECTATIONS OF THE PARTIES?

Mauro Rubino-Sammartano

A. Introduction

5.01 The attitude of arbitrators towards the parties to arbitration proceedings is almost exclusively considered in relation to disclosure of possible conflict of interests and suspicions of bias. It might seem that only new arbitrators are exposed to the risk of not paying sufficient attention to the legitimate expectations of the parties. However, it is suggested that this may occur even to regular arbitrators who are accustomed to sit in such a capacity. It might be wise to accept that this could occur to any of us, even when we have the best intentions. A quick survey of possible—or even involuntary—breaches of the legitimate expectations of the parties may therefore be appropriate.

B. Common Problems

(a) Not allowing sufficient time to the proceedings

5.02 The apparently obvious requirement that the arbitrator devotes to each proceeding the time which it needs is not always met by several arbitrators. This may be due to different reasons. On some occasions this may be due to rush, possibly caused by the arbitrator's other commitments, or by his wish to return quickly to his home or place of business. On other occasions, the arbitrator may have come to the conclusion that what he has heard is sufficient for him to decide. However, even taking into account the understandable wish of the arbitrator not to hear useless repetitions, some submissions or evidence may give rise to further points to be considered. This should not be seen as an invitation for arbitrators either to be slow or to rush. As usual, in *medio stat virtus*.

(b) Not allowing the parties to adequately present their case

5.03 The arbitrator very rarely succeeds in making both parties to a proceeding happy. One might feel that the adequate response to this is that his task is not to make all of them happy, but to decide the dispute. This feeling may also apply to the contents of his decision. However, it does not necessarily apply to another aspect of the proceedings, ie to the right of each party to adequately present his case. In this respect, it is suggested that all parties are entitled to leave the hearing room with the feeling that their right to adequately present their case has been respected.

5.04 If the arbitrator cannot make all the parties happy with his decision, he may—and I would say must—ensure that they are reasonably happy with the opportunity they had to present their case. If the arbitrator is requested to hear many witnesses, this should not justify simply cutting down the list or excluding a new line of examination or cross-examination—unless a point has already been well established in the mind of the arbitrator or is not material, in which event he should say so in order that justice is not only done, but is seen to have been done.

(c) The temptation to rush

5.05 Nobody is immune from the temptation to go quickly through the pleadings, once he has the feeling that he has understood the terms of the problem. The temptation must indeed be very strong when a party repeats fully or largely the same arguments in its subsequent pleadings.

5.06 A serious risk involved in going too quickly through such pleadings is that sometimes—in the middle of the repetition of an argument—one line or one short sentence may be found which is relevant for the decision. The same temptation arises as to documents, and is understandable when a party files documents which are made up of many pages and contain many passages which are totally irrelevant. To avoid this, when I sit as a sole arbitrator or as chairman of the panel, I request the parties to underline and mark the passages of their documents on which each party relies.

(d) Effects of disliking counsel

5.07 It may happen, and it does happen, that an arbitrator does not like the parties (and/or their counsel) in the same way, or that he definitely dislikes one of them. This is human and may be a sort of physical reaction. Of course this feeling is and must remain separate from appreciation of the facts and of the points of law which lead to the decision. Doing otherwise could indeed affect the integrity of the process.

(e) A formalistic approach

5.08 One may wonder why the parties decided to submit a dispute to arbitration rather than to the state courts. Leaving aside transnational disputes (where the parties opt for arbitration to avoid one party to the proceedings having a perceived psychological bias with the courts of its country), I generally volunteer the response that they do so not only because they want something different from what they would usually get from the state courts, but because they expect something better.

5.09 One of these 'better' services they expect is, it is submitted, that the decision is not made just by going by the book and by applying a formalistic approach in establishing the intentions of the parties to a contract, or in appreciating the evidence, or in construing the law. This does not, of course, aim to open the door to subjective criteria, but simply means construing the commitments of the parties and the law by taking into account the real intentions and not just one or two isolated words, and not just coldly applying the law, but seeking a correct interpretation that is much more in line with the intentions of the concerned party.

(f) Lack of a full *de novo* review

5.10 It is not often that immunity produces the result that those who benefit from it become more diligent. On the contrary, immunity tends to induce people to take matters more easily. It is submitted that where there is immunity from errors as to merits, and also as to substantive law, this inevitably creates the risk that such issues are not examined with the same care which is used by the arbitrator when he is aware that in the case of errors his decision would be set aside.

5.11 I personally remain unhappy with this 'partial' conclusion. I have advocated for at least 20 years that since arbitrators are exposed at least as much as a court judge to the risk of mistakes, the remedy of a full *de novo* review, which is available in court proceedings, must also be available in arbitration. This review would be reserved to an appellate arbitral tribunal consisting of three arbitrators, each to be appointed by the arbitral institution. This is the solution to the problem that has been adopted by the European Court of Arbitration.[1]

C. Conclusion

5.12 I have frequently found that the approach of many fellow arbitrators, apart from their legitimate satisfaction with the respect paid to them by entrusting them with this quasi-judicial role, was to render an award which would produce for them respect or even admiration, or the wish, at least in Continental Europe, to write a brilliant intellectual treatise.

5.13 Here, too, I doubt very much that this would be the expectation of the parties. While some parties just wish to always win, in particular when they know they are wrong, to me, the innocent party, the honest man or woman, expects that the arbitrator will decide the dispute with diligence and humanity.[2]

5.14 This final remark brings me back with pleasure to the spirit which I found and liked very much, when—some decades ago—the annual conference of the CIArb was held (twice) in Torquay, under exactly the same rain, with people like Cedric Barclay, Norman Royce, Bertie Vigrass, and many others.

---

[1] Starting from its 1997 Arbitration Rules.
[2] Mauro Rubino Sammartano, *International Arbitration Law and Practice* (3rd edn, Juris 2014).

Part III

INTERNATIONAL ARBITRATION AGREEMENTS

Issues and Perspectives

6

SOME REFLECTIONS ON THE MAKING OF INTERNATIONAL ARBITRATION AGREEMENTS FOR THE RESOLUTION OF COMMERCIAL DISPUTES

Lord Saville

A. Introduction

Many reasons are advanced for the large and increasing use of international arbitration as the means of resolving commercial disputes between parties situated in different countries. Privacy and confidentiality are high on the list, although there are difficulties in enforcing either, and the laws on the subject are far from clear or uniform. The choice of a neutral country rather than recourse to the courts of the country of one party or the other is also high on the list, as is the choice of a neutral tribunal, although in the latter case there is, sadly, sometimes a tendency, in an arbitral tribunal of three, for the arbitrator chosen by a particular party to favour that party. Arbitrators are often chosen for their particular knowledge of the trade or science involved, although here it can be difficult to find a tribunal which is clearly neutral. There are also said to be advantages in reduced costs and speedier processes than those of courts, although this is very far from always being the case. **6.01**

B. The New York Convention

In 1989, Lord Mustill described the New York Convention as the most successful international instrument in the field of arbitration, which as such could perhaps lay claim to be the most effective instance of international legislation in the entire history of commercial law. To my mind, this remains the case 25 years later. **6.02**

The reason is simple. The New York Convention is a treaty that has been adopted to date by over 150 countries throughout the world, and as such provides a simple and effective means of recognizing and enforcing arbitration awards made in one country in any other country that is party to the Convention. It is in truth the bedrock of international commercial arbitration and to my mind the most persuasive reason for choosing this form of international commercial dispute resolution. The bottom line is whether an international arbitral award is enforceable, for if it is not, the process—however private, confidential, neutral, knowledgeable, inexpensive, or quick—will simply be a waste of time and money. **6.03**

6.04 In view of the success of the New York Convention, the choice of arbitration for the resolution of international commercial disputes is today very often the preferable course to take. In addition, the widespread adoption of the UNCITRAL Model Law, either wholesale, or (as in the English Arbitration Act 1996) by incorporation of most of its provisions, has meant that internationally there is now an increasingly level playing field for this form of dispute resolution.

6.05 With the New York Convention and the UNCITRAL Model Law, those considering arbitration as the preferred method of international dispute resolution have sound foundations on which to build an arbitration agreement.

C. Arbitration Agreements

(a) Contract clauses

6.06 The most common form of arbitration agreement is one (known as an arbitration clause) that forms part of a commercial contract, and which provides that any future disputes that may arise under that contract will be resolved through the arbitral process, although of course not infrequently the parties to an existing dispute will by agreement (known as a submission agreement) adopt arbitration as their preferred method of resolution, instead of going to court.

(b) Submission agreements

6.07 Submission agreements tend to set out in some detail how the dispute is to be arbitrated. This is because once a dispute has been identified, it is possible to tailor the arbitral process to that dispute. As far as arbitration clauses are concerned, these vary enormously. At the one extreme the parties may simply stipulate 'Arbitration' without more than perhaps indicating where the arbitration is to take place.

6.08 At the other extreme are lengthy and highly sophisticated provisions, setting out in the fullest detail how and in what circumstances one party can commence an arbitration against the other, how many arbitrators are to be appointed and by whom, where the arbitration should take place or be treated as taking place and how it should be conducted, what law should be applied to the dispute and to the arbitral process itself, how the arbitration should be financed, and so on. Such arbitration clauses can occupy pages of text and are usually the construct of the lawyers negotiating the contract to which the arbitration clause relates. They are often found in large-scale international contracts, such as those concerned with the extraction and marketing of oil and gas.

6.09 These are the two extremes. What occupies much of the middle ground today are institutional arbitration agreements, which are arbitration clauses which specifically incorporate the rules and procedures of arbitral institutions.

D. The Role of Institutions

6.10 There exist today throughout the world a considerable number of arbitral institutions, of which perhaps the widest known is still the ICC in Paris. The function of these institutions is, broadly speaking, to provide specific rules for the conduct of arbitrations, together with administration and management of the arbitral process. They provide model forms of arbitration clause for use in commercial contracts, which have the advantage of incorporating by reference the rules governing the setting up and running of the arbitration, rather than writing them all out in the agreement.

In any substantial international commercial contract where the parties wish to arbitrate rather than litigate any disputes that may arise between them, there is much to be said for using arbitral institutions, rather than seeking to draft specific arbitration clauses, and although of course such use necessarily adds cost to the arbitral process, the benefit is the great experience and knowledge that such institutions possess. **6.11**

In this context it has to be remembered that when commercial entities enter into commercial dealings with each other, they generally do so on the basis that the bargain that they have made will succeed—not that it will fail or lead to disputes. Thus, their minds will not primarily (or, indeed, at all) be directed to what is to happen if they fall out over the performance of their contract, save perhaps a general agreement to arbitrate rather than litigate. In the nature of things, unless well supplied by (expensive) lawyers, they are unlikely to be conversant with important aspects of the arbitral process. **6.12**

An example in the context of international commercial arbitration is the concept of the 'seat' of the arbitration, its juridical place. In general terms, the conduct of the arbitration is governed by the laws of that place, known as the *lex arbitri*. This may or may not in fact be where the arbitration actually takes place, but is where it is treated by the law as taking place. While there have been suggestions that, in some cases at least, an international arbitration should be treated as having no seat at all, and instead float above any municipal laws, there are difficulties in this approach since, for example, an award in an arbitration with no seat may well prove unenforceable under the New York Convention. **6.13**

E. The Role of Law

Such concepts as the juridical seat of an arbitration are unlikely to be at the forefront of the minds of commercial people seeking to make an international bargain, unless they are aided and advised by lawyers versed in the laws of arbitration. The same is true of many other aspects of the arbitral process. However, it is here that much of the UNCITRAL Model Law and statutes such as the English Arbitration Act 1996 are of enormous assistance, for many of their provisions are devoted to setting out what is to happen in the absence of specific agreement by the parties, as are many of the rules of arbitral institutions. **6.14**

(a) The English Arbitration Act 1996

For example, section 3 of the English Arbitration Act 1996 provides that: **6.15**

> 'The seat of the arbitration' means the juridical seat of the arbitration designated:
> (a) by the parties to the arbitration agreement, or
> (b) by any arbitral or other institution or person vested by the parties with powers in that regard, or
> (c) by the arbitral tribunal if so authorised by the parties, or determined, in the absence of any such designation, having regard to the parties' agreement and all the relevant circumstances.

(b) The Model Law

6.16 The Model Law contains similar provisions, although it may be noted that when we were drafting the English Arbitration Act 1996 we added a reference to arbitral institutions, because of their increasing importance.

6.17 The Model Law stipulates that an arbitration agreement should be in writing. Although as a matter of English law an oral arbitration agreement is not entirely ineffective, the English Arbitration Act 1996 contains the same requirement, although it defines 'writing' in rather broader terms than does the Model Law. It seemed to those of us concerned with drafting this Act that it was important to have some permanent record of an arbitration agreement, since such an agreement has the important effect of contracting out of the parties' basic right to go to court in the event of a dispute.

F. Disadvantages to Arbitration

6.18 In some cases, there is a potential disadvantage to agreeing to arbitrate rather than litigate future disputes. This arises where a number of parties are involved, who are not all parties to the same arbitration clause. For example, construction projects often involve a main contractor who makes a number of sub-contracts. The sub-contractor may in turn sub-sub-contract some of the work and so on. Each of these contracts may contain its own arbitration clause.

6.19 A dispute arises between, say, the main contractor and one of the sub-contractors, who seeks in turn to blame one or more of the others. In court proceedings, there is power to order all the involved parties to be heard together, by ordering consolidation or concurrent hearings, or by ordering additional parties to be joined, so that the disputes between all can be resolved at one hearing. However, without the agreement of all, this cannot be done in arbitration. Thus, there is a danger that, in such a case, different arbitral tribunals may reach different and inconsistent conclusions, or at least substantially delay and add to the cost of the resolution of the disputes.

6.20 The reason it cannot be done is that arbitration of the kind under discussion depends upon the agreement of the parties to resolve any disputes arising under their contract by a private tribunal of their choosing. Thus, only those who are party to the arbitration agreement can utilize its provisions (unless of course all concerned agree that this can be done).

6.21 When we were drafting the English Arbitration Act 1996, it was suggested to us that arbitrators (or the courts) be given the power to order that additional parties could be joined, or other arbitral proceedings be consolidated or heard concurrently, but we took the view that (without the agreement of all concerned) this would be contrary to the principle of party autonomy, which underlies this form of arbitration.

6.22 However, this is an example where arbitral institutions can, and in many cases do, provide the solution, by incorporating in their standard forms of contract or their rules suitable clauses permitting the tribunal to consolidate or order concurrent hearings in appropriate cases, so that those who have agreed to an institutional arbitration clause which incorporates such clauses will by doing so have agreed that in appropriate cases other parties may be joined (by consolidation, concurrent hearings, or the like) to the arbitration in question.

In recent years, the IBA has done a large amount of very good work in providing rules and guidance for the conduct of international arbitrations, covering such matters as the taking of evidence in international arbitrations, the requirement of independence and impartiality on the part of arbitrators, and codes of conduct for lawyers appearing for the parties in such arbitrations. Again, it is often and increasingly the case that international commercial arbitration agreements incorporate some or all of this valuable guidance. **6.23**

G. Conclusion

Much has changed with regard to international commercial arbitration since I began practice at the commercial bar in London. For example, in maritime disputes arising out of charterparties where the arbitration was held in London, it was the exception rather than the rule that lawyers would appear before the arbitrators to argue the case. Instead, the attitude was that if a dispute arose, each party appointed an arbitrator and the two were in effect hired to deal with and resolve the dispute themselves, asking for what papers they thought they needed, and meeting on their own to consider the case and their answer to it. Rarely did they disagree, but if they did they put the matter before an umpire. In short, their job was to resolve the dispute, without the need for advocates, pleadings, discovery, and the like. It was a simple, quick, and inexpensive form of dispute resolution. **6.24**

Those days have long gone. The procedure has become much more like that of the London Commercial Court and much more often than not lawyers are called in from the outset. Pleadings, discovery, and the like are commonplace. The arbitral process has become increasingly expensive, notwithstanding substantial efforts by arbitral institutions and others to limit costs. **6.25**

In the English Arbitration Act 1996, we stipulated (in section 33) that it was the duty of the arbitral tribunal to 'adopt procedures suitable to the circumstances of the particular case, avoiding unnecessary delay or expense, so as to provide a fair means for the resolution of the matters falling to be determined'. In the following section, we gave the tribunal wide powers to decide all procedural and evidential matters, subject of course to the right of the parties to agree any matter. **6.26**

My impression is that in international commercial arbitrations where the English Arbitration Act 1996 applies, arbitrators have been slow to use these powers, which include, for example, a power to take the initiative in ascertaining the facts and the law, ie to act inquisitorially. The answer often given to this criticism is that the parties wish to adopt what seem to have become traditional methods, with pleadings, full discovery, oral evidence, cross-examination, pre- and post-hearing briefs, and so on. In some cases, of course, such procedures are required for the proper determination of the dispute, but this is not necessarily the case. **6.27**

I would suggest that, where the tribunal considers that the dispute can be dealt with fairly and more cheaply without the full panoply of such legal procedures as the parties' lawyers propose, it makes sure that the parties themselves, not just their lawyers, are made aware of the tribunal's view. If, of course, the parties are truly in agreement on what procedures should be followed, so be it, but I suspect that in some cases at least, it will be found that what the lawyers propose is not what the parties themselves agree is the way to proceed. To **6.28** my mind, a key to reducing the time and expense of this method of dispute resolution is for arbitral tribunals to be much more proactive in proposing how the arbitration should be conducted. Indeed, to my mind, it is their duty to do so.

6.29 Notwithstanding such points as these, international commercial arbitration has the advantages that I have outlined above. It has truly become a large-scale international service industry. I hope and trust that it will continue to flourish. But it will only do so if it constantly bears in mind that it is a service industry. Such industries only prosper if they provide what the users want. There must accordingly be a constant striving to provide 'a fair means for the resolution of the matters falling to be determined'.

7

ARBITRABILITY DECISIONS BEFORE, DURING, AND AFTER ARBITRATION

John J Barceló III

A. Introduction

The cornerstone of arbitration is the arbitration agreement between the parties. If there is no such agreement, the parties should not be sent to arbitration. If there is such an agreement, one party should not be allowed to obstruct the agreement by litigating in a national court the very issues the parties agreed to arbitrate. But at the outset of a dispute one party may contest the existence, validity, or scope of a putative arbitration agreement. Put another way, that party may claim that there is no arbitration agreement in existence that commits the parties to resolve their underlying merits-based dispute in arbitration. Either there is no arbitration agreement in existence at all, or—what amounts to the same thing—one of the disputing parties is not a party to the putative agreement.

Alternatively, a party may claim that an arbitration agreement entered into by both parties is nevertheless for some reason invalid and hence not enforceable. Or a party may claim that an existing and valid arbitration agreement binding the two contesting parties does not extend in its scope to cover a particular merits-based issue in dispute. These are the questions of the existence, validity, or scope of the arbitration agreement that are characteristically raised in disputes over whether a particular merits-based dispute between the parties is 'arbitrable'—that is, whether the merits-based dispute should be resolved by arbitration instead of by a court.

(a) Defining the term

In using the term 'arbitrability' in this way, I am following the lead of the US Supreme Court. Some commentators object to the US Supreme Court's terminology, because in many countries the term 'arbitrability' is used in a narrower sense to refer to a particular kind of invalidity of an existing arbitration agreement.[1] In these countries the question of 'arbitrability' refers to the issue of whether the underlying merits-based issue falls into the category of questions 'not capable of settlement by arbitration' (to use the terminology of the New York Convention)—in particular because such non-arbitrable issues are so infused

---

[1] See Jan Paulsson, *The Idea of Arbitration* (OUP 2013) 72–7; George A Bermann, 'The "Gateway" Problem in International Commercial Arbitration' (2012) 37 Yale J Int'l L 1, 10–13; Emmanuel Gaillard and John Savage (eds), *Fouchard Gaillard Goldman on International Commercial Arbitration* (Kluwer Law International 1999) 312, para 532.

with public policy concerns that the country whose law applies allows resolution of such issues only in one of its national courts. But, as stated, I will use the concept of 'arbitrability' in the broader sense discussed in the opening paragraph to cover any dispute over whether the parties have validly bound themselves to arbitrate the merits-based issue in dispute.

7.04 The arbitrability issue, understood in this way, can arise at each of the characteristic three stages of the arbitration/litigation process. It can arise at what I have called Stage One,[2] before a national court where one party seeks to litigate the merits of the dispute and the other party petitions to have the dispute sent to arbitration. It can also arise at Stage Two, when the parties are before the arbitrable tribunal itself. In this scenario the objecting party asks the tribunal to declare itself without jurisdiction to decide the dispute because the essential requirement of a binding and valid arbitration agreement is lacking. Finally, it can arise at Stage Three, when the party who wins an award asks a national court to enforce it, or the party who loses asks a national court to set it aside or refuse to recognize and enforce it.

7.05 Discussing the arbitrability issue at each of the three characteristic stages of the arbitration/litigation process is helpful, because the issue is treated differently at each stage. It should be clear, of course, that there may not be a Stage One, because the parties may proceed directly to Stage Two (before the arbitral tribunal) without invoking a national court's jurisdiction to litigate the enforceability of the arbitration agreement. Stages One and Two can also go forward in parallel proceedings at the same time.

7.06 The existence of an arbitrability dispute in a national court at Stage One does not prevent an arbitral tribunal from being seized of the case and proceeding with it simultaneously. It should also be clear that there need not be a Stage Three if the losing party agrees to pay the award. Because of the differences in context and approach that arise at each of the three stages just discussed, it helps to analyse how the arbitrability question is treated and how that treatment differs at each of the three stages, which is how the discussion below is organized.

(b) Substantive arbitrability (jurisdiction) and procedural arbitrability (admissibility)

7.07 Before we begin that discussion, it is important to distinguish between two types of issue that the US Supreme Court calls, on the one hand, 'substantive arbitrability' and, on the other hand, 'procedural arbitrability'. Many civil law jurisdictions, in contrast, refer to these issues as 'jurisdiction' of the tribunal (substantive arbitrability) and 'admissibility' of the claim (procedural arbitrability). 'Substantive arbitrability' in the US Supreme Court's usage refers to whether the arbitral tribunal has good jurisdiction to decide the merits of the dispute. The issue concerns which forum is the proper one to decide the dispute—an arbitral tribunal or a court.

7.08 Thus, substantive arbitrability (whether the arbitral tribunal has good jurisdiction) turns on the existence, validity, and scope of the arbitration agreement. 'Procedural arbitrability' in the US Supreme Court's usage refers to whether the particular claim advanced by the claimant is timely and has been properly handled by the claimant so that it is appropriate for

---

[2] See John J Barceló, 'Who Decides the Arbitrators' Jurisdiction? Separability and Competence-Competence in Transnational Perspective' (2003) 36 Vand J Transnat'l L 1115, 1118–19.

an existing and valid arbitral tribunal to hear this particular claim. Many civil law jurisdictions refer to this issue as one of the 'admissibility' of the claim.

Hence the 'procedural arbitrability' or 'admissibility' issue deals with such questions as whether the claim has been brought too late (after the statute of limitations has run), or too early (because a certain required precondition such as mandatory mediation has not yet occurred), or whether the claimant has waived its right to arbitrate by having sought resolution of its claim in another forum, for example. Thus, 'procedural arbitrability' or 'admissibility' focuses on the claim itself as opposed to which forum, court, or tribunal is the appropriate decision-maker.[3]

7.09

Characterizing an arbitrability dispute as falling within one or the other of these two categories can have a dramatic effect on the outcome of the dispute, as I will discuss below. And although the distinction is often straightforward and easy to make, there can be situations in which making it poses a serious challenge.[4]

7.10

B. Stage One: Arbitrability

A classic dilemma in arbitration typically arises at Stage One and concerns, on the one hand, not wanting to send parties to arbitration unless they have validly agreed to arbitrate a dispute, and, on the other hand, not wanting to allow a party to obstruct a valid arbitration agreement through dilatory litigation tactics before a national court. To deal with this dilemma, courts and legislatures have developed two legal principles that apply very commonly in legal systems throughout the world at Stage One: (i) separability; and (ii) the negative effect of *kompetenz-kompetenz*.

7.11

(a) Separability

Under the concept of separability (or 'severability' or 'autonomy of the arbitration agreement'), if parties enter a transaction that includes an arbitration clause, they are held to have entered two separate and, in many respects, independent agreements: (i) the commercial transaction itself (sale, distribution agreement, licence, transport agreement, construction contract, and so on); and (ii) an arbitration agreement.

7.12

---

[3] For an insightful discussion on the distinction between 'jurisdiction' and 'admissibility', see Paulsson (n 1) 82–90 (s 3.2, 'Jurisdiction Distinguished from Admissibility').

[4] Consider an example drawn from the recent US Supreme Court decision in *BG Group Plc v The Republic of Argentina*, 134 S Ct 1198 (2014). The case involved a claim under the UK–Argentina BIT by a British investor, BG Group, against Argentina for unfair treatment of an investment. The BIT authorized arbitration but provided that the claimant investor must first file the claim in a local Argentinian court and pursue it there for a specified amount of time. The investor did not do so, but the arbitral tribunal found the local court litigation requirement inapplicable because of certain actions Argentina took that the tribunal characterized as obstructing the path to litigation. The question on enforcement of the award was whether the local court litigation requirement was a pre-condition to the formation of the arbitration agreement itself (a question of substantive arbitrability), or a pre-condition on the viability of the claim (a question of procedural arbitrability, or admissibility). In a 7:2 decision, the court characterized the issue as one of procedural arbitrability. Suppose the local court litigation requirement had been included in a clause under the heading of 'Conditions of Consent'. Would the local court litigation requirement then have been a pre-condition applying to the formation of the agreement to arbitrate (substantive arbitrability) or still a procedural pre-condition applying to the viability of the claim (procedural arbitrability)? Sotomayor J's concurring opinion in *BG Group* indicates that on these facts she would probably have changed her characterization, but the majority might not have. One can imagine a variety of factual patterns in which the choice would be difficult to make.

7.13 Thus, a challenge to the validity of the basic commercial agreement will not constitute a derivative challenge to the validity of the arbitration agreement. If a party is resisting arbitration claims before a national court at Stage One on the basis that the basic commercial agreement (let us say a sale) is invalid because the other party fraudulently induced the complaining party into agreeing to the sale, that claim does not on its own terms pose a challenge to the separate arbitration agreement conceived of as independent from the sale contract.

7.14 Therefore, the question of whether the sale contract is invalid because of fraudulent inducement is one that should be sent to the arbitral tribunal for decision. The arbitration agreement does not collapse by derivation from the invalidity of the larger agreement. It maintains a separate existence and therefore requires that an arbitral tribunal should decide whether the commercial agreement (the sale) was in fact invalid.

7.15 We should note an important qualification that applies to the separability principle. If the party resisting arbitration claims that the commercial transaction (the sale) never came into existence, because, for example, the person putatively acting as agent for the respondent had no actual or apparent authority to bind the respondent, then that claim applies equally to the separate arbitration agreement. Thus, if the argument is sound, it undercuts at the same time and directly (not derivatively) the existence of the arbitration agreement. Therefore, the separability doctrine does not apply as a basis for sending such an argument to the arbitration tribunal for decision.[5]

(b) The negative effect of *kompetenz-kompetenz*

7.16 The second principle, the negative effect of *kompetenz-kompetenz*, applies even to claims directly challenging the existence, validity, or scope of the arbitration agreement. The principle operates to cause a national court seized of a dispute, in which there may or may not be a binding arbitration agreement, to stay its hand and send the matter to an arbitral tribunal for an initial decision on the arbitrability of the dispute. The tribunal's arbitrability decision can of course be subject to further judicial review at Stage Three. The applicable standard of review at that stage then becomes a particularly important issue, as we discuss below.

7.17 The term 'negative effect' (of *kompetenz-kompetenz*) refers to the way in which the principle operates to restrain courts from exercising their otherwise legitimate jurisdiction to decide arbitrability at Stage One in deference to a first decision on the issue by the arbitral tribunal. The appropriateness of an arbitral tribunal's exercising competence to decide its own competence is effectively the 'positive side' of the *kompetenz-kompetenz* principle—a principle recognized the world over.

7.18 The force and effect of the 'negative effect' doctrine operates differently in different national legal systems around the world. If we examine the way in which the doctrine operates in two leading arbitration jurisdictions—the United States and France, in particular—we will have an illustration of two major patterns that one sees replicated in other jurisdictions.

---

[5] Generally, a challenge to the *existence* of the main contract also at the same time undercuts the *existence* of the arbitration agreement included in that contract, even if the arbitration clause is conceptualized as a separate agreement. But this 'double function' (or 'double relevance') of an existence challenge does not necessarily always apply. See Gary B Born, *International Commercial Arbitration* (2nd edn, Kluwer Law International 2014) 3457–8.

(c) The US approach to the negative effect of *kompetenz-kompetenz*

7.19 The US Supreme Court has been the principal architect of the negative effect doctrine that applies in the United States, and it has developed that doctrine by asking what the parties would likely have intended when negotiating their arbitration agreement. This approach has led the court to introduce important presumptions. Because the court assumes that parties very rarely even think about who—court or arbitrator—should decide substantive arbitrability questions (the arbitration agreement's existence, validity, or scope), the court sets up a presumption that the parties do not normally intend such questions to be decided by the arbitrator. Thus, at Stage One, a court should decide substantive arbitrability (jurisdiction) issues.[6] This presumption can be rebutted, however, if the parties include in their agreement 'clear and unmistakeable evidence' that they intend substantive arbitrability issues to be decided by the arbitrators.[7]

7.20 The court reverses the pattern just sketched, however, if the arbitrability question falls into the 'procedural arbitrability' (admissibility) category. For procedural arbitrability issues the court presumes that the parties intend the arbitral tribunal to be the principal decision-maker, so that at Stage One a court should not decide such issues, but should send them instead to the arbitrators for initial decision. Once again the presumption can be rebutted if the parties make clear in their agreement that they want a court to decide any emerging procedural arbitrability issues.

7.21 What are 'procedural arbitrability' issues? They are the questions mentioned above that some jurisdictions label as questions of the 'admissibility' of the claim. Hence they include such issues as the timing of the claim, notice requirements, waiver, estoppel, prior mediation requirements, and similar preconditions to bringing a claim.

7.22 In the United States, then, at Stage One substantive arbitrability issues are presumptively for the court to decide and procedural arbitrability issues are presumptively for the arbitral tribunal to decide. These presumptions at Stage One have an important effect on the standard of review applied by a US court at Stage Three when an award is before the court for confirmation or for recognition and enforcement. At Stage Three concerning substantive arbitrability issues (whether the arbitral tribunal has good jurisdiction), a US court should decide the jurisdictional issues *de novo*, with no deference to the arbitral tribunal—unless of course the normal presumption has been rebutted by the parties' explicit agreement to delegate this function to the tribunal. In the latter case, an enforcing court should give deference to the prior decision by the arbitral tribunal. By parallel logic, if the issue is one of 'procedural arbitrability' (admissibility of the claim) where the arbitrator is presumed to be the principal decision-maker, then the normal outcome is for an enforcing court at Stage Three to give deference to the arbitrator's prior decision. Again, this result can be reversed by explicit party agreement.

7.23 When deference is called for, how much deference should be given? In its recent *BG Group Plc v Argentina* decision,[8] the US Supreme Court clarified that issue. In this case, the arbitration agreement (contained in the UK–Argentina BIT) required the claimant

---

[6] *First Options of Chicago, Inc v Kaplan*, 514 US 938 (1995).
[7] ibid 944–5.
[8] *BG Group* (n 4).

(investor) first to litigate in a local Argentinian court for a certain period of time before initiating arbitration. BG Group did not litigate locally, but instead went directly to arbitration with a claim that Argentina had breached the investment treaty by treating BG Group's investment unfairly. The arbitral tribunal rejected Argentina's challenge to its competence by applying the Vienna Convention on the Law of Treaties to interpret the prior litigation requirement in the BIT as being inapplicable under the circumstances. The US Supreme Court characterized the local litigation requirement as a 'procedural arbitrability' question and, therefore, an enforcing US court was required to give deference to the tribunal's decision. In applying the deferential standard, the court asked only whether the arbitral tribunal's resolution of the procedural arbitrability issue had been based on the tribunal's interpretation of the arbitration agreement—as opposed to an application 'of [the tribunal's] own brand of justice'. The court said that it did not necessarily agree with the tribunal's interpretation, but that it was convinced that the tribunal had engaged in an interpretive exercise and had not simply pronounced what it considered to be a just result. Thus, it had acted within its delegated authority, and an enforcing court was required to enforce the resulting award. The deference called for is thus quite sweeping.

7.24 This sweeping deference would presumably also be called for in the case of substantive arbitrability issues whenever the parties include a provision that rebuts the normal presumption privileging the court and that privileges the arbitral tribunal instead as the principal decision-maker. Some recent lower court decisions in the United States have found the normal presumption rebutted whenever the parties choose institutional arbitration rules that include a provision reaffirming the positive *kompetenz-kompetenz* principle.[9] Those cases have so far arisen at Stage One and have resulted in the court's referring the parties to arbitration for an initial decision on substantive arbitrability. The reasoning seems unsound, however, especially because of the sweeping deference that would thereafter be called for at Stage Three. Since institutional rules often contain a provision reaffirming the positive *kompetenz-kompetenz* principle, this means that arbitral tribunals proceeding under such rules will have almost unfettered discretion to decide their own jurisdiction without serious review by a court at Stage Three. Given that arbitrators have a financial incentive to find good jurisdiction in close cases, deferring so completely to the tribunal's decision on jurisdictional issues seems highly questionable. This is especially so when the triggering event is the mere inclusion in institutional rules of a provision reaffirming the positive *kompetenz-kompetenz* principle, which really says nothing at all about the parties' intent concerning who will be the principal decision-maker on substantive arbitrability questions.[10] As we will see, the French approach to these issues avoids this potential pitfall.

---

[9] See, eg, *Republic of Ecuador v Chevron Corp*, 638 F 3d 384, 394 (2d Cir 2011).
[10] The US Supreme Court itself has contributed indirectly to this flawed analysis through its reasoning in *BG Group* (n 4). In that case, having found that the issue of pre-arbitration local court litigation was a procedural arbitrability question on which the arbitral tribunal would normally be privileged (or 'to be normally resolved by arbitrators'), the Court asked whether the parties' agreement contained any indication that they intended to shift that privilege to a court at Stage One or 'that they intended to grant this power to a national court instead'. The court cited as evidence to the contrary that the parties had chosen the UNCITRAL Arbitration Rules 2010, which authorized the arbitrators to decide their jurisdiction, the normal positive *kompetenz-kompetenz* principle. But surely the inclusion of rules containing a positive *kompetenz-kompetenz* principle says nothing at all about the parties' intent concerning who should be the principal decision-maker on substantive or procedural arbitrability questions.

(d) The French approach to the negative effect of *kompetenz-kompetenz*

7.25 The French approach to the negative effect doctrine derives not from court interpretation of expected party intent articulated in an arbitration agreement, but rather from the express provisions of the French CPC. Thus, in good civil law tradition, the applicable rule is given by legislative will and is found in Article 1448 of the 2011 version of the French CPC:

> When a dispute subject to an arbitration agreement is brought before a court, such court shall decline jurisdiction, except if an arbitral tribunal has not yet been seized of the dispute and if the arbitration agreement is *manifestly* void or *manifestly* not applicable.[11]

7.26 By virtue of this provision, at Stage One a French court must send the parties to arbitration if the arbitration agreement has *prima facie* existence and validity and the dispute falls *prima facie* within its scope. Thus, in the vast majority of cases where litigation occurs at Stage One, a French court will not decide the arbitrability question, but will instead send it to the arbitral tribunal for an initial decision. However, the tribunal's decision on arbitrability at Stage Two is not final. In fact, it is entitled to no deference at all at Stage Three. At the enforcement stage a French court will decide on arbitrability *de novo*, on the theory that a court must be the final arbiter of whether the parties have agreed to forego their right to a judicial decision on the merits in favour of arbitration.[12]

7.27 One might wonder why French law would require French courts to abstain from deciding arbitrability at Stage One, only to be the final decision-maker at Stage Three. Why delay if a court will decide the question in the end anyway? French commentators have explained the logic as follows. This approach gives full scope to the 'positive' *kompetenz-kompetenz* principle and deters a party from trying to obstruct arbitration by raising arbitrability questions for extended litigation at Stage One. Instead, most cases go directly to the arbitrators, who, when the arbitrability issue involves strong arguments both ways, may issue a preliminary award on jurisdiction. That award may then be reviewed *de novo* by a French court in a set-aside proceeding (if the seat is in France) with little delay.[13] If the tribunal believes the party objecting to jurisdiction is merely engaged in dilatory or obstructionist tactics, the tribunal may decide to continue with the arbitration proceedings, even while a set-aside proceeding is underway at the arbitral seat. Thus, the obstructionist tactics will not delay the arbitration.

7.28 A number of civil law jurisdictions have followed the French lead on the negative effect of *kompetenz-kompetenz*. For example, a recent amendment to the Mexican Commercial Code adopts this same approach.[14] And some jurisdictions follow this negative effect approach at

---

[11] Although Art 1448 appears in the section of the French CPC applicable to domestic arbitration, Art 1506 of the Code expressly makes Art 1448 applicable to international arbitration as well (emphasis added).

[12] See Gaillard and Savage (n 1) 924–9, para 1605. See also Barceló (n 2) 1125 and sources cited therein.

[13] If the seat is elsewhere, French theory assumes a court at the seat will be available to review the jurisdiction issue *de novo*, since French theory assumes that a court should always be the principal decision-maker concerning whether its jurisdiction has been ousted.

[14] See Art 1465 of the 2011 Mexican Commercial Code:

> When a party petitions a court to stay judicial proceedings and refer the parties to arbitration the remission to arbitration will be denied only
> (a) if there is a judgment or an award holding that the arbitration agreement is null; or
> (b) if, after careful scrutiny, the judge concludes that it is manifest that the arbitration agreement is null, inoperative, or incapable of being performed.
>
> (Translated by the author.)

Stage One even where the code or statutory provisions do not expressly require it. This is the case, for example, in Swiss practice.¹⁵

7.29 We have thus far discussed the French law approach to what the US Supreme Court calls 'substantive arbitrability'. What about procedural arbitrability? In French practice, issues that the US Supreme Court calls 'procedural arbitrability'—timeliness of the claim, or notice, or prior mediation requirements—would generally be referred to as issues of 'admissibility' of the claim. They would not affect the jurisdiction of the arbitral tribunal, but instead would relate only to whether the claim itself was timely and properly presented for decision on the merits. At Stage One, such a claim would be sent to the arbitral tribunal for decision, and at Stage Three a court would not review the tribunal's admissibility decisions. Thus, at Stages One and Three the outcomes would be similar in the United States and France and in other jurisdictions that characterize 'procedural arbitrability' questions as issues of admissibility of the claim.¹⁶

C. Stage Two: Arbitrability Before the Arbitrators

7.30 As we have noted, arbitration proceedings may go forward at Stage Two even if, and while, a challenge to arbitrability has been raised before a court at Stage One. In this situation arbitrators will have to decide whether they have good jurisdiction (issues of the existence, validity, and scope of the arbitration agreement) and whether the claim is admissible. They will do so whether deciding under institutional rules that do or do not expressly give them that power, or whether deciding *ad hoc* under an arbitration statute at the seat that either does or does not expressly grant that power. The concept of *kompetenz-kompetenz* is universally recognized. As we have noted, that does not mean that the arbitrator's decision is final. It means essentially that an arbitrator is entitled to decide on arbitrability and to proceed according to that decision, without having to suspend proceedings until the parties obtain a judicial decision on arbitrability. The judicial decision will come at Stage Three.

7.31 The arbitrability issue before arbitrators at Stage Two raises several important issues. Suppose, for example, a national court has already reached a decision at Stage One that the arbitration agreement is invalid. Will the arbitrators be bound by that decision? Technically, the answer is no, but if the court decision occurs at the arbitral seat, then experienced arbitrators will generally want to heed it. Why? Because if they do not, then any award they render that is inconsistent with that prior arbitrability decision by a court at the seat will presumably be set aside, and thus, because of New York Convention Article V(1)(e)¹⁷ will

---

¹⁵ See Gaillard and Savage (n 1) 409, para 675.
¹⁶ See Solomon Ebere and Blerina Xheraj, 'Who Decides Arbitrability Where a Precondition to Arbitration Has Not Been Satisfied? A Comment on the US Supreme Court's Decision to Hear the Appeal in *BG Group v Argentina*' (2014) 31 J Int'l Arb 101, 106. For the result in France, Ebere and Xheraj cite *Poiré v Tripier*, Cass mixte, 14 February 2003 (2003) 2 Rev arb 403 (pre-arbitration requirement is an admissibility issue) and *Société Nihon Plast Co v Société Takata-Petri Aktiengesellschaft*, Paris Court of Appeal, 4 March 2004 (2005) Rev arb 143 (arbitral tribunal decision on admissibility issue not subject to independent court review). For Germany to the same effect, they cite BGH (1999) Neue Juristische Wochenschrift, Heft 9, 647; BFH (1984) Neue Juristische Wochenschrift, Heft 12, 669.
¹⁷ Art V(1)(e) of the New York Convention lists as a ground for refusing recognition and enforcement of an award the case where the award was set aside 'by a competent authority of the country in which ... that award was made'—that is, at the seat. There is no guarantee that an award set aside at the seat will be refused recognition or enforcement in other New York Convention countries, but this is generally the result. As is well known, awards set aside at the seat of the arbitration will still be enforced in France if they are enforceable

generally be refused recognition and enforcement in other New York Convention countries. A decision on arbitrability by a national court not at the seat will not command the same respect from the arbitral tribunal. The award will not be enforceable in that jurisdiction, but it could still be enforceable in other jurisdictions. So if the arbitrators disagree with the conclusion of the non-seat jurisdiction on arbitrability, they may go forward with their own analysis and conclusions.

Another characteristic issue that arises at Stage Two concerns what law the arbitrators should apply in deciding the existence, validity, and scope of an arbitration agreement. This question cannot be answered definitively, but certain tendencies are common in practice. A dominant tendency among arbitrators is to privilege party autonomy. So if the parties have thought about the question and expressly included a clause choosing a particular national legal system to decide the interpretation and validity of the arbitration agreement, arbitrators will be compelled to apply that law. **7.32**

Some commentators may see this as illogical or as 'bootstrapping'. If the arbitration agreement is invalid, how can one make use of a choice-of-law provision contained in an invalid arbitration agreement? Clearly, privileging party autonomy in this situation effectively treats the parties' choice-of-law agreement in the arbitration clause as separate from the arbitration agreement itself. Thus, that choice-of-law agreement can be valid and effective, even if when applying the chosen law the arbitrators conclude that the arbitration agreement itself is not valid. And even though the New York Convention is not technically addressed to the arbitral tribunal, arbitrators will surely feel supported in this approach by the provision in New York Convention Article V(1)(a) that refers an enforcing court to the law 'to which the parties have subjected [the arbitration agreement]' in deciding the agreement's validity. **7.33**

Another tendency is for arbitrators to favour validating over invalidating law—a validity-preferring approach. Thus, if there are contending arguments for the applicability of two different legal systems, one that invalidates the arbitration agreement and one that validates it, arbitrators will favour the validating law. This approach would not seem well grounded if the issue is the existence itself of the arbitration agreement. It is hard to see any basis for presuming or preferring existence of an arbitration agreement over non-existence. But if the parties have clearly entered an agreement to arbitrate and one party challenges its validity, arbitrators will assume that parties entering an agreement intended a valid agreement. **7.34**

When parties have not explicitly chosen a law to govern the validity of the arbitration agreement, there are usually two contending approaches to the applicable law, each having some basis in party autonomy. The first is to presume that the law governing the basic transaction (eg an international sale) within which an arbitration clause is embedded also applies to the arbitration agreement, which is in one sense just one of the clauses of that basic transaction. If the parties have specifically chosen the applicable law for the basic transaction and that law is presumed to apply as well to the arbitration clause, then at least indirectly party autonomy has decided the law applicable to the arbitration agreement. Even when there is no such clause, the transaction's links to national jurisdictions, links that often determine the applicable law, also emerge out of the parties' negotiation and performance practices and in that sense are also determined by party autonomy. **7.35**

---

under the French national law standards for enforcing foreign awards, standards that are more favourable to enforcement than those of the New York Convention.

7.36 A second approach is to apply the law of the seat. Suppose, for example, a private party agrees to perform services for a governmental entity in Egypt, and the law applicable to this agreement is Egyptian law. The parties nevertheless place the arbitration seat in Geneva, Switzerland. Suppose under Egyptian law the agreement might be considered an administrative contract so that disputes concerning the agreement could not validly be submitted to arbitration. Thus, under Egyptian law the arbitration agreement could arguably be invalid. In a well-known arbitral award involving similar facts, the arbitrator chose not to apply Egyptian law, but the law of the seat, Swiss law, to determine the validity of the arbitration agreement.[18] Under Article 177(2) of the Swiss PIL Act a governmental entity is not allowed to rely on its own law to challenge the validity of an arbitration agreement into which it has entered. Hence, the arbitrator applied this point of the Swiss arbitration law and found the arbitration agreement valid.[19]

D. Stage Three: Arbitrability at Award Enforcement

(a) Setting aside

7.37 If a final arbitral award is brought to a national court at the seat for confirmation or to be set aside, then the national arbitration law at the seat will govern the proceedings, not the New York Convention. If there are questions concerning the arbitrability of the dispute, they will surely be raised here, even though the arbitral tribunal will presumably have already upheld its own jurisdiction as a basis for rendering the award.

7.38 If the arbitral tribunal renders a preliminary award declaring that the tribunal has good jurisdiction to hear the claim, the respondent may again seek to have the preliminary award set aside at the seat. In French practice this way of proceeding—the tribunal's issuance of a preliminary award on jurisdiction followed by a court challenge to the award—has advantages when combined with the strong French doctrine of the negative effect of *kompetenz-kompetenz*. As we have discussed above, under that doctrine most arbitrability issues are not decided by a court at Stage One, but are sent by the court to the arbitral tribunal for an initial decision. If the tribunal upholds its jurisdiction in a preliminary award, the opposing party can get a relatively timely judicial decision on arbitrability before the proceeding advances very far. In the set-aside proceedings (Stage Three), the French court will decide arbitrability *de novo*, with no deference to the arbitral tribunal's prior decision.

7.39 At the same time, the arbitral tribunal, in its discretion, would be free to continue with the arbitral proceedings, even when a set-aside action is underway, in order to thwart any attempt by the opposing party to obstruct arbitration by raising dubious arbitrability issues. If on the other hand the tribunal considers arbitrability to be a close question, it might choose to delay the proceedings to await the court's final decision. The tribunal would presumably abide by a negative court decision, because otherwise the final award would be set aside at the seat and would then be unenforceable in most New York Convention countries on the basis of Article V(1)(e) of the Convention.[20]

---

[18] See *Consultant (France) v Egyptian Local Authority*, Final Award, ICC Case No 6162 (1990) in Albert Jan van den Berg (ed), *Yearbook Commercial Arbitration*, vol XVII (Kluwer Law International 1992) 153.
[19] ibid.
[20] Art V(1)(e) authorizes a New York Convention country to refuse recognition or enforcement of an award that has been set aside at the seat. See n 17.

7.40 Should the tribunal conclude that the dispute is not arbitrable, that award too could be challenged by the claimant in a set-aside action in at least some jurisdictions. France and Switzerland are examples.[21] But countries that have patterned their arbitration law closely on the Model Law do not provide for a court challenge to a tribunal's decision declining jurisdiction.[22]

7.41 In the United States, recall that at Stage Three an enforcing court would decide substantive arbitrability issues (existence, validity, and scope of the arbitration agreement) *de novo*, unless the parties expressed their intent through 'clear and unmistakable evidence' that they wanted the arbitral tribunal to decide arbitrability—a rare occurrence. On procedural arbitrability (admissibility), however, the presumption is reversed. On such an issue (timeliness of the claim, notice, waiver, estoppel, and so on), an enforcing court should give deference to the tribunal's decision, unless the parties rebut the ordinary presumption that they intend the arbitrator to be the primary decision-maker with clear and unmistakable evidence that they prefer a court decision instead.

7.42 In several civil law jurisdictions, 'procedural arbitrability' questions will be analysed as claim admissibility issues. We have discussed the French practice in this respect in Part B(d) above.[23] Germany also follows this approach.[24] In these jurisdictions at Stage One, courts will send admissibility issues to the arbitral tribunal for decision and will not review the tribunal's decision on such issues at all at the Stage Three enforcement level.[25]

7.43 It is worth noting that a party challenging arbitrability at Stage Three must also have raised that challenge before the arbitrators at Stage Two. Otherwise that party will be estopped from raising the claim at Stage Three. Civil law jurisdictions often reach this result on the ground of breach of good faith. One exception to this result would be a case in which the seat considers the arbitration agreement to be invalid because the dispute deals with non-arbitrable subject matter under the seat's law. Because this is a matter of mandatory law—essentially public policy—the parties' actions cannot waive or prevent a court from enforcing the national law *sua sponte*.

(b) Recognition and enforcement

(1) *Non-arbitrable subject matter*

7.44 At Stage Three enforcement under the New York Convention in countries other than the seat country, the same issue of non-arbitrable subject matter is regulated specifically in Article V(2)(a) of the Convention. If the arbitration agreement deals with a subject matter not capable of settlement by arbitration—as determined by the law of the enforcing country—then the award will not be enforced in that country. For other kinds of arbitrability challenges, the analysis is not quite so straightforward.

---

[21] Art 1520(1) of the French CPC provides for the possibility to set aside an award made in France where 'the arbitral tribunal wrongly upheld or declined jurisdiction'. Art 190(2)(b) of the Swiss PIL Act provides for the possibility to set aside an award made in Switzerland 'when the arbitral tribunal wrongly accepted or declined jurisdiction'.

[22] Art 16(3) of the UNCITRAL Model Law provides: 'If the arbitral tribunal rules as a preliminary question that it has jurisdiction, any party may request... the court specified in Art 6 to decide the matter'. The Model Law contains no provision authorizing court review of a tribunal decision declining jurisdiction.

[23] See Ebere and Xheraj (n 16).

[24] ibid.

[25] ibid.

(2) Formal validity

7.45 Formal validity of the arbitration agreement at Stage Three is generally understood to be regulated by Article II of the New York Convention. Under that Article the arbitration agreement must be either signed by all the parties or contained in an exchange of writing coming from all parties. A party seeking to enforce an award under the New York Convention is instructed in Article IV of the Convention to present the award and 'the agreement referred to in Article II'. Thus, a first step in obtaining recognition and enforcement of the award is to present the arbitration agreement, which should conform to the writing requirements of Article II. If the arbitration agreement is not in writing according to the standards of Article II, then the party seeking recognition and enforcement is unable to meet the requirements of Article IV and hence will not succeed.

7.46 However, if the country of enforcement has enacted a national arbitration statute that provides for enforcement of a foreign award under more lenient writing standards than those of Article II, then the 'most favorable right' provision of Article VII of the Convention comes into play, and the enforcing country is required to enforce the award under those more lenient national writing standards. Any country enacting the 2006 revision of the Model Law containing a more lenient writing requirement—or under Option 2 of that revision, no writing requirement at all—will be in this position. As an increasing number of countries adopt more lenient writing requirements for arbitration agreements and expressly provide for recognition and enforcement of foreign awards where the arbitration agreement meets the more lenient national formality standard, the stricter writing standards of Article II of the Convention will be less frequently applicable to block enforcement of a foreign award.

(3) Substantive validity

7.47 A challenge to the substantive validity of the arbitration agreement on grounds other than non-arbitrable subject matter (governed by Article V(2)(a)) is regulated under Article V(1)(a) of the Convention. Thus, an award may be refused enforcement if the arbitration agreement 'is not valid under the law to which the parties have subjected it, or failing any indication thereon, under the law of the country where the award was made'.[26] The *chapeau* of Article V(1) places the burden of proof concerning all Art V(1) grounds to refuse recognition and enforcement on the party resisting enforcement, on the basis that '[r]ecognition and enforcement of the award may be refused … only if [the party requesting refusal] furnishes … proof that: [subparagraph a, b, c, d, or e applies]'.[27]

7.48 The force of party autonomy is evident in this provision, since validity is to be determined by the law to which the parties have subjected their agreement. The law of the seat on substantive validity only comes into play if the parties have not included in their agreement any indication of the law to which they intended to subject their agreement. Hence under Article V(1)(a) the law of the seat is subordinated to the law chosen by the parties. On the other hand, if the arbitration agreement is invalid under the law of the seat, the losing party might be able to get the award set aside by a national court at the seat, and then the award would be unenforceable in most jurisdictions by virtue of Article V(1)(e), which provides, as we have seen, that an award may be refused enforcement if it has been set aside where made. This outcome depends of course on whether a court at the seat would apply the law of the

---

[26] New York Convention, Art V(1)(a).
[27] New York Convention, Art V(1) *chapeau*.

(4) Non-existence of the agreement

7.49 Many countries treat the issue of an arbitration agreement's 'existence'—as between the contending parties—under the same Article V(1)(a) standards that apply to the agreement's 'validity'.[28] Thus, the party resisting enforcement bears the burden of proof. Some countries, however, follow a different approach. Courts in Germany and Spain, for example, consider 'existence' issues under the provisions of Article IV requiring the enforcing party to present the award and the arbitration agreement as an initial step in getting the award enforced.[29] These courts thus conclude that under Article IV the enforcing party must bear the burden of proving that the arbitration agreement has come into existence as between the claimant(s) and respondent(s) as parties. The issue of substantive validity of the agreement is then governed by the provisions of the New York Convention Article V(1)(a).

(5) Scope

7.50 At the enforcement stage, issues of scope will generally be analysed under Article V(1)(c) of the Convention ('the award...contains decisions on matters beyond the scope of the submission to arbitration'). Again, the party resisting enforcement bears the burden of proof. In both France and the United States, the scope issue should normally be decided *de novo* by the enforcing court. In the United States, however, an enforcing court should resolve any doubts in favour of including a disputed issue within the scope of arbitrable issues. Only if the parties have been clear and unmistakable in wanting to exclude a particular issue from the arbitrators' jurisdiction, should an enforcing court conclude that a disputed issue is beyond the scope of submission.[30] This is the correct approach because sending different issues arising from a single controversy to different dispute resolution systems is highly inefficient and would not normally be what the parties had intended.

(6) Procedural arbitrability (admissibility)

7.51 As discussed above, if a disputed issue concerns procedural arbitrability or admissibility of the claim, an enforcing court will normally not review the arbitrators' decision. This is certainly so in France and Germany, for example.[31] This is also the normal result in the

---

[28] The United States and the United Kingdom are examples. For the United States, see ALI, *Restatement (Third) US Law of International Commercial Arbitration* (Tentative Draft No 2) 2012 ss 4–12, comment a ('Article V(1)(a) of the New York Convention...permit[s] a court to deny recognition or enforcement of an award if no arbitration agreement exists'). For the United Kingdom, see the UK Supreme Court's decision in *Dallah Real Estate & Tourism Holding Co v Pakistan* [2010] UKSC 46; [2010] 3 WLR 1472.

[29] See Stefan Kröll, 'The Arbitration Agreement in Enforcement Proceedings of Foreign Awards' in Stefan Kröll and others (eds), *International Arbitration and International Commercial Law: Synergy, Convergence and Evolution* (Kluwer Law International 2011). Professor Kröll cites cases in Germany (eg *Seller v Buyer*, Oberlandesgericht Celle, 4 September 2003 in Albert Jan van den Berg (ed), *Yearbook Commercial Arbitration*, vol XXX (Kluwer Law International 2005) 536) and Spain (eg *Actival International SA v Conservas El Pilas SA*, Tribunal Supremo, 16 September 1996 in Albert Jan van den Berg (ed), *Yearbook Commercial Arbitration*, vol XXVII (Kluwer Law International 2002) 528). He also cites cases in Argentina and Norway that follow the same interpretation.

[30] See *First Options* (n 6) 945 (considering the question of 'whether a particular merits-related dispute is arbitrable because it is within the scope of a valid arbitration agreement', the court cites and quotes *Mitsubishi Motors v Soler Chrysler-Plymouth*, 473 US 614, 626 (1985), which in turn quotes *Moses H Cone v Mercury Construction Corp*, 460 US 1, 24–5 (1983) as follows: 'Any doubts concerning the scope of arbitrable issues should be resolved in favour of arbitration').

[31] See n 16.

United States. In US practice, however, the parties have the power to provide for *de novo* court review of procedural arbitrability issues if they expressly provide in the arbitration agreement that any particular such issues are to be decided by a court.

E. Conclusion

7.52 As we noted at the outset of this chapter, the arbitration agreement is the cornerstone of international commercial arbitration. Disputes over the agreement's existence, validity, and scope—the essential elements for a controversy to be arbitrable—arise at each of the three fundamental stages of the arbitration/litigation process. Moreover, the arbitrability issue is typically subject to different rules and different analytical approaches at each of these three stages. There is also some variability of approach in different national jurisdictions. In all jurisdictions, however, an international commercial arbitration will not yield an enforceable award unless the arbitration agreement exists as between the parties, is valid, and the disputed issues fall within the scope of the agreement.

8

THE DANGERS OF NEGLECT

Governing Law of Arbitration Agreements

Neil Kaplan and Olga Boltenko

A. Introduction

Much scholarly effort has been expended exploring the plethora of avenues and tests that can be applied to determine the law governing the arbitration agreement in the absence of the parties' choice. Running the risk of being accused of 'arbitration revolutionarism', we must admit that this effort is as impressive as it is unnecessary. This chapter explains why. We intend to take a practical approach in the knowledge that elsewhere in this *liber amicorum*, a more scholarly and academic approach can be found.[1] 8.01

B. Model Clauses

(a) Institutional examples

We start by looking at the model arbitration clauses recommended by major arbitral institutions on their websites. It soon becomes apparent that the law governing the arbitration agreement is an unjustly neglected topic: 8.02

Model Arbitration Clause offered by the ICC: 8.03

> All disputes arising out of or in connection with the present contract shall be finally settled under the Rules of Arbitration of the International Chamber of Commerce by one or more arbitrators appointed in accordance with the said Rules.[2]

Model Arbitration Clause offered by the LCIA: 8.04

> Any dispute arising out of or in connection with this contract, including any question regarding its existence, validity or termination, shall be referred to and finally resolved by arbitration under the LCIA Rules, which Rules are deemed to be incorporated by reference into this clause. The number of arbitrators shall be [one/three]. The seat, or legal place, of arbitration shall be [City and/or Country]. The language to be used in the arbitral proceedings shall be [...]. The governing law of the contract shall be the substantive law of [...].[3]

---

[1] Renato Nazzini, 'The Law Governing the Arbitration Agreement: A Transnational Solution?' in Julio César Betancourt (ed), *Defining Issues in International Arbitration: Celebrating 100 Years of the Chartered Institute of Arbitrators* (OUP 2016) ch 9.

[2] Standard ICC Arbitration Clauses <http://www.iccwbo.org> accessed 25 September 2015.

[3] LCIA Recommended Clauses <http://www.lcia.org> accessed 25 September 2015.

8.05 Model Arbitration Clause offered by the SIAC:

> Any dispute arising out of or in connection with this contract, including any question regarding its existence, validity or termination, shall be referred to and finally resolved by arbitration in Singapore in accordance with the Arbitration Rules of the Singapore International Arbitration Centre ('SIAC Rules') for the time being in force, which rules are deemed to be incorporated by reference in this clause. The Tribunal shall consist of [...] arbitrator(s). The language of the arbitration shall be [...].[4]

8.06 This list could be continued. Not one arbitral institution in the world, with one exception, recommends that the parties select the law to govern their arbitration agreements, and yet how many arbitrations have been derailed into a lengthy and costly sideshow as to the law applicable to the arbitration agreement? In the mad rush to finalize the transactional documents, corporate lawyers rarely think through various issues arising out of a poorly drafted arbitration clause, let alone that the absence of the parties' explicit choice of the law governing the arbitration agreement might lead to disastrous delays and substantial legal fees carelessly wasted on debating this topic.

8.07 These poorly drafted clauses are known as 'midnight clauses'. The romanticized name emerges from the process during which these clauses are produced. Having finished hard-fought contract negotiations, transactional lawyers think of the dispute resolution clause at the eleventh hour when 'all is said and done', and they often just copy–paste one of the institutional model clauses—and often inaccurately. As such, the 'midnight clause' lacks specificity regarding the governing law of the arbitration agreement. Just like the rest of the arbitration community, the arbitral institutions may benefit from a reminder of the importance of selecting the law to govern the arbitration agreement.

(b) Moving beyond the 'midnight clause'

8.08 The HKIAC stands out as the first arbitral institution in the world to recommend in its model clause that the parties select the law to apply to their arbitration agreement:

> Any dispute, controversy, difference or claim arising out of or relating to this contract, including the existence, validity, interpretation, performance, breach or termination thereof or any dispute regarding non-contractual obligations arising out of or relating to it shall be referred to and finally resolved by arbitration administered by the Hong Kong International Arbitration Centre (HKIAC) under the HKIAC Administered Arbitration Rules in force when the Notice of Arbitration is submitted.
>
> * The law of this arbitration clause shall be [...] (Hong Kong law).
>
> The seat of arbitration shall be [...] (Hong Kong).
>
> ** The number of arbitrators shall be [...] (one or three). The arbitration proceedings shall be conducted in [...] (insert language).[5]

8.09 The HKIAC goes on to clarify to the unsophisticated who tend to opt for the 'midnight clause' that 'the law of the arbitration clause generally governs the existence, scope, validity, interpretation, performance, breach, termination and enforceability of the arbitration clause. It does not replace the law governing the substantive contract'.[6]

---

[4] SIAC Model Clauses <http://www.siac.org.sg> accessed 25 September 2015.
[5] HKIAC Model Clauses <www.hkiac.org> accessed 25 September 2015.
[6] ibid.

Scholars and judges, as well as arbitrators, have identified at least eight laws that may apply to the arbitration agreement: **8.10**

(1) the law governing the underlying contract;
(2) the law of the arbitral seat;
(3) the law governing the arbitration agreement expressly or implicitly chosen by the parties;
(4) the law of the judicial enforcement forum;
(5) the law of the state with the 'closest connection' or 'most significant relationship';
(6) the law according to the 'validation' principle;[7]
(7) international law; and
(8) the law governing the appointment of the arbitrator.

C. Determining the Correct Law

(a) Mending the omission

Due to this multiplicity, numerous practitioners have complained that determining the law of the arbitration agreement is a complex and confusing process. This complexity creates an unfortunate uncertainty in international arbitration. This uncertainty does nothing to enhance the reputation of arbitration and thus can limit the positive perception of it. The time has come to stop complaining and mend this omission. The simple and obvious way to do so is for the parties to select explicitly the law that will govern their arbitration agreement, and perhaps more importantly, for the institutions to recommend that the parties select the law to govern their arbitration agreements. **8.11**

Attention to this topic has recently been revived by prominent arbitrators and arbitration practitioners. James Spigelman devoted a large part of his 2013 Kaplan Lecture in Hong Kong to the law applicable to arbitration agreements.[8] Gary Born dealt with it in December 2013 in his John E C Brierly Memorial Lecture. The source of all these recent lectures and warnings is arguably a brilliant lecture by Lord Mustill, delivered over 20 years ago, as a part of the Goff Lecture series in Hong Kong. **8.12**

After setting out why this matters, this chapter will explore the various approaches offered by arbitration practitioners on the subject. **8.13**

(b) Why it matters?

The question as to which law governs the arbitration agreement arises in most disputes because, depending on the applicable law, the tribunal may interpret such vitally important **8.14**

---

[7] Gary Born notes that 'some authorities hold that traditional choice of law rules are ill-suited to international arbitration agreements and have instead applied a "validation" principle. The validation principle provides that, if the arbitration agreement is valid under any of several laws which are potentially applicable to it, then the agreement will be upheld. Examples of the validation principle include Art 178(2) of the Swiss PIL Act, providing that an arbitration agreement will be given effect if it is valid under any of the laws chosen by the parties, the law applicable to the underlying contract, or Swiss law'. See Gary B Born, *International Arbitration: Law and Practice* (Kluwer Law International 2012) 56.

[8] James Spigelman, 'The Centrality of Contractual Interpretation—A Comparative Perspective' (Neil Kaplan Lecture, 27 November 2013). This lecture and other series can be found on Neil Kaplan's website <http://www.neil-kaplan.com> accessed 25 September 2015.

issues as existence, formation, and validity of an arbitration agreement in radically different ways. To the list of issues concerning what is governed by the proper substantive law of the arbitration agreement, one must also add at least the following:

(1) the parties' capacity to enter into the arbitration agreement;
(2) the authority of the parties' representatives to bind the parties by signing the arbitration agreement;
(3) the legality of the arbitration agreement;
(4) the non-arbitrability of disputes submitted to arbitration under the arbitration agreement;
(5) the termination and expiration of the arbitration agreement;
(6) the scope of pre-arbitration requirements in multi-tiered clauses;
(7) the assignment of the arbitration agreement and a waiver to arbitrate; and
(8) the scope of the tribunal's jurisdiction as well as other jurisdictional issues.

8.15 The issue of applicable law thus goes to the heart of the arbitration agreement and therefore often to the heart of the tribunal's jurisdiction. In addition to that, different national laws contain different interpretative rules, and if a dispute revolves around a particular point of interpretation of the arbitration agreement, a debate over the applicable law becomes inevitable.

8.16 As one may conclude from the list above, the applicable law may become a vehemently debated part of arbitral proceedings if under one potentially applicable law one of these issues is decided differently from under another potentially applicable law. To add to this complexity, various laws may in fact apply to different issues on that list, so there may in fact be several different laws that apply to one arbitration agreement. In certain situations, it is justified for the parties' counsel to argue the applicability issues in lengthy written and oral submissions before arbitral tribunals and in national courts.

8.17 A few examples as to why the choice of law to govern the arbitration agreement is relevant may be helpful. Let us assume that the main contract is governed by French law. One party can foresee that there might be claims against non-signatories. If that party does not want non-signatories joined, then pushing for English law to govern the arbitration agreement might be wise. Under French law, the 'group of companies' doctrine may assist in joining non-parties, whereas English law takes a stricter approach. In fact, with only rare exceptions, English courts refuse to recognize the 'group of companies' doctrine to extend an arbitration agreement to a non-signatory.[9]

8.18 For example, in *Peterson Farms Inc v C&M Farming Ltd*,[10] Langley J of the Commercial Court applied English law to the arbitration agreement and unequivocally rejected the 'group of companies' doctrine. He said that such doctrine 'forms no part of English law'.[11] On the basis of this and other findings, Langley J set aside for want of jurisdiction that part of the award in which the tribunal awarded payment of losses by other group entities.

---

[9] Stewart R Shackleton (ed), *Arbitration Law Reports and Review: Annual Review of English Judicial Decisions on Arbitration 2011* (OUP 2011) lxii.
[10] *Peterson Farms Inc v C&M Farming Ltd* [2004] EWHC 121 (Comm), [2004] 1 Lloyd's Rep 603.
[11] ibid [62].

With tiered arbitration clauses, English law tends to look for language that can amount to a **8.19** condition precedent to the commencement of the arbitration, while other laws look more to the intent of the parties. In a recent landmark decision by the English Commercial Court in *Emirates Trading Agency LLC v Prime Mineral Exports Private Ltd*,[12] Teare J held that an obligation to 'seek to resolve the dispute or claim by friendly discussion' is 'complete in a sense that no essential term is lacking' and it is therefore enforceable. This decision appears to deviate from how English courts had traditionally treated similar tiered clauses. The previous UK case law led one to believe that an agreement to hold 'friendly negotiations' was nothing more than an unenforceable agreement to agree because it lacked the certainty of a condition precedent.[13] With *Emirates Trading Agency*, this position appears to have changed.

In that regard, a recent New South Wales decision in *United Group Rail Services Ltd v* **8.20** *Rail Corp* is worth noting.[14] In that case, Allsop J had to decide the content and operation of a tiered dispute resolution clause, which provided, among other things, that 'the dispute or difference is to be referred to a senior representative of each of the Principal and Contractor who must... meet and undertake genuine and good faith negotiations with a view to resolving the dispute or difference'.[15] Allsop J found that an obligation to 'undertake genuine and good faith negotiations had sufficient content not to be uncertain'.[16] In reaching his conclusion, Allsop J followed a body of Australian case law on this topic.[17]

This decision deviates from the UK traditional approach in *Walford v Miles*, in which Lord **8.21** Ackner found that an agreement to negotiate is unenforceable because it lacks the necessary certainty,[18] but it is in line with the reasoning in *Emirates Trading Agency*. Much like in that case, Allsop J said that 'an obligation to undertake discussions about a subject in an honest and genuine attempt to reach an identified result is not incomplete. It may be referable to a standard concerned with conduct assessed by subjective standards, but that does not make the standard or compliance with the standard impossible of assessment. Honesty is such a standard.'[19] This case law shows that there is divergence even within common law jurisdictions, which adds to the complexity of the issue.

The authors have had experience of cases where the tribunal had to decide which law applied **8.22** to the arbitration agreement, in one case following four rounds of written submissions and a hearing on the issue. In that case, the importance of the applicable law was tied to a multi-tiered or escalation arbitration clause which, under one potentially applicable law, would

---

[12] *Emirates Trading Agency LLC v Prime Mineral Exports Private Ltd* [2014] EWHC 2104 (Comm), [2014] WLR (D) 293.
[13] See, eg, *Cable & Wireless v IBM* [2002] EWHC 2059 (Comm); and *Holloway v Chancery Mead Ltd* [2007] EWHC 2495 (TCC), [2008] 1 All ER (Comm) 653.
[14] *United Group Rail Services Ltd v Rail Corp (NSW)* [2009] 74 NSWLR 618.
[15] ibid [15].
[16] ibid [24].
[17] *Coal Cliff Collieries Pty Ltd v Sijehama Pty Ltd* (1991) 24 NSWLR 1; *Burger King Corp v Hungry Jack's Pty Ltd* (2001) 69 NSWLR 558; *Alcatel Australia Ltd v Scarcella* (1998) 44 NSWLR 349; and *Con Kallergis Pty Ltd (t/as Sunlighting Australia) v Calshonie Pty Ltd (formerly C W Norris Pty Ltd)* (1998) 14 BCL 201.
[18] *Walford v Miles* [1992] 2 AC 128.
[19] *United Group Rail Services* (n 14) 636.

have considered the pre-arbitration steps as they were worded in the clause to be too vague to be complied with and would have allowed the arbitration to proceed.

8.23 The other potentially applicable law would have upheld the pre-arbitration requirements—however vague they were—and would have disallowed arbitration. This debate took some time and impressive amounts of legal fees were expended on both sides. However, it was an unnecessary side show which would have not been required had the draftsmen applied their minds to the issue we are considering, namely an explicit choice of the law applicable to the arbitration agreement itself.

(c) The *SulAmérica* test

8.24 Our experience with the applicable law issues is not unique. Many others have had to deal with this issue when it could have been avoided. Not only arbitrators, but also judges in national courts, are frequently faced with similar issues. A good example of such a domestic case is *SulAmérica*.[20] In that case, an English judge set out one of the most prominent and often cited tests to determine the law applicable to the arbitration agreement. This test is a threefold enquiry to determine:

(1) whether there is an explicit choice of the governing law by the parties;
(2) whether there is an implied choice by the parties; and
(3) in the absence of explicit or implied choice, what is the system of law with which the arbitration agreement has the closest and most real connection.[21]

8.25 The *SulAmérica* test was considered and confirmed by a number of other judges, notably in *Arsanovia*[22] and *Habas*.[23] While seemingly reducing the unfortunate state of complexity relating to the governing law of the arbitration agreement, this test remains a purely common law test. It inevitably descends the debate into the even more complex debate of conflict of laws, and it allows limited predictability of the outcome. In addition to that, there is a divergence of views on the *SulAmérica* test even within common law jurisdictions.

8.26 For example, in a recent decision in *FirstLink Investments Corp Ltd v GT Payment Pte Ltd*,[24] the High Court of Singapore followed the threefold *SulAmérica* test, but disagreed with the English courts that where the parties have not selected the law to govern the arbitration agreement, the presumption is that the governing law of the underlying agreement is the parties' implied choice of the governing law of the arbitration agreement. In that regard, the Singaporean court found that where the parties had selected the law to govern the underlying agreement but had chosen a different arbitral seat, the presumption should be that the law of the seat takes precedence over the law of the underlying agreement:

> This court takes the view that it cannot always be assumed that commercial parties want the same system of law to govern their relationship of performing the substantive obligations under the contract, and the quite separate (and often unhappy) relationship of resolving disputes when the more commercially sensible viewpoint would be that the latter relationship

---

[20] *SulAmérica Cia Nacional de Seguros SA v Enesa Engenharia SA* [2012] EWCA Civ 638.
[21] ibid.
[22] *Arsanovia Ltd v Cruz City 1 Mauritius Holdings* [2012] EWHC 3702 (Comm), [2013] 2 All ER (Comm).
[23] *Habas Sinai v VSC Steel Co Ltd* [2013] EWHC 4071 (Comm).
[24] [2014] SGHCR 12.

often only comes into play when the former relationship has already broken down irretrievably. There can therefore be no natural inference that commercial parties would want the same system of law to govern these two distinct relationships. The natural inference would instead be to the contrary. When commercial relationships break down and parties descend into the realm of dispute resolution, parties' desire for neutrality comes to the fore; the law governing the performance of substantive contractual obligations prior to the breakdown of the relationship takes a backseat at this moment (it would take the main role subsequently when the time comes to determine the merits of the dispute), and primacy is accorded to the neutral law selected by parties to govern the proceedings of dispute resolution.[25]

It is fascinating how easily this heavy and technical debate can be avoided in any given arbitration if only the parties select the governing law when drafting their arbitration agreements! **8.27**

(d) The 'Lord Mustill' approach

In 1996, at a time when—even though it has been around for millennia—arbitration was on the way to becoming the leading dispute resolution mechanism for resolving international commercial disputes, Lord Mustill explored the tricky avenues of laws governing arbitration during the Goff Lecture in Hong Kong entitled 'Hong Kong 1996—Too Many Laws'. **8.28**

At the outset of the lecture, Lord Mustill explained that Hong Kong was selected for the delivery of the lecture because it is 'a nerve centre of international commercial arbitration as well as a nerve centre of international commerce'.[26] And, indeed, it is no surprise for the reasons so elegantly set out by Lord Mustill that the first reminder of the importance of this topic was delivered in Hong Kong. Lord Mustill explained the choice of the topic by setting out a certain dissatisfaction with the arbitral process that remains relevant today: **8.29**

> The complaint is that where the dispute comes from an international transaction too many domestic laws, and particularly too many domestic procedural laws, are allowed to encumber a process which should be simple and direct, and thus contribute to the complexity, cost and delay which is nowadays so widely deplored.[27]

In addition to being directed at the multiplicity of laws, Lord Mustill's complaint also rebuked arbitration practitioners who see 'too many opportunities to display their techniques' and exploit the plethora of choices to the detriment of the process. **8.30**

One of the ideas explored by Lord Mustill in an attempt to remove this particular uncertainty from the arbitral process was 'transnationalism'. As he explained in his lecture, according to the transnationalism concept, the law governing the arbitration agreement should always remain the same—international law—and it should be isolated from various domestic laws: **8.31**

> The idea behind transnationalism is that the internal procedural law of international arbitrations is a completely self-contained system, insulated from any national law: the concept being that it should make no difference where the arbitration is held, since local procedural laws are irrelevant.[28]

---

[25] ibid [13].
[26] Lord Mustill, 'Hong Kong 1996—Too Many Laws' (1998) 6(1) Asia Pac L Rev 1.
[27] ibid 12.
[28] ibid 14.

8.32 At the same time, Lord Mustill was quick to recognize that the transnationalism idea was as appealing as it was unworkable. The main reason for the failure of the concept is that under the New York Convention, states are to enforce arbitration agreements by staying court proceedings and to enforce foreign awards resulting from such agreements, and this cannot be done in an 'extra-terrestrial bubble' without applying national laws.[29]

8.33 Another alternative that Lord Mustill articulated in his lecture was *lex mercatoria*. He argued that because it is an ' "automatic distillation" of national laws round the world out of which gradually evolves a set of universally accepted rules of law',[30] it is an appropriate and predictable set of rules to be applied universally to arbitration. He then immediately dismissed the idea of this universal applicability on the basis that it is too vague when one is in need of a specific rule and too specific when one is looking for a general rule. He noted as follows:

> I doubt whether many advocates of the lex mercatoria would suggest that it could properly prevail over an express choice of law in the contract: for this would wholly contradict the principle of party autonomy. Since certainty is important above almost everything else in commercial relationships, the parties would be most unwise to enter into any transaction on terms which left the governing law completely blank.[31]

8.34 Lord Mustill dismissed yet another alternative to avoid the multiplicity of applicable laws. This is for arbitrators to engage in 'amiable composition' or decisions *ex aequo et bono*. He dismissed that alternative because, yet again, it is too unpredictable for reasonable business parties to agree to. In that regard, Lord Mustill found it hard to envisage that 'business people will want to entrust their financial futures to a basis of decision about whose outcome no prediction can be made until the arbitral tribunal has actually published its award'.[32] He did specify that this alternative is nevertheless available to the parties if they wish to subject their disputes to the absolute discretion of their arbitrators.

8.35 Lord Mustill concluded quite logically that the most readily available way to avoid the unfortunate confusion resulting from the multiplicity of potential laws is for the parties to write down 'in a clear language what the parties intend'.[33]

(e) The 'Justice Spigelman' approach

8.36 Since Lord Mustill's lecture in 1996, various prominent scholars have considered this issue. Perhaps one of the more recent and notable speeches on this topic is the one delivered by James Spigelman AC QC during the annual Kaplan Lecture in Hong Kong in 2013. In that lecture, much like Lord Mustill 17 years before him, Justice Spigelman acknowledged that the law governing the arbitration agreement may not necessarily be the law of the underlying agreement. Justice Spigelman also complained that it is rare for an arbitration agreement to contain a choice-of-law clause:

> It is rare for an arbitration clause to contain its own choice of law provision. Even where there is a choice of law clause in the relevant contract, if the seat differs from the law so chosen, an issue often arises as to whether the law for the seat should govern the arbitration clause. The

---

[29] ibid.
[30] ibid 19.
[31] ibid.
[32] ibid.
[33] ibid.

cases and the considerable body of literature agonising about the relevant principles, suggest that an express choice is advisable in a case where the governing law of the agreement and the choice of the seat diverge.[34]

Justice Spigelman, again much like Lord Mustill before him, entertained the idea of transnationalism to resolve the complexity of the issue. Also like Lord Mustill, Justice Spigelman rejected this idea, but on a different basis. For him, the recent decisions in *Dallah*[35] and *Astro*[36] were warning signs against the use of transnationalism because of the risk of inconsistent enforcement decisions: 8.37

> I am aware that many arbitral tribunals, in the absence of an express choice of law provision, proceed on the basis that, in an international arbitration, the applicable law should not be national, but 'transnational'. French courts validate this approach. However, as *Dallah* and *Astro* suggest, there are dangers in doing so if enforcement is sought in other jurisdictions which do not accept the concept of a de-localised arbitral system.[37]

Justice Spigelman noted that the failure of arbitral institutions to include choice-of-law provisions in their model arbitration clauses was unfortunate and likely contributed to the parties' failure to select the applicable law. He also noted that 'however desirable it may be to encourage express choice of law in an arbitration clause, it is unlikely to become common practice soon'.[38] 8.38

Like Lord Mustill, Justice Spigelman offered no other ways to improve the situation but for the parties to start including choice-of-law provisions in their arbitration agreements. His predictions are as gloomy as those of Lord Mustill: 'The common failure to include an express choice of law provision in an arbitration clause can lead to uncertainty about the efficacy of the arbitration.'[39] 8.39

(f) The 'Gary Born' approach

In December 2013, the chair of Wilmer Cutler Pickering Hale and Dorr LLP's International Arbitration Group, Professor Gary Born, delivered the annual John E C Brierley Memorial Lecture at McGill University. His talk was titled 'The Law Applicable to International Arbitration Agreements: Past, Present and Future'.[40] In that talk, Professor Born—like Lord Mustill and Justice Spigelman—commented on the unfortunate state of affairs relating to the issue as to what law applied to the arbitration agreement. 8.40

He started off with a historical overview of the issue by noting that early international arbitration conventions 'did not address the question of what law governs the arbitration agreement in any detail'.[41] This historical overview of international instruments with regard to this salient issue is new and refreshing. 8.41

---

[34] Spigelman (n 8) 16.
[35] *Dallah Real Estate & Tourism Holding Co v Ministry of Religious Affairs, Government of Pakistan* [2010] UKSC 46, [2010] 3 WLR 1472.
[36] *PT First Media TBK v Astro Nusantara International BV* [2013] SGCA 57.
[37] Spigelman (n 8) 19.
[38] ibid.
[39] Spigelman (n 8) 18.
[40] Gary B Born, 'The Law Applicable to International Arbitration: Agreements Past, Present and Future' (John E C Brierley Memorial Lecture, 3 December 2013) <http://www.youtube.com/watch?v=5OFfctLM8AM> accessed 25 September 2015. The talk follows closely Gary B Born, *International Commercial Arbitration* (2nd edn, Kluwer Law International 2014) ch 4, 472ff.
[41] ibid, Born, *International Commercial Arbitration*, 477.

8.42 Professor Born noted that one of the earlier conventions, the Geneva Convention, indirectly addressed the issue by providing that one of the conditions for recognition of the award was that the award 'has been made in pursuance of a submission to arbitration which is valid under the law applicable thereto'.[42] The New York Convention later offered more guidance by enhancing the premise that an arbitration agreement is separable and 'subject to specialised international rules of both substantive and formal validity'.[43] He cited Articles II(1) to II(3) of the New York Convention in support of his proposition because they set forth substantive international rules 'of presumptive substantive validity, directly applicable to international arbitration agreements'.[44] More importantly, Article V of the New York Convention specifically refers to the law potentially applicable to the arbitration agreement:

> **Article V(1)(a)**
>
> Recognition and enforcement of the award may be refused, at the request of the party against whom it is invoked only if that party furnishes to the competent authority where recognition and enforcement is sought, proof that:
>
> (a) The parties to the agreement referred to in Article II were, under the law applicable to them, under some incapacity, or the said agreement is not valid under the law to which the parties have subjected it or, failing any indication thereon, *under the law of the country where the award was made*.[45]

8.43 This often-cited provision of the New York Convention establishes a specific international rule to determine the law applicable to the arbitration agreement, and that rule points to the 'law of the country where the award is made' in the absence of the parties' explicit choice. Having examined the various conflict-of-law issues in this respect, Professor Born came to the conclusion that, while of vital importance, the separability presumption has caused the multiplicity of potentially applicable laws to come into play:

> An unfortunate consequence of the separability presumption in the choice-of-law context has been the development of a multiplicity of different approaches to choosing the law governing the formation, validity, and termination of international arbitration agreements. National courts, arbitral tribunals and commentators have adopted a wide variety of choice-of-law approaches to issues of substantive validity, ranging from application of the law of the judicial enforcement forum, to the law of the arbitral seat, to the law governing the underlying contract, to a 'closest connection' or 'most significant relation' standard, to a 'cumulative' approach looking to the law of all possibly-relevant states.[46]

8.44 This observation adds a number of items to the list of laws that can apply to an arbitration agreement, as well as to the number of tests that can be exploited to arrive at the law that should apply. In particular, the 'cumulative' approach is something that has not been often explored in practice. Professor Born noted, though, that the 'cumulative' approach, under which the tribunals will consider all potentially applicable laws, is not helpful in situations in which these various laws yield differing results.

---

[42] Geneva Convention, Art 1(a).
[43] ibid.
[44] Born, *International Commercial Arbitration* (n 40) 478.
[45] Emphasis added.
[46] Born, *International Commercial Arbitration* (n 40) 487 (footnotes omitted).

In his 2014 treatise on international commercial arbitration, which followed his **8.45**
Brierly Lecture, Professor Born added many more potentially applicable laws to this
ever-expanding list:

> Other arbitral awards and national decisions have either applied or considered other choice-of-law standards, including general principles of international law, the law of the place where the arbitration agreement is concluded, the seat of a domestic trade organization which has published a standard form contract/arbitration agreement, or the law of the place where the arbitral award would likely require recognition or enforcement.[47]

These new items bring us to a list of over ten various avenues to be considered to determine **8.46**
which law applies to an arbitration agreement in the absence of the parties' explicit choice.
In this regard, much like Lord Mustill and Justice Spigelman, Professor Born noted the
unfortunate uncertainty that this multiplicity creates:

> This multiplicity of choice-of-law rules potentially applicable to the arbitration agreement does not advance the purposes of the international arbitral process. The existence of multiple choice-of-law rules creates unfortunate uncertainties about the substantive law applicable to arbitration agreements, as well as the risk of inconsistent results in different forums.
>
> In turn, this leads to uncertainty about the extent to which international arbitration agreements can actually be relied upon to provide an effective means of resolving international disputes. The multiplicity of choice-of-law rules leads to delays and expense, resulting from the need to engage in choice-of-law debates, before both arbitral tribunals and national courts, when disputes arise concerning the formation or validity of arbitration agreements. This is inconsistent with parties' expectations of an efficient, centralised dispute resolution mechanism, in entering into international arbitration agreements.[48]

While agreeing with Lord Mustill and Justice Spigelman on the unfortunate state of affairs **8.47**
in relation to this key aspect of international arbitration, Professor Born did not—unlike
them—offer any viable solution to overcome the uncertainty, apart from relying on the
'validation' principle. Instead, he noted with regret that parties rarely select the law applicable to their arbitration agreements, which in turn causes the considerable uncertainty.

D. Conclusion

It is astonishing how a relatively simple matter has mutated into a painfully complex **8.48**
academic subject which has a potential for undermining arbitration as a dispute resolution mechanism by its unnecessary complexity. Despite the unanimous voices of leading
arbitrators and practitioners, the issue of the law applicable to arbitration agreements has
been neglected to such a tremendous extent that even the major arbitral institutions fail
to include the choice-of-law provisions in their model arbitration clauses. Largely as a
result of that oversight, very rarely do the parties include the choice-of-law provision in
their arbitration agreements, and many arbitrations degenerate into unnecessary debates
as to which law applies. It remains astonishing that there still appears to be a huge disconnect between contract drafters and international arbitration experts even within the
same firm.

---

[47] ibid 524 (footnote omitted).
[48] ibid 488.

8.49 On the occasion of the centenary of the CIArb, this chapter is both a wake-up call to the arbitral institutions and a call to all involved to include a choice-of-law provision in the model arbitration clauses and arbitration agreements. Despite this criticism, we should end this chapter, in a book dedicated to the enormous achievements of the CIArb spanning a century, by once again noting the eloquence of Lord Mustill, who recognized the fascinating subject in which we are all involved:

> The world of arbitration is a fascinating mosaic. Lines of fracture run everywhere. Theory and practice. International and domestic. Status and contract. Civilian and common law. Court-free and court-related. Factual and legal. Ritualistic and freewheeling. Macro and micro. Expert and legal.[49]

8.50 This rich diversity will see the CIArb through its second century.

---

[49] Michael J Mustill, 'Foreword—Sources for the History of Arbitration' (1998) 14(3) Arb Int'l 235–6.

9

THE LAW GOVERNING THE ARBITRATION AGREEMENT

A Transnational Solution?

*Renato Nazzini**

A. Introduction

As pointed out elsewhere in this book, parties rarely choose the law applicable to the arbitration agreement. This gives rise to complexities. The obvious solution, but one that, for some reason, is not yet prevalent, is for arbitration clauses to make an express choice of the law applicable to the clause itself, rather than to the matrix contract of which the clause is an element. It is impossible not to endorse this solution. If the parties choose the law applicable to the arbitration agreement, in all but rare cases such a choice will be given effect by arbitrators and courts. The determination of the law applicable to the arbitration agreement will not be problematic. This will be the end of the matter. As in many other areas of international arbitration, precise and clear drafting solves the problem or, rather, prevents the problem from arising in the first place. One does not have to be an 'arbitration revolutionary' to subscribe to this simple proposition. 9.01

The existence of a drafting solution does not mean, however, that the analysis of the legal solution in the absence of clear drafting on the point is an unnecessary effort, as some suggest.[1] The reason is extremely simple: not all arbitration clauses have an express choice-of-law provision concerning the law applicable to the clause itself. And even when everybody has become aware of the need for such a choice, also on the basis of the thoughtful advice given on the matter by practitioners and students of international arbitration, there will no doubt still be arbitration clauses without an express choice-of-law provision concerning the clause itself, because, for example, the parties could not agree on such a law, or simply due to neglect or forgetfulness. After all, there is an enormous amount of literature on arbitration clauses and how to draft them. And yet, there are still problematic clauses that give rise to disputes. The perfect world of perfectly drafted contracts with perfectly drafted arbitration clauses does not yet exist. And problems arise. 9.02

---

  * I am grateful to Elina Zlatanska for her research assistance.
  [1] Neil Kaplan and Olga Boltenko, 'The Dangers of Neglect: Governing Law of Arbitration Agreements' in Julio César Betancourt (ed), *Defining Issues in International Arbitration: Celebrating 100 Years of the Chartered Institute of Arbitrators* (OUP 2016) ch 8.

9.03 This chapter examines one such problem, namely that of the law applicable to the arbitration agreement when there is no express choice of such a law.[2] It does not aim to set out a test, or a set of tests, of universal validity or application. Rather, its objective is to review the current state of play and sketch out a framework for the development of a possible 'transnational'[3] solution to the problem.

9.04 This chapter is structured as follows. First, it explains why a separate enquiry into the law governing the arbitration agreement is necessary and what the implications of such a separate enquiry are. Second, it reviews three possible approaches to determining the law governing the arbitration agreement, namely: (1) the application of the law chosen by the parties to govern their substantive rights and obligations; (2) the application of the law of the seat of the arbitration; and (3) the application of 'transnational' rules. Finally, conclusions are drawn.

B. The Need for a Separate Enquiry into the Law Governing the Arbitration Agreement

9.05 It is trite that a complex matrix of laws applies in international commercial arbitration. Generally, the expressions 'applicable law', 'proper law', and 'governing law' are used as synonymous and interchangeable. In arbitration, the applicable law has three main aspects: (1) the law governing the substance of the dispute (*lex causae* or substantive law); (2) the law governing the arbitration agreement itself; and (3) the law governing the proceedings (*lex arbitri*). Thus, in the *Channel Tunnel* case, Lord Mustill famously explained:

> It is by now firmly established that more than one national system of law may bear upon an international arbitration. Thus, there is the proper law which regulates the substantive rights and duties of the parties to the contract from which the dispute has arisen. Exceptionally, this may differ from the national law governing the interpretation of the agreement to submit the dispute to arbitration. Less exceptionally it may also differ from the national law which the parties have expressly or by implication selected to govern the relationship between themselves and the arbitrator in the conduct of the arbitration: the 'curial law' of the arbitration, as it is often called.[4]

9.06 While Lord Mustill considered it exceptional for the law applicable to the arbitration agreement to be different from the law applicable to the substantive rights and duties of the parties, it is now well established that these two laws may be different and that, whether in the end they are different or not, a separate enquiry into the law applicable to the arbitration agreement itself is necessary.[5] Three reasons may be given for this proposition.

---

[2] The problem may arise in several procedural contexts: see Lawrence Collins, 'The Law Governing the Agreement and Procedure in International Arbitration in England' in Julian D M Lew (ed), *Contemporary Problems in International Arbitration* (Martinus Nijhoff Publishers 1987) 127.

[3] The precise definition of 'transnational' may be complex and falls outside the scope of this chapter. For present purposes, it is proposed to give the adjective 'transnational' the widest possible (negative) meaning of anything that is different from the application of national rules applicable to domestic arbitration.

[4] *Channel Tunnel Group Ltd v Balfour Beatty Construction Ltd* [1993] 1 All ER 664, 682, [1993] AC 334, [357]–[358].

[5] Piero Bernardini, 'Arbitration Clauses: Achieving Effectiveness in the Law Applicable to the Arbitration Clause' in Albert Jan van den Berg (ed), *Improving the Efficiency of Arbitration Agreements and Awards: 40 Years of Application of the New York Convention* (ICCA Congress Series No 9, Kluwer Law International 1999) 201.

9.07 The first is theoretical and is perhaps the least persuasive. The idea is that the arbitration agreement possesses its own specific nature and the nature of the arbitration agreement determines which law applies to it.[6] So, if the nature of the agreement is procedural, it would follow that the law of the seat, as the curial law of the arbitration, should apply to the arbitration agreement. If the nature of the agreement is substantive, this would lead to the conclusion that the substantive law governing the main contract should apply to the arbitration agreement too.

9.08 This approach does not solve the problem, but mutates it into a different question, that of the nature of the arbitration agreement. And this is, of course, a question on which there is no consensus among scholars[7] and which the arbitral tribunals and courts, quite rightly, generally do not address. It is submitted that these metaphysical conjectures are not an efficient way of resolving the problem at hand.[8] The arbitration agreement is, certainly, a contract and, as such, is subject to conflict of laws analysis as any other contract. The question is why the determination of the law applicable to the substantive rights and duties of the parties does not automatically, and without more, apply to the arbitration clause as it does to the rest of the clauses in the contract.

9.09 The second reason rests on the doctrine of separability, according to which the arbitration agreement must be treated as a separate contract from the main agreement, particularly for the purpose of assessing its validity and effectiveness. If the arbitration agreement is separate from the main contract, so the argument goes, then the law applicable to it may be different from the law governing the substantive rights and duties of the parties. In so far as the proposition is that the law applicable to the arbitration agreement may be different from the law governing the main contract, it is difficult to disagree with it. Separability can today be considered a general principle of international commercial arbitration[9] and, in any event, the arbitration clause, even from a purely contractual perspective, has its peculiar scope and function which justify a separate enquiry into the applicable law. This does not mean, however, that the arbitration clause must be treated as a completely stand-alone contract.

9.10 The doctrine of separability means that the existence, validity, and effectiveness of the arbitration clause must be assessed independently of the existence, validity, and effectiveness of the main contract. For other purposes, for example, assignment, the arbitration clause continues to be considered as an integral part of the main contract.[10] Thus, 'the autonomy

---

[6] Alexander J Belohlavek, 'The Definition of Procedural Agreements and Importance to Define the Contractual Nature of the Arbitration Clause in International Arbitration' in Marianne Roth and Michael Geistlinger (eds), *Yearbook on International Arbitration* (Intersentia 2012) 22 and 38.

[7] And, obviously, the choice is not limited to the alternative between a substantive or a procedural nature of the arbitration agreement, as some argue that its nature is both substantive and procedural, which is rather unhelpful as a guide to determining the law applicable to the agreement itself: see Bernardini (n 5) 199–200 and Julian D M Lew, 'The Law Applicable to the Form and Substance of the Arbitration Clause' in van den Berg (n 5) 118.

[8] ibid, Lew.

[9] See Jean-François Poudret and Sébastien Besson, *Comparative Law of International Arbitration* (Sweet & Maxwell 2002) 258. Julian D M Lew and others, *Comparative International Commercial Arbitration* (Kluwer Law International 2003) 106, stating that 'the doctrine of separability is considered one of the... transnational rules in international commercial arbitration'.

[10] *Hussman (Europe) Ltd v Al Almeen Development and Trade Co* [2000] 2 Lloyd's Rep 83.

of the arbitration clause and of the principal contract does not mean that they are totally independent one from the other'.[11]

9.11 The third reason is that, in the body of international, transnational, and domestic arbitration law, special rules apply to the arbitration agreement, which does, therefore, have its own legal regime different from that of the main contract. A few well-known examples will suffice. Article II(1)(2) of the New York Convention sets out the requirement that an arbitration agreement, to be recognized by the Contracting States, must be 'in writing'. This requirement applies regardless of the formal requirements applicable to the main contract. Article V(1)(a) of the same Convention provides that a ground on which a court of a Contracting State may refuse recognition and enforcement of an award is that 'the agreement referred to in Article II … is not valid under the law to which the parties have subjected it or, failing any indication thereon, under the law of the country where the award was made'. Thus, Article V(1)(a) sets out a conflict-of-laws rule specifically applicable to the arbitration agreement. Turning to domestic legislation, Article 178(2) of the Swiss PIL Act provides that 'an arbitration agreement is valid if it conforms to the law chosen by the parties, or to the law governing the subject-matter of the dispute, in particular the main contract, or to Swiss law'. The list could continue and would be a rather long one.

9.12 Thus, there appears to be little doubt that a separate enquiry into the law applicable to the arbitration agreement is needed, if such a law is disputed, and it cannot be automatically assumed that the law governing the substantive rights and duties of the parties applies also to the arbitration agreement. The question is, therefore, how to determine which law applies to the arbitration agreement. The answer could be found, quite easily, in Article V(1)(a) of the New York Convention, which sets out a conflict-of-laws rule specifically applicable to the arbitration agreement. The same rule is adopted in Article 34(2)(a)(i) of the UNCITRAL Model Law.

9.13 However, the conflict rule in question is of limited usefulness in two ways: (1) formally, its application is confined to applications for enforcement under the New York Convention and to applications for setting aside under the Model Law. So, for example, it does not apply when an English court has to rule on an application for stay or for an anti-suit injunction;[12] (2) its meaning is, in itself, unclear. In particular, it is not clear whether 'the law to which the parties have subjected' the arbitration agreement must be a law expressly chosen in relation to an arbitration clause or can be a law impliedly chosen by the parties, for example, by choosing the law applicable to the main contract or by choosing the seat of the arbitration.[13]

---

[11] Yves Derains, 'ICC Arbitral Process: Part VIII. Choice of Law Applicable to the Contract and International Arbitration' (1995) 6(1) ICC Int'l Ct Arb Bull 10, 16–17.

[12] As will be explained later, English courts apply common-law rules when determining the law applicable to the arbitration agreement other than under Art V(1)(a) of the New York Convention, which is given effect in English law by s 103(2)(b) of the English Arbitration Act 1996. However, some national courts apply the conflict-of-laws rules under Art V(1)(a) of the New York Convention also at pre-enforcement stages. See, eg, *Della Sanara Kustvaart-Bevrachting & Overslagbedrijf BV v Fallimento Cap Giovanni Coppola srl* (in liquidation) Genoa Court of Appeal, 3 February 1990 in Albert Jan van den Berg (ed), *Yearbook Commercial Arbitration*, vol XVII (Kluwer Law International 1992) 542–4; and *Insurance Co v Reinsurance Co*, Tribunal Fédéral (Swiss Supreme Court), 21 March 1995 in Albert Jan van den Berg (ed), *Yearbook Commercial Arbitration*, vol XXII (Kluwer Law International 1997) 800–6.

[13] The better view is probably that the choice may be implied: see, eg, *Consortium member A v Consortium member B* (Switzerland), Polimeles Protodikio (Court of First Instance, Multi-Judge Panel), Rodopi, Decision No 84 of 2005 in Albert Jan van den Berg (ed), *Yearbook Commercial Arbitration*, vol XXXIII (Kluwer Law International 2008) 552–4.

Nor could Article V(1)(a) of the New York Convention ever achieve full harmonization, even only at the enforcement stage. Article VII of the Convention allows Contracting States to apply their national law rules if they result in the enforcement of an award the enforcement of which would be refused under the Convention.

Therefore, under the Convention, approaches to the law applicable to the arbitration agreement *in favorem validitatis* coexist with the conflict rule under Article V(1)(a) in enforcement proceedings. In order not to make the analysis excessively complex, the following sections set out, briefly, three possible approaches to determining the law applicable to the arbitration agreement, without distinguishing the various procedural settings in which each approach applies. 9.14

C. The First Candidate Approach: the Law Applicable to the Main Contract

International commercial contracts usually contain a clause specifying the law governing the substance of the dispute.[14] The question is whether the choice of law of the main contract applies, or should apply, to the arbitration agreement. 9.15

Whereas the main authorities following the coming into force of the English Arbitration Act 1996 had initially emphasized the importance of the seat,[15] English law appears now to have answered this question in the affirmative.[16] In *SulAmérica Cia Nacional de Seguros SA v Enesa Engenharia SA*, the Court of Appeal had to decide which law applied to an arbitration clause providing for arbitration under the ARIAS Rules in London. The arbitration clause was part of an insurance policy governed by Brazilian law. The validity of the arbitration clause was a relevant consideration to determining whether an anti-suit injunction should be maintained or discharged. The insured maintained that, under Brazilian law, the arbitration clause could be enforced only with their consent.[17] 9.16

---

[14] Lord Collins of Mapesbury and others (eds), *Dicey, Morris and Collins on the Conflict of Laws*, vol 1 (15th edn, Sweet & Maxwell 2012) r 64, para 16R-001.
[15] *Abuja International Hotels Ltd v Meridien SAS* [2012] EWHC 87 (Comm), [2012] 1 Lloyd's Rep 461; *C v D* [2007] EWCA Civ 1282, obiter, applying the closest connection test to a London arbitration clause in a contract that was expressly governed by New York law; and *XL Insurance Ltd v Owens Corning* [2001] 1 All ER (Comm) 530, applying the implied choice test to a London arbitration clause which made express reference to the provisions of the English Arbitration Act 1996 being applicable and which was therefore found to be governed by English law even if the main contract was governed by New York law.
[16] In line with previous authorities leaning towards the extension of the choice of the law of the matrix contract to the arbitration clause: *Channel Tunnel Group Ltd* (n 4) [357]–[358]; *Sumitomo Heavy Industries v Oil and Natural Gas Commission* [1994] 1 Lloyd's Rep 45; *Sonatrach Petroleum Corp v Ferrell International Ltd* [2002] 1 All ER (Comm) 627. English law is by no means alone in adopting this approach: *National Thermal Power Corp v The Singer Co*, Civ App No 1978, Supreme Court of India (7 May 1992); Albert Jan van den Berg (ed), *Yearbook Commercial Arbitration*, vol XVIII (Kluwer Law International 1993) 403–14; *Eitzen Bulk A/S v Ashapura Minechem Ltd*, AIR 2011 Guj 13; *Aastha Broadcasting Network Ltd v Thaicom Public Co Ltd* [2011] FAO(OS) 411/2011 (High Court, New Delhi); and *Enercon India v Enercon GMBH*, Civ App 2086/7, Supreme Court of India (14 February 2014). See also ICC Case No 2626 (1977), Sigvard Jarvin and Yves Derains (eds), *Collection of ICC Arbitral Awards 1974–1985*, vol I (Kluwer Law International 1994) 316; ICC Case No 6379, Final Award (1990) in Albert Jan van den Berg (ed), *Yearbook Commercial Arbitration*, vol XVII (Kluwer Law International 1992) 212–20; ICC Case No 6752, Final Award (1991) in Albert Jan van den Berg (ed), *Yearbook Commercial Arbitration*, vol XVIII (Kluwer Law International 1993) 54–7.
[17] [2012] EWCA Civ 638, [1]–[6] (Moore-Bick LJ).

9.17 It was common ground before the court that the proper law of the arbitration agreement was to be determined in accordance with the established common law rules for ascertaining the proper law of any contract. These require the court to recognize and give effect to the parties' choice of proper law, express or implied, failing which it would be necessary to identify the system of law with which the contract has the closest and most real connection.[18] Since there was no express choice of the law governing the arbitration agreement, the question was whether the parties had made an implied choice of such a law by choosing Brazilian law as the law applicable to the main contract or whether English law, as the law of the seat of the arbitration, governed the arbitration agreement, either by having been impliedly chosen by the parties or as the law having the closest connection with the arbitration agreement, in the absence of an implied choice.

9.18 Moore Bick LJ, with whom Hallett LJ agreed, said:

> In the absence of any indication to the contrary, an express choice of law governing the substantive contract is a strong indication of the parties' intention in relation to the agreement to arbitrate. A search for an implied choice of proper law to govern the arbitration agreement is therefore likely (as the dicta in the earlier cases indicate) to lead to the conclusion that the parties intended the arbitration agreement to be governed by the same system of law as the substantive contract, unless there are other factors present which point to a different conclusion. These may include the terms of the arbitration agreement itself or the consequences for its effectiveness of choosing the proper law of the substantive contract …[19]

9.19 However, this was only a rebuttable presumption which, on the facts, was displaced by two factors: (1) the choice of England as the seat of the arbitration; (2) the consequences that would follow if Brazilian law were to apply to the arbitration clause.[20] The second factor was particularly powerful. The arbitration clause was clearly drafted so as to bind both parties whereas, under Brazilian law, the clause would have bound only the insurers. Moore-Bick LJ said that this suggested that the parties did not intend Brazilian law to apply to the arbitration clause.[21] Having found that the presumption that the law applicable to the matrix contract also applied to the arbitration clause had been rebutted, Moore-Bick LJ did not, however, go on to consider whether the choice of London as the seat of the arbitration was an implied choice of English law as the law governing the arbitration clause. He assumed that there was no implied choice of such a law. As a consequence, he applied the closest connection test and found that the arbitration agreement 'has its closest and most real connection with the law of the place where the arbitration is to be held'.[22]

9.20 Lord Neuberger MR, as he then was, preferred not to decide, as a matter of general principle, the question of whether the law of the arbitration clause is the chosen law of the contract or the law of the arbitration seat because, on the facts, under either approach the appeal would have been dismissed.[23]

9.21 It has been argued that the decision in *SulAmérica* is correct on the facts of the case. There is no doubt that the ineffectiveness of the arbitration clause under Brazilian law was a

---

[18] ibid [9].
[19] ibid [26].
[20] ibid [29]–[31].
[21] ibid [30].
[22] ibid [32].
[23] ibid [59].

compelling reason against finding that the parties had, impliedly, chosen Brazilian law to govern their rights and obligations under the arbitration clause.[24] Others, however, are critical of the *SulAmérica* approach because of the unpredictability of the outcome of the fully fledged enquiry into the parties' implied choice of the law governing the arbitration clause.[25] When it comes to construction of contractual clauses, absolute certainty is hardly ever achievable. However, whether the approach in *SulAmérica* is correct or desirable in law or policy, its application is sufficiently clear. There is a presumption that an express choice of the law applicable to the main contract is an implied choice of the law governing the arbitration agreement, which can be rebutted on the facts of each individual case.

9.22 In *Arsanovia v Cruz City*,[26] a dispute arose out of a slum clearance programme in India which was subject to considerable delay. There was a suite of contracts in relation to the programme, the relevant shareholders' agreement being governed by Indian law and providing for LCIA arbitration in London. In addition, the arbitration clause in the shareholders' agreement expressly excluded the application of certain provisions of the Indian Arbitration and Conciliation Act of 1996, in particular with regard to the seeking of interim relief in the Indian courts. Two sets of arbitral proceedings were commenced. The same arbitral tribunal was appointed in both sets of proceedings and found against Arsanovia, who challenged the awards under section 67 of the English Arbitration Act 1996. Applying *SulAmérica*, Andrew Smith J decided that the arbitration agreement was governed by Indian law, that being the law governing the main contract. He even suggested, obiter, that the choice of the law of the main contract may be an express, rather than implied, choice of the law of the arbitration clause.[27]

9.23 The question is probably not whether *SulAmérica* gives rise to uncertainties, but whether it gives proper consideration to the expectations of the parties and to the importance that the seat plays in international arbitration. The law of the seat generally governs the arbitral procedure which, according to some, should include the substantive validity of the arbitration agreement given that such an agreement is more closely connected with the curial law than it is with the law governing the substantive rights and obligations of the parties.[28]

D. The Second Candidate Approach: the Law of the Seat

9.24 If the arbitration clause indicates the seat of the arbitration and, according to some commentators, even if the choice of seat is delegated,[29] there are good arguments for holding that the law of the seat applies to the arbitration agreement.[30]

---

[24] Alexander Trukhtanov, 'The Proper Law of Arbitration Agreement—A Farewell to Implied Choice?' (2012) 15 Int'l ALR 140.
[25] Philippa Charles, 'The Proper Law of the Arbitration Agreement' (2014) 80(1) Arbitration 55, 59–60.
[26] *Arsanovia Ltd v Cruz City 1 Mauritius Holdings* [2012] EWHC 3702 (Comm), [2013] 2 All ER (Comm) 1 (QB).
[27] ibid [21]–[23].
[28] Bernardini (n 5) 200; Poudret and Besson (n 9) 258; Lord Collins (n 14) r 64; Lew (n 9) 106.
[29] ibid, Bernadini, 201.
[30] ibid 200. On the role of the seat, see generally Klaus Peter Berger, 'Re-examining the Arbitration Agreement: Applicable Law—Consensus or Confusion?' in Albert Jan van den Berg (ed), *International Arbitration 2006: Back to Basics?* (ICCA Congress Series No 13, Kluwer Law International 2007) 301–34.

9.25 The less controversial case is when there is no choice of the law governing the main contract. This approach has been adopted in England even after the decision of the Court of Appeal in *SulAmérica*, which clearly does not extend the presumption of the applicability of the law of the main contract to the arbitration clause beyond cases in which there is an express choice of the law of the main contract. In *Habas Sinai Ve Tibbi Gazlar Istihsal Endustrisi AS v VSC Steel Co Ltd*,[31] the claimant, Habas, a Turkish company, entered into a contract (through its agents, Charter Alpha Ltd and Steel Park Ltd) with the defendant, VSC, a Hong Kong company, for the sale by Habas of 15,000 mt of steel. No delivery was made and VSC commenced arbitration proceedings. The contract specified ICC arbitration in London, but did not provide for a governing law. Hamblen J held that where the matrix contract does not contain an express governing law clause, the significance of the choice of seat of the arbitration is likely to be 'overwhelming' because the system of law of the country of the seat will usually be that with which the arbitration agreement has its closest and most real connection. On the facts, the arbitration agreement was therefore governed by English law even if the main contract was governed by Turkish law.[32]

9.26 But even when there is an express choice of the law of the matrix contract, the rebuttable presumption established in the *SulAmérica* case is by no means uncontroversial. In fact, Moore-Bick LJ himself in *SulAmérica* emphasized that the arbitration agreement is much more intimately intertwined with the procedural law than it is with the substantive law,[33] which casts doubt on the very foundation of the rebuttable presumption. After all, if the arbitration agreement is separable from the matrix contract and has much more to do with the procedure than with the substance of the dispute, why are the parties presumed to have chosen the law of the substance and not the law of the procedure to govern the arbitration clause?

9.27 In *FirstLink v GT Payment Pte*, Shaun Leong Li Shiong AR in the High Court of Singapore declined to follow the *SulAmérica* approach and held that, when there is a choice of the law of the matrix contract and a choice of seat, the arbitration clause is governed by the law of the seat, even if this law is different from the law of the matrix contract.[34] Singaporean conflict of laws rules are, on this matter, the same as those of English law. Therefore, the Judge applied a three-stage enquiry, exactly as the Court of Appeal in *SulAmérica* had done. The conclusion was, however, that the choice of seat is an implied choice of the law governing the arbitration agreement.

9.28 The reasons given by the judge are the following: (1) there cannot be any inference that the parties want their rights and obligations under the arbitration clause to be governed by the same law that applies to the substance of the dispute because the two, potentially different, laws concern different legal relationships, namely the performance of the contract and the resolution of disputes when the substantive relationship breaks down;[35] (2) the natural inference would be that, when the substantive relationship breaks down, the parties' desire for neutrality comes to the fore and the law chosen as the procedural law of the arbitration takes precedence over the substantive law;[36] (3) 'the arbitral seat is the juridical centre

---

[31] [2013] EWHC 4071 (Comm).
[32] ibid [101]–[103].
[33] *SulAmérica* (n 17) [29] and [32].
[34] *FirstLink Investments Corp Ltd v GT Payment Pte Ltd* [2014] SGHCR 12.
[35] ibid [13].
[36] ibid.

of gravity which gives life and effect to an arbitration agreement';[37] (4) the importance of the seat is recognized internationally, in particular in Article V(1)(a) of the New York Convention and Articles 36(1)(a)(i) and 34(2)(a)(i) of the Model Law;[38] (5) the choice of seat determines the choice of remedies against the award, including the power of the courts to determine the jurisdiction of the arbitral tribunal, and it would be conceivable for the parties to demand consistency between the substantive law and the procedure of determining the validity of the arbitration agreement.[39]

FirstLink is but one of the many cases in different jurisdictions in which the choice of the seat was held to prevail over the choice of the law of the matrix contract.[40] The arguments supporting this approach will no doubt continue to influence courts and arbitration tribunals around the world.   9.29

E. The Third Candidate Approach: Transnational Rules

A third way of answering the question of the law governing the arbitration agreement is to disregard the application of a given state legal system determined on the basis of a conflict of laws analysis and to resort to transnational rules directly applicable to the arbitration clause.   9.30

It is well known that the French courts apply this approach, holding that the validity of the arbitration agreement is governed by *règles matérielles* independent of any national legal system. In the *Dalico* case, the *Cour de Cassation* ruled: 9.31

> According to a substantive rule of international arbitration law, the arbitration clause is legally independent from the main contract in which it is included or which refers to it and, provided that no mandatory provision of French law or international public policy is affected, its existence and its validity depends only on the common intention of the parties, without it being necessary to make reference to a national law.[41]

---

[37] ibid [14].
[38] ibid. The judge considered that the *SulAmérica* approach may determine an inconsistency in the application of the provisions in question because, under *SulAmérica*, the law of the matrix contract may apply to an arbitration agreement which could then be subject to the law of the seat under Art V(1)(a) of the New York Convention and/or Arts 36(1)(a)(i) and 34(2)(a)(i) of the Model Law. However, as explained earlier, it is possible that 'the law to which the parties have subjected' the arbitration agreement under these provisions may denote also an implied choice.
[39] ibid [15].
[40] See *Matermaco SA v PPM Cranes Inc*, Legris Industries SA, Tribunal de Commerce, Court of First Instance (20 September 1999) in Albert Jan van den Berg (ed), *Yearbook Commercial Arbitration*, vol XXV (Kluwer Law International 2000) 641–1164; *Owerri Commercial Inc v Dielle Srl, Gerechtshof*, Court of Appeal, The Hague (4 August 1993) in Albert Jan van den Berg (ed), *Yearbook Commercial Arbitration*, vol XIX (Kluwer Law International 1994) 703–7; and *Petrasol BV v Stolt Spur Inc*, Arrondissementsrechtbank, Court of First Instance, Rotterdam (28 September 1995) in Albert Jan van den Berg (ed), *Yearbook Commercial Arbitration*, vol XXII (Kluwer Law International 1997) 762–5; *Bulgarian Foreign Trade Bank Ltd v AI Trade Finance Inc*, Swedish Supreme Court, T 1881-99 (27 October 2000) in Albert Jan van den Berg (ed), *Yearbook Commercial Arbitration*, vol XXVI (Kluwer Law International 2001) 291–8; *Insurance Co v Reinsurance Co* (n 12) 800–6; *Government of the Republic of the Philippines v Philippine International Air Terminals Co* [2007] 1 SLR 278 (Singapore).
[41] *Municipalité de Khoms El Mergeb v Société Dalico*, Cass 1e civ, 20 December 1993, 1994 Rev arb 116, 117. This case law is now settled in France: see *Société d'études et représentations navales et industrielles v Société Air Sea Broker Ltd*, Cass 1e civ, 8 July 2009, 2009 Rev arb 529; *Société Uni-Kod v Société Ouralkali*, Cass 1e civ, 30 March 2004, 2005 Rev arb 959; *Renault v V2000*, Cass 1e civ, 21 May 1997, 1997 Rev arb 537; *SA Burkinabe des ciments et matériaux v Société des ciments d'Abidjan*, Paris Court of Appeal, 25 November 1999, 2001 Rev arb 165.

9.32 This approach is controversial. Some commentators criticise it because, in their view, its results are unpredictable and arbitrary.[42] Others point out that the 'transnational' principles of law do not represent an autonomous and stand-alone legal system, but depend on their recognition by national law or public international law. Furthermore, they are too general and elementary to enable arbitrators and judges to decide complex issues.[43]

9.33 More importantly, a 'transnational' approach is, currently, risky. If national courts, particularly courts having supervisory jurisdiction over the arbitration, do not recognize such an approach, this may give rise to inconsistent results. One example will suffice. In *Peterson Farms*, an ICC tribunal had awarded damages not only to the party to the contract, and, therefore, to the arbitration agreement, but also to other companies belonging to the same corporate group. The tribunal proceeded on the basis that, even if the contract was expressly governed by Arkansas law, there was no choice of the law governing the arbitration agreement. Because the arbitration agreement is separate from the matrix contract, the tribunal would therefore determine its scope in light of the common intention of the parties. Applying the 'group of companies doctrine' as developed in certain ICC awards[44] and upheld by the French courts,[45] the tribunal found that an arbitration agreement expressed to be made between A and B could be relied upon by companies belonging to the same corporate group as A, provided that the common intention of the parties was to that effect. Langley J, however, considered that the law governing the main contract—that is, Arkansas law—also applied to the arbitration clause and that there was nothing in Arkansas law, which was in all material respects the same as English law, which justified the approach adopted by the tribunal. The principle of privity of contract meant that, unless there was an agency relationship, the tribunal had jurisdiction only on the signatory parties to the contract. On this ground, an application to set aside the award in part for lack of jurisdiction vis-à-vis non-signatory claimants was upheld under section 67 of the English Arbitration Act 1996.[46]

9.34 The current problems surrounding a 'transnational' approach do not mean that such an approach is not desirable as a matter of policy and principle and that, incrementally, it should not become more widely accepted. In particular, the development of a 'transnational' approach may be facilitated by three factors.

9.35 While the French approach may currently be considered too extreme and does not find favour in certain jurisdictions, including England, there are different ways of achieving the same result of excluding the unintended application of peculiar national rules invalidating

---

[42] Marc Blessing, 'Choice of Substantive Law in International Arbitration' (1997) 14(2) J Int'l Arb 39, 40–1.

[43] Beda Wortmann, 'Choice of Law by Arbitrators: The Applicable Conflict of Laws System' (1998) 14(2) Arb Int'l 97, 101–2.

[44] *Dow Chemical Co v ISOVER Saint Gobain*, ICC Case No 4131, Interim Award (23 September 1982) in Pieter Sanders (ed), *Yearbook Commercial Arbitration*, vol IX (Kluwer Law International 1984) 131–7. See also *Pabalk Ticaret Sirketi SA (Turkey) v Norsolor SA*, ICC Case No 3131, Award (26 October 1979) in Albert Jan van den Berg (ed), *Yearbook Commercial Arbitration*, vol IX (Kluwer Law International 1984) 109; and ICC Case No 5103, Award (1998) in Sigvard Jarvin, Yves Derains, and Jean-Jacques Arnaldez (eds), *Collection of ICC Arbitral Awards 1986–1990*, vol II (Kluwer Law International 1995) 361.

[45] See *KIS France SA v SA Société Générale* (France), Paris Court of Appeal, 31 October 1989, 1992 Rev arb 90; *Société Korsnas Marma v Société Durand-Auzias*, Paris Court of Appeal, 30 November 1988, 1989 Rev arb 691; and *Société Ofer Brothers v The Tokyo Marine and Fire Insurance Co Ltd*, Paris Court of Appeal, 14 February 1989, 1989 Rev arb 691.

[46] *Peterson Farms Inc v C&M Farming Ltd* [2004] 1 Lloyd's Rep 603.

arbitration agreements whereby the parties clearly intended to arbitrate. For example, under the FAA, the Fourth Circuit held that the arbitration agreement is governed by a 'body of federal substantive law of arbitrability, applicable to any arbitration agreement within the coverage of the Act'.[47]

9.36 The First Circuit held that the FAA pre-empts parochial policy interests of the states and allows an arbitration agreement to be invalidated only on grounds 'that can be applied neutrally on an international scale'.[48] This more conservative, but still 'transnational', approach could be generalized: it is still necessary to determine a national law that governs the validity of the arbitration agreement, but there is a presumption that the parties do not intend their arbitration agreement to be subject to rules based on specific national policies that would invalidate an otherwise clear agreement to arbitrate. *SulAmérica* itself can be seen as an example of this approach. The Court of Appeal, having set out a presumption according to which the arbitration clause is governed by the choice of law of the matrix contract, was quick to rebut it on the ground that the law of the matrix contract would have made the arbitration agreement ineffective.

9.37 Arbitral tribunals and courts around the world, being presented with an agreement clearly evidencing an unequivocal intention of the parties to arbitrate, will be slow in finding that the agreement is invalid based on the technicalities of the applicable law. When one potentially applicable law has this effect, they will look for another applicable law under which the agreement is valid. This approach is often called the validation principle and is the reflection of a well-established contract law doctrine whereby a clause in a contract must be construed so as to be given effect instead of being invalidated.[49] A statutory example of such an approach is Article 178(2) of the Swiss PIL Act, which provides as follows: '2. As to substance, the arbitration agreement shall be valid if it complies with the requirements of the law chosen by the parties or the law governing the object of the dispute and, in particular, the law applicable to the principal contract, or with Swiss law.' Again, *SulAmérica* is not inconsistent with this approach. While the Court of Appeal applied an orthodox common law conflicts analysis, in practice it looked for the law that gave effect to the arbitration agreement and displaced the law that invalidated it.

9.38 Finally, if, as it is suggested elsewhere in this book, parties increasingly choose the law applicable to the arbitration agreement itself, this will give rise, over time, to a recognizable and well-established body of jurisprudence in the few jurisdictions whose laws will be most frequently chosen. This, together with tighter and clearer drafting, will in itself facilitate the emergence of rules and principles that could over time converge and give more meaningful substance and more precise contours to the admittedly still vague and underdeveloped transnational rules applicable to the validity of the arbitration agreements.

F. Conclusion

9.39 The problem of the law governing the arbitration agreement is more acute than ever. The cases of *SulAmérica* in the English Court of Appeal and of *FirstLink* in the High Court of

---

[47] *International Paper Co v Schwabedissen Maschinen & Anlagen GmbH*, 206 F 3d 411, 417 (4th Cir 2000).
[48] *Ledee v Ceramiche Ragno*, 684 F 2d 184 (1st Cir 1982).
[49] See, extensively, Gary B Born, *International Commercial Arbitration* (2nd edn, Kluwer Law International 2014) 541–8; and Berger (n 30) 312–13.

Singapore demonstrate that leading arbitration jurisdictions around the world can come to diametrically opposite results. In particular, the alternative between the law chosen by the parties to govern their substantive legal relationship and the law of the seat of the arbitration is unlikely to be settled any time soon at international level. This chapter suggests that, without embracing extreme approaches that purport to determine the validity of the arbitration agreement without reference to any national legal system, a more 'transnational' approach should be encouraged and may emerge based on two principles on which some international convergence would be desirable:

(1) there is a presumption that the parties do not intend their arbitration agreement to be subject to rules based on specific national policies that would invalidate an otherwise clear agreement to arbitrate;
(2) the arbitration agreement must be construed so as to be given effect instead of being invalidated. Therefore, among several potentially applicable laws, the arbitration agreement should be governed by a law under which it is valid and most effective rather than by a law under which it is invalidated or rendered less effective.

9.40 *SulAmérica*, in its apparently crystalline legal conservatism, is compatible with both approaches. Over time, legal convergence will also be facilitated by parties choosing, increasingly often, the law applicable to the arbitration agreement, which—it is easy to predict—will often be the law of one of the leading arbitration centres around the world. The emergence of a recognizable and well-established body of jurisprudence in the few jurisdictions, the laws of which will be most frequently chosen, will in itself contribute to the development of a coherent set of 'transnational' rules governing the substantive validity and the effectiveness of arbitration agreements.

10

SILENT TALK

Identifying the Language of an Arbitration When the Arbitration Clause Is Silent

Michael Young

A. Introduction

Language to a lawyer is like an instrument to a musician—without it, we cannot function. **10.01**
Legislation, cases, jurisprudence, analysis, documents, and awards are merely expressions of language. Language, though, is more than a collection of vowels and consonants, of accents and punctuation. It both absorbs and reflects the culture in which it is framed. Language, in short, is elemental.

Despite its importance, the applicable language is addressed rarely in a dispute resolution **10.02**
clause. Given its potent impact, the parties will often disagree over which language (or languages) should apply where the clause is silent. In that situation, how should the language of the arbitration be identified? This chapter seeks to consider and assess the tools available to an arbitral tribunal.

B. The 'Language of the Arbitration' and Its Importance

Before considering those tools, the topic itself needs a proper definition. What, exactly, do **10.03**
we mean by the 'language of the arbitration', and why is it so important?

(a) What does 'language' mean?

There are certain things it is not, or at least not necessarily. It does not have to mean the **10.04**
language of the seat, nor of the substantive law of the contract. It does not have to mean the language of the evidence sustaining any claims. Equally, it is often different from the native language of the parties, their lawyers, or the tribunal. In particular, it has been noted that 'the "internal" language of the arbitral tribunal, in other words the language of deliberation and the language of correspondence between the arbitrators, can be different from the language of the arbitration'.[1]

---

[1] Serge Lazareff, 'The Language of Institutional Arbitration' (1997) 1 ICC Int'l Ct Arb Bull 23.

10.05 Rather, when we talk of the 'language of the arbitration', we mean the official language that the tribunal and parties have adopted for their formal communications, whether in writing or orally. It is that which we are seeking to identify when the dispute resolution clause is silent.

(b) Identifying the language

10.06 Why, though, is it important to identify the language of the arbitration? There are a range of reasons, both practical and substantive. From a purely practical perspective, of course, the choice of language will inform which counsel can act, how well they might represent a party, and which arbitrators can decide the case.[2] The effect of having a Finnish language arbitration is clear: the pool of available arbitrators and counsel would not extend much beyond Finland.

10.07 At the opposite extreme would be a choice of English. Even here, though, the choice of English can have subtle (and often overlooked) consequences. Almost all international practitioners and arbitrators will be able to conduct an arbitration in English. However, if both the tribunal and one party's counsel are non-native speakers of English, counsel who are mother-tongue speakers can fail to adapt. Complex constructions of language (both written and oral), pleasing idioms, or subtle nuances of emphasis might be lost totally on the only audience that matters: the tribunal. Counter-intuitively, that can then place the native speaker at a disadvantage. In becoming the dominant language of global communication, the English language is now owned by the world. Many native speakers of English would do well to appreciate that simple truth.

10.08 Other, obvious practical consequences follow. What translation services will be required for documents drafted in a different tongue (and how much of each document needs translation)? Should any formalities accompany the translation? How will witnesses give evidence if they are not fluent in the chosen language? How can the tribunal make sure that translated testimony is an accurate reflection of what the witness has said, particularly when the latter's native language is unfamiliar to anyone on the panel? That, in turn, places a heavy burden on ensuring that the translators are not just proficient, but impartial and detached (both factually and emotionally) from the process. Few tribunals are involved in the selection of translators, or even in their vetting. Given the importance of making sure that they are the right choice, they should be.

10.09 The choice of language can also have substantive consequences. Not only does it limit the available pool of arbitrators, but it might also affect their background and approach.[3] By choosing, say, English law to govern a Dutch language arbitration, the likelihood is that few English (or other common law) arbitrators would be in a position to sit. While arbitrators often serve in cases governed by applicable laws different from those in which they are qualified, by choosing the Dutch language the parties have made that a near inevitability.

---

[2] Gary B Born, *International Commercial Arbitration* (2nd edn, Kluwer Law International 2014) 2230: 'Among other things, the language of the arbitration affects the choice (and performance) of counsel and arbitrators, the effectiveness of witness testimony and cross-examination, the need for translations and similar matters.'

[3] 'Language clauses can influence choice (and background) of arbitrators, and thus may have considerable practical importance', ibid 1807, fn 356.

10.10 The choice of language can have an even more basic impact on the substantive law. Where there is a disconnect between the language of the arbitration and the language of the applicable law, there is an inevitable risk that concepts are either misunderstood or misapplied. Translation can be an imprecise tool, and false friends are common in any comparative legal analysis. It is all too easy to try and understand an unfamiliar legal principle by approximating it to the closest familiar equivalent, even though the jurisdictional basis of the concept may be fundamentally different:

> [A]... burning issue... is how to translate into Chinese those English legal expressions which find their roots in the English legal system and are based on its socio-cultural context. Where philosophical, moral, ethical, linguistic and cultural values have interacted in the evolution of English law, how is this accurately and fully reflected in a Chinese language version?[4]

10.11 This has prompted some to suggest that the language of the law of the underlying contract should be a key factor in determining the choice of language. In an insightful article authored by the late Serge Lazareff, he noted that the 'problem has been considerably underestimated in the past... and the world of arbitration has only recently realised that language is the expression of culture, and that, as the law of a state is itself clearly the product of that state's culture, the language is an essential key to understanding the law applicable to the substantive issues of the case'.[5]

10.12 But should the language of the substantive law really be given that prominence? Probably not, for reasons I develop below. It does, however, bring us to the central issue under debate: what should be the relevant identifying factors employed by a tribunal when assessing the choice of language?

C. The Choice of Language

10.13 Given the importance of language, to the extent it is in dispute then a determination on the applicable language of the proceedings is likely to be one of the first acts of any tribunal. Ultimately, and subject to public policy exceptions in certain jurisdictions, the choice of language is a question of party autonomy. Given the problems that can arise, it is trite that the parties should try to agree expressly on the language to be adopted in the arbitration clause.[6] Such a choice is, however, relatively rare. The focus here is what happens when the clause is silent on the issue.

10.14 By 'silent', we mean where no express choice of a particular language (or languages) has been made. That does not necessarily mean that the parties have failed to agree on the parameters against which any decision should be made. Most arbitral rules (institutional or otherwise) make provisions, in various forms, to guide the tribunal towards their decision. While the text of those provisions differs between the institutions, the general approach

---

[4] Sally A Harpole, 'Speaking Your Language? What is the Language of Resolution in the Asia Pacific Region?' (Clayton Utz International Arbitration Lecture, Sydney, 16 November 2010).
[5] Lazareff (n 1) 18. Lazareff goes on to say that: '[f]or language is not only a means of expression. It is a medium of communication of a culture' (ibid 19).
[6] As the guidance notes on 'Standard and Suggested Clauses' to the ICC Rules recommend: '[The parties] may also wish to stipulate the language.'

remains the same: a broad assessment of the relevant factors, sometimes with priority given to a particular factor, but always against an overarching discretionary right by the tribunal to determine the issue. As such, the Rules of the ICC talk of 'due regard being given to all relevant circumstances, including the language of the contract'.[7]

10.15 The new LCIA Rules take a slightly different route, giving (interim) default priority to 'the language... of the Arbitration Agreement'.[8] They then go on to provide, among other things, that 'the Arbitration Tribunal shall decide upon the language(s) of the arbitration, after... taking into account the initial language(s) of the arbitration and any other matter it may consider appropriate in the circumstances'. As such, while it may be said that the LCIA Rules afford a greater prominence to the language of the contract, there is no reason to suppose that the end result would be any different from a ruling by an ICC Tribunal (to the extent that a broad discretion is afforded under both sets of rules). Moreover, in either case, the ICC and the LCIA anticipate proceedings in more than one language. Much the same can be said for the Rules of the SCC.[9]

10.16 By contrast, Article 19 of the 2010 UNCITRAL Rules merely requires the tribunal to determine the applicable language (or languages) of the proceedings in the absence of agreement, but provides no guidance as to how that task will be undertaken. A similar approach is taken in the SIAC Rules, where Article 19(1) states: 'Unless the parties have agreed otherwise, the Tribunal shall determine the language to be used in the proceedings'. Very similar language is found in the HKIAC Rules, under Article 15.[10]

10.17 The approach of the various institutional rules is, therefore, somewhat general (at best). A tribunal will need to drill down further to identify which indicia might be useful (or even used) when they exercise their discretionary powers.

D. Potential Indicia in the Exercise of the Tribunal's Discretion

10.18 A number of possibilities arise, some more valid than others (and some not valid at all). We start with the most common reference point: the language of the contract. The language used in the underlying agreement will often point the tribunal in the direction of the language of the proceedings, whether as a priority or as a presumption.

(a) Priorities and presumptions

10.19 Priorities and presumptions can be useful tools, but is this favourite approach too blunt? It certainly has its advantages. It ensures that the interpretation of the underlying contract is carried out in the same language as the proceedings. It is likely to reflect a language in which all parties felt comfortable, at least when the deal was done. It is also simple. But what if the language of the agreement was imposed, rather than adopted by consensus? Alternatively, what if the parties' usual language (or *lingua franca*) is different from that of the contract?

---

[7] 2012 ICC Rules, Art 20.
[8] 2014 LCIA Rules, Art 17.
[9] SCC Rules, Art 21: 'Unless agreed upon by the parties, the Arbitral Tribunal shall determine the language(s) of the arbitration. In so determining, the Arbitral Tribunal shall have due regard to all relevant circumstances and shall give the parties an opportunity to submit comments.'
[10] HKIAC Rules, Art 16.1: 'Subject to agreement by the parties, the arbitral tribunal shall, promptly after its appointment, determine the language or languages of the arbitration.'

10.20 For example, what should happen if the contract is in English, but both parties are equally fluent in German and the applicable law is (say) that of Austria? What if the last time that the parties used that language was when the ink dried on their signatures? The downside of simplicity can be laziness: a haste to adopt this particular approach when other, more powerful indicia point to a different conclusion. As such, reference to the language of the contract might be better approached as a default where there are no other indications, or the other indications are evenly balanced, rather than as a presumption. No tribunal should begin and end with this particular tool.

(b) **The law applicable to the contract**

10.21 What, then, of the other indicia? As noted above, the language of the underlying law is sometimes identified as being a factor (even a key factor) in this exercise. I am not so sure. It is certainly true that legal principles are more readily digested in one's mother tongue. It is also true that law reflects the culture and society in which it has been developed. However, the cultural concerns expressed by certain authors seem more concerned with nationality than with language: the fact that the language is the same is secondary.

10.22 Would an English arbitrator fully understand the cultural and jurisprudential norms of the laws of Alabama? Even assuming that is a relevant (even 'key') factor, I would say not. But the suggestion that he cannot understand and apply those laws—or the laws of any other jurisdiction—is misplaced, or at least overrated. The essence of being a good international arbitrator is being a good comparative lawyer, and neither parties nor institutions would hesitate in appointing tribunal members who have no connection, linguistic or otherwise, with the applicable law.

10.23 That parties approach appointments on this basis betrays another concern in affording too much weight to the language of the substantive law: would it really reflect the parties' intentions and expectations? If Turkish and Czech companies were to agree on Swiss law as the law applicable to the contract, would they have anticipated that being a 'key' factor in the language of a future dispute, leading to the conclusion that it should be French, German, and/or Italian? Parties tend not to think in linguistic terms when choosing the applicable law, which must diminish its relevance in identifying the parties' common intention. Beyond that, of course, is the fact that the choice of law applicable to the contract is often a compromise. To the extent that the parties settle, doubtless with some reluctance, on a particular legal system, it is most unlikely that they also anticipated settling on the applicable language moving forward.

10.24 That is particularly true if the language of the law mirrored the language of one of the parties: were it a German, rather than an Italian, company contracting with a Turkish entity in the example given above, would it really be fair to imply agreement by the Turks to arbitrate in German? In short, therefore, the choice of law applicable to the contract might be a factor in assessing the language of the arbitration, but it should be approached with a degree of circumspection.

(c) **The language of the seat**

10.25 After considering the language of the applicable law, what of the language of the seat? This seems much clearer. Other than in those rare jurisdictions where mandatory rules of law require the language to follow the seat, this should never be a factor. The notion that the choice of Paris as a place of arbitration indicates a preference towards the French language is as nonsensical as suggesting that London militates towards English, Stockholm towards Swedish, and Hong Kong towards Cantonese. International arbitration should be just that, reflecting the fact that parties choose their seat on the basis of its merits as a seat, not on the language spoken by the taxi driver from the airport.

(d) The language of the evidence and other indicia

10.26 Further indicia point to more practical concerns. What impact should the language of the evidence (or merely the language of the underlying project in dispute) have on this exercise? Contrary to the seat, this should be a material factor in a tribunal's assessment. Not only does it support efficiency, but it reflects best the language the parties had themselves considered to be the language of the contract. Were their correspondence all (or largely) to be in one language, the tribunal would have a credible indication of the appropriate language of the arbitration.

10.27 Equally, the fact that the project documentation (such as meeting minutes, technical documents, formal notices, and invoices) were all or predominantly in one language lends genuine support to an argument that this should be the language of the arbitration. Put simply, the language of the arbitration should take proper and careful account of the language of the project under dispute, not least as it is likely to represent an approach with which both parties had (at least once) been comfortable.

(e) The language of witnesses

10.28 A more difficult question arises if one also has to consider the language of certain fact and expert witnesses. To the extent that the language of the fact witnesses is consistent with the language of the documentary record, that clearly lends support to the approach described above. However, is it a factor in itself? That is more difficult, not least where the parties typically can choose which fact witnesses to present, and therefore affect the linguistic balance for tactical reasons. Equally, it will often be difficult at the outset of the proceedings (when the decision on language would normally be taken) to know for certain which witnesses would be produced. As such, one should see fact witnesses as lending support to the broader category of 'evidence', rather than a stand-alone ground in itself. That is particularly so where practical solutions might be found to accommodate testimony in different languages, as typically happens in any international dispute.

10.29 By contrast, expert evidence might give rise to a more subtle analysis. There are certain disputes which are wholly or heavily dependent on expert evidence. Gas market expertise in long-term LNG pricing disputes is a good example. Where there is a limited pool of available experts, and where they either tend to all speak one language or where none speak the likely language of the arbitration, there is a good case for making the proceedings (at least) bilingual. While that is not necessarily the most efficient approach, it can be essential when the parties' right to adduce evidence to substantiate their claims is otherwise prevented on linguistic grounds.

10.30 In a similar vein, should the language of counsel or the tribunal be factors in this analysis? In a word, no. The suggestion that counsel's tongue might be a factor is self-serving and divorced from an objective analysis of the applicable language of the arbitration. Parties choose their counsel; by choosing one with the 'wrong' linguistic background, they should not be able to influence (*ex post facto*) the language of any future proceedings.

The world is not short of lawyers: alternative counsel can always be found. As for the tribunal, their obligation is to exercise this discretion in a fair, impartial, and objective manner. A desire not to lose one's appointment because of an ability to speak the 'proper' language of the arbitration can scarcely be a legitimate factor in this process. In short, the choice of counsel and tribunal should reflect the choice of language, not the other way around.

(f) Equal treatment

10.31 On this point, it has been said that a tribunal should have regard to the principle of equal treatment between the parties. To the extent that a tribunal must exercise their discretion fairly, then that is correct. However, 'fairness' in this context must be defined narrowly. It requires the tribunal to hear the parties on their preferred language, to consider the indicia put forward by them (and to debate with the parties any further factors considered potentially relevant by the arbitrators), and then to weigh those up to select the appropriate language.

10.32 However, it would be dangerous to include a subjective assessment of 'fairness' in the equation. It has, for example, been suggested that (under certain circumstances) 'one party should not succeed with a request that English be chosen as the language of the arbitration on the mere ground that the contract is in English, solely to disadvantage the other party's counsel, whose English is poor'.[11] Nevertheless, if the only potential indicia are (a) the language of the contract and (b) the parties' choice of counsel, why should one party be able to usurp a contemporaneous affirmation of the 'correct' language by a subsequent choice of counsel? Indeed, the relevant strategy there might not be to 'disadvantage the other party's counsel', but rather to make a tactical counsel appointment to influence the language of the proceedings. For the reasons discussed above, that should not be legitimate. Beyond that, it also underscores the difficulties faced by any tribunal in trying to dissect the subjective nature of the parties' 'tactics', and to do so when the proceedings are likely to have only just commenced.

10.33 Are there any other potential factors? Perhaps the language of the likely place of enforcement? One might argue that, given that the award (and proceedings) will need to be translated into the applicable language of that jurisdiction, this would militate towards the use of that language from the outset. At best, however, this would be a minor factor, and one used in support of other indicia identified above. As the place of enforcement might not be known from the start (assuming that there is only 'one' in any event), and given the relative ease of translating documents should enforcement be necessary, it should not be taken as a factor in itself.

10.34 It has also been argued that the tribunal should take into account the 'convenience of the parties' when exercising its discretion: 'the arbitration tribunal has to determine the language which is most appropriate for the proceedings, considering also the convenience of the parties'.[12] To the extent that this refers to factors outside the parties' control when a

---

[11] Tobbias Zuberbühler, Christoph Müller, and Philipp Habegger, *Swiss Rules of International Arbitration* (Kluwer Law International 2004) 160.
[12] Julian D M Lew and others, *Comparative International Commercial Arbitration* (Kluwer Law International 2003), para 21-60.

dispute arises, then I would agree. However, 'convenience' should not be used as a cloak to disguise a party's efforts to influence the language of the proceedings after the event. Rather, 'convenience' should be taken to reflect the relevant indicia discussed above, particularly in the context of documentary and other available evidence. The parties should not be allowed to create their own inconvenience for tactical reasons.

E. Practical Solutions

10.35 Once the tribunal has fixed the language of the arbitration, there should be no ready mechanism for it to change thereafter. While certain practical exceptions might be made (for specific documents or specific witnesses in specific circumstances), the underlying choice of language should not alter. To do so could have a significant impact on the parties' choice of counsel (among other things).

10.36 There are, however, a number of tools available to a tribunal to allow them to maintain the applicable language of the proceedings, while affording the parties flexibility in how they present their cases and ensuring that the matter proceeds efficiently. Most commonly, of course, the tribunal can restrict translations in document-heavy cases, particularly where the tribunal and the parties' counsel are capable of reading that language. The obvious safeguard there is to ensure that counsel is genuinely fluent in that other language. A less subtle issue, however, is if the parties are not fluent in that tongue. That can often be overlooked, but if meaningful instructions cannot be obtained without the delay and cost of a translation, the parties' 'convenience' (within the meaning given above) is not well served. In any case, the challenge with all of these practical measures is to ensure that they do not edge the arbitration towards bilingualism (if bilingual proceedings had not been ordered). To do so would be to change the language of the proceedings long after they have commenced, which (for the reasons explained above) should only rarely be allowed.

F. Conclusion

10.37 Tribunals have available to them a range of potential options to help guide their decision on applicable language, should the dispute resolution clause be silent. As with all discretions, that exercise must be carried out properly and fairly. At the very least that requires the tribunal to evaluate, objectively, what the parties' intentions must have been on the question. In reaching that decision they should not be confined by strict presumptions or priorities; they must assess all of the available indicia, weighing each element in the balance. Equally, however, the tribunal should not take into account actions by the parties after the (potential) dispute arose. The parties should not be able to influence the debate by creating, in effect, their own 'inconvenience' should a decision on language go against them.

10.38 As we have seen, the choice of language can have significant consequences. Any decision by a tribunal needs to be fair. 'Fairness', though, can be an elastic concept. In this context, it should be assessed strictly and objectively. To do otherwise leaves too many possibilities for the parties to influence the debate strategically.

Part IV

ARBITRAL PROCEDURE AND PROCEDURAL MISDEMEANOUR

11

IS INTERNATIONAL ARBITRATION BECOMING TOO CONFRONTATIONAL AND COUNTER-INTUITIVE?

And Some Guidelines as to How Not to Irritate a Tribunal!

Hilary Heilbron

A. Introduction

It is said that Senator Mitchell began his negotiations towards peace in Northern Ireland by asking the warring factions whether they could at least agree on what day it was. It is a ploy arbitrators might consider useful in some arbitrations. Unfortunately, international dispute resolution by way of arbitration is more frequently becoming increasingly fractious, ill-tempered, and combative, as each side deploys tactics—or simply uncompromising lawyers—to argue its case. 11.01

The difference between forceful advocacy on behalf of one's client, on the one hand, and haranguing a tribunal, on the other; between thorough and penetrating cross-examination and an ill-focused shouting match; between arguing for procedural fairness and tactical manoeuvres designed to derail or delay the process, is becoming increasingly blurred in some cases. It is not to say that any of this is unethical, but it is antithetical to what international arbitration should be about. 11.02

All too frequently, lawyers lose sight of the fact that it is the tribunal whom they need to win over to their cause. Aggravating a tribunal, whether by aggressive and combative advocacy or by an ill-presented case, is counter-productive. This chapter addresses the causes of this growing tendency and how to deal with it from the perspective of both oral and written advocacy and presentation. 11.03

B. Consensus

Consensus is the *fons et origo* of international arbitration. Article II of the New York Convention states: 11.04

> Each contracting State shall recognize an agreement in writing under which the parties undertake to submit to arbitration all or any differences which have arisen or which may

arise between them in respect of a defined legal relationship, whether contractual or not, concerning a subject matter capable of settlement by arbitration.

11.05 Article V(1)(d) makes it clear that one of the grounds for refusing recognition and enforcement of the award may include where 'the arbitral procedure was not in accordance with the agreement of the parties or, failing such agreement, was not in accordance with the law of the country where the arbitration took place'.

11.06 The Model Law permits the parties to agree, for example, on the number of arbitrators,[1] the procedure for their appointment,[2] the procedure for challenging arbitrators,[3] the exclusion of the power to grant interim orders,[4] the place of arbitration,[5] the time for service and amendment of pleadings,[6] the procedure to be followed by the tribunal in conducting the arbitral proceedings,[7] and many other matters. The adoption of certain institutional rules provides in many cases such agreement or a framework for such agreement and many such institutional rules similarly provide for procedures subject to the parties' agreement.

11.07 Yet, despite this framework for a consensual approach, arbitrations can turn out to be far from consensual. A fundamental threat to consensus is where the very agreement to arbitrate is in issue. The most obvious case is when the agreement is not sufficiently clear as to amount to a mandatory agreement for binding arbitration. Is the process consensual when all that the parties agree is to arbitrate without reference to any rules or a seat? Was it their intention to leave these issues open to debate for the very reason that they could not agree upon them? What if there is no mechanism for appointing a tribunal—then national courts may have to step in. If the ICC Arbitration Rules are invoked, what is the effect of the ICC, rather than the parties, choosing the seat?

11.08 Perhaps the issue comes into its starkest focus where a non-signatory is brought into the procedure against its will? Whether or not that party is ultimately held to have been a party to the arbitration clause, there is not likely to be a consensus from the outset that it was.

11.09 So one first has to ask, what does 'consensual' mean in the context of the international arbitration process and, if it is not consensual, then should the brakes on confrontation be released? The facile and probably realistic answer is that arbitration is consensual in the sense that the method of dispute resolution is the subject of agreement and thereafter is consensual to the extent that it is consensual! That is, to the extent that the parties are willing to reach agreement whether by reference to institutional rules, a seat, or otherwise. Nonetheless, the fact that the parties cannot reach agreement should not be a justification for changing the whole approach to an established process. By agreeing the form of dispute resolution by way of arbitration, in practice the parties are taken to

---

[1] UNCITRAL Model Law, Art 10(1).
[2] ibid Art 11(2).
[3] ibid Art 13(1).
[4] ibid Art 17(1).
[5] ibid Art 20(1).
[6] ibid Art 23.
[7] ibid Art 19.

have bought into the well-recognized process despite lack of agreement directly between the parties.

C. Why Should the Arbitral Process Be Consensual and not Confrontational?

11.10 A legitimate question might then be why should arbitration be conducted in a non-confrontational manner provided there is nothing unethical or illegal about the way in which the case is presented? After all, the parties are in dispute. If a witness is lying, why should counsel not tear his evidence apart aggressively by excoriating the layers of alleged lies he is mouthing, as might be done for instance before a US jury?

11.11 The answer is that arbitration is a rather different way of resolving disputes. It is in private: there is no public gallery or jury to play to. The tribunal often includes civil law practitioners to whom the adversarial approach to a dispute, with lengthy oral advocacy, is unfamiliar and for whom cross-examination is likewise not the norm in their countries. The tribunal is usually chosen by the parties either directly or indirectly via a chosen institution. The process stems from the agreement of the parties, even though such agreement may later abate once the dispute has started.

11.12 The great success of arbitration, as we know it today, has of course been brought about largely by the impact of the New York Convention, which has led to its rivalling litigation as the means of resolving all manner of disputes, from the relatively small ones to the multi-party billion-dollar international claims. Yet, as claims have become more complex and involve larger sums of money, the scope for a more confrontational and often counter-intuitive approach has increased. Undoubtedly there are several reasons for this, but four are particularly relevant.

D. The Causes of the Problem

(a) A 'one-stop shot at success'

11.13 First and obviously, the resolution of disputes matters hugely to the clients. Enormous sums of money and reputations are often at stake. The client wants his lawyer to put up a show, to fight his corner. He wants his day 'in court'. Given that an award can rarely be appealed, the client faces a one-stop shot at success and wants to throw everything at it, even if misguidedly it may be counter-productive.

11.14 The lawyer obliges, not wanting to disappoint or lose the client for further work. Sometimes the client does not take advice to tone things down. Streams of unnecessary and lengthy argumentative correspondence, fishing expeditions for disclosure, the inability even to agree minor matters are but some examples. Although all this increases costs, what is less frequently said is that the other side of the coin is that it also increases earnings—of the lawyers! But, as explained below, it is not just such tactical manoeuvres that are the cause of the problem in some cases.

(b) Unfamiliar practitioners

11.15 Second, the success of arbitration has encouraged into the field many new players less familiar with the process. In particular, litigation or trial lawyers, more used to jury advocacy in the United States, often find the transition difficult. In so doing, they have sought to introduce elements into the process unsuited to arbitration. Jumping up and down to object every five minutes is but one example. Many a tribunal has had to bite its tongue (or not, as the case may be!) and tell the attorneys it is not a jury.

(c) Different cultural expectations

11.16 Third, a corollary of the second reason, is the very international nature of arbitration with an increasing involvement of parties from emerging markets, which can lead to culture clashes. National procedures and professional rules differ. Opportunities are missed to plead cases fully or to understand what has to be done at a certain time or even to understand the process. Parties and their lawyers view their opponents with a certain scepticism and a desire to browbeat the less sophisticated party or lawyer.

(d) Reluctant tribunals

11.17 Fourth, increasingly wary tribunals are reluctant to curb this rebarbative behaviour, concerned that if they try to curtail some of this manoeuvring, they will produce an unenforceable award as one party yells 'unfair'.

11.18 As a result, there is now often a situation where parties cannot even agree short extensions of time and a tribunal then receives a barrage of correspondence as to why three days will completely scupper the timetable, only to spend four days resolving the issue; or heated correspondence with name-calling designed not to impress the tribunal (for it has the reverse effect), but to impress the clients. Often too, parties cannot agree the ICC Terms of Reference, not appreciating that they are not pleadings, and counsel get very heated during cross-examination or interrupt each other during their submissions.

11.19 A frequent cause of controversy is when a tribunal gives what is viewed as unjust leeway to a respondent, the claimant party being unable to appreciate the fact that the tribunal is assisting the claimant so that if it wins, the award is enforceable.

E. The Right Direction?

11.20 Is this the direction in which arbitration should be moving? Is this consistent with its *raison d'être*? The purpose of arbitration is self-evidently to resolve disputes impartially and finally in a manner which is fair and speedy and as inexpensive as possible. If parties just wanted an answer they could revert to how arbitration was conducted in earlier days and dispense with reasons—that would certainly speed things up and would be music to the ears of most over-worked arbitrators! Instead, today, it is for the tribunal to explain and analyse the arguments and the evidence and to reach a conclusion.

11.21 Yet, aggressive tactics in the conduct of an arbitration aimed at browbeating the other party plays against the ultimate fairness of the process, a process aimed at informing the tribunal where the justice in the case lies. Most tribunals are sufficiently experienced for such tactics to have no impact, but indirectly it can affect the position. The losing party may go away feeling that it has been unnecessarily demeaned and pummelled. Subconsciously some tribunals may react unfavourably to a party behaving in such a manner. Equally, such tactics often add to the delay and costs. Such is the trend that it has spurned a book entitled *Guerrilla Tactics in International Arbitration*.[8]

11.22 It is important to distinguish between improper behaviour of counsel and the behaviour referred to above. The former may embrace the latter, but over-zealous, combative, or aggressive behaviour does not necessarily involve improper conduct and usually does not. Improper behaviour of counsel, such as knowingly presenting false information, is an entirely different scenario and to an extent is addressed by the relatively new IBA Guidelines on Party Representation and is not the subject of this chapter.

11.23 The issue addressed herein is the understanding that international arbitration is a *sui generis* procedure. The tribunal is not composed of impressionable lay jurors swayed by advocacy redolent of a popular television series. Arbitrators are, for the most part, experienced arbitral practitioners who have seen it all before. They know if a witness is prevaricating and not answering the question or is lying; they know where there is a thoroughly disingenuous point being made. They do not need haranguing. As has been said, in international arbitration cross-examination need not be cross!

11.24 Practitioners need to understand that advocacy in international arbitration is most effective and persuasive if it is measured, reasoned, and succinct. The aggressive advocacy and tactics employed by some counsel are, whatever effect they may be intended to have on their own clients, usually counter-productive. Such tactics can lead the tribunal to question the rationale behind them more searchingly.

F. Counter-Productive Advocacy and Presentation

11.25 Unnecessarily confrontational oral advocacy is not the only aspect of case presentation which is likely to irritate most tribunals. Badly presented documentary materials can likewise be counter-productive. Four common problems are addressed: the use of unmeritorious tactical applications, reluctance to agree relatively inconsequential matters, inappropriate advocacy, and the presentation of documentation.

(a) Unmeritorious tactical applications

11.26 First, parties sign up to an arbitration clause. This, however, does not stop attempts to litigate the dispute. Either one party will bring proceedings in a national court only to be met by an application to stay the proceedings or there will be an application for some sort of injunctive relief—either to stop the arbitration or an application for an anti-suit injunction or order. Many of the attempts to litigate are obviously hopeless, yet they entail delay and costs. Then there are applications for security for costs based on flimsy evidence made in the hope that the less financially viable party will cave in. That is not to say that all applications for interim measures are of this order, but a sufficiently large number are made with the probable intention of pressurizing the other side into settlement, more often than not without success. In an informal survey the author carried out among 30 seasoned international

---

[8] Günther J Horvath and Stephan Wilske (eds), *Guerrilla Tactics in International Arbitration* (Kluwer Law International 2013).

arbitration practitioners for a paper at ICCA, Miami, in early 2014, it was found that some 50 per cent of interim applications failed.

(b) A reluctance to agree

11.27 Second, once in dispute resolution mode, some lawyers, particularly those less experienced in international arbitration, are reluctant to agree anything. Order of witnesses, inspection of premises, complaints about a party's response to something, lists of issues, and many more aspects of the procedure can often involve unnecessary time-wasting when the end result is that in these non-critical issues the tribunal will invariably take the route which ensures fairness to all parties and often involves some form of compromise.

(c) The nature of hearings

11.28 Third, the arena where the consensus probably evaporates most directly is in the hearing itself. Once in advocate mode, some lawyers can lose the focus of the need to persuade—rather than aggravate—the tribunal. This is evidenced in many ways: too aggressive cross-examination, constant interruption of an opponent, unnecessary raising of voices, or unwarranted allegations of lack of due process made to the tribunal.

(d) Poor presentation

11.29 Fourth, there is little more irritating to a tribunal than to receive documents presented in an illogical, illegible, and incomplete way. Duplicates and triplicates, binders opening so all documents fall on the floor, documents and schedules in print so small or faded that they are illegible, are all aspects of the same fundamental objective—do not annoy your tribunal unnecessarily. But more importantly, if documents and written submissions and pleadings are not presented in a user-friendly manner, important points may simply be missed.

G. The Way Forward

11.30 What can be done to stop this creeping trend? In desperation, courts have resorted to novel ways to resolve such situations. In a case in Florida, where parties were unable even to agree the location for a deposition to be taken, the judge ordered as follows:

> If counsel cannot agree on a neutral site, they shall meet on the front steps of the [Courthouse.] Each lawyer shall be entitled to be accompanied by one paralegal who shall Act as an attendant and witness. At that time and location, counsel shall engage in one (1) game of 'rock, paper, scissors.' The winner of this engagement shall be entitled to select the location for the 30(b)(6) deposition to be held somewhere in Hillsborough County during the period July 11–12, 2006. If either party disputes the outcome of this engagement, an appeal may be filed.[9]

11.31 Such an approach is unlikely to be emulated in an international arbitration. Change will only occur if tribunals act more uniformly and forcefully. To an extent, some of this is already adopted by many tribunals. The time to act is at the beginning of the arbitration,

---

[9] *Avista Management v Wausau Underwriters Insurance*, US Dist Court Mid Dist Fla (6 June 2006).

before things have become too heated and positions too entrenched. This is the time when tribunals can assert their authority without too much reaction.

11.32 Tribunals, in the first procedural order for the hearing, or appended to it, need to lay down some basic rules. Hitherto these have largely been unspoken as they are assumed to emanate from the general powers of tribunals to conduct arbitrations: they may need to be spelt out in writing so that tribunals can refer back if necessary, particularly if counsel is inexperienced in international arbitration. They fall into two categories.

(a) Oral advocacy

11.33 The first, which lawyers should be compelled to explain to their clients, is to state firmly that the process in the international arbitration should not be combative, but a means of establishing the truth in a fair, just, thorough, and courteous way and that the tribunal will curb unnecessarily confrontational behaviour. The parties should be told to recognize that procedures suitable for litigation may be irrelevant to international arbitration. Cross-examination should be focused, relevant, and interrogatory, but not conducted in an unnecessarily hostile manner unless exceptional circumstances arise. Parties should not constantly make objections during cross-examination. Specific orders can also be added to any (preferably the first) procedural order as befits the particular arbitration, such as requiring parties to speak to each other on the telephone before reaching an impasse on matters such as disclosure, limiting the lengths of submissions, etc.

(b) Document presentation

11.34 A series of bad experiences has led the author to draft and send out with the first procedural order a set of guidelines termed 'Guidelines for Document Presentation'. It is a living instrument and being constantly updated and adjusted to the particular arbitration and individual arbitrators' preferences, which obviously may vary. Some of it can go directly into the first procedural order or the guidelines can be applied by reference or used as a checklist. It is very detailed because the task is often left to non-lawyers who know nothing about the case and tend to approach the matter without thought to the ease of handling the material. For example, a request for large type on the spine of folders so the volume number could be read from a distance, led in one instance to large black type on a dark navy label, so the number was then completely illegible! The author's guidelines[10] read as follows:

> These Guidelines apply to the presentation of written material and documents to the Tribunal during the course of this arbitration and at the hearing subject to any directions to the contrary. They take account of the need for such material to be easily transportable and for the material to be easy to access and user-friendly. They are subject to adjustment to meet the needs of a particular case if so requested by the parties. Additional specific directions of a substantive nature will be given in a separate procedural order(s).
>
> A. **Written pleadings, memorials or submissions**
> 1. All written pleadings, memorials or submissions ('written submissions') should be paginated, the paragraphs should be numbered consecutively and, unless short, they should include a table of contents.

---

[10] © Hilary Heilbron 2016. The Heilbron Guidelines were last updated in September 2015.

2. Footnotes should be confined to references: not argument, evidence or quotations. Any evidence or document extract on which a party wishes to rely should be in the body of the written submissions.
3. Specific directions will be given in each case as to which documents should accompany the written submissions, but unless otherwise directed, it should be assumed that all written submissions should be accompanied by:
   a. all documents on which the party relies;
   b. all witness statements relied upon;
   c. all expert evidence; and
   d. any relevant legal authorities relied upon.
4. A party should, where relevant, indicate which document or documents or legal authority it relies upon in support of each argument (factual or legal) and/or issue in any written submission by reference to the page number in the relevant chronological or alphabetic bundle(s) (see below) even if it also wishes to give it an exhibit number.
5. The Guidelines set out in paragraphs C–J below apply in so far as relevant.

B. Witness statements and experts' reports
1. Witness statements should comply with Article 4(5) and (6) of the 2010 IBA Rules on the Taking of Evidence in International Arbitration revised 2010 (the IBA Rules).
2. Experts' reports, if any, should comply with Article 5(2) of the IBA Rules.
3. The paragraphs of all witness statements and any experts' reports shall be numbered consecutively, the pages paginated and, if lengthy, include a table of contents.
4. Witness statements and any experts' reports should be translated if originally prepared in a language other than English, but both versions should be served.
5. Duplication of testimony should be avoided if possible and, unless otherwise directed, witnesses are at liberty to refer to parts of another witness' witness statement and confirm its accuracy, unless the party producing the witness considers that the second witness should not see the earlier witness' testimony.
6. References in witness statements or experts' reports to documents or legal authorities should be by reference to the page number in the relevant chronological or alphabetic bundle(s) (see below) even if the author also wishes to give it an exhibit number.
7. The Guidelines set out in paragraphs C–J below apply in so far as relevant.

C. Avoidance of Duplication of Documents and Translations
1. Unless bundles are required for an interim or procedural hearing, so far as possible, there should be no duplication of exhibits by a party. Once a document has been exhibited to a written submission, witness statement or expert report, all further references to that document in any contemporaneous or later written submissions, witness statements or expert reports served by such party shall be to the document in the composite bundle provided (see below). In other words there should only be one copy of each document unless a second is required because it shows something different or it is critical to a particular point.
2. Where possible parties should avoid duplicating documents already exhibited by the other party, eg lengthy contracts, but refer instead to the page in the first party's bundle.
3. Similarly, if one party has referred to an authority, the other party need not serve it as well, but refer instead to the page in the first party's bundle.
4. Any documents in a language other than English relied upon by a party should be translated into English, unless otherwise directed or agreed. If the document is a lengthy one of which only part is relevant, only the relevant part or parts need be translated in the first instance, but the receiving party shall be entitled to call for further translation if

necessary. Any dispute as to the extent of any necessary translation should be resolved by the Tribunal.

D. Binders
1. Ring or lever arch files should be used so that documents can be added if necessary, unless otherwise directed.
2. Files should be strong and when delivered should not be packed so tightly that the wire rings bend.
3. Files should not be over-filled so that if the ring is opened the front pages fall out.
4. Files should fit the size of the contents. In other words there should be no half-filled files: either smaller files should be used or more than one topic inserted into larger files and divided with a divider or tab.
5. The volume number should be printed in large felt tip (in excess of 1 cm) or type (min. 48 Font) on the spine of each file on a white or light coloured label so it is easily visible from a distance.
6. Spare files should be provided in case files are damaged in transit.
7. Files should either be A4 or A5 or a mixture (with two or four holes, but not 3 holes), depending on the directions given in the particular case.

E. Indexing and pagination
1. The Tribunal should be provided with one comprehensive index of all documents provided by each party at each stage of the arbitration and, at the hearing, of the agreed hearing bundles.
2. Each bundle should be separately indexed at the front.
3. Any index should give the volume and page number, indicate whether it is a Claimant or Respondent document, and a brief description of the document, and if relevant refer to its exhibit number.
4. All bundles should be clearly paginated.

F. Copying
1. Documents (but not written submissions or skeleton arguments) should be double-sided copied, unless otherwise directed.
2. If double-sided copying is used then:
   a. If a document is large the next document should start on a new page on the right of the bundle.
   b. If the e-mail is a chain, then each chain should start on a new page on the right of the bundle.
3. All documents should be legible and, if not, should be transcribed.

G. General presentation
1. All manuscript appearing on documents should be transcribed if relevant.
2. The font in all written submissions, witness statements and experts' reports should be no less than 12pt. and preferably 1.5 spacing, justified both sides. Long paragraphs should be avoided. Calibri font should not be used as it gets embedded.
3. All schedules should be enlarged onto larger paper if print is small and not easy to read.
4. Documents disclosed by the Claimant should be marked 'C' or 'C1', etc, as appropriate and those disclosed by the Respondent(s) 'R' or 'R1', etc, as appropriate.
5. All references to documents in the pleadings, written submissions, witness statements and submissions must give the date of the document and not refer to the document exclusively by exhibit number.
6. Where documents are translated, both the original and translation should be included in the bundles. If bulky, consideration should be given to putting documents in a foreign language, but which have been transcribed into English, into a separate bundle.

7. All contemporaneous documentation should at all times be provided chronologically in binders (whether pursuant to a party's submissions or in any hearing bundles or otherwise): not according to exhibit or subject order.
8. All legal authorities should at all times be provided alphabetically in binders (whether pursuant to a party's submissions or in any hearing bundles or otherwise): not according to exhibit or subject order and in accordance with C above.
9. Where documents have exhibit numbers these should be clearly identified at the top of the document as well.
10. Directions will be given at a later stage as to any further specific allocation of documentation to bundles for the hearing, eg a separate bundle of written submissions.
11. If bulky, documents such as contracts may be put in a separate bundle.
12. Tabs should not be inserted between correspondence or e-mails, unless otherwise directed.
13. Contemporaneous inter-lawyer documentation should not be provided to the Tribunal unless specifically required for a particular issue or decision, but one copy should be readily accessible and available at the hearing, although this may in the first instance be by electronic means, provided that any copies can be printed if needed.

H. Applications, skeleton arguments and post-hearing briefs

These Guidelines also apply, in so far as relevant, and subject to any specific directions from the Tribunal, to document presentation in relation to any interim applications, skeleton arguments and post-hearing briefs.

I. Referencing

All witness statements, experts' reports and written submissions, etc should be updated prior to the hearing to cross-refer to the pagination in the hearing bundles instead of any earlier bundle referencing.

J. Electronic versions of documents

1. All e-mail communications should state in the subject-line of the e-mail the nature of the issue and/or enclosure for ease of reference at a later date.
2. All documents in excess of 50 pages should also be supplied in hard copy.
3. All pleadings, memorials, submissions and skeleton arguments should also be converted from PDF into Word using appropriate software and supplied in searchable and editable form capable of being copied.
4. Depending on the case, documentation may also need to be made available in searchable electronic form.
5. If so, this should be provided by way of encrypted memory stick or flash drive unless otherwise directed. The Tribunal should be supplied separately with the encryption details.

K. Matters to be determined by further directions

Paragraphs A3; B5; C4; D7; F1; G10 and 12; H; J4 and J5 above.

H. Conclusion

11.35 However experienced in the field of arbitration counsel may be, it is rare for them occasionally not to overstep the mark. An occasional blip, however, is one thing and excusable. The real problem is a developing culture of using the arena of arbitration as a stage to play out the parties' anger against each other, using their lawyers as the means to do so. In so doing, it is sometimes forgotten that the advocate's skill in presentation of his client's case should be directed to persuasion of the tribunal—not its irritation. More importantly, ill-judged oral advocacy and badly presented written advocacy and documentation can lead to important issues or facts becoming obscured in the mire of aggression or ill-organized and ill-presented documentation. As with any culture change, there needs to be a framework to aspire to and it will not happen overnight. But a more robust and circumscribed approach from some tribunals earlier in the process can only be beneficial.

12

PROCEDURAL EFFICIENCY IN INTERNATIONAL COMMERCIAL ARBITRATION

Building It into the Process

*Elizabeth Snodgrass**

A. Introduction

(a) Apologia and caveat

12.01 Anyone practising in the field of international commercial arbitration cannot help but be aware of an increasingly sharp critique of the process on grounds of efficiency, which boils down to the complaint that arbitration generally costs 'too much' and usually takes 'too long'.[1] Participants in the arbitral process and the resulting debate readily share scare stories (usually presented as object lessons) about arbitrations that have gone off the rails in one way or another. Reasons of client confidentiality prevent me from sharing my own here.

12.02 Notwithstanding this critique, arbitration remains a preferred alternative for parties to many international business transactions. Among respondents to a 2013 survey of international arbitration users, 52 per cent identified arbitration as their favoured method for resolving disputes, compared with 28 per cent for litigation.[2] This preference was notably not due to a perceived time and cost advantage; instead proponents of arbitration emphasized the ability to appoint expert decision-makers, neutrality, confidentiality, the enforceability of awards,

---

* This chapter elaborates on remarks delivered at the Chartered Institute of Arbitrators Dispute Appointment Service (DAS) Convention on 15 November 2013. The opinions expressed herein are the views of the author and do not necessarily reflect the views and opinions of the author's employer or any of the firm's clients.

[1] See, eg, 2013 QMUL Survey, 'Corporate Choices in International Arbitration: An Industry Approach' 6 <http://www.arbitration.qmul.ac.uk/research/index.html> accessed 25 September 2015 (referring to 'intense debate surrounding costs and delay' that 'has raised concerns over the satisfaction of some of the largest corporate users of international arbitration'). This echoes findings from the first QMUL Survey that 'expense and the length of time to resolve disputes are the two most commonly cited disadvantages of international arbitration'. 2006 QMUL Survey, 'International Arbitration Study: Corporate Attitudes and Practices' 2 <http://www.arbitration.qmul.ac.uk/research/index.html> accessed 25 September 2015. A 2010 survey among members of the CCIAG revealed that 100 per cent of the corporate counsel surveyed consider that international arbitration 'takes too long' and 'costs too much'. See, eg, Lucy Reed, 'More on Corporate Criticism of International Arbitration' (*Kluwer Arbitration Blog*, 16 July 2010) <http://www.kluwerarbitrationblog.com> accessed 25 September 2015 (reporting on CCIAG Survey).

[2] 2013 QMUL Survey (n 1) 6.

and procedural flexibility as advantages of the process.[3] Thus, the popularity of arbitration appears to be in spite of—not because of—its efficiencies.

It is, however, worth pausing to note the evidence (based on such statistical information as is readily available) that, in the general run of cases, arbitration compares reasonably favourably to litigation in terms of the overall duration of proceedings. The average duration of some 250 arbitrations conducted under various sets of arbitration rules reported on in a 2011 survey conducted by the CIArb was 17 to 20 months from filing of the claim through to award.[4] The LCIA advises that approximately 50 per cent of the cases it administers lead to awards within 12 months of the request for arbitration, and 75 per cent result in an award within 18 months.[5]

12.03

This compares reasonably favourably to the duration of civil litigation proceedings in (for example) the federal trial courts in the United States. The median time from filing to disposition of civil matters in all US Federal District Courts for the 12-month period ending 31 March 2013 was 23.8 months; the median in the Southern District of New York was 28.8 months.[6] Those statistics include disposition prior to trial whether by settlement or summary disposition. A typical duration of 18 to 24 months for an international commercial arbitration, which (as will be discussed in more detail below) generally includes some form of evidentiary hearing prior to award, does not look too out of step by comparison.

12.04

(b) The 'least worst' alternative

But arbitration practitioners and users are—manifestly and quite rightly—not satisfied with a 'least worst' procedural alternative. The procedural flexibility inherent in the arbitral process challenges us to use that flexibility to devise a process that maximizes procedural efficiency without compromising efficacy, in that it is, and is seen to be, legitimate and results in widely enforceable arbitral awards.

12.05

This dual obligation is reflected in applicable arbitration statutes[7] and is amplified in contemporary sets of arbitration rules. For example, Article 22(1) of the 2012 ICC Rules of Arbitration explicitly obliges both the arbitral tribunal and the parties to 'make every effort to conduct the arbitration in an expeditious and cost-effective matter, having regard to the complexity and value of the dispute'. This is echoed in Article 14.4 of the 2014 LCIA Rules, which imposes on arbitrators a 'general duty' 'to adopt procedures suitable to the circumstances of the arbitration, avoiding unnecessary delay and expense, so as to provide a fair, efficient and expeditious means for the final resolution of the parties' dispute'. And

12.06

---

[3] ibid 8.
[4] CIArb, 'Costs of International Arbitration Survey' (2011) 12 <http://www.ciarb.org> accessed 25 September 2015.
[5] See LCIA, 'Frequently Asked Questions' <http://www.lcia.org> accessed 25 September 2015.
[6] Judicial Business of the United States Courts, *Annual Report of the Director 2013*, Table C-5 'US District Courts—Median Time Intervals from Filing to Disposition of Civil Cases Terminated, By District and Method of Disposition' <http://www.uscourts.gov> accessed 25 September 2015.
[7] For example, pursuant to s 33 of the English Arbitration Act 1996, the general duty of the tribunal is both to '(a) act fairly and impartially as between the parties, giving each party a reasonable opportunity of putting his case and dealing with that of his opponent' and to '(b) adopt procedures suitable to the circumstances of the particular case, avoiding unnecessary delay or expense, so as to provide a fair means for the resolution of the matters falling to be determined'. Under s 40(1) of the English Arbitration Act 1996, parties are under a similar general duty to 'do all things necessary for the *proper and expeditious* conduct of the arbitral proceedings' (emphasis added).

Article 14.5 of the 2014 LCIA Rules requires the parties themselves 'at all times' to 'do everything necessary in good faith for the fair, efficient and expeditious conduct of the arbitration'.

(c) **Best practices**

12.07 There is considerable contemporary discourse about best practices in terms of case management techniques that tribunals can use to enhance procedural efficiency. For example, with the 2012 revision of its Arbitration Rules, the ICC included an appendix of case management techniques that should be considered by parties and arbitrators to control the costs and duration of arbitration proceedings.[8] This built on the 2007 report of the ICC Commission on Arbitration and ADR on Reducing Time and Costs in Arbitration, a second edition of which was published in 2012 and offered as an official 'adjunct' to the 2012 ICC Arbitration Rules.[9]

12.08 There is, however, less systematic consideration of the choices parties might make when drafting their arbitration clauses to increase the likely efficiency of an eventual arbitration. This chapter seeks to make a start on filling that gap. The challenge in doing so is to suggest procedural mechanisms that are appropriate *ex ante* for every case when, from the procedural standpoint, experience teaches that 'one size does not fit all'. Parties choose arbitration for different reasons; parties choose arbitration for different disputes; and those differences do and should drive different procedural choices.

(d) **Advantages of arbitration**

12.09 Proponents of arbitration and those seeking to explain why they choose it identify a wide range of different reasons for doing so, including:

(1) neutrality—avoiding any perceived bias in relevant national courts, or simply not according the other side a 'home court advantage';
(2) predictability—avoiding uncertainty, or litigation, over where disputes are to be resolved;
(3) enforceability pursuant to the New York Convention;
(4) the ability to choose decision-makers with relevant expertise;
(5) privacy or confidentiality of arbitral proceedings;
(6) procedural flexibility; and
(7) savings in terms of speed and cost.

12.10 These different 'selling points' for arbitration will be the dominant considerations for different kinds of transactions. Thus, for 'Extractives Inc' entering into a long-term concession with State X, staying out of the courts of State X and having a straightforward mechanism for enforcing awards against State X internationally may be the dominant objectives in agreeing to arbitration. The parties to this transaction will be driven to arbitration primarily by a desire for neutrality, predictability, and enforceability and, possibly—whatever the potential inefficiencies of the arbitral process—relative speed compared to some national courts.

---

[8] 2012 ICC Arbitration Rules, Appx IV <http://www.iccwbo.org> accessed 25 September 2015.
[9] ICC, 'Commission Report: Controlling Time and Costs in Arbitration' (Document No 861-E, 17 March 2014) <http://www.iccwbo.org> accessed 25 September 2015.

12.11 Arbitration will be chosen not because it is necessarily a perfect option, but because it is a less bad alternative to relevant national courts. But for companies entering into repeat transactions for the sale and purchase of cargoes of (say) oranges, arbitration might appeal because it offers a quick and streamlined process that can be conducted by expert decision-makers to resolve disputes arising under standard-form contracts by reference to clear industry practice. These parties will come to arbitration for different reasons, expecting to get different things out of the process.

12.12 The disputes that are likely to arise in the two different settings described above also differ in terms of likely factual and legal complexity, and in potential value. The first might be expected to implicate a complex domestic fiscal regime and issues of political interference in relation to a business worth multiple billions of dollars, while the second will likely turn on the (apparently more straightforward) issue of whether the quantity and quality of goods delivered met relevant specifications.

12.13 Equally importantly, the disputes that in fact do arise in connection with these two different transactions introduce another set of potential variables. What seemed like a straightforward sale and purchase of a cargo of oranges could turn into a dispute about who is liable for the health consequences of contamination affecting third parties—or it could turn into a dispute about whether the contract can be enforced given an economic embargo, or in the face of alleged bribery and corruption, and so on. We should not expect that the same process will necessarily be optimal for every dispute.

12.14 A guiding principle in drafting arbitration clauses is therefore that parties should not pretend the world is more predictable than it really is. Parties should avoid over-engineering a clause to prescribe a process that may be ideal for the dispute they think is likely to materialize, because it might be wholly inappropriate for the dispute that actually does. The best arbitration clauses give parties and arbitrators options, rather than tying their hands.

B. Procedural Options in Clause Drafting

12.15 In the balance of this chapter, in the light of that important caveat, I will briefly assess three techniques that parties might consider when drafting pre-dispute arbitration clauses as techniques *ex ante* to maximize procedural efficiency: (i) appointing a sole arbitrator; (ii) opting for expedited arbitration; and (iii) making express provision for summary dismissal of legally unmeritorious claims.

(a) Appointing a sole arbitrator

12.16 In drafting an arbitration clause, parties generally specify the number of arbitrators, one or three. If parties do not make this choice, there are default rules and provisions for departing from those default rules in the arbitration rules of most arbitration institutions.[10] Choosing

---

[10] See, eg, 2014 LCIA Rules, Art 5.8 ('A sole arbitrator shall be appointed unless the parties have agreed in writing otherwise or if the LCIA Court determines that in the circumstances a three-member tribunal is appropriate ...'); 2012 ICC Rules, Art 12(2) ('Where the parties have not agreed upon the number of arbitrators, the Court shall appoint a sole arbitrator, save where it appears to the Court that the dispute is such as to warrant the appointment of three arbitrators'); 2010 UNCITRAL Rules, Art 7(1) ('If the parties have not previously agreed on the number of arbitrators, and if within 30 days after receipt by the respondent of the notice of arbitration the parties have not agreed that there shall be only one arbitrator, three arbitrators shall be appointed'). The sole arbitrator default rule is also reflected at s 15(3) of the English Arbitration Act 1996.

a sole arbitrator is a straightforward way to reduce the cost of an arbitral process and, potentially, to expedite the proceedings by reducing scheduling complexities, reducing the time needed for deliberation before the award is rendered, and so on.[11]

12.17 Interestingly, while users of arbitration routinely report that they strongly desire to reduce the time and cost of arbitration, it appears that they opt for this straightforward way of doing so relatively infrequently: in a recent survey of arbitration users, counsel, and arbitrators, a significant majority of respondents (73 per cent) had a preference as to number of arbitrators and an even more overwhelming majority (87 per cent) preferred a tribunal of three arbitrators.[12] Clearly, the ability to influence the composition of the tribunal—which 76 per cent of the respondents in a follow-on survey indicated they highly valued[13]—outweighs the potential time/cost savings associated with opting for a sole arbitrator. This reinforces the overriding perception that speed is not the only, or necessarily even the primary, procedural objective for arbitration users.

12.18 Given the unpredictability highlighted in the introduction to this chapter, it may not be appropriate to opt for a sole arbitrator in a pre-dispute arbitration clause in contracts relating to international business transactions of any size or complexity. Instead, parties may wish to draft clauses that keep the option of a sole arbitrator open. This can be done in (at least) one of two ways.

12.19 First, contrary to the usual practice, parties may decide not to specify the number of arbitrators to be appointed in advance, leaving it open for the claimant to make a proposal as to the number of arbitrators when arbitration proceedings are initiated in respect of a specific dispute. This would bring into operation the default provisions of such institutional frameworks as the LCIA and ICC Arbitration Rules, both of which state a soft presumption in favour of a sole arbitrator in appropriate cases.

12.20 It would also provide an opportunity for the parties to consider what number of arbitrators (one or three) is appropriate for the dispute that has actually arisen. In practice, one suspects that parties will still more often prioritize the ability to influence the composition of the tribunal by selecting one arbitrator themselves over the potential time and cost savings of a sole arbitrator once a dispute has arisen, but at least they will not be locked into having a three-person tribunal in every case from the outset.

12.21 A second option would be for parties to seek to agree in advance a category of disputes (or particular characteristics of disputes) that would be submitted to a sole arbitrator, with all other disputes not fitting the specified criteria being submitted to a three-person tribunal. Parties might specify an 'amount in controversy' or similar threshold for a three-person tribunal, the conventional wisdom being that sole arbitrators are 'more appropriate for cases with low amounts in dispute or of lesser complexity'.[14]

---

[11] Nigel Blackaby and others, *Redfern and Hunter on International Arbitration* (5th edn, OUP 2009) 248; Jeffrey Waincymer, *Procedure and Evidence in International Arbitration* (Kluwer Law International 2012) 273.

[12] 2010 QMUL Survey, 'Choices in International Arbitration' 25 <http://www.arbitration.qmul.ac.uk/research/index.html> accessed 25 September 2015.

[13] 2012 QMUL Survey, 'Current and Preferred Practices in the Arbitral Process' 2 <http://www.arbitration.qmul.ac.uk/research/index.html> accessed 25 September 2015.

[14] ibid 25.

Overall, experience suggests that parties are likely to prioritize the perceived benefits of a three-person tribunal, which include a perception of increased neutrality, a lower risk of a 'bad' or idiosyncratic decision, and a more 'balanced' award[15] over the potential time and cost savings of opting for a sole arbitrator. This again suggests that efficiency is not actually the dominant procedural consideration for most arbitration users.

(b) Expedited arbitration

By expedited arbitration, I mean arbitration that is conducted on specified, shorter-than-usual timelines, often against the backdrop of a long-stop date or deadline for the award to be rendered. This is also sometimes referred to as 'fast-track' arbitration.[16]

Parties generally end up in expedited arbitration in one of three ways: (i) they seek to impose *ad hoc* expedited time frames on an existing arbitration framework that does not expressly provide for fast-track arbitration,[17] generally (at a minimum) by specifying an overall deadline for the award to be rendered and (often) by specifying shorter timelines for key procedural steps than otherwise provided for in the chosen arbitration rules; (ii) they opt expressly for expedited proceedings pursuant to existing institutional arbitration rules in a pre-dispute arbitration agreement; or (iii) they agree to apply a set of arbitration rules that contains an option for expedited arbitration and/or elect that option once the dispute arises.

The first of these strategies is procedurally the most challenging, in that it imposes on the parties, in drafting their arbitration agreement, and an institution and/or tribunal, in trying to make sense of their agreement, the obligation to consider and rationalize the various time frames and procedural steps of a typical arbitration in the light of the agreed time constraints. Experience shows that this is possible—particularly if both parties cooperate and share the desire once a dispute arises for the dispute to be resolved expeditiously.[18] But this is the least predictable route to expedited arbitration.

One particular pitfall to avoid when drafting a 'bespoke' expedited clause, rather than using pre-existing institutional expedited rules, is specifying a fixed deadline for completion of the arbitration (ie the issuance of the award) without a mechanism other than subsequent party agreement for that deadline to be extended. In effect this gives one party the power, by delaying the proceedings and preventing the deadline from being met, potentially to render an award given after the deadline unenforceable as an excess of jurisdiction. Relief from such deadlines may be available pursuant to applicable arbitration statutes from courts

---

[15] ibid.
[16] See, eg, Irene Welser and Christian Klausegger, 'The Arbitrator and the Arbitration Procedure—Fast Track Arbitration: Just Fast or Something Different' in Christian Klausegger and others (eds), *Austrian Yearbook on International Arbitration* (Manz'sche Verlags- und Universitätsbuchhandlung 2009) 258; Eva Müller, 'Fast-Track Arbitration: Meeting the Demands of the Next Millennium' (1998) 15 J Int'l Arb 5.
[17] For example, although neither the LCIA nor the ICC have specific sets of 'fast-track' rules, the process pursuant to their standard rules can be adapted to a 'fast-track' procedure. See LCIA, 'Frequently Asked Questions' (n 5); 2012 ICC Rules, Art 38(1) ('The parties may agree to shorten the various time limits set out in the Rules. Any such agreement entered into subsequent to the constitution of an arbitral tribunal shall become effective only upon the approval of the arbitral tribunal').
[18] Reference is made here to the 'Panhandle' and 'Formula One' cases, in which ICC arbitrations were concluded within two and a half months from the request for arbitration (and only two and a half weeks from the evidentiary hearing) in one case and within a matter of days after the hearing, which itself took place after an exchange of submissions within seven-day intervals, in the other. Welser and Klausegger (n 16) 260–1.

of competent jurisdiction (generally the courts at the seat of the arbitration),[19] but it is better practice not to impose an apparently inflexible deadline from the outset.

12.27 Examples of arbitration rules that contain optional expedited arbitration proceedings are the rules of the SCC[20] and the rules of the SIAC,[21] along with several other regional and specialized arbitration institutions.[22]

12.28 Pursuant to the SCC Rules (and several others), the parties have an option to agree on expedited proceedings either in a pre-dispute agreement or once a given dispute arises.[23] Both the SIAC Rules and those of the CIETAC allow for automatic application of the expedited procedures without further express agreement if disputes fall below a certain value threshold.[24] The SIAC Rules also provide that a party can apply to the Registrar to have the Expedited Procedure apply regardless of the amount in controversy if the case is one of 'exceptional urgency'.

12.29 Common procedural features of these expedited arbitration regimes include:

(1) default to a sole arbitrator (this is a requirement under the SCC Expedited Rules, but can be varied by agreement in other regimes);[25]
(2) a limited number of written submissions and short time frames for the same;[26]
(3) limited taking of evidence or examination of witnesses, with an option in some cases for disputes to be resolved on written submissions alone;[27] and

---

[19] See, eg, English Arbitration Act 1996, s 50 ('Where the time for making an award is limited by or in pursuance of the arbitration agreement, then, unless otherwise agreed by the parties, the court may in accordance with the following provisions by order extend that time').

[20] 2010 SCC Rules for Expedited Arbitration <http://www.sccinstitute.com> accessed 25 September 2015.

[21] 2013 SIAC Rules, Art 5 ('Expedited Procedure') <http://www.siac.org.sg> accessed 25 September 2015.

[22] Arbitral institutions offering fast-track or expedited arbitration rules include the 2015 CIETAC Arbitration Rules, ch IV on 'Summary Procedures' <http://www.cietac.org/index/rules.cms> accessed 25 September 2015; DIS Supplementary Rules for Expedited Proceedings <http://www.dis-arb.de> accessed 25 September 2015; JCAA Commercial Arbitration Rules, ch V on 'Expedited Procedures' <http://www.jcaa.or.jp> accessed 25 September 2015; and WIPO Expedited Arbitration Rules <http://www.wipo.int> accessed 25 September 2015.

[23] 2015 CIETAC Arbitration Rules, Art 56(1); DIS Expedited Rules, Art 1.1; SIAC Rules, s 5.1(a).

[24] 2015 CIETAC Arbitration Rules, Art 56(1) (Summary Procedure to 'apply to any case where the amount in dispute does not exceed RMB 5,000,000 yuan', currently approximately £500,000, although parties can opt out of the Summary Procedure by agreement); SIAC Rules, Art 5.1(a) (Expedited Procedure to apply where 'the amount in dispute does not exceed the equivalent amount of S$5 million [currently approximately £2.4 million], representing the aggregate of the claim, counterclaim and any set-off defence').

[25] See SCC Expedited Rules, Art 12; SIAC Rules, Art 5.2(b) (providing for a sole arbitrator 'unless the President [of the SIAC] determines otherwise'); 2015 CIETAC Arbitration Rules, Art 58 (providing for a sole arbitrator 'unless otherwise agreed by the parties'); DIS Expedited Rules, Art 3.1 (providing for a sole arbitrator 'unless the parties have agreed [otherwise] prior to the filing of the statement of claim').

[26] See 2015 CIETAC Arbitration Rules, Art 59 (specifying 20 days); DIS Expedited Rules, ss 4.3 (specifying four weeks) and 5.2 (limiting the number of rounds of pleadings, unless the tribunal indicates otherwise). The SCC Expedited Rules give the sole arbitrator leeway to make procedural directions, see Arts 23 and 24, and the SIAC Rules authorize the Registrar to shorten time limits otherwise specified in the Rules for filing claims and defences, see Art 5.2.

[27] Art 5.2(c) of the SIAC Rules gives parties the option to 'agree that the dispute shall be decided on the basis of documentary evidence only', while according to Art 60 of the 2015 CIETAC Rules this is for the tribunal to decide. The DIS Expedited Rules contemplate, at Art 4.3, that there will be an oral hearing, while pursuant to Art 27(1) of the SCC Expedited Rules this may be dispensed with if the sole arbitrator does not consider it 'necessary'.

(4) less onerous requirements as to the form of the award, including in some cases the ability to dispense with a detailed recitation of the facts[28] or a full statement of reasons for the award.[29]

As stated at the outset, a cardinal feature of expedited or fast-track arbitration is an overall deadline for conclusion of the proceedings. The SIAC Rules specify six months from the date the tribunal is constituted,[30] while the CIETAC Rules provide a time limit of only three months.[31] The DIS Expedited Rules specify that the award should be rendered within six months (in the case of a sole arbitrator) or nine months (for a three-person tribunal) dated from the statement of claim, but they also provide: 'If the arbitral proceeding cannot be concluded within the [specified time frame], the arbitral tribunal shall inform the DIS Main Secretariat and the parties of the reasons in writing. The competence of the arbitral tribunal shall remain unaffected if the time frame set forth ... is exceeded.'[32] The time limit in the SCC Expedited Rules is three months from the date upon which the case was referred to the arbitrator (ie after his selection).[33] **12.30**

One of the advantages of expedited arbitration pursuant to existing institutional rules is that all generally provide a framework for relief from stringent timelines in an appropriate case.[34] This can be critical to obtaining an enforceable award. As noted above, specifying that the tribunal or relevant institution has the discretion to extend time limits, including in particular the long-stop date for rendering an award, is necessary to avoid a situation in which, for legitimate (or at least unavoidable) reasons, the tribunal has not been able to meet this deadline. Strictly speaking, in the absence of any mechanism for relief from the overall deadline, there is a risk that an award rendered after the time limit will be considered to be unenforceable as an excess of the tribunal's jurisdiction. **12.31**

In practice, expedited arbitration appears to be relatively rare—in the survey of arbitration users cited previously, 95 per cent of respondents had either no experience of fast-track arbitration or had experience of it in only a handful of cases.[35] That said, it appears to make up a reasonable, and growing, proportion of the arbitrations handled by some of the institutions that offer the option; while only 8 per cent of the SIAC administered cases in 2011 were pursuant to their Expedited Procedure, in 2014, 27 per cent of the cases administered by the SCC were pursuant to their Expedited Rules.[36] **12.32**

---

[28] DIS Expedited Rules, s 7 ('Unless the parties have agreed otherwise, the arbitral tribunal may abstain from stating the facts of the case in the arbitral award').
[29] SIAC Rules, Art 5.2(e) ('The Tribunal shall state the reasons upon which the award is based in summary form, unless the parties have agreed that no reasons are to be given').
[30] SIAC Rules, Art 5.2(d).
[31] 2015 CIETAC Rules, Art 62(1).
[32] DIS Expedited Rules, ss 1.2 and 6.2.
[33] SCC Expedited Rules, Art 36.
[34] See, eg, 2015 CIETAC Rules, Art 62(2) ('Upon the request of the arbitral tribunal, the President of the Arbitration Court may extend the time period [for rendering the award] if he/she considers it truly necessary and the reasons for the extension are truly justified'); SCC Expedited Rules, Art 38 ('The Board may extend this time limit [for the final award] upon a reasoned request from the Arbitrator, or if otherwise deemed necessary'); SIAC Rules, Art 5.2(d) (contemplating that 'in exceptional circumstances' the Registrar may extend the time for rendering the award).
[35] 2012 QMUL Survey (n 13) 2.
[36] 2014 SCC Statistics <http://www.sccinstitute.com> accessed 25 September 2015.

12.33 In terms of clause drafting, as with the option of a sole arbitrator, it is likely preferable for parties not to commit to expedited arbitration for all disputes in an arbitration clause before a dispute arises, but instead to reserve judgment on whether that will be appropriate for the particular dispute that actually does arise. SIAC arbitration is an attractive option in this respect because it provides a path to expedited arbitration in appropriate cases without requiring further agreement between the parties to get there. In the alternative, parties could include a similar framework in terms in their arbitration clause, selecting 'generic' arbitration rules as a default, but identifying criteria that would lead to the operation of expedited arbitration procedures.

(c) Summary dismissal

12.34 The final technique considered in this chapter is the summary dismissal of legally unmeritorious claims, through such procedural mechanisms as strike-out applications or motions to dismiss, leading to an award prior to a full evidentiary hearing on the issue subject to summary disposition. This is to be distinguished from what is commonly referred to as 'bifurcation', where a tribunal first gives full consideration to one set of issues (such as liability) and renders an award on those issues before turning to a logically sequential set of issues (such as quantum) and rendering an award on those issues.[37] A further distinction is between an early-stage motion to dismiss and a motion for summary judgment. The former proceeds on the basis that a claim as pleaded does not state a legally sufficient ground upon which relief may be granted (to paraphrase the language of the relevant US Federal Court rule).[38]

12.35 By contrast, a motion for summary judgment is made on the basis that, on the extant evidentiary record, there is no genuine dispute as to the material facts such that the movant is entitled to judgment as a matter of law.[39] The key difference for present purposes between what I would call 'summary dismissal' on the one hand, and 'summary judgment' on the other is that the former would not entail any weighing of the evidence, but would broadly accept the facts as pleaded and evaluate their legal relevance. Summary judgment would come after a full evidentiary record has been developed and would involve some evaluation of the sufficiency of that evidence to establish or call into question facts material to the outcome.

12.36 In the balance of this chapter, I will consider the extent to which existing procedural frameworks for international commercial arbitration, in the form of commonly applied sets of arbitration rules, authorize tribunals to award 'summary dismissal' in the sense outlined above in the event of legally unmeritorious claims. I am focusing on this variety of early dismissal instead of 'summary judgment' for three reasons. First, it is the more flagrant omission from the arbitrator's procedural armoury. As one commentator notes, 'Why should a party be allowed to pursue an utterly hopeless claim or defence through possibly years

---

[37] In noting that bifurcation is commonplace, Judith Gill refers to this as 'the acceptable face of early disposition', to be distinguished from a process of early or summary disposition, 'where issues are decided on an expedited, summary basis, [and] the tribunal will reach its conclusion on more limited information and evidence'. Judith Gill, 'Applications for the Early Disposition of Claims in Arbitration Proceedings' in Albert Jan van den Berg (ed), *50 Years of the New York Convention: ICCA International Arbitration Conference* (ICCA Congress Series No 14, Kluwer Law International 2009) 512.
[38] US Federal Rules of Civil Procedure, r 12(b)(6).
[39] cf US Federal Rules of Civil Procedure, r 56.

of proceedings, simply because they inserted an arbitration agreement into their contract rather than providing for the jurisdiction of the national courts?'[40] Second, due process considerations, which are relevant, among other things, to whether an award of summary dismissal is likely to be enforceable, are reduced when the analysis proceeds on the basis that all of the allegations made by the party whose claim was dismissed are to be accepted. Finally, concerns about the time and cost implications of including 'motions practice' in international arbitration can be minimized (though never entirely avoided) by a mechanism that comes into play at an early stage of the proceedings, before the expense of developing a full evidentiary record has been incurred.

12.37 Turning now to the question of whether the power to order summary dismissal is latent in the existing procedural framework for international commercial arbitration: the procedural norms and provisions of international arbitration rules that facilitate bifurcation do not expressly authorize summary dismissal. For example, the 2014 LCIA Rules (like the original LCIA Rules) indicate: 'The Arbitral Tribunal may make separate awards on different issues at different times. Such awards shall have the same status and effect as any other award made by the Arbitration Tribunal.'[41] This is echoed in the SCC Rules[42] and the UNCITRAL Arbitration Rules.[43] This implies that a dispute can be broken up into its constituent parts, but not that any or all parts of that dispute can be dismissed for legal insufficiency at an early stage.

12.38 Numerous sets of institutional arbitration rules explicitly contemplate the possibility of an arbitral process that forgoes an oral hearing and is decided on the basis of written pleadings and evidence only, referred to as a 'documents-only' arbitration. Such an arbitration will generally only happen if the parties expressly agree to it. This option is reflected in many sets of arbitration rules by way of an explicit or implicit presumption that an oral hearing will be held—at least if any party requests it.[44] While a documents-only arbitration can be 'summary' in that it obviates the need for an oral hearing (if the parties agree to it), it still entails a full consideration of the evidence presented by the parties and does not really equate to summary dismissal of a claim in the sense considered here.

---

[40] Gill (n 37) 520.
[41] 2014 LCIA Rules, Art 26.7.
[42] SCC Rules, Art 38 ('The Arbitral Tribunal may decide a separate issue or part of the dispute in a separate award').
[43] 2010 UNCITRAL Rules, Art 34.1 ('The arbitral tribunal may make separate awards on different issues at different times').
[44] With regard to oral hearings, Art 19.1 of the 2014 LCIA Rules, for example, confirms that '[a]ny party which expresses a desire to that effect has the right to be heard orally before the Arbitral Tribunal on the merits of the dispute, unless the parties have agreed in writing on documents-only arbitration'. That provision is echoed in Art 25.2 of the 2012 ICC Arbitration Rules ('After studying the written submissions of the parties and all documents relied upon, the arbitral tribunal shall hear the parties together in person if any of them so requests or, failing such a request, it may of its own motion decide to hear them') and in other commonly used sets of arbitration rules, eg 2015 CIETAC Rules, Art 35(2) ('The arbitral tribunal shall hold oral hearings when examining the case. However, the arbitral tribunal may examine the case on the basis of documents only if the parties so agree and the arbitral tribunal consents or the arbitral tribunal deems that oral hearings are unnecessary and the parties so agree'); SIAC Rules, Art 21.1 ('Unless the parties have agreed on documents-only arbitration, the Tribunal shall, if either party so requests or the Tribunal so decides, hold a hearing for the presentation of evidence and/or for oral submissions on the merits of the dispute, including without limitation any issue as to jurisdiction').

12.39 More generally, subject to any specific agreement of the parties, arbitral tribunals are generally vested with broad procedural discretion to conduct arbitral proceedings as they consider appropriate, consistently with their obligations to provide due process. The 2014 LCIA Rules describe this as 'the widest discretion to discharge its duties allowed under such law(s) or rules of law as the Arbitral Tribunal may determine to be applicable'.[45] The 2012 ICC Arbitration Rules concur that 'the arbitral tribunal, after consulting the parties, may adopt such procedural measures as it considers appropriate, provided that they are not contrary to any agreement of the parties'.[46] And other sets of arbitration rules also generally confer broad procedural powers on arbitral tribunals in similar terms.[47]

12.40 These broad provisions notwithstanding, it is hard to conclude that genuinely 'summary' dismissal is already built into most commonly used sets of arbitration rules. The closest that these rules tend to come is a provision such as Article 16.4 of the SIAC Rules: 'The Tribunal may in its discretion direct the order of proceedings, bifurcate proceedings, exclude cumulative or irrelevant testimony or other evidence *and direct the parties to focus their presentations on issues the decision of which could dispose of all or part of the case*'.[48] Certainly, there is no developed practice of summary dismissal even on the basis of such more tailored procedural provisions.

12.41 Moreover, one sees much clearer grants of authority to effect summary dismissal in domestic court rules and the rules of more specialized tribunals when that mechanism is available. By way of example of the latter, Rule 41(5) of the ICSID Arbitration Rules contemplates dismissal on the basis of a preliminary 'objection that a claim is manifestly without legal merit'. As Rule 41(6) of the ICSID Arbitration Rules makes clear, if the tribunal agrees, 'it shall render an award to that effect' and that is to be the end of the matter.[49]

12.42 The absence of such express provisions from the arbitration rules commonly used in international commercial arbitration would suggest that a mechanism for summary dismissal is not (implicitly) already contained within the procedural framework for the ordinary run of international commercial arbitration cases. It not only would be breaking new ground, but would also give rise to concerns (albeit in the end potentially not insurmountable ones) that a tribunal awarding summary dismissal of a claim had either exceeded its powers or somehow denied the affected party due process. This of course threatens the efficacy of the arbitral process by calling into question enforcement of the award.

---

[45] 2014 LCIA Rules, Art 14.2.
[46] 2012 ICC Arbitration Rules, Art 22.2.
[47] See, eg, SCC Rules, Art 19.1 ('Subject to these Rules and any agreement between the parties, the Arbitral Tribunal may conduct the arbitration in such manner as it considers appropriate'); SIAC Rules, Art 16.1 ('The Tribunal shall conduct the arbitration in such manner as it considers appropriate, after consulting with the parties, to ensure the fair, expeditious, economical and final determination of the dispute').
[48] Emphasis added.
[49] For examples of this provision in operation, see *Global Trading Resources Corp v Ukraine*, ICSID Case No ARB/09/11, Award (1 December 2010) <http://www.italaw.com> accessed 25 September 2015; *RSM Product Corp v Granada*, ICSID Case No ARB/05/14, Order of the Committee Discontinuing the Proceedings and Decision on Costs (28 April 2011) <http://www.italaw.com> accessed 25 September 2015; *Emmis Int'l Holding BV v Republic of Hungary*, ICSID Case No ARB/12/2, Decision on Respondent's Objection under ICSID Arbitration Rules, r 41(5) (11 March 2013) <http://www.italaw.com> accessed 25 September 2015.

12.43 Party autonomy is the antidote to these concerns: if parties want to give arbitrators this power, then in principle there is nothing stopping them from including an explicit authorization to award summary dismissal in their arbitration clause. As has been suggested elsewhere, the most straightforward way to do this would be to track the language of ICSID Arbitration Rules, Rule 41(5) or appropriate domestic court analogues in the arbitration clause itself.[50]

12.44 This might address the efficacy concern, but is this a good idea from the standpoint of procedural efficiency? The concern is that 'importing' into arbitration a species of motion practice from the litigation context will not be a remedy for the perceived inefficiencies of the arbitral process—the cure may be worse than the disease. There are some grounds for concern on this score; the trend in US domestic arbitration over the last several years has been away from encouraging dispositive motions.[51]

12.45 The proof would of course come should a practice of limited motions for summary dismissal develop in the international arbitration context, but three features of international commercial arbitration should help to minimize the risk of abusive motions to dismiss leading to unwarranted delay or additional cost. First, cost and disruption would be minimized by requiring motions to dismiss to be stated in the first substantive pleading and to be addressed on an expedited time frame thereafter. Second, and relatedly, summary dismissal (based on the facts as pleaded, determined prior to the development of a full evidentiary record) should be a more straightforward proposition than summary judgment (occurring after the expense of developing a full evidentiary record has been incurred and requiring a tribunal to engage with and weigh that evidentiary record). Finally, international commercial arbitration already broadly adopts a 'loser pays' or English cost-shifting rule, unlike (say) litigation in the United States, where motion practice gets some of its 'bad name' for being productive of excessive cost and delay. A robust application of the cost-shifting rule should effectively deter the most frivolous motions to dismiss.

C. Conclusion

12.46 In the final analysis, though, what matters is efficacy—would an award of summary dismissal likely be enforced by national courts pursuant to domestic arbitration law and the New York Convention? It is difficult to imagine that summary dismissal that resulted from a process that was expressly consented to by the parties in their arbitration agreement—and that proceeded on the basis of granting to the losing party the benefit of any doubt as to the evidence on which its claim was based—would give rise to meaningful due process or other enforceability concerns simply because, as the parties agreed, there was not a full development of the evidentiary record. Accordingly, arbitration users frustrated with 'procedural inefficiency' in the face of unmeritorious claims may well wish to consider whether, by express agreement, they wish to equip tribunals with additional tools to dismiss such claims. There would seem to be no 'in principle' obstacle to their doing so.

---

[50] See Adam Raviv, 'No More Excuses: Toward a Workable System of Dispositive Motions in International Arbitration' (2012) 28 Arb Int'l 487, 507–8.
[51] See FINRA, 'SEC Approves FINRA Rule to Drastically Limit Motions to Dismiss in Arbitration' (8 January 2009) <http://www.finra.org> accessed 25 September 2015.

13

ETHICS IN ARBITRATION
Party and Arbitral Misconduct

*Lord Hacking and Sophia Berry**

A. Introduction

13.01 International arbitration has been termed the 'new Eldorado for the modern commercial disputes lawyer'.[1] Just as the fable of great riches led the *conquistadores* to flock to the New World in the sixteenth century, practitioners from a multitude of jurisdictions have flocked to the realm of international arbitration. In tandem with these new entrants into the international arbitration community, the claims coming to arbitration are more valuable and more complex. The pressure on party representatives to succeed is ever greater and, in an expanded community of arbitration practitioners, there is less incentive to preserve one's professional reputation and a lower consensus as to what constitutes acceptable or ethical behaviour. Some would say that that we have, in fact, witnessed an 'ethical "race to the bottom"' in international arbitration and the obliteration of any such consensus.[2] Catherine Rogers famously wrote in 2002 that 'international arbitration dwells in an ethical no-man's land'.[3]

13.02 These widely observed trends lend credence to assertions that party misconduct in international arbitrations is on the increase.[4] The level of attention this issue has attracted from practitioners and institutions, as well as scholars, at recent conferences, and in articles, books, and blog posts is a clear indication that party misconduct is a real and pressing problem for international arbitration.[5]

---

* The authors are grateful to Catherine Rogers of Penn State Law and Queen Mary University of London for her assistance with elements of this chapter. The views expressed in this chapter, however, remain those of the authors alone.

[1] Sundaresh Menon, 'Some Cautionary Notes for an Age of Opportunity' (2013) 79(4) Arbitration 393, 394.

[2] Catherine Rogers, 'Guerrilla Tactics and Ethical Regulation' in Günther Horvath and Stephan Wilske (eds), *Guerrilla Tactics in International Arbitration* (Kluwer Law International 2013) 313, 314.

[3] Catherine Rogers, 'Fit and Function in Legal Ethics: Developing a Code of Attorney Conduct for International Arbitration' (2002) 23 Mich J Int'l L 341, 342.

[4] William Rowley, 'Guerrilla Tactics and Developing Issues' in Horvath and Wilske (n 2) 21; Günther Horvath, Stephan Wilske, and Niamh Leinwather, 'Countering Guerrilla Tactics at the Outset, Throughout and at the Conclusion of the Arbitral Proceedings' in Horvath and Wilske (n 2) 33; Peter Rutledge, 'Experiences from Other International Institutions' in Horvath and Wilske (n 2) 250; and Rogers, 'Guerrilla Tactics and Ethical Regulation' in Horvath and Wilske (n 2) 313.

[5] See, eg, V V Veeder, 'The 2001 Goff Lecture: The Lawyer's Duty to Arbitrate in Good Faith' (2002) 18 Arb Int'l 431, 433; Doak Bishop, 'ICCA Keynote Address: Advocacy and Ethics in International Arbitration'

The form party misconduct takes and the steps arbitral institutions and practitioners need **13.03**
to take in order to reclaim no-man's land and put the guerrilla back where it belongs, in the
jungle, are explored in the first half of this chapter.[6] The backdrop to this discussion is the
IBA's adoption of the Guidelines on Party Representation in 2013 and the LCIA's promulgation of the General Guidelines for Parties' Legal Representatives in 2014.

Ethical standards for international arbitrators have attracted similar amounts of commentary **13.04**
and soft law norms. We have seen the promulgation of the 1987 IBA Rules of Ethics,
the 2009 ABA/AAA Revised Code of Ethics for Arbitrators in Commercial Disputes, the
IBA Guidelines on Conflicts of Interest in 2004, and the CIArb Code of Professional
and Ethical Conduct for Members in 2009. Concerns still exist, however, that despite the
existence of detailed codes, rules, and training programmes, arbitrators may engage in
inappropriate interviews with legal representatives or improper delegation of their duties,
charge excessive fees, or fail to disclose important conflicts of interest.[7] The second half of
this chapter will therefore consider the means by which arbitrator misconduct should be
tackled.

B. Party Misconduct

(a) The nature and extent of the guerrilla tactics

In 2010, Edna Sussman and Solomon Ebere conducted a study into party misconduct in **13.05**
international arbitrations.[8] They asked 81 practitioners from around the world whether
they had witnessed 'guerrilla tactics, whether technically unethical or not' being employed
in arbitrations in which they had been involved as either counsel or arbitrator.[9] Out of
those, 55 said that they had and went on to list 10 types of tactics they had witnessed and
would categorize as 'guerrilla' in nature.[10] The tactics most widely reported by participants
in the survey were: attempts to stop hearings progressing; abuse of the document disclosure process; discourteous behaviour; acts to surprise the opposition; and applications for
anti-arbitration injunctions and other approaches to national courts. Less widely reported
were: issues of *ex parte* communications; witness tampering; the creation of conflicts with
arbitrators; frivolous challenges to arbitrators; and the creation of delays.

Examples of more extreme party misconduct such as the use of wiretapping and **13.06**
surveillance,[11] the kidnap of an arbitrator,[12] perjury,[13] and the submission of forged

---

(ICCA Rio, May 2013) <http://www.arbitration-icca.org> accessed 25 September 2015; Toby Landau and
J Romesh Weeramantry, 'A Pause for Thought' in Albert Jan van den Berg (ed), *International Arbitration: The Coming of a New Age?* (ICCA Congress Series No 17, Kluwer Law International 2013).

[6] Günther Horvath and Stephan Wilske, 'Conclusion and Outlook' in Horvath and Wilske (n 2) 341.
[7] Richard Mosk, 'Attorney Ethics in International Arbitration' (2010) 5 Berkeley J Int'l L Publicist 32.
[8] Edna Sussman and Solomon Ebere, 'All's Fair in Love and War—Or Is It? Reflections on Ethical Standards for Counsel in International Arbitration' (2011) 22 Am Rev Int'l Arb 611, 612.
[9] ibid.
[10] ibid 613.
[11] *Libananco Holdings Co Ltd v Republic of Turkey*, ICSID Case No ARB/06/8, Decision on Preliminary Issues (23 June 2008) and Award (2 September 2011).
[12] *Himpurna California Energy Ltd v Republic of Indonesia*, Final Award (16 October 1999) in Albert Jan van den Berg (ed), *Yearbook Commercial Arbitration*, vol XXV (Kluwer Law International 2000) 109.
[13] Affidavit of Floyd Landis in *United States Anti-Doping Agency v Lance Armstrong*, 56 <http://www.d3epuodzu3wuis.cloudfront.net> accessed 25 September 2015.

documents[14] can be found in awards of ICSID and other international tribunals. There is also anecdotal evidence of criminal behaviour, including the physical intimidation of arbitrators, occurring in international commercial arbitrations held in countries such as Russia.[15]

13.07 This list of tactics reported to Sussman and Ebere is a good illustration of the double deontological problem that has concerned the arbitration community for some years.[16] One practitioner's guerrilla tactic may well be another's legitimate practice or even professional obligation. For example, although engaging in *ex parte* communications was a guerrilla tactic reported by five of the practitioners surveyed in 2010 and is generally prohibited under the IBA Guidelines on Party Representation,[17] it is the norm in Chinese arbitrations. Members of arbitral tribunals in China are normally permitted to mediate between the parties.[18] An award issued by the XAC was therefore enforced by the Hong Kong Court of Appeal, despite the fact that the arbitrator had eaten dinner with the winning side (ostensibly to further mediation).[19] The risk of an uneven playing field in relation to document production and the preparation of witness evidence is also patent. Local bar association rules diverge greatly in respect of these aspects of practice.

(b) How tribunals combat misconduct

13.08 The pitch could be levelled by local bar associations harmonizing their conduct rules for practitioners operating in international arbitrations. In the absence of such a shift in approach, however, arbitral tribunals have long been dealing with these matters on an *ad hoc* basis by reference to guidance such as the IBA Rules on the Taking of Evidence. It could be argued that, in any event, this localized model is the best method for dealing with party misconduct.[20]

13.09 Arbitrators can devise guidelines or rules for the conduct of the hearing that are carefully tailored to the counsel in front of them and append them to their first procedural order. They can draft timetables to minimize the parties' ability to make spurious requests for extensions to deadlines and make clear what style of advocacy they expect to see from counsel by setting limits on the length of their cross-examination or written submissions.[21] Tribunals can also deal with misconduct during the hearing itself in a nuanced and graduated manner.

13.10 For example, they might, in the first instance, give an indication of the costs they might award arising out of delay tactics being employed or adverse inferences of fact they might

---

[14] *Maritime Delimitation and Territorial Questions between Qatar and Bahrain (Qatar v Bahrain)* (16 March 2001) ICJ Rep 40.

[15] Günther Horvath, Stephan Wilkse, and Jeffrey Jeng, 'Lessons to be Learned for International Arbitration?' in Horvath and Wilkse (n 2) 278, fn 693.

[16] See, eg, Cyrus Benson, 'Can Professional Ethics Wait? The Need for Transparency in International Arbitration' (2009) 3 DRI 78.

[17] IBA Guidelines on Party Representation, Guidelines 7–8.

[18] The rules of CIETAC, BAC, and all other major Chinese Arbitration Commissions authorize members of the arbitral tribunal or their nominees to mediate between the parties. Hew Dundas and David Bartos, *Dundas and Bartos on the Arbitration (Scotland) Act 2010* (W Green 2014).

[19] *Gao Haiyan v Keeneye Holdings Ltd* [2011] HKCA 459.

[20] Lucy Reed, 'Sanctions Available for Arbitrators to Curtail Guerrilla Tactics' in Horvath and Wilkse (n 2) 93.

[21] This is a problem highlighted by Michael Hwang in 'Why is There Still Resistance to Arbitration in Asia?' (The International Arbitration Club, Table Talk, Singapore, Autumn 2007).

make as a result of one party's behaviour before taking more punitive action.²² Counsel will then know that the tribunal is alert to the possibility of guerrilla tactics being used or an ethical imbalance being exploited and is willing and able to censure such behaviour. This may act as a deterrent. Further, the parties may take more notice of rules or orders that have been produced by their arbitral tribunal with their specific case in mind than of a generic code. There are some examples of cases where this individualized approach has worked well.²³

(c) The use of inherent powers

13.11 In order to address more extreme party misconduct, tribunals may have recourse to the exercise of their inherent (or residual) procedural powers.²⁴ That tribunals possess such powers is apparently universally accepted in the ICSID arena²⁵ and is evidenced by decisions of the Iran–United States Claims Tribunal,²⁶ the Appeal Chamber of the Special Tribunal for Lebanon,²⁷ and the WTO's Appellate Body,²⁸ as well as ICSID tribunals.²⁹

13.12 The source of these powers is best explained by Chester Brown, who views their existence as a necessary condition to any tribunal fulfilling its core function—the effective and efficient administration of international justice.³⁰

13.13 Arbitral tribunals would, of course, need to consider the precise scope of their functions and the express terms of their constitution before concluding that a particular order could be granted pursuant to their inherent or residual powers. They may find that their power to protect the integrity of the proceedings or uphold the interests of justice enables them to change the location of a hearing to protect a witness;³¹ issue an anti-suit injunction to stop the commencement of vexatious parallel proceedings;³² dismiss a claim as an abuse of process;³³ or exclude counsel who have been brought in at the last minute to create a conflict

---

²² ibid. See also Günther Horvath, Stephan Wilkse, and Niamh Leinwather, 'Countering Guerrilla Tactics at the Outset, Throughout and at the Conclusion of the Arbitral Proceedings' in Horvath and Wilkse (n 2) 33.
²³ See, eg, *Adem Dogan v Turkmenistan*, ICSID Case No ARB/09/9, where a recommendation from the tribunal appeared to stop the state from putting further pressure on a witness to sign a back-dated document.
²⁴ Martins Paparinskis, 'Inherent Powers of ICSID Tribunals: Broadly and Rightly So' in Ian Laird and Todd Weiler (eds), *Investment Treaty Arbitration and International Law*, vol 5 (JurisNet 2011).
²⁵ ibid.
²⁶ *Iran v United States*, Iran-United States Claims Tribunal, Decision No DEC 134-A3/A8/A9/A14/B61-FT, Decision Ruling on Request for Revision by Iran (1 July 2011); *E-Systems Inc v Iran*, Interim Award No ITM 13-388-FT (4 February 1983), [1983] 2 Iran-US Claims Tribunal Reports 51.
²⁷ STL (Appeal Chamber) Case No CH/AC/2010/2, Decision on Appeal of Pre-Trial Judge's Order Regarding Jurisdiction and Standing (10 November 2010).
²⁸ WTO, *Mexico: Tax Measures on Soft Drinks and Other Beverages*, Appellate Body Report No WT/DS308/AB/R (24 March 2006).
²⁹ *Hrvatska Elektroprivreda dd v Slovenia*, ICSID Case No ARB/05/24, Tribunal's Ruling regarding the Participation of David Mildon QC in Further Stages of the Proceedings (6 May 2008); *Rompetrol Group NV v Romania*, ICSID Case No ARB/06/03, Decision of the Tribunal on the Participation of a Counsel (14 January 2010).
³⁰ Chester Brown, 'Inherent Powers in International Adjudication' in Cesare Romano, Karen Alter, and Chrisanthi Avgerou (eds), *The Oxford Handbook of International Adjudication* (OUP 2014) 828.
³¹ Victoria Orlowski, 'The Perspective of Arbitral Institutions: Upping the Arsenal—Using the ICC Rules to Counteract Guerilla Tactics' in Horvath and Wilkse (n 2) 54.
³² *E-Systems Inc* (n 26).
³³ *Waste Management Inc v Mexico*, ICSID Case No ARB(AF)/00/3, Decision on Mexico's Preliminary Objection Concerning the Previous Proceedings (26 June 2002). For further discussion on abuse of process, see David D Sandy, 'The Role of Abuse of Process in Protecting the Integrity of Arbitration Awards' in Julio César Betancourt (ed), *Defining Issues in International Arbitration: Celebrating 100 Years of the Chartered Institute of Arbitrators* (OUP 2016) ch 33.

with an arbitrator.[34] Parties in ICSID arbitrations have argued that inherent powers enable tribunals to grant enforceable orders regarding costs (other than awards); non-pecuniary remedies; and conduct investigations into bribery.[35]

13.14 It is difficult to judge how frequently inherent powers are exercised in international commercial arbitrations. However, tribunals should be encouraged to follow their ICSID counterparts and exercise these powers to combat serious misconduct. There might also be scope for the implementation of a set of guidelines to assist tribunals to exercise these powers in a more predictable manner.

(d) The IBA Guidelines on Party Representation

13.15 Anecdotal evidence suggests that the IBA Guidelines on Party Representation have already been referenced in some procedural orders.[36] However, it is not clear how much more assistance they provide to tribunals in addressing party misconduct of the kind described above.

13.16 In the first instance, they appear to have been drafted with the 'double deontology' problem in mind, rather than with a view to addressing more serious party misconduct. The body of the Guidelines is devoted to dealing with issues relating to representatives' submissions to the tribunal, information exchange and disclosure, and witness and expert evidence.[37] While the exclusion of counsel is permitted under Guideline 6, it is tethered to the scenario where a conflict of interest arises because they have been brought into proceedings after the arbitral tribunal has been constituted.

13.17 Exclusion is not a sanction that is expressly included in the list of general remedies for misconduct included at Guideline 26. Tribunals reading these Guidelines together may view them as placing a fetter on the exercise of their inherent powers to exclude counsel for other types of misconduct that fundamentally undermine the arbitral process. Further, there is no mention in the list of general remedies for misconduct of the ability to make costs awards against party representatives personally or give summary judgment.[38] The list of remedies is expressed to be non-exhaustive. However, these tools would be extremely useful additions to the arbitral tribunal's armoury in cases of the most extreme and repeated 'Taliban tactics'.[39] Express reference to such powers could therefore be helpful.

13.18 Eduardo Zuleta, Paul Friedland, and Cyrus Benson, members of the IBA Task Force that drafted the Guidelines, have argued that while experienced practitioners used to dealing with ethical imbalances may not find the Guidelines useful, they will educate newcomers and foster best practice in less developed nations where local bar association rules are less onerous.[40] There must be a danger, however, that they could be used by wily practitioners intent on disrupting proceedings as a means of raising procedural motions.[41]

---

[34] *Hrvatska Elektroprivreda dd* (n 29); cf *Rompetrol Group NV* (n 29).
[35] Paparinskis (n 24).
[36] Sam Chadderton, 'Arbitration: What Does the Future Hold?' <http://www.ibanet.org> accessed 25 September 2015.
[37] IBA Guidelines on Party Representation, Guidelines 9–25.
[38] ibid, Guideline 26.
[39] Horvath, Wilkse, and Jeng (n 15).
[40] Chadderton (n 36); Cyrus Benson, 'The IBA Guidelines on Party Representation: An Important Step in Overcoming the Taboo of Ethics in International Arbitration' (2014) 1 Cahiers arb 47.
[41] Michael Schneider, 'President's Message: Yet Another Opportunity to Waste Time and Money on Procedural Skirmishes: The IBA Guidelines on Party Representation' (2013) 31 ASA Bull 497.

Further, for those concerned by the double deontology problem, the Guidelines will not displace otherwise applicable mandatory laws or professional or disciplinary rules, or vest in arbitral tribunals powers that are reserved to bar associations and other professional bodies.[42] The uneven playing field that exists in some cases will not therefore be eliminated. It is thus difficult to argue against the fact that 'having a new set of different rules, issued by a body different from, and with no authority over those which are responsible for the existing rules, is likely to increase uncertainty and confusion, rather than resolve the issue'.[43]

13.19

(e) The LCIA Rules

Many of the same criticisms could be levelled at the 2014 LCIA Rules. In particular, the sanctions available to arbitral tribunals to punish misconduct are fairly weak. The only measures expressly provided for at Article 18.6 are a written reprimand or caution as to future conduct. These admonishments would remain confidential and may not therefore deter further misconduct by counsel.[44] It is interesting to note that the final version of the LCIA Rules omits a power to exclude counsel from the whole or part of an arbitration for misconduct, in contrast to the IBA Guidelines on Party Representation. Further, there is no reference to any power to refer misconduct to the representative's professional or regulatory authority. These sanctions had both been included in previously circulated drafts of the Rules.

13.20

It is not clear from the LCIA Rules to what extent a counsel's breach of the General Guidelines will rebound on their client.[45] In particular, Article 28.4 of the Rules does not cross-refer to the General Guidelines for the Parties' Legal Representatives when it states that tribunals should take into account the parties' conduct of the arbitration when awarding costs. The IBA Guidelines on Party Representation are far clearer in that respect.[46]

13.21

There are, however, certain features of the LCIA Rules which might assist tribunals in combating party misconduct. Each party to an LCIA arbitration must ensure that its legal representatives have agreed to comply with the General Guidelines pursuant to Article 18.5. This may save tribunal time and argument when drafting their first procedural order. The General Guidelines oblige party representatives not to engage 'in activities intended unfairly to obstruct the arbitration or to jeopardise the finality of any award, *including repeated challenges to an arbitrator's appointment or to the jurisdiction or authority of the Arbitral Tribunal known to be unfounded by that legal representative*'.[47]

13.22

This is an improvement on the IBA Guidelines on Party Representation, which define misconduct as a breach of the specific Guidelines (eg on representatives' submissions to the tribunal, disclosure, and witness evidence) 'or any other conduct that the Arbitral Tribunal determines to be contrary to the duties of a Party Representative'.[48] Further, if the parties

13.23

---

[42] IBA Guidelines on Party Representation, Application of Guidelines, 4.
[43] Schneider (n 41) 499.
[44] Sapna Jhangiani and Khaled Moyeed, 'How Far Do the New LCIA Guidelines for Parties' Legal Representatives and the IBA Guidelines on Party Representation Go?' (*Kluwer Arbitration Blog*, 21 May 2014) <http://www.kluwerarbitrationblog.com> accessed 25 September 2015.
[45] John Zadkovich and Emily Caldwell, 'In the Spotlight: The Parties' Legal Representatives Subject to Conduct Guidelines under the Draft LCIA Rules 2014' (2014) 17(3) Int'l ALR 73.
[46] IBA Guidelines on Party Representation, Guideline 26(c).
[47] General Guidelines for the Parties' Legal Representatives (Annex to the LCIA's Arbitration Rules), para 2 (emphasis added).
[48] IBA Guidelines on Party Representation, Definitions 3.

attempt to add a legal representative to their team, after the formation of the tribunal, the tribunal can withhold its consent to the change.[49] This gives tribunals some control over who appears before them.

C. Arbitral Misconduct

(a) Who regulates the arbitrators?

13.24 Catherine Rogers argues that the market for international arbitrator services is far from a free and transparent one.[50] The pre-eminent qualification for acting as an arbitrator is still one's record of prior appointments. Moreover, it is difficult for parties and their counsel to make a fully informed choice about appointing a particular arbitrator because of the difficulty they will have in ascertaining their track record. International arbitration remains, to some extent, therefore, the domain of what has been termed an 'elite corps' of arbitrators.[51]

13.25 In many states, arbitrators enjoy an absolute or qualified immunity.[52] They can therefore only be held liable in circumstances where they are proven to have engaged in deliberate, bad faith malfeasance or unjustified withdrawal.[53] Further, national courts can normally only protect parties against the worst excesses of arbitrator misconduct at the enforcement stage. That is because national arbitration laws usually give the courts limited grounds on which to refuse enforcement. As a result, the primary regulators of arbitral misconduct are the institutions via their appointment, party selection, and challenge procedures.[54]

13.26 Many of the leading institutions incorporate ethical rules into their arbitration rules that deal with the conduct of hearings and arbitrators' qualifications.[55] These will normally cover the obligation to be impartial and/or independent and to disclose certain information regarding that impartiality or independence obligation. However, very few institutions have clear and comprehensive codes of conduct for arbitrators and there is an inconsistency in the ethical standards required by the institutions.[56]

13.27 It has been argued that the institutions should take a more active role in policing and preventing arbitrator misconduct.[57] In particular, they could improve the mechanisms for investigating complaints of misconduct received from parties and others and strengthen the sanctions that they can impose if misconduct is found to have occurred. International arbitration does not after all have the luxury of impressive courthouses, wigs, and robes and other ceremonial devices that collectively render an appearance of 'correctness' and legitimacy to both the process and the decision-maker.[58] It must bolster public confidence by implementing transparent disciplinary processes for arbitrators.

---

[49] 2014 LCIA Rules, Art 18.
[50] Catherine Rogers, 'The Vocation of the International Arbitrator' (2005) 20 Am U Int'l L Rev 957.
[51] David Hacking, 'Ethics, Elitism, Eligibility: A Response' (1998) 15(4) J Int'l Arb 73.
[52] Rogers (n 50).
[53] ibid.
[54] ibid.
[55] Menon (n 1).
[56] ibid. Menon compares the differing disclosure obligations on arbitrators imposed by the LCIA and ICC Arbitration Rules and the AAA Code of Ethics for Arbitrators.
[57] Rogers (n 50).
[58] Judith Resnik, 'Tiers' (1984) 57 S Cal L Rev 837, 854.

(b) The CIArb disciplinary procedures

13.28 The CIArb disciplinary procedures are a good example of the kind of approach to arbitral misconduct that could and should be taken by all arbitration institutions. A separate Professional Conduct Committee of CIArb exists to investigate complaints from the public and service users, and if necessary, discipline members.[59] The Committee is not formed solely of lawyers, but has lay members. It will not only investigate complaints of breaches of the CIArb Code of Professional and Ethical Conduct, but also accusations that tend to show that an arbitrator's conduct has fallen significantly below the standard expected of a competent professional acting in the private dispute resolution field. The complainant has the right to appeal any decision not to uphold their complaint.

13.29 CIArb disciplinary tribunals have the power to suspend or expel a member, withdraw his chartered status, or make an order for costs against him, if a complaint is made out. For example, John Campbell, a former CIArb President, was expelled from the Institute and ordered to pay £3,000 in costs for failing to deliver an award for four years.[60] CIArb's Board of Trustees also have a discretion to publish a full report of the disciplinary proceedings without anonymizing the names of the individuals involved, although we have found few examples of this in practice.[61]

D. Conclusion

13.30 We should not ignore the fact that 32 per cent of the experienced arbitration practitioners surveyed by Sussman and Ebere in 2010 said that they had not encountered 'guerrilla tactics' or that 'several respondents volunteered that they saw guerrilla tactics employed to a much greater extent in litigation'.[62] However, there are undoubtedly features of international arbitration that make it a uniquely fertile ground for the activities of arbitration guerrillas and terrorists.[63] These include the confidentiality of proceedings, the arbitrators' lack of executive power, and the parties' ability to exploit an uneven ethical playing field.[64] This will continue to be the case, if steps are not taken to combat the guerrillas.

13.31 The IBA Guidelines on Party Representation and the LCIA Rules raise awareness of the issue of party misconduct and may assist less experienced arbitrators in identifying and addressing potential problems of double deontology early on in proceedings. They are, however, no panacea, especially in relation to serious cases of party misconduct. In those situations, the sanctions made available to the tribunal are not as strong as might be hoped for. There is also a risk that both initiatives will deflect arbitral tribunals' attention away from the broad inherent powers that they can already utilize to regulate misconduct and protect the integrity of the proceedings.

---

[59] 2014 Regulations of the Chartered Institute of Arbitrators, Art 10.
[60] *The Chartered Institute of Arbitrators v John D Campbell QC*, Decision of the Disciplinary Tribunal of CIArb (5 May 2011) <http://www.ciarb.org> accessed 25 September 2015.
[61] CIArb, 'How CIArb Investigates Complaints of Misconduct Against its Members' <http://www.ciarb.org> accessed 25 September 2015.
[62] Sussman and Ebere (n 8) 612.
[63] Robert Pfeiffer and Stephan Wilkse, 'The Emergence of the Guerrilla Tactics Phenomenon in International Arbitration' in Horvath and Wilkse (n 2) 16.
[64] ibid.

13.32 Efforts should be focused within arbitration institutions on establishing better means of investigating and sanctioning arbitrator misconduct. This should involve the implementation of a transparent system with real teeth akin to that in place within CIArb. If they do not make such changes, disenchantment may well grow and the golden age of arbitration may be tarnished.

Part V

EMERGENCY ARBITRATORS AND INTERIM RELIEF

14

EMERGENCY ARBITRATORS AND COURT-ORDERED INTERIM MEASURES

Is the Choice Important?

*Doug Jones**

A. Introduction

Parties to a dispute often need urgent relief and may seek interim measures. Interim measures, also known as 'temporary measures of protection' or 'conservatory measures', are orders by courts or arbitral tribunals directed at the preservation of the status quo until a decision on the merits of the dispute is rendered. They are temporary in nature and are designed to ensure that the parties to a dispute suffer minimal damage during the arbitral proceedings, through to the final settlement of the dispute and enforcement of any eventual award. They also seek to preserve the subject matter of the dispute. Usually, interim measures are intended to preserve a factual or legal situation to safeguard rights the recognition and enforcement of which is sought from the court or tribunal.   14.01

The rise of international arbitration has seen the development of many procedures to accommodate the parties' ever-changing needs. One such development that is closely related to interim measures is the concept of the emergency arbitrator—an arbitrator appointed post haste upon the application of a party to a dispute to decide an urgent issue that cannot wait until the constitution of the arbitral tribunal to be decided. Typically, the emergency arbitrator is appointed to issue 'emergency', 'urgent', or 'conservatory' relief, particularly when a party has matters that need to be addressed immediately. These measures, required to protect the interests of a party, can be useful in various circumstances, such as misuse of intellectual property or confidential information, protection against some action by a third party, preservation of assets, being able to sell a property, or obtaining information urgently.[1]   14.02

The emergency arbitrator's jurisdiction and decisions are upheld until the arbitral tribunal is constituted, at which point the arbitrator's jurisdiction and powers cease. Once the arbitral tribunal is constituted, any emergency interim measure granted may be reconsidered, vacated, or modified by the arbitral tribunal. The insertion of emergency arbitrator provisions in the rules of many of the world's leading arbitration institutions has raised   14.03

---

* © Doug Jones 2016. This article was written before the ACICA Arbitration Rules and Expedited Arbitration Rules 2016 came into effect.

[1] N Vivekananda, 'The SIAC Emergency Arbitrator Experience' (SIAC) <http://www.siac.org> accessed 25 September 2015.

considerable interest among the international arbitration community, with many beginning to notice the development of a trend that has the potential to change the face of arbitration on a global scale. It is an especially important development given the recent changes to arbitration legislation in some jurisdictions to provide for the enforceability of emergency arbitrator decisions.

14.04 Against this background, this chapter considers the emergency arbitrator provisions in the rules of selected arbitral institutions, and the interplay between these provisions and a court's ability to order interim measures of protection. The utility of emergency arbitrator provisions in light of issues of enforceability will be discussed, giving way to both legal and practical implications for the choice between seeking emergency arbitration instead of court-ordered interim measures.

B. Emergency Arbitrator Provisions in Institutional Rules

14.05 While many sets of institutional rules have traditionally allowed for the expedient formation of the arbitral tribunal to mitigate any delays, the trend of rules allowing the appointment of emergency arbitrators is recent. A number of institutions have incorporated emergency arbitrator provisions into their rules so that parties may apply for interim relief without having to go to a national court, or having to wait until the main tribunal is appointed.

14.06 The 2012 Arbitration Rules of the ICC, the most widely used and accepted international arbitration institution worldwide,[2] incorporate provisions for the appointment of emergency arbitrators. The SIAC has had emergency arbitrator provisions in its rules since 2010.[3] The ACICA Rules, amended in 2011,[4] now expressly provide for the appointment of emergency arbitrators. Other recent amendments to institutional rules incorporating emergency arbitrator rules include the new HKIAC Rules, which came into force in November 2013, and the new JCAA Rules, which came into force in February 2014. The two most recent additions to the suite of emergency arbitrator provisions are the new Arbitration Rules of the LCIA, which came into effect on 1 October 2014, and the 2015 CIETAC Rules, which entered into force on 1 January 2015.

14.07 Each institutional rule has its own requirements regarding the timing of an application for an emergency arbitrator, as well as the target time frame for appointment and decision. The key features of the emergency arbitrator provisions from each of these sets of institutional rules is outlined at the end of this chapter in Table 14.1.

14.08 Depending on the rule, the emergency arbitrator provisions allow an application for an emergency arbitration together with or after the filing of the notice or request to commence the arbitration. In other words, the provisions enable an emergency arbitrator to be appointed in an arbitration that has 'commenced' (in the way that commencement is defined under the respective rules), but prior to the constitution of the arbitral tribunal. In the case of the ICC and JCAA Rules, an application for an emergency arbitration may be

---

[2] Julian D M Lew and others, *Comparative International Commercial Arbitration* (Kluwer Law International 2003) 37.
[3] 2010 SIAC Rules; 2013 SIAC Rules.
[4] 2011 ACICA Arbitration Rules incorporating the Emergency Arbitrator Provisions.

made before filing the request for arbitration, but a request must be filed within ten days from the date of application.[5]

By accepting arbitration under rules that have emergency arbitrator provisions, parties accept not only arbitration according to the respective rules, but also to be bound by the emergency arbitrator provisions. However, parties adopting the rules may, by agreement, opt out of the emergency arbitrator provisions. **14.09**

C. The Choice between Emergency Arbitration and Court-Ordered Interim Measures

The growth of emergency arbitrator provisions is most likely a function of the increasing expediency with which parties to international arbitrations choose to have their disputes settled, and is a clear indication of the capability of arbitration and the flexibility that it offers to its users. **14.10**

Prior to the widespread availability of emergency arbitrator provisions, parties seeking urgent relief from the arbitral tribunal only had the option of awaiting its constitution. However, depending on the arbitration agreement and the institutional rules it adopts, constituting a tribunal can take a significant amount of time, often months. Although some of the rules provide expedited procedures[6] or provisions for the expedited formation of the tribunal,[7] even the expedited procedures are often not quick enough. In this way, emergency arbitrator provisions have added a new practical dimension to the way in which parties' disputes may be progressed. **14.11**

The other option available for urgent cases is the parties approaching the national courts to obtain interim measures, instead of seeking relief from the arbitral tribunal. Under this option, parties do not need to await the constitution of the tribunal. However, in some jurisdictions, it can take equally as long, if not longer, to obtain interim measures from a court, and parties may be unfamiliar with local procedures. There is also the issue of confidentiality if parties do not wish to have their dispute put in the public domain. Nevertheless, seeking court-ordered interim measures is a viable alternative to appointing an emergency arbitrator. Indeed, many of the emergency arbitrator provisions specifically preserve the parties' right to seek interim relief from the courts.[8] **14.12**

For parties seeking urgent relief which cannot await the constitution of the tribunal, there is therefore an important choice to be made between appointing an emergency arbitrator and seeking interim measures from the courts. This in turn invites the question of whether emergency arbitrator provisions are useful, as compared to court-ordered interim measures. **14.13**

---

[5] 2012 ICC Rules, Appx V, Art 1.6; 2014 JCAA Rules, r 70.7.
[6] See, eg, 2011 ACICA Expedited Arbitration Rules; 2013 HKIAC Rules, Art 41; 2013 SIAC Rules, r 5; 2014 JCAA Rules, ch VI.
[7] 1998 LCIA Rules, Art 9; 2014 LCIA Rules, Art 9A.
[8] See, eg, 2012 ICC Rules, Art 29.7; 2011 ACICA Rules, sch 2, r 7.1; 2013 HKIAC Rules, sch 4, Art 22; 2013 SIAC Rules, r 26.3; 2014 LCIA Rules, Art 9.12.

D. Are Emergency Arbitrator Provisions Really Useful?

14.14 Despite their recent popularity, the emergency arbitrator provisions have been looked upon with a measurable level of doubt by many arbitration practitioners. In particular, the bases of these concerns have revolved around the following three questions:

(1) what, exactly, is the definition and nature of a matter of 'emergency' which might necessitate emergency relief and the appointment of an emergency arbitrator;
(2) does the market actually have much practical use for emergency arbitrators; and
(3) are decisions by emergency arbitrators enforceable?

(a) Definition of 'emergency'

14.15 Every rule has its own requirements as to what constitutes an 'emergency' situation. Take, for example, the ACICA Rules, which have one of the more comprehensive emergency arbitrator provisions. Rule 3.5 in Schedule 2 of the ACICA Rules stipulates that the party requesting an emergency arbitrator to issue an emergency interim measure is required to show that:

(1) irreparable harm is likely to result if the emergency interim measure is not ordered;
(2) such harm substantially outweighs the harm that is likely to result to the party affected by the emergency interim measure if it is granted; and
(3) there is reasonable possibility that the requesting party will succeed on the merits.[9]

14.16 By Rule 1.3 in Schedule 2 of the ACICA Rules, the requesting party is also required to provide details of:

(1) the nature of the relief sought;
(2) the reasons why such relief is required on an emergency basis; and
(3) the reasons why it is entitled to such relief.

14.17 The requirements of Rule 1.3 above are quite rudimentary. However, the use of the phrase 'irreparable harm' in Rule 3.5 calls for the appointment of an emergency arbitrator and the issuance of emergency relief only where there exists an unavoidable and rather dire situation. Some examples of such situations might involve one party wishing to prevent the other party from dissipating its assets or from pursuing a more nefarious agenda, such as destroying evidence.

14.18 In comparison, the ICC Arbitration Rules appear not to make any direct reference to the severity of the circumstances required to justify such an emergency procedure. Article 3 in Appendix V of the ICC Arbitration Rules is in line with Rule 1.3 in Schedule 2 of the ACICA Rules and simply provides that an application for the appointment of an emergency arbitrator shall contain:

(1) a description of the circumstances giving rise to the application and of the underlying dispute referred or to be referred to arbitration; and
(2) the reason why the applicant needs urgent interim or conservatory measures that cannot await the constitution of an arbitral tribunal.

---

[9] These requirements are similar to those under Art 26.3 of the 2010 UNCITRAL Rules for parties requesting interim measures.

14.19 By referring to 'why the applicant needs urgent interim or conservatory measures', the ICC Rules appear to suggest a more party-oriented subjective approach than the ACICA Rules as to the circumstances necessary for the appointment of an emergency arbitrator and the issuance of urgent relief. The same may be said of the SIAC Rules, as Rule 1 of Schedule 1 requires the applicant to provide reasons in support, after which the President may determine whether to accept the application.

14.20 In other words, whereas the ACICA Rules present a more binary distinction between circumstances where the appointment of an emergency arbitrator is necessary and where it is not, the President of the ICC International Court of Arbitration, who is the emergency arbitrator appointing authority under the ICC Arbitration Rules, is afforded more discretion when deciding whether the circumstances require the appointment of an emergency arbitrator.

14.21 The differing requirements of each set of rules leave little wonder as to why so many have questioned when, exactly, the provisions should be invoked.

(b) The market's appetite for emergency arbitrators

14.22 As to the market's call for emergency arbitrators, there are obvious situations (as mentioned above) that would seem appropriate for the appointment of an emergency arbitrator and the dispensation of urgent relief. Whether these situations are, in fact, frequently encountered by parties to international arbitration and worthy of formalized procedure is an entirely different question.

14.23 In an attempt to glean the market's appetite for such emergency procedures, one may look to the statistics published by arbitral institutions regarding the use of emergency arbitrator provisions. The ICC, which annually has over 700 requests for arbitration, has reported a rather low usage of the emergency arbitrator provisions in their rules. The ICC statistics show that there were only two applications in 2012, six applications both in 2013 and 2014.[10]

14.24 While, at first blush, the conclusion from such results might be that the users of international arbitration do not have any great use for emergency arbitrators, it must be recalled that the provisions are recent. As of September 2015, the latest SIAC figures show that there have now been a total of 42 applications for emergency arbitrator appointments since its introduction in 2010,[11] which evidences a steady growth from February 2011, when there had only been three applications.[12] The SCC is another institution which was in 2010 an early adopter of emergency arbitrator provisions. Although the SCC has a much smaller caseload, it has had 13 applications from 1 January 2010 to December 2014.[13]

14.25 Thus, it is possible that international arbitration practitioners and their respective parties have not yet warmed to the concept—and until they do, it could be reasonably expected

---

[10] ICC, 'Statistics' 2014 <http://www.iccwbo.org> accessed 25 September 2015.
[11] SIAC, 'Statistics' (31 December 2013) <http://www.siac.org> accessed 25 September 2015.
[12] Jonathan Leach and Julian Berenholtz, 'The expedited and emergency arbitrator procedures under the SIAC Rules—Six months on, how have they fared?' (Hogan Lovells, February 2011) <http://www.hoganlovells.com> accessed 25 September 2015.
[13] Johan Lundstedt, 'SCC Practice: Emergency Arbitrator Decisions' (Arbitration Institute of the SCC, December 2013) <http://www.sccinstitute.com> accessed 25 September 2015.

that the levels of emergency arbitrator provisions usage would remain low. Further, many of the arbitration agreements governing recent disputes pre-date the incorporation of emergency arbitrator provisions. It is suspected that a greater take-up will occur organically, and so it remains to be seen whether parties will make frequent use of the provisions.

14.26 Another relevant consideration is the effect that an application for the appointment of an emergency arbitrator might have on the remainder of the arbitration proceedings—if party relations are amicable to begin with, will such an application cause any tension, and if tension already exists, will such an application make matters considerably worse? The low number of applications is perhaps a reflection of the 'emergency' nature of the provision and that is not to say that there is a low demand for such procedures to be available.

(c) Enforceability issues

14.27 Thus far there has been a limited number of enforcement cases dealing with emergency arbitrator decisions. There have also been extensive academic discussions on this topic, often without a conclusive answer. There are, however, a number of practical issues that can be anticipated and ought to be borne in mind when dealing with emergency arbitrator procedures.

14.28 One such issue is the question of whether the decision is a final and binding 'award' for the purposes of the New York Convention. It is similar to the issue encountered by tribunal-ordered interim measures, which has been the subject of academic analysis and judicial decisions around the world. Emergency arbitrator decisions are in a slightly different position as emergency arbitrators decide on the merits of the particular application brought before them and make a decision that is final.[14] That said, all of the rules allow the arbitral tribunal, once constituted, to modify or annul the decision of the emergency arbitrator,[15] which could pose a problem for characterizing the decision as final and binding.

14.29 It is worth noting that the finality aspect is not an issue under the UNCITRAL Model Law, as Article 17H now recognizes interim measures issued by an arbitral tribunal as binding.[16] There is, however, an added problem with emergency arbitrator decisions as to whether they can be considered as decisions of an 'arbitral tribunal'. Recognizing this issue, the Singapore International Arbitration Act is a leading example as it clarifies that 'arbitral tribunal' includes emergency arbitrators, and that 'award' includes any interim, interlocutory, or partial award deciding on the substance of dispute.[17]

14.30 Further, recent amendments to the Hong Kong Arbitration Ordinance specifically included a provision allowing Hong Kong courts to enforce relief granted by an emergency arbitrator, whether made in or outside Hong Kong.[18] Accompanying the proliferation of emergency

---

[14] Rainer Werdnik, 'The Award and the Courts: The Enforceability of Emergency Arbitrators' Decisions' in Christian Klausegger and others (eds), *Austrian Yearbook on International Arbitration* (Manz'sche Verlags- und Universitätsbuchhandlung 2014) 249, 276.

[15] 2012 ICC Rules, Art 29.3; 2011 ACICA Rules, sch 2, r 5.2; 2013 HKIAC Rules, sch 4, Art 18; 2013 SIAC Rules, sch 1, r 7; 2014 LCIA Rules, Art 9.11.

[16] However, many jurisdictions have not adopted the 2006 amendments. See UNCITRAL, 'Status—UNCITRAL Model Law on International Commercial Arbitration (1985), with amendments as adopted in 2006' <http://www.uncitral.org> accessed 25 September 2015.

[17] Singapore International Arbitration Act 1994 (amended in 2002), ch 143A, s 2 (definition of 'arbitral tribunal' and 'award').

[18] Hong Kong Arbitration Ordinance (Ch 609) 2011, s 22B.

arbitrator provisions, the emergence of such legislative amendments is a welcome development in the interest of the practice of international arbitration.

In some jurisdictions, there is also the issue of whether the award can be enforced urgently. In an ideal world, enforcement of arbitral awards within the New York Convention framework will minimize jurisdictional differences. The reality is, however, that the judiciary in some jurisdictions may not enforce emergency arbitrator decisions within the time frame desired by the applicant.

14.31

From a different perspective, there may also be the potential for a party to be found to be in breach of contract if it fails to comply with an emergency arbitrator's award or order. The rules of ACICA,[19] ICC,[20] SIAC,[21] HKIAC,[22] and JCAA[23] all require parties to give an undertaking to comply with any emergency interim measure issued by an emergency arbitrator without delay. Some emergency arbitration provisions, for example in the ICC Arbitration Rules, allow arbitral tribunals to take into consideration any non-compliance with an emergency arbitrator's decision in finalizing costs and damages.[24] Therefore, in addition to the legislative amendments, the arbitral institutions have implemented other mechanisms in their rules to deal with enforcement issues for emergency arbitrator decisions.

14.32

E. Evaluating the Choice

Generally, emergency arbitration is an efficient and useful process. It requires arbitral institutions to appoint an arbitrator promptly, a procedural timetable is immediately established, and a decision must be made within a short but reasonable period of time.

14.33

As mentioned previously, there are clear advantages to appointing an emergency arbitrator instead of approaching the national courts. The enforcement of arbitral decisions, subject to the enforcement issues outlined above, are more streamlined. The issues parties may encounter are more predictable regardless of the jurisdiction in which enforcement is sought. Approaching the national courts may not be an issue in some jurisdictions, however: it is often the parties' desire to avoid jurisdiction-specific issues that led them to refer their disputes to arbitration in the first place. Confidentiality is another perceived advantage of choosing emergency arbitration over the courts, as it is purported to be a major attraction of arbitration in general.

14.34

As with all things, however, emergency arbitration is not without its limitations, particularly when compared with the court-ordered interim measures. For example, once it is established that urgent relief can be obtained from the courts, there are no additional issues with enforcement that exist for arbitral awards. Emergency arbitrators are also unable to bind third parties, such as a bank, against which a court may issue a freezing order. The other advantage of approaching the courts is the ability to seek relief on an *ex parte* basis. Emergency arbitrator procedures usually require the applicant to file a notice of arbitration

14.35

---

[19] 2011 ACICA Rules, Art 4.2.
[20] 2012 ICC Rules, Art 29.2.
[21] 2013 SIAC Rules, sch 1, Art 9.
[22] 2013 HKIAC Rules, sch 4, Art 16.
[23] 2014 JCAA Rules, rr 66.8 and 70.1.
[24] 2012 ICC Rules, Art 29.4.

to the other party. This essentially defeats the purpose of seeking urgent relief if notifying the opposing party leads to that party taking the very action that the applicant is seeking to prevent.

14.36 Another issue with emergency arbitration is that there can be a perception that courts are better placed to deal with urgent matters. When there is an application for emergency arbitration, the parties, institution, and arbitrator are all required to act promptly, which can be seen to affect the quality of the process. This will not be an issue if a suitable arbitrator with the requisite qualities is appointed. For this reason, there is an added responsibility for arbitral institutions to take care when administering emergency arbitrator cases.

F. Conclusion

14.37 Both choices therefore have their advantages and their drawbacks, depending on the circumstances. However, in urgent cases, speed, predictability, and confidentiality are paramount, all of which are strong points of emergency arbitration. The emergency arbitrator provisions of institutional rules have the proper mechanisms inbuilt so that a suitable arbitrator is appointed, a procedural timetable is established, and an award is issued, all in a prompt manner. As jurisdictions clarify the issues surrounding the enforcement of emergency arbitrator decisions, as has been done in Hong Kong and Singapore, there will be a greater role to be played by emergency arbitrators. There is in any event a continuing role for courts to play notwithstanding the availability of emergency arbitrator provisions. There are obvious circumstances, such as where enforcement against a third party is sought, under which parties should approach the courts and keep the choice in mind.

Table 14.1 Outline of key features of emergency arbitrator provisions from selected arbitral institutions

Rules of institution	ICC 2012	SIAC 2013	ACICA 2011	HKIAC 2013	JCAA 2014	LCIA 2014
Relevant emergency arbitrator provisions	Article 29; Appendix V	Rule 26; Schedule 1	Article 28; Schedule 2	Article 23; Schedule 4	Rules 70–74	Article 9B
Date of commencement of emergency arbitrator provisions	1 January 2012	1 July 2010	1 August 2011	1 November 2013	1 February 2014	1 October 2014
Timing of application	Before, with, or after filing request for arbitration	With or after filing notice of arbitration	With or after filing notice of arbitration	With or after filing notice of arbitration	Before, with, or after filing request for arbitration	Together with request for arbitration (claimant) or the response to the request (respondent)
Time frame for appointment by institution	To appoint within as short a time as possible, 'normally' within two days	To 'seek to appoint' within one business day	To use 'best endeavours' to appoint within one business day	To 'seek to appoint' within two business days	To use 'reasonable efforts' to appoint within two business days	To appoint no later than three days or 'as soon as possible thereafter'
Decision time from appointment	No later than 15 days	Schedule to provide 'reasonable opportunity to all parties to be heard'	No later than five business days	Within 15 days	Within two weeks	No later than 14 days
Cost of procedure	Administration fee: US$10,000

Arbitrator's fee: US$30,000 | Administration fee: S$5,000 (S$5,350 for Singapore party)

Arbitrator's fee: Capped at 20 per cent of the maximum fee in schedule | Administration fee: AU$2,500

Arbitrator's fee: AU$10,000 | HKIAC to determine administration and arbitrator's fees by reference to hourly rate and in accordance with schedule | Administration fee: ¥216,000

Emergency arbitrator's remuneration: ¥2,100,000 | LCIA Court to determine 'special fee' covering emergency arbitrator and administrative fees in accordance with schedule |

15

LEGAL STANDARDS APPLICABLE TO DECIDING APPLICATIONS FOR INTERIM RELIEF

Grant Hanessian*

A. Introduction

15.01 In international arbitration—as in all disputes—it is sometimes critical for a party to obtain relief prior to the final disposition of the case. Such relief—in international arbitration variously termed 'interim measures of protection'; 'conservatory measures'; or 'provisional', 'preliminary', or 'temporary' relief—may be necessary to preserve the status quo (eg by ordering continued performance of a contract during the arbitral proceedings), to facilitate conduct of arbitral proceedings (eg by ordering the preservation of evidence or inspection of goods, property, or documents), or to ensure enforcement of a future award (eg by freezing assets).[1]

15.02 In national courts, the substantive and procedural law applicable to deciding requests for interim relief is well developed. In international arbitration, however, the matter is more complicated.

15.03 First, there is usually no arbitration tribunal in place at the commencement of the dispute to which a party may direct a request for provisional relief. Prior to the recent development of emergency arbitrator provisions by many arbitration institutions, parties to arbitration agreements had no choice but to resort to national courts prior to the formation of the arbitral tribunal, and this of course remains the case with respect to *ad hoc* arbitration. Where a request for interim relief involves a third party—such as a financial institution holding disputed assets or a witness outside the control of the parties—recourse to national courts may be necessary because the arbitral tribunal has no jurisdiction to order or enforce the requested relief. In some jurisdictions, the law of the place of arbitration may significantly circumscribe the power of arbitrators to grant interim relief.

15.04 Also, and now coming to the subject of this chapter, historically there has been little authority to guide arbitral tribunals and parties with regard to the legal standards applicable

---

* The author thanks Justin Marlles, an associate in the Houston office of Baker & McKenzie LLP, for his assistance in the drafting of this chapter.

[1] See, eg, Nigel Blackaby and others, *Redfern and Hunter on International Arbitration* (5th edn, OUP 2009) paras 5.24–5.36.

to requests for interim relief. Arbitration rules and *leges arbitri* typically provide little, if any, direction. In recent years, however, the subject has received more attention and it has become increasingly possible to identify international standards applicable to applications for interim relief. This chapter considers these emerging standards, with particular emphasis on contributions made by the decisions of investor-state tribunals[2] and emergency arbitrators.[3]

B. Arbitral Rules and *Leges Arbitri*

Virtually all international arbitration rules now provide arbitral tribunals with power to order interim relief.[4] Most rules provide a broad grant of power to arbitral tribunals to order interim relief without restriction or qualification as to the nature or types of interim relief, subject only to a finding that the relief is 'appropriate'[5] and/or 'necessary'.[6] Emergency arbitrators are usually provided with broad authority to grant interim measures, but none of the rules speaks to the appropriate standard to be applied to determine when such authority should be exercised.

15.05

---

[2] The ICSID Convention, unusually among international arbitration conventions, explicitly provides for interim relief. The ICSID Convention, at Art 47, states: 'Except as the parties otherwise agree, the Tribunal may, if it considers that the circumstances so require, recommend any provisional measures which should be taken to preserve the respective rights of either party.' Consistent with most institutional rules, the ICSID Rules, r 39(1), state that 'a party may request that provisional measures for the preservation of its rights be recommended by the Tribunal. The request shall specify the rights to be preserved, the measures the recommendation of which is requested, and the circumstances that require such measures'. Notwithstanding the word 'recommend' instead of 'prescribe', ICSID tribunals 'increasingly have ordered binding measures (finding creative ways to enforce them) in order to preserve critical rights at stake in their proceedings'. Caline Mouawad and Elizabeth Silbert, 'A Guide to Interim Measures in Investor-State Arbitration' (2013) 29 Arb Int'l 381, 383. This remedy is particularly important in ICSID cases since the ICSID Convention, at Art 26, provides that parties that consent to arbitration before ICSID do so to the exclusion of any other remedy. This provision, intended to eliminate or stay parallel national court proceedings, is generally thought to exclude applications for interim relief before national tribunals in ICSID cases. See Georgios Petrochilos and others, 'ICSID Arbitration Rules, Rule 39' in Loukas A Mistelis (ed), *Concise International Arbitration* (Kluwer Law International 2010) 275–8; Lucy Reed and others, *Guide to ICSID Arbitration* (Kluwer Law International 2010) 145–6.

[3] The following institutional rules provide for the appointment of an emergency arbitrator prior to the constitution of the arbitration tribunal: 2012 ICC Rules, Art 29(1) and Appx V; 2014 LCIA Rules, Art 9B; 2014 ICDR Rules, Art 37.1; 2013 SIAC Rules, r 26(2) and sch 1; 2010 SCC Rules, Appx II; 2013 HKIAC Rules, Art 23.1 and sch 4; 2013 KLRCA Rules, r 7(2) and sch 2; 2012 Swiss Rules, Arts 42–3; 2008 CANACO Rules, Arts 36 and 50; 2010 NAI Rules, Arts 42a and 42b; and 2015 CIETAC Rules, Art 23. Towards the end of 2013, the ICDR appointed 37 emergency arbitrators, the SIAC 30, the SCC nine, and the ICC seven; the average time to resolve these requests appears to be about two weeks from the date of application to award or order. For a discussion of the various rules and their implementation, see Grant Hanessian, 'Emergency Arbitrators' in Lawrence Newman and Richard Hill (eds), *The Leading Arbitrators' Guide to International Arbitration* (Juris 2014).

[4] Some commentators consider the ability to grant interim relief an inherent part of arbitrators' adjudicatory powers. See, eg, Gary B Born, *International Commercial Arbitration* (2nd edn, Kluwer Law International 2014) 2453–5.

[5] Among rules permitting a tribunal to order 'appropriate' relief are those of the ICC (Art 28(1)), the 2-11 KCAB (Art 28(1)), the SCC (Art 32(1)), the CAM (Art 30(1)), and the SIAC (Art 26(1)).

[6] The rules of the AAA (Art 34(a)) and its international entity, the ICDR (Art 21(1)), JAMS (Art 26.1), DIAC (Art 31.1), the WIPO (Art 46(a)), and the 2015 CIETAC Rules (Art 23(3)) require a determination that the interim relief requested be 'necessary'.

15.06 Unusually, the CIArb Arbitration Rules (2000 edition)[7] and the LCIA specify certain types of interim relief as within the power of a tribunal to grant. Article 25(1) of the LCIA Rules provides that a tribunal may order: (i) a party to provide security for all or part of the amount in dispute; (ii) the preservation, storage, sale, or other disposal of any property or thing under the control of a party and relating to the subject matter of the arbitration; and (iii) any relief, on a provisional basis and subject to final determination in an award, that the arbitral tribunal would have the power to grant in an award. Similarly, Article 7.8 of the CIArb Arbitration Rules (2000 edition) provides that the tribunal has the power to grant provisional orders for: (i) the payment of money or the disposition of property as between the parties; (ii) interim payment on account of the costs of the arbitration; and (iii) the grant of any relief in the arbitration.[8]

15.07 An arbitral tribunal's authority to grant interim relief, of course, is also subject to restrictions imposed by the law of the place of arbitration (*lex arbitri*),[9] since the courts of the place of arbitration will have supervisory jurisdiction over the conduct of the arbitration.[10] Thus, even where the parties have expressly agreed to confer on the arbitrators power to grant interim relief by agreeing to arbitration rules that provide for such relief, such authority may be circumscribed where the arbitration has its legal seat in a jurisdiction that does not permit arbitrators to issue injunctions—such as Argentina, Greece, Italy, Thailand, or the Province of Quebec, Canada[11]—or certain types of interim relief, such as China.[12] In addition, certain

---

[7] Although see the new 2015 CIArb Arbitration Rules, Art 26.

[8] It has been suggested that these provisions of the LCIA and the 2000 CIArb Arbitration Rules may be influenced by the fact that s 38 of the English Arbitration Act 1996 grants an arbitral tribunal certain specific powers to order interim relief, such as the powers to order a claimant to provide security for costs for the arbitration and to issue orders for the preservation of property and evidence that is the subject matter of the proceedings. Simon Nesbitt, 'LCIA Arbitration Rules, Article 25 [Interim and conservatory measures]' in Mistelis (n 2) 447–50. However, s 39 of the English Arbitration Act 1996 also provides that parties are 'free to agree that the tribunal shall have power to order on a provisional basis any relief which it would have power to grant in a final award' (eg by selecting rules of arbitration that provide for such powers).

[9] See, eg, Jean-François Poudret and Sébastien Besson, *Comparative Law of International Arbitration* (2nd edn, Sweet & Maxwell 2007) para 606; Blackaby and others (n 1) para 5.08; Julian D M Lew and others, *Comparative International Commercial Arbitration* (Kluwer Law International 2003) paras 23.8–23.9. Presumably if no place of arbitration is specified in the parties' arbitration agreement, in the typical case the institution, arbitral tribunal, or emergency arbitrator will determine the legal situs, in accordance with the institutional rules (and applicable law, as the case may be), prior to issuing an interim award or order.

[10] See Blackaby (n 1) 167–88.

[11] See J Brian Casey, 'Emergency Interim Relief under the ICDR Rules: Practical and Legal Considerations' (2013) 6(1) NY Disp Res Law 17; Born (n 4) 2439.

[12] Chinese arbitration law permits conservatory measures regarding assets and evidence to be ordered only by the Chinese courts and thus not by arbitral tribunals. For commentary on the former 2012 CIETAC Rules, see Song Lu, 'The New CIETAC Arbitration Rules of 2012' (2012) 29(3) J Int'l Arb 306; Phillip Landolt and Barbara Reeves Neal, 'Provisional Measures Concerning Competition Law in International Arbitration' in Gordon Blanke and Phllip Landolt (eds), *EU and US Antitrust Arbitration: A Handbook for Practitioners* (Kluwer Law International 2011) 670, para 19-012; Christopher Boog, 'The Laws Governing Interim Measures in International Arbitration' in Franco Ferrari and Stefan Kröll (eds), *Conflict of Laws in International Arbitration* (Sellier European Law Publishers 2011) 414–16. But see the new 2015 CIETAC Rules, which make provisions for interim measures. It has been said that 'the Rules appear to have developed faster than reform in Chinese national arbitration law': Allen & Overy, 'CIETAC's New Arbitration Rules 2015' 7 January 2015, <http://www.allenovery.com> accessed 25 September 2015. As Gary Born has observed, where parties have chosen in their arbitration agreement international arbitration rules that broadly permit the arbitrators to grant interim relief and a situs that regulates, or prohibits, interim relief, it may be appropriate for arbitrators to consider that the parties' specific choice (the rules) supersedes the general (the *situs lex arbitri*). In practice, of course, few arbitrators will grant interim or other relief prohibited by the *lex arbitri*, whether or not such *lex arbitri* would violate the New York Convention and such orders may be enforceable in jurisdictions other than the *situs*. See Born (n 4) 2558–60.

procedural requirements may be considered applicable to applications for interim relief, eg Article 24(1) of the UNCITRAL Model Law, which requires an arbitrator to hold an oral hearing upon the request of either party prior to granting any requested relief.

15.08 With regard to the standards to be applied by a tribunal in deciding a request for interim relief, of the major arbitration rules only the *ad hoc* UNCITRAL Arbitration Rules—and the identical provisions of the CRCICA and the KLRCA—set forth such standards. These Rules provide as follows:

> The party requesting an interim measure ... shall satisfy the arbitral tribunal that:
> (a) Harm not adequately reparable by an award of damages is likely to result if the measure is not ordered, and such harm substantially outweighs the harm that is likely to result to the party against whom the measure is directed if the measure is granted, and
> (b) There is a reasonable possibility that the requesting party will succeed on the merits of the claim. The determination on this possibility shall not affect the discretion of the arbitral tribunal in making any subsequent determination.[13]

15.09 Additionally, these rules provide that the above requirements apply 'to the extent the arbitral tribunal considers appropriate' where the interim relief sought relates to the preservation of evidence that may be relevant and material to the resolution of the dispute.[14]

15.10 The *lex arbitri* is usually thought not to include the legal standards applied by national courts in deciding applications for interim relief,[15] although such national judicial standards are sometimes agreed to by the parties and applied by arbitrators, presumably because such standards are relatively accessible and familiar to parties and arbitrators. In their recent survey of ICC emergency arbitrator cases, ICC Secretary General Andrea Carlevaris and Deputy Secretary General José Ricardo Feris[16] report that ICC emergency arbitrators have taken other approaches:

> In ... other cases, the emergency arbitrators relied more heavily on international arbitral practice. In one case, the emergency arbitrator held that the law governing the contract did not apply, and turned instead for guidance to practice generally followed by international arbitrators, mentioning also the procedural law at the place of arbitration. Another emergency arbitrator found that neither the law governing the contract nor the law governing court procedure at the place of the emergency arbitrator proceedings was applicable and, after finding that the law governing arbitral proceedings at the place of the emergency arbitrator proceedings was silent on standards applicable to the granting of interim relief, he

---

[13] Art 26(3) of the UNCITRAL, CRCICA, and KLRCA Rules. The UNCITRAL Model Law is almost identical, providing at Art 17A that the party requesting an interim measure shall satisfy the arbitral tribunal that: '(a) Harm not adequately reparable by an award of damages is likely to result if the measure is not ordered. Such harm substantially outweighs the harm that is likely to result to the party against whom the measure is directed, if the measure is granted; and (b) There is a reasonable possibility that the requesting party will succeed on the merits of the claim.'

[14] Art 26(4) of the UNCITRAL, CRCICA, and KLRCA Rules.

[15] See Born (n 4) 2558–60. In the United States, the traditional test for an interim injunction requires the applicant to establish that it is likely to succeed on the merits and likely to suffer irreparable harm in the absence of preliminary relief, that the balance of the equities tips in its favour, and that an injunction is in the public interest. See Tod Gamlen and Christina Wong, 'Emergency Relief in International Arbitrations' *The Recorder* (California, 15 January 2013). In the United Kingdom and Canada, the applicant needs only to establish that there is a serious issue to be tried, damages would not be an adequate remedy, and the balance of convenience lies in granting an injunction. See Casey (n 11) 17–18.

[16] Andrea Carlevaris and José Ricardo Feris, 'Running in the ICC Emergency Arbitrator Rules: The First Ten Cases' (2014) 25(1) ICC Int'l Ct Arb Bull 25.

ultimately found guidance in international sources such as arbitral awards grounded in common principles of law in developed states. In another case, the emergency arbitrator similarly disregarded the law governing the contract, noted that the parties had not chosen a law applicable to the arbitral procedure, and concluded that the law of the seat did not require him to take into account any national law; he consequently turned to scholarship and arbitral precedents and emphasized the importance of the factual circumstances of the case.[17]

15.11 Further to the notion that international arbitral procedure is not bound by national judicial standards of interim relief, two recent US court decisions held that arbitrators are not required to adhere to interim relief standards applicable in US courts. In *CE International Resources Holdings LLC v SA Mineral Ltd Partnership*,[18] the court was asked to enforce an arbitrator's order freezing respondents' assets *pendente lite*. The respondent sought to set aside the New York arbitrator's order on the grounds that the arbitrator had acted in manifest disregard of the law, as New York's procedural law does not permit a plaintiff in an action for a money judgment to obtain pre-judgment security. The court enforced the arbitrator's order, holding that the parties had agreed to arbitrate under the ICDR Rules, and the ICDR Rules gave the arbitrator jurisdiction to order interim relief that might not be available from a court under New York law.

15.12 Similarly, in *Rocky Mt Biologicals Inc v Microbix Biosystems Inc*, a federal court in Montana refused an application by a non-party to the arbitration to set aside the order of an ICDR emergency arbitrator in New York,[19] on the basis that under New York procedural law applicable to applications for interim relief the applicant third party was a necessary party to the emergency arbitrator proceeding.

C. Harm, Urgency ... and Other Factors

15.13 In the absence of direction from arbitral rules and/or *lex arbitri*, it is of course for the arbitral tribunal to determine the standards applicable to a request for interim relief.[20] It is generally said that an applicant for interim relief in international arbitration must establish: (i) a risk of serious or irreparable harm to the party seeking interim relief that outweighs any risk of harm to the party against which the interim relief will be granted; (ii) that the risk of such harm is imminent; (iii) that granting the interim relief will not amount to a pre-judgment on the merits of the case; and that the applicant has established a *prima facie* case or likelihood of success on (iv) the merits of the dispute and (v) the tribunal's jurisdiction.[21]

15.14 These requirements are of course not applicable in all circumstances, nor are they necessarily exhaustive. In considering the public decisions on interim relief, it seems that two factors dominate: harm and urgency, with the other factors playing important but subsidiary roles depending on the relief requested and the circumstances of the application.

---

[17] ibid 36 (footnotes omitted).
[18] 2012 US Dist LEXIS 176158, Case No 12 Civ 8087(CM) (SDNY 2012).
[19] 2013 US Dist LEXIS, Case No CV 13-73-M-DLC (D Mont, 30 October 2013). The emergency arbitrator's order was annexed to Rocky Mountain's moving papers and is publicly available on PACER, the US judiciary's electronic filing system. The author served as emergency arbitrator in this case.
[20] See, eg, Peter Turner and Reza Mohtashami, *A Guide to the LCIA Arbitration Rules* (OUP 2009) para 6.110; Jason Fry and others, *The Secretariat's Guide to ICC Arbitration* (ICC Publication No 729E, 2012) paras 3.1037–3.1038.
[21] See, eg, Born (n 4) 2467–82.

The standards for granting relief and the applicant's burden of proof and persuasion with regard to such standards are of obvious importance in considering whether evidentiary hearings are required in order to fairly adjudicate a request for interim relief. If the applicant need only establish a *prima facie* showing of urgency and likelihood of success on jurisdiction and the merits, the need for evidentiary hearings and cross-examination is reduced. If, on the other hand, the applicant must show 'irreparable injury' and that it is 'likely to succeed on the merits', this may require a more rigorous determination of the facts underlying the request.

(a) Harm and urgency

15.15　The precise definition of a 'serious or irreparable harm' factor varies somewhat from case to case, although it usually 'does not require mechanical application of particular levels of probability'.[22] Some investment treaty tribunals, such as the *Chevron v Ecuador* panel, have adopted a US-style approach by interpreting this factor to require a showing of 'a sufficient likelihood that such harm ... may be irreparable in the form of monetary compensation'.[23]

15.16　Increasingly, however, arbitral tribunals, as in *Paushok v Mongolia*, consider the irreparable harm factor to have a 'flexible meaning':[24] referencing the decision of the Iran-US Claims Tribunal in the *Behring* case, the *Paushok* panel stated that 'the concept of "irreparable prejudice" does not necessarily require that the injury complained of be not remediable by an award of damages'.[25] There is some evidence that commercial tribunals may utilize an even more relaxed approach, with one ICC tribunal opining that 'any non marginal risk of aggravation of the dispute is sufficient to warrant an order for interim relief'.[26]

15.17　An ICC emergency arbitrator determined that while international arbitration practice normally requires a risk of irreparable harm, the applicant was entitled to relief despite the absence of such a risk, as the dispute would otherwise have become more aggravated and granting the request would not cause irreparable harm to the responding party.[27]

15.18　This reasoning is consistent with one of the principal purposes of interim relief: protection of the status quo pending the tribunal's resolution of the dispute. In the investor-state context, this may be traced to the ICJ's jurisprudence on interim measures, according to which these types of measures may be granted even in the absence of irreparable harm. In *Pulp Mills on the River Uruguay*, the ICJ, quoting Article 41(1) of the ICJ Statute, stated that 'the power of the Court to indicate provisional measures has as its object to permit the Court to preserve the respective rights of the parties'.[28]

---

[22] ibid 2472.
[23] *Chevron Co and Texaco Petroleum Co v Republic of Ecuador*, UNCITRAL, PCA Case No 2009-23, Second Interim Award on Interim Measures (16 February 2012) [2].
[24] *Sergei Paushok v The Government of Mongolia*, UNCITRAL, Order on Interim Measures (2 September 2008) [69]. See Caline Mouawad and Elizabeth Silbert, 'A Guide to Interim Measures in Investor-State Arbitration' (2013) 29 Arb Int'l 381, 392 (citing cases).
[25] ibid, *Sergei Paushok*, [68] (citing *Behring Int'l Inc v Islamic Rep Iranian Air Force, Iran Aircraft Indus, and Gov't of Iran*, Award No ITM/ITL 52-382-3 (21 June 1985), 8 Iran-US Claims Tribunal Reports 238, 276).
[26] *Distrib A v Mfg B*, ICC Case No 1596, Interlocutory Award (2000) in Albert Jan van den Berg (ed), *Yearbook Commercial Arbitration*, vol XXX (Kluwer Law International 2005) 66, 71.
[27] Carlevaris and Feris (n 16) 36.
[28] *Pulp Mills on the River Uruguay (Argentina v Uruguay)*, Provisional Measures (13 July 2006), 2006 ICJ Rep 113, 159.

15.19 This criterion has now been adopted by a number of investment disputes panels (which are, of course, not governed by the ICJ Statute). In their survey of interim measures in investor-state cases, Caline Mouawad and Elizabeth Silbert explain that: '[s]everal investor-state tribunals have ordered interim measures on the basis of these well-accepted principles of preserving the *status quo*, preventing the aggravation of the dispute, and preserving the integrity of the arbitral proceedings'.[29]

15.20 The concept of balancing the harm between the parties has been increasingly seen as part of the international standard since the 2006 revisions to the UNCITRAL Model Law and 2010 revisions to the UNCITRAL Rules, both of which require that a party requesting interim relief satisfy the tribunal that the harm it faces 'substantially outweighs the harm that is likely to result to the party against whom the measure is directed if the measure is granted'.[30] Investor-state tribunals applying the UNCITRAL Rules have begun to take this factor into consideration,[31] although it remains to be seen whether this will influence cases decided under other rules.

15.21 As to urgency, in investor-state cases this consideration 'appears to have evolved and relaxed somewhat over the years, morphing from a requirement that the harm be immediately likely and imminent to the seemingly more widespread standard today that the harm occur prior to the tribunal's issuance of the final award'.[32] This approach is also based significantly on ICJ jurisprudence. Referencing Article 41(2) of the ICJ Statute,[33] the ICJ stated in the 1991 *Great Belt* case that interim measures are 'only justified if there is urgency in the sense that action prejudicial to the rights of either party is likely to be taken before [a] final decision is given'.[34]

15.22 The ICJ further observed in the 2006 *Pulp Mills on the River Uruguay* case that 'the power of the Court to indicate provisional measures to maintain the respective rights of the parties is to be exercised only if there is an urgent need to prevent irreparable prejudice to the rights that are subject of the dispute before the Court has had an opportunity to render its decision'.[35] The tribunal in the *Chevron v Ecuador* arbitration used language almost identical to that of the ICJ statute in granting Chevron's second request for interim relief, stating that Chevron had established 'a sufficient urgency given the risk that substantial harm may befall the Claimants before this Tribunal can decide the Parties' dispute by any final award'.[36]

---

[29] Mouawad and Silbert (n 2) 395–6. These include *Tokios Tokelés v Ukraine*, ICSID Case No ARB/02/18, Procedural Order No 1 (1 July 2003); *City Oriente Ltd v Republic of Ecuador and Petroecuador*, ICSID Case No ARB/06/21, Decision on Provisional Measures (19 November 2007); *Perenco Ecuador Ltd v Ecuador*, ICSID Case No ARB/08/6, Decision on Provisional Measures (8 May 2009); *Burlington Resources Inc v Ecuador*, ICSID Case No ARB/08/5, Procedural Order No 1 (29 June 2009); and *Biwater Gauff (Tanzania) Ltd v Tanzania*, ICSID Case No ARB/05/22, Procedural Order No 1 (31 March 2006).

[30] 2006 UNCITRAL Model Law, Art 17A(a) and 2010 UNCITRAL Arbitration Rules, Art 26(3)(a).

[31] See *Guaracachi America Inc and Rurelec Plc v Bolivia*, PCA Case No 2011-17, Procedural Order No 14 (11 March 2013) [9].

[32] Mouawad and Silbert (n 2) 386.

[33] Statute of the ICJ (26 June 1945), Art 41, 59 Stat 1055, 33 UNTS 933:

1. The Court shall have the power to indicate, if it considers that circumstances so require, any provisional measures which ought to be taken to preserve the respective rights of either party.
2. Pending the final decision, notice of the measures suggested shall forthwith be given to the parties and to the Security Council.

[34] *Passage through the Great Belt (Finland v Denmark)*, Provisional Measures (29 July 1991), 1991 ICJ Rep 12, 17.

[35] *Pulp Mills on the River Uruguay* (n 28).

[36] *Chevron* (n 23) [2].

15.23 Emergency arbitrators—by the necessity of their limited office—have been rigorous in requiring that the applicant demonstrate urgency.[37] ICC Arbitration Rules regarding emergency arbitration particularly stress urgency, stating that the emergency arbitrator provision is available only to parties 'that cannot await the constitution of an arbitral tribunal'.[38] Carlevaris and Feris report that ICC emergency arbitrators 'have generally avoided defining what is meant by this requirement and referred instead to the particular circumstances of the case'.[39] One ICC emergency arbitrator considered whether applications for emergency measures required a greater showing of urgency than applications for ordinary interim relief, but did not decide the question, denying the application on grounds of failure to show the necessary harm.[40] Out of the seven SCC emergency applications denied in 2013, the arbitrator stated in five cases that there was insufficient urgency.[41]

(b) Other factors

15.24 Following considerations of harm and urgency, other considerations include some showing that the applicant is likely to succeed on the merits of the case and that the tribunal has jurisdiction (if this has not been previously established).

15.25 An analysis of the likelihood of success on the merits, as this subject is known in common law jurisdictions, is noticeably absent from many of the ICJ cases on interim relief,[42] although this criterion appears increasingly present in investor-state decisions. In the recent *Tethyan v Pakistan* case, an ICSID tribunal observed:

> The question of whether the right to be preserved exists goes to the merits of the case which will not be decided at this preliminary stage of the proceedings. It therefore suffices that the party requesting the provisional measure establishes a prima facie case that it owns a legally protected interest.[43]

15.26 Similar sentiments were expressed by tribunals in two widely circulated ICC commercial decisions on interim relief.[44] There is evidence that emergency arbitrators also consider likelihood of success. In four out of the seven SCC cases in which the applications were denied, the emergency arbitrator found that the applicant had demonstrated a *prima facie* case, or reasonable possibility of success, on the merits.[45] Similarly, ICC emergency arbitrators

---

[37] See Johan Lundstedt, 'SCC Practice: Emergency Arbitrator Decisions 1 January 2010–31 December 2013' <http://www.sccinstitute.com> accessed 25 September 2015.
[38] ICC Rules, Art 29.1.
[39] Carlevaris and Feris (n 16) 35.
[40] ibid.
[41] See Lundstedt (n 37).
[42] See *The Great Belt*, Provisional Measures (n 34) 16–17; *Pulp Mills on the River Uruguay* (n 28) 159–60. This is generally thought to be attributable to a reluctance by the court to appear to pre-judge the case. See, eg, Jerrod Wong, 'The Issuance of Interim Measures in International Disputes: A Proposal Requiring a Reasonable Possibility of Success on the Underlying Merits' (2005) 22 Ga J Int'l & Comp L 606.
[43] *Tethyan Copper Co v Pakistan*, ICSID Case No ARB/12/1, Decision on Provisional Measures (13 December 2012) 145, 154; see also *Sergei Paushok* (n 24) [55]–[56]. See also Mouawad and Silbert (n 2) 398.
[44] See *Trust C (Isle of Sark) v Latvian Group (Latvia)*, ICC Case No 10973, Interim Award (2001) in Albert Jan van den Berg (ed), *Yearbook Commercial Arbitration*, vol XXX (Kluwer Law International 2005) 82 ('It is a general rule in international arbitration that a claimant must prove the fumus boni juris, ie, that there exists a probability that his claims, regarding the question(s) as to the merits of the case, will be successful'); *Distrib A* (n 26) 68 ('The first requirement for interim relief is that the applicant render plausible that it has a prima facie contractual or legal right to obtain the relief it seeks').
[45] See Lundstedt (n 37).

have usually considered whether there was a *prima facie* case for the measures requested and failure to meet this requirement has generally been considered sufficient to reject the application.[46]

15.27 As to a *prima facie* case on jurisdiction, in its decision in the *Great Belt* case, the ICJ explained that 'on a request for provisional measures the Court need not, before deciding whether or not to indicate them, finally satisfy itself that it has jurisdiction on the merits of the case, yet it ought not to indicate such measures unless the provisions invoked by the Applicant appear, *prima facie*, to afford a basis on which the jurisdiction of the Court might be founded'.[47] Investment treaty tribunals seem to have adopted this rather low bar set by the ICJ, and considered whether claimants had *prima facie* demonstrated the right to claim as investors under the ICSID Convention and the relevant treaty.[48]

15.28 In international commercial arbitration, the practical application of this factor may simply require a high-level assessment of whether: (a) there is a valid arbitration clause that binds the parties, and (b) the rules of arbitration chosen by the parties allow the arbitral tribunal to provide interim relief.[49]

D. Conclusion

15.29 Standards applicable to requests for interim relief are continuing to evolve and, it would appear, are increasingly becoming more uniform and predicable. Whether or not investment treaty awards and publicly available decisions by international commercial and emergency arbitrators serve as 'precedent'[50] in any technical sense, this developing consensus is the inevitable result of the increasing use and importance of international arbitration, and the fundamental role of interim relief in any successful dispute resolution system.

---

[46] Carlevaris and Feris (n 16) 36.

[47] *The Great Belt*, Provisional Measures (n 34) 15. Notably, identical language appears to have been used in *Military and Paramilitary Activities in and against Nicaragua (Nicaragua v USA)*, Provisional Measures (Order of 10 May 1984), 1984 ICJ Rep 169, [24].

[48] See *Sergei Paushok* (n 24) [47]–[48] (quoting *Military and Paramilitary Activities in and against Nicaragua* (n 47) [24]); *Tethyan Copper Co* (n 43) 122 (finding *prima facie* jurisdiction under Art 25(1) of the ICSID Convention and the applicable BIT); *Churchill Mining Plc v Republic of Indonesia*, ICSID Case No ARB/12/14, Procedural Order No 3 (4 March 2013) 36ff (finding *prima facie* jurisdiction on the basis of several jurisdictional tests).

[49] See *Trust C (Isle of Sark)* (n 44).

[50] Most commercial awards remain confidential and, unlike decisions by the highest court in a particular judicial system, arbitral tribunals cannot know whether a particular award or reasoning has, or should have, widespread acceptance. See, eg, Emmanuel Gaillard and Yas Banifatemi (eds), *Precedent in International Arbitration* (IAI International Arbitration Series No 5, Juris Publishing 2008). For advocacy of a system of *stare decisis* in international commercial arbitration, see Thomas E Carbonneau, *The Law and Practice of Arbitration* (3rd edn, Juris Publishing 2002) 427; and Klaus Berger, 'The International Arbitrator's Application of Precedent' (1992) 9 J Int'l Arb 4, 19. An opposing view is offered in Tom Ginsburg, 'The Culture of Arbitration' (2003) 36 Vand J Transnat'l L 1335, 1340.

Part VI

DISCOVERY AND DOCUMENT PRODUCTION

16

DISCOVERY IN ARBITRATION

Can Parties Use 28 USC § 1782 to Circumvent the Process Ordered by the Arbitral Tribunal?

Alexander A Yanos

A. Introduction

The title of this chapter may seem like a misnomer. After all, one of the stated purposes of 28 USC § 1782 ('section 1782') is to provide 'judicial assistance to foreign or international tribunals'. In that light, how could the statute be used to subvert the procedures ordered by an arbitral tribunal? However, the profound differences between the broad form of discovery available under section 1782 and the narrow form of discovery generally available in international arbitration may well create the possibility of conflicts between the process envisioned by the arbitral tribunal and the process made available to parties by the US judiciary.[1] **16.01**

First, section 1782 allows litigants in an arbitration to obtain discovery from persons that are not party to the underlying arbitration, relief that arbitral tribunals cannot generally order because they only have jurisdiction over the parties before them. Second, under section 1782, depositions are available even though they are generally considered anathema to arbitral proceedings. Third, and most fundamentally, the breadth of document discovery available under section 1782 is, generally speaking, well beyond the scope of discovery ordered in all but the most 'americanized' international arbitrations. **16.02**

For example, parties seeking discovery under section 1782 may request 'any' or 'all' documents in a subpoena recipient's 'possession, custody or control' relating to a given subject matter[2]—a practice that is rarely permitted in arbitral proceedings, where requested categories of documents (and the issues to which they are material) must generally be described with specificity. Finally, discovery applications under section 1782, unless filed under seal (a process that is subject to strict judicial supervision and rarely allowed when no threats to life or limb or specific confidential agreements are present), can be used to reveal to the public the existence of a dispute that was otherwise confidential. The discovery mechanisms **16.03**

---

[1] Note that the US Federal Rules of Civil Procedure govern discovery ordered under s 1782 unless the court's order provides otherwise.
[2] US Federal Rules of Civil Procedure, r 34; see also US Federal Rules of Civil Procedure, r 26, which defines 'relevance' very broadly.

available under section 1782 have great potential to clash with the procedures applied by most arbitral tribunals.

B. Conflict Resolution: the Hard Line

16.04 Courts have worked to resolve these conflicts in different ways. Early cases from the Second and Fifth Circuits sidestepped potential conflicts by barring applications made in support of all arbitration proceedings. They did so on statutory grounds—on the basis that such proceedings did not constitute proceedings before a 'foreign or international tribunal' within the meaning of the statute.[3] In dicta, these courts expressed concern that US-style discovery mechanisms could endanger the values of efficiency and cost-effectiveness that commercial arbitration is designed to further.[4] But it would be a mistake to suggest that these courts were motivated by deference to arbitral process or procedure.

16.05 After all, applications were denied on statutory grounds; if they signalled deference at all, it was to congressional intent, not the authority of arbitrators. And by barring applications on statutory grounds, these courts effectively closed the door to direct requests from arbitral tribunals—not just to participants in arbitral proceedings. In any event, the approach has been applied unevenly. Whilst denying the application of section 1782 to commercial arbitration proceedings, courts, including those in the Second and Fifth Circuits, have allowed applications in support of investment arbitration proceedings, with or without the consent of the arbitral tribunal.[5] US discovery mechanisms pose the same challenges to those arbitral proceedings as they do in commercial arbitration proceedings.

C. The Functional Approach

16.06 In 2004, the landscape shifted with the Supreme Court's decision in *Intel Corp v Advanced Micro Devices Inc*.[6] Although *Intel* did not concern arbitration proceedings, the Supreme Court cast doubt on the strict prohibition that had been employed by the Second and Fifth Circuits, and injected a measure of flexibility into the assessment. First, the court established a test of general application for courts to apply when determining whether

---

[3] See *NBC v Bear Stearns & Co*, 165 F 3d 184 (2d Cir 1999) (Congress intended the phrase 'foreign or international tribunal' to extend only to 'governmental entities ... *acting as state instrumentalities* or with the *authority of the state*'—that is, 'governmental or intergovernmental arbitral tribunals', 'conventional courts', and 'other state-sponsored adjudicatory bodies') (emphasis added); *Republic of Kazakhstan v Biedermann International*, 168 F 3d 880 (5th Cir 1999).

[4] *NBC* (n 3) ('If the parties to a private international arbitration make no provision for some degree of consensual discovery *inter se* in their agreement to arbitrate, the arbitrators control discovery, and neither party is deprived of its bargained-for efficient process by the other party's tactical use of discovery devices'); *Republic of Kazakhstan* (n 3) ('Arbitration is intended as a speedy, economical, and effective means of dispute resolution ... s 1782 need not be construed to demand a result that thwarts private international arbitration's greatest benefits').

[5] *In re Chevron Corp*, 749 F Supp 2d 141 (SDNY 2010); *In re Republic of Ecuador*, No C-10-80225 Misc CRB (EMC), 2010 WL 3702427 (ND Cal 15 September 2010); *Republic of Ecuador v Bjorkam (Chevron)*, 801 F Supp 2d 1121 (D Colo 2011); *In re Mesa Power Group, LLC*, No 2:11-MC-270-ES, 2013 WL 1890222 (DNJ 19 April 2013).

[6] 542 US 241 (2004).

or not a foreign proceeding qualifies for assistance under section 1782,[7] making it more difficult for courts to simply sidestep conflicts between arbitral procedures and the statute by relying on a per se statutory bar.[8] Second, the court expanded on the discretionary factors that courts may apply in deciding whether an application that satisfies the statutory requirements should nonetheless be permitted to proceed. Among the factors identified by the court were: (i) whether the person from whom discovery is sought is a participant in the foreign proceeding; (ii) the nature of the foreign tribunal, the character of the foreign proceedings, and the receptivity of the foreign entity to federal judicial assistance; and (iii) whether the request conceals an attempt to circumvent foreign proof-gathering restrictions or other policies of a foreign country or the United States.

Following *Intel*, only the Fifth Circuit has affirmed its earlier ruling, and continued to deny the application of section 1782 to foreign commercial arbitration proceedings. The Second Circuit has not revisited the issue.[9] The Eleventh Circuit initially took the opposite approach, but has since changed course, leaving the question open as to whether section 1782 applies to commercial arbitration proceedings.[10] A number of district courts have allowed section 1782 discovery in support of foreign commercial arbitration proceedings in the wake of *Intel*.[11] Bizzarely, some courts have drawn a distinction between commercial arbitrations governed by the UNCITRAL Arbitration Rules and arbitrations governed by the LCIA or ICC on the ground that UNCITRAL is a public body, but the ICC and LCIA are not.[12]   **16.07**

D. Deference-Plus?

In the wake of *Intel*, most courts have adopted a case-by-case approach in respect of section 1782 applications, scrutinizing the features of the arbitral tribunal in question—its governing rules and evidentiary practices, and any statements that the tribunal has made concerning the application—to determine whether assistance ought to be granted. The availability of discovery is generally treated as a discretionary matter: courts choose to permit or deny assistance based on the application of one of the discretionary factors identified in *Intel*, most prominently: (i) the receptivity of the foreign tribunal to the evidence sought; and (ii) whether or not the application constitutes an attempt to circumvent a foreign proof-gathering restriction.[13]   **16.08**

---

[7] Under that analysis, a tribunal qualifies if: (i) it acts as an adjudicatory first-instance decision-maker; (ii) it is capable of producing a dispositive ruling; and (iii) its ruling is subject to judicial review.

[8] See *El Paso Corp v La Comision Ejecutiva Hidroelectrica Del Rio Lempa*, 341 Fed Appx 31 (5th Cir Tex 2009), affirming 1999 ruling in *Republic of Kazakhstan* (n 3).

[9] *Intel* (n 6) 265.

[10] Compare *Consorcio Ecuatoriano de Telecomunicaciones SA v JAS Forwarding (USA) Inc*, 685 F 3d 987 (11th Cir Fla 2012) with *Application of Consorcio Ecuatoriano de Telecomunicaciones SA v JAS Forwarding (USA) Inc*, 747 F 3d 1262, 1770 n 4 (11th Cir Fla 2014).

[11] See *Comision Ejecutiva v Nejapa Power Co LLC*, No 08-135-GMS, 2008 WL 4809035 (D Del, 14 October 2008); *In re Roz Trading Ltd*, 469 F Supp 2d 1221, 1226-27 (ND Ga 2006); *In re Application of Hallmark Capital Corp*, 534 F Supp 2d 951, 954-55 (D Minn 2007). But see *In re An Arbitration In London, England Between Norfolk Southern Corp v ACE Bermuda Ltd*, 626 F Supp 2d 882 (ND Ill 2009).

[12] *In re Matter of the Application of Oxus Gold Plc*, No 06-82, 2006 WL 2927615 (DNJ 11 October 2006).

[13] District courts in the Southern District of New York have also made it clear recently that they will exercise their discretion to deny discovery where the party purports to locate financial information for use in a foreign arbitral proceeding, but in reality seeks to determine whether to initiate a proceeding. See, eg, *In re Asia Maritime Pacific Ltd*, No 15-CV-2760 (VEC), 2015 WL 5037129, at *3 and n 6 (SDNY 26 August 2015); *In re Harbour Victoria Inv Holdings Ltd Section 1782 Petitions*, No 15-MC-127 (AJN), 2015 WL

16.09 The problem, of course, is that most applications filed pursuant to section 1782 are brought by one of the parties to the arbitral proceeding—and not the arbitral tribunals themselves. Thus, the courts often have no direct information concerning the attitude of the arbitral tribunal to the application for discovery pursuant to section 1782. Perhaps, as a result, courts have set a very high bar when reviewing any evidence concerning the arbitral tribunal's receptivity to evidence sought under section 1782. The party opposing discovery generally bears the burden of proof with regard to the discretionary factors, and silence on the part of the tribunal will rarely suffice.[14] Nor is it typically sufficient that a foreign tribunal lacks the power to order the discovery sought—the lack of power to make such an order is not generally equated with a lack of receptivity. The common retort when respondents make these arguments is that there is no foreign discoverability requirement under section 1782;[15] and no exhaustion requirement.[16]

16.10 In fact, under *Intel*, applications may proceed even in cases where the foreign tribunal expresses formal reservations about the application—even strong ones.[17] In *Intel*, the Supreme Court went so far as to discount a statement by the European Commission, in an *amicus curiae* brief to the district court, that it did not need or want the district court's assistance.[18] Rather than deferring to the Commission's statement on the issue, the Court concluded that it lacked clarity: 'It is not altogether clear ... whether the Commission, which may itself invoke § 1782(a) aid, means to say "never" or "hardly ever" to judicial assistance from United States courts'.

16.11 In the court's view, a foreign tribunal's discovery limits do 'not necessarily signal objection to aid from United States federal courts'. Rather, a foreign tribunal's 'reluctance to order production of materials present in the United States similarly may signal no resistance

---

4040420, at *5 (SDNY 29 June 2015); *Jiangsu Steamship Co v Success Superior Ltd*, No 14-CV-9997 (CM), 2015 WL 3439220, at *5 (SDNY 6 January 2015).

[14] *In re Mesa Power Group, LLC*, 878 F Supp 2d 1296, 1304 (SD Fla 2012) ('the party requesting judicial assistance does not have to prove receptivity to show that they are not attempting to circumvent foreign proof-gathering mechanisms'); *Gov't of Ghana v ProEnergy Servs, LLC*, No 11-9002-MC-SOW, 2011 WL 2652755 (WD Mo 6 June 2011) ('Balkan has not shown that the arbitral tribunal or High Court of Ghana would be unreceptive to the materials discovered under Ghana's s 1782 request'); *In re Roz Trading Ltd*, No 1:06-CV-02305-WSD, 2007 WL 120844, at *2 (ND Ga 11 January 2007) ('Respondent's claim that the arbitral panel might not be receptive to the aid of this Court is purely speculative. Thus, it appears the Centre is fundamentally "receptive" to such aid for the purposes of this *Intel* criteria'); but see *In re Chevron Corp*, 762 F Supp 2d 242, 252 (D Mass 2010); *In re Babcock Borsig AG*, 583 F Supp 2d 233, 241–42 (D Mass 2008) (under s 1782 a discovery request was denied 'until ... the ICC provides some affirmative indication of its receptivity to the requested materials').

[15] See, eg, *In re Chevron Corp*, 633 F 3d 153, 163 (3d Cir NJ 2011) citing *Intel* (n 6) at 2473 ('there is no requirement that the material be discoverable in the foreign country for it to be discoverable pursuant to a section 1782 request in the United States'); *In re Republic of Kazakhstan*, No 15 Misc 0081 (SHS), 2015 WL 3855113, at *5 (SDNY 22 June 2015).

[16] See, eg, *In re Application of Euromepa*, 51 F 3d 1095, 1098 (2d Cir 1995) (quoting *In re Malev Hungarian Airlines*, 964 F 2d 97, 100 (2d Cir 1992)) (courts have 'refused to engraft a "quasi-exhaustion requirement" onto s 1782 that would force litigants to seek "information through the foreign or international tribunal" before requesting discovery from the district court'); *In re Imanagement Servs, Ltd*, No Misc 05-89 (FB), 2005 WL 1959702, at *5 (EDNY 2005); *Infineon Techs AG v Green Power Techs Ltd*, 247 FRD 1, 5 (DDC 2005); *In re Veiga*, 746 F Supp 2d 8, 24 (DDC 2010); *In re Republic of Kazakhastan*, No 15 Misc 0081 (SHS), 2015 WL 3855113, at *5 (SDNY 22 June 2015).

[17] See *In re Chevron Corp*, 762 F Supp 2d 242, 250 (D Mass 2010) (*Intel* factors weighed in favour of granting a section 1782 application even though it was 'not entirely clear that the Ecuadorian criminal court [wa]s receptive to such "discovery assistance"').

[18] ibid 266.

to the receipt of evidence gathered pursuant to § 1782(a)'.[19] The bottom line is that the standard for lack of receptivity is a high one. In order to block an application in reliance on this discretionary factor, the foreign tribunal must oppose the application loudly and unequivocally. What is typically required is an express statement from the foreign tribunal that it would disallow the evidence sought.[20] Without such vigorous opposition, courts will generally come down on the side of the applicant.

The second of the discretionary factors that courts rely upon in this context—whether the application conceals an attempt to circumvent a foreign proof-gathering restriction—is also subject to a very high standard. As with lack of receptivity, courts generally place the burden on respondents.[21] And in determining whether a petition represents an effort to circumvent a foreign proof-gathering restriction, courts generally require some showing of bad faith or surreptitious conduct on the part of the applicant,[22] such as the deliberate concealment of a restriction in the applicable foreign rules.[23]

16.12

E. Conclusion

In the end, the courts' shift towards greater doctrinal flexibility has not resulted in an increase in deference towards arbitral tribunals or procedures. The aims of section 1782—assistance to foreign litigants on the one hand, and assistance to foreign tribunals on the other—often come into conflict with one another. The statute is subject to a strong presumption in favour of discovery. When a foreign litigant wants discovery, but the foreign tribunal may not, courts typically err on the side of the foreign litigant.

16.13

---

[19] ibid 261–2.
[20] See, eg, *In re Microsoft*, 428 F Supp 2d 188, 194 (SDNY 2006) (granting motion to quash discovery because the tribunal 'vehemently opposed the judicial aid, the tribunal's rules governing discovery guaranteed equal document access, and "a decision by this Court would either pre-empt or contradict a decision by the" tribunal').
[21] *In re Mesa Power Group, LLC*, No 2:11-MC-270-ES, 2013 WL 1890222, at *18–19 (DNJ 19 April 2013) (permitting discovery in support of NAFTA proceedings because there was 'nothing in the record to suggest that [the] application … is an attempt to side-step proof-gathering or other restrictions in the NAFTA Arbitration'); *In re Thai-Lao Lignite (Thail) Co*, 821 F Supp 2d 289, 297 (DDC 2011) (there was no indication that petitioners were trying to circumvent foreign proof-gathering restrictions by applying for, and being barred from similar assistance in France, application denied on other grounds).
[22] *In re Chevron Corp*, No 7:10-MC-00067-JCT, 2010 WL 4883111, at *3 (WD Va 24 Nov 2010); *Minatec Fin SARL v SI Group Inc*, No 1:08-CV-269 (LEK/RFT), 2008 WL 3884374, at *8 (NDNY 18 August 2008).
[23] *In re Caratube Int'l Oil Co, LLP*, 730 F Supp 2d 101, 108 (DDC 2010) (application concealed an attempt to circumvent a foreign proof-gathering restriction where it failed to disclose a provision of the governing arbitral rules that required disclosure decisions to be taken by the tribunal only).

17

MEETING THE REQUIREMENTS OF ARTICLE 3(3) OF THE IBA RULES

Recommendations for Successful Requests for Document Production

Mark McNeill and Margaret Clare Ryan

A. Introduction

17.01 The IBA Rules on the Taking of Evidence, first issued in 1999, were designed as a tool for parties and for arbitrators to promote 'an efficient, economical and fair process for the taking of evidence in international arbitration'.[1] Article 3 of these Rules concerns the taking and presentation of documentary evidence, and is arguably the central provision of the Rules given the important role played by documentary evidence in international arbitral proceedings as compared to other means of evidence.

17.02 While Article 3 of the IBA Rules on the Taking of Evidence is now routinely applied in the setting of international arbitration,[2] its practical application and interpretation is often the subject of debate between disputing parties. This is particularly true as it relates to Article 3.3, which sets forth the positive requirements that a party must meet when submitting a request to produce documents that are in the control of an opposing party (a 'Request to Produce').[3] Indeed, while the Rules were designed as a principled approach to disclosure that reflects a compromise between procedures in use in different legal systems,[4] certain standards under Article 3.3 remain uncertain and subject to conflicting views, with the

---

[1] 2010 IBA Rules on the Taking of Evidence, foreword, 2.

[2] A survey conducted in 2012 by the School of International Arbitration of QMUL found that the IBA Rules on the Taking of Evidence are used in 60 per cent of arbitrations. See 2012 QMUL Survey, 'Current and Preferred Practices in the Arbitral Process' 2 <http://www.arbitration.qmul.ac.uk/research/index.html> accessed 25 September 2015.

[3] The IBA Rules on the Taking of Evidence define a 'Request to Produce' as 'a written request by a Party that another Party produce Documents' (see IBA Rules, 5). Art 3.3 of the Rules provides that a Request to Produce shall contain: '(a)(i) a description of each requested document sufficient to identify it; (a)(ii) a description in sufficient detail (including subject matter) of a narrow and specific requested category of Documents that are reasonably believed to exist ... ; (b) a statement as to how the Documents requested are relevant to the case and material to its outcome; (c)(i) a statement that the requested documents are not already in [the party's] possession, custody or control ... ; (c)(ii) a statement of the reasons why the requesting Party assumes the Documents requested are in the possession, custody or control of another Party.'

[4] See IBA Rules on the Taking of Evidence (n 1).

17.03 result that the document production phase of an arbitration remains highly contentious, and all too often costly and time consuming.

This chapter will briefly explore the most debated criteria of Article 3.3 of the IBA Rules on the Taking of Evidence with a view to identifying the characteristics of a well-drafted Request to Produce. Meeting the requirements of Article 3.3 will assist a party in advancing its case by obtaining the production of vital and specific documents in an adversary's possession, and more generally, will promote an efficient and cost-effective process of taking evidence in international arbitration.

B. The Requirement to Identify Individual Documents or Limited Categories with Sufficient Specificity

17.04 Article 3.3(a) of the IBA Rules on the Taking of Evidence provides that a Request to Produce shall contain a description of 'each requested document' or 'a narrow and specific category of documents'.[5]

17.05 It is widely commented that the 'narrow and specific' requirement of Article 3.3(a) distinguishes document production under the Rules from the practices of certain domestic legal systems.[6] The IBA Working Group explained that these Rules were intended to avoid 'expansive American or English style discovery', which it considered 'generally inappropriate in international arbitration'.[7] Article 3.3 does not contemplate a process of American-style discovery which would require a party to submit any and all documentary evidence in its possession, regardless of whether it would support its adversary's case. At the same time, the IBA Working Group expressly recognized that some level of document production is appropriate in international arbitration, even in procedures involving practitioners from civil law countries where such practices remain highly restrictive.[8]

17.06 It should also be noted that the presumption under the IBA Rules on the Taking of Evidence is that a party will substantiate its allegations based primarily on documents already within its own possession. This is reflected in Article 3.1, which obliges parties to submit those documents in the procedure on which they rely.[9] In light of this presumption, the scope of document production ordered by an arbitral tribunal will typically be restrictive.

17.07 While the exact meaning of 'narrow and specific' is ultimately a matter of interpretation by an arbitral tribunal, the generally accepted meaning of this requirement may be gleaned by reference to case law and commentary on the IBA Rules on the Taking of Evidence. As

---

[5] IBA Rules on the Taking of Evidence, Art 3.3(a).
[6] See, eg, Peter Ashford, *The IBA Rules on the Taking of Evidence in International Arbitration* (CUP 2013) para 3.34; Nathan O'Malley, 'Document Production under Art 3 of the 2010 IBA Rules of Evidence' (2010) Int'l ALR 186, 187.
[7] 1999 IBA Working Party and 2010 IBA Rules of Evidence Review Subcommittee, 'Commentary on the revised text of the 2010 IBA Rules on the Taking of Evidence in International Arbitration' (2010) 8–9 (hereinafter, 'IBA Commentary').
[8] ibid 7.
[9] Art 3.1 of the IBA Rules on the Taking of Evidence provides: 'Within the time ordered by the Arbitral Tribunal, each Party shall submit to the Arbitral Tribunal and to the other Parties all Documents available to it on which it relies, including public Documents and those in the public domain, except for any Documents that have already been submitted by another Party'.

the drafters of the Rules note, the 'narrow and specific' requirement is designed to enable a party's adversary to decide whether it wishes to voluntarily comply with a document request pursuant to Article 3.4, or to raise objections to some or all of the documents requested pursuant to Article 3.5, as well as to make it possible for the arbitral tribunal to decide whether or not it should grant the request.[10]

17.08 A well-drafted request for an individual document is relatively straightforward. As its drafters note, the IBA Rules 'simply require that a description be "sufficient to identify a document"'.[11] A member of the IBA Working Party has explained that a request for an individual document should normally identify the presumed author/recipient of the document, the date or presumed time frame within which the document was established, and the presumed content of the document.[12]

17.09 The IBA Rules on the Taking of Evidence contemplate that parties are often unable to specifically identify documents despite the fact that such documents may be relevant and material.[13] Pursuant to Article 3.3(a)(ii) of the Rules, accordingly, a party may request a 'narrow and specific category of documents' relating to a certain topic or contention which the requesting party wishes to prove. As explained by the NAFTA tribunal in *International Thunderbird v The United States*:

> In accordance with article 3.3(a) of the IBA Rules, the categories of documents to be produced shall be 'narrow and specific', which the tribunal interprets to mean narrowly tailored, ie reasonably limited in time and subject matter in view of the nature of the claims and defenses advanced in the case.[14]

17.10 A request for a narrow and specific category of documents must be 'carefully tailored' in order to meet the requirements of Article 3.3(a). A request should thus clearly tie the time frame of the requested category of documents to the relevant chronology of the case. Where possible, a description of the subject matter of the requested category should identify its technical or commercial function (eg business plan, or meeting minutes) as well as the authors and possible recipients of the documents targeted.[15]

17.11 Despite the fact that the IBA Rules on the Taking of Evidence were expressly intended to preclude 'fishing expeditions', parties often submit requests for overly broad and vaguely defined categories of documents. A party who seeks broad and sweeping categories of documents should expect its adversary to object in writing to the request, in its entirety or in part. Article 3.5 of the Rules provides that the reasons for an objection shall be any of those set out in Article 9.2, or a failure to satisfy the requirements of Article 3.3. Parties typically object to overly broad requests on the grounds that it would be unreasonably burdensome to produce the requested documents as provided by Article 9.2(a), and that the request fails to meet the 'narrow and specific' standard of Article 3.3(a).

---

[10] IBA Commentary (n 7) 8.
[11] ibid.
[12] Hilmar Raeschke-Kessler, 'The Production of Documents in International Arbitration—A Commentary on Article 3 of the New IBA Rules of Evidence' (2002) Arb Int'l 411, 417.
[13] IBA Commentary (n 7) 9.
[14] *International Thunderbird Gaming Corp (United States of America) v United Mexican States*, NAFTA/UNCITRAL, Procedural Order No 2 (31 July 2003) 3.
[15] Nathan O'Malley, *Rules of Evidence in International Arbitration: An Annotated Guide* (Informa 2012) para 3.35.

17.12 In the event that a party objects to a document request, the tribunal will decide on the issue in accordance with Article 3.7, which provides:

> Either Party may, within the time ordered by the Arbitral Tribunal, request the Arbitral Tribunal to rule on the objection. The Arbitral Tribunal shall then, in consultation with the Parties and in timely fashion, consider the Request to Produce and the objection. The Arbitral Tribunal may order the Party to whom such Request is addressed to produce any requested Document in its possession, custody or control as to which the Arbitral Tribunal determines that (i) the issues that the requesting Party wishes to prove are relevant to the case and material to its outcome; (ii) none of the reasons for objection set forth in Article 9.2 applies; and (iii) the requirements of Article 3.3 have been satisfied. Any such Document shall be produced to the other Parties and, if the Arbitral Tribunal so orders, to it.

17.13 If a tribunal considers that a request fails to meet the 'narrow and specific' requirement of Article 3.3, the question arises whether Article 3.7 of the IBA Rules on the Taking of Evidence permits a tribunal to reformulate or narrow the request by its own initiative in order to elicit documents that appear to be relevant and material.

17.14 It is uncontroversial that an arbitral tribunal has broad powers to control the arbitral procedure. In the words of one commentator, 'the power on the part of the arbitral tribunal to require the parties to produce documentary or other materials, relevant and important to resolving a dispute, is a venerable and highly important aspect of the arbitral process'.[16] Moreover, certain institutional rules which the parties may choose to govern their arbitration expressly provide the tribunal with discretion to establish the facts of a case by the means it considers necessary.[17] If after reviewing a Request to Produce that is overly broad and fails to meet the requirements of Article 3.3(a) as drafted, a tribunal has a clear idea of which of the requested documents it wishes to see, it would theoretically be within its power to reformulate the Request, and to order the opposing party to produce documents responsive to the reformulated request.

17.15 In *Vito G Gallo v Canada*, for instance, a US claimant filed a claim against Canada under the NAFTA, alleging to be the owner of a Canadian company that had been expropriated as a result of the promulgation of certain legislation restricting the company's business activities.[18] Canada objected to the jurisdiction of the tribunal on the ground that the claimant was not the legal owner of the company (and thus a protected investor under NAFTA) at the time of the alleged measures. During the document production phase, Canada requested broad categories of documents, many without time limitations, which would clarify the links between the claimant and the Canadian company. In its procedural order, the tribunal narrowed several of Canada's requests, and ordered the claimant to produce only documents that the tribunal expressly considered relevant, such as documents demonstrating

---

[16] Gary B Born, *International Commercial Arbitration* (2nd edn, Kluwer Law International 2014) 2319.
[17] See, eg, Art 25(1) of the 2012 ICC Rules ('The Arbitral Tribunal shall proceed within a short time frame to establish the facts of the case by all appropriate means'); Art 22.1(iii) of the 2014 LCIA Rules ('The Arbitral Tribunal shall have the power, upon the application of any party or (save for sub-paragraphs (viii), (ix) and (x) below) upon its own initiative, but in either case only after giving the parties a reasonable opportunity to state their views and upon such terms (as to costs and otherwise) as the Arbitral Tribunal may decide ... to conduct such enquiries as may appear to the Arbitral Tribunal to be necessary or expedient, including whether and to what extent the Arbitral Tribunal should itself take the initiative in identifying relevant issues and ascertaining relevant facts and the law(s) or rules of law applicable to the Arbitration Agreement, the arbitration and the merits of the parties' dispute').
[18] *Vito G Gallo v The Government of Canada*, NAFTA/UNCITRAL, Award (15 September 2011) [121].

the identity of the ultimate shareholders of the company for a six-year period beginning on the date of its incorporation, and agreements or contracts signed by the company during the same time frame.[19] Given the specific jurisdictional issues in that case, the tribunal was well placed to identify the documents that would inform its decision, and by narrowing Canada's document requests it was able to promote a more efficient and streamlined disclosure process.

17.16 In certain circumstances, however, a tribunal's decision to narrow or reformulate a party's document requests will be more controversial. Where parties agree that the IBA Rules on the Taking of Evidence should strictly govern their procedure, there would normally be no expectation that the tribunal would grant a requesting party a 'second chance' to obtain documents despite its failure to meet the requirements of Article 3.3(a).[20] In this connection, the Rules contain no express provision that contemplates the power of the tribunal to reformulate document requests. The drafters of these Rules rather specified that the burden is placed on the requesting party to 'identify the document or documents sought, described in sufficient detail', and to put the tribunal in a position to decide if the requested documents are in fact appropriate proof for the allegations it advances.[21] A tribunal's decision to unilaterally reformulate a party's document request could also raise concerns of procedural unfairness, particularly where parties are not granted any further opportunity to raise objections to those document requests that the tribunal redrafted.[22]

17.17 Furthermore, in complex cases where the issues in dispute are not sufficiently clear during the early phases of the procedure, an arbitral tribunal may be ill-placed to redraft a request for documents. Crucially, a tribunal does not have access to the same facts as the disputing parties, and justifications that accompany a Request to Produce are normally the tribunal's principal reference point. A tribunal that reformulates or narrows a request without guidance from the parties risks turning what appears to be an innocuous exercise (for example, providing a date range for a request lacking a time limitation) into a decision that inadvertently imposes a significant and unjust burden on one or more of the parties.

C. The Requirement to Explain the Relevance of the Documents to Disputed Issues and Their Consequence on the Outcome of the Case

17.18 Article 3.3(b) of the IBA Rules on the Taking of Evidence also provides that a Request to Produce must contain 'a statement as to how the Documents requested are relevant to the case and material to its outcome'. The requirements of this Article are essential to ensure the probative value of a document request under these Rules.[23] Under the 1999 version of

---

[19] ibid, Procedural Order No 2 (amended), 10 February 2009, 10.
[20] It is worth noting that the Procedural Orders in *Vito G Gallo v Canada* specified that Art 3 of the IBA Rules on the Taking of Evidence would function only as a 'guideline' for the exchange of documents, and that the tribunal would order the production of documents in its 'discretion'. ibid, Procedural Order No 1 (4 June 2008) [41]–[44].
[21] IBA Commentary (n 7) 9.
[22] In this connection, Art 3.10 of the IBA Rules on the Taking of Evidence, which empowers a tribunal to 'request any Party to produce Documents', is subject to the same objection process as if documents had been sought in a Request to Produce by the other party. See IBA Commentary (n 7) 11.
[23] The official IBA Commentary explains that '[t]he content of the requested documents needs to relate to the issues in the case, and the relationship between the documents and the issues must be set forth with

the Rules, this requirement was formulated as 'relevant and material to the outcome of the case'. With the adoption of the new formula in the 2010 Rules, 'relevant to the case, and material to its outcome', it is clear that the requesting party must satisfy the distinct requirements of both prongs of this standard.[24]

17.19 The requesting party has the burden to clearly demonstrate the relevance of the requested documents to the case as presented by the parties. Document production under the IBA Rules on the Taking of Evidence cannot be used as a means of identifying new allegations or claims, but is rather aimed at obtaining evidence that is relevant and material to existing claims and issues in dispute between the parties.[25] A well-drafted request should, wherever possible, tie the requested documents to specific allegations made in the parties' written submissions so as to show how obtaining the requested document would assist it in discharging the requesting party's burden of proof. An ICC arbitral tribunal thus described in an unpublished award:

> The request for production must establish the relevance of each document or each specific category of documents sought in such a way that the other party and the Arbitral Tribunal are able to refer to factual allegations in the submissions filed by the parties to date. Obviously, this shall not prevent a party from referring to upcoming factual allegations (subsequent memorials) provided such factual allegations are made or at least summarized in the request for the production of documents. In other words, the requesting party must make it clear with reasonable particularity what facts/allegations each sought document (or category of documents) will establish.[26]

17.20 In this connection, when determining whether requested documents are relevant to the case, a tribunal will normally perform only a *prima facie* analysis of the matter based on facts known by the tribunal and the representations of counsel.[27] The requirement to tie the document requests to the parties' specific allegations (and not simply vague issues in dispute between the parties) becomes even more important in this context.

17.21 Furthermore, it may be advisable for parties to agree that the document production phase of their arbitration should take place only after the filing of the first submissions. As noted in the IBA Commentary: 'The specificity required in the request to produce makes it likely that a request will be made only after the issues have become sufficiently clear in the case.'[28] After the first submissions have been filed, the arbitral tribunal will presumably be more informed of the issues in dispute, and will have a better understanding as to whether the requested materials are relevant and material to the parties' allegations.

---

sufficient specificity so that the arbitral tribunal can understand the purpose for which the requesting party needs the document'. IBA Commentary (n 7) 9–10.

[24] O'Malley (n 15) para 3.68.

[25] See Born (n 16) 2309 ('Tribunals are generally very unwilling to permit parties to engage in "fishing expeditions", aimed at identifying possible claims or sources of further inquiry, rather than at adducing evidence in support of existing claims').

[26] Quoted in Virginia Hamilton, 'Document Production in ICC Arbitration', ICC Int'l Ct Arb Bull, 2006 Special Supplement, Document Production in International Arbitration, 70. The IBA Working Group similarly explained that '[t]he content of the requested documents needs to relate to issues in the case, and the relationship between the documents and the issues must be set forth with sufficient specificity so that the arbitral tribunal can understand the purpose for which the requesting party needs the requested documents'. IBA Commentary (n 7) 9–10.

[27] ibid, Hamilton, 69; O'Malley (n 15) para 3.69; Ashford (n 6) para 3.37.

[28] IBA Commentary (n 7) 10.

17.22 As noted above, under the 2010 version of the IBA Rules on the Taking of Evidence, the requirement of 'materiality to the outcome of the case' is a separate requirement aimed at avoiding 'wasteful duplication and the provision of unnecessary material'.[29] The materiality requirement pertains to 'the tribunal's right to evaluate the requested records in light of whether such documents will bear upon the final award'.[30] This additional requirement is another feature that distinguishes document production in international arbitration from that in civil litigation. As Redfern and Hunter comment:

> Most legal practitioners are accustomed to the obligation to satisfy a court, or arbitral tribunal, as to the question of relevance of documents or other information that they are seeking from the opposing party. But the requirement of showing 'materiality to the outcome of the case' is a greatly increased burden. It also enables arbitral tribunals to deny document requests where, although the requested documents would clearly be relevant, they consider that the production of them will not affect the outcome of the proceedings.[31]

17.23 The requirement of materiality under Article 3.3(b) would thus allow a tribunal to reject a request to produce that would unduly delay the arbitral procedure without yielding any additional evidence that would bear on its final award. For instance, an ICSID tribunal in *El Paso v Argentina* rejected document production requests filed after a jurisdictional hearing, on the grounds that the evidence already before the tribunal was 'sufficient to decide the jurisdictional issues raised by the Respondent'.[32]

17.24 Requiring a party to demonstrate that requested documents are material to a tribunal's decision could be considered unduly burdensome. In most international arbitrations, regardless of their complexity, a tribunal cannot know the extent of the evidentiary record of both parties. Furthermore, as noted above, at the time of the document production phase a tribunal is normally not in a position to fully understand the relative importance of the parties' contentions to its final award. All of these considerations call for arbitrators to be effective case managers and to interpret the materiality requirement practically in light of the issues of the particular case. In the words of one commentator:

> The tribunal needs to be as reasonably familiar as possible with the case as then presented to make decisions on such issues. A tribunal will need to consider how much it asks the applicant to explain in demonstrating materiality. To the extent that the tribunal itself considers this question, the aim is not to prejudge the ultimate issue but only to deal fairly with the production request.[33]

17.25 In the event that a tribunal is unsure whether documents requested by a party would be material to the outcome of a dispute, but does not wish to foreclose that possibility, it may postpone a decision on a document request to a later stage of the proceeding. This was the approach adopted by the tribunal in *El Paso v Argentina* which, when ruling on the Respondent's document requests, held: 'If the proceedings reach the merits of the

---

[29] Jeffrey Waincymer, *Procedure and Evidence in International Arbitration* (Kluwer Law International 2012) 859.
[30] O'Malley (n 15) para 3.73.
[31] Nigel Blackaby and others, *Redfern and Hunter on International Arbitration* (5th edn, OUP 2009) para 6.109.
[32] *El Paso Energy International Co v Argentina*, ICSID Case No ARB/03/15, Procedural Order No 1 (28 July 2005), quoted in the Decision on Jurisdiction (27 April 2006) [9].
[33] Waincymer (n 29) 859.

dispute, it will be open to the Respondent to reiterate the above request for the production of documents.'[34]

D. The Requirement to Address Possession, Custody, and Control

17.26 Article 3.3(c) of the IBA Rules on the Taking of Evidence provides that a Request to Produce must contain '(i) a statement that the Documents requested are not in the possession, custody or control of the requesting Party or a statement of the reasons why it would be unreasonably burdensome for the requesting Party to produce such Documents, and (ii) a statement of the reasons why the requesting Party assumes the Documents requested are in the possession, custody or control of another Party'.

17.27 Fulfilling the requirements of Article 3.3(c) is generally straightforward. For instance, where a party requests an individual document that was authored by or communicated to its adversary, or a narrow category of documents that would clearly be contained in its adversary's company files, there would be little debate as to whether or not such documents are in the requesting party's possession, custody, or control.

17.28 The question of possession, custody, or control is in other cases more difficult, for instance where the requesting party seeks documents that are not in the possession of its adversary, but rather in the possession of a third party such as its adversary's corporate affiliates or advisors. The question then arises whether the party should be deemed to have 'control' over such documents and should be compelled to obtain them from those third parties.

17.29 Under English law, courts have analysed these requirements by reference to Rule 31.8(1) of the English CPR, which provides that 'a party's duty to disclose documents is limited to documents which are or have been in his control'. Rule 31.8(2) of the English CPR specifies that 'a party has or has had a document in his control if (a) it was in his physical possession; (b) he has or has had a right to possession of it; or (c) he has or has had a right to inspect or take copies of it'.

17.30 In the 2012 decision *North Shore Ventures Ltd v Anstead Holdings Inc*, the English Court of Appeal held that 'in determining whether documents in the physical possession of a third party are in a litigant's control for the purposes of CPR Rule 31.8, the court must have regard to the true nature of the relationship between the third party and the litigant'. On the facts of that case, the court held that documents in the possession of certain trustees were in the 'control' of the settlors of trusts within the meaning of Rule 31.8 of the English CPR, and that the settlors would be required to produce those documents. According to the court, 'the concept of "right to possession" covers ... a situation where a third party is in possession of documents as agent for a litigant'. The Court of Appeal further noted that the concept of 'control' for the purposes of disclosure was not limited to the three circumstances outlined in Rule 31.8(2) of the English CPR and, 'even if there were, on a strict legal view, no "right to possession" ... it would be open to the English court in such circumstances to find that, as a matter of fact, the documents were nevertheless within the control of that party within the meaning of CPR 31.8(1)'.[35]

---

[34] *El Paso* (n 32) [133].
[35] *North Shore Ventures Ltd v Anstead Holdings Inc* [2012] EWCA Civ 11, [40].

17.31 When determining whether the duty of disclosure extends to documents in the possession of third parties to a proceeding, arbitral tribunals have likewise interpreted the requirements of Article 3.3(c) liberally and practically and have looked beyond strict legal definitions of 'control'. For instance, an ICC arbitral tribunal composed of North American and European arbitrators expressed the requirement as follows:

> 'Possession, custody or control' shall include documents to the extent Claimant or Respondent has actual knowledge, without an obligation to do any research or inquiry, that a document responsive to a request for production is in the possession, custody or control of a person or entity (i) within the same group as Claimant or Respondent, as the case may be, or (ii) from which the Claimant or Respondent, as the case may be, has a contractual right to obtain such document… An entity shall be deemed to belong to the same group as Claimant or Respondent if such entity directly or indirectly owns or controls such Claimant or Respondent, or is directly or indirectly owned or controlled by the same entity as Claimant or Respondent.[36]

17.32 Arbitral tribunals in investment treaty cases have applied a similar standard, and have required parties to search the records of affiliated entities, their advisors, and/or their agents. In *CME v Czech Republic*, for example, the tribunal ordered that 'documents of advisors to Claimant shall be disclosed to the extent that these documents are in the possession of the Claimant and/or its affiliated companies or should have been transmitted by the advisor to the Claimant in the ordinary course of business'.[37] In *Vito G Gallo v Canada*, the tribunal considered that 'the duty of production extends to entities controlled by each party', and required that Canada seek to obtain documents from its municipalities and that the claimant do the same in relation to documents in the possession of a successor company to its investment vehicle.[38]

17.33 The 2010 Rules also impose an express duty on the parties to act in good faith in the taking of evidence.[39] In the words of one NAFTA tribunal, 'for a party to claim that documents are not in its control, it must have made its "best efforts" to obtain documents that are in the possession of persons or entities with whom that party has had a relevant relationship'.[40] While under the IBA Rules on the Taking of Evidence a party is required to use its 'best efforts' to obtain documents in the possession of third parties, it may nonetheless object to a request for documents and seek to convince the tribunal that the requested evidence would be 'unreasonably burdensome' to produce, as provided by Article 9.2(c).

17.34 As drafters of the IBA Rules explain, an 'unreasonable burden can take many forms, and the nature of the burden is purposely left to the discretion of the arbitral tribunal'.[41] What 'burdensome' means is therefore largely dependent on the facts of each case. According to one commentator: 'When considering the burden of production arbitral tribunals are likely to have in mind the potential use of the documents, the relevance and materiality, the costs

---

[36] Quoted in Hamilton (n 26) 74.
[37] *CME Czech Republic BV (The Netherlands) v The Czech Republic*, UNCITRAL, Final Award, 14 March 2003, [65].
[38] *Vito G Gallo* (n 18) [8]–[9].
[39] See IBA Rules, Preamble 3. See also Amy Cohen Kläsener, 'The Duty of Good Faith in the 2010 IBA Rules on the Taking of Evidence in International Arbitration' (2010) Int'l ALR 160, 160.
[40] *Clayton and Bilcon v Government of Canada*, UNCITRAL/NAFTA, Procedural Order No 8 (25 November 2009) 1.
[41] IBA Commentary (n 7) 26.

of production, the reasonableness of each party's position and the likely probative value.'[42] A party who submits requests for documents in the possession of third parties should take all of these factors into account in assessing the likelihood of their acceptance by a tribunal.

E. Conclusion

The foregoing discussion has sought to define some best practices for parties seeking to draft effective Requests to Produce that meet the requirements of Article 3.3 of the IBA Rules on the Taking of Evidence. A well-drafted Request to Produce will ultimately enable a party to obtain the vital and specific documents for its case, and will promote an efficient and economical process of taking documentary evidence in the setting of international arbitration. **17.35**

---

[42] Ashford (n 6) para 3.42.

Part VII

WITNESSES AND PERJURY

18

CROSS-EXAMINATION OF FACT WITNESS STATEMENTS IN INTERNATIONAL ARBITRATION

Lawrence W Newman

A. Introduction

18.01 International arbitrations are, to a great extent, made up of paper—or, more accurately, words in electronic form that may or may not be reproduced on paper. Documents memorialize that which gives rise to the dispute being heard—the contract. Similarly, there is a variety of other documents that bear on issues in the case, including financial documents and correspondence. These can be, and are, dealt with by the parties and the arbitrators through the exchange and submission of further documents—memorials with reproductions are important supporting documents. In spite of the great importance of documents, there are hearings held—and not just for the purpose of hearing oral arguments from the parties' representatives. Witnesses are heard in hearings, both fact witnesses and expert witnesses.

B. Fact Witnesses

(a) Witness statements

18.02 Time was when fact witnesses were presented through direct testimony in international arbitration, just as they are in court, particularly in courts within the Anglo-American tradition. But as time has passed, there has come into almost universal use the presentation of the direct testimony of witnesses in the form of their written statements—called 'witness statements'.

18.03 It is widely understood and accepted that fact witness statements are—if not prepared by— supervised or vetted by counsel for the party presenting the witness. There is, therefore, considerable scepticism as to whether such statements are truly the same kind of testimony that the witness would give if he were testifying orally on direct examination before an arbitral tribunal. Accordingly, it can be accepted that any witness statement that represents the best effort of the party presenting the witness will limit its coverage to what the party's counsel considers to be helpful and will avoid touching on subjects that are not helpful to the party's case.

18.04 Certain witness statements can be more helpful than others to the party presenting them. Some can be fairly innocuous, perhaps referring to or commenting on documents in the record. Others may represent an effort by the party to make an executive speech about the importance of the case to the party and the merits of that case—presenting in effect a certain kind of advocacy to supplement that of counsel. Other witness statements fall into a different category. Not only may they touch on certain subject-matter areas, leaving out areas that are harmful to that party's case, but they may also distort accounts of certain meetings or other events, or even lie about them.

18.05 Witness statements falling into the first category are not troublesome and do not require dealing with. Those in the second category, however, can, if left alone and taken seriously by the tribunal, have a deleterious effect on the case of the opposing party. Therefore, they must be dealt with.

(b) Assessing harm

18.06 But how? An assessment must be made, often only a few days prior to the hearing, as to the ways in which a harmful statement by a fact witness may be responded to. One way is to rely on one's own witnesses and the accounts they will give of the events in question. These witnesses for the opposing party might be regarded as likely to be more persuasive to the tribunal, thereby obviating the need to question the witness concerning his witness statement.

18.07 Under these circumstances, a decision not to question the witness may be justified, particularly if much of what he has said is in fact accurate or if the would-be cross-examiner knows that the witness could add even more troubling testimony when questioned. In such cases, there is little to be gained by addressing the witness statement through questions to the witness.

18.08 The reality is, however, that witness statements are often sufficiently troublesome and sufficiently inaccurate or incomplete, that they should be made subject to efforts to blunt their effectiveness.

18.09 What to do? First, the cross-examiner must assess not only the content of the witness statement, but also the background and attitude of the witness. The witness may not be wholeheartedly hostile even though he may have been called by one of the parties or even be an employee of that party. One should usually assume, at least at first, that the witness, when questioned on cross, will answer questions in a civil and non-obstructive manner. He will probably have been instructed to do so lest naked hostility to the cross-examiner undercut the credibility of the testimony contained in the witness statement.

18.10 Thus, a good approach to cross-examination is to start the questioning of the witness in a friendly, non-confrontational manner, asking questions that seek to clarify and supplement what is contained in the witness statement. One has to be careful, however, in putting such questions to the witness that they seek information that is helpful to the cross-examiner, rather than testimony that supports what is contained in the witness statement.

18.11 Herein lies the biggest potential danger in cross-examination: reinforcing the other side's case. When one cross-examines a witness on a certain subject, one is highlighting that subject for the tribunal, whose members may have glossed over this portion of the witness statement in preparing for the hearing and may not have grasped its negative impact on the cross-examiner's side. But when the arbitrators hear the cross-examiner raise questions about the subject, their interest will be piqued and they will be listening with more attention than they may have paid to it when they read the witness statement. There is a real danger that the witness, when confronted with certain kinds of questions by a cross-examiner, will repeat in other words what he said in the witness statement—and perhaps even reinforce and embellish the point made in the statement. This is obviously disastrous for the cross-examiner—just how disastrous depends on how important the point being discussed is. One thing is clear: it is better not to have questioned the witness at all than to bring out testimony that favours the witness.

Therefore, one must be careful in questioning a witness presented by the other side. The questions must not, in most instances, be so open-ended as to permit the witness to engage in verbal excursions on his own; such excursions are almost always in the witness's favour and in support of his testimony. **18.12**

(c) **Cross-examination**

There have been negative comments made about cross-examinations, in particular about the use of closed or leading questions that are intended to control the witness by eliciting 'yes' or 'no' answers. To some civil lawyers' ears, the asking of such questions shows hostility and is an undesirable legacy from the common law. But such questions need not be hostile in tone or content. Instead, the approach can be conversational rather than confrontational. Even with a friendly approach, the questions can call for answers that very often have to be 'yes' or 'no'. A questioner in sufficient command of the facts and with a sensitivity to the witness's personality and disposition may be able to lead a conversation in which the witness willingly agrees to a narrative that flows, through a series of questions eliciting yes or no answers, in a direction favouring the questioner. **18.13**

Questioning using this approach—that of the friendly leading questioner—may not always result in a nice, easy flow. The witness may not like where the conversation is going and may try to distract or resist. If the goal is worth pursuing, the cross-examiner may have to take a tougher approach with the witness. It helps if the questioning is done in such a way as to bring the tribunal along in the quest for clarification. That is, the tribunal members should be interested in what the questioner is seeking to do and not offended by or impatient with a more insistent line of questioning. **18.14**

Accordingly, the cross-examiner has to be sensitive to the cultural and other attitudes of the tribunal members, some of whom may regard the notion of cross-examination with hostility. Moreover, it is not uncommon in international arbitration for limited, often short, time periods to be allowed for cross-examination. Such time limits give an advantage to the obfuscating witness and give all the more reason for closed questioning to be put to the witness so as to avoid bloviating responses that consume time. **18.15**

When getting tough with the witness, one has to have a goal in sight—one that is attainable. Sometimes a series of denials by the witness or answers that are palpably untrue may be all that is required—and all that is readily obtainable. **18.16**

Nonetheless, the cross-examiner should prepare a plan for cross-examination that anticipates denials, obstruction, and obfuscation by the witness. Indeed, the witness may be expected to lie about certain points. Few things can be as effective in a hearing as the exposure of a witness as a liar in front of the arbitrators. Such exposure cannot only result in a finding by the tribunal that the testimony about which the witness has misspoken is regarded as untruthful but—particularly if this kind of problem of prevarication should **18.17** occur more than once—the tribunal may disbelieve much of the other testimony presented by the witness.

18.18 This is, of course, the best of all possible worlds for the cross-examiner and devoutly to be wished. Exposing a witness as a liar is, however, not easy. Before a lie is exposed, its true dimensions must be established. That is, the witness's untruthful statement must be pinned down. The statement set out in writing in the witness statement should first be validated by the witness orally in front of the arbitrators. Once the existence and scope of the lie is established, there can be the confrontation—with the truth. The most effective expression of the truth is a prior statement of the witness to the contrary of what is in his witness statement. Such statements are not always available, but frequently they are.

C. Taking the Process Seriously

18.19 A sociological phenomenon of international arbitration is that, often, witnesses do not take the testimonial process as seriously as they should because they are too busy on other, seemingly more important, business activities. They therefore allow too little time to familiarize themselves with the record, which often contains many documents, several of which may have been authored by or copied to the witness. The executive witness may not have spent the time necessary to read over these documents or may even not have paid a great deal of attention to them at the time of their creation. Indeed, he may not have given a great deal of thought to the content of the witness statement. This phenomenon of the executive who is too important to take the time to prepare can be deadly to the side on whose behalf he testifies.

18.20 There is another species of untruthful witness. This comprises employees of large corporations, private or state-owned, or of government agencies—those who have no choice but to toe the party line and say what they know they have to say, at the risk of possible loss of job or worse if they do not. Being untruthful is, for them, a rational alternative to lying and suffering the adverse consequences of being caught, which may, on balance, be less important to them and their employer.

18.21 So, if a cross-examiner is lucky and works hard, he will be able to have an important effect on the arbitrators' perception of the merits of the case. But, even if one has the ammunition and has nailed down an untruthful statement, there is still the question of how best to utilize contradicting evidence. This is a judgment call for the cross-examiner. Time may be short, the arbitrators' attention may be fading, or the arbitrators may have shown themselves to be impatient with cross-examination. Under such circumstances, the cross-examiner has to go straight to the point and proceed in a more abbreviated way to confront the witness with the contradictory testimony.

18.22 When there is time available and the matter is important enough, one should not waste good cross-examination material by failing to extract the maximum value from it. Thus, an opportunity is wasted when a cross-examiner does no more than refer the witness to his existing statement and then engage in a confrontation. At worst, a cross-examiner might, without referring to the prior statements except in a general way, simply show the witness a document containing the inconsistent statement and ask if he was the author.

18.23 It is more effective and not much more time-consuming to lay a foundation by having the witness validate the prior written statement before asking the witness whether he ever took a different position or described the matter in question in a materially different way—perhaps paraphrasing what is in the inconsistent statement. The witness may well reiterate his most recent statement and deny having said something different. The cross-examiner can then ask the witness if it were not true that he made a contradictory statement in the prior document. The contrast between the two statements should be made manifest. The inconsistent statement can then be read or shown to the witness, who is asked to admit its authenticity. Of course, it goes without saying that this exercise should focus only on inconsistencies that are material to issues in the case. Focusing the attention of the arbitrators and the witness on minor inconsistencies can be counterproductive.

18.24 There are experienced trial lawyers in the United States who maintain that the ability to cross-examine is a gift one is born with and that cross-examination is therefore a skill that cannot be learned. Although it is true that there are persons who have greater natural abilities than others in various activities in human life, cross-examination is a skill that *can* be learned. Sometimes, it must be learned in practice. One must learn, for example, how to listen carefully to the answers to the questions that one puts to a witness and one must learn how, on the appropriate occasion, to use those answers to deviate from one's planned line of questioning to go into a different area that may be fruitful. One must learn that too rigid an outline of questions to be asked can prevent the cross-examiner from taking advantage of opportunities afforded by the witness's answers. It is by going through the experience of 'thinking on one's feet' and thoroughly focusing on the subject matter that one develops the skill.

D. Conclusion

18.25 No cross-examiner, no matter how practised and skilled, can do without the thorough preparation by immersion in the record—and even outside the record—needed to prepare a flexible outline of cross-examination.

18.26 In days of yore, there was more guesswork involved in preparing to cross-examine witnesses in international arbitration, particularly if there was not—as was usually the case—pre-hearing questioning of witnesses in depositions. In today's international arbitration world, however, witness statements give the cross-examiner a clear framework within which to work—and there are still poorly prepared witnesses who can be profitably cross-examined. There are thus rewards to be had in cross-examining a witness on his written statement—even if it is prepared by a lawyer.

19

THE EXPERT WITNESS IN INTERNATIONAL ARBITRATION

Bernardo M Cremades

A. Introduction

19.01 In his 1995 'Access to Justice: Interim Report', Lord Woolf identified expert evidence as the major cause of cost increases in civil litigation, particularly by reason of its excessive or inappropriate use and the partisanship of experts. The aim of this chapter is to raise the question of whether this also applies today in international arbitration—that is, whether experts are necessary or indeed appropriate given the frequent criticism as to the high costs they generate and the inevitable delays caused by their participation in arbitration proceedings.

B. Party and Tribunal-Appointed Experts

19.02 Parties, when presenting their claims, often have recourse to expert witnesses. Sometimes, they are appointed when a problem arises that may lead to arbitration. They are also often approached at the preparation stage of the claim, or again, when the arbitration proceedings are underway.

19.03 The party experts' positions are sometimes so divergent that the tribunal needs to appoint an independent expert to assist it in assessing the parties' respective positions. This raises the question of how the tribunal should appoint these experts: should it seek the approval, or at least the opinion, of the parties? The tribunal should set the qualifications required of the expert. Needless to say, it should only appoint the expert once the facts of the case are known so that it is better able to determine the expert's exact mission.

19.04 The role that the expert witness should play is a perennial debate. Two very specific examples taken from procedural reform come to mind—namely, the reform of the English CPR in 1998 in England and Wales, and the introduction of the new Civil Procedure Law in Spain in 2000. In the United Kingdom, the solution lay in bringing expert evidence under the control of the judge. The Anglo-Saxon tradition of each party presenting their experts was, from the perspective of this reform, the root of the problem in civil procedure. The reform aimed at introducing the figure of a single joint expert, appointed by common accord and coming under judicial control—thus making the evidentiary phase more efficient. The aim was to secure greater impartiality, a reduction in costs, increased efficiency, party equality, and the potential to facilitate the settlement of disputes.

19.05 In contrast, in Spain the historical position was to use court-appointed experts in civil proceedings. Judges tended to accept their conclusions, and on occasion without discussion. The delays involved in using the official lists of experts drew the proceedings out interminably and inevitably rendered them less efficient. For this reason, there is an increasing tendency towards party-appointed expert witnesses as well as an expert witness appointed by the judge of the hearing.

19.06 Consequently, the solutions in comparative law are aligned, but moving in opposite directions: in England and Wales, there is greater court control over expert evidence; while in Spain, the inefficiencies inherent in court-appointed experts have led to an increased participation by the parties in presenting expert evidence. In short, we are moving towards flexibility in the handling of expertise today, with greater objectivity resulting from the duties of transparency and disclosure of the circumstances surrounding the preparation of expert evidence, communication between the experts, and tribunal monitoring of the presentation of expert evidence.

19.07 Recently, attempts have been made to introduce the Australian practice of 'expert conferencing' as the solution to concerns about partisanship and the costs and delays attributed to expert evidence. Such Anglo-Saxon marketing initiatives are surprising when our procedural system has long been familiar with the practice of the confrontation of experts. This technique, however, is ever-more present in contrasting opinions, and cross-examination before the tribunal and in the presence of the parties.

C. The Function of the Expert Witness in International Arbitration

19.08 The expert has the dual role of witness and expert in their field. As a witness, their role differs from that of an auditor, consultant, and, above all, party-appointed counsel. The auditor's mission is to verify the company books and their opinion is a guarantee to third parties. Company investors and creditors feel secure in the knowledge that the accounts are accurate. The expert witness, in contrast, alerts the tribunal to any doubts that may exist regarding the accounting or financial situation of the company. They assist in the calculation of any losses or damages that may derive from any contractual agreement. Whereas the auditor attests the veracity of book entries, the expert witness's role is to assist in the assessment of evidence.

19.09 The role of the expert also differs from that of the consultant. The consultant's mission is to assist the employer in finding the solution most in line with their business strategy. That is why it is difficult to reconcile the presence of the consultant—who in some cases is virtually an integral part of the company—in the preparation of arbitration claims. Natural resources and construction companies, for example, are the major client base of international consulting firms. In many cases they are already present at the outset of the dispute advising on how to prevent or organize the strategy of a future arbitration. Then, once arbitration proceedings commence, they appear as expert witnesses in the field.

19.10 The expert's role in arbitration proceedings is to testify and assist the tribunal—not to instruct it. It is all too common to see party-appointed experts taking a position that is far more radical even than counsel's. The expert is obliged to tell the truth in accordance with their professional ethics. Expert opinions, consequently, are subject to party questioning to check the veracity of the line of argument and conclusions. It is also true, however, that where there are lawyers with an Anglo-Saxon background, there is a risk that the lawyer's desire to shine may predominate. Sometimes the Anglo-Saxon lawyer seems to consider more the written record than the efficiency of the expert questioning. Further, if his client is present he may be thinking more of the client's satisfaction than the probative value of the expert evidence.

19.11 The expert is a witness, but, in contrast to the legal framework for experts in court proceedings, in international arbitration they do not have to be independent of the parties. The majority of experts appearing before arbitral tribunals are employees or habitual subcontractors of one of the parties. The reason for this is that nobody is more familiar than they are with the circumstances surrounding the matter at hand. They are obliged to give full disclosure before the tribunal and the other party of the nature of the special relationship. The object of expert evidence is to place all possible elements of evidence before the arbitral tribunal so that it may undertake its assessment of the case.

19.12 Accordingly, this begs the question of whether an expert witness can be challenged, either for their disclosures in and of themselves or for any connections that come to light that were not initially disclosed. I am of the opinion that they should not. The tribunal, when the time comes, will assess the possible lack of objectivity that the special relationship with the appointing party may have given rise to and whether this has conditioned the expert evidence in any way. The possible challenge of a tribunal-appointed expert may have other connotations and above all different consequences.

19.13 Expert evidence, when proposed by a party, must be credible, and when designated by the tribunal, must additionally be prudent. On this basis, it is a great mistake for the expert to adopt the stance of a 'guru' whose mission it is to instruct the tribunal, believing it to be composed of three jurists unequipped with a technical mindset. This does not only happen with technical matters, however. Examples proliferate in accounting or legal issues with the 'Taliban' or 'fundamentalist' approach to the interpretation of FIDIC contracts. The expert's role is not to impose their criteria or to instruct the tribunal, but rather to assist its members in their assessment of the circumstances surrounding the litigation.

D. The Challenge of Expert Witnesses

19.14 The expert is a highly qualified witness and furthermore an expert in the particular field. Accordingly, a detailed CV reflecting specialist qualifications should be attached to his report. An engineer, for example, cannot be an expert in all areas, but rather only in those in which he has pursued his professional activity over the years. However, costs of the proceedings may oblige a party to request an expert to issue an expert opinion on technical matters beyond the scope of his usual specialty. The financial constraints of each of the parties determine the reach of the expertise. The tribunal must be alert to this fact to prevent the financially stronger party potentially submitting overwhelming evidence where the financially weaker party has had to limit expenditure in hiring and controlling the expert. The arbitrators here must exercise care and acknowledge that the only objective of evidence in arbitral proceedings is to convince the tribunal as to specific facts or assessments of this evidence.

19.15 International arbitration today requires that the experts adopt a collaborative rather than a combative stance in their dealings with each other. They have to be aware that their role consists of assisting the tribunal in reaching a decision. For this reason, then, a seasoned arbitrator will strive to ensure that the party-appointed experts work together, or, failing that, at least work in collaboration with the tribunal-appointed expert(s). Experts are required to show the tribunal and the parties all the documentation used in the preparation of their reports, so as to fully understand the reality of the expertise.

19.16 At times, relations between the party-appointed expert and the appointing party are less than simple. Counsel pursuing a particular line of argument may restrict the information provided to the appointed experts with a view to retaining control over strategy. This is a big mistake. Sometimes during the arbitration proceedings a critical opinion of the expert might turn out to be in direct conflict with the position of the party that appointed them, thus necessitating the party's in-house lawyer to step in to smooth over a conflict that could have potentially devastating effects. This has, on occasion, led to the replacement of the expert, although it is difficult to understand why such a substitution might negate all the opinions and interpretations of the former expert already admitted by the tribunal. And if, in the interim, a partial award has been issued, it could also be considered that the former expert evidence, for the very nature of its inclusion in the award, could constitute *res iudicata*. Any error that may be detected in the expert reports may constitute sufficient basis to request the correction of the award or even its annulment.

E. The Rise of the So-Called Star Expert

19.17 The 'artisan' style of arbitration that I experienced at the beginning of my career has become an important and often very lucrative industry. Today, we are increasingly witness to mega commercial and investment arbitrations. Some decades ago, natural resources arbitration acquired very great importance. Much more recently, it is investment protection arbitration based on bilateral and multilateral treaties which has given arbitration its extraordinary economic, cultural, and even political thrust.

19.18 The players in these mega-arbitrations form an extraordinarily competitive market. Today, the figure of the individual expert is giving way to the organizational expert. Many employers find it much more convenient to propose to the board of directors the appointment of a well-reputed team of professionals. If things do not work out, it will not be the employer's fault or that of their internal advisors. They prefer to pay the high costs of an external organization that will allow them to shift any eventual responsibility.

19.19 It is not uncommon now to find expert evidence in the hands of a team of experts. The manager of the team which the company in question habitually hires distributes the work among the team members. Part of the team is in charge of drafting the expert report, working alongside the team of lawyers appointed by the company to defend its interests in the arbitration. In the hearing itself, an expert giving oral testimony will have the technical know-how, but also possess excellent communication skills and be adept at convincing arbitral tribunals. In short, there are experts who are skilled report drafters and others who have the powers of persuasion. The expert who invariably appears before the tribunal as the 'star' witness is simply presenting the efforts of the whole team.

19.20 With this backdrop, it is worth asking whether the expert's participation in the design of the strategy for the arbitration, and the fact that the same counsel and expert appear repeatedly in different proceedings, do not call into question the true function of the expert witness both as witness and as an expert collaborating with the tribunal in its mission to ascertain the truth on which to base its decision.

F. Conclusion

19.21 I do not know if Lord Woolf in his 1995 analysis was right or not. What is clear, however, is that today arbitration is losing sight of its original function as it becomes a major industry. Arbitration proceedings are both protracted and costly. If we wish to guarantee access to arbitral justice we must reconsider arbitration as it is today, bearing in mind the very significant role played by expert evidence.

19.22 The work of an arbitrator and an expert witness is often inseparable. The sectors with which the arbitrator comes into contact most frequently are construction, energy, telecommunications, and concessions. Regardless of an arbitrator's background, they will require the support of an expert in the field. However, within this new industry of arbitration, we are losing sight of the personal and truly artisan character of the expert. The proliferation of expert witnesses in arbitration proceedings, and above all the teams of experts, is often the cause of confusion and, of course, delays. Based on my own experience of excessively lengthy and costly arbitration proceedings, I can't help but feel that we are killing the goose that has laid the golden eggs. This tension between the arbitrator and the expert witness brings to mind a *huapango* written by Rubén Fuentes and popularized by Miguel Aceves Mejía, which goes:

> With you or without you
> my troubles have no cure.
> With you, because you kill me
> and yet without you, I'd die for sure.

20

OATHS AND PERJURY

Audley Sheppard

A. Introduction

Section 38(5) of the English Arbitration Act 1996 states that the tribunal 'may direct that a party or witness shall be examined on oath or affirmation, and may for that purpose administer any necessary oath or take any necessary affirmation'. **20.01**

This chapter examines the law and practice of oaths and affirmations in international arbitration, particularly in England and Wales. **20.02**

At the start of my arbitration career (last century, but not a century ago), it was common for witnesses to swear an oath or make an affirmation (for those who did not believe in a god) before giving their oral evidence. These days, it is very uncommon. There may be various reasons for this, including increased secularization of society generally, recognition that oaths/affirmations are unlikely to cause a witness to be more honest, and the influence of arbitrators from countries where oaths/affirmations are rarely administered (or, in some jurisdictions, not allowed). **20.03**

An oath (of Old English origin, *āth*[1]) is a solemn or formal declaration invoking God (or a god, or other object of reverence) as witness to the truth of a statement, or to the binding nature of a promise or undertaking. The essence of a divine oath is an invocation of divine agency to be a guarantor of the oath taker's own honesty and integrity in the matter under question. By implication, this invokes divine displeasure if the oath taker fails in their sworn duties. It therefore implies greater care than usual in the act of the performance of one's duty. **20.04**

References to oaths are found in the Jewish tradition in the Book of Numbers: 'When a man voweth a vow unto the Lord, or sweareth an oath to bind his soul with a bond, he shall not break his word; he shall do according to all that proceedeth out of his mouth';[2] and the Muslim faith: 'Allah forbids you to swear by your fathers. If anyone swears, let him swear by Allah or keep silent.'[3] They often occur in the Christian tradition, albeit the Gospel of Matthew records Jesus as saying: 'I say to you: "Swear not at all"';[4] **20.05**

---

[1] *Concise Oxford English Dictionary* (12th edn, OUP 2011), and before that Old German <http://www.oed.com> accessed 19 October 2015.
[2] Book of Numbers 30:2.
[3] Book 22, Hadith 14.
[4] Gospel of Matthew 5:34–7.

and the Book of James states: 'Above all, my brothers, do not swear—not by heaven or by earth or by anything else. Let your "Yes" be yes, and your "No", no, or you will be condemned.'[5]

20.06 The oath historically had a central place in a system of justice based on a belief that God would punish the liar. In this form, the oath was a traditional 'self-curse' which could be used as security for a promise.[6] With certain exceptions, evidence would not be admissible in common law courts unless given upon oath.[7] This view is illustrated by the comments of an American judge in 1828: 'A man of the most exalted virtue, though judges and jurors might place the most entire confidence in his declarations, cannot be heard in a court of justice without oath. This is a universal rule of the common law, sanctioned by the wisdom of ages, and obligatory upon every court of justice whose proceedings are according to the course of the common law.'[8] In England, before the Evidence Act 1869, the testimony of atheists was wholly inadmissible.[9]

20.07 A century later, there was far greater realism and/or scepticism. The Criminal Law Revision Committee (CLRC) recognized in its report in 1972 that oaths had not prevented 'an enormous amount of perjury in the courts'.[10] In 1977, the English Court of Appeal noted that: 'It is unrealistic not to recognise that, in the present state of society, among the adult population the divine sanction of an oath is probably not generally recognised.'[11] In its 1996 report, *Evidence in Criminal Proceedings*, the English Law Commission noted that oaths provide no guarantee that the witness will tell the truth, and that there is widespread scepticism about their utility.[12] It noted that 'many responsible organisations in England and Wales have called for the oath to be abolished'.[13] However, the English courts have continued to require the administering of oaths or affirmations.

B. Oaths Act

20.08 Legislation concerning the administering of oaths in legal proceedings has existed in England since at least 1775.[14] The current legislation is the Oaths Act 1978. It provides that for persons of the Christian or Jewish faiths, oaths are to be administered as follows:

> The person taking the oath shall hold the New Testament, or, in the case of a Jew, the Old Testament, in his uplifted hand, and shall say or repeat after the officer administering the oath the words 'I swear by Almighty God that …', followed by the words of the oath prescribed by law.[15]

---

[5] Epistle of James 5:12.
[6] Mark Weinberg, 'The Law of Testimonial Oaths and Affirmations' (1976) Monash Uni LR 25.
[7] *Regina v Emanuel Tew* (1855) 169 ER 766, 792; (1855) Dears 429.
[8] *Atwood v Welton*, 7 Conn 66, 72 (1828).
[9] Hodge M Malek (ed), *Phipson on Evidence* (18th edn, Sweet & Maxwell 2013) para 9.28.
[10] CLRC *Evidence (General), Report 11* (Cmd 4991, 1972) para 280(vi).
[11] *R v Hayes (Geoffrey)* [1977] 1 WLR 234, 237 (Bridge LJ).
[12] English Law Commission, *Evidence in Criminal Proceedings: Hearsay and Related Topics* (Law Com No 245, 1996) 26–27.
[13] ibid 27.
[14] Oaths Act 1775. An example of even earlier legislation concerning documents is the Oaths of Minors Act 1681.
[15] Oaths Act 1978, s 1(1).

20.09 The prescribed words for factual witnesses are the following: 'the evidence I shall give shall be the truth, the whole truth, and nothing but the truth'.[16] The Oaths Act further provides that for persons that are neither Christian nor Jewish, oaths shall be administered 'in any lawful manner'.[17]

20.10 A Guidance Note[18] for English Coroners provides advice on acceptable forms of oaths for persons of other faiths:

(1) *Muslim*. Members of the Muslim faith will omit the words 'I swear by Almighty God' and substitute the words 'I swear by Allah'.
(2) *Hindu*. Members of the Hindu faith will omit the words 'I swear by Almighty God' and substitute the words 'I swear by Gita'.
(3) *Sikh*. Members of the Sikh faith will omit the words 'I swear by Almighty God' and substitute the words 'I swear by Guru Nanak'.

20.11 The Oaths Act goes on to provide that any person who objects to swearing an oath shall be permitted to make his solemn affirmation. The wording of the affirmation should be: 'I do solemnly, sincerely and truly declare and affirm ...', and this should be followed by the words of the oath as prescribed by law (ie 'the evidence I shall give ...', etc).

20.12 Although the Oaths Act provides details of the wording to be spoken while swearing an oath or making an affirmation, the Court of Appeal has held in *R v Chapman* that the words in section 1 are directive, but that a failure to comply with them does not necessarily invalidate the oath.[19] The test of whether or not the oath is administered in a lawful manner is whether the oath appears to the court to be binding on the conscience of the witness and whether the witness himself considers the oath to be binding on his conscience.[20] In *Hampshire County Council v Pendragon*, a defendant who claimed to be a Druid was allowed to read aloud a Druidic oath while holding a broadsword, but only after the judge had made enquiries in order to satisfy himself that this was regarded as a binding oath by Druids.[21]

20.13 There is no prescribed wording for interpreters or independent expert witnesses, but they are usually asked to swear/affirm that they will interpret or give their evidence honestly and to the best of their professional skill and judgment. As to who may administer an oath, the Evidence Act 1851 at section 16 provides that 'every court, judge, justice, officer, commissioner, arbitrator, or other person, now or hereafter having by law or by consent of the parties authority to hear, receive, and examine evidence, is hereby empowered to administer an oath to all such witnesses as are legally called before them respectively'.[22]

---

[16] These words were approved by a resolution of the judges of the King's Bench Division on 11 January 1927, and the form approved for all courts, civil and criminal. See further Malek (n 9) para 9.32.
[17] Oaths Act 1978, s 1(3).
[18] Courts and Tribunals Judiciary, 'Chief Coroner Guidance No 3: Oaths and Robes', 16 July 2013 <http://www.judiciary.gov.uk> accessed 19 October 2015.
[19] *R v Chapman* [1980] Crim LR 42; see also Malek (n 9) para 9.30. Recently it was reported that a judge was forced to discharge a jury and order a retrial after a Muslim witness was sworn in on the Bible and not the Koran, saying 'I cannot accept his evidence and neither can you'. See *The Times*, 28 February 2015.
[20] *R v Kemble* [1990] 1 WLR 1111, 1114 (Lane LCJ). In some circumstances, it may be permissible to enquire why the witness chose to affirm rather than swear an oath: *R v Mehrban* [2001] EWCA Crim 2627.
[21] See *Hampshire CC v Pendragon* (unreported 2003) and *R v Pendragon* (unreported 1997) referred to in Malek (n 9) para 9.34 and fns 180 and 181. See also 'Druid does battle over poll tax bill' 25 January 1994 <http://www.independent.co.uk> accessed 21 October 2015.
[22] See also English CPR, Part 32 Practice Direction, para 9.1.

20.14　The requirement of an oath or affirmation also applied to written witness evidence, with any affidavit having to be sworn before a qualified person. Written witness evidence no longer needs to be sworn; however, witness statements should contain a statement or declaration of truth.[23] Nevertheless, before giving evidence at an oral hearing, the witness will be asked to confirm under oath the truthfulness of his witness statement.

C. Perjury Act

20.15　English legislation has also for many years prescribed a sanction for not telling the truth (presumably on the premise that any punishment meted out by the god to whom the oath was made is not sufficient).[24] The current legislation is the Perjury Act 1911.[25] The 1911 Act, at section 1, provides:

> (1) If any person lawfully sworn as a witness or as an interpreter in a judicial proceeding wilfully makes a statement material in that proceeding, which he knows to be false or does not believe to be true, he shall be guilty of perjury, and shall, on conviction thereof on indictment, be liable to penal servitude for a term not exceeding seven years, or to imprisonment ... for a term not exceeding two years, or to a fine or to both such penal servitude or imprisonment and fine.
> (2) The expression 'judicial proceeding' includes a proceeding before any court, tribunal, or person having by law power to hear, receive and examine evidence on oath.
> (3) Where a statement made for the purposes of a judicial proceeding is not made before the tribunal itself, but is made on oath before a person authorised by law to administer an oath to the person who makes the statement, and to record or authenticate the statement, it shall, for the purposes of this section, be treated as having been made in a judicial proceeding.
> [...]
> (6) The question whether a statement on which perjury is assigned was material is a question of law to be determined by the court of trial.[26]

20.16　To obtain a conviction for perjury, the prosecution must prove the following: '(a) that the witness was lawfully sworn as a witness; (b) in a judicial proceeding; (c) that the witness made a statement wilfully, that is to say deliberately and not inadvertently or by mistake; (d) that that statement was false; (e) that the witness knew it was false or did not believe it to be true; (f) that the statement was, viewed objectively, material in the judicial proceeding.'[27]

20.17　Accordingly, the false statement must be made wilfully or knowingly, and recklessness is not sufficient. Furthermore, the false statement must be objectively material.

20.18　The evidential requirements for securing a conviction for perjury are prescribed in section 13 of the 1911 Act, entitled 'Corroboration', as follows:

---

[23] English CPR, Parts 22 and 32 Practice Directions require a witness statement to be verified by a statement of truth; Criminal Procedure Rules 2015, Part 16.2 requires a witness statement to contain a declaration of truth.

[24] Crimes of perjury and perverting the course of justice are described as 'offences against justice'.

[25] See Susan S M Edwards, 'Perjury and Perverting the Course of Justice' (2003) Crim LR 525.

[26] The Perjury Act is also concerned with: false statements on oath made otherwise than in a judicial proceeding (s 2); false statements as to births and deaths (s 4); false statutory declarations and other false statements without oath (s 5); and false declarations to obtain registration for carrying on a vocation (s 6).

[27] Peter Richardson, *Archbold Criminal Pleading, Evidence and Practice* (Sweet & Maxwell 2014) para 28.141, which notes that by virtue of s 1(6) of the Perjury Act 1911, requirement (f) is a matter to be decided by the judge (see *R v Millward* [1985] QB 519, 80 Cr App R 280).

A person shall not be liable to be convicted of any offence against this Act ... solely upon the evidence of one witness as to the falsity of any statement alleged to be false.

The courts have observed that to obtain a conviction for perjury 'there must be one witness and something else in addition',[28] meaning at least two pieces of evidence would be required to establish the falsity of a statement.[29]   **20.19**

Judges used to have the power to order the prosecution of persons for perjury.[30] However, this power was removed in 1985[31] and now when a judge comments on an instance of alleged perjury, a report of the judge's comments, including an account of the circumstances giving rise to them, is submitted promptly by the case manager at the court to the Unit Head at the CPS and reported to the Chief Crown Prosecutor (Sector Directors London).[32] Consideration will be given as to whether the CPS or the SFO should request an investigation. In due course, either the CPS or the SFO will decide whether or not to prosecute and the judge will be notified of the decision once it is taken.[33]   **20.20**

The courts have regularly expressed views on the seriousness of perjury, for example: **20.21**

> Parker LCJ: Perjury is a very serious offence; justice could not be administered unless people spoke the truth on oath. Again it is very difficult to prove, and accordingly it must be understood that perjury, when proved, attracts a severe penalty;[34]
>
> Chapman J: Perjury is one of the most serious offences on the criminal calendar, because it wholly undermines the whole basis of the administration of justice ... and that is why it is a matter which must carry a sentence of imprisonment;[35] and
>
> Popplewell J: [Perjury] strikes at the root of our system of justice.[36]

Given this perspective and also given that most criminal trials and many civil disputes are decided on the veracity of witness evidence, with a decision in favour of one party often implying that the evidence of one or more witnesses for the other party is not accepted, there are surprisingly few prosecutions for perjury.   **20.22**

Professor Susan Edwards in her review of the ten-year period 1991 to 2000 records that 1,024 defendants stood trial for perjury in the Crown Court (ie an average of 102 per year), with 830 convictions (an average of 83 per year, and 81 per cent of the total prosecutions).[37]   **20.23**

The maximum sentence for perjury in England and Wales is seven years' imprisonment.[38] The question of culpability is of central consideration, thus a deliberate lie in the face of the   **20.24**

---

[28] *Rex v Threlfall* [1914] 10 Cr App R 112.
[29] The Court of Appeal has interpreted this as imposing a requirement for corroboration of the falsity of the relevant statement: see *R v Hamid and Hamid* [1979] 69 Cr App R 324.
[30] Perjury Act 1911, s 9.
[31] Prosecution of Offences Act 1985, s 28.
[32] CPS Prosecution Policy and Guidance, 'Judicial Comments' <http://www.cps.gov.uk> accessed 19 October 2015.
[33] SFO Guidance on Perjury <http://www.sfo.gov.uk> accessed 19 October 2015.
[34] *R v Simmonds (George Lewis James)* (1969) 53 Cr App R 488; see also ibid.
[35] *R v Warne* (1980) 2 Cr App R (S) 42; see also SFO Guidance (n 33).
[36] *R v Healey* (1990) 12 Cr App R (S) 297.
[37] Edwards (n 25) 529. See also Keith Soothill and others, 'Perjury and False Statements: A Criminal Profile of Persons 1979–2001' (2004) Crim LR 926.
[38] CPS Prosecution Policy and Guidance <http://www.cps.gov.uk> accessed 19 October 2015.

court is regarded as more serious than perjury or perverting the course of justice committed on the spur of the moment.[39] Other factors have been said to include the number of offences committed, the timescale over which they are committed, whether they are persisted in, whether the lies which are told or the fabrications which are embarked upon have any actual impact on the proceedings in question, and whether the activities of the defendant draw others in.[40] The courts have also held that the sentences for perjury and perverting the course of justice must be proportionate to the wrong or harm of the index offence to which the offence against justice was perpetrated.

20.25 Professor Edwards records that between 1991 and 2000, of the 830 persons convicted, 437 were sentenced to imprisonment (an average of 43 per year, and 52 per cent of the total convictions), with 171 for four months or under (39 per cent), 78 for four to six months (18 per cent), 133 for 6 to 12 months (30 per cent), and 28 for 12 to 18 months (6 per cent) (ie 94 per cent in total), leaving only 27 with sentences of over 18 months (6 per cent).[41]

20.26 One notable example of a longer sentence during this period was Lord Jeffrey Archer, the former deputy chairman of the Conservative Party and best-selling author, who was convicted in 2001 on two counts of perjury (along with two counts of perverting the course of justice) in relation to a libel case against the *Daily Star* newspaper which took place in 1987, in which he lied about the contents of his diary. Archer was sentenced to three years' imprisonment for the first count of perjury, and four years for the second, the sentences, which were confirmed on appeal, to run concurrently.[42] Jonathan Aitken, the former MP, was sentenced to 18 months for perjury (and perverting the course of justice) in relation to a libel case against the *Guardian* newspaper, in which he lied about payment of a bill for his stay in the Paris Ritz hotel.[43]

20.27 More recent statistics indicate a decline in prosecutions, but an increase in conviction rates and lengths of sentence. Between 2009 and 2013, 356 people stood trial for perjury (an average of 89 per year), and 334 of those were convicted (an average of 67 per year, which is 94 per cent of total prosecutions), with 90 per cent sentenced to imprisonment of up to 18 months, ie 10 per cent for more than 18 months.[44]

D. The English Arbitration Act 1996

20.28 As mentioned in the Introduction to this chapter, section 38(5) of the 1996 Act provides that the arbitral tribunal has the power to direct that a party or witness shall be examined on oath or affirmation, and may for that purpose administer any necessary oath or take any

---

[39] Edwards (n 25) 533–4. The Criminal Justice Act 2003 further endorsed the importance of harm and culpability when determining sentencing. That Act put in place a number of reforms from the *Halliday Review* (John Halliday, *Making Punishments Work: A Report of a Review of the Sentencing Framework for England and Wales* (July 2001)).
[40] *R v Archer (Jeffrey)* [2002] EWCA Crim 1996, [63] (Rose LJ).
[41] Edwards (n 25) 529.
[42] *R v Archer (Jeffrey)* (n 40). The false evidence was relevant to whether Archer had spent a particular night with a prostitute.
[43] *The Financial Times*, 8 June 1999. The false evidence was relevant to whether or not he was present in Paris and met with alleged arms dealers.
[44] See *Criminal Justice Statistics 2013* <http://www.gov.uk> accessed 19 October 2015.

necessary affirmation. It replaced section 12(3) of the English Arbitration Act 1950.[45] In respect of the new section 38(5), the DAC simply stated in its report that the provision was self-explanatory.[46]

Section 1(2) of the Perjury Act 1911 states that the expression 'judicial proceeding' includes a proceeding before any court, tribunal, or person having by law power to hear, receive, and examine evidence on oath. Accordingly, any person who is lawfully sworn (ie in compliance with the Oaths Act 1978) as a witness or an interpreter in an arbitration in England may be prosecuted for perjury.[47] In such circumstances, the tribunal itself would have to make a report to the Unit Head at the CPS and the Chief Crown Prosecutor. 20.29

Merkin and Flannery comment that it is a 'rare occurrence' when an arbitrator requires a witness to swear evidence on oath or affirmation, although the authors add that it 'often takes place where some wrongdoing is alleged, or there is a direct conflict of oral testimony'.[48] Accordingly, as noted in *Russell on Arbitration*,[49] as modern practice is not generally for witnesses to be examined on oath in arbitration, prosecutions are therefore very rare indeed. In fact, I am not aware of any prosecution in England arising out of an international commercial arbitration. 20.30

Where perjury is alleged after the award is issued, it may nevertheless form the basis of a challenge, on grounds of serious irregularity under section 68(2)(g) of the English Arbitration Act 1996 ('the award being obtained by fraud or the way in which it was procured being contrary to public policy'). A recent example is *Chantiers de l'Atlantique SA v Gaztransport & Technigaz SAS*.[50] The applicant applied to the High Court to have an ICC award of a tribunal seated in London set aside, on grounds that it was obtained by fraud on the part of the other party. Flaux J considered that where a party to an arbitration (not just a witness for one of the parties[51]) had deliberately given misleading evidence to the arbitrators, that would amount to fraud for the purposes of section 68(2)(g). The application was, however, refused on grounds that there was nothing to indicate that the fraud had caused 'substantial injustice': if the true position had been disclosed to the arbitrators, that would not in all probability have affected the result of the arbitration. 20.31

E. Arbitral Procedural Rules

Some institutional procedural rules provide for the provision of evidence on oath. The 1998 LCIA Rules provided that the testimony of a witness may be presented by a party in written 20.32

---

[45] s 12(3) provided: 'An arbitrator or umpire shall, unless a contrary intention is expressed in the arbitration agreement, have the power to administer oaths to, or take the affirmations of, the parties to and witnesses on a reference under the agreement.'
[46] *DAC Report*, para 199.
[47] There is a curious inconsistency between the English Arbitration Act 1996 (which refers to a party or a witness being examined on oath) and the Perjury Act (which refers to witnesses and interpreters).
[48] Robert Merkin and Louis Flannery, *Arbitration Act 1996* (5th edn, Informa Law 2014) 155.
[49] David Sutton and others, *Russell on Arbitration* (23rd edn, Sweet & Maxwell 2007) para 5.154.
[50] [2011] EWHC 3383 (Comm).
[51] It was held in *Elektrim SA v Vivendi Universal SA* [2007] EWHC 11 (Comm) that the phrase 'obtained by fraud' in s 68(2)(g) had to refer to an award being obtained by the fraud of a party to the arbitration, or by the fraud of another to which a party to the arbitration was privy; it could not refer to the fraud of anybody involved in the arbitral proceedings irrespective of whether or not the fraud was committed with the knowledge of the relevant party to the arbitration.

form, either as a signed statement or 'as a sworn affidavit' (Article 20.3). The new 2014 Rules amended this provision to refer to a signed statement or 'like document' (Article 20.2), thus making sworn affidavits/witness statements even less likely. Neither version of the Rules refers to administering of oaths before giving oral evidence, so that it is left to the discretion of the tribunal and/or the parties.

20.33 Similarly, Article 54(d) of the 2014 WIPO Arbitration Rules provides that the testimony of witnesses may, either at the choice of a party or as directed by the tribunal, be submitted in written form, whether by way of 'signed statements, sworn affidavits or otherwise'.

20.34 The 2012 ICC Rules, the 2013 UNCITRAL Rules, and the 2014 ICDR Rules make no mention of oaths or affirmations.

20.35 By contrast, the 2006 ICSID Rules do provide for administering of affirmations. They state that '[e]ach witness shall make the following declaration before giving his evidence: "I solemnly declare upon my honour and conscience that I shall speak the truth, the whole truth and nothing but the truth"'. In relation to expert witnesses, the last clause of this sentence is replaced with 'that my statement will be in accordance with my sincere belief'.[52]

20.36 Similarly, the IBA Rules on the Taking of Evidence provide that: 'A witness of fact providing testimony shall first affirm, in a manner determined appropriate by the Arbitral Tribunal, that he or she commits to tell the truth' or in relation to an expert witness that it is his or her 'genuine belief in the opinions to be expressed'.[53]

20.37 Where the institutional rules do not provide for the administering of oaths or affirmations, arbitral tribunals should nevertheless be mindful of the law of the seat, in case it requires oaths to be taken. Even if there is no requirement, tribunals may choose to administer an oath or affirmation, unless they are prohibited from doing so. One example of this is an ICC award seated in New York where the arbitrators (from mixed common law and civil law backgrounds) described the procedure they considered appropriate: 'Prior to testifying each witness and expert read either a "witness declaration" or an "expert declaration" aloud, as appropriate: [Fact Witness Declaration] I am aware that in my testimony I have to tell the truth and nothing but the truth. I'm also aware that if I do not comply with this obligation, I may face severe legal consequences.'[54]

20.38 In my experience, it is increasingly common for tribunals to refer to potential legal consequences of not telling the truth, but without saying (or probably knowing) what those consequences might be at the arbitral seat or the witness's domicile.[55]

F. Other Jurisdictions

20.39 There is a wide variety of approaches concerning the administering of oaths by arbitral tribunals in other jurisdictions.[56] Unsurprisingly, other jurisdictions in the common law

---

[52] rr 35(2) and (3).
[53] Art 8(4). See also Art 8(3) of 1999 Rules.
[54] *Mobil Cerro Negro v PDVSA and PDVSA-CN*, ICC Case No 15416/JRF/CA (2011) fn 85, [37] in Nathan D O'Malley, *Rules of Evidence in International Arbitration: An Annotated Guide* (Informa Law 2012) 261.
[55] ibid. See also Peter Ashford, *The IBA Rules on the Taking of Evidence in International Arbitration* (CUP 2013) 134.
[56] See, eg, Jeffrey Waincymer, *Procedure and Evidence in International Arbitration* (Kluwer Law International 2012) 919.

family typically give arbitral tribunals a discretion whether or not to administer oaths/affirmations.[57] Some civil law jurisdictions also follow this approach, for example the Netherlands, where a Dutch court, upon consideration of testimony heard by an arbitral tribunal without the administration of an oath, said 'in the court's judgment, the testimony offered under oath and one given while not under oath should in principle be given the same weight'.[58]

20.40 Certain jurisdictions do not permit oaths in arbitral proceedings—for example, Belgium, where legislation prescribes that an arbitral tribunal should hear a person 'without oath'.[59] In Sweden, an arbitral tribunal may not administer oaths or 'truth affirmations' and therefore criminal sanctions for perjury cannot apply;[60] however, where a party wishes a witness or an expert to testify under oath, or a party to be examined under truth affirmation, the party may, after obtaining the consent of the arbitrators, submit an application to such effect to the District Court.[61]

20.41 In Germany, an arbitral tribunal cannot require a witness to take a formal oath (but may request court assistance), but the tribunal can and generally does issue an admonition or reminder of the obligation to tell the truth subject to criminal sanction.[62] In Switzerland, an arbitral tribunal is required to inform the witness of their duty to tell the truth and of the possible criminal consequences of failing to do so.[63]

20.42 By contrast, some jurisdictions continue to compel the use of oaths in arbitral proceedings. For example, Article 211 of the UAE Civil Procedure Code 1992 states: 'The arbitrators shall cause the witnesses to take oath. Whoever makes a false statement before the arbitrators shall be deemed to have committed the crime of perjury.'[64] Failure to administer an oath can have serious consequences for the enforceability of an award and has led to a domestic award being set aside. In *Bechtel Co Ltd v Department of Civil Aviation of the Government of Dubai*, which was seated in Dubai, it was agreed that the oath administered on His Excellency Sheikh Ahmed Bin Saeed Al-Maktoum should be less stringent than normal, taking into account his 'position in society'.[65] The Dubai Court of Cassation set aside the award, holding that Article 211 was mandatory and could not be waived by the parties.[66]

---

[57] eg Hong Kong Arbitration Ordinance (Cap 609) 2011, s 56(8); Singapore International Arbitration Act 2002, s 12(2); and New York Civil Practice Law and Rules, Art 7505. The practice of Indian parties is often to file affidavits sworn before an Oaths Commissioner, pursuant to the Indian Oaths Act 1969.
[58] *Rechtbank Groningen* (Groningen Court of First Instance), Case No 49632/HA ZA 00-915, 24 January 2002; see further O'Malley (n 54) 261.
[59] Belgian Judicial Code, Art 1700(4) as amended in 2013.
[60] Swedish Arbitration Act 1999, s 25(3); Finn Madsen, *Commercial Arbitration in Sweden* (2nd edn, OUP 2006) 178.
[61] Swedish Arbitration Act 1999, s 26(1).
[62] Karl-Heinz Böckstiegel and others (eds), *Arbitration in Germany: The Model Law in Practice* (2nd edn, Kluwer Law International 2015) 283.
[63] Tobias Zuberbühler and others, *Swiss Rules of International Arbitration* (Schulthess 2013) 248. Criminal sanctions will apply only when the witness has been made aware of such sanctions in advance of their testimony and he/she still intentionally provides false testimony: Swiss Criminal Code 2014, Arts 307 and 309.
[64] See translation at <http://www.diac.ae> accessed 19 October 2015.
[65] In England and Wales, the Sovereign is probably immune from taking an oath or affirmation, but a foreign head of state would probably not receive such dispensation: see Malek (n 9) para 9.38; and the State Immunity Act 1978, s 20.
[66] For a full account of arbitration in the UAE, see Gordon Blanke, 'Arbitration in the UAE: Demystifying the Myths' in Julio César Betancourt (ed), *Defining Issues in International Arbitration: Celebrating 100 Years of the Chartered Institute of Arbitrators* (OUP 2016) ch 34.

The award was nevertheless enforced in France, which declined to recognize the Dubai annulment decision.[67]

20.43 However, compliance with Article 211 may not be necessary in order to enforce a foreign award. In *Maxtel International FZE v Airmec Dubai LLC*,[68] the successful claimant sought to enforce a London award between two Dubai entities. The award debtor resisted enforcement on the grounds that the tribunal had not administered an oath. The Dubai Court of First Instance concluded that it need only be satisfied that a foreign award did not conflict with the Federal Decree under which the UAE had acceded to the New York Convention, which did not include a requirement that an oath be administered. An appeal was made to the Dubai Court of Cassation, but was rejected.[69]

G. Conclusion

20.44 In so many areas of arbitral practice, much has changed over the last 100 years. In my experience, it is now very rare for arbitral tribunals sitting in England to ask a witness to swear an oath or affirmation. However, most tribunals ask the witness to confirm that he will tell the truth. Some go further (influenced by German and Swiss arbitration practice) and say that failure to tell the truth may lead to potential legal consequences; but that would not be the case in England if the witness had not been lawfully sworn. Whether sitting in England or elsewhere, it is important for tribunals and counsel to check what rules apply, as graphically indicated by the *Bechtel* case.

---

[67] Enforcement was also sought in the United States, but stayed. See, eg, *Bechtel Co Ltd v Department of Civil Aviation of the Government of Dubai*, 300 F Supp 2d 112 (DDC 2004) <http://www.leagle.com> accessed 19 October 2015.

[68] *Maxtel International FZE v Airmec Dubai LLC*, Commercial Action No 268/2010, Court of First Instance (12 January 2011).

[69] *Maxtel International FZE v Airmec Dubai LLC*, Case No 132/2012, Dubai Court of Cassation (18 October 2012).

Part VIII

ARBITRATORS' DECISION-MAKING POWER AND ARBITRAL TRIBUNALS' CESSATION OF FUNCTIONS

21

INHERENT AND IMPLIED POWERS OF ARBITRATORS

Margaret L Moses

A. Introduction

(a) Agreement-based powers

The powers of arbitrators in international commercial arbitration are based on the agreement of the parties, usually set forth in an arbitration clause contained in a contract between the parties or in a separate agreement to arbitrate. Increasingly, however, arbitrators are exercising powers that are not derived specifically from a party agreement, but rather may be implied or inherent. The terms 'implied' and 'inherent' are frequently used rather loosely, and sometimes interchangeably.[1] But there are differences, even if sometimes the meanings appear to be overlapping. 21.01

This chapter will attempt to develop a framework for understanding and using the terms, so that parties, arbitrators, and courts can employ common meanings and concepts when considering arbitral powers. It is important for a tribunal to understand the scope of its powers in order to ensure that its use of those powers does not jeopardize award enforcement. This understanding is also important to counsel who may need to defend an award for which enforcement is challenged on the ground that the tribunal exceeded its powers. Finally, the understanding of the terms and their use can be critical to a court that must decide whether the powers of the tribunal were employed in an appropriate manner within the scope of the arbitral agreement, the laws, and the rules. 21.02

An arbitrator must always keep in mind his duty to try to render an enforceable award.[2] In carrying out that duty, the arbitrator may find that some necessary powers have not been clearly spelled out in the arbitration agreement. Importantly, the arbitrator must not cross 21.03

---

[1] See, eg, Robert Wachter, 'On the Inherent Powers of Arbitral Tribunals in International Commercial Arbitration' in Gerold Zeiler and others (eds), *Austrian Yearbook on International Arbitration* (Manz'sche Verlags- und Universitätsbuchhandlung 2012) 68, fn 16 ('For purposes of this paper the author used the terms *inherent powers* and *implied powers* interchangeably').

[2] See Yves Derains and Eric Schwartz, *A Guide to ICC Rules of Arbitration* (Kluwer Law International 2005) 385 ('Enforceability of the award ... is ... the raison d'être of the arbitration process'). Some institutional rules impose an explicit obligation. Art 41 of the ICC Rules states that 'the Court and the arbitral tribunal ... shall make every effort to make sure that the award is enforceable at law'. The 2014 LCIA Rules state in Art 32.2 that 'the LCIA Court, the LCIA, the Registrar, the Arbitral Tribunal and each of the parties ... shall make every reasonable effort to ensure that any award is legally recognized and enforceable at the arbitral seat'.

the line that circumscribes his powers, because acting in excess of authority could render the award unenforceable.[3] When dealing with a novel problem not clearly within his enumerated powers, an arbitrator risks being challenged for bias or for acting beyond the scope of the arbitration agreement.

(b) Sunshine and shadow

21.04 On the spectrum of proper arbitrator powers, there is an area of sunshine, and an area of shadow. In the sunny area are any powers defined in the arbitration agreement of the parties, in any rules of an arbitral institution adopted by the parties, and in any arbitration law at the seat of the arbitration. From these three sources, certain powers of the arbitrator can be clearly discerned.

21.05 Nonetheless, there will always be some areas of shadow, because even the most complete agreement, laws, or rules cannot cover every situation where an arbitrator may be required to act. For that reason, many of the laws and rules give broad discretion to the arbitrator with regard to various procedures that must be followed if the arbitration is to proceed to a final, enforceable award. But as will be discussed below, there will often be areas that cannot be squarely placed within the discretionary powers that are provided, and must therefore come from some source other than the governing laws and rules.

21.06 Part B of this chapter will focus on possible definitions of the terms 'implied' and 'inherent' and will consider whether there is any critical difference in the taxonomy of these terms between international commercial arbitration and international investment arbitration. Part C will consider different applications of implied powers, and the unlikely possibility that such applications will cause enforceability problems. Part D will deal with the sources and uses of inherent powers, and the need to balance the use of such powers with the risk of their leading to an unenforceable award. The chapter will conclude with some thoughts on why distinguishing the meaning of implied powers and inherent powers may be useful in supporting the enforcement of an award.

B. Definitions

(a) Inherent and implied powers

21.07 The ILA's Committee on International Commercial Arbitration has recently grappled with the concepts and the practice of inherent and implied powers, and issued a thoughtful and comprehensive report on the subject.[4] The ILA Report has acknowledged that proper application of inherent and implied powers is highly contextual, and may depend on both the particular circumstances of a case as well as the relevant laws, rules, and legal culture.[5] Nonetheless, the Report has attempted to come up with a workable framework for understanding the terms. It has suggested three different categories: implied powers, discretionary

---

[3] An award can be refused enforcement if 'it contains decisions on matters beyond the scope of the submission to arbitration' (Art V(1)(c) of the New York Convention).
[4] ILA, International Commercial Arbitration Committee, 'Report for the Biennial Conference in Washington DC' (April 2014) <http://www.ila-hq.org> accessed 25 September 2015.
[5] ibid 14.

powers, and inherent powers.⁶ Implied powers can be discerned from express provisions in the laws and rules governing the arbitration.

Thus, if certain objectives or duties are expressly imposed on the arbitrators, one could imply that they have the authority to take steps to implement those objectives. An example given by the Report is that if there is a provision requiring the arbitration to be conducted efficiently, then an arbitrator's implied powers could include limiting the scope of document production, and perhaps even bifurcating the proceedings.⁷   **21.08**

With regard to discretionary powers, when arbitrators are specifically given broad discretion to make certain determinations, then the specific powers the arbitrator exercises within that grant of discretion can be said to be implied.⁸ For example, the rules may state that the tribunal may conduct arbitration in such manner as it considers appropriate.⁹ Such a broad grant of discretionary power provides the arbitrator with a great deal of flexibility to organize and carry out the various procedural steps leading up to and including the hearing and any post-hearing activity.   **21.09**

Finally, with regard to inherent powers, the ILA Report describes these as very limited powers that can only be exercised in circumstances so compelling that failure to exercise such power would risk subverting the integrity of the tribunal or the arbitral process or endangering the enforceability of the award.¹⁰ Thus, with regard to the source of the arbitrators' powers, implied powers are derived from either the necessity to take steps to accomplish express objectives, or the obligation to comply with the discretion explicitly provided to the arbitrators. The source of inherent powers, however, is less clear, and will be dealt with below in Part D.   **21.10**

(b) A useful distinction?

Although the categories discussed in the ILA Report are helpful for focusing one's thinking on the different kinds of powers exercised by arbitrators, it is not altogether clear that making a distinction between two kinds of implied powers—those derived from express provisions and those derived from discretionary grants of power—is particularly useful at a pragmatic level.¹¹ Perhaps it would be better to consider these two categories of implied powers as one, and to focus on the difference in function between implied and inherent powers.   **21.11**

Implied powers, whether implied from the text of agreement, rules, or laws, or from the broad discretion given the arbitrator, are gap fillers that move the arbitral process forward, consistent with the expectations of the parties and consistent with generally accepted arbitration practice. Inherent powers, on the other hand, come into play when some conduct   **21.12**

---

⁶ ibid.
⁷ ibid 15.
⁸ ibid. The Report notes, however, that discretionary powers 'also resonate as having an "inherent" quality, because arbitrators are widely understood to have some inherent degree of control over the efficient conduct of procedure'.
⁹ See, eg, 2010 UNCITRAL Rules, Art 17; 2012 ICC Arbitration Rules, Art 22(2); 2014 ICDR Arbitration Rules, Art 31(1).
¹⁰ See ILA Report (n 4) 14: 'There exists a limited authority to exercise truly inherent powers, which arbitrators may employ only if presented with compelling circumstances that risk undermining a tribunal's integrity or compromising the enforceability of its award.'
¹¹ The Report acknowledges that there is an overlap between the categories. See ILA Report (n 4) 15.

that is generally unexpected and unusual must be dealt with in order to prevent the arbitral process from being undermined.[12]

21.13 The ILA Report noted that in considering various situations where implied or inherent powers might be relevant to international commercial arbitration, the drafters needed to draw on analogues from the investment dispute context as well as from ICJ and *ad hoc* arbitral bodies.[13] Because of the confidentiality of international commercial arbitration, the application of inherent and implied powers in publicly available awards was a necessary proxy.[14] This raises the question of whether there are or should be differences between commercial arbitration and investor-state arbitration in terms of the proper use of inherent or implied powers.

21.14 Some commentators and courts find that inherent powers in investment arbitrations are derived in large part from a particular treaty and its interpretation,[15] from arbitration rules,[16] from public international law,[17] and from the need to fulfil international judicial functions.[18] Treaty-based arbitrations are sometimes considered to have not only a private function of regulating disputes between parties, but also a public aspect in the sense of administering justice and developing international law.[19] Commercial arbitrations, being based on contract, have a different jurisdictional foundation, and have generally functioned simply to resolve private disputes.[20] Thus, the treaty basis of investment arbitration, as opposed to the contract basis of commercial arbitration, may suggest to some a different and perhaps more substantial authority for the use of inherent arbitral powers.

21.15 However, basic issues remain the same in both forms of arbitration. The ILA Report takes the position that although there are important differences between investment arbitration

---

[12] This is a simplified and useful distinction, but not a universal one. Other, more complex concepts abound. For example, Martins Paparinskis, 'Inherent Powers of ICSID Tribunals: Broad and Rightly So' in Ian A Laird and Todd J Weiler (eds), *Investment Treaty Arbitration and International Law*, vol 5 (JurisNet, LLC 2011) 4, asserts that inherent powers may be 'either implied or expressly set out' (citations in this article are to the electronic version <http://www.ssrn.com/abstract=1876705> accessed 25 September 2015).

[13] See ILA Report (n 4) 6.

[14] ibid.

[15] See, eg, Paparinskis (n 12) 9, stating that 'exercise of inherent powers by ICSID Tribunals is put on safe legal ground by the explicit language in the constitutive instruments', specifically ICSID Convention, Art 44 and 2006 ICSID Rules, r 19.

[16] See ibid, referring to ICSID Rules, r 19.

[17] See, eg, *Hrvatska Elektroprivreda dd v Slovenia*, ICSID Case No ARB/05/24, Tribunal's Ruling Regarding the Participation of David Mildon QC in Further Stages of the Proceedings (6 May 2008), where the tribunal stated that '[i]t considers that as a judicial formation governed by public international law, the Tribunal has an inherent power to take measures to preserve the integrity of its proceedings'.

[18] See, eg, Chester Brown, 'The Inherent Powers of International Courts and Tribunals' (2005) 76 BYIL 228 ('A better view of the source of the inherent powers of international courts is their need to ensure the fulfillment of their functions').

[19] See Wachter (n 1) 67.

[20] Arguably, as international commercial arbitrations deal with more statutory-based issues such as antitrust claims, arbitrators in these cases have more responsibility to uphold the public interest and not just to decide the dispute between the parties. In her article 'Transparency in International Arbitration', Professor Catherine Rogers proposed that there is a need to monitor how well arbitrators uphold the policy interests at stake in the applicable laws. See Catherine A Rogers, 'Transparency in International Commercial Arbitration' (2006) 54 U Kan L Rev 1301, 1333. In the labour context, J Joseph Lowenberg has argued that arbitrators must become familiar with public policy and judicial standards and, if they do not do so, 'they imperil the award and the federal policy favoring arbitration for the resolution of disputes'. See J Joseph Lowenberg, 'The Neutral and Public Interests in Resolving Disputes' (1992) 13 Comp Lab L & Pol'y J 488, 503.

and commercial arbitration, those differences are not material to understanding inherent and implied powers.[21] Both forms of arbitration are consent-based, and perform an important adjudicatory function, which must be accomplished in accordance with standards of good faith, fairness, and efficiency.[22] In both kinds of arbitration, the arbitrators have obligations to safeguard the arbitral process and to ensure the proper administration of justice.[23] They should not abdicate their responsibility for determining a dispute simply because they cannot find the specific authority spelled out for them. Increasingly, arbitrators in both investment arbitrations and commercial arbitrations find that when there is silence regarding an arbitrator's power to deal with a certain issue, the implication is not that there is no authority to act, but rather that there is no prohibition on acting in ways that are called for in the circumstances.[24] There are, however, limits on such powers, which will be discussed below.

The broader interpretation of arbitrators' inherent and implied powers follows the evolution of arbitration in the direction of giving more express power to arbitrators and to arbitral institutions.[25] One result of this evolution is that because express coverage of many matters has expanded, the concepts of inherent and implied powers have become circumscribed within a smaller conceptual space and can therefore be understood in a more simple fashion. Powers that may have been viewed as inherent or implied in the past are today frequently expressed as part of the rules chosen by the parties, or are generally considered   **21.16**

---

[21] See ILA Report (n 4) 6.

[22] See Gary B Born, *International Commercial Arbitration* (2nd edn, Kluwer Law International 2014) 1253.

[23] Just as an international court such as the ICJ refers to the basis of its inherent powers as the need to safeguard its judicial functions (see, eg, Brown (n 18) 228), so, too, international tribunals must be able to call upon inherent powers when necessary to perform their adjudicatory functions. Brown notes that inherent powers for international courts might be said to derive ultimately from the consent of the states, when they formed the constitutive instruments of international courts (ibid 229). This could also be said of investor-state or state-to-state tribunals. There is also an argument that states that are party to the New York Convention have consented to inherent powers of commercial arbitrators to carry out arbitrations in a way that will render awards enforceable under the Convention. Having agreed under the Convention that awards that meet certain standards will be enforced—in essence, authorizing the arbitral process—states could be presumed to have agreed that arbitrators must have the powers to take the necessary steps that will enable parties to receive enforceable awards. But cf Wachter (n 1) 78, who argues that the Convention and the Model Law are not sources of inherent power, but simply operate as a boundary on the arbitral tribunal's inherent authority. Whether or not inherent power is ultimately derived from state consent, however, the obligation of a tribunal to properly carry out the adjudicatory function entrusted to it should suffice as a proper source of its inherent power.

[24] See *Abaclat v Argentina*, ICSID Case No ARB/07/5, Decision on Jurisdiction and Admissibility (4 August 2011), where the tribunal found that silence under the ICSID Convention concerning collective proceedings was a gap that the tribunal could fill by permitting the mass claims of approximately 60,000 claimants to proceed in arbitration. See also Wachter (n 1) 81, fn 73.

[25] For example, the UNCITRAL Model Law, in the 2006 amendments, added a substantial new Art 17 giving arbitrators extensive power to order interim measures and issue preliminary orders. The most recent ICC Rules include a new section giving the ICC Court more authority with regard to issues of joinder, multiple contracts, and consolidation. The 2014 LCIA Rules provide express power for the arbitrator to sanction counsel. The Rules include an Annex, 'General Guidelines for the Parties' Legal Representatives', setting forth specific rules of conduct for counsel in an LCIA arbitration. Moreover, LCIA Rules, Art 18.6 provides express powers for the tribunal to impose sanctions against counsel who do not comply with the Guidelines. The LCIA Arbitration Rules also provide that a tribunal may order consolidation if the parties have agreed in writing and if the LCIA Court has approved (Art 22.1(ix)). Moreover, even without the agreement of the parties, the tribunal may, with the approval of the LCIA Court, order consolidation of multiple arbitrations involving the same parties if only one tribunal has been appointed, or if all appointed tribunals are composed of the same arbitrators (Art 22.1(x)).

within the parties' expectations of what an arbitrator is allowed to do. For example, the concept of competence-competence, which provides that arbitrators can determine their own jurisdiction, was not always as widely accepted as it is today, and parties could dispute whether an arbitrator had such power.[26]

21.17 Today, however, many laws and rules expressly provide for competence-competence.[27] Even in the United States, where the FAA does not specifically provide for competence-competence, court decisions have essentially provided that if arbitral rules chosen by the parties provide for competence-competence, then arbitrators may determine their own jurisdiction.[28] Thus, by reason of parties having adopted specific rules that provide for competence-competence, or by the application of laws that provide for it, the doctrine of competence-competence no longer needs to be based on inherent or implied powers of the arbitrators.

21.18 Moreover, if implied powers are considered to be those that are needed to move the arbitration forward in a reasonable and expected manner, they are unlikely to cause a risk of unenforceable awards. Part C below will consider the kinds of powers that should be considered implied, and should not cause arbitrators concern in exercising them, even though they are not completely spelled out in the arbitration agreement or in the pertinent rules and law.

C. Implied Powers

(a) Scope

21.19 If the concept of implied powers is that they follow from textual provisions, or from broad discretionary powers, and that they are the usual, expected powers of an arbitrator based on laws, rules, and arbitration practice, what kinds of powers fall within this term? First of all, powers relating to the conduct of the arbitral proceedings would be included. The arbitrators' powers to make necessary determinations with regard to specific aspects of the proceedings may not be precisely stated in the applicable laws and rules. Matters typically determined by the tribunal, for example, include the schedule for exchanging documents or memorials, the question of bifurcating the proceedings, the amount of time each side will have at the hearing, the number of witnesses, whether any depositions will be permitted, whether a change of venue will be permitted, and whether certain evidence will be admitted or excluded.[29]

21.20 Second, powers relating to various kinds of arbitral decision-making can also be considered implied powers. For example, even without specifically stated powers, a tribunal is generally considered to have the authority to determine the applicable law, if it has not been chosen

---

[26] See ILA Report (n 4) 6.
[27] See UNCITRAL Rules, Art 23; ICDR Rules, Art 19; LCIA Rules, Art 23.1.
[28] See, eg, *Republic of Ecuador v Chevron Corp*, 638 F 3d 384, 393–4 (2d Cir 2011), where the court held that because the parties had agreed to the UNCITRAL Rules, the arbitrators would have the power to rule on their jurisdiction.
[29] Some of these powers may be expressly provided for in the arbitration rules. For example, the ICDR Arbitration Rules provide in Art 20(2) that: 'The tribunal may in its discretion direct the order of proof, bifurcate proceedings, exclude cumulative or irrelevant testimony or other evidence, and direct the parties to focus their presentations on issues the decision of which could dispose of all or part of the case'.

by the parties.[30] Moreover, in determining its jurisdiction, a tribunal may need to decide if certain issues are irrelevant or moot, or it may need to award declaratory or injunctive relief, or even in some instances to summarily dismiss a case.[31]

(b) Limitations

These kinds of implied powers should remain well within the proper scope of implied authority of the arbitrator. There are, of course, limitations on the arbitrator's implied powers. While implied powers are broad and give the arbitrator a great deal of flexibility, he should exercise those powers in consultation with the parties and with a goal of meeting overall objectives of fairness and expediency. In addition, whatever power the arbitrator exercises must not contradict any mandatory limitation provided by the arbitration agreement or the law or rules.[32] **21.21**

Moreover, the arbitrator should not exercise powers in a way that would create reasons for non-enforcement under the New York Convention.[33] Assuming the arbitrator does not overstep these boundaries, there should be little danger of the exercise of such powers resulting in an unenforceable award. In general, courts are quite deferential to arbitral decisions, and a court is unlikely to second-guess an arbitrator who has largely followed accepted arbitration practice. It is when the actions of the arbitrator challenge the notions of usual and normal practice that the risk of unenforceability rises. Thus, when calling upon inherent powers in situations that go beyond what parties might typically expect, an arbitrator must tread more cautiously. **21.22**

D. Inherent Powers

Although some definitions of inherent powers may appear complex and unsettled, the ILA Report puts forward a comprehensible framework for the concept. It asserts that if a power **21.23**

---

[30] Some arbitration rules expressly provide this power. See, eg, ICC Rules, Art 21(1), 2010 SCC Rules, Art 22(1); LCIA Rules, Art 22.3.

[31] See ILA Report (n 4) 9. The ILA Report refers to an example of a case of summary dismissal where the tribunal described the powers it was exercising as inherent rather than implied powers. *Rio Grande Irrigation and Land Co Ltd (Great Britain) v United States*, Award of the United States–United Kingdom Mixed Claims Commission (28 November 1923) reprinted in 1990 (IV) RIAA 131. Because implied powers can be ascribed to the steps an arbitrator must normally carry out for the arbitration to move forward (or not) in a fair and expeditious way, it is not unreasonable to consider a summary dismissal as based on powers implied from the tribunal's obligation to determine its own jurisdiction to hear the claim. If, on the other hand, the circumstances are highly unusual, and involve situations where an arbitrator might not normally tread, the power called upon might be considered inherent. In this 1923 case, in referring to its power as inherent and viewing the issue as jurisdictional, the tribunal stated: 'Whatever the proper construction of the instruments controlling the Tribunal or of the rules of procedure, there is inherent in this and every legal Tribunal a power, and indeed a duty, to entertain, and, in proper cases, to raise for themselves, preliminary points going to their jurisdiction to entertain the claim.' However, a tribunal today, if it viewed the issue as jurisdictional, would probably be more likely to consider this power implied, and derived from its express power to determine its own jurisdiction to hear the claim.

[32] Although parties normally can, by agreement, derogate from arbitration rules, there are some rules that an arbitral institution may consider non-derogable, particularly with regard to meeting its administrative requirements.

[33] See New York Convention, Art V, which lists the grounds for non-enforcement. These include, *inter alia*: that the party was unable to present his case; that the award deals with matters beyond the scope of the arbitration agreement; and that recognition and enforcement would be against the public policy of the enforcing state.

derives from the nature and function of a tribunal as constituted, the power should properly be labelled inherent to the tribunal.[34] This is contrasted with an implied power, which derives from a particular rule or provision of the parties' agreement.[35] With the Report's framework in mind, one should focus on the nature and function of the tribunal which will give rise to such an inherent power.

(a) Fulfilling its adjudicatory function

21.24 While various commentators have identified different sources for inherent powers,[36] in essence, all sources eventually support the very basic requirement that a tribunal must be able to fulfil its adjudicatory function. A tribunal is supposed to settle disputes between the parties in a manner that is fair and just.[37] It must have the power to take steps necessary to carry out its mandate in an equitable and efficient manner. As the role of arbitration in international dispute settlement has grown and expanded, courts have increasingly supported and deferred to arbitral decision-making. In the process, arbitration has assumed many of the same functions as a court system, and concomitantly has assumed many of the same duties and obligations. Like a court, an arbitral tribunal must ensure that the parties are treated fairly, that the proceedings are conducted efficiently and effectively, and that it can at all times properly discharge its functions. Thus, in functioning as an adjudicatory body, a tribunal has powers as well as responsibilities, in order to meet its obligation to safeguard the credibility and integrity of the adjudicatory process.[38]

21.25 The topic of inherent powers of arbitrators has in recent times moved to the forefront of many discussions, in part because of the growing need for such powers. Arbitration has evolved from an elite group of arbitrators whose judgment, neutrality, and expertise were highly respected and who resolved disputes quite civilly with a minimum of acrimony between the parties,[39] to a modern, more diverse, and more global process, where arbitrators must deal with a far more contentious practice.[40] The change is reflected in the recent concerns about guerilla tactics of arbitration counsel,[41] and the resulting need for arbitrators to

---

[34] See ILA Report (n 4) 14.

[35] ibid. See also Paparinskis (n 12) 4, who similarly asserts that *inherent* 'relates to the nature of the powers', while *implied* 'explains the manner of their exposition in the particular instrument'.

[36] See Brown (n 18) 223. Brown asserts that four possible sources of inherent powers can be discerned in the jurisprudence of international courts and the writings of publicists: the concept of general principles of law, the doctrine of implied powers, the identity of international courts as judicial bodies, and a functional justification.

[37] ibid. Brown states that international adjudication has a public function that can help in the 'creation of norms which can generate obedience among members of the community being regulated by that system of norms'. ibid 230.

[38] See ILA Report (n 4) 13, citing the dissent in *ConocoPhillips Petrozuata BV v Bolivarian Republic of Venezuela*, ICSID Case No ARB/07/30, Decision on Respondent's Request for Reconsideration (10 March 2014).

[39] See Yves Dezalay and Bryant G Garth, *Dealing in Virtue* (University of Chicago Press 1996) 8, 34–6.

[40] See Gunther Horvath, 'Guerrilla Tactics in Arbitration, an Ethical Battle: Is There Need for a Universal Code of Ethics?' in Nikolaus Pitkowitz and others (eds), *Austrian Yearbook on International Arbitration* (Manz'sche Verlags- und Universitätsbuchhandlung 2011), 297–8 ('In its youth, international arbitration was run by a small group of professionals. Ethical conflicts were rare because of the importance of maintaining one's reputation, and ethical codes were unnecessary as practitioners understood that their peers expected strict professionalism').

[41] ibid. See also Edna Sussman and Solomon Ebere, 'All's Fair in Love and War—Or Is It? Reflections on Ethical Standards for Counsel in International Arbitration' (2011) 22 Am Rev Int'l Arb 611; Stephan Wilske, 'Arbitration Guerrillas at the Gate: Preserving the Civility of Arbitration Proceedings When the Going Gets

have a firm hand and sufficient power to control egregious conduct that thwarts a reasonable dispute resolution process.[42]

(b) Imposing sanctions

Arbitrators today need the power to impose sanctions and to require parties to honour their obligation to act in good faith.[43] While some institutional rules grant arbitrators express powers to impose a range of sanctions,[44] most say little that is specific. Moreover, arbitrators lack the coercive powers of a court, such as being able to put someone in jail for persistent misconduct.[45] Nonetheless, the inherent powers of the tribunal to preserve the integrity of the process should be useful in dealing with conduct of counsel that is considered beyond the pale. 21.26

There are a number of different kinds of situations in which arbitrators have called upon their inherent powers, but because of limited space, this chapter can only mention a few. One area is the problem of witness intimidation, which is not dealt with expressly in governing arbitration laws and rules.[46] Although witness intimidation may be hard to prove, a tribunal convinced that it may occur or is occurring should be able to bring its powers to bear to stop such conduct. There are a number of sanctions that a tribunal could impose. 21.27

For example, it could grant interim measures of protection or cease and desist orders.[47] If its orders are not complied with, it could draw adverse inferences, or refuse to admit evidence obtained through intimidation, or impose costs against the offending party.[48] If witnesses 21.28

(Extremely) Tough' in Nikolaus Pitkowitz and others (eds), *Austrian Yearbook on International Arbitration* (Manz'sche Verlags- und Universitätsbuchhandlung 2011).

[42] For a discussion, see Lord Hacking and Sophia Berry, 'Ethics in Arbitration: Party and Arbitral Misconduct' in Julio César Betancourt (ed), *Defining Issues in International Arbitration: Celebrating 100 Years of the Chartered Institute of Arbitrators* (OUP 2016) ch 13.

[43] See Born (n 22) 1253 ('The most fundamental objective and effect of an international arbitration agreement is to obligate the parties to participate cooperatively and in good faith in the resolution of their disputes by arbitration pursuant to that agreement ... Simply put, an agreement to arbitrate necessarily entails a commitment to cooperate in good faith in the arbitral process, with both the arbitral tribunal and other parties to the arbitration, in resolving the parties' disputes in a fair, objective and efficient manner'). See also Anne Peters, 'International Dispute Settlement: A Network of Cooperational Duties' (2003) 14 EJIL 1–34 ('While the dispute itself implies disagreement and non-cooperation, some kind of cooperation, in procedure or in substance, between the parties is needed for its resolution. Without cooperation, no settlement. Therefore a general, customary law-based duty of cooperation with a view to a settlement is inherent in the obligation to settle disputes peacefully'); V V Veeder, 'The Lawyer's Duty to Arbitrate in Good Faith' (2002) 18(4) Arb Int'l 431, 439.

[44] See, eg, the 2014 ICDR Rules, Art 20(6) ('The arbitral tribunal may allocate costs, draw adverse inferences, and take such additional steps as are necessary to protect the efficiency and integrity of the arbitration'); JAMS Rules, r 29 ('... [S]anctions may include, but are not limited to, assessment of Arbitration fees and Arbitrator compensation and expenses; assessment of any other costs occasioned by the actionable conduct, including reasonable attorneys' fees; exclusion of certain evidence; drawing adverse inferences; or, in extreme cases, determining an issue or issues submitted to Arbitration adversely to the Party that has failed to comply').

[45] Abba Kolo suggests that tribunals should have the inherent power to impose fines for misconduct. See Abba Kolo, 'Witness Intimidation, Tampering and Other Related Abuses of Process in Investment Arbitration: Possible Remedies Available to the Arbitral Tribunal' (2010) 26 Arb Int'l 68. The broad description of possible sanctions in the 2014 LCIA Rules, Art 18.6, also appears to permit the imposition of fines.

[46] ibid 65–6. See also Wilske (n 41) 59–60 (citing *Kensington Int'l Ltd v Republic of Congo*, Slip Copy, 2007 WL 2456993 (SDNY 24 August 2007)).

[47] A number of institutional rules provide expressly for such measures, but in the absence of such rules, the tribunal should be able to draw on its inherent adjudicatory authority. See Kolo (n 45) 65–6.

[48] ibid 65.

(or counsel or the arbitrators themselves) are being intimidated locally, the tribunal may also be able to move the venue to another jurisdiction.[49]

21.29 Another area where a tribunal may need to call upon inherent powers is when it perceives that fraud or corruption are tainting the arbitral process. It is conceivable that if the tribunal believed that the arbitration process was being used as a means of laundering money or engaging in some form of fraud or corruption, it would have the inherent power to conduct an investigation.[50] This power would come not only from its basic responsibilities to ensure that the proceedings were conducted in good faith, and that the adjudicatory function was properly discharged in a way that did not undermine the integrity of the process, but also from its duty to render an enforceable award. Under the New York Convention, an award tainted by fraud or corruption would likely be unenforceable on the ground of violating public policy.[51]

(c) **Disqualifying counsel**

21.30 Tribunals have also been called upon to disqualify counsel, a task that has traditionally been viewed as only possible by a court.[52] In *Hrvatska Elektroprivreda dd v Slovenia*,[53] a tribunal invoked its inherent powers to preserve the integrity of its proceedings to disqualify a British QC who shared chambers with the tribunal's President, and who was brought in as counsel right before the hearings began.

21.31 However, not all tribunals are willing to rely on inherent powers to disqualify counsel, or at least not without very compelling circumstances. In *Rompetrol Group NV v Romania*,[54] the tribunal denied a request to disqualify a newly added counsel for the claimant who, a year earlier, had been employed in the same law firm as the arbitrator appointed by the claimant. The tribunal referred to the *Hvratska* tribunal as having exercised powers that should only be exercised in extraordinary circumstances, 'these being circumstances which genuinely touch on the integrity of the arbitral process as assessed by the Tribunal itself'.[55]

21.32 The *Rompetrol* decision may be a touchstone for how tribunals will determine whether to call upon inherent powers to make a decision where there is no express authority and few examples of similar applications. The tribunal indicated a reluctance to use inherent powers

---

[49] See, eg, Matthias Scherer, 'The Place of the "Seat of Arbitration" (Possibility and/or Sometimes Necessity of its Transfer?): Some Remarks on the Award in ICC Arbitration No 10.623' (2003) 21(1) ASA Bull 112. See also ILA Report (n 4) 18.

[50] See ILA Report (n 4) 18. See also Christian Albanesi and Emmanuel Jolivet, 'Dealing with Corruption in Arbitration: A Review of ICC Experience' (2013) ICC Int'l Ct Arb Bull 27, 34–5 ('If an arbitral tribunal suspects the existence of corrupt practices in the underlying transaction, it should make the necessary enquiries, while ensuring that the parties are given an opportunity to comment and respond on the matter').

[51] See New York Convention, Art V(2)(b).

[52] US courts, including state and federal courts, have held that a court and not an arbitral tribunal is the proper forum to address attorney disqualification. See *Northwestern Nat'l Ins Co v Insco, Ltd*, 2011 WL 4552997 (SDNY 2011); *Bidermann Industries Licensing, Inc v Avmar NV*, 570 NYS 2d 33 (1st Dept 1991).

[53] *Hrvatska Elektorprivreda dd v Slovenia* (n 17).

[54] ICSID Case No ARB/06/3, Decision of the Tribunal on the Participation of a Counsel (14 January 2010).

[55] ibid [15]. The *Rompetrol* tribunal also noted that the late arrival in the proceedings of the counsel in *Hvratska*, with no prior disclosure, influenced the decision, such that 'the *Hvratska* Decision might better be seen as an *ad hoc* sanction for the failure to make proper disclosure in good time than as a holding of more general scope'. ibid [25].

in a novel way, unless there were compelling circumstances, as well as a risk that inaction might undermine the arbitration process.[56]

However, some new arbitration rules may ease the pressure on arbitrators with regard to their powers to deal with newly added counsel in situations like in *Hvratska* and *Rompetrol*. Article 18 of the 2014 LCIA Rules provides that once the tribunal has been formed, any intended change or addition by a party to its legal representatives is subject to the approval of the arbitral tribunal, which may withhold approval if the change could 'compromise the composition of the Arbitral Tribunal or the finality of any award'.[57]

21.33

(d) Limitations of power

In the absence of such express rules, tribunals will continue to struggle with the proper exercise of their inherent powers. Because tribunals generally are concerned about their duty to try to render an enforceable award, they are likely to engage in self-restraint, which is a form of limitation of their power. Another limitation is that the exercise of inherent power must be necessary to the proper functioning of the arbitral process,[58] and must not impinge upon fairness to the parties, or the parties' ability to present their case.[59] A final limitation is that the tribunal must not claim as an inherent power anything that contradicts a stated prohibition in the pertinent agreement or rules.[60]

21.34

However, if parties want to place a limitation on the power of the arbitrator, they must make such limitation very clear. In *ReliaStar v EMC National Life Co*,[61] the parties had included a provision in their arbitration clause that limited the arbitrators' ability to allocate costs. The clause provided that each party would pay its own costs and fees. Nonetheless, the arbitrators awarded costs and fees against the respondent, on the grounds that the respondent had acted in bad faith. The Second Circuit Court of Appeals in New York affirmed the award.[62] The court reasoned that the arbitrators' power was not limited by the arbitration clause because when the parties provided in the clause that each would pay its own costs and fees, there was a presumption that both parties would act in good faith. Because one party did not act in good faith, the tribunal, according to the court, had inherent authority to sanction that party by an award of attorney's fees.[63]

21.35

The court stated further that if the parties had meant that they would each pay their own costs and fees even if the other party acted in bad faith, they could have said that in the agreement,[64] but they did not. Thus, this case demonstrates that if parties want to put a

21.36

---

[56] ibid [16] and [22].
[57] See LCIA Arbitration Rules, Arts 18.3 and 18.4.
[58] See Brown (n 18) 78–81. See also Paola Gaeta, 'Inherent Powers of International Courts and Tribunals' in Lal Chand Vohrah and others (eds), *Man's Inhumanity to Man: Essays on International Law in Honour of Antonio Cassese* (Martinus Nijhoff 2003) 365–8.
[59] See New York Convention, Art V(1)(b).
[60] See *Aguas Argentina SA v The Argentine Republic*, ICSID Case No ARB/03/19, Amicus Curiae Order (12 February 2007), 6 ('Although the Tribunal ... does have certain inherent powers with respect to arbitral procedure, it has no authority to exercise such power in opposition to a clear directive in the Arbitration Rules').
[61] 564 F 3rd 81 (2d Cir 2009).
[62] ibid.
[63] ibid 86.
[64] ibid 89 ('As sophisticated commercial entities, the parties were certainly capable of stating clearly any intent to exclude attorney's and arbitrator's fees from the broad range of sanctions generally available to arbitrators upon an identification of bad faith').

restriction on arbitrators' power, they need to do so quite clearly. With regard to these particular circumstances, however, parties will probably not race to put a provision limiting sanctions based on bad faith in their arbitration agreements. It is hardly in one party's interest to give the other party a licence to act in bad faith with impunity as to costs.

21.37 These are only a few of the kinds of situations where arbitrators have had to determine whether they had inherent powers to act. It is likely that a number of factors will converge in the future to make it more common that arbitrators will be called upon to determine the scope of powers they can assert. The increasing participation in the arbitral process by parties from many different legal cultures, the unfortunate use of guerilla tactics, and the amount of corruption that infects global business all put stresses on a tribunal's ability to render a fair, efficient, and untainted final award. There is thus a need to have a good understanding within the arbitral community of when it is proper for an arbitral tribunal to call upon its inherent powers.

E. Conclusion

21.38 Arbitrators need to be able to exercise their powers in novel situations when circumstances risk endangering the integrity of the process or the enforcement of the award. They are not likely to use such powers without a careful balancing of their duties and obligations against the risk that if they are considered to have exceeded their powers, the award may not be enforced. When an unexpected or unusual situation arises, it may matter which label—'implied power' or 'inherent power'—is used.

21.39 As noted earlier, some commentators use the terms interchangeably or lump them together.[65] And in many cases, it will not be easy to determine in which specific category a power may be said to belong. There may well be substantial overlap. However, for a tribunal that does not want an award to be refused enforcement, and for counsel resisting the challenge to enforcement of an award for an arbitrator's excess of authority, it may be important to give some thought to framing the kind of power that is used.

21.40 From a pragmatic and strategic point of view, it would probably be worthwhile, particularly if the source of the power is not entirely clear, to start by trying to see if the power can be asserted as an implied power. Thus, if the action taken by the arbitrator can somehow be tied to or related to an express provision in the text of the arbitration agreement or the applicable rules or the *lex arbitri*, then it may make the expression of that power seem less controversial and less subject to challenge.

21.41 However, if the ties are weak, or perhaps even if they are not, it would make sense to point out alternatively, if there appears to be a basis for it, that the powers exercised by the arbitrator are inherent to the adjudicatory function, such that if not exercised, the arbitration process itself will be tainted, and the award at risk. Arbitrators should have the courage and should acknowledge the power to stand up against corruption, guerilla tactics, and other attempts to improperly delay or impede the arbitration. In today's evolving arbitration world, they may find it helpful that broader interpretations are being given to their powers. The ILA Report noted in its Introduction that:

---

[65] See, eg, Wachter (n 1).

Arbitrators who creatively employ inherent or implied powers to achieve efficient and successful outcomes may take some comfort from the fact that actions previously perceived as novel have now become integral to the fabric of international commercial arbitration, and have even been given express incorporation into arbitral rules.[66]

Implied and inherent powers, properly exercised, can help ensure that the arbitral process fulfils its promise of providing a fair, ethical, and reasonable way to resolve disputes. **21.42**

---

[66] See ILA Report (n 4) 6.

22

GOOD (AND BAD) INITIATIVES OF ARBITRATORS
Where to Draw the Line between Activism and Passivity?

Sébastien Besson

A. Introduction

22.01 Those acting as counsel and as arbitrator may have noted that the role they play has an impact on their mindset. The counsel tends to be factually oriented and will inevitably be and become influenced by the story of the facts as partly experienced and partly created by his client. The arbitrator tends to be more legally oriented. He will naturally place more focus on the terms of the contract and of the law, and will not integrate the facts as much as the counsel.

22.02 These different perspectives may lead to misunderstandings. At virtually every hearing, the arbitral tribunal will speak about the counsel and say 'Why did they not develop that point?', and when receiving the award, the counsel will most often ask 'Why did the arbitral tribunal not consider more carefully that argument?'

22.03 A possible way of limiting such misunderstandings is to foster interactions between the arbitral tribunal and the parties' counsel. Such interactions imply that arbitrators do not remain passive, but take initiatives. Initiatives of arbitrators may, however, have drawbacks. They may notably lead to additional costs and extra procedural activities.

22.04 The purpose of this chapter is to explore the power of arbitrators to take initiatives. Does the arbitral tribunal have a power to take initiatives? If so, when is it appropriate to have a proactive attitude?

22.05 Any initiative may result in new elements—of facts or of law—being added to the file. As a rule, the parties' counsel should hence be given an opportunity to comment on the result of the arbitrators' initiatives. The present chapter will not, however, address this aspect of the arbitrators' initiatives. It will not examine to what extent the parties must be heard and must be provided with an opportunity to comment on the new issues or evidence brought into the debate as a result of arbitrators' initiatives. It will assume that the parties' right to be heard is respected and that the initiatives comply with the notion of due process.

B. Legal Basis and Sources of the Arbitrators' Power to Take Initiatives

(a) Initiatives to establish the facts and to collect evidence

As Landolt has observed, one seeks 'in vain' a 'binding norm of universal application in international arbitration expressly providing that arbitrators have the power to take initiatives to obtain evidence of fact and law'; however, it is 'in fact almost universally the case' that 'arbitrators do have such powers'.[1]

22.06

The arbitrators' power to take initiatives is rarely addressed in arbitration legislation. Interestingly, the English Arbitration Act 1996 is one of the rare arbitration laws expressly and specifically empowering the arbitrators to 'take initiatives'. Under the heading 'Procedural and Evidential Matters', section 34(2)(g) of the Act empowers the arbitrators to determine 'whether and to what extent the tribunal should itself take the initiative in ascertaining the facts and the law'.

22.07

According to Merkin and Flannery, this provision permits the arbitrators to 'dispense with the adversarial process and adopt instead an inquisitorial approach whereby the initiative is taken by the arbitrators', which was not permissible under the previous Act without the agreement of the parties.[2]

22.08

The DAC report accompanying the Arbitration Bill stressed that, during the consultation process, 'some anxiety was expressed' at the 'power to act inquisitorially ... on grounds that arbitrators are unused to such powers and might, albeit in good faith, abuse them'.[3] However, the DAC was supportive of such power and was confident that it would be used within the frame of section 33 of the Act.[4] The DAC added that 'in suitable cases an inquisitorial approach to all or some of the matters involved may well be the best way of proceeding' provided that the arbitrators 'give all parties a reasonable opportunity' of commenting on the points covered by the arbitrators' initiative.[5]

22.09

In France, scholars consider that the arbitrators' power to take initiatives finds a statutory basis in Article 1467 of the French CPC, which is applicable in international arbitration by virtue of Article 1506(3).[6] This provision would in particular empower the arbitrators to

22.10

---

[1] See Phillip Landolt, 'Arbitrators' Initiatives to Obtain Factual and Legal Evidence' (2012) Arb Int'l 180.
[2] Robert Merkin and Louis Flannery, *Arbitration Act 1996* (4th edn, Informa Law 2008) 89.
[3] DAC Report, para 171.
[4] English Arbitration Act 1996, s 33(1) reads as follows:

   (1) The tribunal shall—
      (a) act fairly and impartially as between the parties, giving each party a reasonable opportunity of putting his case and dealing with that of his opponent, and
      (b) adopt procedures suitable to the circumstances of the particular case, avoiding unnecessary delay or expense, so as to provide a fair means for the resolution of the matters falling to be determined.

[5] DAC Report, para 172.
[6] French CPC, Art 1467 reads as follows:

   The arbitral tribunal shall proceed with the necessary steps for the taking of evidence unless the parties authorise the tribunal to assign such task to one of its members.
   The arbitral tribunal may hear any person. Such hearing shall take place without the taking of oath.
   If a party is in possession of an item of evidence, the arbitral tribunal may order that party to submit such evidence according to the terms and conditions the tribunal decides and, as need be, under penalty.

take initiatives to establish the facts and obtain evidence. As Seraglini and Ortscheidt put it: '*Parce qu'il [l'arbitre] ne doit pas seulement trancher un différend, mais aussi faire oeuvre de justice, il dispose de pouvoirs d'initiative qui lui permettent d'introduire dans le débat des faits que les parties n'auraient pas spécialement invoqués ou allégués*' ('Because he [the arbitrator] does not only have to resolve a dispute, but also to render justice, he has the powers to take initiatives allowing him to introduce into the debate facts that the parties have not specifically raised or alleged').[7]

22.11 This statutory basis is, however, less clear than section 34(2)(g) of the English Arbitration Act 1996. It is worth stressing that Article 10 of the French CPC, which expressly provides that the judge in France has the power to order on his own motion all means of evidence legally admissible, is not applicable in international arbitration, but only in domestic arbitration in France.[8]

22.12 Section 1042(4) of the German ZPO provides that the arbitral tribunal shall, failing an agreement between the parties, conduct the arbitration 'in such manner as it considers appropriate' and that it is 'empowered to determine the admissibility of taking of evidence, take evidence and assess freely such evidence'.[9]

22.13 According to German scholars, the arbitrators' power to take initiatives to obtain evidence and to establish the facts is not controversial and is merely confirmed by this provision. In their commentary, Sachs and Lörcher state that the rights of arbitrators to take evidence are 'self-evident' and that they are 'nevertheless expressly stated in the new German arbitration law in order to emphasise for common law and other users not familiar with German procedural law that the arbitral tribunal, unless otherwise agreed by the parties, has the discretion to play an active role in the taking of evidence and to actively manage the case'. They add that the wording would make clear that 'the arbitral tribunal may also determine the specific issues on which it wants to hear evidence'.[10]

22.14 Although not referring specifically to section 1042(4) of the German ZPO, Rützel, Wegen, and Wilske agree with the existence of the arbitrators' power to take initiatives to establish the facts. They state that German arbitration law leaves it 'to the arbitral tribunal to decide on how it approaches fact-finding and the gathering of evidence if there is no specific agreement by the parties'.[11] They further state that the arbitral tribunal 'is not limited by the submissions and offers to produce evidence by the parties' as it is allowed 'to establish the facts of the case by all appropriate means'.[12]

---

[7] Christophe Seraglini and Jérôme Ortscheidt, *Droit de l'arbitrage interne et international* (LGDJ 2013) 335, para 375.

[8] Art 10 of the French CPC is applicable in domestic arbitration by virtue of the reference made in the French CPC, Art 1464(2), to the general principles of the trial (*principes directeurs du procès*), but Art 1464(2) is not applicable in international arbitration (see Art 1506).

[9] Translation from Stefan Rützel and others, *Commercial Dispute Resolution in Germany: Litigation, Arbitration, Mediation* (CH Beck 2005) 326.

[10] Klaus Sachs and Torsten Lörcher, 'Commentary to § 1042 ZPO' in Karl-Heinz Böckstiegel and others (eds), *Arbitration in Germany: The Model Law in Practice* (Kluwer Law International 2007) 290–1, para 34; and s 1042 ZPO; I fail to see how the 'wording' of s 1042(4) ZPO would make clear that the arbitral tribunal has specifically the power to determine 'the specific issues on which it wants to hear evidence', but this debate is without interest, as such power is undisputed in Germany.

[11] Rützel and others (n 9) 132.

[12] ibid 133.

22.15 These authors expressly confirm that German arbitration law allows both an adversarial system and a more inquisitorial system, stressing that the arbitral tribunal 'can either leave it up to the parties to collect the necessary evidence and present it to the arbitral tribunal, or it can actively manage the proceedings by deciding on issues of evidence from the beginning, and only ordering the taking of relevant and material evidence', adding that in arbitration proceedings 'with mainly German participants, the second procedure will usually prevail'.[13]

22.16 Article 184(1) of the Swiss PIL Act provides that 'the arbitral tribunal shall itself take the evidence'. In my opinion, such provision is not relevant and merely provides that the taking of evidence shall be under the control of the arbitral tribunal and should in principle not be delegated to a third party (which does not, of course, prevent the appointment of experts for clarifying certain issues).[14]

22.17 However, it is not controversial among Swiss scholars that the arbitrators have the powers to take initiatives to establish the facts and to obtain evidence.[15] Veit has expressed the view that the arbitral tribunal is 'not required—but permitted—to take evidence on its own which has not been offered by the parties'.[16] Berger and Kellerhals stress that it is 'the arbitral procedure'—to be determined by the arbitral tribunal in the absence of an agreement between the parties—that determines 'whether the presentation and the taking of evidence shall follow the "adversarial" system of common law, or instead the continental European-style "inquisitorial" system' and that 'the arbitral tribunal may also want to consider that the consequences of the principle [that it is primarily the task of the parties to present their case] are mitigated in Swiss legal tradition by more or less far-reaching obligation of the judge to examine the facts of the case on his own initiative'.[17]

22.18 Schneider and Scherer mention a decision of the Swiss Federal Tribunal recognizing the applicability of the court's duty to ask for clarifications (*Fragepflicht*) in international arbitration,[18] but they rightly consider that the application of such principle is 'doubtful'.[19]

22.19 The arbitrators' power to take initiatives to establish the facts or to obtain factual evidence on their own motion has been recognized in other countries despite the absence of an express basis in the arbitration legislation.[20]

22.20 I have in fact found only one exception worth being mentioned. In his commentary on international arbitration in Sweden, Hobér states that, under the Swedish Arbitration Act (SAA), the 'initiative with respect to evidence is exclusively in the hands of the parties'.[21] He bases this statement on section 25(1) of the SAA, which provides that 'the parties shall

---

[13] ibid.
[14] Jean-François Poudret and Sébastien Besson, *Comparative Law of International Arbitration* (2nd edn, Sweet & Maxwell 2007) para 642; Bernhard Berger and Franz Kellerhals, *International and Domestic Arbitration in Switzerland* (2nd edn, Sweet & Maxwell 2010) para 1197.
[15] Marc D Veit, 'Commentary on Chapter 12 PILS, Article 184' in Manuel Arroyo (ed), *Arbitration in Switzerland: The Practitioner's Guide* (Kluwer Law International 2013) 128; Michael E Schneider and Maxi Scherer, 'Commentary on Article 184 SPIL' in Heinreich Honsell and others (eds), *Basler Kommentar* (3rd edn, Internationales Privatrecht 2013) 1876, para 10; Berger and Kellerhals (n 14) 340, para 1198.
[16] ibid, Veit, 128.
[17] Berger and Kellerhals (n 14) 340, para 1198 and 292–3, para 1017.
[18] Decision of the Swiss Federal Tribunal (18 August 1992) ATF 118 II 359, para 5b (unpublished).
[19] Schneider and Scherer (n 15) 1844, para 55.
[20] Landolt (n 1) 180.
[21] Kaj Hobér, *International Commercial Arbitration in Sweden* (OUP 2011) 220, para 6.93.

supply the evidence', and on the explanatory notes of the government on the Arbitration Bill.[22] However, I respectfully doubt that the passage referenced by Hobér can be given such a categorical interpretation, and I would hesitate to follow the learned author in his proposition that, in Sweden, evidence 'is exclusively in the hands of the parties'.[23]

22.21 The arbitrators' power to establish the facts and to collect evidence on their own motion may also find basis in the arbitration rules of some institutions.

22.22 Mirroring section 34(2)(g) of the English Arbitration Act 1996, Article 22.1(iii) of the LCIA Rules provides that the arbitral tribunal has the power 'to conduct such enquiries as may appear to the Arbitral Tribunal to be necessary or expedient, including whether and to what extent the Arbitral Tribunal should itself take the initiative in identifying relevant issues and ascertaining relevant facts and the law(s) or rules of law applicable to the Arbitration Agreement, the arbitration and the merits of the parties' dispute'. Article 22.1(v) further empowers the arbitral tribunal 'to order any party to produce to the Arbitral Tribunal and to other parties documents or copies of documents in their possession, custody or power which the Arbitral Tribunal decides to be relevant'. The very same provisions were already contained in the 1998 version of the LCIA Rules.

22.23 Under the heading 'Establishing the Facts of the Case', Article 25 of the ICC Arbitration Rules confers broad powers on arbitrators in ICC arbitrations. Article 25(1) of the ICC Rules provides that the arbitral tribunal shall 'proceed within as short a time as possible to establish the facts of the case by all appropriate means'. Article 25(2) of the ICC Rules empowers the arbitrators to decide to hear the parties on their own motion. More importantly, Article 25(5) of the Rules provides that: 'At any time during the proceedings, the arbitral tribunal may summon any party to provide additional evidence.' The same powers were already contained in the 1998 ICC Rules (Article 20).

22.24 In their commentary on the Rules, Fry, Greenberg, and Mazza note that the exercise of the discretion, in practice, will 'depend on the manner in which the case is conducted generally and will be strongly influenced by the parties' and individual arbitrators' preferences'.[24]

22.25 Other commentators have expressed different views as to the meaning and impact of Article 25—previously Article 20—of the ICC Rules. Bühler and Jarvin consider that Article 20 'reflects the inquisitorial element of the civil law tradition', that it is 'the arbitrator's—not the parties'—responsibility to establish the facts' and that a 'leading idea is that the arbitrator shall manage the case, take initiatives, be active'.[25]

---

[22] ibid 220, fn 66.
[23] See, in particular, s 8.7 of the government's Bill concerning procedural management stating, ie, that arbitrators—in the same way as judges—should take action in order to make the parties clarify their claims and the circumstances invoked in support of such claims, that the arbitrators should endeavour to clarify the evidence invoked by the parties, and that, if the arbitrators consider that a rule of law not raised by the parties may be relevant, they should draw the parties' attention to such rule (Prop 1998/99:35) 120ff <http://www.riksdagen.se> accessed 25 September 2015.
[24] Jason Fry, Simon Greenberg, and Francesca Mazza, *The Secretariat's Guide to ICC Arbitration* (ICC Publication No 729E, 2012) 268, para 3.942.
[25] Michael W Bühler and Sigvard Jarvin, 'Commentary on Article 20 ICC Rules' in Frank-Bernd Weigand (ed), *Practitioner's Handbook on International Commercial Arbitration* (OUP 2009) 1290–1, para 15.779.

22.26 However, in the very next paragraph of their commentary, they add that establishing the facts of the case 'depends basically on the evidence provided by the parties and their counsel', and that an arbitral tribunal 'will rarely take the initiative to collect and review evidence from sources other than the parties, other than at the request of a party or through a tribunal-appointed expert'.[26] I see a possible contradiction between these two positions and, in any event, an evolution in the way they perceive the inquisitorial 'bias' of ICC Rules.[27]

22.27 Craig, Park, and Paulsson have also noted that the ICC Rules 'suggest approval of the continental civil law approach under which judges have a duty to "instruct" the case and actively investigate the facts'.[28]

22.28 Other commentators have taken different views. In particular, Derains and Schwartz have, in my opinion, rightly, stressed that the rules do not manifest any 'procedural bias', that they are intended 'for universal use', and that many ICC arbitrations 'have been conducted over the years by common law lawyers in the manner to which they are accustomed'.[29] These authors stress, however, that Article 25(1)—formerly Article 20(1)—of the ICC Arbitration Rules assumes 'that the Arbitral Tribunal will play a more active role in managing and conducting the proceedings than might be the custom in certain common law jurisdictions' and that, even in those jurisdictions, arbitrators 'are being urged to become more involved in directing the proceedings, in the interest, among other things, of increased efficiency'.[30]

22.29 Fry, Greenberg, and Mazza also stress that Article 25 of the ICC Rules does not provide 'specific guidance on how to establish the facts' and that the process 'will be strongly influenced by the parties and individual arbitrators' preferences'.[31] Observing the reality of ICC cases, the authors note that 'the parties will bear primary responsibility for locating and presenting the evidence that is necessary to establish the facts upon which they seek to rely' and that '[d]epending on the cultural backgrounds and preferences of the arbitrators', the arbitrators 'may or may not probe for further information or clarification from the parties on points of fact'.[32]

22.30 Bühler and Webster also stress that 'establishing the facts of the case depends basically on the evidence provided by the parties and their counsel in the ICC arbitration' and that it would be 'seldom that a Tribunal will take the initiative to collect and review evidence from sources other than the parties'.[33]

22.31 As Derains and Schwartz have made clear, I believe that the ICC Arbitration Rules do not contain any 'procedural bias' and that it would be beyond the language and spirit of

---

[26] ibid 1291, para 15.780.
[27] See their previous commentary, Michael W Bühler and Sigvard Jarvin, 'Commentary on Article 20 ICC Rules' in Frank-Bernd Weigand (ed), *Practitioner's Handbook on International Arbitration* (OUP 2002) 238–9.
[28] W Laurence Craig, William W Park, and Jan Paulsson, *ICC Arbitration* (3rd edn, Oceana Publication 2000) 416, para 23.01.
[29] Yves Derains and Eric A Schwartz, *Guide to the ICC Rules of Arbitration* (2nd edn, Kluwer Law International 2005) 272.
[30] ibid.
[31] Fry and others (n 24) 268–9, paras 3.940 and 3.943.
[32] ibid 269, para 3.943.
[33] Michael W Bühler and Thomas H Webster, *Handbook of ICC Arbitration* (2nd edn, Sweet & Maxwell 2008) 286–7.

Article 25 of the Rules to see in this provision an invitation to favour the 'inquisitorial element of the civil law tradition'.

22.32 Based on Article 27(3) of the UNCITRAL Arbitration Rules, Article 24(3) of the Swiss Rules provides that at any time during the arbitral proceedings, the arbitral tribunal 'may require the parties to produce documents, exhibits, or other evidence within a period of time determined by the arbitral tribunal'.[34] Commentators on both the UNCITRAL Rules and the Swiss Rules have stressed that arbitrators have the power to take initiatives in establishing the facts and obtaining evidence.[35]

22.33 The DIS Arbitration Rules are more explicit on this question. Under the heading 'Establishing the facts', section 27 provides that the arbitral tribunal 'shall establish the facts underlying the dispute' and that, '[t]o this end, it has the discretion to give directions and, in particular, to hear witnesses and experts and order the production of documents'. This provision further adds that the arbitral tribunal 'is not bound by the parties' application for the admission of evidence'.

22.34 In his commentary, Risse stresses that this provision clarifies that the arbitral tribunal 'may, on its own initiative, appoint an expert or summon a witness to testify' and that it would reflect the 'general approach arbitrators shall pursue in DIS arbitrations', namely 'that of an active case manager and not the one of a passive judge who only listens to the parties without giving any directions'.[36]

22.35 Risse further submits that the 'more active role' of the arbitrators is emphasized by 'the duty to establish the facts of the disputes' and by the 'two main elements of the inquisitorial style', namely 'the right to give directions' and the 'tribunal's own right to collect evidence, ie independent from any respective motions by the parties'.[37] He also stresses that section 27.1 of the DIS Rules implies that an arbitrator who 'actively exercises those rights' cannot be 'challenged on these grounds for lacking impartiality'.[38] Describing the 'practice', he softens his statements and notes that 'most DIS arbitral tribunals will be reluctant to run the proceedings too proactively and to investigate without a corresponding request by at least one party' and that arbitral tribunals 'will consider the parties responsible for presenting their case', some giving directions to 'focus the parties' attention on the relevant areas of the dispute and to avoid wasting time by discussing irrelevant facts'.[39]

22.36 Finally, one may mention Article 43(1) of the 2015 CIETAC Rules, which provides that '[t]he arbitral tribunal may undertake investigations and collect evidence as it considers necessary'.

---

[34] Note that Art 27(3) of the UNCITRAL Rules has not changed when compared to the initial version of the Rules of 1976 (former Art 24(3)).

[35] Gabrielle Nater-Bass and Christina Rouvinez, 'Commentary on Article 24 Swiss Rules' in Tobias Zuberbühler, Christoph Müller, and Philipp Habegger (eds), *Swiss Rules of International Arbitration Commentary* (2nd edn, Kluwer Law International 2013) 268, paras 28–9; David D Caron and Lee M Caplan, *The UNCITRAL Arbitration Rules: A Commentary* (OUP 2006) 574.

[36] Joerg Risse, 'Commentary on Section 27 of the DIS Rules' in Böckstiegel and others (n 10) 755.

[37] ibid 756; among the 'directions' that an arbitrator can give, Risse mentions the 'preliminary assessment of the case' or the 'request for specific information'.

[38] ibid.

[39] ibid.

22.37 The IBA Rules on the Taking of Evidence also envisage the arbitrators' powers to take initiatives to obtain evidence. Article 3(10) of these Rules provides that '[a]t any time before the arbitration is concluded, the Arbitral Tribunal may (i) request any Party to produce Documents, (ii) request any Party to use its best efforts to take or (iii) itself take any step that it considers appropriate to obtain Documents from any person or organization'. Article 4(10) further provides: 'At any time before the arbitration is concluded, the Arbitral Tribunal may order any party to provide for, or to use its best efforts to provide for, the appearance for testimony at an evidentiary hearing of any person, including one whose testimony has not yet been offered'. The arbitrators' power to appoint independent experts is also provided for in Article 6(1).

22.38 In an article on witnesses before arbitral tribunals, Oetiker has submitted that the power provided for by Article 4(10) is 'too broad' and that it must be left 'to the discretion of the parties as to which arguments and evidence they wish to present in support of their position', the only 'valid exceptions' being those 'in which an arbitral tribunal must consider certain aspects *"ex officio"* and the parties have not, or at least not adequately, commented on these aspects', but with the arbitral tribunal remaining 'cautious, since it runs the risk of exceeding its powers'.[40]

22.39 It follows from this review of arbitration legislation and arbitration rules that the arbitrators' power to take initiatives as to the establishment of the facts and the collection of evidence finds some support in different texts, but is rarely based on a comprehensive and detailed provision. Even without an explicit statutory or conventional basis, I submit that arbitrators enjoy the power to take initiatives to establish the facts or to obtain evidence on their own motion, unless the parties have agreed otherwise. Such power is an aspect of the general power of the arbitral tribunal to conduct the proceedings as it deems appropriate in the absence of an agreement to the contrary between the parties.[41] It also finds a justification in the arbitral tribunal's duty to resolve the dispute.[42]

22.40 In that respect, I do not share the views of the authors of the ILA's *Final Report on Ascertaining the Contents of the Applicable Law in International Commercial Arbitration* of 2008, who expressed the view that 'both common and civil law acknowledge that arbitrators do not have independent fact-finding powers'.[43] In my opinion, such a statement is too broad and categorical.

(b) Initiatives to ascertain and to apply the law

22.41 As noted by Landolt, there is 'remarkably little commentary on arbitrators' initiatives to obtain factual evidence', but there is a 'substantial body of commentary on arbitrators' initiatives to obtain evidence of law'.[44] However, the debate has been rendered confused by

---

[40] Christian Oetiker, 'Witnesses before the International Arbitral Tribunal' (2007) 25(2) ASA Bull 263.
[41] See Landolt (n 1) 181–2, 190; Antonias Dimolitsa, 'The Equivocal Power of the Arbitrators to Introduce Ex Officio New Issues of Law' (2009) 27(3) ASA Bull 427.
[42] Such duty implies, in my opinion, that the arbitrators can take initiative whenever they feel it necessary for understanding the factual basis supporting the parties' legal position.
[43] ILA, *Final Report on Ascertaining the Contents of the Applicable Law in International Commercial Arbitration* (Rio de Janeiro Conference, 2008) 5, fn 10 <http://www.ila-hq.org> accessed 25 September 2015.
[44] Landolt (n 1) 174.

the uncertainty of the principle of *iura novit curia*. Terms such as this are used to express two different concepts.

22.42 In a broad sense, *iura novit curia* is 'a power or duty of an adjudicator to ascertain the law independently of party submissions'[45] or, as another author puts it, it is the authority to 'determine the contents of the *lex causae* beyond the parties' submissions'.[46] In a much narrower sense, *iura novit curia* is the power to determine the contents of the law beyond the parties' submissions and to apply the law so determined without inviting the parties to comment on the contents of the law.[47]

22.43 Such uncertainty in the terminology is reflected in the case law of the Swiss Federal Tribunal, which recognizes the principle of *iura novit curia* in international arbitration.[48] The Swiss Federal Tribunal finds that 'by virtue of the rule "*iura novit curia*", it [the court or the arbitral tribunal] is in principle not bound by the legal arguments developed by the parties—except for the case where they would have agreed to limit the mission of the tribunal to legal arguments that they would raise'; this is *iura novit curia* in the broad sense. However, the Swiss Federal Tribunal continues by stating that 'the judge [or the arbitrator] can hence apply *ex officio* another provision of substantive law to grant the claimant's prayers for relief, without having to draw the parties' attention to the existence of such or such legal problem';[49] this is *iura novit curia* in the narrow sense.

22.44 It is submitted that, in the broad sense, *iura novit curia* is widely recognized and is applicable in international arbitration. Most jurisdictions empower the arbitrators to take initiatives 'in ascertaining the law'[50] and, accordingly, to establish the contents of the law on their own motion if they find it appropriate. As Dimolitsa correctly notes: 'The power—and not the obligation—of arbitrators to ascertain such contents on their own initiative constitutes a facet of their jurisdictional mission and cannot be questioned as such. Either under the maxim *iura novit curia*, which is accepted for arbitrators as well in civil law jurisdictions though under differing attenuations and conditions, or on the basis of explicit provisions of a national law or of arbitration rules,[51] this power should be considered as generally accepted.'[52]

22.45 The true difference in approach concerns only *iura novit curia* in the narrow sense, namely the extent of the arbitral tribunal's duty to invite the parties to comment on the application of the law.

22.46 Two trends can be identified. In England, the rule is that the parties have the right to be heard also on legal issues.[53] In Switzerland, the rule is that the parties do not have the right

---

[45] ibid 174, fn 2.
[46] Gisela Knuts, 'Jura Novit Curia and the Right to Be Heard—An Analysis of Recent Case Law' (2012) Arb Int'l 670, 669.
[47] See Manuel Arroyo, 'Which is the Better Approach to Iura Novit Arbiter—the English or the Swiss?' in Christoph Müller and Antonio Rigozzi (eds), *New Developments in International Commercial Arbitration* (Schulthess 2010) 45.
[48] Decision 4P 100/2003, Swiss Federal Tribunal (30 September 2003) DTF 130 III 35, (2004) 3 ASA Bull 574–82, [5].
[49] ibid.
[50] See English Arbitration Act 1996, s 34(2)(g).
[51] English Arbitration Act 1996, s 34(2)(g); 2014 LCIA Rules, Art 22.1(c).
[52] Dimolitsa (n 41) 427–8.
[53] Christian P Alberti, 'Iura Novit Curia in International Commercial Arbitration: How Much Justice Do You Want' in Stefan M Kröll and Loukas A Mistelis (eds), *International Arbitration and International*

to be heard on legal issues, unless the legal provision or reasoning that was not pleaded and that the arbitral tribunal envisages applying is 'unpredictable'.[54] As correctly noted by Meier and McGough, 'the main difference between the Swiss and the English approach seems to be the extent to which the parties have a right to be heard on legal issues. Under English case law, new legal arguments contemplated by the arbitral tribunal should generally be submitted to the parties for comments prior to the making of the award. Under Swiss case law, the right to comment is limited to cases in which the legal assessment would take the parties by surprise.'[55] French law appears to be somewhere in between the English and the Swiss positions.[56]

22.47 It is not the objective of this chapter to explore further these issues and nuances. For present purposes, it is sufficient to note that the power of the arbitral tribunal to take initiatives in ascertaining the law is widely recognized even in common law jurisdictions.

22.48 Having established the principle of the arbitrators' power to take initiatives, in particular to establish the facts, to obtain factual evidence, and to go beyond the legal arguments presented by the parties, I am conscious that we have not been very far. The most important issue to determine is how the arbitrators should exercise their discretion and there are very few studies concerning this question.[57]

C. Exercise of the Arbitrators' Discretion

22.49 Most scholars merely stress that the arbitrators enjoy a broad discretion to exercise their power to take initiatives, or they refer to very abstract and undefined factors. As an example, Fry, Greenberg, and Mazza refer to the 'cultural backgrounds and preferences of the arbitrators'.[58]

22.50 It is recognized that the exercise of the arbitrators' power to take initiatives is to be examined on a case-by-case basis and that it will depend on a variety of factors. However, I propose to take a step further and try to identify the most relevant factors that may influence the exercise of the arbitrators' discretion.

22.51 As a preliminary remark, I do not believe that there should be a general presumption against arbitrators' initiatives. There are good and bad initiatives, and the latter should be avoided. However, the modern practice of international arbitration does not suffer from arbitrators' exacerbated activism. On the contrary, arbitrators' prudence and passivity have sometimes

---

Commercial Law: Synergy, Convergence and Evolution (Kluwer Law International 2011) 23. See also Arroyo (n 47) 38–44.

[54] Decision 4A_108/2009, Swiss Federal Tribunal (9 June 2009), ASA Bull 3 (2010) 511, [2.1]; see also DTF 130 III 35 (n 48) [5].

[55] Andrea Meier and Yolanda McGough, 'Do Lawyers Always Have to Have the Last Word? Iura Novit Curia and the Right to Be Heard in International Arbitration: An Analysis in View of Recent Swiss Case Law' (2014) 32(3) ASA Bull 492.

[56] Teresa Isele, 'The Principle Iura Novit Curia in International Arbitration' (2010) 13(1) Int'l ALR 14, 15; Jeffrey Waincymer, 'International Arbitration and the Duty to Know the Law' (2011) J Int'l Arb 205; Alberti (n 53) 11; Rainer Hausmann, 'Pleading and Proof of Foreign Law: A Comparative Analysis' (2008) 1 European Legal Forum I.1.I, I.4.

[57] As far as I am aware, the article by Landolt (n 1) is the most detailed analysis and I will often refer to it, although I do not share all of the views expressed by the author.

[58] Fry and others (n 24) 299, para 3.943.

been criticized.⁵⁹ I hence disagree with Landolt when he submits that 'a great deal more reserve is usually indicated than is widely supposed' in respect of arbitrators' initiatives to obtain evidence of facts and law, that there is 'much in general to recommend arbitrator passivity as regards the obtaining of factual and legal evidence', that '[a]ny arbitrators' initiatives will encroach upon party autonomy', that arbitrators' initiatives 'usually add to the time and costs of the arbitration', and that such initiatives 'will usually result in favour to one party and disfavour to the other' and 'inject uncertainty into the arbitration'.⁶⁰

22.52 This preliminary remark does not mean that the arbitrators should not respect the traditional division of role between counsel and adjudicator. The starting point will always be for the arbitrators to analyse the parties' submissions. This also applies to legal issues. In arbitration and, specifically, in international arbitration, the parties are expected to make legal arguments and the arbitrators are expected to consider them in the first place. In its Report, the ILA Committee stresses this point and states that '[a]rbitrators should primarily receive information about the contents of the applicable law from the parties' (Recommendation 5).⁶¹

22.53 The factors that I will address below are not meant to be exhaustive. They leave room for interpretation and may overlap. Nevertheless, I hope that they can assist in the exercise of the arbitrators' discretion as to whether a proactive approach or a passive attitude is to be preferred.

(a) Agreement of the parties

22.54 The arbitrators are bound by the parties' procedural agreement. If the parties have established procedural rules addressing the arbitrators' initiatives, eg by excluding the principle of *iura novit curia*, such rules must be respected by the arbitrators.⁶² However, procedural agreements concerning arbitrators' initiatives are rare and hence unlikely to play a role in practice.

(b) The parties' expectations

22.55 The arbitrators should not take initiatives that would run against the parties' expectations.⁶³ This proposition is likely to be undisputed. However, it will be difficult to identify what these expectations are in a given case. These expectations are usually related to the parties' legal background, to which I now turn.

(c) Legal background of the parties

22.56 This is an important factor. The arbitrators should be mindful of the legal background of the parties' counsel and pay attention to it. All other things being equal, an arbitrator

---

⁵⁹ See Landolt (n 1) 218–19.
⁶⁰ ibid 197, 204, and 222.
⁶¹ ILA, *Final Report* (n 43) 23.
⁶² Decision 4A_46/2011, Swiss Federal Tribunal (16 May 2011) (2011) 3 ASA Bull 643, [5.1.1]; DTF 130 III 35 (n 48) [5]. See also Joachim Knoll, 'Commentary on Article 182 PILS' in Arroyo (n 15) 102; Veit (n 15) 128; Manuel Arroyo, 'Commentary on Article 190 PILS' in Arroyo (n 15) 239; Schneider and Scherer (n 15) 1850, para 69. The case where the rule to be applied is of a public policy nature should, however, be reserved.
⁶³ Mauro Rubino-Sammartano, 'How Easy Is It Not to Take Adequate Care of the Proper Expectations of the Parties?' in Julio César Betancourt (ed), *Defining Issues in International Arbitration: Celebrating 100 Years of the Chartered Institute of Arbitrators* (OUP 2016) ch 5.

can afford to take more initiatives when the parties involved have a civil law background because such parties are more used to the inquisitorial approach.

22.57 Importantly, it is submitted that the parties' legal background is in fact the legal background of their counsel. If two Russian oligarchs retain two London firms in an LCIA arbitration, the relevant legal background will be common law rather than Russian law. The choice of counsel gives a message to the arbitrators and it is not inappropriate for them to adapt their behaviour to the expectations of the chosen counsel.

(d) Nature of the arbitration

22.58 This factor is related to the previous one. The international or domestic nature of the arbitration is an important consideration to take into account. In an international context, the arbitrator should avoid creating an unbalanced situation by adopting a procedural behaviour inspired by court-proceedings techniques with which only one of the parties is familiar. In a domestic context, this risk is less important and court techniques common to all participants are likely to prevail, including those techniques with an inquisitorial element. In a domestic arbitration in Germany before a retired German judge acting as arbitrator, for example, it is likely that the arbitrator will take a very proactive approach in terms of establishing the facts and, in particular, that the questioning of the witnesses will be led by the arbitrator. There is nothing wrong in such approach in a German domestic law environment, although it would be at odds with the usual practice of international arbitration.

(e) Expertise of the arbitrator

22.59 The arbitrator is more likely to take good initiatives concerning issues within his field of expertise. The parties are likely to expect such initiatives when appointing a specialized arbitrator.

22.60 If the arbitrator is an engineer, it is appropriate for him to take a proactive approach in relation to technical issues in which he is a specialist, notably by asking questions, or for further information or documents from the parties. A passive attitude would be in conflict with the parties' expectations.

22.61 Similarly, if the arbitrator is a Swiss contract law professor charged with a dispute subject to Swiss substantive law, it would be unreasonable to limit the arbitrator's understanding of the scope of Swiss law to excerpts of legal authorities translated into English and presented to him by a US or UK counsel. The arbitrator is likely to establish the law on his own initiative, including by doing additional legal research (possibly into his own publications!).

22.62 By contrast, the arbitrator should be more prudent when taking initiatives in relation to issues outside of his field of expertise. I have seen several cases of inappropriate initiatives taken by legally trained arbitrators with regard to technical issues that they were manifestly not mastering.

(f) The parties' procedural experience

22.63 The parties' procedural experience is also a relevant factor. It encompasses that of their counsel. The more experienced the parties, the less initiative is needed from the arbitrators, and vice versa.

22.64 In extreme cases, where the parties are unable to present their case, the arbitrators cannot simply dismiss the claims. They have a duty to understand the facts and to apply the law, and this may lead them to adopt an inquisitorial and proactive attitude, eg by establishing a detailed list of factual and legal issues to be addressed by the parties.

22.65 The balance is particularly delicate to strike when the parties are unequally represented. Landolt submits that it would be 'inappropriate' for the arbitrator to 'sub-consciously redress the balance where the parties' respective counsel prove to be of unequal effectiveness although both are perfectly competent'.[64] I agree that it would be improper to assist a party weakly represented. However, the arbitrators may take a proactive approach in order to make sure that they understand properly the position of that party, and that they have enough elements to make a meaningful confrontation of the positions of both parties.

(g) Procedural efficiency

22.66 The arbitrators should be mindful of the procedural impact, in particular, in terms of the costs of their initiatives.

22.67 The scope of their initiative will play a role. It is one thing to invite the parties to produce an email, the existence of which was discovered during the hearing; it is quite another to embark on a neutral expertise procedure that neither of the parties has requested. Initiatives concerning specific points that are within the frame of the issues in dispute are much less problematic than initiatives concerning entirely new sets of issues.

22.68 In its Report, the ILA Committee made a distinction between initiatives designed to '*introduce* legal issues' and those concerning the determination of the contents of the applicable law within the frame of legal issues already pleaded by the parties.[65] Under Recommendation 6, the Committee stresses that 'in general … arbitrators should not introduce legal issues—propositions of law that may bear on the outcome of the dispute—that the parties have not raised'; under Recommendation 7 and in contrast, the Committee finds that '[a]rbitrators are not confined to the parties' submissions about the contents of applicable law' and that they may 'question the parties about legal issues the parties have raised and about their submissions and evidence on the contents of the applicable law, may review sources not invoked by the parties relating to those legal issues and may, in a transparent manner, rely on their own knowledge as to the applicable law as it relates to these legal issues'.[66] The timing is also key and the arbitrators' initiatives are likely to be more efficient sooner than later.

22.69 Initiatives reducing the scope of the dispute or the evidentiary process, eg refusing to hear witnesses on issues that are considered irrelevant, are by essence fostering procedural efficiency. Landolt has referred to 'negative initiatives' and characterized them as 'a sort of approximate pre-decision'.[67] From a Swiss perspective, such a decision to exclude certain facts from the evidentiary process or to limit the means of evidence is characterized as anticipatory assessment of evidence, which is perfectly admissible.[68] For Landolt, such 'negative' initiatives 'save costs and time' and they are respecting 'the relevant values, notably party autonomy'.[69] I note, however, that decisions reducing the scope of the dispute or limiting the evidentiary

---

[64] Landolt (n 1) 212.
[65] ILA, *Final Report* (n 43) 23 (emphasis added).
[66] ibid. With regard to introducing legal issues (Recommendation 6), the ILA Committee reserves, however, Recommendation 13, which deals with rules of public policy.
[67] Landolt (n 1) 178.
[68] Knoll (n 62) 112; Arroyo, 'Commentary on Article 190 PILS' (n 62) 237.
[69] Landolt (n 1) 178.

process are likely to be badly perceived by the parties and the reality of international arbitration shows that arbitrators are very reluctant to take such 'negative initiatives'.

(h) Procedural fairness

22.70 The initiatives should respect procedural fairness, and should not create undue advantages to one of the parties. To some extent, I agree with Landolt that any initiative, if related to a relevant point of fact or law, is likely to influence the outcome and 'will usually result in favour to one party and disfavour to the other'.[70] However, this is not a reason to ban initiatives (and the point could be made that the absence of initiatives will also, ultimately, favour one party and disfavour the other party). The difficulty is to strike the correct balance between good initiatives favouring the arbitral process as a whole and impermissible assistance to one party to the detriment of the other. Initiatives may in particular be improper if they aim at broadening the case presented by one party.

22.71 A few examples may illustrate the line of division, which will always remain a matter of discretion for the arbitral tribunal. If a party has produced an expert report for calculating its damages, the arbitrator can question the expert and ask for clarifications or additional information that are not contained in the report. If a party has not produced any expert report, it would be improper for the arbitrator to draw that party's attention to the notion of burden of proof and invite it to produce an expert report.

22.72 If a party has not availed itself of a specific legal defence—eg statute of limitation, lack of standing—it would be improper for the arbitrator to raise such defence on his own motion. Defences pertaining to public policy must be reserved because interests other than those of the parties are at stake.[71] The applicable substantive law may provide additional and specific restrictions to the ability of the arbitrator to raise defences that were not invoked by a party. For example, Swiss substantive law provides that the statute of limitation or set-off defences must be invoked by the party.[72] Otherwise, the judge, or the arbitrator, cannot consider such defences.

(i) Issues pertaining to public policy or raising matters of public interest

22.73 The parties' expectations must be respected if they are legitimate. The parties cannot abuse the arbitral process and the arbitrators cannot entirely disregard 'valid interests other than those of the parties'.[73]

22.74 It is outside the scope of this chapter to discuss the justification for and the precise extent of the arbitrators' duty to apply mandatory norms and rules of public policy. For present purposes, it is sufficient to stress that it is widely recognized that arbitrators have such a duty to apply mandatory norms and norms pertaining to public policy.[74] In particular, they must consider and apply competition law.[75]

---

[70] ibid 222.
[71] See Section C(i) of this chapter.
[72] Swiss Code of Obligations, Arts 142 and 124(1).
[73] Landolt (n 1) 215.
[74] Nigel Blackaby and others, *Redfern and Hunter on International Arbitration* (5th edn, OUP 2009) paras 3.128–3.135; Waincymer (n 56) 236–7.
[75] ibid paras 3.128–3.135; Niko Hukkinen, 'Application of Competition Law Ex Officio' in Tobias Zuberbühler and Christian Oetiker (eds), *Practical Aspects of Arbitrating EC Competition Law* (Schulthess 2007) 43–57.

22.75 As a result, arbitrators also have a duty to take a more active approach vis-à-vis mandatory norms and norms of public policy compared to norms protecting only private interests. In its Report, the ILA Committee stressed the following in Recommendation 13: 'In disputes implicating rules of public policy or other rules from which the parties may not derogate, arbitrators may be justified in taking measures appropriate to determine the applicability and contents of such rules, including by making independent research, raising with the parties new issues (whether legal or factual) and giving appropriate instructions or ordering appropriate measures in so far as they consider this necessary to abide by those rules and to protect against challenges to the award.'[76]

22.76 Typically, the arbitrators will invite the parties to supplement their legal case or may even apply the relevant mandatory norms *ex officio*. They may also take initiatives to establish the facts relevant for assessing defences or legal arguments pertaining to public policy or mandatory norms.[77] This is in particular the case with corruption. The *Metal-Tech v Republic of Uzbekistan* case[78] offers a good example of a proactive approach by an ICSID arbitral tribunal (Professor Gabrielle Kaufmann Kohler, President, Mr John Townsend and Mr Claus von Wobeser, arbitrators). Faced with an admission at the hearing that substantial payments had been made in relation to the contract, the arbitral tribunal sought to understand 'what services these payments were intended to compensate'.[79] It gave the claimant 'an opportunity to substantiate the reality and legitimacy of the services for which payments were made' and, taking a step further, requested on its own motion evidence, including categories of information and documents, as well as a new witness statement addressing some relevant questions.[80] In its assessment on evidence, the arbitral tribunal then took into account the claimant's failure to comply with these requests.

(j) Default proceedings

22.77 Arbitrators should take more initiative when one of the parties refuses to take part in the proceedings.[81] In such situation, the adversarial process does not operate and it is hence normal that the inquisitorial approach plays a more important role. In particular, without becoming the advocate of the non-participating party, the arbitrators may wish to test the claimant's arguments by asking specific questions or by inviting the claimant to adduce further evidence when the respondent's determinations are missing.[82]

22.78 The arbitrators also have a duty to examine their jurisdiction if the respondent does not proceed, and may take initiatives in that respect. For instance, they may invite the claimant to deal with or develop this question.[83]

22.79 The nature of the proceedings has also been identified as a relevant factor by the ILA Committee in its Report, which stresses under Recommendation 14 that 'in applying the

---

[76] ILA, *Final Report* (n 43) 23.
[77] Landolt (n 1) 215.
[78] *Metal-Tech v Republic of Uzbekistan*, ICSID Case No ARB/10/3, Award (4 October 2013).
[79] ibid [246].
[80] ibid [246]–[254].
[81] Landolt (n 1) 218; Knoll (n 62) 116; Judith Butchers and Philip Kimbrough, 'The Arbitral Tribunal's Role in Default Proceedings' (2006) Arb Int'l 237–8.
[82] ibid.
[83] ibid.

foregoing Recommendations, arbitrators may take into account the nature of the proceeding, in particular regarding default and expedited interim relief proceedings, and may take a more active role than might otherwise be the case in questioning legal submissions'.[84]

(k) Different standards for initiatives as to both the facts and law

22.80 In his study, Landolt wonders whether 'arbitrators should be more robust in their initiatives concerning evidence of law than concerning evidence of fact', since arbitration law systems and arbitration rules place 'an obligation upon arbitrators to apply the law'.[85] He reaches the conclusion that 'no difference in approach is indicated' between initiatives to obtain factual evidence and initiatives to obtain evidence of law.

22.81 I have a different view. As seen above, the principle of *iura novit curia* (in the broad sense) is widespread and there are good arguments justifying the arbitral tribunal's application of the law—including the contract—in its entirety. By contrast, the parties' factual presentations will necessarily be a selection of some facts deemed relevant by each side. In complex cases, one cannot examine the factual situation in its entirety and the facts contained in the file will always be an incomplete, biased, and approximate description of the reality.

22.82 As the facts cannot be established 'in their entirety' and as the facts will always be the result of a selection made by the parties, there are in my view fewer reasons for the arbitrators to take initiatives as to the facts than as to the law. Unless the facts are unclear, suspect, not sufficient to understand the situation, or related to the application of mandatory norms or norms of public policy, the arbitrators should as a rule remain within the scope of the factual framework presented to them. The initiatives concerning the application of the law can go beyond these situations and can, in particular, be related to the correct application of the law. Hence, it is submitted, to paraphrase Landolt, that arbitrators should be more robust—ie less shy—in their initiatives concerning evidence of law than of fact.

D. Initiatives to Clarify or to Correct the Parties' Request

22.83 The arbitrators' initiatives—or absence of initiatives—play an important role in relation to defective requests of the parties, in particular, and most importantly, in relation to defective prayers for relief. The factors that I have identified above are relevant for assessing to what extent the arbitrators should be more inclined or less inclined to draw the parties' attention to defective requests and offer them an opportunity to improve their submissions. One can nevertheless try to formulate the following general principles:

(1) it is appropriate for the arbitral tribunal to seek clarification if the parties' requests or prayers for relief are unclear or ambiguous;[86]
(2) it is appropriate for the arbitral tribunal to invite a party to complete its requests or prayers for relief if such requests or prayers for relief have manifestly and inadvertently omitted an aspect of the case effectively argued by that party;

---

[84] ILA, *Final Report* (n 43) 23.
[85] Landolt (n 1) 220.
[86] Waincymer (n 56) 222.

(3) it is inappropriate to invite a party to complete its requests or prayers for relief in all other circumstances; and[87]

(4) it is inappropriate to invite a party to correct the substance of its requests or prayers for relief, eg to draw that party's attention to the fact that the requested amount is not in the appropriate currency in view of the circumstances and of the applicable law.

E. Conclusion

22.84 It follows from this review that arbitrators indisputably have the power to take initiatives concerning the facts and the law. They may also take initiatives in relation to defective requests presented by the parties. Some initiatives are appropriate, some are not. This chapter has tried to identify the most relevant factors that will play a role in the arbitral tribunal's discretion. In the end, the distinction between good and bad initiatives will always imply a balancing of interests and will require the careful judgment of the arbitrators.

---

[87] ibid 230.

23

THE LAW IS WHAT THE ARBITRATOR HAD FOR BREAKFAST

How Income, Reputation, Justice, and Reprimand Act as Determinants of Arbitrator Behaviour

Thomas Schultz and Robert Kovacs*

A. Introduction

In arbitration, the law is what the arbitrator says it is—against the background, granted, of what courts whisper at the seat of the arbitration and the places of enforcement. And as the view classically attributed to legal realism has it, what the judge (or arbitrator) says depends on what he had for breakfast.[1] So, on this view, the law in arbitration depends on what the arbitrator had for breakfast. This, in substance, is the subject of this chapter. 23.01

No, it does not mean that we will entertain profound discussions on the relative merits of sunny-side up v poached, pancakes v croissants, tea with milk v cappuccino, or even the critically important debate over full English v full Irish breakfast (sorry if you are already hungry). What it does mean is that we will take the idea seriously that if we better comprehend what influences and motivates the behaviour of arbitrators, we can better understand arbitration, and the law that applies and should apply to it, and the law created by it. 23.02

(a) An intuitive sense of right and wrong

The point is simple: as Brian Leiter puts it, describing a central line of thought in legal realism: 'What causes judges to decide as they do'—and the same applies to arbitrators—'is not legal rules, but a sense of what would be fair on the facts of the case at hand'.[2] For evidence, he points us to statements of judges such as this: 'the vital, motivating impulse for the decision is an intuitive sense of what is right and wrong for that cause'.[3] 23.03

Now what, exactly, is 'that cause', in the preceding sentence, which is to be advanced by the decision? Canons of the law and economics approach would tell us that it is not the 23.04

---

* Particular thanks for useful comments go to Andrea Bianchi and Fuad Zarbiyev. Many occasional discussions with the late Pierre Lalive informed the narrative of this chapter.

[1] This is merely jurisprudential lore, but the metaphor is useful in making our point. See Brian Leiter, *Naturalizing Jurisprudence* (OUP 2007) 62.

[2] ibid 76–7.

[3] Joseph C Hutcheson, 'The Judgment Intuitive: The Function of the "Hunch" in Judicial Decision' (1929) 14 Cornell L Rev 274, 285.

human context per se of the case, but rather the arbitrators' own expected 'utility'—what best satisfies their own needs, wants, desires, and aspirations. Arbitrators, like everyone else, are maximizers of their own utility. The pursuit of that maximization influences how they decide cases. The components of their utility are determinants of their behaviour.

23.05 No doubt, Leiter's perceived fairness on the facts is one component of that utility. But there are others. Put differently, the so-called 'moral reason-for-action' (a reason focused on advancing other people's interests) that makes an arbitrator care for the human context of a case is just one of his reasons-for-action. 'Prudential reasons-for-action' (reasons focused on advancing one's own interests) are also inevitably present.[4] This is not a point of reproach, merely a recognition of human realism. To be sure, what really determines arbitrator behaviour is much more complex than just the law and what would be fair on the facts of the case at hand. That, in essence, is what the metaphor of the arbitrator's breakfast refers to. And that is what we examine in this chapter.

(b) Incentives and constraints

23.06 Our hope is that we will come to better understand arbitrator behaviour, and thus arbitration itself, by considering certain salient incentives and constraints that the current socio-legal system of arbitration places on arbitrators. This type of ambition is not new. Many similar forays have been made, notably from the law and economics camp, into the territory of judicial behaviour.[5] What determines the behaviour of judges? What do they seek to maximize? What incentives do they follow? How do these incentives differ from the average practising lawyer? These are the sorts of questions that have been asked in these studies.

23.07 How do these questions play out in relation to arbitrators? That is the question we want to answer. And we, too, draw on law and economics methods, though rather lightly, as a conditionally useful set of instruments, not as a school of thought. The explanandum, here, is not the full variegatedness of the components of an arbitrator's utility—the full set of incentives and constraints that amount to determinants of arbitrator behaviour. We rather focus on a laconically selective array of incentives and constraints, principally those that are usually shrouded in conventional wisdom.

23.08 Why do this? It is not done for the purposes of an evaluative investigation eventually aimed at what Pierre Schlag calls 'norm-selection' or 'norm-advocacy':[6] we do not seek to say that the law—any law—should be interpreted or crafted in a certain way. It is not, then, the habitual juridical project of academic articles in law that is pursued here.[7] The purpose

---

[4] Matthew H Kramer, 'On the Moral Status of the Rule of Law' (2003) 63 Cambridge LJ 65, 66: 'Somebody's prudential reasons-for-action are focused exclusively or primarily on his own interests and only derivatively if at all on the interests of other people. Somebody's moral reasons-for-action are focused exclusively or primarily on other people's interests and only derivatively if at all on his own interests (apart from interests, such as a concern for acting in a morally proper fashion, which are themselves defined by reference to the well-being of other people)'.

[5] See, for instance, Richard A Posner, 'The Role of the Judge in the Twenty-First Century' (2006) 86 BUL Rev 1049; Richard A Posner, 'Judicial Behavior and Performance: An Economic Approach' (2004–05) 32 Fla St UL Rev 1259; Gordon R Foxall, 'What Judges Maximize: Toward an Economic Psychology of the Judicial Utility Function' (2004) 25 Liverpool L Rev 177; Richard A Posner, *Overcoming Law* (HUP 1995) 109–44; Richard A Posner, 'What Do Judges and Justices Maximize (the Same Thing Everybody Else Does)' (1993) 3 Sup Ct Econ Rev 1; Richard S Higgins and Paul H Rubin, 'Judicial Discretion' (1980) 9 J Leg Stud 129.

[6] Pierre Schlag, 'A Comment on Thomas Schultz's Editorial' (2014) 5 JIDS 235.

[7] Pierre Schlag, 'The Faculty Workshop' (2012) 60 Buff L Rev 807.

of this chapter is primarily to better understand arbitration, to be a piece in the realm of 'thinking about law' as opposed to 'doing law'.[8]

Yet the practice of law is not spared. Not quite. The practice of arbitration law is, inevitably, informed by the parties' understanding of arbitration. Altering the understanding of the determinants of arbitrator behaviour likely changes—and hopefully improves—the way counsel approaches a case. The purpose of counsel, after all, is to be yet another determinant that contributes to orienting what arbitrators do: if counsel believe they only play against the law and the facts, they might well be playing a different game than they think—or at least under a different set of rules. 23.09

(c) Behavioural determinants

But what does it mean, exactly, to talk about determinants of arbitrator behaviour? Let us see first how this works for judges. As Richard Posner puts it, most people tend to maximize a combination of 'income, leisure, family relationships, work satisfaction, [a sense of] personal integrity, reputation, and felt achievement'.[9] The combination varies from one person to another, as some people weight certain elements more than other people do. Clearly, some people value income more than felt achievements; others accord more importance to reputation than personal integrity; yet others hold family relationships more dearly, or less, than the pleasure derived from doing a good job. 23.10

Judges, Posner maintains, tend to maximize a specific combination of these objectives. These objectives thus become determinants of the behaviour of judges—of judges taken as an abstract, generalized ideal-type. For instance, people who become judges tend to favour public recognition and leisure more than the average practising lawyer does. If we know that, we know what sort of people tend to become judges, how judges tend to behave once they are appointed, and how they tend to make decisions. We can then better understand the functioning of the judiciary as a socio-legal institution. This allows us to see more clearly into how judges make law, and thus what the law likely is or will be in a particular jurisdiction. And again, as we said above, understanding this helps counsel make their case in court. 23.11

The same reasoning applies to arbitration: arbitrators tend to maximize a specific combination of the objectives mentioned above, and of certain others. The way arbitrators respond to incentives and constraints, and the identity of these incentives and constraints, form the determinants of their behaviour. Seeing these determinants helps us understand the functioning of arbitration as a socio-legal institution, including the decisions and norms it produces. 23.12

Consider a quick example: in investment arbitration, it is beyond cavil that arbitrators make law, and that they do so to a significant degree.[10] This is not necessarily a good thing (in the relative sense that less might be better than more, as it is barely a credible proposition to maintain that arbitrators should not make law at all). It is not necessarily a good thing 23.13

---

[8] Thomas Schultz, 'Doing Law and Thinking about Law' (2012) 3 JIDS 217.
[9] Posner, 'Judicial Behavior and Performance' (n 5) 1260.
[10] There are many examples here. Consider, for instance, Alec Stone Sweet and Giacinto della Cananea, 'Proportionality, General Principles of Law, and Investor-State Arbitration: A Response to Jose Alvarez' (2014) 46(3) NYU J Int'l L & Pol 911.

because more law is not necessarily better than less.[11] Now, whether it actually is a good thing, or is likely to be so, depends in part on whether arbitrators are appropriate people for lawmaking in the particular context. That, in turn, depends in part on the determinants of their behaviour.

23.14 In the discussion that will follow, our arguments are not grounded in scientifically measured evidence, but proceed from a humanistic affinity, relying on commonsensical, necessarily subjective insights. We do not invoke armchair confidence in the correctness of our view. We merely submit that the plausibility of our view is more than occasional, and that systematic empirical studies would be welcome in the places we mark.

23.15 The chapter follows a simple path: it mirrors the main steps taken by classical law and economics studies on judicial behaviour. It takes the main types of incentives and constraints identified in these studies and applies them to the behaviour of arbitrators.

B. Income

(a) Lessons from the judiciary

23.16 With regard to judges (more precisely US federal judges, and the point can only be transposed with care to other judges), Richard Posner has this to say: he 'can be lazy, lack ... temperament ... berate without reason the lawyers who appear before him, be reprimanded for ethical lapses, verge on or even slide into senility ... hold under advisement for years cases that could be decided perfectly well in days or weeks, leak confidential information to the press, pursue a nakedly political agenda [and yet] he will retain his office'.[12]

23.17 Now, is it any different for arbitrators? To what extent can the behaviour of arbitrators, and more specifically their decisions, influence their income, their keeping their job? One of the points of providing judges with such extraordinary tenure was to avoid them having to respond to market forces, to economic incentives—their decisions should have no or little effect on their income. The rules governing compensation and terms and conditions of judicial employment usually take away financial 'carrots and sticks'.[13] Judges are typically paid a set salary which cannot be lowered. Once appointed it is difficult to remove them. Most judges are only allowed to work as judges and do not have to source work, as cases are supplied through the operation of the state judicial system.

(b) Influencing market value

23.18 This objective is, precisely, not replicated in the nature of the office of an arbitrator. Arbitration is strongly regulated by market forces. Robert Cooter, one of the torchbearers of the law and economics movement, made the obvious point in an early paper on private judges: arbitrators, he said, are subject to the same 'market pressures as anyone who sells a service'.[14] Arbitrators are private actors who perform their function for private gain.[15] To do

---

[11] Thomas Schultz, 'Against Consistency in Investment Arbitration' in Zachary Douglas and others (eds), *The Foundations of International Investment Law* (OUP 2014) 297.
[12] Posner, 'What Do Judges and Justices Maximize' (n 5) 4–5.
[13] ibid 2.
[14] Robert D Cooter, 'The Objectives of Private and Public Judges' (1983) 41 Publ Ch 107, 107.
[15] Andrew T Guzman, 'Arbitrator Liability: Reconciling Arbitration and Mandatory Rules' (2000) 49 Duke LJ 1279, 1302–3.

that, they must attract business.¹⁶ Again: whereas judges can exert only limited influence on their income through their decisions in court, arbitrators, on the other hand, are likely to be able to influence their market value, and thus their income, through their decisions.

23.19 So what sorts of decisions increase the market value and income of arbitrators? Intuitively, one may think that good decisions on the merits do precisely that, and that they do so rather significantly. Do we not want, as arbitrators, great lawyers who make great legal decisions, who render great awards on the merits? Cooter certainly thought so: for an arbitrator to maximize demand for his services, he must—and Cooter thought this was an 'obvious' point on which to build—'acquire a reputation for deciding cases on the merits', and for being particularly good at it.¹⁷ This led Cooter to believe that a good economic strategy for an arbitrator is to 'pick a speciality and acquire skill at interpreting that particular body of law': an arbitrator should focus on making great awards, on the merits, in this particular area of law because he is particularly proficient in this area of the law¹⁸—a line of thought quite able to hold water.

23.20 And yet ... does that really happen? Does the market want, as arbitrators, great lawyers who make great legal decisions, great awards on the merits? How can we know? One way to form a hunch might be this: one would expect, in a market where there is considerably more supply, or offers, than demand, that conspicuous failures in providing a service would lead to a fairly quick and strong reaction of the market in moving to other offers. In commercial arbitration, the market remains mostly unaware of any such failure because awards are generally not published and therefore are not subject to independent scrutiny. But in investment arbitration, awards are routinely published and dissected ad nauseam by a variety of actors in the arbitration market. Accordingly, in this market, there would seem to be no reason why unfortunate substantive decision-making should not lead to an immediate market reaction, possibly commensurate to the unfortunateness of the decision.

23.21 Now consider that even an author as considerate and balanced as Federico Ortino identifies a number of arbitral decisions as 'egregious failures', produced by legal reasoning on the part of the arbitrators that is 'manifestly contradictory, inconsistent or practically non-existent'.¹⁹ Yet the relevant arbitrators seem to have faced no immediate and commensurate decrease in their appointments, even after having been thus hauled over the coals. And investment arbitration is often considered to be a luxury class of arbitration—one of its more demanding, high-profile, high-value varieties.

23.22 All in all, it is surprisingly difficult to find empirical evidence positively associating a lack of substantive decision-making proficiency, as elucidated through scholarly commentary on its manifestations, with a decrease in the apparent market value of the relevant arbitrators.

23.23 But should that difficulty really be surprising? William Park makes the obvious point in a recent article: 'Publicly, lawyers talk about the proverbial good arbitrator who will be honest and intelligent. Yet in evaluating candidates to sit in their own cases, they doubtlessly hope

---

¹⁶ Christopher R Drahozal, 'Privatizing Civil Justice: Commercial Arbitration and the Civil Justice System' (1999–2000) 9 Kan JL & Pub Pol'y 578, 588.
¹⁷ Cooter (n 14) 109–10.
¹⁸ ibid.
¹⁹ Federico Ortino, 'Legal Reasoning of International Investment Tribunals: A Typology of Egregious Failures' (2012) 3 JIDS 31, 31.

for someone well-disposed to their arguments'.[20] Put bluntly, there is no such thing as an unproficient arbitrator who sees the dispute the way you, the party, see it. What is wrong with a foolhardy decision that lets you win the case (assuming it does not raise grounds for annulment)?

23.24 Park takes the argument to its inevitable next step: 'one might ask why it matters that the arbitrator be relatively free from bias'.[21] Park's question, though, is not entirely as rhetorical as the context of its quote here might suggest: it is often not quite so easy to gauge how the arbitrator sees the dispute before he is appointed.

(c) Social capital

23.25 Sergio Puig looks at the question from a different angle, leading him to a yet more radical view. In a recent study using an empirical method called 'network analysis', he suggests this: the overwhelming trigger for appointments in investment arbitration is the arbitrators' social capital (the preferential treatment accorded between members of a group or, brutally put, who they know) combined with market collusion (keeping new entrants at arm's length to reduce competition on the supply side).[22] The trigger is neither proficiency in legal interpretation, nor sensitivity for the fairness of the facts of the case.

23.26 And the situation is self-reinforcing: because of the importance of social capital, even when proficiency in legal interpretation and sensitivity for fairness obtain to a great degree, they are dampened by 'conformity pressures'.[23] This means that conformity pressures displace, constrain, and possibly override proficiency and sensitivity, making them less consequential in the decision-making process and thus yet less germane to the selection of the arbitrator.

23.27 In an earlier study on commercial arbitration, we found that neither specialization of an arbitrator in the substantive area of law relevant to the dispute, nor an arbitrator's past decisions are primary factors in the selection of arbitrators. Participants in commercial arbitration, our findings suggested, seem to be primarily looking for dispute resolution managers.[24] In other words, it may be (and hedging is appropriate, as more dedicated empirical investigation would be welcome on this point) that there is little noticeable economic incentive for arbitrators to produce good decisions on the merits. Or put with yet more caution: this incentive seems significantly less strong than popular lore has it.

23.28 There is, however, one way in which decisions on the merits (though this does not only relate to merits) are likely to connect to appointments. It is more precisely a question of reasoning than one of outcome. The point is this: given the importance of social capital underscored by Puig, it would seem plausible that following arbitral precedents positively contributes to getting appointments. Indeed, who does not like to see one's decisions endorsed by other tribunals? Following precedents nurtures social relations and thus creates social capital.

---

[20] William W Park, 'A Fair Fight: Professional Guidelines in International Arbitration' (2014) 30(3) Arb Int'l 409, fn 15.
[21] ibid.
[22] Sergio Puig, 'Social Capital in the Arbitration Market' (2014) 25(2) EJIL 387.
[23] ibid 389. As Puig explains, this is not unique to investment arbitration, and is in fact fairly frequent in institutions that contribute to global governance, as argued by David Kennedy, 'Challenging Expert Rule: The Politics of Global Governance' (2005) 27 Syd LR 18.
[24] Thomas Schultz and Robert Kovacs, 'The Rise of a Third Generation of Arbitrators? Fifteen Years after Dezalay and Garth' (2012) 28 Arb Int'l 161.

Hence, it is economically sensible for arbitrators to follow prior cases decided by arbitrators most likely to influence future appointments: decisions of individuals often selected as co-arbitrators, for instance, become particularly worthy of attention.

(d) Specialization

23.29 The economic value, for arbitrators, of their decisions on procedural questions is a different matter. For instance, in our earlier study already mentioned, we found that specialization in the law and practice of arbitration and management abilities were the two most significant factors for the selection of arbitrators. Both factors relate to decisions on procedural questions. As we just said: parties, counsel, and arbitrators, when choosing other arbitrators, seem to place a great deal of importance on managerial skills. They appear to want dispute resolution managers who do not mess up the procedure. People who do not allow the arbitration to get derailed. People who make good procedural decisions.

23.30 Notice also that it is comparatively easier to discriminate between derailed and non-derailed arbitrations, than to discriminate between substantively good and bad arbitration outcomes. Put differently, it is generally easier to assess the quality of procedural decisions than to assess the quality of substantive decisions. This comparative ease in turn facilitates the diffusion of information regarding the decisions.[25] The effects of confidentiality in arbitration are here attenuated: it is less difficult for the market to ascertain the value of arbitrators in regard to their procedural abilities, than in regard to their ability to apply substantive law to the essential facts of the case.

23.31 In addition, there is typically far less room for antinomy between procedural regularity and conformity pressures than between a substantive decision on the merits and conformity pressures. Put bluntly, conformity pressures are much less likely to get in the way of good, managerially sound, efficient procedural decisions. Hence, Puig's point mentioned above about the 'tweaking effects' of conformity pressures remains compatible with the argument that the variegated procedural decisions made by arbitrators have direct, 'un-tweaked' market value and can as such influence an arbitrator's income.

(e) Increasing income

23.32 Now consider two ways in which procedural decisions can increase the income of arbitrators. The first way is to increase the chance of the arbitrator in question to get a slice, or a bigger slice, of the existing pie. This amounts to competitively improving the offer while demand stays constant. The second way is to increase the size of the pie itself.

23.33 This means increasing demand. The first way has been the object of our attention thus far: increasing one's proficiency in running clean, efficient arbitrations is a way to competitively improve one's offer of arbitration services. But it does not increase, at least not directly, the demand for arbitration.

23.34 To the second way: increasing the demand for arbitration. This can, for instance, be achieved by allowing entire new breeds of cases to go to arbitration, by making it easier for certain types of disputes, or indeed for all types of disputes, to go to arbitration. This,

---

[25] In the proverbial locker rooms of the local tennis club, one is more likely to hear statements to the effect that X messed up the procedure again, than judgments on Y's decision on the merits.

in turn, can for example be attained by taking the edge off jurisdictional or admissibility requirements.[26]

23.35 A modicum of knowledge of the recent history of investment arbitration, for instance, is enough to recollect decisions on jurisdiction that were, from a black-letter law perspective, 'interesting' (think of small bondholders, or of most favoured nation (MFN) clauses), but that were in any event good for arbitrators' business. From a law and economics perspective, relaxing jurisdictional and admissibility requirements is, in most situations, a very sensible thing to do for arbitrators.

23.36 The resulting situation might be unfortunate for certain parties (consider, for instance, the measurable harm in investment flows caused to states by letting investment arbitrations pass the jurisdictional phase even when they have no case on the merits).[27] But it is good for arbitration business. So if this is to be changed, some market intervention might be required: this means altering the sundry incentives and constraints that the current socio-legal system of investment arbitration places on arbitrators.

23.37 Increasing income has its limits. From a perspective that isolates income, and discounts other objectives, the optimal number of cases an arbitrator should take on depends on the relationship between: on the one hand, the marginal income generated by a case; and on the other, the expected loss of future cases due to a loss in reputation caused by a decreased quality of (particularly procedural, it seems) decision-making.

23.38 Here it bears noting that, much against conventional wisdom, it appears that the world of arbitration is barely opposed, in practice, to arbitrators delegating work. In our earlier study already quoted, we found indeed that two-thirds of interviewees (arbitrators and lawyers practising in arbitration) did not mind an arbitrator delegating his preparation for hearings, issuing procedural orders, and even writing the award. This, of course, significantly displaces the constraints created by physical limits and must move upwards the optimum number of cases mentioned above.

23.39 Our argument so far has followed a simple path: we have focused on the economic incentives implied by arbitrators seeking to be 'picked and picked again', as Christopher Drahozal puts it.[28] But there is a major side road off this path: for many arbitrators, being picked does not create the greatest economic incentive. Most arbitrators have other sources of income, typically legal counsel work, which usually are more lucrative, both in total and for equal time and effort. For such arbitrators, which likely form the great majority of arbitrators, it makes no economic sense to engage in certain behaviour (typically making certain decisions) that increases their chance of being picked, but reduces their chance of being used as counsel. If potential future clients represent a dominant share of an arbitrator's long-term income—an income greater than the income generated by appointments—then it is in most cases economically sensible to privilege these clients' interests over those of the parties

---

[26] For an overview of jurisdiction and admissibility requirements, see John J Barceló III, 'Arbitrability Decisions Before, During, and After Arbitration' in Julio César Betancourt (ed), *Defining Issues in International Arbitration: Celebrating 100 Years of the Chartered Institute of Arbitrators* (OUP 2016) ch 7, Part A(b).

[27] Todd Allee and Clint Peinhardt, 'Contingent Credibility: The Reputational Effects of Investment Treaty Disputes on Foreign Direct Investment' (2011) 65 Int'l Org 401.

[28] Drahozal (n 16) 588.

to the case. This, however, assumes that these interests are antagonistic, which is not necessarily the case.

23.40 These are some of the salient ways in which the maximization of income—a routine business objective, we are not being judgmental here—connects to the behaviour of arbitrators. There is, however, one narrative about economic incentives that tells an implausible story. Admittedly, it is a dead horse, but it requires flogging to ensure it stays dead. It is the argument that arbitrators should, from an economic viewpoint, split the baby. Recall the argument: in order to maximize their income, arbitrators should make decisions that are pair-wise efficient for the plaintiff and the defendant. To do that they should divide the stakes so as to keep both parties happy, or in other words 'split the baby' with regard to awarding damages sought. This is meant to increase their chances of being reappointed by either party in the future.[29] This is a dead horse because empirical investigations have shown that arbitrators do not in fact do this, or only marginally.[30]

23.41 To be sure, there could be other incentives and constraints that systematically offset this particular incentive, thwarting its empirical manifestations. But the more plausible explanation is that parties tend to over-evaluate their chances of winning the case. Hence, if the expectation is to get half the baby, it is lower than what they would expect to obtain from an arbitrator who, in their view, competently applies law to facts (not to speak of an arbitrator who sees the dispute their way), since on average each party believes that they have more than 50 per cent chances of winning.

23.42 On our way to discussing reputation, which forms the substance of Part C below, we should pause to consider an important distinction. Certain forms of reputation are purely instrumental: they only serve to achieve other objectives, typically, but not necessarily, the maximization of income. These forms of reputation may, but also may not, be perceived as positive, or appealing, by the average participant in the system: one may not wish to have a certain reputation per se, but it serves an ulterior purpose. For these forms of reputation, we may use the word 'publicity'. Now let us ask the customary marketing question about publicity: is there such a thing as bad publicity for an arbitrator or is there only publicity?

23.43 We delineated above a few ways in which it makes economic sense for an arbitrator to be known. Then again, even many bad decisions, on the merits or the procedure, are in fact good for someone. Deralling an arbitration may actually be what the respondent wants. Abilities to massage the law until it relaxes may be prized. Being open to bribes cannot fail to effectively seduce certain parties. What is certain is that someone who is not known at all is very unlikely to be suggested, and thus appointed, as an arbitrator. Is it not so, then, that what counts above all is to be on the map? That there are economic reasons to prefer being a generally unpalatable somebody than a generally palatable nobody?

23.44 Let us not, of course, deform the argument to the point of making it inane—there are many characteristics for which an arbitrator may be known that are not appealing to anyone and

---

[29] ibid; Cooter (n 14) 125.
[30] Bruce L Benson, 'Arbitration' in Boudewijn Bouckaert and Gerrit de Geest (eds), *Encyclopedia of Law and Economics* (Elgar 2000) 159, 181–2.

serve no ulterior purpose. But the point we tried to develop is that the pool of these characteristics is much smaller than conventional wisdom has it. And that pool is likely to be even smaller when the arbitrator's primary economic objective is to source clients for his counsel work: certain arbitrations are great platforms for publicity. In sum, being famous, even if only for being famous, has economic value, and thus creates economic incentives to strive for it.

C. Reputation, Fame, and Prestige

23.45 But money is not everything in life. In fact, as we said, being an arbitrator is not even the highest paying activity for many practising lawyers. So if someone chooses to become an arbitrator, it is either because he cannot enter one of the higher paying activities or because he does not want to.[31] In the latter case, when someone chooses to become an arbitrator because he prefers it to other more lucrative activities within reach, and assuming there is no problem of information asymmetry, we may assume the following: that person derives more satisfaction from the pursuit or realization of other objectives than he loses in satisfaction from the loss in income.

(a) Reputation

23.46 There is nothing surprising here. There are vastly more credible situations in which people care about their reputation for reasons that are existentially independent of their instrumentality in generating income, thus granting reputation independent value, than credible situations in which people simply do not care about their reputation. In plain English: for most people, maintaining a positive reputation is an objective in itself, independently of its usefulness in generating income.

23.47 The same point has been made with regard to judges. We already mentioned in the introduction that economic analyses of the judiciary suggest that judges tend to care more about reputation than the average practising lawyer.[32] More precisely, they entertain a different ratio of the value they accord to reputation to the value they accord to income. Posner finds support for this view in the fact that many judges are sensitive to statistics even if they have no tangible effect on their career.[33] Who, indeed, is entirely insensitive to peer recognition?[34]

---

[31] Let us leave aside, here, the hypothetical already chalked out above, in which someone becomes an arbitrator only for instrumental reasons, for instance using the publicity that being an investment arbitrator generates in order to obtain income from other sources, through counsel work or academic appointments or anything else.

[32] Posner, 'Judicial Behavior and Performance' (n 5). Note that becoming a judge, at least in most national courts, excludes other sources of revenue, while being an arbitrator does so only to the degree that the same time and energy cannot be used for other remunerative activities. Let us put this differently: a difference between choosing to work as an arbitrator and choosing to become a judge in a state court is that the decision to become a judge typically excludes all other forms of work, whereas one can work as an arbitrator while still maintaining a professional practice as legal counsel, or in any other vocation. The economic cost, then, of choosing to work as an arbitrator is significantly less than the cost of choosing to become a judge.

[33] Posner, 'Judicial Behavior and Performance' (n 5) 1271.

[34] Arguably, this behaviour of judges is in fact best explained as an indirect, fairly unconscious way to measure the implicit demand for their services, as Cooter maintains (Cooter (n 14) 107). It would thus be a way to measure their economic value for society. Yet it is not a direct economic, income-maximizing incentive.

(b) Fame

23.48 Now, what is the extent of an arbitrator's reputation? Let us linger just a little longer on judges to make the case for arbitrators. Some judges, clearly, acquire a reputation that amounts to fame. Importantly, though that much should be obvious, we are addressing ourselves here to positive reputation that amounts to fame, not just to any form of publicity as we contemplated above. So, Posner, a judge himself, considers that for some judges fame is in fact an important objective when conducting judicial behaviour.[35]

23.49 What about arbitrators? Do some of them acquire a level of reputation that amounts to fame, in the sense we understand it here? The answer depends of course on how high we place the bar on reputation before it becomes fame. And it depends on the community we consider.

23.50 The best-known arbitrators are clearly known to other arbitrators and to people acting as counsel in arbitration. So much would be true in mostly every professional community. But in many cases, their fame extends beyond these circles, in the first place to people who would like to join these circles: typically practising lawyers and law students who want to work in the field of arbitration and therefore have to acquaint themselves with the social mechanics in that field.

23.51 Arbitrators may also be famous in communities that are interested in the effects of their work: for example, international organizations, non-governmental organizations (NGOs), academics beyond the field of law, and even journalists often are interested in the contributions of investment arbitrators to investment law, to general international law, to the economics of foreign investments, to the international political economy of foreign investments, and so on.

23.52 But we said above that we are considering here positive reputation that amounts to fame: so are these contributions necessarily, or even just mostly, positive? Let us briefly park the question, and return to it after we have entered a quick clarification.

(c) Prestige

23.53 We should make it plain that we are moving here to a specific form of reputation: prestige, which in the context we discuss is the type of instantaneous reputation that attaches to an individual merely because he serves as an arbitrator, regardless how that activity is actually performed by the individual in question. Prestige, again, is a positive type of reputation, which entails respect and admiration. So the question here is: do respect and admiration attach to the function of an arbitrator?

23.54 From a 30,000 foot view, there is something inherently prestigious in every dispute resolution function. This is, in fact, often taken as a given in behavioural economic work on the judiciary.[36] Granted, it seems commonsensical that one of the motivating

---

[35] Posner, 'The Role of the Judge' (n 5) 1056.
[36] Linz Audain, 'The Economics of Law-Related Labor V: Judicial Careers, Judicial Selection, and an Agency Cost Model of the Judicial Function' (1992–93) 42 Am UL Rev 115, 120–1 ('Because prestige, power and high incomes are commonly available amenities for partners in large law firms and because those partners are willing to take substantial reductions in income to become judges, it follows that the judiciary confers more prestige (and power) on these individuals than is available to them in the law firm context'); Cooter (n 14) 129 ('In the absence of a compelling alternative, a reasonable hypothesis is that self-interest judges seek prestige').

factors for becoming a judge in a state court is the prestige that is associated with the position. Holding a position as a judge does indeed confer a certain level of respect and prestige and social standing in many societies. These are caused by the community's recognition that this individual exhibits the requisite symbolic capital to exert a function that has significant socio-legal consequences for individual parties and, in the aggregate, for the community as a whole. Likewise, there is something inherently respectable in being chosen by members of the international commercial community to decide their disputes.

23.55 But let us start the descent from our 30,000 foot view. Consider the prestige that comes with being associated to a certain group of people, or more specifically to certain Weberian ideal-types, in our case ideal-type arbitrators. Recall that the so-called 'first generation' of arbitration, in the 1970s, was cast by Yves Dezalay and Bryant Garth as 'Grand Old Men'.[37] Such individuals were chosen because of their personal prestige acquired before becoming an arbitrator. They brought that prestige to the collective representation of what it is to be an arbitrator. To put it simply, who would not want to be associated with a group of Grand Old Men (assuming you are a man, that is)?

23.56 The second generation of arbitrators, in the 1990s, was cast as 'technocrats'. These were acrobats, if you will, of arbitration law and procedure—highly specialized experts in the technical intricacies of arbitration. Garth and Dezalay considered this to be still 'rather glamorous'.[38]

23.57 How about today? If our prior study, to which we keep referring, holds true in that the current generation of arbitrators is best described as 'Dispute Resolution Managers', the question becomes: how much glamour, inherent respect, and admiration do managers typically get? Does it differ, to take extremes, from the prestige of being a Grand Old Man (or Woman)? The question probably does not need to be answered. All of this is very much simplified, of course, as the very nature of ideal-types is to be analytical constructs, but the point remains: the greatness thrust on individuals (to use a bit of Shakespeare terminology) by virtue of being an arbitrator may well be quite different today than it was 40 years ago.

23.58 Let us consider investment arbitration again. To be sure, investment arbitration has conspicuously altered the relation between arbitrators and reputation and fame. For a long time, the majority of people who know about arbitration would look up to arbitrators: admire them, merely because they were arbitrators. The rise of investment arbitration gave arbitrators an extraordinary platform for publicity. Notice how the website of ICSID, where it lists current and past arbitrations, is used as a Who's Who in arbitration.

23.59 Today, indeed, even the layperson can very easily find out who arbitrates disputes between household-name companies and states. And notice how investment arbitrators decide, again very often in cases in which the arbitrators' identity is public and publicized, matters of great import: the financial stakes are often high, and so are sometimes the social, environmental, and public health stakes.

---

[37] Yves Dezalay and Bryant Garth, *Dealing in Virtue: International Commercial Arbitration and the Construction of a Transnational Legal Order* (University of Chicago Press 1996) 21.
[38] ibid 8.

(d) A changing view?

23.60 This is a double-edged sword. As the world at large came to realize that certain effects of investment arbitration can be devastating, the notorious backlash against investment arbitration developed and grew.[39] The very word 'backlash' is probably suggestive enough to point out the changing social view of arbitration.

23.61 Here, we must return to a distinction we sketched above between two different communities, or constituencies, that arbitrators appeal to: on the one hand, arbitration practitioners and would-be arbitration practitioners; on the other, the public at large that looks at arbitration. These are two different groups of people in which arbitrators build the sort of reputation and fame we are discussing here, which has value independently of its ability to generate income.

23.62 The first constituency, clearly, is narrower than the second. It is composed essentially of lawyers—law practitioners, law students, even academic lawyers. In this group, to put it bluntly, there is no backlash. Backlash stories are simply misunderstandings of arbitration (a textbook case of Bourdieusian symbolic violence if there ever was one). In this group, one may be (or, more precisely, one may carefully build a reputation for being) investor friendly, or well disposed to state public interest, or a neutral player, but one is not against the system itself of arbitration. In this group, the métier of 'arbitrator' is still a high achievement.

23.63 But, arguably, the perceived identity of arbitrators is no longer so exclusively shaped by this natural habitat. The perception of outsiders starts to matter: the perception of this second community we flagged, the public at large, which is becoming a constituency. Notice, for instance, the unnecessary force with which arbitrators and would-be arbitrators have reacted to reports of campaign groups, empirical studies of political scientists, and stories of journalists. They could just have been oblivious to all this. Instead, they seemed to react to something that went through to their perceived identity. The constituencies of an arbitrator's reputation are expanding.

23.64 Let us not kid ourselves: investment arbitration (and arbitration in general is all too easily assimilated to it) is despised in many social circles.[40] There are areas in this world, social and geographic areas, where it is probably advisable not to say that one is an investment arbitrator, and stick to discussing the weather. Whether this disagreeableness is justified or not is irrelevant.[41] What is relevant is that it exists.

23.65 In certain situations it is understandable. Consider the following: imagine you have lost a family member, a friend, to lung cancer due to smoking; imagine an investment arbitral tribunal significantly stifles the efforts of one nation directly, and of several nations indirectly, to curb smoking; imagine you are aware of this and your daughter comes home one night saying she just became an investment arbitrator. Who would not have reservations in their pride?

---

[39] See, for instance, Osgoode Hall Law School, 'Public Statement on the International Investment Regime' (31 August 2010) Art 14, according to which states 'should take steps to replace or curtail the use of investment treaty arbitration; and should strengthen their domestic justice system for the benefit of all citizens and communities, including investors'. See also Michael Waibel and others (eds), *The Backlash against Investment Arbitration* (Kluwer Law International 2010).

[40] See the classic *cri de coeur* by Pia Eberhardt and Cecilia Olivet, *Profiting from Injustice: How Law Firms, Arbitrators and Financiers Are Fuelling an Investment Arbitration Boom* (Corporate Europe Observatory and Transnational Institute 2012).

[41] For a study that nibbles at the question, see Thomas Schultz and Cédric Dupont, 'Investment Arbitration: Promoting the Rule of Law or Over-Empowering Investors? A Quantitative Empirical Study' (2014) 25(4) EJIL 1147.

23.66 Now, this is an extreme situation, of course. But the point is that resolving purely commercial disputes between commercial actors is incomparably less likely to elicit strong sentiments in those who watch, than 'interfering' in agreeable social and health policies, with a sword used primarily to champion investor interests.

23.67 What does this mean? It means that the publicity arbitrators get from practising their trade grows, but that the social reputation they acquire in doing so might—just might—be decreasing rather than increasing. It might be becoming less appealing, rather than more. Can it go so far that the reputation individuals acquire from being an arbitrator shifts from being a gain, a utility, to being a cost?

D. Doing Justice

23.68 Doing justice is often an objective for an individual in charge of resolving a dispute. An objective in the sense of something having inherent value if it is attained or approached, as opposed to something required by others. Doing justice is thus likely to figure, sometimes prominently, sometimes marginally, in the matrix of incentives that make dispute resolvers behave the way they do. But what does it mean to do justice? Can we at least rough out a typology of what this may mean for arbitrators?

(a) Changing the world

23.69 Studies on judges provide, again, a useful starting point. Certain such studies accent the importance for judges of their power to promote their own conception of justice or political vision on society.[42] One of the reasons why lawyers seem to choose to become judges, in defiance of the economic disadvantages outlined above, is a desire to 'change the world for the better'.[43]

23.70 Can this be transposed to arbitrators? The classical argument one encounters when suggesting mostly anything of that kind is that the authority of arbitrators is derived from the agreement of the parties and as such the arbitrators' duty is to the parties and to the parties only. Arbitrators get their instructions from the parties, and if these instructions do not call for 'justice', only for refereeing, then there shall be no pursuit of justice. (Let us, *ex hypothesi*, exclude refereeing from the realm of justice.)

23.71 Among black-letter lawyers, such arguments may do. But if we overcome our legal reflexes and consider even just a glimpse of the psychological and sociological aspects of human conduct, it seems fairly unlikely that this is a sufficiently elaborate explanation of the relation arbitrators entertain with justice.

(b) Community stakes

23.72 To start with a simple point, many arbitrations are not only the parties' business. They are often also society's business. As William Park puts it: 'The general community often has a stake not only in the outcome of arbitration, but also in the way proceedings have been conducted.'[44] There is no need for advanced moral philosophy to suggest that arbitrators, as

---

[42] Foxall (n 5) 181.
[43] Posner, 'The Role of the Judge' (n 5) 1056.
[44] William W Park, 'Arbitration in Autumn' (2011) 2 JIDS 287, 304.

members of society, should not remain systematically impervious to externalities that may exist in connection with their cases. But more importantly, the point can also be made as a descriptive matter: arbitrators, at least sometimes, are indeed concerned by general ideals of justice that transcend the case at hand.

For instance, who has not heard investment arbitrators openly claim that the world needs a strong hand, that investment arbitration is to investment flows what the United States is to international security, that it gets rogue states to walk the straight and narrow? Or, on the other end of the spectrum, investment arbitrators expressing the belief that the priority in regulating the international economy, including through the arbitration of disputes, is to end poverty? These are not unpoliticized views devoid of justice symbolism.[45] **23.73**

Investment arbitration, you might say, is special. But even in commercial arbitration, for many arbitrators, a heightened sense of fairness in the way they handle a dispute seems to matter a great deal. Consider William Park, for instance, whose many writings insist on 'the right way to do things' and on arbitration's role in the search for truth; and his many references, direct and indirect, to Christian morality.[46] Do they not point to something more profound than the need to comply with the applicable law or professional rules or codes of conduct? **23.74**

A more classical example: the role of ideologies of justice in an arbitrator's home legal culture (for instance, formalism v informalism, or legalism v Confucianism) influence that arbitrator's belief about how often settlement is an appropriate outcome.[47] Justice, in other words, is done differently depending on one's home legal culture, and its attendant representations of the right ways to do justice. Of course, disputation can be had endlessly about the appropriateness of all these variegated references for the pursuit of justice in arbitration. But that is not the point. **23.75**

The point is that it is plausible that, on average, doing justice is a value that figures prominently enough in the decision-making matrix of the average arbitrator for it to be taken into account in the general analytical construct we are putting together here. So again the question: can we at least sketch a rough typology of what doing justice might mean for arbitrators? And sketch it in a way that allows us to think about how it may influence their decision-making? **23.76**

(c) Ways to do justice

One such typology could be this. Arbitrators, and mostly every other dispute resolver, have at least three broad ways to do justice.[48] **23.77**

First, they can seek to maximize the cumulated satisfaction (subjective) or interests (objective) of the parties to the instant case. In other words, both parties should get the best possible deal out of the arbitration, even if it is only the best possible loss. A typical incarnation **23.78**

---

[45] For a philosophical, normative (not descriptive) account of this question, see Thomas Pogge, 'International Law between Two Futures' (2014) 5(3) JIDS 432.
[46] For instance, William W Park, 'Arbitrators and Accuracy' (2010) 1 JIDS 25.
[47] See the classical work of Simon Roberts and Michael Palmer, *Dispute Processes: ADR and the Primary Forms of Decision-Making* (2nd edn, CUP 2005).
[48] Thomas Schultz, 'The Three Pursuits of Dispute Settlement' (2011) 1 CYArb 227.

of this ideal is to disregard prior cases which offer themselves as possible precedents to follow. Obiter dicta are avoided. The focus is on the case, not on past or future cases.

23.79 Second, they can seek to further the rule of law, in the sense of aiming at the greatest possible predictability. Here, the arbitrators reward the parties for the plans they have made and permit other, future parties to make meaningful plans. This may, but need not, lead to a decision in the arbitration that does not advance the current interests of the parties to the greatest extent possible. *Dura lex sed lex*. A classic example of this ideal is to treat prior cases as precedents to the greatest reasonable degree.

23.80 Third, they can seek to further certain substantive societal values, such as, quite classically, the protection of the environment, human rights, the protection of property (including, perhaps, intellectual property) as a cornerstone of our economy, decreasing poverty as a cornerstone of global justice, etc. This may, but need not, lead to arbitral decisions that make neither of the parties particularly happy nor are particularly predictable, but may be good for the community at large. Under this conception of justice, prior cases, future cases, rules, and even the case at hand are all instruments—means but not ends—used by the arbitrators to achieve their societal goal.

23.81 In each case in which one of these pursuits is somewhat advanced, the arbitrator may reasonably derive some satisfaction, from having advanced a certain conception of justice, from having done justice. This may well have independent value for the arbitrator. To be clear, seeking to maximize this value acts like a vector that reinforces, weakens, or displaces the effects on the behaviour of arbitrators of other vectors such as the maximization of income or reputation.

23.82 One concrete example might help: creating and following precedents. The classical economic theory on precedents, for instance, suggests that it makes little economic sense for arbitrators to relate one case to another: arbitrators are hired and paid by the parties to resolve the dispute between them, not to clarify the law or help future parties anticipate what will happen.[49] From this perspective, for an arbitrator to write an obiter dictum amounts to working for free (or to billing the parties for something he was not required to do). Seeking to do justice, on the other hand, may create an incentive that is strong enough to alter the arbitrator's view in this regard.

E. Avoiding Reprimand by an Annulment or Denial of Enforcement

23.83 And the law, the obdurate lawyer at the end of his tether may now cry out, this surely creates determinants of arbitrator behaviour too?

23.84 We entered the caveat in the introduction that we would not review the full scope of incentives and constraints that determine the behaviour of arbitrators, but rather focus on a selected few determinants. We certainly acknowledge the variegated effects of law's

---

[49] Robert D Cooter and Daniel L Rubinfeld, 'Economic Analysis of Legal Disputes and Their Resolution' (1989) 27 J Econ Lit 1067, 1093; Drahozal (n 16) 586; William M Landes and Richard A Posner, 'Adjudication as a Private Good' (1979) 8 J Leg Stud 235, 238, 245; Foxall (n 5) 180. The little economic sense that it does make comes from the fact that, under certain circumstances, an arbitrator's work may gain in efficiency by following precedents with little discussion.

perceived authority (law being obeyed, and thus acting as a determinant, merely because it is 'law')[50] and we recognize the likely Bourdieusian *habitus* to use legal rules and 'soft-law' rules as the first port of call for arbitrators to orient themselves. Professional liability, to some degree, is also likely to come into the mix. A full map of the ways in which law acts as a determinant of arbitrator behaviour would need to elaborate on these points.

23.85 We want to focus on one thing in particular that assuredly directs the behaviour of arbitrators, and may well be one of the most important: the objective of avoiding the reprimand elicited by an annulment of the award or its unenforceability.

23.86 Only a brief discussion is warranted here, because the subject is fairly straightforward. To our usual point of departure: classical economic theory accents the importance for judges not to have their decisions overturned by superior courts.[51] Arbitrators have a similar worry—let us not fret here over the distinction between appeal (of judgments) and annulment (of arbitral awards), for this is a difference that makes no difference for the argument we want to make.

23.87 The point really is simple: arbitrators are almost inevitably in effect reprimanded when their awards are annulled, set aside, or even, with many qualifications, denied enforcement. In ICSID arbitrations, *ad hoc* annulment committees often make a point of castigating the arbitral tribunal for what the committee sees as a reproachable lack of interpretive proficiency of the applicable legal provisions.

23.88 The question, of course, is not whether the reprimand is justified or not—certain annulments are barely disguised political actions, or deplorable manifestations of judicial incompetence. Essentially, barely anyone likes to see their work, in this case often months if not years of work, thrown to the winds, with accompanying implicit if not express scolding.

F. Conclusion

23.89 The deference arbitrators receive during hearings is likely to have value for most individuals, and is thus likely to attract people to the job of arbitrator and to guide their behaviour when on the job. Arbitrators can decide on the life and death of companies, and order forbidding dictators to pay up tens and hundreds of millions of dollars in compensation. This is real power, and deference tends to follow. Arbitrators may also find consumption value in hearing the case and making a decision, or casting a vote on its outcome.

23.90 Arbitrating cases is more intellectually stimulating than many other areas of legal practice and business. Arbitrators may consume the arbitration as if a spectator at a play or theatre performance, or as a detective seeking to unravel mysteries. They may even find joy in keeping a poker face as the parties try to read their thoughts about the case they are pleading. And we should not forget the importance of mimetic desires: desires are borrowed from others, modelled on the desires of others, with whom one identifies and seeks to copy. The fulfilment of what were originally other people's desires has value for us and directs our

---

[50] For a discussion of these effects, see Thomas Schultz, *Transnational Legality: Stateless Law and International Arbitration* (OUP 2014) chs 1 and 2.
[51] See, eg, Andrew J McClurg, 'The Rhetoric of Gun Control' (1992) 42 Am UL Rev 53, 62; see also Posner, 'What Do Judges and Justices Maximize' (n 5) 14 (arguing that judges do not like to be reversed).

behaviour. Certain people want to become arbitrators, and to behave in a certain way when being an arbitrator, because other people want it too. The greater the rivalry, the greater the value of the desired object.

23.91 And the list could go on. All of these objectives may act as determinants of arbitrator behaviour. Our endeavour was merely to point out certain salient features of the matrix of arbitrator decision-making. What the arbitrator had for breakfast will of course not feature prominently in this matrix—unless the breakfast was really quite peculiar.

23.92 Admittedly, it is clearly crucially important, in order to do arbitration, to conduct detailed analyses of the legal and quasi-legal rules governing arbitration. The customary black-letter law works on arbitration are, there, worthy of commendation. But such works—that skip breakfast, as it were—will take us only so far if we want to think about arbitration.

23.93 An approach grounded in legal realism and borrowing law and economics methods gets us one step further. It at least tells those who think that the behaviour of arbitrators is directed solely by a proficient interpretation of the applicable law that they might want to think again.

23.94 And a final word to those who rely on the paradigm of arbitration being a strict legal-rational institution, an actor whose rationality only comprises legal commands:[52] we encounter too many anomalies that this paradigm cannot explain. They cannot be brushed away as acceptable levels of error. The paradigm has to change.

---

[52] This paradigm is, for instance, occasionally used to deny the possibility that investment arbitration causes regulatory chill: see, eg, the discussion in Kyla Tienhaara, 'Regulatory Chill and the Threat of Arbitration: A View from Political Science' in Chester Brown and Kate Miles (eds), *Evolution in Investment Treaty Law and Arbitration* (CUP 2011).

24

FUNCTUS OFFICIO?

Greg Fullelove

Iudex posteaquam semel sententiam dixit, postea iudex esse desinit ... semel enim seu male seu bene officio functus est.

The Digest of Justinian, 42.1.55

A. Introduction

The words of Ulpian quoted above, and recorded in Justinian's Digest, remind us that the principle of *functus officio* is of considerable antiquity.[1] In the third century AD, Ulpian noted that once a judge has given his judgment, he ceases to be a judge in that case. The judge cannot return to correct the judgment once handed down since, 'for better or for worse', he has discharged his duty: *officio functus est*. **24.01**

In international arbitration today, the expression *functus officio* is similarly used to refer to the point when the arbitral tribunal has discharged its duty in full and can no longer act.[2] This point is generally held to be when the tribunal has concluded all matters with which it has jurisdiction to deal pursuant to a particular arbitration agreement. A tribunal may fulfil its mandate in stages by making more than one award,[3] each being final and binding as to the claims disposed of therein.[4] However, the principle that a tribunal is *functus officio* (subject to limited exceptions) in an arbitration once it has delivered its final award including as to costs has been described by one commentator as 'sacrosanct'.[5] **24.02**

---

[1] The principle of functus officio was doubtless of some antiquity by the time of Ulpian as well, whose commentaries synthesized the work of his predecessors. See Peter Stein, *Roman Law in European History* (OUP 1999) 20–1. For further discussion, see Derek Roebuck and Bruno de Loynes de Fumichon, *Roman Arbitration* (Holo 2004) 41.

[2] The principle of functus officio may therefore be clearly distinguished from other instances in which the arbitrator ceases to act, for example, because he is removed or resigns. In such cases the mandate terminates, but is not completed. See Gary B Born, *International Commercial Arbitration* (2nd edn, Kluwer Law International 2014) 3116.

[3] An arbitral tribunal must ensure that all the relevant issues have been fully determined before rendering the 'final award'. In some cases, a 'partial' or 'interim' award will be appropriate, eg where a costs issue remains unresolved. See Nigel Blackaby and others, *Redfern and Hunter on International Arbitration* (6th edn, OUP 2015) 507–8.

[4] For a discussion of the finality of an interim award as to what it decides, see *Emirates Trading Agency LLC v Sociedade de Fomento Industrial Private Ltd* [2015] EWHC 1452 (Comm) [32].

[5] Thomas H Webster, 'Functus Officio and Remand in International Arbitration' (2009) 27(3) ASA Bull 41. This view was endorsed by Teresa Giovanni in her article, 'When Do Arbitrators Become Functus Officio?' in Laurent Lévy and Yves Derains (eds), *Liber Amicorum en l'honneur de Serge Lazareff* (A Pedone 2011) 313.

24.03 As we shall see, while the principle itself may be superficially straightforward, its scope and application in certain cases have raised issues. This is in part explained by a (relative) dearth of authority on the subject in some jurisdictions and contradictory and/or unhelpful authorities or commentary in others.[6] As discussed below, the way in which the Latin label *functus officio* is sometimes used can also be confusing. Does it make any sense to describe a tribunal as *functus*? And is the perception of *functus officio* as a 'state' into which a tribunal passes and from which it can on occasion be recalled correct?

24.04 These are questions of some practical importance.[7] As a lengthy international arbitration draws to its close and the arbitrators prepare to sign the award, they may believe (or hope) that their work is done. But when can the tribunal be sure that its mandate is complete, ie *officio functus est*? When, if ever, can the arbitrators definitively say that they are 'free' of their duties in an arbitration?

B. *Functus Officio* and Finality

24.05 As set out below, the principle (or as sometimes described 'doctrine') of *functus officio* is generally reflected and/or encoded in arbitration laws, rules, and instruments[8] worldwide to some extent. The precise content and scope of the principle may therefore differ depending on the particular laws applicable to a dispute. That said, the essential rationale for the principle in any system is not hard to see.

24.06 Arbitration is (or is meant to be) cloaked in finality. The tribunal's mandate is to issue an award or awards which finally dispose of the claims submitted by the parties. Such awards are typically subject to limited challenge or appeal. The principle of *functus officio* is consistent with this finality and reinforces it. It is closely linked conceptually to the *res iudicata* doctrine. Indeed, to decide whether a tribunal's mandate has been fulfilled, a first step will be to determine which claims have been finally decided by the tribunal.

24.07 Arbitrators, like the parties, require certainty about when a matter is closed. At some point documents need to be disposed of and the position on potential conflicts updated. If there were no certainty on this point, the arbitrator's life could be somewhat complicated. As a US judge once noted, at the end of a hearing arbitrators return to their private lives and as such are less 'sheltered' than domestic judges.[9] If there were endless routes of appeal, correction,

---

[6] In a recent English case on the point, the court prefaced its own findings with the observation that '[t]he efforts of experienced Counsel have failed to locate much of relevance by way of authority as to when and how an arbitrator becomes *functus officio*'. This, as the judge went on to note, was probably since parties tend to be happy not to have to revert back to a tribunal after a final award is given. See *Martin Dawes v Treasure & Son Ltd* [2010] EWHC 3218 (TCC) [26].

[7] For an illustration of the problems that may arise where a tribunal makes an award as to costs in its final award but does not provide for any further proceedings relating to the quantification of such costs, see *Union of India v Cairn India Ltd*, CS(OS) No 2445/2015 [14]. In that case, the High Court of Delhi found that, applying the principle of functus officio, the tribunal could not hold further proceedings relating to quantification having not provided for such proceedings in its final award.

[8] It is often noted that the New York Convention does not contain any provision directly referring to or dealing with the principle of functus officio. This is perhaps not surprising. Unlike the UNCITRAL Model Law, for example, the New York Convention does not deal directly with the termination of the underlying proceedings.

[9] See the comments of Judge Posner in *Glass, Molders, Pottery, Plastics and Allied Workers Int'l Union AFI-CIO, CLC, Local 182B v Excelsior Foundry Co*, 56 F3d 884, 847 (7th Cir 1995).

challenge, and the like which they had to deal with, they would potentially be bombarded with communications and applications from the parties (both *inter partes* and *ex parte*). Without the structure and mechanisms of a court, this could become impossible to manage.

It is unsurprising, therefore, that the principle of *functus officio* is reflected—and often 'encoded' to some extent—in national arbitration laws and other arbitral rules and instruments in provisions which deal with the 'termination of proceedings'. Article 32 of the UNCITRAL Model Law provides, *inter alia*, that: **24.08**

(1) *The arbitral proceedings are terminated by the final award* or by agreement of the parties or by an order of the arbitral tribunal in accordance with the parties or by an order of the arbitral tribunal in accordance with paragraph (2) of this article.[10]

...

(3) *The mandate of the tribunal terminates* with the termination of the arbitral proceedings, subject to the provisions of articles 33 and 34(4).[11]

Article 32(3) clarifies that, subject to certain so-called 'exceptions', which we consider below, the mandate of the arbitral tribunal terminates with the arbitral proceedings themselves. Similar provisions are found in a considerable number of national arbitration laws around the world.[12] By contrast, the English Arbitration Act 1996 makes no specific reference to the termination of proceedings, albeit that the principle of *functus officio* is established as part of the English law on arbitration.[13] **24.09**

As noted above, Article 32(3) of the Model Law indicates that the mandate of the arbitral tribunal terminates with the proceedings subject to 'exceptions'. These exceptions (again reflected in leading arbitration rules and national laws[14]) concern: (i) the correction of any clerical or typographical errors in the award; (ii) requests for interpretation of a specific point or part of the award;[15] and (iii) requests for an additional award regarding claims presented in the arbitration, but omitted from the award.[16] An exception not present in the **24.10**

---

[10] Art 32(2) provides (in summary) that the arbitral tribunal shall issue an order for the termination of the arbitral proceedings when: (i) the claimant withdraws his claim; (ii) the parties agree on a termination of proceedings; or (iii) the arbitral tribunal finds that the continuation of the proceedings has for any other reason become unnecessary or impossible.
[11] Emphasis added.
[12] Including, for example, those of France, Singapore, Hong Kong, Germany, and Scotland.
[13] See, eg, *Martin Dawes* (n 6) [27] (Aikenhead J).
[14] With regard to arbitral rules see, eg: UNCITRAL Rules, Arts 37–8; ICC Rules, Art 35; 1998 LCIA Rules, Art 27; ICSID Rules, rr 49–55; and ICSID Additional Facility Rules, Arts 55–7. The relationship of the functus officio principle to such rules has been considered in the ICSID case of *Gold Reserve Inc v Venezuela*, ICSID Case No ARB(AF)/09/1.
[15] A request for interpretation of an award is not an opportunity for the merits of the case to be reconsidered, but is simply a request for an explanation of the award. In the inter-state arbitration *Case Concerning the Delimitation of the Continental Shelf between the United Kingdom of Great Britain and Northern Ireland and the French Republic*, Decision (14 March 1978) XVIII RIAA 271 [29], the tribunal explained it as follows: '"Interpretation" is a process that is merely auxiliary, and may serve to explain but may not change what the Court has already settled with binding force as *res iudicata*. It poses the question, what was it that the Court decided with binding force in its decision, not the question what ought the Court now to decide in the light of fresh facts or fresh arguments. A request for interpretation must, therefore, genuinely relate to the determination of the meaning and scope of the decision'.
[16] s 57(3)(b) of the English Arbitration Act 1996 contains an equivalent provision. In *Torch Offshore LLC v Cable Shipping Inc* [2004] EWHC 787 (Comm), the court held that this provision applies to claims which have been presented to the tribunal, but not dealt with in the award. It would not apply to an 'issue' which was undetermined as part of a claim. A claim would be, say, a head of claim for damages. Therefore, this section provides recourse when an award has been issued *infra petita*.

Model Law but found in other arbitral instruments is the right to request a revision of the award.[17]

24.11 As you might expect, such powers are generally only available for a short time (if it were otherwise, there would be significant room for 'tactical' and/or 'dilatory' applications being made). Under the English Arbitration Act 1996, for example, although the parties may agree otherwise, any application for the exercise of such powers must be made within 28 days of the award and any corrections must be made within 28 days of the receipt of the application by the tribunal.[18] Where an additional award is required, the tribunal should render this within 56 days of the original award, unless the parties agree to an extension of time.[19]

24.12 The tribunal's powers to correct, interpret, revise, or issue additional awards have also generally been narrowly construed by both arbitrators and courts to avoid: (i) the tribunal revisiting its reasoning and the decision after the final award; and (ii) the finality of the proceedings being thereby endangered.[20]

24.13 However, there are always exceptions. The US case of *T Co Metals LLC v Dempsey Pipe & Supply, Inc*[21] provides an illustration of where the arbitrator went beyond his post-award powers in his 'correction' of the final award, albeit that the US Court of Appeals for the Second Circuit (surprisingly) supported his approach. In this case, the original arbitration had been decided under the 2009 ICDR Rules. Upon receipt of the original final award, both parties submitted applications to the arbitrator to amend the award under Article 30(1) of the ICDR Rules.[22]

24.14 In summary, T Co Metals alleged that there were a number of errors in the arbitrator's damages calculations, which arose from his misreading and/or misunderstanding of certain invoices. The arbitrator concluded that Article 30(1) of the ICDR Rules dealing with corrections allowed him to go beyond 'rote computation' (ie merely correcting clerical errors)

---

[17] See, eg, ICSID Arbitration Rules, r 51(1). This rule applies in situations where a party has become aware of a new fact that is 'of such a nature as decisively to affect the award' and where a party can show that its 'ignorance of that fact was not due to negligence'. There is a time limit for any application of 90 days after the discovery of the new fact and in any event within three years after the date on which the award was rendered (or any subsequent decision or correction). See *Victor Pey Casado and President Allende Foundation v Republic of Chile*, ICSID Case No ARB/98/2, Decision on Revision (18 November 2009).

[18] Where the correction is made by the tribunal on its own initiative, any correction should be made within 28 days of the award, save where the parties agree otherwise (see English Arbitration Act 1996, s 57(4)).

[19] English Arbitration Act 1996, s 57(6).

[20] For example, when considering an application for revision pursuant to ICSID Arbitration Rules, r 51(1), the tribunal in *Victor Pey Casado* (n 17) noted that '[t]he requirements for admissibility of a request for revision … make it clear that the revision is not an appeal of the award, a proposition with which the parties agree, even if it appears that the Respondent considered that, in this particular case, the Application constituted in reality a type of appeal in disguise'. Similarly, in a decision of the High Court in Delhi, India, it was noted (in relation to the limited powers granted to the tribunal under the UNCITRAL Rules, Arts 36 and 37, and the UNCITRAL Model Law, Arts 32 and 33) that 'after passing of an award, [the] arbitration tribunal becomes *functus officio* except either for making corrections to the Award which are in the nature of clerical or arithmetic or some mistakes or for passing of an additional award. With respect to making corrections or with respect to making of an additional award it [is to] be noted that such proceedings take place without leading of any further evidence by the parties'. See *Union of India* (n 7) [11].

[21] 592 F3d 329 (2d Cir 2010).

[22] 2009 ICDR Rules, Arts 30(1)–(2), provide that the tribunal may upon request of a party 'correct any clerical, typographical or computation errors or make an additional award as to claims presented but omitted from the award'.

and to change the conclusions that he had reached based on his clerical errors. This led to a reduction in the damages awarded to Dempsey from US$420,537 to US$340,587.

24.15 Following a challenge to the award, the US district court agreed with Dempsey that these errors were not evident on the face of the award and were not obvious errors in mathematical computation. Accordingly, the court found that such errors could not be corrected as they would 'violate the *functus officio* doctrine'; the arbitrator had exceeded his powers and vacatur of the amended award was warranted on this basis.[23] This decision would appear to have been orthodox and what most arbitration practitioners would expect. However, the US Court of Appeals for the Second Circuit afforded a high level of deference to the arbitrator's construction of Article 30(1) of the 2009 ICDR Rules, which the arbitrator concluded allowed him to make the wider amendments.

24.16 This decision has been widely criticized—and rightly so.[24] Dempsey's submission (referred to by the court in its decision), correctly sums up the need for a restrictive interpretation of provisions dealing with post-award corrections, viz: '[i]f Arbitrators' interpretations of [Article] 30(1) (and similar rules) were entitled to deference, then on a case-by-case basis they could expand their powers to permit reconsideration of their initial decisions'.[25] As Dempsey submitted, the approach that the court ultimately endorsed seems to be one that could effectively introduce 'back-door appeals'. That would indeed be a violation of the principle of *functus officio* and an unwelcome 'enhancement' of the reduced powers of the tribunal post-final award.

C. *Functus* or Defunct: Do Tribunals 'Return from the Dead'?

24.17 There is a tendency among some commentators (and indeed courts) when describing acts of the tribunal post-award to suggest that they are a 'resuscitation' of the arbitral body.[26] In other words, the arbitral tribunal essentially 'ceased to be' when it rendered its final decision, but 'returns from the grave' to make some typographical amendment, interpretation, or additional award. This equates to seeing *functus officio* as a 'state' into and out of which a tribunal passes: one day the tribunal is *functus officio*, and the next it is not.[27]

24.18 Perhaps a better way of understanding matters (and one consistent with the main arbitral laws, rules, and instruments, including the Model Law) is that at the point the final award is issued, the tribunal's duty is not fully discharged, but reduced.[28] The tribunal should in principle have completed its mandate to decide finally on the claims referred to

---

[23] *T Co Metals LLC v Dempsey Pipe & Supply, Inc*, No 07-civ-7747 (SDNY 8 July 2008), slip op, 8. As Jennifer Kirby correctly noted in an article on the case: 'Just because a tribunal has the power to interpret the parties' chosen procedural rules does not mean it has the power to rewrite them to give itself powers the parties never intended.' See Jennifer Kirby, '*T Co Metals LLC v Dempsey Pipe & Supply, Inc*: Are There Really No Limits on What an Arbitrator Can Do in Correcting an Award?' (2010) 27(5) J Int'l Arb 527.

[24] See ibid, Kirby.

[25] *T Co Metals LLC* (n 21) 23.

[26] On the ways in which functus officio is sometimes understood and interpreted, see the following Swiss case: Decision 4A_14/2012, Swiss Federal Supreme Court (2 May 2012), (2013) 2 ASA Bull 322, [3.1.1].

[27] Descriptions such as 'the tribunal was functus' are commonplace, but arguably unhelpful. The past participle 'functus' is active in meaning ('having fulfilled') and governs 'officio' ('the duty'). Saying that a tribunal is functus is understandable, but incorrect.

[28] On this point, see Born (n 2) 3124.

it. However, there is a continuing (albeit narrower) mandate during the period when corrections, interpretation, and additional awards may be made and/or while those powers are being exercised. Accordingly, during the period when it may be called upon to exercise the powers that remain to it to correct, etc, the tribunal cannot say definitively that *officio functus est*.

24.19 Moreover, even when the time for corrections, etc is past, a tribunal still cannot safely say that it has entered into a state of *functus officio* from which it will never return. This would be to ignore the possibility of 'remand' or as it is sometimes called 'remittal' of some or all of the award by a national court for reconsideration by the tribunal. It is to this issue that we now turn.

D. Remand: The Award Returned

24.20 Article 34 of the Model Law provides that, in the context of an application for the setting aside of an award, the court may where appropriate and so requested by a party suspend the setting-aside proceedings for a period of time in order to give the arbitral tribunal an opportunity to 'resume the arbitral proceedings' or (alternatively) to take such other action as in the arbitral tribunal's opinion will eliminate the grounds for setting aside.[29] There is a time limit on such setting-aside applications being made (three months).[30]

24.21 As stated earlier, the return of the award for further consideration by a court to the tribunal is often referred to as 'remittal' or 'remand'. Again, it is a feature of many domestic laws and a provision upon which courts do rely.[31] The English Arbitration Act 1996 includes particularly involved provisions relating to remittal of arbitration awards upon challenge to an award in sections 68 (challenge on grounds of serious irregularity)[32] and 69 (appeal on a point of law).[33]

24.22 The power to remit is regularly exercised by the English courts, including in relation to appeals on a point of law. In the 2014 case of *NYK Bulkship (Atlantic) NV v Cargill International SA*, for example, the Court of Appeal endorsed the lower court's decision to remit a question on causation to the arbitrators having found in favour of the appellant. The Court of Appeal emphasized that the court's discretion to remit (rather than, for example, itself vary the award) was broad.[34]

---

[29] UNCITRAL Model Law, Art 34(4).

[30] Pursuant to Art 34(3) of the Model Law, an application for setting aside may not be made after three months have elapsed from the date on which the party making the application had received the award or, if a request had been made under Art 33, from the date on which that request had been disposed of by the arbitral tribunal. As noted above, Art 33 deals with correction and interpretation of the award and additional awards.

[31] Where an award is annulled there is generally no objection to the same arbitrators hearing it on remand. This would not, however, be the case where, eg, the annulment was for lack of independence or impartiality. On this point, see Swiss Decision (n 26) [3.1.1].

[32] s 68(3) of the English Arbitration Act 1996 provides that '[i]f there is shown to be serious irregularity affecting the tribunal, the proceedings or the award, the court may—(a) remit the award to the tribunal, in whole or in part, for reconsideration, (b) set the award aside in whole or in part, or (c) declare the award to be of no effect, in whole or in part'.

[33] s 69(7) provides, *inter alia*, that on an appeal under that section, the court may by order '(c) remit the award to the tribunal, in whole or in part, for reconsideration in the light of the court's determination, or (d) set aside the award in whole or in part'.

[34] *NYK Bulkship (Atlantic) NV v Cargill International SA* [2014] EWCA Civ 403 [45].

24.23 Here again, therefore, where remittal/remand is provided for in the applicable arbitral law, a tribunal's mandate cannot be considered finally concluded simply upon delivery of the final award (ie that *officio functus est*). The reward may return and the tribunal be asked to consider some or all of the claims anew.

24.24 The structure and drafting of, for example, the Model Law appear to clarify this. As noted above, the mandate of the arbitral tribunal terminates 'subject to' Article 34(4), which deals with remand. The UNCITRAL 'analytical commentary' on the draft text of the Model Law states that '[t]he Court ... would invite the arbitral tribunal, whose *continuing mandate* is thereby confirmed, to take appropriate measures for eliminating a certain remediable defect'.[35] The description of a 'continuing mandate' is apt.[36] The tribunal's *officium* cannot be said to be complete until the point when the award may no longer be returned to the tribunal for further consideration under the applicable laws and rules and is in that sense 'final'. Only thereafter can it be safely said that, absent extraordinary circumstances, *officio functus est*.[37]

24.25 In extreme cases, remand can result in tribunals being asked to resume the arbitral proceedings some years after the original 'final award' was rendered. A notable example of this is the case of *M&C Corp v Erwin BEHR GmbH & Co, KG*, which after two decades of proceedings was described in 2012 by the US Court of Appeals for the Sixth Circuit as litigation of 'Dickensian proportions'.

24.26 The background to the original arbitration proceedings was a claim that Behr had breached a 1985 contract under which M&C was to be Behr's exclusive agent for the sale of wood interior panelling for luxury cars. In a 1994 award, the sole arbitrator in ICC proceedings with a London seat ordered, *inter alia*, that Behr pay future commissions to M&C. This was, therefore, a 'forward-looking order of specific performance'.[38] The parties disputed which orders were included within the scope of the award and therefore what payments were due. Applications and cross-applications went between the district and appeal courts in the United States for some time, but ultimately the case was remanded to the original arbitrator for clarification and a hearing was held on 11 to 31 April 2005. This led to the arbitrator issuing a letter 'clarifying' the award in June 2005.

24.27 The *M&C v Behr* case has been (understandably) seized on by commentators writing about post-award issues.[39] In relation to the principle of *functus officio* and the question of when an arbitrator can say that he is truly 'free' of a case, the facts that: (i) the arbitrator had the award remanded to him for 'clarification' some ten years after the original award; and (ii) a two-day hearing was held a decade after the original one are notable. Further, the remand was accepted despite it being from a court other than that of the seat (London,

---

[35] Emphasis added.
[36] 'UNCITRAL Analytical Commentary on Draft Text of a Model Law on International Commercial Arbitration: Report of the Secretary General', UN GAOK 9th Comm, 18th Sess, UN Doc A/CN9/264 (1985) 74.
[37] See Webster (n 5) 463 ('Many arbitrators assume that they are *functus officio* thirty days after they have signed what they have entitled a final award. Arbitral institutions tend to take the same approach. However, reality is that arbitrators are *functus officio* when the national court at the place of arbitration—and exceptionally the place of enforcement—decides that they have finally completed their task').
[38] *M&C Corp v Erwin Behr GmbH & Co KG*, No 06-2344, 8.
[39] See in particular Andrew Foyle, 'Extension and Resumption of the Arbitral Tribunal Function after the Final Award' in Pierre Tercier (ed), *Post Award Issues* (ASA Special Series No 38, Juris 2011) 113–26.

England)⁴⁰ and the ICC Arbitration Rules (in common with other leading rules at the time) not expressly permitting or providing for remand.⁴¹

24.28 That said, there is a risk of reading too much into *M&C v Behr* or drawing general conclusions about the length of time that could elapse before a remand might be made. Most arbitrators would likely regard *M&C v Behr* as essentially *sui generis*, turning on its own facts and circumstances. Complex litigation can result in anomalies and we should note that satellite litigation was on foot as late as December 2013, with attempts being made to draw other parties into the dispute. This tells us something about the particular facts of the matter. Few disputes are likely to be of the Dickensian proportions to result in a remand ten years 'after the event'.⁴² Also, as noted, the remand did not (as one would expect) come from the seat of the arbitration (being London, England). In the normal course, the time for the English courts to have made an equivalent order would have been long past.

E. *Hussman*: Reconstitution Without Remand

24.29 Remand is therefore a further example of where a tribunal may find that it is called upon again after issuing what it intended to be its final award. In this regard, the English case of *Hussmann* is worthy of mention.⁴³ *Hussmann* provides an example of where an arbitral tribunal was reconstituted after a successful challenge to a supposedly final award even in the absence of a court's remand. *Hussmann* explored the question of what happens if a tribunal makes its final award in favour of a party which, it turns out, should never have been deemed a party to the original reference. Where that original award was subsequently found to be of no effect, could the original tribunal be reconstituted? Or would the principle of *functus officio* prevent this?

24.30 The facts in *Hussmann* are somewhat involved, but for present purposes may be summarized as follows. The underlying distribution contract had been made directly between Mr Pharaon 'trading as' Al Ameen Development and Trade Establishment (the 'Trade Estabishment') and Mr Hussmann. Under (the applicable) Saudi Law, the Trade Establishment had no legal

---

⁴⁰ The court recognized that there was a question over its power to remand the award. Behr had argued that the US court (London was the seat) had no power under the New York Convention to remand the award. The court held that the Convention was 'utterly silent' on the issue. The court accepted that it had no power to 'vacate' (ie set aside) the award, but that a power of remand was not inconsistent with the New York Convention. See *M&C Corp v Erwin Behr GmbH & Co KG*, 326 F 3d 772 (6th Cir 2003) 11. The court's order was followed. If it had not been, it is hard to see how the English courts would have given an order to the same effect compelling the arbitrator to 'clarify' an award ten years after it was rendered.

⁴¹ This point was raised by the court in *M&C Corp* (n 40) [70]. M&C pointed to Art 35 of the 1998 ICC Rules, which provides that '[i]n all matters not expressly provided for in these rules, the court and the Arbitral Tribunal shall act in the spirit of these Rules'. The court concluded that it read 'this provision to permit remand in this case, given that clarification by the original arbitrator is critical in order to make the Eighth Award enforceable at law'. The ICC Arbitration Rules in Art 35(4) now specifically deal with the situation where an award is remitted by a court for reconsideration by the tribunal.

⁴² The contested part of the final award related to an order for specific performance. Such orders can by their nature lend themselves to either the need for 'further supervision' or later clarification, which often leads tribunals to be wary of providing this form of equitable relief. One solution is to express specific performance awards as 'partial awards'—something often seen in construction cases—which gives the tribunal some measure of 'control' or 'supervision' of proceedings. For further discussion, see Robert J Gemmell, 'To Order Specific Performance?' (2010) 76(3) Arbitration 467.

⁴³ *Hussmann (Europe) Ltd v Ahmed Pharaon* [2003] EWCA Civ 266.

personality. Subsequently, Mr Pharaon incorporated Al Ameen Development & Trade Co ('the Al Ameen Company') in Saudi Arabia to carry on his business. Mr Hussmann brought arbitration proceedings under the contract. The question of which entity was the correct respondent is at the heart of the case.

24.31 The arbitrators ultimately made a first award in the name of and largely in favour of Al Ameen Company, although it was Mr Pharaon trading as the Trade Establishment that was the named party to the contract (Mr Hussmann was awarded *c*. US$57,000, while the respondent was awarded *c*. US$660,000 for its counterclaim). Mr Hussmann applied to the court under section 67 of the English Arbitration Act 1996 for the setting aside of the first award on the grounds that the tribunal had no jurisdiction to make an award in favour of the Al Ameen Company.[44] Ultimately, the court made an order declaring that the first award be 'of no effect' (in other words, the award was not expressly 'set aside'). The court concluded that the award had been made in favour of the wrong party; there was no doubt that the intended respondent was Mr Pharaon trading as the Trade Establishment.

24.32 The court in this case had no power to remit the award. However, the parties did themselves return to the arbitrators. The arbitrators considered that the declaration of 'no effect' rendered the first award a 'nullity'. Accordingly, the arbitration was 'revived'; the reference remained where it had been before the first award since the tribunal had not discharged its duty by rendering an effective award.[45] The tribunal restored the 'outcome' of the first award in a second award, this time in favour of Mr Pharaon trading as the Trade Establishment. Mr Hussmann returned to the English courts. He argued, *inter alia*, that the second award should be set aside as it had been made without jurisdiction: the arbitral tribunal had been *functus officio* following issuance of the first award.

24.33 However, in a judgment which was both (a) logical and (b) consistent with the principle of *functus officio*, the Court of Appeal dismissed the challenge. While there was no prior authority determinative of the issue, the court found that there was no good reason in principle why an invalid final award in excess of jurisdiction should exhaust the arbitrators' jurisdiction. The arbitration had therefore properly 'revived' after the finding that the first award was of 'no effect'.

24.34 This must be correct. There was, it appears, no doubt about the identity of the intended respondent. When an award was originally made in favour of another entity, the tribunal had not fulfilled its *officium* to adjudicate and finally decide upon the claims submitted to it by the parties to the reference. There were accordingly no grounds for the claimant to rely on the principle of *functus officio*.[46]

---

[44] s 67(1) of the English Arbitration Act 1996 provides that '[a] party to arbitral proceedings may (upon notice to the parties and to the tribunal) apply to the court—(a) challenging any award of the arbitral tribunal as to its substantive jurisdiction; or (b) for an order declaring an award made by the tribunal on the merits *to be of no effect*, in whole or in part, because the tribunal did not have substantive jurisdiction' (emphasis added).

[45] See *Hussmann* (n 43) [53], which records the arbitrators' finding that '[w]e hold therefore that the Tribunal has jurisdiction, is not *functus officio*, remains seized of the reference and the position now is that the reference reverts to the position in which it stood immediately before we signed the Award on 11th June 1999'.

[46] Other arguments might have been taken before the tribunal itself when it was 'revived', eg that Mr Pharaon had waived the right to have an award in the name of the Trade Establishment and that the attempt to seek a second award was an abuse of process (see *Hussmann* (n 43) [82]). However, this was not the case.

F. *Functus Officio* and Settlement

24.35 At the outset of the chapter we posed the question of when an arbitrator can be confident that his mandate is at an end. Unsurprisingly, a further question that has arisen in the context of *functus officio* has been its relationship with the parties' decision to settle. Can settlement of itself discharge the appointment of an arbitrator? And what is the position where there is a dispute over whether there has been a settlement at all (or its scope)? Will the tribunal retain jurisdiction to decide such disputes? The English case of *Martin Dawes v Treasure & Son Ltd* and the later Singaporean case of *Doshion* have considered these issues.

24.36 In *Martin Dawes*, the claimant (Mr Dawes) had engaged the respondent (Treasure & Son) to carry out construction work. The contract provided for arbitration under the JCT/CIMAR Arbitration Rules 2005,[47] to which certain contractual disputes were referred. However, before the arbitrator rendered his final award, the parties 'settled' the dispute (save as to costs). Neither the parties nor the arbitrator drew up any award or order to reflect the terms of the settlement. Costs orders did, however, follow. Mr Dawes then subsequently attempted to commence fresh arbitral proceedings, alleging defects in the work carried out by Treasure and proposing a different arbitrator. Treasure submitted that the settlement covered all of the allegations made by Dawes and served a 'Notice of Arbitration No 2' which referred, *inter alia*, that dispute to the original arbitrator. He in turn ruled that he was not *functus officio* and was therefore able to act.[48]

24.37 The English court agreed. The court began by noting that one must look to the parties' arbitration agreement under which the arbitrator was appointed to determine what the parties have agreed (expressly or by implication) about when the arbitrator's jurisdiction becomes exhausted.[49] While the court does not say so explicitly, this would include considering the parties' choice of seat and institutional rules. Here, the court found that the arbitrator was not *functus officio* following the settlement between the parties: a settlement of itself does not terminate the arbitrator's mandate.[50]

24.38 There was no dispute in this case as to whether a settlement had been agreed (it had been). However, had there been such a dispute, the court held that the original arbitrator would have retained jurisdiction to resolve it. He would still have been the arbitrator to resolve the underlying disputes, which would have included hearing a defence that the claim had been settled.[51] A settlement agreement could of course limit such jurisdiction, but that was not the case here.[52]

---

[47] These are the JCT/CIMAR Construction Industry Model Arbitration Rules 2005.
[48] The arbitrator made this ruling under s 30 of the English Arbitration Act 1996, which reflects the principle of competence-competence.
[49] *Martin Dawes* (n 6) [29]. See also Masood Ahmed, 'When an Arbitrator Becomes Functus Officio and the Impact of This on Settlement of an Arbitration' (2011) 77(3) Arbitration 371.
[50] The court found support for its position in s 51(2) of the English Arbitration Act 1996, which provides that where during arbitral proceedings the parties settle, '[t]he tribunal shall terminate the substantive proceedings and, if so requested by the parties and not objected to by the tribunal, shall record the settlement in the form of an agreed award'. This provision clearly shows that mere settlement of a dispute will not render the tribunal functus officio. At that point the tribunal has still to 'terminate' the substantive proceedings and record the settlement in an 'agreed award', ie its mandate continues albeit its end is envisaged.
[51] *Martin Dawes* (n 6) [32].
[52] ibid.

In sum, the court concluded that it would only be upon issuance of a final award that the arbitrator would be *functus officio*. As the court correctly noted, in the normal course where settlement issues were raised, the publication of a final consent award (absent in this case) would usually bring an end to the arbitrator's jurisdiction.[53]

24.39

In the later Singaporean case of *Doshion*,[54] it was held that *Martin Dawes* had been correctly decided. Doshion claimed that the parties had reached a binding settlement and sought, *inter alia*, an injunction to restrain Sembawang from continuing with the arbitration. The court considered that an argument that the tribunal had become *functus officio* amounted to a challenge to the tribunal's jurisdiction (which the tribunal would be entitled to hear as an exercise of competence-competence). That was so even where the settlement agreement was a separate contract. As the court put it, 'the determination of the existence of the Settlement Agreement is for the arbitral tribunal and should not be stolen from its hands by an injunction'.[55] In short (and again consistent with the principle of *functus officio*), the tribunal was not *functus officio* where it had not even begun to hear the case and determine its own jurisdiction.

24.40

G. Conclusion

In the 1995 US case of *Glass, Molders, Pottery, Plastics and Allied Workers*,[56] Judge Posner said that the principle of *functus officio* was, in the context of US labour law at least, 'riddled with exceptions ... hanging on by its fingernails'. Judge Posner regarded *functus officio* as a throwback to the 'bad old days' when judges were hostile to arbitration and ingenious in 'hamstringing' the process. He considered that denying arbitrators the right to revisit their awards ultimately gave them an 'ill-fitting mantle of infallibility'.

24.41

As we have seen above, the principle of *functus officio* has done significantly better than 'hang on by its fingernails' in international arbitration. It has been accepted as a core principle and accordingly encoded in international instruments such as the Model Law and domestic legislation worldwide. Aside from the occasional anomalous decision, the so-called 'exceptions' to the principle of *functus officio* are typically narrowly construed. An aversion to arbitrators going back to their awards is not so much a statement of 'arbitral infallibility' as an arbitral imperative. The perceived finality of the process is often why arbitration is chosen in the first place.

24.42

Above, we have considered the question of when a tribunal can safely consider itself to have discharged its mandate—the point when it can say that *functus officio est*. As we have seen, it

24.43

---

[53] The court also relied upon the 'consolidation' wording in JCT/CIMAR Arbitration Rules 2005, r 3.3. This provision allowed either party to give a further notice of arbitration referring any other dispute which falls under the same arbitration agreement to the arbitrator in existing proceedings and that arbitrator a power of 'consolidation'. There was no time limit as to when the referral could be made or consolidation ordered. Here, Treasure had served its Arbitration Notice No 2 before the arbitrator had issued a final award or the parties had agreed a settlement that discharged the tribunal or otherwise limited its jurisdiction. The arbitrator was, therefore, entitled under r 3.3 to deal with Treasure's Arbitration Notice No 2 by 'consolidating it' with the original dispute, which is what he effectively did.

[54] *Doshion Ltd v Sembawang Engineers and Constructors Pte Ltd* [2011] SGHC 46.

[55] The court made specific reference to Art 16 of the UNCITRAL Model Law, which has force of law in Singapore.

[56] *Glass, Molders, Pottery, Plastics and Allied Workers* (n 9).

would be wrong to consider that a tribunal has certainly finished its work when it sends the final award including as to costs to the parties. In many jurisdictions and under the leading arbitration rules, there will still be a continuing but reduced mandate to correct, interpret, and/or revise the award and perhaps to issue additional awards.

24.44 In some cases there may also be other more minor 'offices' to be fulfilled following the signing of the award, eg the notification and/or deposit of the award and the settling of accounts with the parties in respect of final fees and amounts advanced.[57] And then there is the possibility that a court might remand the final award back to the tribunal for reconsideration. It is only when the possibility of such remand has passed that a tribunal might conclude that the award is final and its mandate discharged. Even then, duties of confidentiality to keep awards, orders, submissions, and evidence confidential will not automatically terminate.[58]

24.45 To conclude, it is commonplace in judgments and commentary to find the principle of *functus officio* being used as an adjectival label in phrases such as 'the tribunal was *functus officio*'. The Romans, for reasons of grammar alone, would never have done the same. In Justinian's Digest, there was instead a reference to when the arbitrator had 'ceased to be': *arbiter esse desierat*.[59] Our modern day usage can tempt us to overlook the precise content and scope of the principle itself. As we have seen, whether in the context of correction, interpretation, revision, settlement, or remand, what constitutes the tribunal's *officium* may be fuller than we had imagined. We must be wary of declaring too early that a tribunal has ceased to be.

---

[57] The post-award life of the tribunal has received increased attention of late, in particular, in Pierre Tercier (ed), *Post Award Issues* (ASA Special Series No 38, Juris 2011). On notification and deposit of the award and ongoing confidentiality obligations post-award, see also Bernhard Berger, 'Notification and Deposit, Publication, Confidentiality and Preservation of the File' in Pierre Tercier (ed), *Post Award Issues* (ASA Special Series No 38, Juris 2011) 75.
[58] See ibid, Berger.
[59] See Roebuck and de Loynes de Fumichon (n 1) 178.

Part IX

COSTS, FUNDING, AND IDEAS FOR OPTIMIZATION

25

THE HARMONIZATION OF COSTS PRACTICES IN INTERNATIONAL ARBITRATION

The Search for the Holy Grail

Michael O'Reilly

A. Introduction

Justice V K Rajah's[1] foreword to the book *Costs in International Arbitration*[2] described the 'making of more principled decisions whilst addressing costs issues' and 'harmonising practices in this critical aspect of decision making' as 'the Holy Grail'. In this chapter, the prospect of reaching this Holy Grail will be considered.

The question of costs arises in each of the many thousands of arbitrations commenced every year worldwide. Even when proceedings do not reach a final award, anticipated costs will be a factor when deciding whether or not to initiate proceedings, whether to continue or discontinue when adverse information is received (eg following discovery/disclosure), and when deciding on a settlement strategy.

The 'problem of costs' can be divided into two distinct components. First, there is the overall cost of arbitration. Commentators have accepted that 'arbitration proceedings—particularly where the dispute is complex and there are large amounts at stake—can be extremely costly'[3], and '[i]t used to be said that arbitration was a speedy and relatively inexpensive method of dispute resolution. This is no longer so, at least where international arbitrations are concerned.'[4]

In a survey of users of international arbitration by the School of International Arbitration at Queen Mary University of London, respondents were asked to identify advantages and disadvantages of international arbitration. The summary was:

> The expense of the international arbitration process (including the costs of arbitration lawyers, arbitrators, and the arbitration institution that may be involved) was the most widely recognised disadvantage. Out of 80 respondents, 70 cited it as one of their top three concerns, with 50% of respondents ranking it as their primary concern. This challenges one

25.01

25.02

25.03

25.04

---

[1] Attorney General of Singapore since June 2014.
[2] Colin Ong and Michael O'Reilly, *Costs in International Arbitration* (Lexis Nexis 2013).
[3] Emmanuel Gaillard and John Savage (eds), *Fouchard Gaillard and Goldman on International Commercial Arbitration* (Kluwer Law International 1999) 686.
[4] Nigel Blackaby and others, *Redfern and Hunter on International Arbitration* (5th edn, OUP 2009) 315, para 1.100.

of the common myths surrounding international arbitration, namely that it is less expensive than transnational litigation.[5]

25.05 Much of the concern in this area relates to a number of ills which have been identified, including over-lawyering, aggressive representation, vague/prolix statements of case, excessive applications, over-extensive disclosure and discovery, taking weak points, failure to adhere to the timetable, etc.

25.06 The second component concerns the allocation of costs liability under the award. Given the significant costs that can be incurred, the parties are concerned with whether those costs will lie where they fall (no cost shifting) or whether one party will be required by the award to pay the reasonable costs of the other (cost shifting) and if so, what the tribunal will consider amounts to reasonable costs. This is the question at the heart of this chapter. This second question is a 'Holy Grail' because it provides the opportunity not only to solve one of the two main components of the problem of costs, but also because it can help to solve both simultaneously.

25.07 The development of a principled and consistent approach to costs can operate to moderate overall costs. If a successful party will recover its costs—but only that proportion which is reasonable, it will be incentivized away from the types of behaviours which have been identified with increasing costs. If a successful party will only recover its reasonable costs—but at the same time have to compensate the losing party in the event that the successful party has acted unreasonably, it will be discouraged from acting in this way.

25.08 However, in order for this incentive to work properly, the rules have to be understood by both parties from the outset and applied consistently and predictably by tribunals. This discipline—both the communication of the costs principles to be applied and the consistent application of those principles—represents one of the major challenges to the international arbitration community. This is the topic of the author's recent book (*Costs in International Arbitration*),[6] and which will be referred to at points within this chapter.

B. Some Preliminary Observations as to Costs

25.09 The award as to costs 'completes the mission of the arbitral tribunal [and] renders the arbitral tribunal *functus officio*'.[7] While the tribunal will generally have the power to correct slips, the making of an award as to costs is usually its final action in the proceedings. The award as to costs may be included in the substantive award or, where the provisions applicable to the conduct of the proceedings permit, may be in a separate subsequent award.

25.10 Authors and rules (and hence the tribunals which apply those rules) draw a distinction between two classes of costs:

(1) central costs: those costs which relate to the central administration of the proceedings. They include the fees and expenses of the tribunal and those of any appointing authority

---

[5] 2006 QMUL Survey, 'International Arbitration Study: Corporate Attitudes and Practices' 2 <http://www.arbitration.qmul.ac.uk/research/index.html> accessed 25 September 2015.

[6] Ong and O'Reilly (n 2).

[7] Blackaby (n 4) para 9.18. For further discussion, see Greg Fullelove, 'Functus Officio?' in Julio César Betancourt (ed), *Defining Issues in International Arbitration: Celebrating 100 Years of the Chartered Institute of Arbitrators* (OUP 2016) ch 24.

or relevant arbitral institution. They include the costs of any services properly commissioned directly by the tribunal or arbitral institution, such as tribunal-appointed experts; and

(2) party costs: those expenses incurred directly by the parties. They include each party's expenditure on investigations, witnesses, representation in the proceedings, and so on.

The utility of this classification is widely recognized, but a range of expressions is used to distinguish between them. A sample of these include: 'The costs of international arbitration are two-fold and consist of the costs of the proceeding and the costs of the parties.'[8] 'The term "costs" in the context of arbitration may be divided into two broad categories: the costs of the arbitration and the costs of the parties.'[9] 'Costs related to arbitration can be divided into two main groups: arbitration costs and legal costs.'[10]

25.11

The main terminological confusion relates to what is described above as 'central costs'. Expressions such as 'costs of the arbitration' or 'arbitration costs' bear a range of meanings in international arbitration rules and legislation—including, confusingly, the legal costs of the parties[11] from which they are to be distinguished. For this reason, it is suggested that it may be appropriate to introduce a new term, hence 'central costs' which is not used in any other sense.

25.12

A number of features of costs in international arbitration are worthy of preliminary note. First, the applicable law of costs is generally part of the procedural law of the seat of the arbitration. Second, the remedy of costs is an incidental or derivative remedy. Third, the award of costs is generally discretionary. But, fourth, in line with the principle of party autonomy, an agreement by the parties as to costs will generally be acceptable by virtually all seats and applied by the parties. These points, while correct in their generality, have a number of exceptions, or potential exceptions.[12]

25.13

The third and fourth points lead to the following scheme: the costs will be in the discretion of the tribunal—but if the parties have agreed on the principles by which that discretion is to be exercised, tribunals will generally give effect to those principles.

25.14

C. Discretion and Principles

Subject to any agreement and to the laws of the seat and procedural rules, the decision as to costs is in the discretion of the tribunal. However, with few exceptions, the provisions of the seat or procedural rules are largely permissive or provide outline guidance only, and hence, even in these cases, a wide discretion is preserved largely intact.

25.15

---

[8] John Y Gotanda, 'Attorneys' Fees Agonistes: The Implications of Inconsistency in the Awarding of Fees and Costs in International Arbitrations' in Miguel Ángel Fernández-Ballesteros and David Arias (eds), *Liber Amicorum Bernardo Cremades* (La Ley 2010).
[9] Blackaby (n 4) 545, para 9.87.
[10] Julian D M Lew, Loukas A Mistelis, and Stefan Kröll, *Comparative International Commercial Arbitration* (Kluwer Law International 2003) 652, para 24-80.
[11] 2012 ICC Rules, Art 37(1): 'The costs of the arbitration shall include ... the reasonable legal and other costs incurred by the parties for the arbitration'. 2010 UNCITRAL Rules, Art 40(1): 'The arbitral tribunal shall fix the costs of arbitration ... (2) The term 'costs' includes only ... (e) The legal and other costs incurred by the parties ...'. English Arbitration Act 1996: '(1) References in this Part to the costs of the arbitration are to ... (c) the legal or other costs of the parties ...'.
[12] For fuller discussion, see Ong and O'Reilly (n 2).

25.16 The arbitration procedural laws of a number of jurisdictions expressly refer to the discretionary nature of costs.[13] Published awards frequently include relevant comments which show that tribunals correctly apprehend the nature of the exercise: 'As both Parties recognise in their written submissions, this Arbitral Tribunal enjoys a broad discretionary power in deciding the allocation of party (and other arbitration) costs between the Parties and (as regards party costs) assessing their recoverable amount.'[14] 'It is accepted that this rule gives the Arbitral Tribunal broad discretion in deciding on the costs of the arbitration.'[15] 'As pointed out by the prevailing doctrine "this wording is intended to permit the arbitrators the greatest possible discretion in fixing the costs of the arbitration pursuant to Art 31(3)".'[16] 'Under Article 61(2), the Tribunal is granted discretion in making its determination with respect to the allocation of costs.'[17] 'Both the Convention and the Arbitration Rules give a tribunal broad discretion in the awarding of costs.'[18]

25.17 Although the discretion may be wide, the tribunal should make its decision on the basis of principle. In one investment arbitration, the *ad hoc* committee hearing annulment proceedings stated: 'the Committee has broad discretion in determining costs. However discretion may not be capricious or arbitrary. It must be the result of rational consideration of relevant factors.'[19] There is, further, clear national court authority for the desirability of exercising the discretion in a broadly predictable way.

25.18 Bingham LJ articulated this clearly: 'While the exercise of any discretion necessarily means that there is an area within which the judge's discretion is final and unchallengeable, it is highly desirable that the general lines on which a familiar discretion will be exercised should be generally known and broadly predictable.'[20] This important point translates directly into arbitration practice because the same obligation of fairness to the parties applies both in litigation and arbitration.

25.19 Where a common practice may be identified, it is appropriate for the tribunal to have regard to that practice when exercising its discretion; thus where the expectation of all parties is, for instance, that costs should reflect the degree of success, it is important for the tribunal to have regard to that principle;[21] and where it decides to depart from that principle, it must do so for a proper reason that it is able to justify.[22]

---

[13] For example, British Columbia International Arbitration Act 1996, s 31(8): 'Unless otherwise agreed by the parties, the costs of an arbitration are in the discretion of the arbitral tribunal ...'; Australian International Arbitration Act 1974 (as amended in 2010), s 27(1): 'The costs of an arbitration (including the fees and expenses of the arbitrator or arbitrators) shall be in the discretion of the arbitral tribunal.'

[14] ICC Case No 14108, Final Award (2011) in Albert Jan van den Berg (ed), *Yearbook Commercial Arbitration*, vol XXXVI (Kluwer Law International 2011) 135–201, [260].

[15] ICC Case No 12745, Final Award (2010) in Albert Jan van den Berg (ed), *Yearbook Commercial Arbitration*, vol XXXV (Kluwer Law International 2010) 40–128, [273].

[16] ICC Case No 14046, Final Award (2010) in Albert Jan van den Berg (ed), *Yearbook Commercial Arbitration*, vol XXXV (Kluwer Law International 2010) 241–71, [77].

[17] *Toto Costruzioni Generali SpA v Republic of Lebanon*, ICSID Case No ARB/07/12, Award (7 June 2012), [258].

[18] *Swisslion DOO Skopje v The Former Yugoslav Republic of Macedonia*, ICSID Case No ARB/09/16, Award (6 July 2012), [354].

[19] *ATA Construction, Industrial and Trading Co v The Hashemite Kingdom of Jordan*, ICSID Case No ARB/08/2, Annulment Proceedings (11 July 2011).

[20] *K/S A/S Bani v Korea Shipbuilding and Engineering Corp* [1987] 2 Lloyd's Rep 445, 448 (Bingham LJ).

[21] In *The Erich Schroeder* [1974] 1 Lloyd's Rep 192, Mocatta J said: 'In exercising his discretion judicially an umpire/arbitrator must have regard in the first place to the primary principle guiding courts and arbitral tribunals in the exercise of their discretion in relation to costs, namely, that costs follow the event'.

[22] *Reinhard Hans Unglaube and Marion Unglaube v Republic of Costa Rica*, ICSID Case No ARB/09/20 and No ARB/08/1, Award (16 May 2012), fn 255 ('While the Arbitration Rules (Art 44) suggest that these determinations are left to the discretion of the Tribunal, this discretion should be exercised in a justified manner').

(a) Success/outcome as the primary factor for the exercise of discretion

25.20 The state courts in many jurisdictions apply a success-based costs regime.[23] International arbitration lawyers often commence their careers in state court litigation and this may influence their arbitration practice. There is frequently a presumption that similar principles apply in both forums. In the rare instances where an arbitrator's decision on costs comes for review by the courts, it is generally taken as read that similar principles apply in arbitration as they do in court.[24] Commentators on practice in a number of jurisdictions generally apply similar principles as apply in the state courts to arbitration practice.[25]

25.21 Some arbitration legislation specifically refers to success or outcome. The German legislation provides that 'the arbitral tribunal shall allocate ... the costs of the arbitration ... it shall do so at its discretion and take into consideration the circumstances of the case, in particular the outcome of the proceedings'.[26] The Austrian legislation uses similar wording.[27] The Finnish Arbitration Act provides that 'the arbitral tribunal may, in its award ... order a party to compensate, in whole or in part, the other party for his normal legal costs, in accordance with the provisions of the Code of Judicial Procedure'. The Code provides that '[t]he party who loses the case is liable for all reasonable legal costs incurred by the necessary measures of the opposing party', although there are exceptions to this principle.[28]

25.22 Mexican legislation stipulates that: 'Except as provided in the following paragraph, the costs of arbitration shall be borne by the unsuccessful party. However, the arbitral tribunal may apportion each of such costs between the parties if it determines that apportionment is reasonable, taking into account the circumstances of the case. With respect to the costs of legal representation and assistance, the arbitral tribunal, taking into account the circumstances of the case, shall determine which party shall bear such costs or may apportion such

---

[23] This includes Singapore, Malaysia, Hong Kong, Australia, New Zealand, Canada, and many of the European jurisdictions (see Sir Rupert Jackson, *Interim Report*, vol 2, which reviews a number of jurisdictions).

[24] For example, in the Singapore case of *VV v VW* [2008] 2 SLR 929, Prakash J noted at [13]: 'The arbitrator's decision was that the principle that costs should follow the event should apply'. This was not controversial; the complaint in that case was about whether the quantum was disproportionate and/or whether there was jurisdiction to award costs in respect of the counterclaim. In the Hong Kong case of *Kin Shing (Leung's) General Contractors Ltd v Chinese University of Hong Kong* [2011] HKEC 284, the question in issue was whether the arbitrator was entitled to take into account an offer of settlement when he awarded costs; this debate presupposed that costs will ordinarily be linked to the outcome, a point that was not controversial. Deputy Judge Chan stated at [24]: 'I regard the Arbitrator's decision on costs as entirely fair and reasonable.' See also Singapore Court of Appeal in *Chin Yoke Choong Bobby v Hong Lam Marine Pte Ltd* [2000] 1 SLR 137, which also confirmed that the Singapore courts follow the principle of 'costs follows the event'.

[25] Om Prakash Malhotra and Indu Malhotra, *The Law and Practice of Arbitration and Conciliation* (2nd edn, Lexis Nexis Butterworth 2006): 'the practice which is sometimes followed in commercial arbitrations, of leaving each party to pay his own costs, possibly on the ground that any other order appears too "litigious" is not correct; unless the special circumstances of the case justify such an order'. See also Robert Merkin and Johanna Hjalmarsson, *Singapore Arbitration Legislation Annotated* (Informa Law 2009): 'The position in Singapore, as in England, is that unless the parties agree to the contrary the arbitrators are entitled to award costs, and that costs follow the event ... For the operation of the principle in judicial proceedings, see RC, Ord 59. There is nothing in the IAA or the Model Law which refers to the award of costs, other than s 21, which is concerned with their taxation.'

[26] German ZPO, s 1057(1).

[27] Austrian ZPO, s 609. See also Jenny W T Power and Christian W Konrad, 'Costs in International Commercial Arbitration: A Comparative Overview of Civil and Common Law Doctrines' in Christian Klausegger and others (eds), *Austrian Yearbook on International Arbitration* (CH Beck, Stämpfli & Manz 2007) 261–74.

[28] Finnish Code of Judicial Procedure, ch 21 'Legal costs' (1013/1993), s 1(368/1999).

costs between the parties if it determines that apportionment is reasonable.'[29] The English legislation provides that 'the tribunal shall award costs on the general principle that costs should follow the event except where it appears to the tribunal that in the circumstances this is not appropriate'.[30]

25.23 Provisions in many leading arbitration rules expressly indicate a link between the exercise of the discretion as to costs award and the outcome of the case. The 2010 UNCITRAL Rules provide, for example: 'The costs of the arbitration shall in principle be borne by the unsuccessful party or parties. However, the arbitral tribunal may apportion ... taking into account the circumstances of the case.'[31] Similar sentiments permitting the tribunal to exercise a success-based approach are expressed in most other rules, a selection of which includes the LCIA,[32] TOMAC,[33] WIPO,[34] SCC,[35] ACICA,[36] Swiss,[37] and CIETAC[38] Rules.

25.24 Surveys of awards in practice also confirm that a primary factor in international practice is success. Derains and Schwartz describe an unpublished study of costs awards published between March 1989 and September 1991, which concluded in summary:

(1) that where the claimant's case was predominantly successful, so that one would say the claimant had prevailed in the case as a whole: (a) as to central costs, the tribunal apportioned these so that the unsuccessful respondent would pay all or high proportion in about 80% of cases. Where the tribunal did not do this, the tribunal in most cases

---

[29] Mexican Commercial Code, Title IV 'Commercial Arbitration', s 1455.
[30] English Arbitration Act 1996, s 61(2).
[31] 2010 UNCITRAL Rules, Art 42.1: 'The costs of the arbitration shall in principle be borne by the unsuccessful party or parties. However, the arbitral tribunal may apportion ... taking into account the circumstances of the case.'
[32] 1998 LCIA Rules, Art 28.4: 'the general principle that costs should reflect the parties' relative success and failure in the award or arbitration, except where it appears to the Arbitral Tribunal that in the particular circumstances this general approach is inappropriate'.
[33] TOMAC Rules, Art 44(2): 'Upon application by a party for recovery from the other party of attorneys' fees and other procedural costs of the arbitration, the Tribunal may in the arbitral award or by a separate order permit, to a reasonable extent and in consideration of the contents of the arbitral award, such recovery.'
[34] 2014 WIPO Rules, Art 73(c): 'The Tribunal shall, subject to any agreement of the parties, apportion the costs of arbitration and the registration and administration fees of the Center between the parties in the light of all the circumstances and the outcome of the arbitration.'
[35] 2010 SCC Rules, Art 44: 'Unless otherwise agreed by the parties, the Arbitral Tribunal may in the final award upon the request of a party, order one party to pay any reasonable costs incurred by another party, including costs for legal representation, having regard to the outcome of the case and other relevant circumstances.'
[36] 2011 ACICA Rules, Art 41.1: 'Except as provided in Article 41.2, the costs of arbitration shall in principle be borne by the unsuccessful party. However, the Arbitral Tribunal may apportion each of such costs between the parties if it determines that apportionment is reasonable, taking into account the circumstances of the case.' Art 41.2: 'With respect to the costs referred to in Article 39(e) [the costs of the successful party], the Arbitral Tribunal, taking into account the circumstances of the case, shall be free to determine which party shall bear such costs or may apportion such costs between the parties if it determines that apportionment is reasonable.'
[37] 2012 Swiss Rules, Art 40(1): 'Except as provided in Article 40(2), the costs of the arbitration shall in principle be borne by the unsuccessful party. However, the arbitral tribunal may apportion any of the costs of the arbitration among the parties if it determines that such apportionment is reasonable, taking into account the circumstances of the case.' Art 40(2): 'With respect to the costs of legal representation and assistance referred to in Article 38(e), the arbitral tribunal, taking into account the circumstances of the case, shall be free to determine which party shall bear such costs or may apportion such costs among the parties if it determines that an apportionment is reasonable.'
[38] 2015 CIETAC Rules, Art 52(2): 'The arbitral tribunal has the power to decide in the arbitral award, having regard to the circumstances of the case, that the losing party shall compensate the winning party for the expenses reasonably incurred by it in pursuing the case'.

explained its reason for not doing so, implying that it appreciated that this was against the trend; (b) as to party costs, the tribunal directed the unsuccessful respondent to pay the successful claimant's reasonable costs or a significant proportion of them in about 50% of cases;

(2) where the claimant had some success but recovered approximately half the amount claimed or less, the most common outcome was to require both parties to pay central costs equally and to pay their own party costs although in some cases, the respondent was directed to pay a greater proportion of central costs and to meet some of the party costs of the claimant; and

(3) where the claimant's claims were dismissed or the tribunal had no jurisdiction, the most common outcome was to order the claimant to pay the central costs and to pay the respondent's reasonable party costs.[39]

25.25 This represents practice approximately a quarter of a century ago, but even then the principle of success-based awards as to costs was already becoming embedded. This trend had moved on further by 2009. In a review of 100 ICC awards published by Webster in 2009, he concluded that 'the principle that the "costs follow the event" was generally applied',[40] although with considerable adaptation to the circumstances. In particular, central costs were awarded to the clearly successful party in 78 per cent of the awards and party costs awarded in 63 per cent. According to the survey, 'tribunals consider various factors, such as procedural behaviour, when allocating costs'.

25.26 Webster notes that 'One of the most striking aspects on review of these 100 cases is that, although parties are ordered to share costs on an equal basis on a number of occasions, there is not a single instance in which the tribunal expressly disagreed with the basic principle that costs should follow the event. The starting point for an ICC tribunal from whatever background is basically that costs should follow the event, subject to the exercise by the tribunal of its discretion'. The following excerpt from an ICC award illustrates the standard case—and more importantly the recognition that success is a primary factor: 'In coming to its decision on which party should bear the costs or what proportion of the costs should be recoverable, the Tribunal follows the general principle that costs should normally follow the event, viz the party that prevails should normally be entitled to the costs incurred.'[41]

25.27 Finally, in a review published in Ong and O'Reilly, the authors carried out a review of 30 ICSID decisions[42] and identified that even in these cases the majority of tribunals had regard to success when making their decision as to costs. A number of tribunals expressed the view strongly that this was essential where large claims were made with little merit.

---

[39] Yves Derains and Eric Schwartz, *Guide to the ICC Rules of Arbitration* (2nd edn, Kluwer Law International 2005) 369–73.

[40] Thomas H Webster, 'Efficiency in Investment Arbitration: Recent Decisions on Preliminary and Costs Issues' (2009) 25(4) Arb Int'l 469. The 100 ICC awards were being used as a control population: 'Since one of the points of comparison on costs issues is the practice in international commercial arbitration in general, Table 2 is a summary of review of a random sample of 100 awards rendered in ICC international commercial arbitration between 2006 and 2008 with respect to costs, preliminary decisions on jurisdiction and bifurcation of proceedings.'

[41] ICC Case No 13676, Final Award (2010) in Albert Jan van den Berg (ed), *Yearbook Commercial Arbitration*, vol XXXV (Kluwer Law International 2010) 168–217, [115].

[42] Ong and O'Reilly (n 2) ch 13.

(b) Conduct in the proceedings as an important subsidiary factor

25.28 Although success is the primary consideration, the tribunal may take account of any relevant factors or considerations. These will include, in particular, objectionable conduct. The rationale for this is obvious. When parties agree to arbitration, it by no means follows that they have consented to suffer their opponents' delaying and diversionary tactics which prevent the matter being dealt with quickly, effectively, and fairly. While arbitration agreements may not explicitly refer to the requirement to act reasonably and in good faith during proceedings, in many cases it may be appropriate to imply such an obligation. This provides a suitable jurisprudential basis for sanctioning in costs a party which has conducted the proceedings other than reasonably and in good faith, even where that party has prevailed.

25.29 One important expression of the relevance of conduct in relation to costs is in the IBA Rules on the Taking of Evidence. Preamble 3 provides: 'The taking of evidence shall be conducted on the principle that each Party shall act in good faith and be entitled to know, reasonably in advance of any Evidentiary Hearing or any fact or merits determination, the evidence on which the other Parties rely.'

25.30 Although restricted to matters of evidence, it expresses a wider principle. Article 9(7) provides: 'If The Arbitral Tribunal determines that a Party has failed to conduct itself in good faith in the taking of evidence, the Arbitral Tribunal may, in addition to any other measures available under these Rules, take such failure into account in its assignment of the costs of the arbitration, including costs arising out of or in connection with the taking of evidence.'[43] This provision has generally been welcomed by leading practitioners. Doug Jones, for instance, describes it as 'a powerful disincentive for parties to refrain from dilatory tactics which ensures that the process will proceed in the most timely and cost effective manner'.[44]

25.31 In cases under the 1998 ICC Rules, conduct was a matter to which reference was frequently made. For example, in one award, the outcome and conduct were both referred to as the main factors: 'A common method [ie principle by which liability for costs is allocated] is to award costs to the party having won the arbitration or, where there is no clear winner, to allocate costs in proportion to the outcome of the parties' claims ("costs follow the event"). Another criterion adopted by arbitral tribunals under the 1998 ICC Rules is the general conduct of a party.'[45]

25.32 The 2012 version of the ICC Arbitration Rules now expressly includes reference to conduct. Article 40(5) provides: 'In making decisions as to costs, the arbitral tribunal may take into account such circumstances as it considers relevant, including the extent to which each party has conducted the arbitration in an expeditious and cost-effective manner.' Note that the rule refers specifically to: (i) conduct in the arbitration, not conduct in the performance of the underlying contractual obligations; and (ii) expedition and cost-effectiveness, so that what is being targeted is poor conduct that leads to impact on the opponent. We do not

---

[43] ibid.
[44] Doug Jones, 'The Cost, Time and Process Implications of the New IBA Rules of Evidence' (Financial Review International Dispute Resolution Conference, Sydney, 15 October 2010).
[45] ICC Case No 12745, Final Award (2010) in Albert Jan van den Berg, *Yearbook Commercial Arbitration*, vol XXXV (Kluwer Law International 2010) 40–128, [274].

understand the draftsperson to suggest that the outcome—who won and who lost, etc—is of lesser importance than hitherto. The draftsperson must be assumed to have been aware of practice among ICC arbitrators and did not seek to realign it.

The 2014 LCIA Arbitration Rules also explicitly refer to conduct and reflect a growing confidence and consensus in this area. **25.33**

As to the conduct which may affect costs, this will differ from case to case. Examples may include: **25.34**

(1) the winning party did not act reasonably in the period leading up to commencement (eg a successful claimant may have commenced proceedings precipitately without offering a chance to consider settlement, or a successful respondent may have refused to discuss the matter, or, where appropriate, to engage in a reasonable form of mediation or conciliation);
(2) the respondent to a claim did not answer it appropriately;[46]
(3) objections were made inappropriately and/or were not withdrawn in a timely fashion;[47]
(4) the winning party may have drawn up its case in an unhelpful way, eg by failing to give proper particulars or alternatively by overloading the case with prolix pleadings with a myriad of irrelevant allegations;
(5) the winning party may have made unreasonable applications[48] or excessive requests for disclosure/discovery or to strike out parts of the opponent's case, etc;

---

[46] For instance, in the Final Award in ICC Case No 14108 the tribunal remarked at [264]: 'It was not merely a question of the Joint Venture reasonably bringing its claims in these proceedings, but rather the reverse. It was only at the main hearing that the substance and strength of Respondent's Defence to the claims emerged, for the first time, with the oral testimony of certain of Respondent's factual witnesses. Until then, in the Arbitral Tribunal's view, there was no sufficient answer clearly advanced by Respondent which could reasonably have led the Joint Venture to have concluded that its full claims were or might be unsustainable. By the time of the hearing, however, the course of these page proceedings was firmly set; and there could be no question of the Joint Venture changing that course then or after that hearing.' At [265]: 'In these circumstances, for all these reasons, the Arbitral Tribunal considers that Respondent should bear all the legal costs incurred by the Joint Venture in regard to both the Counterclaims and the Claims.' Reported in Albert Jan van den Berg (ed), *Yearbook Commercial Arbitration*, vol XXXVI (Kluwer Law International 2011) 135–201.

[47] ICC Case No 14020, Final Award (2011) in Albert Jan van den Berg (ed), *Yearbook Commercial Arbitration*, vol XXXVI (Kluwer Law International 2011) 119–34. In setting out the reasons for its decision on costs, the tribunal included at [55] the fact that the '[b]uyer just days before the final hearing and after all written pleadings abandoned its objections to jurisdiction'.

[48] ICC Case No 13507, Final Award (2010) in Albert Jan van den Berg (ed), *Yearbook Commercial Arbitration*, vol XXXV (Kluwer Law International 2010) 158–67. In this case, the claimant withdrew his claim and the tribunal decided that the central costs of the discontinued proceedings should be borne by the claimant. However, as to the party costs, the tribunal had regard to the conduct of the respondents, at [19]: 'However, the issue of general legal costs, fees and expenses should be viewed differently and in light of other fairness considerations. Claimant has succeeded in overcoming numerous and repeated applications by both Respondents to obtain a stay of these arbitral proceedings and to challenge the jurisdiction of the Sole Arbitrator to hear this case. Such applications—proven without merit—substantially slowed down the pace of these arbitral proceedings and unnecessarily delayed, among other things, the completion of the Terms of Reference and the general organization of this arbitration, including the timing for the submission of memorials, production of evidence and scheduling of a hearing on the merits. It is not to be excluded that had such disruptions not taken place, these arbitral proceedings would have ended by a final award on the merits before or shortly after the initiation of the liquidation of First Respondent. Under such circumstances, the Sole Arbitrator concludes that each Party shall support its own general legal costs, fees and expenses.'

(6) the winning party may have extended the hearing beyond what was required, eg by making prolix submissions, excessive examination of witnesses, calling inappropriate or irrelevant evidence, etc; and

(7) the winning party may have acted dishonestly either itself (which makes the matter extremely serious) or by its employees acting unilaterally (for which it should still bear some culpability).

25.35 Where the winning party's conduct was unreasonable in some respect, the questions for the tribunal should be: (a) did that unreasonable conduct lead the opponent to incur additional costs; and (b) is the conduct worthy of censure independently of any impact it may have on the other party? It will be in the discretion of the tribunal to consider how it will take account of conduct.

(c) **Trends identified in academic and scholarly writing**

25.36 A number of authors have identified emerging trends in the field of apportionment and allocation of costs. A leading text from 1999 states that: 'It is increasingly common for the arbitral tribunal to order the party which is defeated on the merits of a dispute to pay all or a substantial part of the costs of the arbitration. That is traditionally the practice in some common law countries and now frequently occurs when the arbitral tribunal has its seat in continental jurisdictions, such as France or Switzerland. In reaching their decision on the allocation of costs between the parties, arbitrators may take into account the attitude of the parties during the arbitral proceedings.'[49]

25.37 The term 'attitude' appears to equate to 'conduct', in that conduct is the outward manifestation of the attitude. In a study from 2003, the same trends are identified: 'An emerging trend can be recorded for the arbitration tribunal to order the losing party to pay all or the substantial part of the costs of the arbitration. This tradition is widely accepted and can be seen, for example, in England, in France and Switzerland. The other emerging trend in allocating costs between the parties is to take into account their attitude during the proceedings.'[50] More recently, in 2011, an experienced practitioner reports: 'Some arbitral decisions hold that the principle of "costs should follow the event" is becoming a governing principle in international arbitration. There is an emerging trend for arbitral tribunals to order the losing party to bear both the procedural costs and the legal costs of the other party unless the circumstances of the case warrant a departure from such rule.'[51]

25.38 These emerging trends are consistent with the 2004 Principles of Transnational Civil Procedure,[52] drawn up by UNIDROIT and approved by the ALI,[53] which establish 'standards for adjudication of transnational commercial disputes'.[54] These principles also apply

---

[49] Gaillard and Savage (n 3) 686.
[50] Julian D M Lew and others, *Comparative International Commercial Arbitration* (Kluwer Law International 2003) 654, para 24-82.
[51] José Rosell, 'Arbitration Costs as Relief and/or Damages' (2011) 28(2) J Int'l Arb 115.
[52] ALI/UNIDROIT Principles of Transnational Civil Procedure (2004) 4 Unif L Rev 758–808.
[53] The ALI is a non-profit body based in Washington DC and established in 1923 to foster harmonization and clarification of the law.
[54] ALI/UNIDROIT Principles of Transnational Civil Procedure, Scope and Implementation (n 52) 758.

to arbitration.[55] The provisions are available on the UNIDROIT website in a range of languages.[56] The provisions as to costs are as follows:

> **25. Costs**
>
> 25.1 The winning party ordinarily should be awarded all or a substantial portion of its reasonable costs. 'Costs' include court filing fees, fees paid to officials such as court stenographers, expenses such as expert-witness fees, and lawyers' fees.
>
> 25.2 Exceptionally, the court may withhold or limit costs to the winning party when there is clear justification for doing so. The court may limit the award to a proportion that reflects expenditures for matters in genuine dispute and award costs against a winning party who has raised unnecessary issues or been otherwise unreasonably disputatious. The court in making cost decisions may take account of any party's procedural misconduct in the proceeding.

25.39 The commentary supplied with the principles notes that '[a] fee-shifting rule is controversial in certain types of litigation but is generally considered appropriate in commercial litigation'.[57]

D. Complicating and Ancillary Issues

25.40 The analysis above relates to the main themes, but the difficulty in individual cases often arises from the very particular circumstances. It will rarely be the case that one party is an absolute winner and there are no factors which complicate the situation. These will often include partial success, the effect of counterclaims, and amendments to case. In these cases, the tribunal may—and arguably should—make an award which takes these factors into account. A number of difficult considerations apply, which are addressed in detail in Ong and O'Reilly.[58]

(a) Offers of settlement and security for costs

25.41 Likewise, in any developed system of costs, two additional aspects need to be considered: offers of settlement and security for costs. These are not, as has sometimes been suggested, solely related to English-influenced jurisdictions. They are a logical and necessary adjunct of any system of costs in which a party which has been successful and has conducted the proceedings reasonably can expect to be reimbursed an element of costs.

25.42 The significance of offers of settlement is readily illustrated. Suppose the claimant C claimed $x and the respondent offered at the outset to settle the proceedings by paying $¾ x to C; if C rejects that offer, presses on with the arbitration and recovers $½ x under the award, how is the relative success of each party to be evaluated? Are we to say that C has been substantially successful, when he has caused substantial costs to be needlessly incurred recovering a sum less than was offered to him at the outset? This illustrates that where costs are apportioned or allocated by reference to the outcome in the substantive award, there needs to be consistent practice around making offers of settlement.

---

[55] ibid P–E, 759. See also the ALI website <http://www.ali.org> accessed 25 September 2015: 'Principles of Transnational Civil Procedure can be used in judicial proceedings as well as in arbitration. The result is a work that significantly contributes to the promotion of a universal rule of procedural law.'

[56] The principles are available on the UNIDROIT website in English, French, Chinese, German, Japanese, Persian, Spanish, and Turkish; a Russian version is also available. UNIDROIT website <http://www.unidroit.org> accessed 25 September 2015.

[57] ALI/UNIDROIT Principles of Transnational Civil Procedure, Principle 25, Commentary P-25A <http://www.unidroit.org> accessed 25 September 2015.

[58] Ong and O'Reilly (n 2).

25.43 Likewise, where an impecunious claimant advances a speculative claim, the respondent may feel confident of winning, but correctly considers that any costs award made against the claimant will be worthless. If the claimant—for example, a shell company belonging to a large successful group—is funded in the claim by its owners or associates who will benefit from a successful outcome, but will not be at risk of having to pay costs, this creates an imbalance. One solution is to require a claimant in such a position to provide security for the costs. This is a controversial point, but one that needs to be addressed in any developed system of costs. All of these various matters are fully discussed in Ong and O'Reilly.[59]

(b) Agreements as to costs

25.44 Although there is an emerging consensus as to the rules for costs application, we have not yet arrived at a consistent practice. We remain in a situation where the domestic practice of arbitrators can influence their approach. The factors which a tribunal may take into account are unlimited and the weight they can apply to each is for them to decide. However, the parties may create additional certainty by agreeing a costs protocol. A typical example is set out in Ong and O'Reilly and is reproduced in the appendix below.[60]

E. Conclusion

25.45 Few will quibble with the view that '[a]part from the ultimate outcome and the time that may be required for the conduct of an arbitration, there is usually no aspect of the arbitration process that is of greater concern to the parties than its cost'.[61] In arbitrations at the high end of the value scale, and which involve an array of complex matters, the costs can be very substantial indeed—many millions of dollars. At the other end of the value scale, the costs will generally be very much less, but can be a significant proportion of the sums in substantive dispute and will often exceed them; so while the question of costs may be less significant in absolute terms, in relative terms the question of costs can dominate the outcome.

25.46 So, what about the prospects of attaining what the Attorney General of Singapore has described as the Holy Grail? The prospects look extremely positive. There is a growing consensus that costs should generally reflect success, but that conduct is also important. The latest LCIA Arbitration Rules reflect this new confidence:

> 28.4. The Arbitral Tribunal shall make its decisions on both Arbitration Costs [ie central costs] and Legal Costs [ie party costs] on the general principle that costs should reflect the parties' relative success and failure in the award or arbitration or under different issues, except where it appears to the Arbitral Tribunal that in the circumstances the application of such a general principle would be inappropriate under the Arbitration Agreement or otherwise. The Arbitral Tribunal may also take into account the parties' conduct in the arbitration, including any co-operation in facilitating the proceedings as to time and cost and any non-co-operation resulting in undue delay and unnecessary expense. Any decision on costs by the Arbitral Tribunal shall be made with reasons in the award containing such decision.

---

[59] ibid, ch 7 deals with offers of settlement and ch 9 deals with security for costs.
[60] Ong and O'Reilly (n 2) ch 3. This protocol may be used without restriction, provided its source is acknowledged.
[61] Derains and Schwartz (n 39) 328.

25.47 Article 28.3 further provides that the arbitral tribunal shall 'decide the amount of such Legal Costs on such reasonable basis as it thinks appropriate'. Even in investment arbitrations, where there has been a marked reluctance by some tribunals to shift costs, it is becoming the norm to award costs to the successful party unless there is some other overriding interest—such as the access of individuals to justice.

25.48 However, growing confidence about these general propositions—that costs awards should reflect success and that conduct should be taken into account—should not obscure the reality that there are many details and nuances which still need to be worked through. Some of these have been touched upon in this chapter—partial success, offers of settlement, security for costs to name but a few. Ong and O'Reilly[62] consider the various points which may arise and which can often be the most difficult issues. Perhaps we should temper our confidence by clarifying that while we can certainly glimpse the Holy Grail in the middle distance, the difficulty in closing out the last few miles should not be underestimated.

Appendix*

In the matter of an arbitration between ... (Claimant) and ... (Respondent), together the Parties

Protocol as to Costs

1. This protocol has been agreed by both Parties [and endorsed by the Tribunal] and supplements the arbitration agreement. It shall prevail over any inconsistent terms. The Tribunal has exclusive jurisdiction to construe the protocol's meaning and effect and shall give such directions, including as to the time available for any step necessary or convenient to implement it.

Conduct

2. Parties shall conduct the proceedings in good faith, in compliance with orders of the tribunal and cooperate where appropriate with their opponent to ensure that the proceedings are conducted time- and cost-effectively.

Offers of settlement

3. Parties may at any time make a formal written offer 'without prejudice save as to costs' to settle the proceedings as a whole, which offer should not be disclosed to the tribunal until substantive issues have been decided. Should such an offer be accepted without reservation before it is withdrawn the matter shall be settled on the offered terms which shall be incorporated into a consent award. Any offer may include a provision that the question of costs is to be referred to the tribunal; and in that case the tribunal will seek submissions and make its costs decision, which will also form part of the award.

4. If the proceedings are not settled, the following provisions apply.

Awarding costs at the conclusion of the proceedings

5. Within 14 days of the close of submissions on the merits of the substantive case, the parties shall exchange on an open basis as between themselves and supply to the tribunal in a password protected file brief submissions on costs ('Submissions as to Costs') with annexes as follows:
   (i) Annex 1. A schedule of the costs which that party seeks to recover from the other, including for experts and witnesses and for representation identifying the fee earners involved, the dates, time spent by each, the work done and the reasonable recovery claimed in respect of that work;
   (ii) Annex 2. Copies of any offers made 'without prejudice as to costs' or associated correspondence to which the tribunal may properly be invited to have regard when considering the question of costs.

---

[62] Ong and O'Reilly (n 2).

* Protocol on Costs, from Ong and O'Reilly (n 2).

(iii) Annex 3. A statement of any conduct in and about the proceedings which the party invites the tribunal to take into account when making its decision as to costs.
6. Within 14 days of exchange of submissions in accordance with paragraph 5 above, each party may if so advised exchange between themselves on an open basis and file with the tribunal in a password protected file a reply ('Reply as to Costs') with points raised by the opponent in their primary Submissions as to Costs.
7. When it has completed its decision on the merits/substantive issues, the tribunal shall request the passwords, open the submissions and take them into consideration when making its decision as to costs.
8. When deciding how the tribunal's fees and expenses shall be apportioned and liability for party costs shall be allocated the tribunal shall take into account the submissions of the parties and in particular:
    (i) the outcome of the proceedings and in particular the degree of success of each party, in respect of the substantive issues including by reference to any offer made without prejudice save as to costs;
    (ii) any failure to conduct the proceedings in good faith including in taking of evidence in accordance with the 2010 IBA Rules on the Taking of Evidence or other conduct including conduct referred to in paragraph 82 of the '2012 ICC Commission Report: Controlling Time and Costs in Arbitration'.
9. The costs recoverable by a party shall be limited to those costs claimed and satisfactorily explained in its sealed submissions and in respect of party costs which are:
    (i) within those classes of costs referred to in Article 41.2 of the UNCITRAL Rules 2010
    (ii) reasonable and not disproportionate to the sums in dispute (save for costs necessary for the proper resolution of the disputes or which arose from the unreasonable actions of the other party).
10. The tribunal shall state in its award its decision on costs with brief reasons and shall state clearly the net sum payable in respect of costs and which party is to pay it.

Signed as agreed by:

_____
[] acting for the Claimant

_____
[] acting for the Respondent

26

THE COSTS AND FUNDING OF INTERNATIONAL ARBITRATION

Joe Tirado, Daniel R Meagher, and Arpan Gupta

A. Introduction

The costs and the funding of international arbitration are fundamental considerations for anyone contemplating international arbitration. Cost is likely to be one of the first issues discussed between a potential claimant and its counsel, often even before any detailed discussion of the merits.[1] Increasingly, a discussion on costs will also be coupled with how to fund a particular matter.

26.01

The costs and funding of international arbitration are, therefore, an integral part of the dispute process and not mere consequence. As the costs for the end-users of international arbitration continue to rise, there is 'a greater emphasis on recovering them, a dismay about how arbitration is "out of control", together with a variety of efforts at reforms designed to reduce costs and foster efficiency'.[2]

26.02

As a leading commentator has noted:

26.03

> Arbitration practitioners need to understand—in a more nuanced way than ever before—their clients' commercial objectives and the level of service they expect and are prepared to pay for ... How a case is run will have a substantial impact on costs. When considering the size of a team working on a case there is a trade-off between managing costs and timing/service ... The use of sophisticated financial software and management processes can increase efficiency and reduce time spent and therefore costs.[3]

The first part of this chapter considers the different cost elements involved in international arbitration proceedings. The second part explores the funding mechanisms which are increasingly available to parties in international arbitration.

26.04

B. The Costs of International Arbitration

It is clear from recent surveys that the overall costs of an international arbitration are at the forefront of in-house counsels' minds.[4] Indeed, although the cost of an international

26.05

---

[1] Philippe Cavalieros, 'In-House Counsel Costs and Other Internal Party Costs in International Commercial Arbitration' (2014) 30(1) Arb Int'l 145.
[2] Nicolas C Ulmer, 'The Cost Conundrum' (2010) 26(2) Arb Int'l 221.
[3] Judith Gill QC, *Legal and Arbitration Costs* (Session Abstracts, ICCA Singapore Congress 2012) 77.
[4] See, eg, the 2013 QMUL Survey, 'Corporate Choices in International Arbitration: Industry Perspectives' <http://www.arbitration.qmul.ac.uk/research/index.html> accessed 25 September 2015.

arbitration 'is the last thing to be dealt with in any arbitration, it is usually the first thing on the client's mind'.[5] Many users view international arbitration as a process which 'costs too much'.[6]

(a) Institutional charges

26.06 Institutional charges tend to be relatively modest in comparison to the broader cost of international arbitration proceedings.[7] The ICC estimates institutional charges to make up approximately 2 per cent of the overall costs of an international arbitration.[8]

26.07 Almost all of the leading arbitration institutions calculate their fees on an *ad valorem* basis (ie a predetermined percentage based on the value in dispute), taking into account claims and counterclaims. The LCIA, on the other hand, charges an hourly rate for work on the administration of the arbitration, together with a set percentage (currently 5 per cent) of the tribunal's overall fees.[9]

(b) Arbitral tribunal fees and expenses

26.08 According to the ICC, the fees and expenses of the arbitral tribunal account for approximately 16 per cent of the overall costs of an international arbitration.[10] The tribunal's fees can be calculated on either an hourly basis or an *ad valorem* basis.[11] While the hourly basis is in line with more traditional methods of recording and billing a lawyer's time spent on a given matter, the *ad valorem* basis provides a level of predictability and transparency which some users find preferable. As a result, the *ad valorem* approach has become the predominant method for calculating arbitrators' fees in many of the leading arbitral institutions. Nearly all arbitral institutions produce a fee schedule which is updated from time to time.

26.09 Some arbitral institutions, such as the ICC and the SCC, provide online fee calculators which can help a party anticipate the likely institutional and arbitrators' fees to be incurred in a given dispute based upon the value of the dispute and number of arbitrators.

26.10 In addition to the prescriptive fee schedules, there is often room for adjustments in the case of exceptionally high-value claims, in cases which are terminated or settle at an early stage of the proceedings, and in any other unusual proceedings. In all cases, the arbitral institution retains a certain level of control over the arbitral tribunal with regard to the setting and/

---

[5] Michael O'Reilly, 'The Problem of Costs in International Arbitration' (RAIF Conference on International Arbitration 2012, Bali, Indonesia, 5–6 May 2012).

[6] CCIAG Survey results: 56 per cent of respondents strongly agree that international arbitration 'takes too long', and 69 per cent of respondents strongly agree that international arbitration 'costs too much'. Lucy Reed, 'More on Corporate Criticism of International Arbitration' (*Kluwer Arbitration Blog*, 16 July 2010) <http://www.kluwerarbitrationblog.com> accessed 25 September 2015.

[7] For Karl-Heinz Böckstiegel's insights on the functioning of arbitral institutions, see Karl-Heinz Böckstiegel, 'Experiences and Suggestions Regarding the Functioning of International Arbitration Institutions' in Julio César Betancourt (ed), *Defining Issues in International Arbitration: Celebrating 100 Years of the Chartered Institute of Arbitrators* (OUP 2016) ch 2.

[8] ICC, 'Commission Report: Controlling Time and Costs in Arbitration' (Report No 861-1 ENG, ICC Dispute Resolution Library, 2007).

[9] LCIA Schedule of Costs (effective 1 January 2014), s 1.

[10] 'Commission Report' (n 8).

[11] Interestingly, the 2013 HKIAC Administered Arbitration Rules allow parties to agree upon either *ad valorem* or hourly.

or review of the arbitrators' fees, which can help to prevent anomalies and may also help to ensure consistency of approach across different cases.

(c) External counsel's fees

26.11 Legal fees (ie the cost of external counsel) make up the significant majority of the costs of any international arbitration. Indeed, according to a survey conducted by the CIArb, 74 per cent of the costs of the arbitral process relate to external legal costs.[12] The ICC has estimated them to be as high as 82 per cent of the overall costs.[13]

26.12 Those external legal fees will cluster around certain parts of the procedure—most often (a) in the earliest stages as external counsel learn about the background of the dispute and explore all relevant background evidence with the client; (b) during the preparation of pleadings and supporting evidence; and (c) in preparation for and in the conducting of the substantive hearing. There may also be occasional spikes in external legal fees for procedural events such as interim applications, the disclosure/discovery process, and any other procedural developments.[14]

(d) Costs of witnesses

26.13 Expert witnesses can take many forms. A lawyer or a professor from a particular jurisdiction may be invited to opine upon a point of that jurisdiction's law; an industry expert might comment upon common practice within a particular industry; a specialist accountant might conduct a forensic analysis of a set of transactions to calculate damages or value a business at a particular point in time.

26.14 The expert's involvement might consist of simply one written statement, or it could involve several written statements/reports, meetings with the corresponding expert appointed by the other side, production of a joint report outlining points of agreement and disagreement, and attendance and cross-examination at the hearing itself. The level of involvement of the expert witness will, in turn, impact upon the total fees of the expert witness.

26.15 It is generally accepted that a witness of fact may have his disbursements and lost earnings for attending the hearing for cross-examination reimbursed.[15] More controversial is whether in certain circumstances it is acceptable to pay a 'reasonable' fee to a witness of fact in exchange for the presentation of testimony by that witness. This will depend largely upon the ethical rules of a given jurisdiction and may impact upon the weight to be given to that witness's testimony. The new IBA Guidelines on Party Representation and the Annex to the 2014 LCIA Rules of Arbitration address this issue.

26.16 Perhaps rarely quantified is the amount of time spent on an arbitration by in-house counsel, managers, and staff of a corporate entity that is party to an arbitration.[16] As noted by leading commentators, the overall costs of arbitration:

> rarely include any allowance for the time spent on the case by senior officials, directors or employees of the parties themselves and the indirect costs of disruption to their ordinary

---

[12] CIArb, 'Costs of International Arbitration Survey' (2011) 12 <http://www.ciarb.org> accessed 25 September 2015.
[13] 'Commission Report' (n 8).
[14] See CIArb Costs Survey (n 12).
[15] Guideline 25 of the IBA Guidelines on Party Representation.
[16] Cavalieros (n 1).

business. The hidden costs of such 'executive' or 'management' time may be very high. Indeed, it may occasionally exceed the direct costs.[17]

26.17 The amount of time spent can vary significantly depending upon the level of involvement by in-house counsel in the day-to-day affairs of the arbitration, including aspects of the proceedings such as document preservation and production and interface with the rest of the business's management. Other staff may become closely involved in the arbitration proceedings, most often as witnesses of fact and expert support.

26.18 The cost of such time spent could be quantified not only based on an hourly rate, but on any opportunities lost for the business as a whole as a result of increased time spent by individual members of the business on the arbitration proceedings rather than any new ventures (or, similarly, any liabilities incurred by the business as a result of in-house counsel diverting attention from other potential liabilities to the arbitration proceedings). While traditionally these costs were not viewed as recoverable, parties are increasingly seeking to recover such costs.

(e) Miscellaneous costs

26.19 There will be additional costs incurred by the parties, in particular in the lead-up to the hearing. These may include the cost of a document management electronic database and document review software, printing and copying, venue hire for the hearing, a transcriber and interpreter, travel to and from the hearing, together with accommodation, meals, and local transport for all individuals involved.

C. The Funding of International Arbitration

26.20 There exist a number of options by which funding can be arranged—usually in exchange for either a portion of any winnings, or an upfront insurance premium.

(a) Types of funding

26.21 While the terminology used herein has a particular focus on common practice in the London market, the concepts and funding options can be found in various jurisdictions. Attorney-led products can largely be separated into two categories:

(1) a discounted fee, with an uplift in the event of success; or
(2) a discounted fee in exchange for a percentage of any amount won in the dispute.

26.22 In England, the former are commonly known as conditional fee arrangements (CFAs), and the success percentage is capped at 100 per cent of a lawyer's standard rate.

26.23 The latter is referred to as damages-based agreements (DBAs) in England. DBAs have had particular prominence in US litigation for decades, and have been increasingly relied upon in a number of other jurisdictions, including, for example, Australia and Canada. DBAs have only recently been allowed in England, from 1 April 2013 onwards, following the so-called Jackson reforms. The maximum percentage which can be charged as

---

[17] Nigel Blackaby and others, *Redfern and Hunter on International Arbitration* (5th edn, OUP 2009) para 9.91.

to the compensation obtained is 50 per cent for matters not concerning employment or personal injury.

Insurance products can cover a range of situations for a party to a dispute. A pre-existing policy may provide insurance for any judgment or award made against the insured, and/or may insure against the costs of participating in the dispute proceedings. Depending upon the circumstances, the insurer can take varying levels of control over the case.[18] 26.24

Furthermore, specialized forms of insurance exist to protect against either or both of the insured's own legal expenses and a potential costs award against the insured. These specialized insurance products are commonly used in the context of English litigation and are often known as before-the-event (BTE) and after-the-event (ATE) insurance products.[19] 26.25

Finally, third-party funding consists of an arrangement whereby a funder agrees to cover some or all of the legal costs and expenses of the client in exchange for a percentage of any future compensation or damages in the dispute.[20] The funder's interest in the progress and outcome of the dispute is often purely financial.[21] 26.26

These three general categories of products can be creatively combined depending upon the client and the circumstances of the case. The rules on alternative fee arrangements, legal expenses insurance, and third-party funding vary by jurisdiction. 26.27

The movement of third-party funding began in Australia in the late 1980s and early 1990s and has spread into Germany, Austria, Switzerland, the United States, and the United Kingdom. Leading funders include Burford Capital, Calunius Capital, Fulbrook Management LLC, Harbour Litigation Funding, and Juridica Investments Ltd. There are also brokers, such as TheJudge, who work with multiple funders in order to source the most appropriate funding arrangement. 26.28

(b) Third-party funding—current practices, benefits, and challenges

As a practical matter, third-party funders view a claim (or counterclaim) as an investment. Therefore, before agreeing to put forward money in support of such claims, funders will undertake extensive due diligence. This will include, under cover of a non-disclosure agreement, a thorough analysis of the merits of the claim, the likely amount of damages, and the enforcement prospects.[22] Certain factors may weigh particularly heavily in certain circumstances, for example issues such as jurisdictional obstacles, any defence to the claim, the nature and length of the proceedings, the possibilities of settlement, and the 26.29

---

[18] Lisa Bench Nieuwveld and Victoria Shannon, *Third-Party Funding in International Arbitration* (Kluwer Law International 2012) 3–18. See also Maya Steinitz, 'Whose Claim Is This Anyway? Third-Party Litigation Funding' (2011) 95 Minn L Rev 1268, 1275–6.
[19] ibid, Nieuwveld and Shannon, 5. See also Bristows, 'Guide to Litigation Costs Funding and Insurance' <http://www.zorinlegal.com> accessed 25 September 2015.
[20] Bernardo M Cremades, 'Third Party Litigation Funding: Investing in Arbitration' (2012) 13 Spain Arbitration Review/Revista del Club Español del Arbitraje 155–87.
[21] Jeremy Morgan, 'Third Party Funding—Legal Aspects' (The London Common Law and Commercial Bar Association, 12 March 2008) <http://www.39essex.com> accessed 25 September 2015.
[22] Niccolò Landi, 'The Arbitrator and the Arbitration Procedure: Third Party Funding in International Commercial Arbitration—An Overview' in Christian Klausegger and others (eds), *Austrian Yearbook on International Arbitration* (Manz'sche Verlags- und Universitätsbuchhandlung 2012) 85–104.

lawyers acting on behalf of the funding applicant (and the compensation structure for such lawyers).[23]

26.30 Anecdotal evidence suggests that the percentage sought by third-party funders is often between 30 and 50 per cent of the relevant compensation or proceeds. Sometimes funders will calculate their compensation on the basis of a multiple of the costs incurred by the funder throughout the course of the dispute. There can also be a staging of the payments to the funder which is dependent on success at various stages of the dispute.

26.31 The benefits of third-party funding, and the challenges it creates, have been the subject of intense discussion and debate within the international arbitration community in recent years. Supporters of third-party funding argue that such funding can support access to justice in arbitration—a process which is exclusively financed by the parties to the dispute. Access to justice measures exist within national procedural frameworks, allowing relatively equal access to courts.[24] Funding, its supporters say, helps to level the playing field. This in turn may also have a positive impact on the prospects of settlement.

26.32 Another benefit of third-party funding put forward by supporters of such funding is that funders can provide a unique perspective and approach to applying risk assessment devices or analysis methods in order to complete an early and independent evaluation of a claim. This analysis, some funders argue, goes a step beyond the often purely legal analysis conducted by law firms.[25]

26.33 However, there are some criticisms levelled at third-party funding and its impact on the disputes market. Funding might lead to frivolous and abusive claims which have little merit, but are used as a method of creating disruption and extracting settlement. Furthermore, funders might impose unfair terms on a client, or may force early resolution of the claim (which may not be in the client's best interests). These problems stem from the fact that funders may not be regulated in the same way in which lawyers and insurers are regulated with regard to other funding products.[26]

26.34 Another criticism of third-party funding is that it can create ethical concerns. There exists between lawyer, client, and funder a very high potential for conflicts of interests. Lawyers may be tempted to be influenced more by the funder than the client given that the funder pays the bills.[27] Furthermore, the funder may take strategic decisions in the case on the basis of its duties to its investors, which may conflict with the best interests of the client.[28] While these risks impose challenges for all parties involved, many of the concerns surrounding

---

[23] Cremades (n 20) 155–87. Different funders give a sense from their online materials as to what types of claims they look for; for example, Juridica Investments states that it 'seeks to invest in claims that are likely to be resolved through settlement in a reasonable time frame' <http://www.juridicainvestments.com> accessed 25 September 2015.

[24] ibid 155–87.

[25] This due diligence is considered to be additional examination for success of the claim and the third-party funder usually funds claims that are meritorious. See Eric De Brabandere and Julia Lepeltak, 'Third-Party Funding in International Investment Arbitration' (2012) 27(2) ICSID Rev 379, 398.

[26] For a discussion of these issues, see Susana Khouri and others, 'Third Party Funding in International Commercial and Treaty Arbitration—A Panacea or a Plague? A Discussion of the Risks and Benefits of Third Party Funding' (2011) 4 TDM <http://www.transnational-dispute-management.com> accessed 25 September 2015.

[27] ibid.

[28] Cremades (n 20) 155–87.

conflicts of interest can and should be addressed in the funding agreement, for example by recognizing that the lawyer owes its professional and fiduciary duties to the client.

26.35 There is also a risk—depending upon which rules of privilege apply—that communications between funder and client, or funder and lawyer, may not be privileged and therefore may be subject to a later disclosure order. Another risk is that a conflict of interests may arise for a lawyer acting as arbitrator in one dispute and counsel in another—both of which are funded by the same funder. That lawyer will undoubtedly have close contact with the funder in the matter where he is acting as counsel—the question then arises whether that creates any risk of bias in the matter where the lawyer is acting as arbitrator, and whether the arbitrator must disclose the relationship.[29]

26.36 The risks and challenges posed by the presence of third-party funders, and the corresponding impact upon the arbitration process, have led to a significant debate as to whether parties should be obliged to disclose the existence of third-party funding arrangements in arbitration proceedings. As a starting point, many funding agreements will contain a confidentiality clause, and so it will be for the arbitral tribunal to order the disclosure, if the tribunal determines that such disclosure would be appropriate.[30] Disclosure of such arrangements might bolster the opposition's chances of obtaining security for costs, and might significantly influence the arbitral tribunal in assessing and apportioning costs. Furthermore, disclosure of such arrangements might assist in ensuring arbitrators are independent and impartial.[31]

26.37 In the recent case of *Oxus Gold Plc v Republic of Uzbekistan*,[32] because the claimant was a listed company, the claimant voluntarily announced that there was a funding agreement between the claimant and a third-party funder (Calunius Capital). Following this announcement, the claimant's share price increased by 200 per cent and became the top performing stock of the London Stock Exchange.[33]

D. Conclusion

26.38 International arbitration is a practice area which has flourished, and continues to do so, with the rise of cross-border trade and cross-border disputes. With that growth come challenges. The challenges include costly proceedings and how best to control those costs and apportion them between the parties. Meanwhile, a relatively unregulated market of third-party funding has arisen in which investors seek out international arbitration claims with a view towards making a profitable return.

---

[29] See discussion of this scenario in Maxi Scherer, 'Third-party Funding in International Arbitration. Towards Mandatory Disclosure of Funding Agreements?' in Antonias Dimolitsa and Bernardo M Cremades Román (eds), *Third-Party Funding in International Arbitration* (Dossier X of the ICC Institute of World Business Law, 2013).
[30] Brabandere and Lepeltak (n 25).
[31] Scherer (n 29).
[32] *Oxus Gold Plc v Republic of Uzbekistan, the State Committee of Uzbekistan for Geology & Mineral Resources, and Navoi Mining & Metallurgical Kombinat*, UNCITRAL Case, Award (1 January 2012). See the press release in which the funding agreement was disclosed. Oxus Gold Plc Press Release, 'Litigation Funding' (1 March 2012) <http://www.lse.co.uk> accessed 25 September 2015.
[33] Georges Affaki, 'A Financing is a Financing is a Financing …' in Dimolitsa and Cremades Román (n 29).

26.39 At the centre of these new developments are the various participants in the international arbitration process, including the parties to the dispute, their legal advisors, the arbitrators, the arbitral institution, the courts of the seat of the arbitration, any insurers or funders, and perhaps national regulators.

26.40 With the rise of funding options, each participant's engagement will be necessary to ensure that the quality of international arbitration as a dispute settlement process is maintained and perhaps enhanced. The risks and challenges which funding can bring to international arbitration will need to be addressed, for it is difficult to imagine a future for an expansive field of international arbitration without some component of funding.

27

'OTHER COSTS' IN INTERNATIONAL ARBITRATION

A Review of the Recoverability of Internal and Third-Party Funding Costs

*Marie Berard**

A. Introduction

It is trite to say that international arbitration proceedings frequently result in the incurrence of substantial fees and expenses.[1] The questions of how a tribunal awards those costs which are incurred by the parties, and how such costs should be allocated between the parties, entail difficult decisions in practice. Determining the 'winner' of a dispute, or whether certain actions were spurious or unreasonable, is not always straightforward, especially where multiple points are in issue.

27.01

A related, but less discussed matter, which forms the subject matter of this chapter, is the nature of the costs which a successful party should rightfully be able to recover. Money spent by parties on legal counsel, witnesses, and experts is widely accepted to be recoverable. However, most arbitral rules are silent as to internal costs and third-party funding costs, leaving the question of recoverability of such costs at the discretion of the tribunal.

27.02

In practice, more and more work is being undertaken by teams of in-house lawyers instead of external counsel, with disputes consuming substantial resources.[2] Cases can also demand the regular attention of a party's senior management or executive board, resulting in lost management time and driving up the overall cost of the arbitration to the parties. Should these costs be recoverable? What about a party whose costs have been paid by a third-party funding arrangement; should they, or their funder, be reimbursed if successful?

27.03

---

* The author would like to thank her Clifford Chance colleagues Carla Lewis and Richard Robinson for their assistance in the preparation of this chapter, which was written in October 2014.

[1] The measures that have been taken by institutions (in particular) to try and reduce those costs are well known. See, eg, the 2012 ICC 'Commission Report: Controlling Time and Costs in Arbitration' (Report No 861-1 ENG, ICC Dispute Resolution Library, 2007).

[2] For discussion, see Philippe Cavalieros, 'In-House Counsel Costs and Other Internal Party Costs in International Commercial Arbitration' (2014) 30(1) Arb Int'l 145, 146 ('Nowadays, especially in a post-financial crisis context, in light of the need for companies to better control outside counsel costs and to tackle an ever-increasing complexity of disputes, both from a technical and legal perspective, in-house counsel, senior officials, and in-house specialists increasingly are taking a strategic role, before, during, and after the arbitration process').

27.04 This chapter will explore the types of costs that may be awarded in arbitral proceedings, analyzing the underlying principles governing the recoverability of costs in international arbitration. In particular, it will focus on how claims relating to the costs of: (i) in-house legal counsel; (ii) staff and senior management; and (iii) third-party funding arrangements, are generally decided by arbitral tribunals.

B. Underlying Principles Governing Recovery of Costs

27.05 Before considering what categories of costs may be claimed at the end of arbitration proceedings, it is worth recalling the underlying principles governing recoverability. For a party to recover a specific cost it must fulfil three general criteria: (i) that the cost was incurred; (ii) that it specifically related to the arbitration; and (iii) that it was reasonable and necessary. The burden of proof rests with the party claiming its costs.

27.06 Taking each of these criteria in turn, in order to be recoverable, first, a party must be able to show that the costs sought are genuine and demonstrable.

27.07 Second, parties must further demonstrate that the cost in question was incurred for the specific purpose of the arbitration. An arbitral tribunal will not, for example, grant a party their costs of defending parallel court proceedings brought in breach of an arbitration agreement in an attempt to torpedo the arbitration process, although this could form the basis of a damages claim brought in the arbitration.[3]

27.08 Third, the cost sought must be both reasonable and necessary. Although common to many arbitral rules, reflecting growing concerns over the cost and efficiency of proceedings, the concept of reasonableness is generally undefined in international arbitration. Guidance provided by the CIArb suggests that reasonableness should include an element of proportionality. In determining whether costs have been reasonably incurred, arbitrators should consider various factors, such as the sums at stake, the conduct of the parties, and the importance or complexity of the matters in dispute.[4]

C. Standard Costs: Arbitration and External Counsel's Costs

27.09 As well as having to satisfy these underlying principles, only certain categories of costs are generally recognized as recoverable.

27.10 Reflecting the consensual nature of arbitration, most domestic arbitration laws and institutional rules allow parties to agree between themselves precisely what costs can be recovered. In the absence of any such agreement, the decision usually falls to the arbitral tribunal. For example, section 63 of the English Arbitration Act 1996 states that 'parties are free to agree

---

[3] *Company A (Italy) v 6 Respondents (Italy)*, ICC Case No 14046, Final Award (2010) in Albert Jan van den Berg (ed), *Yearbook Commercial Arbitration*, vol XXXV (Kluwer Law International 2010) 241–71.
[4] CIArb Practice Guideline 9: Guideline for Arbitrators on Making Orders Relating to the Costs of the Arbitration, paras 5.2.3–5.2.4.

what costs of the arbitration are recoverable'; failing any such agreement, the arbitral tribunal may determine the issue on 'such basis as it thinks fit'.[5]

27.11 While generally permitted, in practice parties rarely exercise this right to determine issues of costs before a dispute actually arises. As a result, more often than not, such questions are a matter of discretion for the arbitral tribunal. Few domestic laws set out precisely which costs may be recovered. However, some direction can be derived from the definition of 'costs' adopted within the majority of institutional arbitration rules.[6]

27.12 Most institutional rules allow the recovery of two distinct categories of costs, namely: (i) the administrative and procedural costs of convening an arbitration; and (ii) the legal costs associated with defending or pursuing a claim in arbitration.[7]

27.13 This first category of procedural costs covers costs ranging from hiring arbitrators and booking arbitral facilities to paying the fees and expenses of tribunal-appointed experts. For example, under Article 37(1) of the 2012 ICC Arbitration Rules, the fees and expenses of the arbitrators and any tribunal-appointed experts, along with any administrative expenses incurred by the ICC Court, are 'costs of the arbitration'.[8]

27.14 The legal fees that parties incur defending or pursuing claims make up the second accepted category of recoverable costs. In general, this is taken to mean the professional fees levied by external legal counsel. Whether such costs can be recovered is usually at the discretion of the tribunal. For example, Article 28(3) of the 2014 LCIA Arbitration Rules allows an arbitral tribunal to award a party 'all or any part of the legal or other expenses [it has] incurred ... on such reasonable basis as it thinks appropriate'. Many other arbitration rules have similar wording.[9]

---

[5] In the absence of a decision by the tribunal, either party may apply to the English courts to determine the recoverable costs of the arbitration on such basis as it thinks fit, s 63(4). Similar provisions can be found within the Irish Arbitration Act 2010 and the German ZPO, s 1057(1), as well as the ICSID Convention, s 61(2), and the 2014 LCIA Arbitration Rules, Art 28(3).
[6] See, eg, 2012 ICC Rules, Art 37(1).
[7] Michael O'Reilly refers to these costs as 'central costs' and 'party costs' respectively. See Michael O'Reilly, 'The Harmonization of Costs Practices in International Arbitration: The Search for the Holy Grail' in Julio César Betancourt (ed), *Defining Issues in International Arbitration: Celebrating 100 Years of the Chartered Institute of Arbitrators* (OUP 2016) ch 25.
[8] Art 40 of the 2010 UNCITRAL Rules similarly allows for these costs to be recovered.
[9] See, eg, 2012 ICC Rules, Art 37.1 ('reasonable legal and other costs incurred by the parties for the arbitration'); 1998 ICC Rules, Art 31.1 ('reasonable legal and other costs incurred by the parties for the arbitration'); 2014 LCIA Rules, Art 28.3 ('the legal or other expenses incurred by a party'); 2008 DIFC-LCIA Rules, Art 28.3 ('legal or other costs incurred by a party'); 2013 VIAC Rules, Art 44.1.3 ('the party's costs, ie the reasonable expenses of the parties for their legal representation; and other expenses related to the arbitration'); 2013 SIAC Rules, Art 33 ('the legal or other costs of a party'); 2005 SIArb Rules, Art 17.2 ('the legal or other costs of one party'); 1999 SCC Rules, Art 41 ('legal representation and other expenses'); 2013 HKIAC Rules, Art 33.1 ('reasonable costs for legal representation and assistance'); 2010 UNCITRAL Rules, Art 40.(e) ('legal and other costs incurred by the parties in relation to the arbitration'); 2013 KLRCA Rules, Art 40(2)(e) ('legal and other costs incurred by the parties in relation to the arbitration'); 2012 PCA Rules, Art 40.2(e) ('legal and other costs incurred by the parties in relation to the arbitration'); 2011 CRCICA Rules, Art 42.2(g) ('legal and other costs incurred by the parties'); 2011 ACICA Rules, Art 39(e) ('legal and other costs directly incurred by the successful party'). The 2007 DIAC Rules stand out by their omission of the 'legal or other costs' provision: 'The costs of the arbitration shall include the Centre's administrative Fees for the claim and any counterclaim and the fees and expenses of the Tribunal fixed by the Centre ... and shall include any expenses incurred by the Tribunal, as well as the fees and expenses of any experts appointed by the Tribunal.'

D. Contested Costs: In-House Counsel
(Management and Third-Party Funding Costs)

27.15 In addition to these two generally accepted types of recoverable costs, many arbitral rules allow parties to recover their 'other costs' associated with the arbitration.[10] Such language gives the arbitral tribunal broad discretionary powers to allow parties to recover their other legitimate costs arising from proceedings.

27.16 However, what these legitimate costs might include is unclear. In particular, the extent to which parties can rely on these provisions in order to recover fees incurred by in-house counsel and other staff and management, or within third-party litigation funding arrangements, remains highly contentious.

(a) In-house counsel costs

27.17 Companies increasingly employ large in-house legal teams, preferring to enhance their internal capabilities to resolve disputes in order to reduce their expenditure on external counsel. According to a study published by PwC in 2013,[11] approximately 90 per cent of the corporations surveyed had their own legal departments, of which 49 per cent included a dedicated disputes team. While this survey showed that most corporations still retained outside counsel when involved in full-blown arbitration, a number sought to do part of the legal work internally, splitting tasks (such as drafting submissions and collecting documents) between the two teams. The potential level of costs incurred under this category could be significant in any given case.

27.18 Whether the arbitral tribunal can award costs for in-house counsel is subject to debate. Traditionally, the costs of in-house counsel have been treated as part of the normal running costs of a business. The view was held that the costs for in-house counsel exist irrespective of the arbitration in question and are thus not recoverable at all, least of all in addition to external lawyers' fees.

27.19 The rationale behind this position is that in-house counsel receive their salary irrespective of their work on a particular arbitration fought by their employer, and there is no direct causal link between the work of in-house counsel and a particular arbitration. There are also concerns that where a company retains external legal counsel while continuing to use its own in-house lawyers, there will, inevitably, be a certain degree of overlap between their respective work-streams, resulting in unnecessary duplication. If this is avoided, the argument follows that any internal case management required would not exceed that which forms part of the ordinary course of business of an in-house legal department.[12]

---

[10] See, eg, Art 34 of the 2014 ICDR Rules.
[11] 2013 QMUL Survey, 'Corporate Choices in International Arbitration: Industry Perspectives' <http://www.arbitration.qmul.ac.uk/research/index.html> accessed 25 September 2015. For example, in 2012, Shell set up its Legal Services Global Litigation group comprising over 70 lawyers, a fully integrated in-house dispute team to handle all of its litigation and arbitration. See 'Shell kicks off global litigation group with Fulbright hire', *The Lawyer* (7 May 2012).
[12] Unpublished Award in ICC Case No 17333 (2011), quoted by Anne-Carole Cremades and Alexandre Mazuranic, 'Costs in Arbitration' in Elliott Geisinger and Nathalie Voser (eds), *International Arbitration in Switzerland: A Handbook for Practitioners* (2nd edn, Kluwer Law International 2013) 173, 190 ('where a sole arbitrator refused to award costs for time spent by the successful party's in-house personnel, in light of

27.20 However, this argument is losing support. There are a number of compelling reasons why costs incurred by in-house counsel should be recoverable in arbitral proceedings. If a party relies solely on in-house counsel for its legal representation before an arbitral tribunal, the work of the in-house counsel is both necessary and directly related to a particular arbitration. In that case, there should be little doubt that costs for the in-house counsel's work on the arbitration are recoverable. But even in cases where in-house counsel work alongside external counsel, the trend is for such costs to be recoverable.[13]

27.21 First, there is an apparent lost opportunity cost borne by companies; as a result of the arbitration, in-house legal teams may be required to perform work outside of their normal mandate, preventing them from undertaking tasks that are normally required in these traditionally advisory roles. This is especially true where a company is the respondent in proceedings; in such circumstances the business could be considered disrupted by these new unanticipated work-streams. It is misguided to suggest that companies would have incurred these in-house costs by virtue of the lawyers being on their permanent payroll regardless of the arbitration having arisen.

27.22 Second, the costs of internal and external counsel cannot be objectively distinguished where both are undertaking work required by the arbitration. Were it not for the existence of this internal capacity, the tasks undertaken by these in-house lawyers would need to be completed by external counsel. Why should the latter's fees be recoverable and the former's costs not, simply because the work was completed by a party's own employees? To proceed in this manner would penalize a party for trying to streamline its legal team to keep costs down. Allocating appropriate work, such as the collection of documents and gathering of evidence, to an in-house legal team is usually cheaper (and more cost-effective) than using external counsel.

27.23 In-house counsel have better access to information within the company represented before the arbitral tribunal. They devote substantial time to the case, play a key role in gathering documents, control the work of external counsel, and will often attend the hearing as client representative.[14] In assisting external lawyers, in-house counsel render arbitral proceedings more

---

the fees of that party's external legal counsel which had been awarded in full. The sole arbitrator first stated that: "Managing disputes is part of everyday business, in particular for in-house legal departments. The costs related to this particular activity are recoverable, but only to the extent that they exceed the ordinary level of legal and litigation risk inherent to any business" ').

[13] ICC Case No 6564 (1993) quoted in Eric Schwartz, 'The ICC Arbitral Process, Part IV: The Costs of ICC Arbitration' (1993) 4 ICC Int'l Ct Arb Bull 45–6 ('In the Arbitral Tribunal's view in-house legal costs may well form part of a party's normal legal cost incurred in the conduct of a case. It is for each party to decide whether it wishes to retain outside counsel or prepare and argue the case by its own staff. There is no justification to privilege a party in terms of costs for the sole reason that it retained outside counsel'); ICC Case No 8786, Final Award (1997) (2002) ASA Bull 68, in which the claimant was awarded 80 per cent of its legal costs, including '*in-house legal costs*'; ICC Award No 16879 (2013) quoted in W Laurence Craig, William W Park, and Jan Paulsson, *International Chamber of Commerce Arbitration* (3rd edn, Oceana Publication 2000) 394, fn 8 ('The Tribunal finds that the amounts claimed for the [in-house] translators and in-house counsel are costs of the arbitration. Although they were employees of [the claimant], they performed specific tasks for the arbitration which would otherwise have been performed by outside lawyers and professional translators. This finding is consistent with the observation by Craig, Park and Paulsson that "some Awards have … allowed the recoupment of costs of in-house legal counsel" ').

[14] CIArb, 'Guidelines for Arbitrators on Making Orders Relating to Costs of the Arbitration' (2003) 69(2) Arbitration 130, 139 ('The staff of a company or firm involved in an arbitration often dedicate substantial time to the case, including the generation of figures and attendance at the hearing').

27.24 This is in line with recent developments in procedural rules that are aimed at reducing costs in arbitration. When making decisions as to cost, the ICC Rules permit the tribunal to take into account the extent to which parties have conducted themselves in an expeditious and cost-effective manner.[15] The 2014 LCIA Rules also allow any 'co-operation in facilitating the proceedings as to time and cost' to be taken into account in costs awards.[16] These provisions certainly relate to decisions that tribunals make as to the allocation of costs between the parties, and arguably relate to the decisions made by the tribunal as to the recoverability of certain categories of costs. By this token, any efforts by the parties to streamline the process from an economic perspective should be welcomed.

27.25 It is not unknown for money spent on internal legal resources to be recoverable where parties have been able to evidence clearly the time spent by their in-house counsel specifically working on the arbitration.[17]

27.26 There appears to be a growing acceptance that parties should, as a matter of principle, be able to recover such costs where properly incurred. However, for those costs to be recoverable, the successful party must be able to evidence and quantify such costs in sufficient detail. Tribunals will often expect cost claims to be subject to full proof just like damages claims. This may be achieved through the use of comprehensive schedules summarizing contemporaneous detailed time records of the work, itemizing the work undertaken and how it related to the arbitration.[18]

(b) Management and staff costs

27.27 Management and other members of staff of the parties will often be expected to give substantial time and attention to the proceedings. It is therefore unsurprising that companies frequently seek to recover the cost and expense of this lost time.

27.28 While the recently introduced Paris Arbitration Rules (which provide a structure for *ad hoc* arbitration) do make express provision for the recovery of management and staff costs,[19] this is somewhat of an atypical position; in general, arbitral rules are silent regarding the recovery of these costs, leaving the issue in most cases to the discretion of the tribunal.

27.29 As is the case for in-house counsel's costs, the traditional view has resisted the recoverability of management and executive time, on the basis that they are an inevitable cost of initiating or defending a claim in arbitration.[20] The rationale behind this view is that it is precisely the

---

[15] Art 37(5).
[16] Art 28.4.
[17] See cases referred in n 13.
[18] See ICC Case No 6564 (n 13) 45–6 ('There is, however, an important difference between the costs for outside counsel and those incurred in-house: the former are expenditures and can be clearly identified and evidenced; in the case of the latter this is not always the case. In view of this difference it appears justified to require some substantiation, *inter alia* with respect to the nature of the cost, the personnel involved and type of work performed').
[19] Art 7(6).
[20] See, eg, ICC Case No 5759, Final Award (1989) in Albert Jan van den Berg (ed), *Yearbook of Commercial Arbitration*, vol XVIII (Kluwer Law International 1993) 34 (the Tribunal ruled that 'Claimant's internal costs for management, employees, [and] travel … cannot be qualified as arbitration costs'); ICC Case No 5029, Award (1991) in Schwartz (n 13) 32 ('Legal costs do not include any allowance for time spent on the arbitration

role of management to help the company to deal with the risks of doing business and therefore the costs of pursuing arbitration fall within their existing role. On this view, legal risks are no different from any other type of risk being faced by a company. They are part and parcel of the normal costs of running an enterprise. Why should a party be compensated simply because its managers did their jobs? These employees would still have been on the company's payroll irrespective of the arbitration.

27.30 But there are valid arguments in favour of being able to recover management and staff costs in arbitral proceedings. Members of management and staff are usually required to devote considerable time to the proceedings; their participation is required in order to understand the factual circumstances underlying a dispute, produce witness statements, explain the technical elements at issue, and generally to assist counsel in framing a party's case. This time spent on the arbitration represents a significant indirect cost to the business; it is time these employees could have spent furthering the objectives of their companies. This lost opportunity cost incurred by parties can be significant, especially in highly technical fields (such as energy or construction), where the outcome of a dispute can turn on complicated factual issues.

27.31 Both of these views are reflected to some extent in the CIArb Practice Guideline 9.[21] Although stated to be generally irrecoverable, these guidelines do suggest that such costs may be reimbursed in commercial cases if the arbitrator is 'satisfied that the work done internally obviated the need for others to do it and hence led to an overall saving of costs'. The guidelines also provide that '[r]easonable compensation may normally be allowed for a person who represents himself or his employer in an arbitration'.[22]

27.32 Indeed, in the context of litigation, similar logic has been applied by the English courts, resulting in the successful recovery of management costs. The Court of Appeal in *Aerospace Publishing Ltd v Thames Water Utilities Ltd*[23] held that the cost of employees diverted from

---

by the party itself or its directors, employees, representatives and agents. Arbitrations inevitably take up time of the parties themselves and their staff, but the cost of any such time is in the Arbitral Tribunal's opinion not part of the legal costs of the proceedings'); ICC Case No 9797 (2000), (2000) 15(8) Mealey's IAR (the arbitrator dismissed a US$15 million claim for internal employee costs 'because the allocation of their employees' time and effort to the present arbitration is a decision dependent entirely on the [Respondents'] discretion ...'); ICC Award No 6293, Final Award (1990) in Schwartz (n 13) 43 (the tribunal rejected the claimant's claim for compensation for the time of its personnel involved in the preparation of its case on the basis that 'it does not in [the tribunal's] view form part of the costs of the arbitration, in the sense of being part of the Claimant's "normal legal costs" ... The *per diem* sum claimed for each employee, whether for salary alone or salary plus overhead, does not represent a special cost incurred by it for the purposes of the arbitration but is part of its normal operating expenses. It is for the same reason that such amounts, cannot in [the tribunal's] opinion, form party [sic] of its legal costs'); ICC Award No 16879 (2013), unpublished ('The Tribunal has concluded that the "reasonable legal and other costs incurred by the parties" referred to in Article 31 of the [1998] ICC Rules cannot include [Claimant's] staff costs. [Claimant] was unable to put before the Tribunal any previous decision of a court or an arbitral tribunal to the contrary. The Tribunal concurs with the observation of Redfern and Hunter that "traditionally such costs have been regarded as part of the normal cost of running ... a business enterprise"'). See also Nigel Blackaby and others, *Redfern and Hunter on International Arbitration* (5th edn, OUP 2009) para 9.91 (stating that recoverable costs 'rarely include any allowance for the time spent on the case by senior officials, directors, or employees of the parties themselves, and the indirect costs of disruption to their ordinary business' and that it is 'unusual to recover the costs of executive time, particularly if this includes—as it frequently does—the cost of "in-house" counsel or of an internal legal department').

[21] CIArb Practice Guideline 9 (n 4) para 5.7.3.2.
[22] ibid 5.7.3.1.
[23] [2007] EWCA Civ 3.

their usual revenue-generating activities was recoverable. In that case, it was important that the party claiming its costs had established with sufficient detail that employees (in particular, senior employees) had been diverted from their usual tasks. The claimant also had to establish that the diversion caused significant disruption to its business. If such diversion and disruption were established, then the court could reasonably infer that, had their time not been thus diverted, staff would have applied it to activities which would, directly or indirectly, have generated revenue for the claimant in an amount at least equal to the costs of employing them during that time. Of course, a good evidential trail of costs incurred is pivotal to the recovery of such costs. Parties need to keep detailed records of the time spent by their staff on the arbitration, and of how and why the staff are diverted from their regular work activities.

27.33 While there may be issues in practice with the recovery of management costs, authorities suggest that, at least as a matter of principle, it may be possible to recover costs for time spent by management and staff in arbitration.[24]

(c) Third-party funding costs

27.34 Costs incurred under third-party funding arrangements probably constitute the most contentious head of 'other costs' that parties may seek to claim in arbitral proceedings. Typically involving a funder with no prior connection to or interest in the dispute, under these arrangements, the legal fees and disbursements incurred by a party are paid (in whole or in part) by a funder in exchange for a proportion of the party's proceeds (if successful).

27.35 Before addressing issues of recoverability, third-party funding agreements must first be distinguished from other sources of support available to disputing parties, such as 'after-the event-insurance' and 'contingency fee arrangements'.

27.36 After the event (ATE) insurance is a form of insurance whereby a party pays a fee to an insurer in exchange for an assurance that they will be compensated if their claim proves unsuccessful. The cost of procuring this insurance is generally irrecoverable in arbitral proceedings.

27.37 Contingency fee arrangements (CFAs) are agreements between disputing parties and their external counsel whereby the latter's fees are partially or wholly contingent upon the outcome of a dispute. Such fees are generally deemed to amount to a reward granted to external counsel for their success, as opposed to an accurate representation of the party's costs, and are rarely recoverable in practice over and above the normal level of fees.

---

[24] See, eg, ICC Award No 6564 (n 13) ('A claim for a party's internal cost is admissible in principle also in those cases where outside counsel had been retained. A party must be free in allocating the work between its outside counsel and its own services. A party which decides to perform most of the preparatory work for the case by its own legal and technical departments should not be placed at a disadvantage compared to one which confers all work to outside counsel and experts'). See also ICC Award No 6959, Final Award (1992) in Schwartz (n 13) 49 (the tribunal awarded the reasonable costs and expenses of the steering committee of the winning party, stating: 'It would seem that in France costs awarded to the winning parties may include not only fees and costs paid or payable to lawyers or costs incurred by the winning party's legal departments but also other expenses incurred by the winning party'); Final Award, ICC Case No 10329 (2000) in Albert Jan van den Berg (ed), *Yearbook Commercial Arbitration*, vol XXIX (Kluwer Law International 2004) 108–32 (' "legal costs" do not encompass only attorneys' fees but also the costs of a party itself provided that they are reasonable and incurred in connection with the preparation and presentation of the arbitration case').

27.38 Third-party funding in international arbitration usually involves a commercial funder agreeing to pay some or all of the claimant's legal fees and expenses, in return for reimbursement of the funder's direct costs and a share of any damages recovered by way of settlement or award.

27.39 In the context of English litigation, Jackson LJ considered the recoverability of CFA success fees and ATE premiums led to disproportionate costs and were key drivers behind the escalating costs of civil litigation. From April 2013, these are no longer recoverable in English litigation. However, Jackson LJ approved of third-party funding, as he viewed it as having no impact on costs.[25]

27.40 Traditionally, third-party funding arrangements were reserved for mass tort claims or class action law suits in the United States. However, this model is increasingly being applied in commercial litigation and also in international arbitration. For example, such a funding arrangement was used in the ICSID case of *S&T Oil Equipment and Machinery Ltd v Romania*.[26] Whether a party to arbitral proceedings may be able to recover any costs in such circumstances, though, is strikingly unclear, a fact compounded by the private nature of arbitration.

27.41 The majority of domestic arbitration laws and institutional rules are underpinned by the concept of party consent. This emphasis on the consensual nature and privity of arbitration has proved problematic in practice for parties seeking to recover the costs of third-party funders. Section 61(1) of the English Arbitration Act 1996 provides that tribunals may make an award 'allocating the costs of the arbitration as between the parties'. Article 61(2) of the ICSID Convention similarly empowers tribunals to 'assess the expenses incurred by the parties in connection with the proceedings'. A third-party funder is not privy to the arbitration agreement from which jurisdiction is fundamentally derived. As a result, funders lack the necessary standing needed to recoup their costs from a tribunal; tribunals similarly cannot compel a third-party funder to pay an adverse costs order.

27.42 As stated above, in the absence of an express agreement between the parties identifying the categories of recoverable costs, the decision falls to the tribunal. In making this decision, arbitrators are free to take into account any relevant circumstances.[27] This raises the important question of whether a party should inform its tribunal of the existence of any third-party funding arrangements.

27.43 Is the mere existence of a third-party funder a relevant circumstance which should be taken into account by the arbitral tribunal? What about the conduct of a funder actively engaged in procedural warfare in order to wear out an economically weaker opposing party? At present, none of the most commonly used arbitral rules (for example, ICC, LCIA, and UNCITRAL) imposes an obligation on parties to disclose the existence of third-party funders.

---

[25] Jackson LJ, *Review of Civil Litigation Costs: Final Report* (CIArb, December 2009).
[26] ICSID Case No ARB/07/13, Order of Discontinuance of the Proceeding (16 July 2010).
[27] See, eg, the English Arbitration Act 1996, s 61(2), which reads: 'Unless the parties otherwise agree, the tribunal shall award costs on the general principle that costs should follow the event except where it appears to the tribunal that in the circumstances this is not appropriate in relation to the whole or part of the costs'. Similar wording can be found in Art 28(4) of the 2014 LCIA Rules and Art 37(5) of the 2012 ICC Rules.

27.44 A third-party funding arrangement raises two main questions relating to the recoverability of costs in arbitration. The first question is whether the funded party can be awarded the costs borne by its funder—ie, could the losing party argue that the successful funded party has incurred no costs and should therefore not be awarded any costs? The second question is whether the tribunal may award to the successful funded party the success fee due to the third-party funder over and above the costs actually borne. In the author's view, the second question should be treated similarly to CFAs, and should not be recoverable.[28] If the third-party funder's premium was recoverable, this would substantially and unfairly increase the amounts owed by the losing party.

27.45 The first question has divided arbitral tribunals. An ICC tribunal held that, had a respondent been successful in the arbitration, its legal costs that had been paid by a third-party insurer would have been recoverable.[29]

27.46 In *Ioannis Kardassopoulos & Ron Fuchs v Georgia*,[30] the respondent sought to resist liability for the claimant's costs on the grounds that the claimant had been funded by Allianz Litigation Funding. This argument was rejected, with the tribunal holding that the existence of a funder did not affect recoverability: 'The Tribunal knows of no principle why any such third-party financing arrangement should be taken into consideration in determining the amount of recovery by the Claimants of their costs'.[31] The tribunal therefore ordered the respondent to pay approximately US$8 million in costs.

27.47 The opposite conclusion was reached in *Quasar de Valores v Russia*.[32] In this case, the claimants were awarded US$2 million in damages and sought to recover approximately US$14 million in legal costs. The tribunal, chaired by Jan Paulsson, declined to award any costs to the successful claimants (Spanish minority shareholders in Yukos) on the grounds that proceedings had been funded entirely by the majority shareholder, Menatep. In the tribunal's view, the claimants had incurred no costs. The costs were borne by a third party which, the tribunal held, had no standing before it—the tribunal could not award such costs.

---

[28] Most commentators deny the recoverability of a funded party's costs over and above normal legal fees (conditional fees, ATE-premium, litigation funder's return): see Daniel Wehrli, 'Contingency Fees/Pactum de palmario "Civil Law Approach"' (2008) 26 ASA Bull 241, 253–4; Michael O'Reilly, *Costs in Arbitration Proceedings* (2nd edn, Informa Law 1997) 67–8; Bernard Hanotiau, 'The Parties' Costs of Arbitration' in Richard H Kreindler and Yves Derains (eds), *Evaluation of Damages in International Arbitration* (Dossier IV of the ICC Institute of World Business Law, 2006) 213, 219; Jeffrey Waincymer, *Procedure and Evidence in International Arbitration* (Kluwer Law International 2012) 1246; Micha Bühler, 'Awarding Costs in International Commercial Arbitration: An Overview' (2004) 22 ASA Bull 249, 272; Markus Jäger, *Reimbursement for Attorney's Fees* (Eleven International Publishing 2010) 137.

[29] *Supplier v First distributor, Second distributor*, ICC Case No 7006, Final Award (1992) in Schwartz (n 13) 49, noting that costs paid by the third-party insurer are recoverable 'at least from the point that Defendants rather than the [third party insurer], mandated counsel to represent them in the arbitration. By so doing, they incurred the primary obligation to pay such counsel's fees and expenses—one not negated by the fact that someone else, through prior arrangement, paid them on their behalf. The counterpart to this determination is that Defendants would be obliged to reimburse their indemnifier any costs they recovered from the arbitration'.

[30] ICSID Case Nos ARB/05/18 and ARB/07/15. See also *RSM Production Corp v Grenada*, ICSID Case No ARB/05/14, Order of the Committee Discontinuing the Proceeding and Decision on Costs (28 April 2011).

[31] ibid, *Ioannis* [691].

[32] *Quasar de Valores SICAV SA v The Russian Federation*, SCC Arbitration No 24/2007, Award (20 July 2012).

Further, the tribunal found that the 'usual arguments about the recoverability of costs **27.48** where a party's participation in a case has been financed by a third party are inapposite here, because such third-party financing is typically part of a legally enforceable bargain under which the prevailing party in the arbitration has given up something in return for that support. Here, it is conceded that there is no legal duty on the part of the Claimants to hand over any recovery on account of costs to [the third-party funder]'.[33]

The *Quasar de Valores* case is likely to be earmarked as an exception on the basis of the **27.49** unusual nature of the third-party funding arrangement in that case. As noted by the tribunal, the claimants were under no legal duty to compensate the funder for their costs or to share in any recovery. However, commercial third-party arrangements will expressly provide for such legal duty. In such cases, and where English law is applicable, it is expected that arbitral tribunals would find that the presence of third-party funding does not affect the recoverability of legal costs, and should be regarded just in the same way as bank loan funding.

One should also note that third-party funding arrangements are illegal as a matter of public **27.50** policy in many jurisdictions. Recoverability, therefore, will depend on the legality of such arrangements under the laws of the place of performance, the seat of the arbitration, and any countries in which enforcement of an arbitral award may be sought.

E. Conclusion

While most arbitral rules expressly allow for the recovery of arbitral costs and reasonable **27.51** legal fees incurred by external counsel, the position is less clear where the fees of in-house lawyers, lost management time, or third-party funding arrangements are concerned.

In theory, in-house counsel fees should be recoverable where parties are able to demonstrate **27.52** the reasonableness and necessity of these costs—subject also to being able to evidence and quantify costs, which requires that contemporaneous time recording be put in place.

A more controversial issue is the recoverability of management costs incurred in support of **27.53** the arbitration, which has typically been resisted. However, changing trends and practice in litigation suggest that, if sufficiently evidenced, a party should in principle be able to recover such costs in arbitration if time spent on the arbitration caused substantial disruption to its business.

Costs underwritten by a third-party funding arrangement should, in principle, be similarly **27.54** recoverable provided the funding arrangement was agreed at arm's length and is permitted under the applicable laws.

The forthcoming report of the ICC Task Force on Decisions as to Costs co-chaired by **27.55** Bernard Hanotiau and Julian Lew will be welcomed by arbitration users as it is expected to provide multi-jurisdiction insights and data on the recoverability of internal and third-party funding costs in international arbitration.

In a context where the spotlight is increasingly focused on the escalating cost of arbitration **27.56** proceedings, clarity on the recoverable nature of the parties' internal costs in international

---

[33] ibid [223].

arbitration is to be welcomed. If parties were assured of the recoverability of their in-house counsel and other staff costs, they would be more likely to rely on their own internal resources during the arbitration process, which would ultimately decrease the overall cost of the arbitration.

28

OPTIMIZING THE USE OF MEDIATION IN INTERNATIONAL ARBITRATION

A Cost–Benefit Analysis of 'Two Hat' Versus 'Two People' Models

Jeffrey Waincymer

A. Introduction

Leading arbitration practitioners are highly supportive of mediation, with the CIArb being at the forefront of mediation training in the United Kingdom. This support is natural, as like arbitration, mediation is based on consent, with successful mediation involving not only consent to the form of dispute settlement process, but also to the specifics of the outcome. For similar reasons, if parties choose to settle arbitral proceedings, this should be supported, as the consent to continue the arbitration no longer exists.[1] A consensual outcome of mediation is in that sense fair, being an agreed outcome of an agreed process. In most instances it should also be efficient, reducing the dead-weight transaction costs of dispute resolution, often leading to a more harmonious end-state position than would be the case after a 'winner-takes-all' arbitral decision. 28.01

While most would thus support some role for mediation as an adjunct of arbitration, it is still necessary to identify the optimal way in which arbitration and mediation should inter-relate. In doing so, it is necessary to consider the impact of both successful and unsuccessful mediation. If unsuccessful, ADR processes have time and cost implications and can be particularly problematic if they undermine any ensuing adjudicative process. Problems can arise in terms of confidentiality, privilege, and admissibility of evidence from the mediation and also as a result of challenges to an arbitrator based on actions as mediator. These problems can be more significant in international arbitration disputes, where arbitrator challenges are becoming more common and where there can be conflicts of law questions about these matters, with no consensus as to the way in which evidentiary principles should apply in the international arena. 28.02

These questions of optimal design can arise in a range of alternative scenarios. There are cases where parties first try mediation and then proceed to arbitration if the mediation fails; 28.03

---

[1] Many rules and statutes expressly provide for settlement, but even if this is not the case, this would generally be 'implied' into any contract with the arbitrator and/or the institution.

cases where an arbitrator suggests mediation in the middle of the arbitral process, either in whole or in part; and cases where the parties establish a staged process, typically with negotiation followed by mediation, followed by arbitration.

28.04 Perhaps the most polarizing question flows from a further division of the above scenarios, between cases where the same person acts as mediator and arbitrator, whether concurrently or sequentially, and conversely, cases where different persons are utilized for each process. The aim of this chapter is to compare these alternative models. To this end, each of the former scenarios is referred to as involving a dual-role neutral.[2]

28.05 To some, there is a gateway philosophical question as to whether an arbitrator may adopt a mediation function or whether the dual roles are antithetical.[3] This chapter does not purport to engage in this debate, although its cost–benefit conclusions may impact upon those observations. In the author's view, there is nothing antithetical about dual-role neutrals provided that informed consent is present, a view not shared by all from a common law background. Yet, as Neil Kaplan observed many years ago, if the parties agree to provide such power to an arbitrator, 'it [is] difficult to see why the law should not oblige'.[4] In his view, it depended upon the trust and respect that the parties had in the person with that power.[5]

28.06 While the possible use of dual-role neutrals is accepted by a majority, or close to it, this does not mean that it will be optimal in all or most scenarios and it is the purpose of this chapter to test that hypothesis by engaging in a cost–benefit analysis of differing scenarios when mediation is utilized in an arbitral context. The prime comparison is between parallel mediation with a separate neutral and the alternative of a dual-role neutral. The essential three-part thesis of the chapter is that: (1) there should be much

---

[2] Various notations, such as med-arb, arb-med, or arb-med-arb, have been used by commentators to denote the order in which the dual-role neutral addresses each of the respective functions. These distinctions will only be referred to separately if they impact upon the cost–benefit analysis.

[3] See Jacob Rosoff, 'Hybrid Efficiency in Arbitration: Waiving Potential Conflicts for Dual Role Arbitrators in Med-Arb and Arb-Med Proceedings' (2009) 26(1) J Int'l Arb 89. Hilmar Raeschke-Kessler, 'The Arbitrator as Settlement Facilitator' (2005) 21(4) Arb Int'l 525; Harold I Abramson, 'Protocols for International Arbitrators Who Dare to Settle Cases' (1999) 10 Am Rev Int'l Arb 4; Gerald Aksen, 'Comments on Enforceability of Awards on the Role of Arbitrators as Settlement Facilitators' in Albert Jan van den Berg (ed), *New Horizons in International Commercial Arbitration and Beyond* (ICCA Congress Series No 12, Kluwer Law International 2005) 565–6; Michael Collins, 'Do International Arbitral Tribunals Have Any Obligations to Encourage Settlement of the Disputes before Them?' (2003) 19(3) Arb Int'l 341; Pierre Lalive, 'The Role of Arbitrators as Settlement Facilitators: A Swiss View' in van den Berg, *New Horizons*, ibid, 562–3; Christian Bühring-Uhle, *Arbitration and Mediation in International Business: Designing Procedures for Effective Conflict Management* (Kluwer Law International 1996) 366; Michael E Schneider, 'Combining Arbitration with Conciliation' in Albert Jan van den Berg (ed), *Planning Efficient Arbitration Proceedings: The Law Applicable in International Arbitration* (ICCA Congress Series No 7, Kluwer Law International 1996) 88; Gabrielle Kaufmann-Kohler, 'When Arbitrators Facilitate Settlement: Towards a Transnational Standard: *Clayton Utz/University of Sydney International Arbitration Lecture*' (2009) 25(2) Arb Int'l 197; Tania Sourdin, 'Facilitative Judging' (2004) 22(1) L Context 64.

[4] Quoted in Lucy Greenwood, 'A Window of Opportunity? Building a Short Period of Time into Arbitral Rules in Order for Parties to Explore Settlement' (2011) 27(2) Arb Int'l 199, 206.

[5] Consent may also come via *lex arbitri* and arbitral rules, as accepted by the parties. Some legal systems strongly endorse the dual-role neutral, with China being the leading example. Jun Ge, 'Mediation, Arbitration and Litigation: Dispute Resolution in the People's Republic of China' (1996) 15 UCLA Pac Basin LJ 122.

more mediation occurring at the international level, both in respect of potential and actual arbitral disputes; (2) a commercially minded arbitrator concerned for the parties' good faith should encourage mediation where appropriate, in particular, when an adjudicated outcome will not be in the interests of either, usually because the dispute is a small part of a long-term relationship that can risk that relationship no matter who wins; and (3) while informed party autonomy should always support a dual-role neutral, in the vast majority of factual permutations, informed parties could be expected to prefer parallel mediation as long as there is full cooperation between mediator and arbitrator.

The chapter contends that the relative benefits of the use of dual-role neutrals would invariably be greatly outweighed by the costs in fairness and efficiency and the inevitable need for a suboptimal design of either or both dispute processes. The benefits would also be separately outweighed by the risks of significant disruption to any ensuing arbitration if a dual-role neutral fails to achieve a settlement. 28.07

B. The Right to Act as Mediator or Conciliator in Facilitating Settlement

Before considering what ought to be done, it is necessary to consider what is permissible to be done. This chapter presumes that most *leges arbitri* and arbitral rules allow for settlement, and, in many cases, go so far as to impose some obligations on an arbitrator to assist in that regard.[6] While few expressly stipulate that an arbitrator can act as a mediator, *leges arbitri* and rules that are silent are better seen as impliedly allowing for this power, always subject to the parties' consent in that regard.[7] 28.08

While that is the better view, an important consideration is to see how a dual-role neutral might exercise such a function in the context of the overriding arbitral obligations to provide for equal treatment and to provide a reasonable opportunity for each party to present its case. This chapter considers the various techniques typically used by mediators and looks at whether these may compromise the arbitration in some way, or whether these overriding arbitral obligations would constrain the mediator in terms of utilization of otherwise desirable mediation techniques. The chapter concludes that both problems are likely to arise. 28.09

---

[6] See, eg, New Hong Kong Arbitration Ordinance (Cap 609) s 33; Indian Arbitration and Conciliation Act, Art 30(1); Singapore International Arbitration Act, s 17; DIS Arbitration Rules, s 32.1; Austrian ZPO, Art 204; German ZPO, s 278; Netherlands Code of Civil Procedure, Art 1043; Japanese Arbitration Law of 2003, Art 38(4); The Arbitration Law of the People's Republic of China 1995. See also 2014 IBA Guidelines on Conflicts of Interest, General Standard 4(d), which indicates that an arbitrator may assist the parties in reaching a settlement subject to express agreement of the parties.

[7] There are arguments either way in terms of implied powers, absent any guidance in the *lex arbitri* or Rules. The argument in favour would be that settlement by way of consent is complying with procedural directions of the parties. The contrary argument is that the procedural powers are to be for the purposes of the arbitration itself and not for separate mediation purposes. The former view is to be preferred. See Margaret L Moses, 'Inherent and Implied Powers of Arbitrators' in Julio César Betancourt (ed), *Defining Issues in International Arbitration: Celebrating 100 Years of the Chartered Institute of Arbitrators* (OUP 2016) ch 21. Some rules expressly prohibit dual-role neutrals: r 1(4) of the ICSID Rules and Art 19 of the 1980 UNCITRAL Conciliation Rules prevent a mediator from acting as an arbitrator in the same dispute.

C. Facilitative v Evaluative Mediation

28.10 Before addressing the relative costs and benefits of the alternative approaches, it is important to outline the two main forms of mediation, as the analysis varies significantly depending on the type of mediation involved. The two main types of mediation are commonly described as facilitative and evaluative, respectively. Evaluative mediation will at some stage involve the neutral providing views on the merits of the case or on the appropriateness of settlement offers. Importantly, however, there is no need to conduct mediations in this manner and the dominant theoretical and training model is facilitative or interest-based. Such mediation does not engage in the debate on the dispute itself, but looks for overlapping interests that might be identified as an alternative to pursuance of the dispute.

28.11 Critics of dual-role neutrals typically presume that any mediation would be evaluative. Such critics find it antithetical for a person, who may ultimately decide the dispute as arbitrator, to provide an indication of a likely future determination during the mediation. While purely facilitative mediation can overcome many of the criticisms of the dual-role model, the very fact that different mediators have biases in favour of one or other approach, adds to the conflicts facing dual-role neutrals, absent clear guidance from informed parties. The following cost–benefit analysis will consider the two models in making the comparative assessment between dual-role and separate-neutral approaches.

D. Advantages and Disadvantages of a Dual-Role Neutral

(a) Cost

28.12 The most obvious advantage of utilizing a dual-role neutral, either a mediator who then acts as arbitrator or an arbitrator attempting to mediate, is the saving of cost. Only one person needs to understand the dispute in order to engage in both functions. While some cost saving might be inevitable with a dual-role neutral, it is too easy to overstate this potential benefit. The cost of any mediator needs to be looked at as a percentage of total cost and might also be looked at as against the value of the dispute. Because commercial and investment arbitration typically involves vastly bigger amounts than domestic litigation, the importance of any absolute cost saving is likely to be reduced.[8]

28.13 It could be presumed that an arbitrator who adopts a mediation function is well prepared for the latter. Bringing in a separate mediator would require discrete preparation time, but this will often be less than arbitrators would imagine, particularly if the mediator adopts a facilitative approach, looking to have the parties identify their long-term interests rather than seeking to come to grips with the minutiae of the actual dispute. The saving in preparation time might even be outweighed by the extra time taken in finding a suitable person to perform adequately as a dual-role neutral. There may be delays in terms of such a person's availability as they are likely to be part of a much smaller pool than is the case with single-role professionals. Few will have equal skills in both, particularly if facilitative mediation

---

[8] Often estimated at 80 per cent of the total. Gerald Aksen, 'Arbitrability of Disputes' in Gerald Asken and others (eds), *Global Reflections on International Law, Commerce and Dispute Resolution: Liber Amicorum in Honour of Robert Briner* (ICC Publishing 2005) 17.

is to be the first option. Even if the skill set is there, it is also necessary to have the parties understand why different processes are being adopted and why the dual-role neutral might be interested in very different factors in each. There can even be problems for the parties in determining how to approach a potential dual-role neutral, for example if there would ethically be a need to interview jointly.[9]

There is also a problem in selecting the relevant dual-role neutral if there is a three-person arbitral panel, a problem that does not arise if a single mediator is selected to work in parallel. Where multi-person tribunals are concerned, all three would not normally act as conciliators. If they sought to do so, there may be problems with perceived bias as to the way in which party-appointed persons operated, and in such circumstances, some compromise or undue pressure on the role of the Chair. While party appointment is natural in arbitration, it seems antithetical to voluntary conciliation. 28.14

(b) An authoritative figure may more readily promote settlement

A second suggested advantage of the dual-role neutral is that a prospective arbitrator proposing settlement might be more likely to engender agreement. Merely enquiring about settlement can help overcome the reluctance of each party to make the first move lest they appear weak.[10] That is not an argument in favour of a dual-role neutral, but instead is an argument in favour of imposing some obligation on the tribunal to promote settlement and to raise the issue *sua sponte*, now allowed for in a number of rules. 28.15

It has also been suggested that med-arb leads to a higher percentage of settlements,[11] but it is virtually impossible to compare that to the alternative proposed in this chapter, namely, parallel mediation. A related possibility is that the parties may be more ready to accept a figure or line of discussion proposed by an authoritative arbitrator.[12] That is not necessarily so and is not necessarily desirable even if true. First, if it is simply the stature of the arbitrator, the parties can have a mediator of equal or greater stature. If it is because of a concern not to offend the arbitrator lest arbitration ensue, this suggests acceptance of a figure that is not seen as inherently correct, which is problematic. The more that the dual-role neutral directs attention towards a particular result, the more that there could be a challenge for pre-judgment. 28.16

(c) Coordination benefits

Another suggested benefit is in relation to coordination. It would seem reasonable to suggest that one person could more easily switch between the roles than two, where the latter must agree from time to time. A dual-role neutral could move back and forth between processes whenever it was seen as desirable, although again, there is no reason why a distinct arbitrator could not stay the arbitration proceedings for a parallel mediation or continue with other parts of the arbitration that are discrete. There could also be regular dialogue with the mediator with a view to a consensus between them on process, referrals to the 28.17

---

[9] Edna Sussman, 'Developing an Effective Med-Arb/Arb-Med Process' (2009) 2(1) NY Disp Res Law 73.
[10] Schneider (n 3) 71.
[11] Richard Hill, 'Med-Arb: New Coke or Swatch' (1997) 13(1) Arb Int'l 105. See also JCAA Newsletter No 22 (2009) claiming successful solutions in 25 out of 48 cases where arbitrators sought to assist settlement.
[12] Louise Otis J and Eric Reiter, 'Mediation by Judges: A New Phenomenon in the Transformation of Justice' (2006) 6 Pepp Disp Resol LJ 351.

parties where there is no such consensus, and residual direction by the arbitrator if agreement is otherwise lacking.

28.18 A further problem with a dual-role neutral can arise where interim measures are sought during the currency of the mediation. It would seem preferable to have discrete persons address these issues, particularly where the interim measure decision must consider chances of success and rule on interim injunctions and applications for undertakings as to damages. It would be difficult to mediate successfully while making such interventionist determinations. It would also be harder to mediate a dispute about the future variation of interim measures granted by the same neutral.

(d) Timing

28.19 A related coordination argument in favour of dual-role neutrals is that an arbitrator may best be able to identify the optimal time for mediation. This does not require that person to have a dual role, but simply to conduct the arbitration in a way that is supportive of settlement, for example adjourning by consent for such purposes. Counsel may also be less willing to advocate settlement before they understand the weaknesses in their own case, which may occur after seeing their opponent's evidence via document production and witness statements. Good arbitrators may help this by ensuring openness about each party's case from the outset and by organizing targeted and staged evidence production.

28.20 There is even a consent concern with a dual-role neutral who decides when to move between processes, as mediation normally involves direct consent at the relevant time by the parties and not the neutral. An early attempt at settlement is no problem for a distinct mediator, but can be problematic for a dual-role neutral, although this will depend on whether facilitative or evaluative mediation is proposed. Where the dual-role neutral is concerned, the earlier that settlement occurs in the life of an arbitration, the less unique knowledge that person has and the more reluctant they may be to try and encourage settlement before they truly understand the case, unless they are simply engaging in facilitative mediation. In the latter event, there is no problem with early settlement attempts, but there is also little saving in having a dual-role neutral as they are engaging in a distinct function with distinct considerations to that which pertain when they act as arbitrator.

28.21 Issues of timing are not a concern when the parties choose to change processes, for example by way of an escalation clause, but such clauses add to the challenges for a dual-role neutral if it is that person who has to decide when a new stage is appropriate or required, if the parties are not in agreement. For example, there is a complex question as to who calls an end to mediation when this occurs within an arbitral context. There is little problem with differing neutrals, as the arbitrator is not compromised by such decisions. Where a dual-role neutral is concerned, what if he disagrees with a view taken by the parties? A dual-role neutral might be seen as having a conflict if they are too quick to form a view that mediation is a waste of time.

28.22 There is also a timing problem for a dual-role neutral in that they have a separate duty of arbitral efficiency and it is not just a contractual issue as and when empowered solely as a mediator. On the other hand, there are distinct problems with separate neutrals in terms of this duty of arbitral efficiency. Absent clear agreement of the parties, it may be difficult for an arbitrator to stay the proceedings while mediation is on foot, given general duties to promote a timely conclusion to an arbitration.

(e) Negative incentives as to party behaviour

28.23 There are a number of negative incentives that use of a dual-role neutral provides in terms of mediation behaviour. If the parties know that, where the mediation is unsuccessful, the mediator will ultimately be the adjudicator, there is a greater incentive to use the time to try to sway the neutral rather than seek a successful settlement. Even a facilitative mediator will face this problem while trying to tell the parties that he is not interested in the merits of the case. It may also provide undesirable inducements to have the parties seek to ingratiate themselves with the mediator/arbitrator and paint the other party as unreasonable.

28.24 Another serious disincentive would be in relation to information release. If one knows that one is mediating in front of a dual-role neutral, one may be circumspect and selective in the material and information that is provided, again with a view to swaying them if and when they become an adjudicator. There is an incentive to be as strategic as one would be in the arbitration, although it should also be conceded that there might be reluctance to be too selective if it meant that there would be a loss of trust by the dual-role neutral.

(f) Dealing with improper conduct in the mediation

28.25 Another difficulty is that a dual-role neutral will have greater difficulty in dealing with parties that are perceived to have behaved badly in the mediation. A mediator with no adjudicatory power can admonish someone for suboptimal behaviour in the mediation or even walk away, but a dual-role neutral could be accused of prejudging the outcome, should the mediation fail.

28.26 A further problem arises in seeking to exclude counsel. In some cases, a mediator may find that the parties are somewhat intransigent because of their lawyers. In other instances, a mediator may find that the parties simply are unwilling to engage personally and, instead, take a back seat behind their counsel. It is not uncommon in such circumstances for a mediator to consider temporarily excluding the lawyers to see if the parties can break the impasse. A dual-role neutral would have some greater difficulty in doing so without clear consent, particularly if the mediation was simply based on an implied arbitral power. Similarly, a dual-role neutral may face some difficulties in mediation if only one party is represented by counsel.

(g) Jurisdictional ambit

28.27 Another problem might arise with a dual-role neutral if the mediation power was seen as deriving from general arbitral procedural powers, but the mediation considers issues outside of arbitral jurisdiction. That would be a potential problem with all forms of facilitative mediation. It would be suboptimal if the arbitrator/mediator felt limited to the issues within the arbitral mandate when engaging in the mediation, a view apparently taken at one time in Germany.[13]

28.28 That would not be a problem for a discrete mediator with a direct mandate, although concerns could still arise if the mediated solution was sought to be incorporated within a consent award. In the latter event, it would still be possible to have the parties extend their

---

[13] Schneider (n 3) 65.

arbitral jurisdiction to overcome any potential concerns. Similar problems would arise with a dual-role neutral dealing with multiple contracts or multiple party scenarios. Mediation by consent is needed, whether for separate or dual-role neutrals, but discrete enforcement challenges again arise in such scenarios.

(h) Conflicting powers and duties

28.29 Any mediation process within the context of arbitration must also comply with all relevant laws on confidentiality, privilege, ethics, and enforceability. There may also be discrete laws on the mediation itself that might apply, for example where the parties have selected the 1980 UNCITRAL Conciliation Rules. A dual-role neutral will have more potential conflicts between such norms where they are not adequately drafted with the dual-role neutral in mind.

28.30 Even the mediation consent may be problematic when a dual-role is suggested by an arbitrator, if the parties are not in support but do not wish to say so for fear of offending. The parties can always walk away from the mediation, but there are problems either way with any ensuing arbitration. If they can walk away from that as well, the dual approach will almost certainly undermine more arbitration than it will help. If they cannot walk away, true party autonomy in mediation is in large part undermined.

(i) Immunity

28.31 There can also be problems of arbitrator immunity and the extent to which this applies to a dual-role mediation function. There may be problems of coverage with insurance policies. Attempts to clarify these uncertainties or contract against them could undermine the ambience of the mediation.

(j) Reality testing

28.32 A further problem arises for the dual-role neutral in helping reality test the parties' positions in terms of what negotiation theory describes as BATNA and WATNA analysis. A mediator may typically invite each party to consider both their best alternative (BATNA) and their worst alternative (WATNA) to a negotiated agreement in helping understand whether they should make more effort towards a resolution. Yet, in many instances, BATNAs and WATNAs may need to consider the likely results of arbitration, making it hard for the dual-role neutral to discuss these processes. They may need to touch on particular evaluative aspects such as applicable substantive laws, other conflicts of laws issues and arbitral discretions in that regard, place of assets, and the enforcement behaviour of domestic courts, all matters upon which it would be difficult for the dual-role neutral to opine.

28.33 A related issue is the greater tendency of international arbitrators to award close to indemnity levels of costs, at least in commercial—as opposed to investment—arbitration. This increases the difference between each party's BATNA and WATNA and itself provides a disincentive to settlement for a party who thinks it will win. Another difficulty is that mediation often involves trying to help the parties see that litigation primarily operates in counsels' interest, with excessive transaction costs being inevitable. How would the dual-role neutral try and explain how arbitration should be avoided for this reason? Top-flight arbitrators naturally think they can be trusted to run cases efficiently, and the parties consented to arbitration in any event.

(k) Caucusing

28.34 An important tool in a mediator's strategic array of options is caucusing. This occurs on an *ex parte* basis. This has to be considered in the context of the prohibition on *ex parte* communications in arbitration that might then impact on certain aspects of otherwise optimal mediator behaviour. Uncertainty is itself a problem. Few jurisdictions give any guidance on this, the exceptions being Hong Kong and Singapore which allow for *ex parte* communications with the parties, subject to contrary agreements by them.[14] In other jurisdictions this might be seen as *prima facie* evidence of bias.[15]

28.35 A dual-role neutral has a problem either way. In the event of any uncertainty as to the power to engage in caucusing, any decision could be challenged as improper procedure. In terms of effectiveness, deciding not to engage in caucusing would be adopting a potentially suboptimal mediation model. Caucusing allows parties to be open about the strengths and weaknesses of their case and allows the arbitrator to better deal with emotional and psychological factors.

28.36 Yet, where arbitration is concerned, caucusing without express power to do so could be argued to offend against equal treatment and the opportunity to fully or reasonably prepare one's case, the latter where issues are discussed without the other side hearing what is being said. The better view is that private caucusing does not breach due process concerns, at least where it is only about attempts to bring the parties' interests closer together and does not involve arguments or evidence admissible in any ensuing arbitration, but this does not alleviate all problems and possible challenges.

28.37 Even where caucusing is permitted, there will be a strong disincentive to presenting one's 'bottom-line' if one knows that that would effectively put a cap on what one would obtain should that person be asked to adjudicate in due course. Yet the less the neutral knows the true bottom lines, the harder it is to be effective. This also negates the potential value that the mere presence of a dual-role neutral might have in inducing the parties to appear to take the mediation seriously. The parties are more likely to be looking for hints from the dual-role neutral as to what their BATNAs might be, than offering their own views.[16]

(l) Evaluative mediation

28.38 While many of the above problems could be obviated through the use of facilitative mediation alone, it must be acknowledged that this is not the norm and that many parties would wish to have some evaluation occur. Whether an arbitrator exercising a mediation function can express a preliminary view on the merits relates in part to whether an arbitrator may also act in this way. Certain civilian statutes expressly allow for settlement proposals to be made by arbitrators.[17]

---

[14] New Hong Kong Arbitration Ordinance (Cap 609), s 33; Singapore International Arbitration Act, s 17.
[15] See *The Duke Group Ltd (in liq) v Alamain Investments Ltd* [2003] SASC 272; *Glencot Development & Design Ltd v Ben Barrett & Son (Contractors) Ltd* [2001] EWHC Technology 15 (13 February 2001); *Gao Haiyan v Keeneye Holdings Ltd* [2011] HKEC 514 (2 December 2011).
[16] Brian A Pappas, 'Med-Arb: The Best of Both Worlds May Be Too Good to be True' (2013) 19(3) Disp Resol Mag 42.
[17] See, eg, Austrian ZPO, Art 204; German ZPO, s 278; Netherlands Code of Civil Procedure Art 1043; Japanese Arbitration Law 2003, Art 38(4); JCAA Arbitration Rules, r 47 and JCAA International Commercial Mediation Rules, rr 8 and 11. The French CPC, Art 21, references domestic norms, by requiring arbitrators 'to assist the parties towards a settlement between themselves of their dispute ... in a way similar to that of the judge in a French court'.

28.39 Even where the parties have called for this, there is a potential for challenges for pre-judgment should the mediation not succeed. There is a due process and consent concern if the dual-role neutral refuses to answer an evaluative query for fear of derailing any arbitration. There is an added concern where a dual-role neutral begins with facilitative mediation, but decides along the way that some evaluation would be required to break an impasse.

28.40 While some leading arbitrators argue that it is quite proper in an arbitration to give the parties a preliminary indication of one's view,[18] this is somewhat distinct from evaluative mediation. In the latter case, the evaluation is intended to lead to an immediate negotiated solution consistent with the evaluation. In the arbitral context, a preliminary indication of view would always be presented on the understanding that it is only preliminary and that while it may be presented in part to aid settlement, more importantly, the aim is to guide the parties as to how best to continue with the case in order to consolidate or vary such preliminary indications or otherwise concentrate on the matters of most interest to the tribunal. There is also a difference between a preliminary view on law and on evidence, particularly when a dual-role neutral would almost always be mediating before the hearing and before cross-examination.

28.41 There are other important differences in providing an evaluation in mediation as compared to a preliminary indication in the arbitration. In the latter event, it is provided to both parties concurrently. There will be a transcript that clearly indicates the words used by the tribunal. Conversely, where mediation is concerned, evaluative reality testing usually works best during caucusing in the absence of the other party and without any transcript. Reality testing is also problematic in a mediation in front of all the parties, if one party has a more unrealistic position, but the dual-role arbitrator wishes to appear neutral.

28.42 There are also problems in seeing an inherent value in settlements that flow from some evaluative behaviour by a dual-role neutral. A party may reluctantly settle simply to save transactions costs, knowing that the evaluative view of the dual-role neutral is the most likely arbitral outcome if settlement is not achieved. Settlement proposals may also not be objectively optimal, with the suggestion that arbitrators/mediators may try to give each party 'something'.[19]

(m) Confidentiality

28.43 There are a number of potential problems with confidentiality, privilege, and waiver that face dual-role neutrals. The first is whether confidential information obtained during caucusing must be disclosed. Very few statutes seek to clarify this, with Singapore and Hong Kong again being the exceptions, each requiring disclosure of confidential material.[20] Even if that is thought to be the proper approach in arbitration, such norms mean that there is no true confidentiality in the mediation if a dual-role neutral is used, which renders it

---

[18] For an example of a leading arbitrator advocating the possibility of early indications, see David W Rivkin, 'Towards a New Paradigm in International Arbitration: The Town Elder Model Revisited' (2008) 24(3) Arb Int'l 382.

[19] Jacob Grierson, 'Commentary on the CEDR Rules for the Facilitation of Settlement in International Arbitration' (2010) 15(1) IBA Arb News 122, 124; see also Pierre Mayer, 'Reflections on the International Arbitrator's Duty to Apply the Law' (2001) 17(3) Arb Int'l 235.

[20] Singapore International Arbitration Act, s 17(3); Hong Kong Arbitration Ordinance (Cap 609), s 33.

suboptimal in that sense. One further problem is that the parameters of permitted behaviour will vary depending on which arbitration law applies. Without such guidance, uncertainty is again a problem.

The second issue is whether an arbitrator has a duty to disclose the fact that confidential information may give rise to justifiable doubts as to ongoing impartiality. A dual-role neutral may find some conflict between the duty of confidentiality in mediation and such general duty of disclosure. It would be difficult to adopt an effective waiver of the duty of disclosure or prevent even unmeritorious challenges aiming to disrupt the process. The dual-role neutral can never ensure that inappropriate confidential material will not be presented or that positional assertions might not be made which could ground a subsequent impartiality challenge. **28.44**

Where confidential material is properly put in the mediation but would not be presented in the arbitration, how would the dual-role neutral respond? Can it ever be the case that material is presented in the mediation, but not produced in the arbitration? While judges and juries are often asked to disregard evidence that is inadmissible, at least in the common law environment, that is easier said than done.[21] **28.45**

Problems may also arise as to whether the release of confidential material to a dual-role neutral could be said to constitute waiver in relation to its admissibility at a subsequent arbitral hearing. There may be questions as to whether waiver applies in mediation; which law of waiver applies where the parties come from different jurisdictions; who decides on waiver allegations; what evidence of waiver is possible; and whether waiver rules in arbitration statutes apply to mediation processes as well. Even more problematic would be the fact that evidence of waiver might need to come from the dual-role neutral in terms of what was or was not said by the parties during the mediation process. **28.46**

Once again, the dual-role neutral is compromised whichever way they proceed. If they are unduly cautious in seeking to shelter themselves from confidential material in the mediation, they may be conducting it suboptimally. Conversely, if they too readily allow confidential material to be presented, they may compromise the ultimate arbitration should that prove to be required. **28.47**

(n) Enforcement

Another suggested advantage of dual-role neutrals is the ability to render a mediated agreement as an enforceable award, but there seems no reason why a mediated solution by a parallel mediator could not also be converted in this way. In each case, the arbitrator must consider whether the agreed position can properly constitute a legitimate award. **28.48**

There could also be enforcement problems arising from a dual-role function given that enforcement challenges can look at all aspects of procedural behaviour by the tribunal, which would include behaviour in private mediation sessions.[22] Uncertainty can also arise **28.49**

---

[21] Andrew J Wistrich, Chris Guthrie, and Jeffrey J Rachlinski, 'Can Judges Ignore Inadmissible Information? The Difficulty of Deliberately Disregarding' (2005) 153 U Pa L Rev 1251, 1323.
[22] An extreme example was seen in *Gao Haiyan v Keeneye Holdings Ltd* [2011] 3 HKC 157 (12 April 2011) and *Gao Haiyan v Keeneye Holdings Ltd* [2011] HKCA 459. For a discussion of the case, see Friven Yeoh and Desmond Ang, 'Reflections on Gao Haiyan—Of "Arb-Med", "Waivers", and Cultural Contextualisation of Public Policy Arguments' (2012) 29(3) J Int'l Arb 285–97.

where there has been a decision to defer complaint about the conduct of the mediation, or the conflicts arising from it, until the results of the arbitration are known. Such a decision may then lead to debate about waiver, with no certainty as to the result.[23]

28.50 A further problem with a dual-role neutral could arise if counsel cannot readily agree on settlement terms and seek the assistance of the dual-role neutral. Problems may arise where the dual-role neutral is asked to encapsulate what he considers was agreed into written form where the parties then do not both agree.

E. Conclusion

28.51 It cannot be presumed a priori that there are significant cost savings in the use of a dual-role neutral. Even where this would occur, these would be relatively low in terms of percentage figures.

28.52 The above analysis suggests that there are serious problems in terms of compromise in optimal mediation techniques through use of a dual-role neutral. In addition, the need to be concerned with potential guerrilla tactics means that there is significant scope for frustration of any ensuing arbitration as a result of the behaviour of a dual-role neutral. Prudent arbitrators might draw up special contractual provisions, but these themselves could add costs and debate about terms, with the arbitrator being unable to make rulings on their own contract drafts.

28.53 Conversely, parallel mediation, with the full involvement and support of the arbitrator, can overcome each of the above problems whether as to confidentiality, caucusing, or the disincentives to optimal mediation behaviour. Parallel processes could involve staying all or part of proceedings while mediation occurs, or operating a dual track, with mediation dealing with less important issues or gateway issues that would in due course streamline the arbitration. Parallel processes could see the arbitrator briefing the mediator on salient issues to minimize operation time. It can also protect the arbitrator from accusations of bias where there is any evaluative discussion. An arbitrator providing some indication of the potential strengths and weaknesses of the arguments to the mediator where that is kept confidential from the parties is less likely to be challenged for bias.

28.54 While this chapter has sought to argue for parallel mediation as the better option, circumstances will certainly exist where a hybrid is preferred. A typical scenario might be a major arbitration with CEOs present for a hearing where there is a narrow window of opportunity for a settlement and no time to identify and utilize a separate neutral. Even in such a scenario, the person should have sufficient dual expertise and obtain clear guidance in terms of consent, the type of mediation intended, the appropriateness or otherwise of caucusing, the role of confidentiality, questions of timing, potential for challenges, and waiver.

28.55 Whatever approach is ultimately recommended, informed consent is the key and arbitrators should think carefully about their ability to operate as dual-role neutrals.

---

[23] Kaplan J (as he then was) held accordingly in *China Nanhai Oil Joint Service Corp, Shenzhen Branch v Gee Tai Holdings Co* [1994] 3 HKC 375.

Part X

JUDICIAL REVIEW, JUDICIAL PERFORMANCE, AND ENFORCEMENT

29

JUDICIAL REVIEW OF THE MERITS OF ARBITRATION AWARDS UNDER ENGLISH LAW

Sir Bernard Rix*

> There must be no Alsatia in England where the King's writ does not run ...
>
> *Czarnikow v Roth, Schmidt & Co* [1922] 2 KB 478, 488 (Scrutton LJ)
>
> I have always wished to see arbitration, as far as possible, and subject to statutory guidelines no doubt, regarded as a freestanding system, free to settle its own procedure and free to develop its own substantive law—yes, its substantive law.
>
> Lord Wilberforce during the second reading of the Arbitration Bill in the House of Lords, 18 January 1996, cited with emphasis by Lord Steyn in *Lesotho Highlands Development Authority v Impregilo SpA* [2006] 1 AC 221, 231

A. Introduction

What has caused such a shift in the views of great commercial judges of English law in the space of some 70 years? The CIArb was founded in 1915 and celebrated the first centenary of its foundation in 2015, a period well embracing the time span just referred to above.[1] I am honoured to have been invited to contribute to this *liber amicorum* in commemoration of that centenary. It was only a generation before the Institute's foundation that the Commercial Court was founded in 1895, in order to bring judicial expertise to the decision-making of commercial cases. In this context, I propose to write as much as a historian of law as a lawyer, and to consider the history of judicial review of the merits of arbitration awards in the courts of England. That is a large subject for a short chapter, and my canvas must therefore be painted in somewhat impressionistic style.[2]

29.01

---

* I am grateful to my legal assistant, Muin Boase, for his help, particularly with the footnotes.

[1] Tony Marks and Julio César Betancourt, 'The Chartered Institute of Arbitrators' in Julian D M Lew and others (eds), *Arbitration in England, with Chapters on Scotland and Ireland* (Kluwer Law International 2013) ch 5.

[2] For an overview, see Michael J Mustill and Stewart C Boyd, *The Law and Practice of Commercial Arbitration in England* (2nd edn, Butterworths 1989); William W Park, 'Judicial Supervision of Transnational Commercial Arbitration: The English Arbitration Act of 1979' (1981) 21 Harv Int'l LJ 87; Julian D M Lew and Melissa Holm, 'Development of the Arbitral System in England' in Lew and others (n 1).

B. Before the Nineteenth Century

(a) The medieval era

29.02 The history of arbitration is probably older still than the history of courts of law. It is far older than the history of English law and the King's courts.[3] In medieval times, merchants, both English and foreign, no doubt found their own solutions to their own problems, and arbitration was among those solutions.[4] Talk of the *lex mercatoria* comes down to us from such medieval times, if not before. Gradually, however, as the nation states began to coalesce and strengthen what today might be called the rule of law, the two systems of arbitration and court justice lived side by side, with the state seeking to bring the private, mercantile, world of arbitration within its control.[5]

29.03 By 1609 in *Vynior v Wilde*, Lord Coke enunciated the poor doctrine that an agreement to arbitrate was analogous to an authority given to an agent and could be revoked.[6] That sounded a note of confidence in the courts' own jurisdiction and reflected also a feeling of uncertainty about the separate world of arbitration.

(b) Legislative attention

29.04 The first statute to concern itself with arbitration was the English Civil Procedure Act of 1698, but that sought to regulate the enforcement of submissions to arbitrate by making them a rule of court and to empower the court to set aside an award if 'procured by corruption or other undue means', rather than to provide a remedy by way of an appeal on the merits.[7] Within the protection of the courts, the use of arbitration was supported: among the Act's objects were 'promoting trade, and rendering the awards of arbitrators more effectual'. Outside the purview of the Act, however, the common law's attitude to arbitration continued to sound an uncertain note.[8]

29.05 By the middle of the nineteenth century, the position as to review on the merits appears to have been that, in the absence of an admission by the arbitrators themselves of an error, and in the absence of a material and patent error of law on the face of the award or apparent from documents incorporated within it, an award could not be reviewed in the courts, but that with such patent error, it could be. In this state of the law, a practice developed whereby parties could by agreement ask the arbitrators to state their award in such a way as to render any error patent upon it. That was the origin of the 'special case' which came to be recognized in later statutes.[9]

---

[3] Derek Roebuck, 'Sources for the History of Arbitration: A Bibliographical Introduction' (1998) 14 Arb Int'l 237.
[4] Derek Roebuck, *Early English Arbitration* (The Arbitration Press 2008).
[5] Lord Parker of Waddington, *The History and Development of Commercial Arbitration* (Lionel Cohen Lectures 5th Series, The Hebrew University of Jerusalem, Magnes Press 1959) 19.
[6] *Vynior v Wilde* (1609) 8 Coke Rep 81b, 77 ER 595 (KB).
[7] 9 & 10 Will III c 15. *Lesotho Highlands Development Authority v Impregilo SpA* [2006] 1 AC 221, 231.
[8] *Corneforth v Geer* (1715) 23 ER 1038; *Hutchins v Hutchins* (1738) 95 ER 406; *Kill v Hollister* (1746) 1 Wils KB 129; *Kent v Elstob* (1802) 102 ER 502. See also Andrew Tweeddale and Keren Tweeddale, *Arbitration of Commercial Disputes: International and English Law and Practice* (OUP 2005) 477–93.
[9] Mustill and Boyd (n 2) 439–40.

29.06 The first of such statutes was the Common Law Procedure Act of 1854, which covered the field of civil procedure, including arbitration.[10] This gave statutory force to the special case practice by its section 5, as long as the power to state such a case for the opinion of the court was not excluded by contrary agreement. The common law power to set an award aside for error of law on its face continued alongside this new statutory power. That power operated in an erratic and technical manner, since everything depended on what was regarded as patent on the face of the award. The only remedy was to set aside the award, whereupon the parties had to begin again.

29.07 The 1850s was a decade of significance in the history of English arbitration also because of two important decisions which firmly stated a principle in favour of arbitration and against the idea that it was contrary to public policy.[11]

29.08 From then on, arbitration statutes were enacted at regular intervals, although some have been more important than others. The English Arbitration Act 1889 repealed section 5 of the 1854 Act and re-enacted the arbitrators' power to state an award in the form of a special case in its section 7.[12] As in the case of the 1854 Act, that power was expressed to be subject to contrary agreement.

29.09 However, the 1889 Act added under section 19 a power to state a special case at any stage of the reference, thereby also permitting a consultative case prior to a final award, but, significantly, no longer referred to this additional power being subject to contrary agreement.[13] Albeit there was no express reference to this statutory language, this absence of a proviso in favour of contrary agreement was critical to the decision in *Czarnikow v Roth, Schmidt & Co* where the Court of Appeal held that a contract to exclude the parties from applying to the arbitrator to state a special case was contrary to public policy as an invalid attempt to oust the jurisdiction of the court.[14]

(c) The *Czarnikow* decision

29.10 I have cited Scrutton LJ's famous remark from *Czarnikow* in the heading of this chapter.[15] It arose from a standard exclusion of the rules of the Refined Sugar Association, one of the numerous commodity associations in London which provided standard form contracts and arbitration rules on which a great proportion of the world's international commodity trades had come to be transacted. The Court of Appeal comprised that famous trio, Bankes, Atkin, and Scrutton LJJ, 'whose combined authority in matters of commercial law is probably unequalled'.[16]

29.11 Their judgments were reserved. It appears that the party which had applied to the arbitrators for a special case had done so both under section 7 and section 19 of the 1889 Act (although primarily under section 19), but the arbitrators considered that they were bound

---

[10] 17 & 18 Vict c 125.
[11] See *Scott v Avery*, 10 ER 1121, (1856) 5 HL Cas 811; and *Russell v Pellegrini*, 6 E&B 1020 (KB 1856).
[12] 52 & 53 Vict c 49, s 7.
[13] English Arbitration Act 1889, s 19: 'Any referee, arbitrator, or umpire may at any stage of the proceedings under a reference, and shall, if so directed by the Court or a judge, state in the form of a special case for the opinion of the Court any question of law arising in the course of the reference'.
[14] *Czarnikow v Roth, Schmidt & Co* [1922] 2 KB 478.
[15] ibid 488 (Scrutton LJ).
[16] Commercial Court Committee, *Report on Arbitration* (1977–78 Cmnd 7284) para 13.

by the contrary agreement expressed in the arbitration rules and issued their award in final form and not in the form of a special case, and without giving the applicant party a chance, which it had if necessary requested, to make an application to the court before issue of an award.[17] The award was set aside and remitted to the arbitrators to decide anew on an application to state their award in the form of a special case.

29.12 It seems that the Court of Appeal must have regarded the application for a special case as essentially being made under section 19, for there is no mention in any of the judgments of section 7 and its express authority for contrary agreement. In such serendipitous way did the Court of Appeal give itself freedom to vent powerful statements of the public interest in arbitration according to English law. Those statements have continued to influence arbitration law in England to this day, although, as will appear below, in much attenuated form. It is worth setting out part of the court's reasoning, from which it appears that extraneous political views were not altogether absent.

29.13 Thus, Bankes LJ said:

> The importance of maintaining in its integrity the rule of law in reference to public policy is in my opinion a matter of considerable importance at the present time. Powerful trade organizations are encouraging, if not compelling, their members and persons who enter into contracts with their members to agree, so far as they can lawfully do so, to abstain from submitting their disputes to the decision of a Court of law. The present case is a case in point. There have been others before the Courts. Among commercial men what are commonly called commercial arbitrations are undoubtedly and deservedly popular. That they will continue their present popularity I entertain no doubt, so long as the law retains sufficient hold over them to prevent and redress any injustice on the part of the arbitrator, and to secure that the law that is administered by an arbitrator is in substance the law of the land and not some home-made law of the particular arbitrator or the particular association. To release real and effective control over commercial arbitrations is to allow the arbitrator, or the Arbitration Tribunal, to be a law unto himself, or themselves, to give him or them a free hand to decide according to law or not according to law as he or they think fit, in other words to be outside the law. At present no individual or association is, so far as I am aware, outside the law except a trade union. To put such associations as the Refined Sugar Association in a similar position would in my opinion be against public policy. Unlimited power does not conduce to reasonableness of view or conduct …[18]

29.14 Mustill and Boyd comment that:

> The writers have personal experience of instances where arbitrators who disapproved of particular rules of law established by judicial decision, which the arbitrators regarded as ill-conceived and commercially unsound, would have ignored the rules and decided according to their own ideas of fairness, if not restrained by an intimation that a special case would be called for.[19]

29.15 In the light of the strong judicial steer found in *Czarnikow v Roth, Schmidt & Co*, it is not surprising that the provision for contrary agreement which had survived since the 1854 Act fell out of the English Arbitration Act 1934, section 9(1) of which combined the provisions of both sections 7 and 19 of the 1889 Act, but did so in the terms of the latter's section 19,

---

[17] *Czarnikow* (n 14) 480.
[18] ibid 484.
[19] Mustill and Boyd (n 2) 450.

that is to say without the proviso in favour of contrary agreement. That remained the situation in the English Arbitration Act 1950, a major piece of legislation which rewrote much of England's arbitration law (see section 21).

C. The English Arbitration Act 1979

(a) An inconsistent course

29.16 The policy of the law was not reconsidered until the English Arbitration Act 1979. In the meantime, judicial review of the merits of an arbitration award had followed an inconsistent course, and the special case procedure had fallen into abuse which threatened the well-being of English arbitration.

29.17 The course was inconsistent because at one and the same time it became harder to disturb an award on the ground of patent error of law, and increasingly easy to obtain a review through the machinery of a special case. As for error of law, the courts would not permit extrinsic evidence to be adduced in order to demonstrate an error of law. And even though matters of contractual construction could be described as errors of law, the courts would not review arbitral decisions of interpretation just because they as judges would have decided differently.[20]

(b) The *Halfdan Grieg* decision

29.18 As for the special case procedure, however, the courts inconsistently showed an unwillingness to circumscribe the circumstances in which a 'question of law' would be ordered to be made the subject matter of a special case. The matter came to a head in the Court of Appeal decision in *Halfdan Grieg & Co A/S v Sterling Coal & Navigation Corp ('The Lysland')*.[21] There a dispute arose under a time charter's very much one-off provision for quantifying the compensation to be paid to owners (via the mechanism of a deposit and deductions from it) according to whether the vessel earned more or less over the balance of the time charter period. The arbitrators had been asked for a special case and had refused. No authorities on the point of construction had been cited to them. The arbitrators said:

> We did not feel that this was a proper case to be so stated. Whilst it may well be that there is a question of law, it is our feeling that, whilst we do not presume to usurp the functions of the court, it is more suitable for decision by a commercial arbitration tribunal than by the courts since its interpretation is so closely allied to commercial practice and the interpretation that commercial men would give it.

29.19 In the Commercial Court, Kerr J agreed and refused to direct a special case. He emphasized that the question of construction in that case involved no consideration of legal authorities and no identifiable question of principle, and that the arbitration had itself been subject to delay on the part of the party who held the disputed funds. However, he spoke as though his refusal still remained exceptional, and he said that borderline cases should be decided

---

[20] *Kelantan Government v Duff Development Co* [1923] AC 395, 409 (HL): 'But where a question of construction is the very thing referred for arbitration, then the decision of the arbitrator upon that point cannot be set aside by the Court only because the Court would itself have come to a different conclusion' (Lord Cave LC).
[21] [1973] 1 QB 843.

in favour of stating a case.[22] He was also prepared to accept that the great majority of cases would satisfy criteria put forward by the applicant, namely a clear-cut question of law which was seriously arguable, important for the resolution of the parties' dispute, and raised *bona fide* and not merely for the purposes of delay.[23]

29.20 In the Court of Appeal, however, Kerr J's decision was reversed. The essential reasoning appears to have been that any other decision would be taken as altering the practice previously adopted, something that even Kerr J had said that he would be unwilling to do.[24] The Court of Appeal was composed of Lord Denning MR, and Megaw and Scarman LJJ, a strong court.

29.21 After *Halfdan Grieg*, there was no holding the tide in favour of the special case. Writing when he was chairman of the Law Commission, Kerr J referred to that decision as opening the floodgates to what was already an increasing trend.[25] In *The Kavo Peiratis*, Kerr J had previously stated that concern judicially, and made an unusual order for costs to mark what he considered had been a respondent's abusive request for a special case, made in order to achieve delay.[26] It also so happened that in the 1970s there was a great expansion of work in the Commercial Court, in part because of the number of cases proceeding from arbitrations arising out of the prohibition on export of US soya beans. These arbitrations led to innumerable special cases. Whereas at the beginning of that decade the Commercial Court sat with only a single judge in any year, by the end of that decade the modern practice of using a complement of judges had begun.[27]

(c) Calls for change

29.22 There were other events within the 1970s which were also catalysts of change. There was an exponential growth of so-called 'one-off' development and investment contracts, a trend which in still more modern times has only accelerated. Such contracts differ from the more familiar and standardized contracts of international trade which existed for the sale of commodities or for the chartering of vessels. The parties to such contracts are often consortia made up of companies from many different countries and include governments and their agencies. Such parties had become wary of submitting their arbitral disputes to review by any national government.[28]

29.23 By the end of the 1970s, there were calls within the legal profession, from senior judges, from arbitrators and parliamentarians, for a reconsideration of the terms on which judicial review of the merits of awards could be achieved. The 'Story of the Arbitration Act 1979' from the insider's point of view of a parliamentarian interested in arbitration has been told by Lord Hacking.[29] The 1979 Act arose out of a *Report on Arbitration* published by a Commercial Court Committee comprising the commercial judges and the users of the

---

[22] ibid 852H/853A.
[23] ibid 855.
[24] *Halfdan Grieg* (n 21) 863G.
[25] Michael Kerr, 'The Arbitration Act 1979' (1980) 43 MLR 45, 46.
[26] *Granvias Oceanicas Armadora SA v Jibsen Trading Co ('The Kavo Peiratis')* [1977] 2 Lloyd's Rep 344, 349, 353.
[27] Nowadays, it is not uncommon to have up to eight commercial judges sitting at any one time hearing different cases, and that is so despite far less judicial review of the merits of arbitration awards.
[28] William W Park, 'Judicial Supervision of Transnational Commercial Arbitration' (1980) 21 Harvard Int'l LJ 87.
[29] Lord David Hacking, 'The Story of the Arbitration Act 1979' (2010) 76(1) Arbitration 125. For other contemporaneous accounts, see: Kerr (n 25); David W Shenton and Gordon K Toland, 'London as a Venue

Commercial Court.[30] Their recommendations were to abolish the special case procedure, to abolish as well the power to set aside an award for error of law on the face of the award, but to permit appeal to the courts on a question of law although only with the leave of the court or the consent of the parties.

To assist in that new process, arbitrators would be encouraged to give reasons for their awards. Consultative references to the court in the course of a reference would be permitted only at the request of the arbitrators or with the consent of the parties. The right to judicial review would be entrenched by limiting the circumstances in which parties could agree to exclude it: thus parties would be able to agree to exclude such review after a dispute had arisen; and parties to what were called 'supranational agreements', ie the one-off contracts referred to above, could exclude the right of review at any time, after or before a dispute had arisen; but before a dispute had arisen parties to 'special category disputes', viz shipping, commodity, and insurance disputes, would not be entitled to exclude judicial review for a trial period of two to three years. **29.24**

It was contemplated that leave to appeal 'should only be given if the High Court is satisfied that the question of law in issue might be determined on appeal in a way which would affect the rights of the parties under the award', but that the 'right of further appeal from the High Court to the Court of Appeal should be strictly limited.[31] It would arise only on a certificate of a judge of the High Court that the question of law was one of general importance' to the trade in question, and only with the leave of the judge or the Court of Appeal.[32] **29.25**

It is interesting to note that the entrenchment of the right of appeal was still much influenced by *Czarnikow v Roth, Schmidt & Co*, 'a decision of such importance' that relevant extracts from the judgments were reproduced in an appendix;[33] and a decision whose public policy considerations 'greatly impressed' the Committee.[34] **29.26**

In the result, the 1979 Act did not reproduce the recommendations of the Report in their entirety, but in the main it did. Thus, after repealing section 21 of the English Arbitration Act 1950 (which provided for the special case procedure) and removing jurisdiction to set aside or remit awards 'on the ground of errors of fact or law on the face of the award', section 1 went on to provide that 'an appeal shall lie … on any question of law arising out of an award' with the consent of all the parties to the reference or with the leave of the court. Leave could not be granted by the court, however, 'unless it considers that, having regard to all the circumstances, the determination of the question of law could substantially affect the rights of one or more of the parties'. Section 1(5) gave the court power to order the arbitrator 'to state the reasons for his award in sufficient detail to enable the court, should an appeal be brought under this section, to consider any question of law arising out of the award'. Leave to appeal could not be granted **29.27**

---

for International Arbitration: The Arbitration Act 1979' (1980) 12 Law & Pol'y Int'l Bus 643; Reuben Clark and Dieter G Lange, 'Recent Changes in English Arbitration Practice Widen Opportunities for More Effective International Arbitrations' (1980) 5 Bus Law 1621; Lord Kenneth Diplock, 'Use and Abuse of the Case Stated' (1978) 44(3) Arbitration 107; David Hacking, 'The "Stated Case" Abolished: The United Kingdom Arbitration Act of 1979' (1980) 14 Int'l Law 95; William W Park, 'Judicial Supervision of Transnational Commercial Arbitration' (1980) 21 Harv Int'l LJ 21; D Rhidian Thomas, *The Law and Practice Relating to Appeals from Arbitration Awards: A Thematic Analysis of the Arbitration Act 1979* (Lloyds of London Press 1994).

[30] *Report on Arbitration* (n 16).
[31] ibid para 35.
[32] ibid para 37.
[33] ibid para 13.
[34] ibid para 42.

in the absence of reasons unless a party had given notice to the arbitrators that a reasoned award would be required.[35] No appeal would lie to the Court of Appeal unless leave was given and the question of law was certified by the judge to be 'one of general public importance or ... one which for some other special reason should be considered by the court of appeal'.[36]

29.28 A question of law arising in the course of the reference could be referred to the court, but only with the consent of the arbitrators or the parties.[37] Exclusion agreements could prevent resort to the courts, save in the case of statutory arbitrations; or domestic arbitrations where the exclusion agreement was made before the commencement of arbitration; or any arbitrations which related to a claim falling within the admiralty jurisdiction or disputes arising out of a contract of insurance or a commodity contract, unless the exclusion agreement was entered into after the arbitration commenced or the governing law of the underlying contract was a law other than the law of England and Wales. The entrenchment of judicial review of maritime, insurance, and commodity contract arbitrations was not, however, limited to a few years by a sunset clause, but provision was made allowing for the Secretary of State by order to alter the provisions relating to the entrenchment of appeals arising from such contracts. And there was no special provision relating to the so-called 'one-off' supranational contracts, possibly because there was no need to, since few if any of them would concern maritime, insurance, or commodity contracts.

29.29 It might be observed that the 1979 Act contained no rules as to how the matter of leave to appeal from the arbitrators to the court should be handled, other than that leave could only be granted on a question of law (that had long been the classic position with regard to the special case), that the question of law had substantially to affect the rights of one of the parties (ie the question of law must not be rendered moot or relatively unimportant by reason of other unappealable decisions in the award, not in itself a novel departure), and that at the next stage of leave to appeal to the Court of Appeal the question of law had to be certified as one of public importance or one that ought for some special reason to be considered by the Court of Appeal.

29.30 It is important to remember that at this time leave to appeal to the Court of Appeal in ordinary litigation was only required in interlocutory matters: a trial judgment could be taken to appeal as a matter of right. So, at the Court of Appeal stage there was a new departure in this respect, which did not apply at the level of the High Court. There is no real suggestion in these provisions that the 'right of appeal' as the Committee had termed it, and as it continued to be referred to, should be 'strictly limited' (another phrase used by the Committee) other than at the Court of Appeal stage, or that a doctrine of 'general public importance' or other 'special reason' should be introduced at any stage earlier than the Court of Appeal.

D. *The Nema* Decision

(a) Background of the case

29.31 The question of the principles on which the discretion to grant leave to appeal to the courts might be exercised fell to be considered for the first time in *The Nema*, a case which

---

[35] English Arbitration Act 1979, s 1(6).
[36] ibid s 1(7).
[37] ibid s 2.

concerned the possible frustration of a seven-voyage consecutive voyage charter by reason of a prolonged strike at the loading port. The strike lasted from 6 June to 5 October 1979, a major part of the open season for the performance of the seven voyages within April to December 1979. In the meantime, by an addendum to the charter, the shipowners were permitted to perform an intermediate voyage for another charterer and the charter was extended for a further seven voyages in 1980. The owners were unable to fix the vessel elsewhere, so in a still further addendum the charterers agreed to compensate the owners for their lost voyage and to grant permission to the owners again to fix an intermediate voyage elsewhere, which they did. Subsequently, the owners wanted to perform what was in effect a third intermediate voyage and fixed her for one, but the charterers wanted her by now to go to the loading port in case the strike ended, and obtained an interim injunction from the courts to prevent this further voyage's performance. Under the charter, time lost by reason of strikes was at the owners' risk. In mid-August 1979, the parties agreed to an early arbitration, which took place on 26 September 1979. The award was rendered on 3 October 1979, saying that the 1979 charter had been frustrated and that no consideration had been given to the addendum for the 1980 season. The strike ended on 5 October 1979. Thus, the charterers lost the vessel for the rest of the 1979 season, and a question mark arose about the status of the 1980 season. The charterers sought leave to appeal from the arbitrator's award.

Although it is true that questions of frustration are to a large extent fact-sensitive, it is nevertheless an exceptional doctrine of law which excuses the parties from further performance of their contracts, and it arose in circumstances where, *inter alia*, the owners had expressly accepted the risk of delay through strikes, had been largely shielded from loss so far by means of their intermediate voyages (two agreed, the third not), and had been compensated with an extension of the charter into 1980. Moreover, there was a potential issue whether the 1979 and 1980 voyages could be separated, which the award left in an awkward state of indecision, despite a post-award request to the arbitrator to clarify the matter. In his response, the arbitrator said that his decision was that the charter had become frustrated, and that an issue as to whether the 1979 and 1980 seasons were severable had not been adequately argued.[38] Cases on frustration had become (and as it happens continue to be) quite rare. So, it was not perhaps surprising that an eminent commercial judge, Goff J, gave leave to appeal[39] and subsequently allowed the appeal.[40] He also gave leave to the owners to appeal to the Court of Appeal, on the basis that the case was of general importance to the maritime community and thus of general public importance within the meaning of section 1(7)(b) of the 1979 Act, and he so certified.[41] **29.32**

(b) **The Court of Appeal**

In the Court of Appeal, however, the mood was very different.[42] The decision of the Commercial Court on the merits was reversed, albeit not without a substantial judgment from Lord Denning MR, and a shorter but still substantial judgment from Templeman LJ. **29.33**

---

[38] See the facts stated by Goff J in the Commercial Court: *BTP Tioxide Ltd v Pioneer Shipping Ltd and Armada Marine SA (The Nema) (No 2)* [1980] 2 Lloyd's Rep 83, 88.
[39] *BTP Tioxide Ltd v Pioneer Shipping Ltd (Leave to Appeal) (No 1)* [1980] 1 Lloyd's Rep 519 (Note).
[40] *BTP Tioxide Ltd v Pioneer Shipping Ltd (No 2)* (n 38).
[41] The question of certification and leave was considered in full in a separate short judgment reported at [1980] 2 Lloyd's Rep 83. Goff J pointed out, *inter alia*, that 'this is the first case on frustration of a consecutive voyage charter-party' at 94 lhc.
[42] *Pioneer Shipping Ltd v BTP Tioxide Ltd (The Nema) (No 2)* [1980] QB 547.

Fifteen authorities were cited in those judgments. The decision was to uphold the arbitrator's award which was interpreted to be that the charter for the 1979 season had been frustrated, but to clarify that the addendum for the 1980 season had not been frustrated (that had been left in the air by the arbitrator). In effect, an argument of severability of the seasons (or severability of the original charter and one of its addenda) was upheld, even though the arbitrator had not ruled on that argument and in his response to the request for clarification had said that that argument (on which the owners prevailed in the Court of Appeal) had not been sufficiently advanced for him to decide it. Lord Denning went on to observe that:

> Under the new approach the judge should not have given leave at all ... The judge, however, did give leave; and he did certify the case as one of general importance. As such, I have come to the conclusion that the judge was in error. He should have adopted the new approach. He ought not to have reversed the decision of the arbitrator—which the parties had agreed should be 'final'—unless it was clearly wrong.

29.34 The appeal committee of the House of Lords speedily allowed a petition by the charterers for leave to appeal;[43] but at the hearing of that appeal the charterers were told that leave had only been granted in order to emphasize how the new regime under the 1979 Act was to work—so as not to permit appeals save under the most stringent conditions. That must have been a disappointment to the charterers, since they must have thought that permission had been granted because they had a reasonable prospect of succeeding on the merits. As Lord Roskill was to accept in his speech in the House of Lords,[44] only one case of frustration of a charter due to a strike was known 'and in that case the underlying reasoning of the judgment is far from easy to follow'.[45]

(c) The House of Lords

29.35 In the House of Lords, the charterers' appeal nevertheless failed on the merits, but their Lordships' decision is famous rather for the judicial development of the so-called *Nema* guidelines.[46] Lord Diplock confirmed in his speech that leave to appeal had been given only in order to instruct the commercial judges as to the considerations which should influence them in deciding how to exercise their discretion under section 1 of the 1979 Act.[47] As Lord Diplock remarked:

> This [leave to appeal] was not because of any intrinsic general importance of the points of law involved in the arbitrator's award. If ever there were a case which under the new procedure ought never to have been allowed to get any further than the arbitrator's award, this was one.

29.36 It appears that the essential reason advanced for this attitude was the factor that the parties had wanted a speedy arbitral decision for an ongoing emergency.[48] That was true. But the owners had fixed their intermediate voyage before the reference to arbitration, the strike had ended within two days of the award, the award had left the overall contractual situation up in the air, and the Commercial Court had granted leave to appeal, so that the overall situation was much more complex than was allowed. Indeed, Goff J pointed out that it was the

---

[43] ibid 575.
[44] *Pioneer Shipping Ltd v BTP Tioxide Ltd (The Nema) (No 2)* [1982] AC 724, 754D.
[45] *The Penelope* [1928] P 180.
[46] *Pioneer Shipping Ltd* (n 44).
[47] ibid 734C–E.
[48] ibid 735F.

owners (who submitted that leave should not be granted, but who obtained leave to go to the Court of Appeal, and there, and in the House of Lords, again submitted that the original leave should never have been granted) who had first asked the arbitrator to give reasons for his award. He observed that 'reasons of course are particularly relevant to the question of appeal'.[49]

Lord Diplock went on to explain, by reference to *Czarnikow v Roth, Schmidt & Co*, the importance still ascribed in English law to the ability to refer questions of law on standard contract forms from arbitration to the courts. He said: **29.37**

> It is only if parties to commercial contracts can rely upon a uniform construction being given to standard terms that they can prudently incorporate them in their contracts without the need for detailed negotiation or discussion. Such uniform construction of standard terms has been progressively established up to 1979, largely through decisions of the courts upon special cases stated by arbitrators. In the result English commercial law has achieved a degree of comprehensiveness and certainty that has made it acceptable for adoption as the appropriate proper law to be applied to commercial contracts wherever made by parties of whatever nationality.[50]

Lord Diplock nevertheless derived from the terms of the 1979 Act itself a parliamentary intention to restrict that general availability of appeals on a question of law which had previously existed under the abused special case procedure. In that he was undoubtedly right. What, however, the Act was generally silent about was a judicial strategy for the post special case world. In this respect, Lord Diplock effectively legislated for the narrowest of gateways from the finality of an award. In the case of a 'one-off' clause, leave to appeal should not be given unless the judge of his own motion upon mere perusal could see that the arbitrator was 'obviously wrong'. Otherwise leave should be refused.   **29.38**

In the case of standard clauses, however, leave might be granted for the sake of the 'clarity and certainty of English commercial law', but only if there was a 'strong *prima facie* case' that the arbitrator was wrong, and the circumstances in which the standard clause came to be construed were not in themselves 'one-off'. If they were, the 'obviously wrong' test should be used even in the case of standard clauses.[51] It is not clear what role general principles of law, such as frustration itself, play within these guidelines.   **29.39**

The *Nema* guidelines went far to shut down the avenue of judicial review of the legal merits of arbitration awards in English law. They went as far as they could possibly go in denying access to the court while still allowing for the theoretical possibility of leave to appeal, which the 1979 Act of course allowed. It was as if their Lordships had repented of the Act which they had promoted in Parliament, and had rejected along the way much of the reasoning of the Commercial Court Committee's Report.[52]   **29.40**

There was at that time, and remains, a profound disagreement between many users of arbitration and of English commercial law as to whether any recourse on the merits to the court   **29.41**

---

[49] *BTP Tioxide (No 1)* (n 39) 522 lhc.
[50] *Pioneer Shipping* (n 44) 737G–H.
[51] ibid 742H–743F.
[52] As Lord Saville's *DAC Report on the Arbitration Bill*, leading to the English Arbitration Act 1996, was to say (at para 287): 'Many of those abroad who do not have ready access to our case law were unaware that the Arbitration Act 1979 had been construed by the House of Lords in a way that very much limited the right of appeal, and which was not evident from the words of the Act themselves'.

from the finality of an arbitral award should be allowed at all. Ever since 1955, the institutional arbitration rules of the ICC did not allow for any such appeal.[53] In 1978, the institutional rules of the LCIA governing international arbitrations sought to overcome the defects of the special case procedure by providing that recourse to law could only be made provided the arbitrator 'certified that the dispute between the parties involves (a) a question of considerable legal difficulty; or (b) a legal principle of general interest'.[54]

29.42 By 1985, the LCIA Rules provided for a waiver of 'any form of appeal or recourse to a court'.[55] Moreover, during the years when *The Nema* was making its way through the courts, what was to emerge in 1985 as the UNCITRAL Model Law was being developed and drafted.[56] And this, by its Article 34, permitted recourse to the courts only on the limited grounds permitted by the New York Convention, which do not extend to challenges on the merits (other than on the basis of public policy).[57]

29.43 There may well, therefore, have been a growing feeling that English law was out of step with international practice: and a fear, already expressed at the time of the 1979 Act, that England would lose out in the international competition for arbitration appointments in the modern world.[58]

E. Section 69 of the English Arbitration Act 1996

29.44 The question of leave to appeal was revisited in section 69 of the Act. There, the *Nema* guidelines were effectively enacted into statutory form, but with some change of language. The *DAC Report on the Arbitration Bill* considered the call from certain quarters for the abolition of any right of appeal on the substantive issues in an arbitration: on the ground that '[t]o substitute the decision of the Court ... would be wholly to subvert the agreement the parties had made'.[59] However, the Report rejected that approach on the familiar ground that an express choice of English law brought with it the desire that the law be properly found and applied.

29.45 Nevertheless, the new Act permitted the parties to contract out of the right to appeal without any of the limitations placed on that right of contracting out to be found in the 1979 Act. That reflected the 1996 Act's philosophy of putting the autonomy of the parties at the forefront of policy considerations. The right of appeal was, moreover, to be limited along *Nema* lines. There had to be a question of law, which the arbitrator had been requested to determine, which substantially affected the rights of the parties, and on which the arbitrator's decision was either obviously wrong or which, being a question of general public

---

[53] Art 29.2 of the 1955 ICC Rules ('By submitting their disputes to ICC arbitration, the parties undertake to carry out the subsequent award without delay and waive their right to any form of appeal, insofar as such waiver may be valid').
[54] Art 19 headed 'Special Case Procedure' of the 1978 LCIA Rules.
[55] Art 16.8 of the 1985 LCIA Rules.
[56] 'Report of the Secretary-General: possible features of a model law on international commercial arbitration' (A/CN.9/207, 1981) 12 UNCITRAL Yearbook 90, which rejected the English 'special case procedure'.
[57] Michael Kerr, 'Arbitration and the Courts: The UNCITRAL Model Law' (1985) 34 ICLQ 1; L Steyn, 'England's Response to the Model Law of Arbitration' in Julio César Betancourt and Jason A Crook (eds), *ADR, Arbitration, and Mediation: A Collection of Essays* (Author House 2014) 369–97.
[58] Lord David Hacking (n 29).
[59] DAC Report (n 52), para 284.

importance, was one the decision on which was at least open to serious doubt; and on top of all that, it had to be just and proper for the court to determine the question.[60]

29.46 The critical court decision on these provisions is *The Northern Pioneer*.[61] Lord Phillips of Worth Matravers MR there emphasized that section 69 must now be interpreted on its own terms freed of the still tighter shackles of earlier jurisprudence on the 1979 Act.[62] Therefore, the statutory phrase, in a case where a question of general public importance is in issue, is 'at least open to serious doubt', not, as previous jurisprudence would have had it, 'a strong *prima facie* case … that the arbitrator had been wrong'.[63] Ultimately, however, these phrases leave scope for the wisdom of the commercial judges who hear applications for leave to appeal in the Commercial Court.

29.47 Since 1996, there has continued to be concern whether English arbitration law has managed to get the issue of appeal to the courts from an arbitration award in the right place. There are voices on both sides of the argument, but the majority appear to say that the situation is about right. For instance in 2006, in a survey chaired by a leading London maritime arbitrator, Bruce Harris, the majority of consultees thought that the present appeals regime was satisfactory.[64] However, while no real case had been made for altering the statutory tests, the report concluded that a pragmatic solution to the controversy could be found in a 'slightly more liberal approach' to the application of the regime.[65] A few years later, V V Veeder QC, a distinguished international arbitrator, reported, under the aegis of Lord Mance's advisory committee on the workings of section 69, on a survey of applications for leave to appeal to the Commercial Court in the three years 2006, 2007, and 2008.[66]

29.48 The report comes to no conclusions and is essentially a statistical survey: it appears to have been a preliminary study for further work which in the event did not take place. It points out, however, that the parties, or more importantly associations which develop standard arbitration clauses for their own trades, or arbitration institutions which promulgate their own rules, are free under the 1996 Act to permit appeals, as a matter of contract, under their own less stringent terms, if they so desire. The 2010 QMUL Survey found London to be one of the most popular places in the world in which to arbitrate, in large part because of the favoured view which is taken of English law and of the legal infrastructure in London.[67]

29.49 In 2012, with the help of my then judicial assistant, Olivia Jackson, I conducted my own survey of section 69 appeals under the 1996 Act, at any rate as demonstrated by cases

---

[60] English Arbitration Act 1996, s 69(3).
[61] *CMA CGM SA v Beteiligungs-KG MS 'Northern Pioneer' Schiffahrtsgesellschaft-mbH & Co* [2002] EWCA Civ 1878; [2003] 1 WLR 1015.
[62] Such as was to be found in *The Nema* itself, or for instance in *The Antaios, Antaios Cia Naviera SA v Salen Rederierna AB* [1985] AC 191, where Lord Diplock screwed the *Nema* tourniquet still tighter.
[63] Lord Phillips at [60]–[61], where he explained that the statutory test was 'broader than Lord Diplock's requirement'.
[64] Bruce Harris, 'Report on the Arbitration Act 1996' (2007) 23 Arb Int'l 437. The Report was produced by a committee chaired by Bruce Harris and prepared for the Commercial Court Users' Committee, the BMLA, the LSLC, and other bodies.
[65] ibid para 75.
[66] LMAA, 'First Interim Report on the Workings of Section 69 of the 1996 Act in Regard to Maritime Arbitrations in London before the Commercial and Admiralty Court' (2009) <http://www.lmaa.org.uk> accessed 25 September 2015.
[67] 2013 QMUL Survey, 'International Arbitration Survey: Choices in International Arbitration' <http://www.arbitration.qmul.ac.uk/research/index.html> accessed 25 September 2015.

reported in Lloyd's Reports down to the end of 2011. This suggests that some 72 cases have been granted leave to appeal, although an unknown number of these, probably very small, if any, may have come forward as consensual appeals. Moreover, some of the 72, in the earlier years covered by the survey, are not clearly identified as arising under either the 1979 or the 1996 Acts. Of those 72, only 12 have reached the Court of Appeal, and of those 12, two have reached the House of Lords or Supreme Court.

29.50 Both of those cases, as it happens, raise questions under the general law of damages, namely *The Golden Victory*[68] and *The Achilleas*.[69] As for the 72 appeals taken as a whole, the great majority appear to be maritime disputes, with a fair sprinkling of shipbuilding and international sale of goods disputes among them. There appear to be no, or hardly any, appeals from large construction or infrastructure disputes, possibly because these are often arbitrated under institutional rules which do not allow recourse to the courts at all.[70]

29.51 It may be interesting to note that, using the year of the report as a guide, which is somewhat inaccurate, the biggest year for appeals was 2008, which is one to two years after the Harris Report had suggested that the courts could perhaps apply the section 69 test with a 'slightly more liberal approach'. Thus, my research finds one appeal reported in 1999, three in 2000, five in 2001, two in 2002, seven in 2003, four in 2004, five in 2006, four in 2007, 12 in 2008, six in 2009, nine in 2010, and ten in 2011.

29.52 That suggests a slow start (as awards under the 1996 Act took time to reach any possible appeal stage), a tight rein for the first few years, rising to seven in 2003, possibly influenced by *The Northern Pioneer* (which was decided in December 2002), and rising further to 12 in 2008 (following the Harris Report in 2006), and then falling back somewhat, but still at a higher level than in earlier years. It looks as though there has been something of a pendulum, with the Commercial Court ultimately finding an equilibrium with the help of *The Northern Pioneer* and some empirical research.

F. Conclusion

29.53 I conclude this historical survey with a reference to Lord Wilberforce's parliamentary observation cited by Lord Steyn in *Lesotho Highlands* and set out at the beginning of this chapter.[71] *Lesotho Highlands* did not arise as an appeal under section 69, but raised an issue under section 68(2)(b) of the 1996 Act as to whether the arbitral tribunal had 'exceed[ed] its powers'. The House of Lords held that an erroneous exercise of a power that was possessed was a mere error of law and not the same thing as acting in excess of powers that were not possessed; and that therefore the award could not be challenged. Their Lordships were not, however, unanimous, for Lord Phillips dissented.

29.54 I suspect that, as a matter of principle, it might be difficult to distinguish between an error of law and an excess of power, as might be demonstrated for instance in the different context of judicial review in administrative law. But in the context of arbitration, the House

---

[68] *The Golden Victory* [2007] 2 AC 353.
[69] *Transfield Shipping Inc v Mercator Shipping Inc (The Achilleas)* [2009] AC 61 (HL).
[70] 2014 LCIA Rules, Art 26.8; 2012 ICC Rules, Art 34.6.
[71] *Lesotho Highlands Development Authority v Impregilo SpA* [2006] 1 AC 221, 231.

of Lords was determined to allow no possibility that errors of law might be dressed up as decisions in excess of powers. That would have opened the floodgates to the opportunities for judicial intervention in the merits of disputes. Lord Steyn was having none of it.

29.55 One could see the way the wind was blowing when he quoted Lord Wilberforce during the debate on the Arbitration Bill from Hansard. That quote is as good a plug for arbitration as one could desire, even if it seems to have had little direct reference to the section 68(2)(b) issue before their Lordships. But it was expressive of the desire to free arbitration from the control of the courts as far as possible, so it was at any rate spiritually relevant to the issue at hand.

29.56 What is remarkable is how far Lord Wilberforce's observation stands from the mood of the Court of Appeal in *Czarnikow v Roth, Schmidt & Co*, a decision repeatedly cited in modern times as underpinning English law's concern that those who contract to arbitrate under English law should still be entitled, at any rate within strict limits, to a result required by English law. It is true that Lord Wilberforce qualified his language with the phrase 'subject to statutory guidelines no doubt'.

29.57 Nevertheless, his interest in arbitration's freedom to 'develop its own substantive law' harks back to the ideas of a *lex mercatoria* which preceded the emergence of national commercial law.[72] The difficulty about the development of an arbitral *lex mercatoria*, however, is that the concept of confidentiality means that, generally speaking, and outside the area of investment arbitration, arbitration awards are not published and thus the development of arbitration's own substantive law remains hidden and uncertain.[73] That, however, is another topic.

---

[72] Julian D M Lew, 'Achieving the Dream: Autonomous Arbitration?' in Lew and others (n 1); Michael J Mustill, 'The New Lex Mercatoria: The First Twenty-five Years' (1988) 4 Arb Int'l 86; cf Gunther Teubner, 'Breaking Frames Economic Globalization and the Emergence of *Lex Mercatoria*' (2002) 5(2) EJST 199, 210.
[73] Ralf Michaels, 'Dreaming Law without a State: Scholarship on Autonomous International Arbitration as Utopian Literature' (2013) 1 Lond Rev Int'l Law 35.

30

IMPROVING JUDICIAL PERFORMANCE IN MATTERS INVOLVING INTERNATIONAL ARBITRATION

S I Strong

A. Introduction

30.01　Participants in international arbitration often consider national courts to be the 'weak link' in the chain of arbitral practice and procedure. Although parties can and often do contract in advance for experienced arbitrators and efficient procedures, all of that planning and forethought can come to naught if a judge refuses to enforce an arbitration agreement or award.

30.02　Recalcitrant courts are often branded as parochial, a move which suggests that the judges in question know what the proper course of action is, but simply prefer to protect national interests or parties. However, what appears to be a conscious desire to thwart the international arbitral regime could actually be nothing more than a judicial misunderstanding of a particularly complex area of law.

30.03　While not perhaps as blameworthy as bias, the prospect of judicial confusion is nevertheless disturbing, not only for the parties' sake, but also for the public at large, since society has a vested interest in a well-informed judiciary. However, significant questions exist as to how judges should be educated and on what issues or procedures.[1]

30.04　While every country has its own philosophy regarding the way in which judges are to be trained, most judicial education programmes focus on procedural and administrative concerns.[2] Relatively little training is offered on substantive matters, on the grounds that a well-prepared bar is the best means of ensuring a well-informed bench.[3] This sort of indirect method of judicial education can lead to problems in cases involving international

---

[1] See Diane E Cowdrey, 'Educating into the Future: Creating an Effective System of Judicial Education' (2010) 51 S Tex L Rev 885; Emily Kadens, 'The Puzzle of Judicial Education: The Case of Chief Justice William de Grey' (2009) 75 Brooklyn L Rev 143; Symposium, 'Judicial Education and the Art of Judging: From Myth to Methodology' (2015) J Disp Resol 1–190.

[2] See John Clifford Wallace, 'Globalization of Judicial Education' (2003) 28 Yale J Int'l L 355, 356–7.

[3] Judges from civil law jurisdictions receive some substantive training as part of their formal judicial education, since civil law judges choose their career path while still in law school. Common law judges are considered to have less of a need for training on substantive matters, since they are not elevated to the bench until after they have already had a distinguished career at the bar. ibid.

arbitration, since such disputes arise relatively infrequently in comparison to other types of matters and sitting judges tend to have very little independent experience with arbitration.[4]

30.05 Because most legal systems rely on skilled advocates to educate judges regarding the substantive law, the arbitral community has made considerable efforts to inform practitioners about the nuances of international arbitration.[5] Although a vast and ever-increasing number of professional conferences are currently being offered around the world on matters relating to international commercial and investment arbitration, this approach has not been entirely successful as a means of educating national court judges about the intricacies of this field.

30.06 One reason why educating lawyers has not proven entirely effective in transforming the quality of judicial decision-making stems from the fact that advocates are required to make the most advantageous argument possible for their clients, even if that argument could create disarray in the field at some point in the future. While not every jurisdiction embraces the principle of binding legal precedent, many legal systems still attempt to achieve a certain degree of consistency in their jurisprudence so as to provide parties with the type of predictability that is necessary in commercial practice. Therefore, even a small number of questionable decisions can lead to problematic legal analysis for years to come.

30.07 Another reason why an emphasis on practitioner education has limited value relates to the rapid expansion of international arbitration in the last 10 to 20 years. Whereas the field was once populated entirely by specialists, a significant number of generalist practitioners are now entering the market. Although well intentioned, these lawyers are not as well informed as specialists are about the nuances of international arbitration and are often unable to provide judges with top-notch advocacy about the special nature of international arbitration.

30.08 These phenomena suggest that attempting to educate judges indirectly through practitioners is not the most effective means of ensuring quality decision-making about international arbitration. However, there are other ways to improve judicial performance. First, a state may restructure its judicial system so as to allow for specialization of judges in arbitral matters. Second, a country may attempt to educate its judges directly about issues involving international arbitration.[6] Both mechanisms are being adopted with increasing frequency.

B. Structural Efforts to Improve Judicial Decision-Making

30.09 Every country structures its judiciary differently. Some jurisdictions provide for judicial specialization, while other states have adopted a more generalist approach. This dichotomy is evident in the world of international arbitration, with several of the leading jurisdictions (most notably France and England) giving certain courts exclusive competence over arbitral

---

[4] For example, judges who come to the bench after an established career at the bar are unlikely to have specialized in arbitration, since that background is unlikely to have led to their appointment or election to a judgeship. Judges who have spent their entire careers on the bench will never have practised as an advocate or arbitrator and thus will never have seen the arbitral process from the inside.

[5] A considerable amount of effort has also been aimed at educating law students, in the hopes that they will have at least a basic understanding of international arbitration by the time they get into practice.

[6] Some commentators have supported direct education of judges in other areas of law as well. See Jeffrey W Stempel, 'Refocusing Away from Rules Reform and Devoting More Attention to the Deciders' (2010) 87 Denver UL Rev 335, 359–60.

matters[7] while other countries (such as the United States) allow disputes relating to arbitration to be considered by courts of general jurisdiction.[8]

30.10 Interestingly, a number of jurisdictions that have traditionally adopted a generalist approach have begun to shift towards the use of specialist courts, apparently as part of a strategic effort to establish themselves as centres of arbitral excellence. For instance, Australia and India have both moved towards increased judicial specialization, as have several US states.[9]

30.11 Specialization can occur in a variety of ways. For example, some jurisdictions have created special subsections within their existing court systems and given those subsections exclusive jurisdiction over matters relating to international arbitration.[10] Other jurisdictions have designated a single judge to handle all matters relating to international arbitration.[11]

30.12 Proponents of judicial specialization take the view that channelling arbitration-related disputes to a limited number of judges allows for adjudicatory competence in a particularly challenging area of law. Because judges are hearing certain matters more frequently, they can develop an increased understanding of the issues relating to arbitration. This approach is said to benefit parties by facilitating the development of a predictable and internationally defensible body of jurisprudence and decreasing the number of judicial appeals.

---

[7] For example, a special chamber of the Court of Appeal in Paris (where most French arbitrations are seated) hears disputes relating to international arbitration, and subsequent appeals are heard by the First Chamber of the *Cour de Cassation*, which specializes in matters of private international law, including those associated with international arbitration. See Jean-Christophe Honlet, Bart Legum, and Anne-Sophie Dufêtre, 'Commercial Arbitration—France' (2010) Global Arbitration Review Know-How <http://www.globalarbitrationreview.com> accessed 25 September 2015. England sends matters relating to international arbitration to the Commercial Court, which is generally perceived as having special expertise in this field. See Nigel Rawding and Elizabeth Snodgrass, 'Commercial Arbitration—England and Wales' Global Arbitration Review Know-How <http://www.globalarbitrationreview.com> accessed 25 September 2015.

[8] See Mark Becket and others, 'Commercial Arbitration—United States' Global Arbitration Review Know-How <http://www.globalarbitrationreview.com> accessed 25 September 2015 (discussing US federal courts). Switzerland adopts a hybrid approach whereby most arbitral matters are heard by courts at the seat of arbitration, although efforts to set aside an award are only heard by the Swiss Federal Tribunal. See Dominique Brown-Berset and Dominique Ritter, 'Commercial Arbitration—Switzerland' Global Arbitration Review Know-How <http://www.globalarbitrationreview.com> accessed 25 September 2015.

[9] See Barry Leon, 'To Specialize or Not: How Should National Courts Handle International Commercial Arbitration Matters?' (*Kluwer Arbitration Blog*, 2 September 2010) <http://www.kluwerarbitrationblog.com> accessed 25 September 2015.

[10] This approach was recently adopted by the Eleventh Judicial Circuit of the US state of Florida. See Administrative Order, Eleventh Judicial Circuit, Miami-Dade, Florida, dated 3 December 2013 <http://www.globalarbitrationreview.com> accessed 25 September 2015 (creating the new subsection within the Complex Business Litigation Section (section 40)). The administrative order creating the new subdivision indicates that:

> WHEREAS, international commercial arbitration is a specialized area of law; and
> WHEREAS, designated particular *trained* judges to hear all international commercial arbitration matters will foster greater judicial expertise and understanding in this area of law, will lead to more uniformity in legal decisions, and help establish a consistent body of case law [emphasis added].

This new subsection would address matters arising out of arbitrations seated in Miami, Florida, which is perhaps the leading jurisdiction for Latin American arbitrations. The High Court of Mumbai in India adopted a somewhat similar approach through the creation of a special court within the High Court.

See Leon (n 9).

[11] This is the mechanism adopted by the US state of New York. See Administrative Order of the Chief Administrative Judge of the Courts dated 16 September 2013 <http://www.nycourts.gov> accessed 25 September 2015 (naming Judge Charles E Ramos to the post). Some Australian courts have adopted a modified form of this approach. See Leon (n 9).

However, it is not clear whether specialized courts always lead to high quality decision-making.[12] One feature that may be important to a determination about the value of specialized courts relates to the number of judges that are sitting in a specialist capacity. For example, naming a single judge to be the arbitral specialist minimizes the possibility of conflicting case law, but also runs the risk of allowing one person to develop the law in a highly idiosyncratic manner. Creating a special subsection allows for a diversity of viewpoints, which could be useful in developing a sophisticated understanding of arbitration law. However, this latter scenario could experience difficulties if the various judges adopted widely divergent views of particular issues.

30.13

The uncertain benefits of judicial specialization suggest that structural reforms provide only a partial solution to the problem of judicial decision-making in international arbitration. Therefore, many states have found it helpful to consider other means of improving the quality of judicial decisions in this field. The most popular of these measures involves direct education of judges themselves.

30.14

C. Educational Efforts to Improve Judicial Decision-Making

(a) Conferences and seminars

On first glance, educating judges about international arbitration would appear to be a relatively simple task, given the ever-increasing number of conferences and seminars offered around the world on investment and international commercial arbitration. However, sitting judges seldom attend these events. To some extent, this phenomenon may be due to the fact that judges believe that arbitration is entirely separate from court proceedings and therefore outside the realm of judicial competence or concern. However, other factors also appear to play into judges' willingness to attend practitioner conferences.

30.15

For example, some judges believe that only another judge can truly understand the factors that are relevant to the judicial process and therefore will only attend educational programmes taught by judges.[13] Other judges hesitate to attend industry-sponsored events due to concerns about potential conflicts of interest.[14] As a result, many judges will only attend training programmes aimed exclusively at judges.

30.16

Judicial education programmes are offered by a variety of organizations, some affiliated with local, state, or regional organizations and others existing independently. Interestingly, a number of these organizations have recently increased their efforts to educate national judges about the intricacies of international arbitration.[15]

30.17

---

[12] Indeed, there is some debate about this issue. See Leon (n 9). Some critics might view these developments as simple examples of rent-seeking by local lawyers keen to attract arbitral business to their home jurisdictions. See S I Strong, 'International Litigation—Arbitration' in Jürgen Backhaus (ed), *Encyclopedia of Law and Economics* (Springer 2014).

[13] See Wallace (n 2) 359.

[14] See Bruce A Green, 'May Judges Attend Privately Funded Educational Programs? Should Judicial Education Be Privatized? Questions of Judicial Ethics and Policy' (2002) 29 Fordham Urb LJ 941, 942–3.

[15] Of course, there is often an element of self-selection in this process, since judges in most, if not all, jurisdictions are typically allowed to choose the subject matter of any educational programmes that they attend. This feature can reduce the number of judges who are exposed to training on international arbitration, since many judges prefer to focus on practical skills (such as opinion-writing or case management) rather than on what is perceived by some jurists to be a somewhat arcane field of law. See Stempel (n 6) 360; Wallace (n 2) 358–9.

(b) Judicial outreach efforts by governmental organizations

30.18 Over the last few years, governmental organizations have increased their efforts to provide judges with training on international arbitration. Some initiatives focus on live, in-person programming. Courses may be offered by national bodies, as was the case with a recent conference hosted by the Law and Justice Commission of Pakistan,[16] or by regional bodies, as was the case with a seminar offered by the Court of Justice for the Common Market for Eastern and Southern Africa (COMESA).[17]

30.19 Sometimes, judges from one country travel to another jurisdiction to help raise judicial consciousness regarding international arbitration. Thus, the US Department of Commerce[18] and the International Judicial Relations Committee of the US Judicial Conference[19] have both sponsored a number of judicial exchanges that see US federal judges visiting various countries to discuss international arbitration with other judges.

30.20 Governmental efforts to educate judges about international arbitration can also take the form of various guidebooks and monographs, referred to in some jurisdictions as 'benchbooks'. One such item, entitled 'International Commercial Arbitration: A Guide for US Judges', was recently published by the FJC, which is the research and education arm of the US federal judiciary.[20] That guide was subsequently translated into Chinese and published by the Press of the People's Court of China. Benchbooks and similar publications are often highly persuasive to judges because they provide a neutral perspective on certain matters.[21]

30.21 Indeed, two US federal courts—the District Court for the Southern District of New York and the District Court for the Southern District of California—have already cited the FJC guide on international commercial arbitration as persuasive authority.[22] Although the FJC publication is aimed primarily at US judges, it provides information that is useful to readers in other jurisdictions as well. The US Department of Commerce has generated a number of benchbooks on international arbitration for judges outside the United States.

30.22 UNCITRAL has also commissioned a text that is meant to assist judges in the area of international commercial arbitration. This guide compiles information on how the New York

---

[16] See Secretariat, Law and Justice Commission of Pakistan, 'Report on International Judicial Conference' (International Judicial Conference, 13–15 April 2012) <http://www.ljcp.gov.pk> accessed 25 September 2015 (noting the conference was usually national in scope, but became international on this occasion).

[17] See Common Market for Eastern and Southern Africa, 'Court of Justice Explores International Arbitration' <http://www.comesa.int> accessed 25 September 2015.

[18] Many of the Commerce Department programmes have focused on the Middle East. See US Department of Commerce, Commercial Law Development Program <http://www.cldp.doc.gov> accessed 25 September 2015.

[19] See Committee on International Judicial Relations, US Judicial Conference <http://www.fjc.gov> accessed 25 September 2015. The Judicial Conference is the governing body of the US federal courts.

[20] See S I Strong, 'International Commercial Arbitration: A Guide for US Judges' (FJC 2012) <http://www.fjc.gov> accessed 25 September 2015. The title is part of a larger series published by the FJC on matters relating to international litigation. Other judicial guides address matters as diverse as The Hague Convention on the Civil Aspects of Child Abduction, the US Foreign Sovereign Immunities Act 1976, discovery in transnational civil litigation, international extradition, and mutual legal assistance treaties. See FJC, Publications <http://www.fjc.gov> accessed 25 September 2015.

[21] All FJC publications are subject to extensive editorial scrutiny, including review by one or more federal judges, so as to ensure objectivity. As a result, FJC publications are cited routinely in US courts. For example, a search of the terms 'Federal Judicial Center', 'FJC', 'Manual for Complex Litigation', and 'Manual on Scientific Evidence' in the Westlaw 'all federal cases' database yielded 4,000 different cases.

[22] See *Freaner v Valle*, 966 F Supp 2d 1068, 1075 (SD Cal 2013); *Yukos Capital SARL v OAO Samaraneftegaz*, 963 F Supp 2d 289, 296 (SDNY 2013).

Convention is interpreted by various courts around the world.[23] While the UNCITRAL text is not intended to provide binding rules of interpretation that are to be followed in all circumstances, the guide is nevertheless meant to offer judges a neutral and authoritative means of understanding how international arbitration works.

(c) Judicial outreach efforts by inter-governmental and non-governmental organizations

30.23 Governmental bodies are not the only entities that are involved in judicial education regarding international arbitration. Intergovernmental organizations and NGOs are also active in this field. Again, efforts include both in-person programming and written materials.

30.24 Live programming is offered on both a national and regional level. For example, the Organization of American States (OAS), an intergovernmental organization operating in the Americas, has held a number of educational programmes for judges, magistrates, academics, and high-level government officials from various countries in the OAS.[24] Meetings have been held in a variety of countries, including Chile, Costa Rica, the United States, and Uruguay. The IJA, which is an NGO dedicated to judicial education, recently organized a similar programme on international commercial arbitration for Chinese judges.[25]

30.25 NGOs also provide various types of publications aimed at judges. One project that has garnered a great deal of attention is the ALI's Restatement (Third) of the US Law of International Commercial Arbitration.[26] Although Restatements are not precisely analogous to benchbooks, US judges nevertheless find Restatements to be highly persuasive and useful sources of information.[27] Courts outside the United States also find Restatements to be helpful in describing how particular issues are (or might be) considered under US law.[28] The Restatement on international commercial arbitration may be particularly useful to judges because it focuses primarily on matters that arise in the judicial context rather than on those that arise within the arbitration proceeding itself.[29]

---

[23] See UNCITRAL, Settlement of Commercial Disputes, 'UNCITRAL Guide on the Recognition and Enforcement of Foreign Arbitral Awards' (New York, 1958), UN Doc A/CN.9/814 (25 March 2014), para 8 (noting the guide is meant to assist national court judges, as well as others). Scholars specializing in international arbitration have argued that '[w]hen investment arbitration is introduced into a local legal environment, it becomes integrated with international commercial arbitration, and often domestic arbitration' and can 'provide not only concrete, effective guidance but also an internationally established sense of legitimacy and access to an extensive international arbitration network that can be valuable' in developing judicial and practitioner competence in international arbitration. See Catherine A Rogers, 'International Arbitration, Judicial Education, and Legal Elites' (2015) J Disp Resol 71, 72.
[24] See OAS <http://www.oas.org> accessed 25 September 2015.
[25] See IJA <http://www.ijaworld.org> accessed 25 September 2015.
[26] See ALI, Current Projects <http://www.ali.org> accessed 25 September 2015.
[27] Notably, a Restatement is not considered law unless and until it is adopted by a particular US state or federal court.
[28] See George A Bermann and others, 'Restating the US Law of International Commercial Arbitration' (2009) 113 Penn St L Rev 1333, 1341. Some caution must be exercised when relying on a Restatement, since some Restatements focus on summarizing existing law, while other Restatements take a slightly more aspirational approach. See George A Bermann, 'Restating the US Law of International Commercial Arbitration' (2009) 42 NYU J Int'l L & Pol 175, 191.
[29] The Restatement is expected to address matters such as: the enforcement of arbitration agreements; judicial assistance in cases where an arbitration is seated in the United States and where it is seated abroad; recourse from and enforcement of international arbitral awards rendered both in and outside the United States; and the preclusive effect of international arbitral awards.

(d) Judicial outreach efforts by private organizations

30.26 Private organizations are also interested in helping judges appreciate the intricacies of international arbitration. One of the more ambitious programmes in recent years involves a series of judicial colloquia for state and federal judges undertaken by the NYIAC in conjunction with the US Federal-State Judicial Council.[30] The inaugural session of the series was co-hosted by the Chief Judge of the US District Court for the Southern District of New York, Loretta Preska, and New York State Court of Appeals Judge Victoria Graffeo. Yale Law School professor and former Legal Advisor of the US Department of State Harold H Koh acted as the keynote speaker.

30.27 Other private organizations have also been active in judicial education initiatives. For example, the ICCA has hosted a series of programmes for judges in a number of countries in Asia, the Middle East, and the Americas.[31]

D. Conclusion

30.28 Concerns about judicial competency in international arbitration have led to a worldwide effort to increase judges' knowledge of and familiarity with the principles and practices of international commercial and investment arbitration. Some states have attempted to address this issue through structural reforms, whereas other jurisdictions have done so through educational initiatives. Although it is difficult at this point to know which approach will be the most effective in improving the quality of judicial decision-making, it is clear that legal systems around the world are becoming more aware of the importance of informing their judges about the special challenges of international arbitration.

---

[30] See NYIAC International Arbitration Initiatives <http://www.nyiac.org> accessed 25 September 2015.
[31] See ICCA, New York Convention Roadshow <http://www.arbitration-icca.org> accessed 25 September 2015.

31

THE PRINCIPLED ENGLISH AMBIVALENCE TO LAW AND DISPUTE RESOLUTION BEYOND THE STATE

Alex Mills

A. Introduction

In the century since the CIArb was founded, London has become firmly established as the leading centre for the non-judicial (and indeed judicial) resolution of international commercial disputes. A number of reasons are commonly given for this, not least the knowledge and skill of London-based arbitrators and counsel—an expertise which the CIArb has helped to promote and develop, both in England and around the globe. A further reason which is frequently put forward is that the English legal system is reputed to have a favourable disposition towards the private resolution of disputes through non-state forms of law and dispute resolution. 31.01

Is this reputation deserved? There is no doubting that English courts can and do provide significant support for arbitral proceedings in numerous ways, including through making various orders (such as anti-suit injunctions,[1] asset freezing injunctions, and disclosure orders) which can also be made in support of judicial proceedings.[2] This chapter examines what appears, however, to be an ambivalence in English law towards non-state forms of law and dispute resolution. 31.02

First, it focuses on the fact that an English court will not recognize the validity of a choice of non-state law in a contract, but will nevertheless recognize and enforce an arbitral award based on the application of non-state law, identically chosen by the parties. Second, it deals with the attitude of the English courts to the recognition and enforcement of a foreign arbitral award which has been set aside by the courts of the seat of the arbitration, under which the arbitral award is neither voided, nor necessarily still enforceable. 31.03

While the approach of English law in both contexts might appear to leave it open to charges of inconsistency, there are good arguments of principle in favour of the ambivalent positions adopted in each case, reflecting the reality of a world in which both private and public power coexist. 31.04

---

[1] Although an anti-suit injunction in support of a jurisdiction or arbitration agreement is no longer available in EU national courts to restrain potential proceedings in other European Member States, following the decisions of the CJEU in Case C-159/02 *Turner v Grovit* [2004] ECR I-3565 and Case C-185/07 *Allianz SpA v West Tankers* [2009] ECR I-663.
[2] English Arbitration Act 1996, s 44; Senior Courts Act 1981, s 37; see further *Ust-Kamenogorsk Hydropower Plant JSC v AES Ust-Kamenogorsk Hydropower Plant LLP* [2013] UKSC 35.

B. Choice of Non-State Law

(a) Choice of non-state law in litigation

31.05 One of the foundations of modern private international law is the widespread acceptance that parties are generally free to choose the law which governs their contractual relations, as part of the phenomenon known as party autonomy.[3] A key question concerning the limits of party autonomy is whether individuals may choose non-state law to govern their contractual relations, and thus avoid (or evade) the law of any national legal system. Under the common law,[4] the Rome Convention,[5] and now the Rome I Regulation,[6] it has long been established that if a contract is litigated before the English courts, the courts will only give effect to a choice by the parties of the law of a 'state'.[7] If parties choose non-state law to govern a contract, that choice is simply considered to be invalid.

31.06 It is true that courts have endeavoured in at least some cases to give effect to the intentions of such parties, by taking into consideration their chosen non-state system of law—such as a choice of religious law—in the interpretation of their contract.[8] However, this secondary role for the chosen law can only be of limited effect—it cannot, for example, affect questions of the material validity of the contract. It is, rather, the equivalent of finding that parties have incorporated by reference certain (non-state) rules or principles of contractual interpretation as terms of their contract—as indeed is expressly permitted under Recital 13 of the Rome I Regulation, which provides that parties are not precluded 'from incorporating by reference into their contract a non-State body of law or an international convention'.

31.07 The choice of law rules applicable in English courts thus implicitly provide that the public interests of at least one state must have a role to play in resolving the dispute between the parties. Party autonomy is constructed as a limited choice between the laws of states, accepting pluralism of state legal orders, but not of legal orders beyond the state. Under this perspective, non-state law is not considered to be truly law, and a contract is not a contract without a law to give it that status—it is, to paraphrase Lord Diplock in the House of Lords, just a piece of paper.[9]

31.08 Choice-of-law rules are generally products of state law-making,[10] and as such it is perhaps unsurprising that they have traditionally been committed to what might be called

---

[3] See, eg, Regulation (EC) No 593/2008 of the European Parliament and of the Council of 17 June 2008 on the law applicable to contractual obligations (Rome I), OJ L 177/6 (4 July 2008) ('Rome I Regulation') Art 3.

[4] See, eg, *Musawi v RE International (UK) Ltd* [2007] EWHC 2981 (Ch).

[5] Convention on the law applicable to contractual obligations (opened for signature 19 June 1980, entered into force 1 April 1991), OJ L 266, 9 October 1980, Art 3.

[6] Rome I Regulation, Art 3.

[7] See, eg, *Beximco Pharmaceuticals Ltd v Shamil Bank of Bahrain EC* [2004] EWCA Civ 19. More accurately, the choice is limited to a law which constitutes or is part of a state legal order—it might be doubted whether either English law or New York law, for example, are strictly laws of a 'state'.

[8] See, eg, *Halpern v Halpern* [2007] EWCA Civ 291; [2007] 3 All ER 478.

[9] *Amin Rasheed Shipping Corp v Kuwait Insurance Co* [1984] AC 50, 65 (Lord Diplock): 'Contracts are incapable of existing in a legal vacuum. They are mere pieces of paper devoid of all legal effect unless they were made by reference to some system of private law'.

[10] Which is not to deny that they may reflect underlying obligations or limitations of public international law, see generally Alex Mills, *The Confluence of Public and Private International Law* (CUP 2009).

the regulatory monopoly of the state.[11] States have thereby lent their public enforcement resources to each other (willingly applying the laws of a foreign state in civil disputes, as directed by rules of private international law), but have been less inclined to lend them to purely private sources of rules, which would not necessarily take into account any public interests. This monopoly of the state as a sovereign actor has also traditionally been supported by public international law—classically expressed in the 1929 decision of the PCIJ in the *Serbian and Brazilian Loans* case:

> Any contract which is not a contract between States in their capacity as subjects of international law is based on the municipal law of some country.[12]

31.09 The classical model of international law which underlies this perspective, under which states are considered the exclusive bearers of international legal personality, is no longer generally adopted in modern international law.[13] Many would argue, for example, that individuals are bearers of direct rights under human rights law, and that investors are the bearers of direct rights under international investment treaties.[14] The (still much-debated) emergence of this 'new' international law, which recognizes the importance of private as well as public actors and interests, raises questions about the traditional exclusivity of states as sources of normative authority—if states are not the only actors whose agency is recognized and valued in international law, then why should they claim a monopoly over lawmaking? These broader developments thus link back to the question as to whether non-state law generated by private actors should be accepted as a valid form of law.

(b) Choice of arbitration and non-state law

31.10 The general effectiveness of arbitration agreements, and thus of privatized 'non-state' dispute resolution, has of course long been accepted at a national level and further supported internationally under the New York Convention. Part of the reason for the near-universal acceptance of arbitration is that it has various policy justifications which reinforce each other. It can be argued that arbitration allows parties to choose and customize the most efficient dispute resolution system for their dispute, for example, or that a possible choice of arbitration makes courts work harder to compete with ADR systems.

31.11 Supporting arbitration can be attractive to states, as it takes some of the burden of resolving disputes away from public courts, reducing their drain on public resources. If the parties are willing to arbitrate their issues, public taxes do not have to go towards resolving what might be a purely private dispute. Of course, the question of when—if ever—a dispute

---

[11] It is notable that a different position has recently been proposed under The Hague Principles on Choice of Law in International Commercial Contracts, Art 3, a model law prepared by an expert group rather than government representatives, although approved by the Member States of The Hague Conference on Private International Law on 19 March 2015. The Principles are available at <http://www.hcch.net> accessed 25 September 2015.

[12] *Case Concerning the Payment in Gold of the Brazilian Federal Loans Issued in France (French Republic v Kingdom of the Serbs, Croats and Slovenes)*, PCIJ Series A Nos 20/21, Judgments 14 and 15 (12 July 1929) 41.

[13] See further, eg, Alex Mills, 'Rethinking Jurisdiction in International Law' (2014) 84 BYIL 187; 'Agents of Change: The Individual as a Participant in the Legal Process' (2012) 1(3) CJICL <http://www.joomla.cjicl.org.uk> accessed 25 September 2015.

[14] See, eg, *Occidental Exploration & Production Co v Republic of Ecuador* [2005] EWCA Civ 1116, [18]; *Corn Products International v Mexico*, ICSID Case No ARB(AF)/04/01, Decision on Responsibility (15 January 2008) [168]–[169] ('It is now clear that States are not the only entities which can hold rights under international law; individuals and corporations may also possess rights under international law').

should be considered to be purely private remains a key controversy, but in any case issues of public policy and arbitrability may be raised at the stage of judicial enforcement of an arbitral award.

31.12 The success of arbitration in attracting the acceptance and indeed support of states is not only a consequence of these policy arguments, but also a reflection of the realities of private power. To the extent that private parties prefer arbitration as a means to resolve their disputes, they will look less favourably on a state to the extent that it does not recognize arbitration or arbitral awards, either as a place to do business or as a place to carry out dispute resolution. The global system of privatized dispute resolution which has emerged in the form of international commercial arbitration thus also reflects the realities and preferences of a globalized economy in which private actors wield significant power—not the sovereign power of states, but genuine power nonetheless.

31.13 The exclusion of the possibility of a choice of non-state law in the English courts, as discussed above, is notably distinct from the way in which a choice of non-state law is dealt with in arbitral proceedings, including those conducted in England under the supervision of the English Arbitration Act 1996. Article 46 of the Act provides as follows:

> Rules applicable to substance of dispute.
> (1) The arbitral tribunal shall decide the dispute—
>   (a) in accordance with the law chosen by the parties as applicable to the substance of the dispute, or
>   (b) if the parties so agree, in accordance with such other considerations as are agreed by them or determined by the tribunal.

31.14 As an arbitration does not need to apply 'law' to be valid, an arbitrator may confidently recognize a choice of non-state rules—the question of whether non-state law is 'truly' law is rendered moot. Arbitrators are indeed commonly and perhaps increasingly prepared to treat contracts as governed exclusively by such international codifications as the UNIDROIT Principles of International Commercial Contracts,[15] or even by an uncodified *lex mercatoria*, and not by any national law, where, for example, the parties have indicated that they wish their contract to be governed by 'principles of international business', or some similar non-state designation.[16]

31.15 Arbitration is a system of dispute resolution which competes with state systems, and it is natural enough that arbitrators would allow parties to achieve their desired objective of escaping both state procedural and substantive rules. Arbitrators also derive their authority contractually—and therefore (at least from one perspective) must apply the rules designated by the parties, as a matter of contract,[17] regardless of theoretical questions about whether the *lex mercatoria* is or is not a 'legal system'.

---

[15] For further information, see the publications of UNIDROIT <http://www.unilex.info> accessed 25 September 2015.

[16] ICC Arbitration Rules, Art 17; 2010 UNCITRAL Rules, Art 33; UNCITRAL Model Law, Art 28; European Convention on International Commercial Arbitration (opened for signature 31 April 1961, entered into force 7 January 1964) ('1961 European Arbitration Rules'), Art VII. Also reflected in Resolution on Transnational Rules adopted at the 65th ILA Conference (Cairo, 26 April 1992). See generally, eg, Thomas Schultz, *Transnational Legality: Stateless Law and International Arbitration* (OUP 2014); and Klaus Peter Berger, *The Creeping Codification of the New Lex Mercatoria* (2nd edn, Kluwer Law International 2010).

[17] Which law governs the contract between the parties and the arbitrator(s)—and whether this might itself be non-state law—is a further complication which is beyond the scope of this chapter.

Of course arbitrators will frequently apply national laws in resolving contractual disputes, even those in which the parties have not designated a national law or have designated a non-state law such as the *lex mercatoria*. To some extent this is a recognition of the existence of state interests which may override party autonomy, although it may also be simply a pragmatic recognition by the arbitrator that their award, in order to be ultimately enforceable, must be accepted by at least one national court system—sometimes described as a duty to render an enforceable award.[18] This raises the key question, then, of whether or to what extent an arbitral award based on non-state law will be capable of recognition and enforcement. 31.16

(c) Judicial enforcement of arbitral awards based on non-state law

Given the traditional state hostility towards choice of non-state law in contracts, it might be expected that courts would also be hostile to arbitral awards decided on the basis of non-state law. This is, however, generally not the case. The English courts have long been prepared to enforce arbitral awards based on a variety of non-state law sources (provided the parties intended to create legally binding relations, and designated a sufficiently certain 'law' which does not violate English public policy).[19] This practice was further implicitly endorsed in the English Arbitration Act 1996, which does not provide for non-enforcement of arbitral awards based on an application of unrecognized systems of law, but rather (in section 46) endorses the application of non-state law, as noted above. 31.17

This anomaly creates a disconnect between the worlds of judicial dispute resolution and arbitration—two worlds which collide in the context of the judicial enforcement of an arbitral award. Here, the policy of not recognizing non-state sources of law comes into conflict with the policy of recognizing arbitration agreements and arbitral awards, and the latter triumphs, at least in England. A court which is itself interpreting a contract which purports to be governed by the *lex mercatoria* must (applying the Rome I Regulation) find that this is an invalid choice of law, and that the contract is governed by some state system of law. A court which is determining the validity of an arbitral award which is the product of an application by the tribunal of the *lex mercatoria*, even based on the interpretation of the very same contract, must (applying section 46 of the English Arbitration Act 1996) recognize that this is a valid choice of law. 31.18

Arbitration under the *lex mercatoria* is thus viewed by the English courts with sympathy, even if the choice of law itself would not be—although an arbitral award may be based on a law which the courts would not themselves recognize as even a valid legal system, it is nevertheless entitled (at least presumptively) to judicial recognition and enforcement. 31.19

---

[18] See, eg, 2012 ICC Rules, Art 41, which provides that: 'In all matters not expressly provided for in the Rules, the Court and the arbitral tribunal shall act in the spirit of the Rules and shall make every effort to make sure that the award is enforceable at law'; see also the 2014 LCIA Rules, Art 32.2—although requiring only 'every reasonable effort'.

[19] *Deutsche Schachtbau- und Tiefbohrgesellschaft mbH v The Government of the State of R'as Al Khaimah and The R'as Al Khaimah Oil Co ('The Rakoil Case')* [1987] 2 All ER 769 (reversed on other grounds at [1990] 1 AC 295); *Channel Tunnel Group Ltd v Balfour Beatty Constructions Ltd* [1993] AC 334; *Musawi v RE International (UK) Ltd* [2007] EWHC 2981 (Ch); *Dallah Real Estate & Tourism Holding Co v Pakistan* [2010] UKSC 46. See generally Schultz (n 16).

(d) Inconsistency or principled ambivalence?

31.20 This apparent inconsistency is, however, arguably merely an ambivalence which is supported by solid principle. As noted above, there are good reasons for states to accept arbitration agreements in general—essentially, arbitration resolves disputes efficiently and without using public resources. There are also respectable reasons why states generally refuse to accept a choice of non-state law—essentially, it would put public resources (courts) at the service of what may be characterized as purely 'private' norms.

31.21 When it comes to the enforcement of arbitral awards based on non-state law, these policies must be weighed against each other. Enforcement of an arbitral award based on non-state law does involve using some public resources (through court enforcement proceedings) to serve private norms. But those resources are less than what would be required in full litigation of the dispute, and they give support to an efficient, flexible, and party-centred system of arbitration which is attractive to private commercial actors. And in determining the enforceability of an arbitral award, there is the opportunity to bring public policy to bear, if there are public interests in the case.

31.22 There is, therefore, a principled basis for the seemingly inconsistent attitude of the English courts towards a choice of non-state law. Its effect is that the validity of a choice of non-state law may depend on the context in which the question will be addressed—on whether the question arises in litigation or arbitration. The answer to the 'substantive' validity question may notably depend on the 'procedure' through which it is determined.

C. Non-State Dispute Resolution

(a) The 'independence' of an arbitral award

31.23 This part of the chapter deals with a distinct issue concerning the status which is afforded in English law to an arbitral award. An arbitral award may be viewed through two contrasting lenses—indeed, the tension between these two perspectives is a definitive theme underlying the history and theory of international commercial arbitration.[20] First, an award may be viewed as an act whose legal status is conferred by or derived from the law of the seat of arbitration, which will also at least partially regulate the conduct of the arbitral proceedings. Second, an award may be viewed as a resolution of a dispute which should be binding between the parties, regardless of its location or territorial connections—a private act which operates distinctly from the law of any state. One critical question in the law governing arbitration arises where these two perspectives necessarily depart—the question of what effect should be given, if any, to an arbitral award which has been set aside by the courts of the seat of arbitration.[21]

31.24 On one view, the legal status of the arbitral award is a product of the 'public' national legal order under which that status is conferred, and an award set aside by the courts of that legal

---

[20] See generally Walter Mattli and Thomas Dietz (eds), *International Arbitration and Global Governance: Contending Theories and Evidence* (OUP 2014); Emmanuel Gaillard, *Legal Theory of International Arbitration* (Martinus Nijhoff 2010); Emmanuel Gaillard, 'The Representations of International Arbitration' (2010) 1 JIDS 271.

[21] See, eg, William W Park, 'Arbitration in Autumn' (2011) 2 JIDS 287, 313–14. cf, eg, Albert Jan van den Berg, 'Enforcement of Annulled Awards?' (1998) 9 ICC Int'l Ct Arb Bull 16 (against enforcement of annulled awards); Jan Paulsson, 'Enforcing Arbitral Awards Notwithstanding a Local Standard Annulment

order is thus effectively null and void. On a contrary view, the arbitral award has a 'private' free-standing status independent of national law which is unaffected by any decision of the courts of the arbitral seat. The uncertainty has not been decisively resolved in international practice, nor by Article V of the New York Convention or its implementation in section 103 of the English Arbitration Act 1996, which provide (in relevant part) only that an arbitral award may be refused recognition if set aside by a competent authority of the country in which it was made.[22]

(b) *Yukos Capital SARL v OJSC Rosneft Oil Co*

The 2012 Court of Appeal decision in *Yukos Capital SARL v OJSC Rosneft Oil Co*[23] addressed these issues directly. The origins of the dispute lay in arbitrations in Russia, in which four damages awards totalling US$425 million were made in favour of Yukos Capital against OJSC Yugansknefregaz ('YNG'). Yukos Capital and YNG had entered into various loan contracts with exclusive arbitration agreements when they had been part of the same Russian corporate group, but by the time of the arbitration YNG had come under the control of the state-owned Rosneft company. Shortly after the awards, YNG was amalgamated with Rosneft who succeeded to its rights and obligations. On application by Rosneft, the Russian courts declared the arbitral awards to be annulled, finding the contracts between Yukos Capital and YNG to be part of an unlawful tax avoidance scheme. **31.25**

Yukos Capital nevertheless pursued enforcement of the arbitral awards in the Dutch courts, against Rosneft assets in the Netherlands. The action was dismissed at first instance because of the Russian decision setting aside the arbitral award, but on appeal the Dutch courts decided that the awards should indeed be enforced despite the declaration of the Russian courts, accepting Yukos Capital's argument that the Russian judicial proceedings were 'partial and dependent' because of state interference. The Dutch courts thus took the view that the arbitral award should be viewed as having an independent existence, despite its rejection according to the law of the place of arbitration.[24] Yukos Capital then brought English proceedings seeking enforcement of the awards plus an additional US$160 million in post-award interest. Following a failed appeal to the Dutch Supreme Court, the awards were enforced against security put up by Rosneft in the Netherlands—thus, only the post-award interest claim remained. The central issue facing the English courts was whether to recognize and give effect to the decision of the Russian courts setting aside the arbitral awards, or the arbitral awards themselves.[25] **31.26**

(LSA)' (1998) 9 ICC Int'l Ct Arb Bull 14 (in favour of enforcement of some annulled awards). A similar issue, not discussed in this chapter, arguably arises on the question of what status to accord to an arbitral award which does not comply with mandatory rules of the law of the seat of arbitration.

[22] On this issue, and the different approaches taken in other jurisdictions, see further, eg, *Dallah Real Estate & Tourism Holding Co v Pakistan* [2010] UKSC 46, [129]–[130]; Gary B Born, *International Commercial Arbitration* (Kluwer Law International 2009) 2672ff; Claudia Alfons, *Recognition and Enforcement of Annulled Foreign Arbitral Awards: An Analysis of the Legal Framework and Its Interpretation in Case Law and Literature* (Peter Lang 2010).

[23] [2012] EWCA Civ 855, [2013] 1 All ER 223. The analysis here in Part C(b) is based on Alex Mills, 'From Russia with Prejudice? The Act of State Doctrine and the Effect of Foreign Proceedings Setting Aside an Arbitral Award' (2012) 71(3) CLJ 465.

[24] The decision is criticized by Albert Jan van den Berg, 'Enforcement of Arbitral Awards Annulled in Russia, Case Comment on Court of Appeal of Amsterdam April 28, 2009' (2010) 27 J Int'l Arb 179.

[25] A further issue concerned what effect, if any, should be given to the Dutch decision that the Russian judicial proceedings were 'partial and dependent'. Overturning the decision at first instance, the Court of

31.27 The approach of the Court of Appeal in this case was to adopt something of a pragmatic middle ground. The court effectively held that, in principle, an arbitral award set aside in the courts of the place of arbitration might nevertheless be enforced in the English courts—accepting the independent and private nature of arbitration. On the other hand, the court also acknowledged the possibility that a foreign national court decision annulling an arbitral award ought to be followed as a matter of comity, therefore precluding enforcement of the award in the English courts. The principal ground on which Yukos Capital sought to argue that the decision of the Russian courts should not be recognized, was that the outcome of those proceedings was dictated by bias and state interference, as part of a campaign to effectively 're-nationalize' Yukos Capital and its assets. The Court of Appeal determined that this was a justiciable question, and that the question of whether the Russian proceedings were tainted by state interference, or whether they should instead be followed as a matter of comity precluding enforcement of the arbitral awards, was thus one which would have to proceed to trial.[26]

(c) Inconsistency or principled ambivalence?

31.28 Two somewhat contrasting conclusions can be derived from this case. First, in the English courts an arbitral award is not null and void because it has been set aside by the foreign court of the seat of arbitration. An arbitral award is therefore different from a foreign judgment which has been overturned on appeal, and which therefore no longer exists as a legally enforceable determination of the parties' rights and obligations. It is true that in the recent case of *Merchant International Co Ltd v Natsionalna Aktsionerna Kompaniya Naftogaz Ukrayiny*[27] the Court of Appeal determined that a foreign appellate court decision overturning a judgment need not be given effect—but in this exceptional case, the initial foreign judgment had already been enforced in the English courts, and thus had 'vested' as a matter of English law.

31.29 The second conclusion is that an arbitral award may be refused enforcement in the English courts because it has been set aside by the courts of the seat of arbitration—the arbitral award, despite having a 'private' or 'independent' status, nevertheless remains subject to national law, and is not entirely 'free floating'. The key question then becomes whether the foreign annulment decision has a status and character which is capable of recognition and enforcement before the English courts, to be adjudged according to the usual standards on recognition and enforcement of foreign judgments.

31.30 There is, again, an apparent ambivalence under this approach when it comes to the 'status' accorded to the foreign arbitral award, which exists in a 'legal limbo' until such time as the courts of the place of enforcement determine whether to enforce the judgment setting it aside, or the award itself. The award has a 'mixed public/private' character, which is (it seems) semi-independent of the system of law under which it was created. However, this

---

Appeal held that the Dutch judgment did not give rise to an estoppel in England, as it was concerned with the question of whether the Russian judgment was contrary to Dutch public policy. This decision might perhaps be criticized on the basis that the Dutch decision could nevertheless have given rise to an issue estoppel concerning the *factual* question of whether the Russian proceedings were 'biased'.

[26] See further, essentially confirming and applying this approach, *Yukos Capital SARL v OJSC Rosneft Oil Co* [2014] EWHC 2188 (Comm).

[27] [2012] EWCA Civ 196, [2012] 1 WLR 3036.

apparent ambivalence is once again arguably justifiable. The arbitral award is recognized as having a status beyond the law of the state under which it is created, accepting the reality of a globalized private system of dispute resolution.

At the same time, the approach continues to recognize and respect the reality of territorial state power—the regulatory capability of states to determine the rights and obligations of parties and events within their territory, including arbitral proceedings, which should at least in certain circumstances be accepted by other states through recognition and enforcement of their judicial decisions. It might be debated whether the English rules on the recognition and enforcement of judgments do define these circumstances entirely appropriately[28]—the rules may be criticized for accepting foreign jurisdiction as valid in cases in which the English courts would never assert jurisdiction themselves, and for refusing to recognize foreign jurisdiction in cases in which the English courts would happily assert jurisdiction themselves.[29] Regardless of where exactly the line is drawn, the point remains that an arbitral award is given a hybrid or intermediate status—it is not simply a product of the foreign legal order under which it was created, but nor is it entirely independent of that order. **31.31**

D. Conclusion

It is perhaps trite these days to note that we live in a world of legal pluralism—the existence of a range of normative orders, within, between, and beyond states. In both of the contexts examined in this chapter—the question of the validity of a choice of non-state law, and the question of the enforceability of an arbitral award set aside by the courts of the arbitral seat—the underlying issue is the extent to which English law and courts are receptive to non-state norms and normative processes, and the extent to which they remain in a paradigm under which states are the exclusive sovereign actors. In both contexts, the English legal system strikes a balance. **31.32**

On the one hand, it recognizes that states are no longer the only sheriff in town. Private parties may establish their own legal standards, and apply those legal standards through privatized dispute resolution processes which do not depend on recognition by the territorial state in which they take place for their legal validity. On the other hand, the English legal system recognizes that states are still sheriffs, and they are still in town. The courts will not lend their public enforcement powers to claims based on purely private norms, but will insist on applying the law of some state, and the powers of foreign states to regulate acts of private parties within their territory continue to be recognized. While this all may appear as legal ambivalence, what is really at play in these contexts is a delicate and principled balance struck in the face of the reality of a world in which, sometimes competing and sometimes cooperating, public and private power, rules and dispute resolution coexist. **31.33**

---

[28] A different balance, more deferential to foreign courts, is struck in the ALI Restatement (Third) of the US Law of International Commercial Arbitration, ss 5–12 Tentative Draft, September 2010. Comment 'd' provides: 'In extraordinary circumstance, an award that has been set aside may also be recognized or enforced ... when it is shown that the set-aside court knowingly and egregiously departed from the rules governing the set-aside in that jurisdiction [or] substantial and justifiable doubts [exist] about the integrity or independence of the rendering court with respect to the judgment in question'. See discussion in Park (n 21) 314.

[29] See, eg, Adrian Briggs, 'Crossing the River by Feeling the Stones: Rethinking the Law on Foreign Judgments' (2004) 8 Sing YIL 1.

Part XI

PUBLIC POLICY AND ABUSE OF PROCESS

32

PUBLIC POLICY RULES IN ENGLISH ARBITRATION LAW

*Stavros Brekoulakis**

A. Introduction

Public policy is a key concept for international arbitration, being both theoretically complex and practically relevant. It is theoretically complex because any discussion about public policy necessarily implicates the foundations of arbitration and its relationship with state interests. It is practically relevant because public policy is enshrined in the New York Convention and almost all national laws as a ground to resist enforcement or to annul an arbitral award. Above all, public policy is a dynamic concept that constantly evolves. 32.01

It is perhaps because of its theoretical complexity and dynamic nature that the public policy exception 'has been interpreted erratically by the courts and is probably the most misused ground of all [in the New York Convention]'.[1] Equally, arbitration literature on public policy seems to be informed more by conventional wisdom than critical examination. It is interesting to see that the majority of arbitration literature as well as all the main textbooks in international arbitration offer broadly the same account of public policy, as a general principle almost exclusively associated with 'basic notions of morality and justice'.[2] It is also amusing to note that almost all articles on public policy cannot resist reiterating Burrough J's famous description of public policy as an unruly horse from almost two centuries ago,[3] a phrase which apparently highlights the open-ended and constantly evolving nature of the doctrine. 32.02

Has the discussion on public policy in international arbitration settled then? We believe not. In fact, we think that there are a number of areas related to the doctrine of public policy that must be revisited, including the very concept of public policy, its function, and its limitations. As explained in Part D below, it is posited that the doctrine of public policy that is currently adopted by legal discourse in arbitration is conceptually and 32.03

---

* This chapter is a part of the forthcoming book Audley Sheppard and Stavros Brekoulakis, *Public Policy and Mandatory Laws in International Arbitration: A Common Law Perspective* (OUP 2016).

[1] Jan Paulsson, 'The New York Convention in International Practice—Problems of Assimilation' in Mark Blessing (ed), *The New York Convention of 1958* (ASA Special Series No 9, 1996) 100, 113.

[2] Julian D M Lew and others, *Comparative International Commercial Arbitration* (Kluwer Law International 2003) 26–114. See also ILA, Committee on International Commercial Arbitration, *Final Report on Public Policy as a Bar to Enforcement of Public International Awards* (New Delhi Conference, 2002).

[3] In *Richardson v Mellish* (1824) 2 Bing 229, 252.

methodologically confusing, and outdated. It is conceptually confusing because there is usually no explanation about how the content of public policy is ascertained or whether the doctrine functions as a legal principle or a set of legal rules. Furthermore, the arbitration discourse on public policy primarily takes place in a transnational terrain. Here, the influence of Lalive's seminal work on the concept of truly transnational public policy (or *ordre public international*) has been so dominant that we often forget that the concept of public policy has always had strong associations with national states, and its primary purpose was to give effect to public interests of states. Despite extensive research on the field of transnational business communities and law, the corroborative concept of transnational public policy lacks coherence and remains more desired than real. We believe that the doctrine of public policy, as a structured set of legal rules, can be better conceived of as a doctrine of national law.

32.04 Equally, it is believed that the rules of public policy can be ascertained from a careful analysis of the historical context and jurisprudential development of the doctrine. Accordingly, for the purposes of our study, we first look into the concept and function of public policy in English law and jurisprudence and then narrow the focus of our examination on the role of public policy in English private international law, before we finally ascertain the rules of public policy in English arbitration law. Such a broad approach to the subject of our study not only allows us to ascertain clear rules of public policy in English arbitration law, but it also enables broader conclusions about the suitability of the concept of transnational public policy that currently prevails in international arbitration.

B. Public Policy in English Law

(a) Historical development of public policy in English law

32.05 The enquiry into public policy in English law brings us directly into the centre of a broader jurisprudential debate.[4] Is public policy a general principle of an open-ended nature or a legal rule identified with the policy of the law? Judicial function would differ considerably in these two different jurisprudential accounts of public policy. In the former, judges would be accorded a wide range of discretion to ascertain the content of public policy.

32.06 Judges would even have the authority to decide on questions of political expedience, which are typically left for the legislature. In the latter account, judges would need to ascertain the content of the doctrine by reference to more precise legal rules, as embodied in the text of law. To understand the present state of English law on public policy we must first look into the historical development of the doctrine, whose conceptual origins are traced back many centuries ago.

32.07 Public policy's antecedent might be found as early as in 1413 where a condition in suit was declared to be 'encounter common ley'.[5] Winfield, in his seminal study on the subject, noted that the concept of public policy was unconsciously or half consciously pervading, albeit under several different names, the whole English legal system at a time when little

---

[4] See John Shand, 'Unblinkering the Unruly Horse: Public Policy in the Law of Contract' (1972) 30(1) CLJ 144.
[5] W S M Knight, 'Public Policy in English Law' (1922) 38 LQR 207.

statutory or common law existed and the majority of cases would raise new legal matters for English judges. In those times, when English judges laid down a new rule or moderated existing rules that were harsh, they did it for nothing else but for the benefit of the public.[6] Even in the sixteenth and seventeenth centuries, the concept of public policy remained in disguise under widely abstract terms which allowed judges to fill gaps in the law on the basis of considerations of what was good for the community.[7]

32.08 Public policy started to acquire more precise meaning and technical shape, albeit not a definite conception, much later. In the eighteenth century, case law and statutes were becoming increasingly dense and they were covering increasingly more ground in English law which was previously occupied by abstract legal concepts, such as reason, convenience, and policy. As a result, the idea of public policy ceased being a pervasive concept underpinning English law as a whole, and started shrinking to certain legal fields,[8] such as agreements in restraint of law,[9] the rule against perpetuities,[10] contracts tainted by fraud, and marriage contracts.[11] At the same time, terms such as 'public utility' and 'public offices' began to appear in decisions more often.[12]

32.09 But although it had lost its all-pervasive nature, public policy in the eighteenth century remained an open-ended concept that was largely considered as a valid basis for judicial legislation.[13] So wide was the range of discretion accorded to English judges in the eighteenth century that they had authority to invalidate a contract, which was otherwise not prohibited by law or legal precedent, if they considered the contract to be against principles of morality or sound policy.

32.10 For example, in *Jones v Randall* (1774),[14] an action was brought for the recovery of money won upon a wager. The wager was prohibited neither by statute nor previous case law. Nevertheless, said Lord Mansfield, the validity of a contract that is prohibited by neither positive law nor precedent will be decided upon 'principles of morality' and 'sound policy'.

32.11 He noted:

> The law of England would be a strange science indeed if it were decided upon precedents only. Precedents serve to illustrate principles, and to give them a fixed certainty. But the law of England, which is exclusive of positive law, enacted by statute, depends upon principles; and these principles run through all the cases according as the particular circumstances of each have been found to fall within the one or other of them.[15]

32.12 These principles, Lord Mansfield declared, are either 'principles of morality' or 'principles of sound policy'. Being such an open-ended concept, public policy made it difficult

---

[6] Percy Winfield, 'Public Policy in the English Common Law' (1928) 42 Harv L Rev 77.
[7] Knight (n 5) 207.
[8] Winfield (n 6) 84.
[9] *Michel v Reynolds* (1711) 1 P Wms 181.
[10] *Howard v Duke of Norfolk'* (1681–5) 3 Ch Cas 1.
[11] *The Earl of Chesterfield v Sir Abraham Janssen* (1750) 1 Atk 301.
[12] ibid 353 ('So in bargains to procure offices, neither of the parties is defrauded or unapprized of the terms, but it serves to introduce unworthy objects into publick offices; and therefore, for the sake of the public, the bargain is rescinded').
[13] Winfield (n 6) 86.
[14] (1774) I Cowp 37.
[15] ibid [39].

to distinguish legal reasoning from political expedience. In *The Earl of Chesterfield v Sir Abraham Janssen*, the court held that:

> Political arguments, in the fullest sense of the word, as they concern the government of a nation, must, and have always been of great weight in the consideration of this court, and tho' there may be no dolus malus, in contracts as to other persons, yet if the rest of mankind are concerned as well as the parties, it may properly be said, that it regards the publick [sic] utility.[16]

32.13 As English statutory and case law further evolved in the nineteenth century, giving clear shape to legal principles and laying down legal rules, the account of public policy as a form of judicial legislation was about to be challenged. This was a period during which judges started looking at public policy in more critical terms, and began to realize that the wide scope and fluid nature of the doctrine had to be constrained 'unless it was to thrust them into a position which Parliament alone could occupy, or to infect with a virus of uncertainty principles which had long been settled by case law'.[17] It is no coincidence that the famous reference to public policy as an 'unruly horse' was made at that time.[18] Burrough J aptly articulated a general feeling of unease among the majority of judges of the time that the doctrine of public policy as a general principle of law had the potential to disturb the delicate balance of powers between the parliament and the judiciary.

32.14 Against this background of judicial disquiet towards public policy, the outcome of the landmark decision in *Egerton v Brownlow*,[19] in the middle of the eighteenth century, came as a surprise. In his will, the Earl of Bridgewater had devised large real estates in favour of Lord Alford with the caveat that if he died without having acquired the title of Duke or Marquis of Bridgewater, the gift would be void. While the legal question was whether the caveat was valid or void as against public policy, the stakes in Egerton were much higher, namely whether public policy was to be reduced to a mere legal construct for judges to ascertain the policy of any particular statutory or common law rule or whether public policy was to operate as a general legal principle whereby judicial function would border on judicial legislation. The judges were summoned by the House of Lords to give their views. The vast majority of them opined that public policy was the policy of the law only. They noted that an activity or a contract would be illegal as against public policy only when it is contrary to principles established by law, rather than when it is considered inexpedient by judges. Baron Parke expressed this view forcefully, observing:

> Public policy is a vague and unsatisfactory term, and calculated to lead to uncertainty and error, when applied to the decision of legal rights. It is the province of the statesman, and not the lawyer, to discuss, and of the Legislature to determine, what is best for the public good, and to provide for it by proper enactments. It is the province of the judge to expound the law only ... [W]e are not ... authorised to establish as law everything which we may think for the public good, and prohibit everything which we think otherwise.[20]

32.15 However, the view of the majority of the judges was dismissed. Instead, the House of Lords endorsed the view of Lord Chief Baron Pollock who offered an account of public policy that amounted to a legal principle allowing judges wide discretion to decide any new case that may arise on the basis of what judges consider to be good for the 'public welfare':

---

[16] *The Earl of Chesterfield* (n 11) [352].
[17] Winfield (n 6) 86.
[18] *Richardson* (n 3) [28.02] (Burrough J).
[19] *Egerton v Brownlow* (1853) 4 HL Cas 1.
[20] ibid 123.

My Lords, after all these authorities, am I not justified in saying that, were I to discard the public welfare from my consideration, I should abdicate the functions of my office—I should shrink from the discharge of my duty? I think I am not permitted merely to follow the particular decisions of those who have had the courage to decide before me, but in a new and unprecedented case to be afraid of imitating their example. I think I am bound to look for the principles of former decisions, and not to shrink from applying them with firmness and caution to any new and extraordinary case that may arise.[21]

32.16 To appreciate why the House of Lords chose political expedience over statutory law and legal precedent, we must remember that Egerton was decided at a time when the majority of Peers were not judges. It was only after the law reform of 1873 and the Appellate Jurisdiction Act 1876 that the House of Lords was placed on proper judicial footing, and provisions were made for senior and experienced judges to be appointed as Lords of Appeal.[22] The law reform in the 1870s and the shift in the judicial function of the House of Lords may also explain why, Egerton notwithstanding, judges in the late nineteenth century remained doubtful and increasingly sceptical of a fluid concept of public policy, akin to political expedience.[23]

32.17 Such scepticism against an open-ended concept of public policy soon found its way into jurisprudence, as is apparent from a number of cases in the beginning of the twentieth century,[24] most notably *Janson v Driefontein Consolidated Mines*.[25] Here, Lord Halsbury shrunk the scope of the doctrine to the confines of the law when he stated that public policy:

> Does not leave at large to each tribunal to find that a particular contract is against public policy … you may say that it is because [certain things] are contrary to public policy they are unlawful, but it is because these things have been either enacted or assumed to be by the common law unlawful, and not because a Judge or Court have a right to declare that such and such things are in his or their view contrary to public policy.

32.18 In the course of the twentieth century, the concept of public policy evolved away from the generalizations of the earlier years into a much more structured doctrine. English courts not only kept public policy confined to certain areas of law; they also developed certain public policy rules and tests for each of those areas.

32.19 For example, the public policy rule in the field of restraint of trade is that contracts that unreasonably purport to restrain a person as to how he will exercise his trade in the future are against public policy.[26] The test of reasonableness, which allows English courts to perform a balancing exercise taking account of the interests of the parties concerned and the interests of the public, was pronounced by Lord Macnaghten in *Nordenfelt v Maxim Nordenfelt Guns and Ammunition*:

> The true view at the present time, I think, is this: The public have an interest in every person's carrying on his trade freely: so has the individual. All interference with individual

---

[21] ibid 149.
[22] I am grateful to HH Humphrey Lloyd for this observation.
[23] Knight (n 5) 212–13 and John Bell, *Policy Arguments in Judicial Decisions* (OUP 1983) 157.
[24] See, eg, *Elliman v Carrington* [1901] 2 Ch 275: 'It is said that the contract is against public policy; but that phrase merely embodies, for the present purpose, the great principle of restraint of trade, and to say that it is to prevent [the Claimant] from exercising their own discretion seems to me to be applying a well-settled principle of law to facts to which it cannot have any possible application.'
[25] [1902] AC 484, 491.
[26] See Bell (n 23) 157ff.

liberty of action in trading, and all restrains of trade of themselves, if there is nothing more, are contrary to public policy and therefore void. That is the general rule. But there are exceptions: restraints of trade and interference with individual liberty of action may be justified by the special circumstances of a particular case. It is a sufficient justification and indeed it is the only justification, if the restriction is reasonable—reasonable that is, in reference to the interests of the parties concerned and reasonable in reference to the interests of the public, so framed and so guarded as to afford adequate protection to the party in whose favour it is imposed, while at the same time it is in no way injurious to the public.[27]

32.20 In the field of illegal contracts the underpinning justification of public policy stems from the Latin maxim *ex turpi causa non oritur action*, so that 'no court will lend its aid to a man who founds his cause of action upon an immoral or an illegal act'.[28] While the *ex turpi* principle (or 'policy' according to Lord Hoffmann in *Gray v Thames Trains Ltd*[29]) is helpful as a guideline, its scope and content is abstract. Accordingly, English courts have evolved and applied more specific public policy tests, including the test of 'reliance',[30] the test of 'inextricable link',[31] and more recently the 'test of consistency' to decide the illegality defence.[32] In *Gray v Thames Trains Ltd*, the House of Lords laid down the public policy rule that a claimant is precluded from claiming loss of earnings and general damages he has suffered in consequence of his criminal act; the civil law must be consistent with any criminal sentence already imposed. Lord Hoffmann observed that this public policy rule is justified 'on the ground that it is offensive to public notions of the fair distribution of resources that a claimant should be compensated (usually out of public funds) for the consequences of his own criminal conduct'.[33]

32.21 Overall, English courts over the course of the last two centuries have developed public policy rules which are mostly clear and well defined, to the point that the modern concept of public policy has been criticized as inflexible and unjust.[34] While it may serve as a useful reminder of the remarkable evolution of the doctrine from a nebulous concept to a set of structured legal rules, such criticism is mostly unfounded for two reasons. First, as is generally accepted, public policy applies not only in cases where common law rules are settled, but also in new situations.[35] When new situations raise novel legal points, public policy will still operate as a general legal principle, rather than a rigid legal rule. Second, although the concept of English public policy has taken a visible, even technical, shape, many of the underpinning justifications and public policy tests are broad, allowing a considerable

---

[27] [1894] C 535, 565.
[28] See Lord Mansfield's well-known dictum in *Holman v Johnson* (1775) 1 Cowp 341, 343: 'The principle of public policy is this; *ex dolo malo non oritur actio*. No court will lend its aid to a man who founds his cause of action upon an immoral or an illegal act'.
[29] *Gray v Thames Trains Ltd* [2009] 1 AC 1339, 1370 F.
[30] In *Tinsley v Milligan* [1994] 1 AC 340, the House of Lords held that the illegality defence applies when the claimant needs to plead or lead evidence of illegality in order to establish his claim in the first place.
[31] As Beldam LJ stated in *Cross v Kirkby*, *The Times*, 5 April 2000: 'Claimant's claim is so closely or inextricably bound up with his own criminal or illegal conduct that the court could not permit him to recover without appearing to condone the conduct'.
[32] See Paul Davies, 'The Illegality Defence and Public Policy' (2009) 125 LQR 556.
[33] *Gray* (n 29).
[34] See Shand (n 4) 165: 'For the judges have themselves reacted from the broad and vaporous concept of public policy and reduced it to a set of rules whose operation is predictable and whose application is obligatory and not a matter of discretion.'
[35] See Bell (n 23) 157.

degree of discretion to the courts to adapt the rules of public policy to changes in economic and social conditions.[36]

32.22 In this regard, one of the most important tenets of *Egerton* is still alive today. The Lords in Egerton rejected the view of the majority of the judges that the concept of public policy was nothing more than the policy of the law. Despite the limitations they placed upon the doctrine over the course of the last century in particular, English courts never returned to such a narrow conception of public policy. Accordingly, judges riding the horse of public policy can go well beyond the policy of the common or statutory law, and consider, for example, that a contract is void as against public policy, even if such a contract is not against a legal rule.[37]

32.23 Of course, and this is where the modern concept of the doctrine has deviated from Egerton, judges have bounded discretion to decide what is against public policy. This is not a decision that will be taken on the basis of 'opinions of men of the world as distinguished from opinions based on legal learning'.[38] Rather, it is a decision that will be taken on the basis of certain legal principles and with the benefit of jurisprudentially developed tests on public policy.

(b) Public policy in English private international law

32.24 In English private international law, public policy operates as a ground for English courts to refuse to apply a foreign law or to recognize or enforce a foreign judgment on the grounds that the foreign law or the foreign judgment are inconsistent with certain aspects of English public policy. Thus, the private international law function of public policy differs from the ordinary function of public policy in English domestic law. Whereas in domestic law public policy typically invalidates a contract by overriding party autonomy, in private international law public policy overrides the act of a foreign legislature or judiciary.

32.25 This observation underscores the sensitivity of the judicial function of English courts when deciding whether to exclude a foreign law, or refuse to enforce a foreign judgment. Thus, the question of public policy in English private international law becomes a matter of the acceptable degree of tolerance of different legal traditions or values.[39] It requires English courts to examine the content of a foreign law or a foreign judgment, which in itself is a highly exceptional power, and make a value assessment of the foreign law and foreign judgment on the basis of the legal values and conceptions of English law.

32.26 We can roughly distinguish between two groups of foreign contracts and judgments that require a private international law (or conflict-of-laws) analysis. First, when a contract is legal under foreign law, but illegal under English law. In this case and unless the contract is unacceptably repugnant, such as the sale of slaves or the sale of illegal drugs, English courts will not necessarily refuse enforcement of the ensuing judgment. As is generally accepted, English courts may enforce a foreign judgment even if the outcome of the foreign judgment

---

[36] ibid 158.
[37] Hugh G Beale, *Chitty on Contracts* (31st edn, Sweet & Maxwell 2012) para 16.004.
[38] *Rodriguez v Speyer Bros* [1919] AC 59 (Lord Haldane).
[39] Alex Mills, 'The Dimensions of Public Policy in Private International Law' (2008) 4 J Priv Int'l L 213.

is different from that which would be under English law.[40] As has been held, 'the [English] court will be even slower to invoke public policy in the field of conflict of laws than when a purely municipal legal issue is involved'.[41]

32.27 Second, when a contract is illegal under foreign law, but legal under English law. In these circumstances, and unless the underlying contract is a contract to commit a criminal offence in a foreign country,[42] English courts will normally give effect to the policy favouring the enforcement of foreign judgments.[43] English courts have repeatedly held that under private international law rules they are mainly concerned with the enforcement of the foreign judgment, not the underlying contract.[44]

32.28 In the rare circumstances where a foreign contract was refused enforcement on the ground of violating English public policy, the underlying contract was illegal under both English law and the law of the place of performance. For example, in the leading case of *Lemenda Trading Co Ltd v African Middle East Petroleum Co Ltd*,[45] the defendants, a company registered in London, entered into an agreement with the claimants, a company registered in Nassau, under which the claimants agreed in return for a substantial commission fee to procure the renewal of the contract between the defendants and the national oil corporation of Qatar for oil supply. Under the agreement, the claimants' task was to use personal influence within the Qatari national oil corporation. The oil supply contract was renewed and the claimants brought an action in England to recover commission.

32.29 The English Court noted that had such an agreement been made to procure a contract from a British government body, English courts would refuse to enforce it as against English public policy.[46] However, this was a foreign contract and therefore English courts had to give regard to other policies, including the public policy of the place of performance (in this case Qatar) and international comity. The court accepted evidence that an agreement for the payment of commission to an agent or broker in respect of the negotiation or renewal of any oil supply contract was prohibited by Qatari law and was contrary to public policy in Qatar. Thus, the court held that the agreement was not only against the public policy of

---

[40] See *Cablevision Systems Development Co v Shoupe* (1986) 39 WIR 1; cf P B Carter, 'The Role of Public Policy in English Private International Law' (1993) 42 ICLQ 2 ('The automatic injection of standards applicable in a domestic situation into a transnational situation may be seen, at best as an exercise in mechanical jurisprudence, and at worst as blatant judicial chauvinism').

[41] *Vervaeke v Smith* [1983] 1 AC 145, 164; cf *Kuwait Airways Corp v Iraqi Airways Co* [2002] UKHL 19, 140.

[42] See *Foster v Driscoll* [1929] 1 KB 470.

[43] See Waller LJ in *Westacre Investments Inc v Jugoimport-SDPR Holding Co Ltd* [2000] 1 QB 288, 304G: 'There is also an implied recognition as it seems to me that if all that can be said of a contract is that performance in a foreign country will be contrary to the domestic public policy of that state, enforcement will only be refused if performance would be contrary to the domestic public policy in England. If that were not so, consideration of English public policy would not in fact have been necessary or relevant'.

[44] See *Soinco SACI v Novokuznetsk Aluminium Plant*, The Times, 29 December 1997 and *Westacre Investments Inc v Jugoimport*, ibid 305: 'It would be for example legitimate for a foreign tribunal to take the view (indeed consistent with the English court's own view if I am right on the above implication), that albeit performance was contrary to domestic public policy in its place of performance, since it was not contrary to the domestic public policy either of the country of the proper law and/or the curial law, enforcement should be allowed. It is in this context, in my view, that albeit the award is not isolated from the underlying contract, it is relevant that the English court is considering the enforcement of an award, and not the underlying contract.'

[45] [1988] QB 448.

[46] ibid 458.

English law, but also against the public policy of the place of performance, which in this case was a 'friendly country'.

Phillips J considered that: **32.30**

> The English courts should not enforce an English law contract which falls to be performed abroad where: (i) it relates to an adventure which is contrary to a head of English public policy which is founded on general principles of morality, and (ii) the same public policy applies to the country of performance so that the agreement would not be enforceable under the law of that country. In such a situation international comity combines with English domestic public policy to militate against enforcement.[47]

(c) Public policy in arbitration law

What can the above analysis of public policy in English law tell us for arbitration? First, it shows us that public policy operates in the form of legal rules that are ascertained from a careful analysis of the decisions of English courts. Although the underpinning justifications and tests used by English courts are typically broad, the rules of public policy are mostly clear and well defined. This is the approach that one has to take to ascertain the rules of public policy in arbitration law, at least under English law. Indeed, as is discussed in detail in Part C below, the public policy rules for English arbitration law are mainly drawn from English public policy rules on illegality and private international law. **32.31**

Second, it can enable broader conclusions to be drawn about the function of public policy in law and, by implication, about the suitability of the concept of transnational public policy that currently prevails in international arbitration. If public policy is not a general principle of morality, but a set of structured rules, the concept of transnational public policy or *ordre public international* is ill-defined and unwarranted. This is discussed in Part E of this chapter. **32.32**

C. Public Policy in English Arbitration Law

The notion of public policy in English arbitration law is typically used as a defence against the enforcement of a foreign arbitral award, involving allegations of illegality in respect of the underlying contract. While there are only a limited number of arbitration cases decided on public policy, English courts have drawn on case law and public policy rules in respect of illegal contracts and enforcement of foreign judgments to lay down public policy rules for the enforcement of arbitral awards. It must be noted that, although English courts will usually have regard to the public policy provisions in both the New York Convention and the English Arbitration Act 1996,[48] the rules which English courts will primarily consider and apply are common law rules on public policy. **32.33**

The public policy rules which English courts will apply to decide whether to enforce an award based on an illegal contract are as follows. **32.34**

First, when it is alleged that the underlying contract is illegal as against public policy, the interposition of an arbitral award does not insulate the claim to enforce an award from **32.35**

---
[47] ibid 461D.
[48] See New York Convention, Art V(2)(b) and English Arbitration Act 1996, s 103(3).

the illegality that gave rise to it.⁴⁹ A contract to pay a bribe is unenforceable or void *ab initio* under English law, and consequently an award that enforces a contract to pay a bribe would be unenforceable as contrary to English public policy. Thus, when allegations of illegality contravening English public policy are raised at the enforcement proceedings, English courts will consider the nature of the underlying contract. This does not suggest that English courts will review how arbitrators decided the merits of the case; rather, they will look into the facts as they appear from the award and its reasons.

32.36 In *Soleimany v Soleimany*, the defendant agreed to sell quantities of carpets in the United Kingdom or elsewhere, which the claimant had exported illegally out of Iran. When a dispute over the division of the proceeds of the sale arose between the parties, the dispute was referred to arbitration before the *Beth Din*, which applied Jewish law. The award was issued in favour of the claimant, who then proceeded to enforce the award. At first instance, Langan J allowed enforcement of the award, holding that a contract which is unenforceable due to illegality, becomes enforceable if the procedural law of the arbitration has no regard to the illegality. The Court of Appeal overturned the decision and refused enforcement. The Court of Appeal held that although the arbitrator considered that the illegality of the underlying contract was of no relevance under the law governing the merits of the dispute, it was apparent from the face of the award that the contract was an illicit enterprise.⁵⁰ Apparent evidence of illegality will invite English courts to further enquire into the nature of the underlying contract, and possibly refuse enforcement of the ensuing award.

32.37 Waller LJ stated that:

> An enforcement judge, if there is prima facie evidence from one side that the award is based on an illegal contract, should inquire further to some extent... We do not for one moment suggest that the judge should conduct a full-scale trial of those matters in the first instance. That would create the mischief which the arbitration was designed to avoid. The judge has to decide whether it is proper to give full faith and credit to the arbitrator's award. Only if he decides at the preliminary stage that he should not take that course does he need to embark on a more elaborate inquiry into the issue of illegality.⁵¹

32.38 Second, if the underlying contract or activity violates principles of public policy which are 'of the greatest importance',⁵² the ensuing award will be unenforceable under English law. According to English courts, examples of such universally condemned activities include terrorism, drug trafficking, paedophilia, fraud, or corruption in international commerce.⁵³ In these circumstances, the primary justification for public policy are fundamental principles of morality, so that the award will be unenforceable in England irrespective of whether such an activity is expressly prohibited by law, or what the governing law or the law of the place of performance provide, and despite the policy of the English law favouring the enforcement of arbitral awards. As the Court of Appeal has noted:

---

⁴⁹ *Soleimany v Soleimany* [1999] QB 785, 800A; also accepted by *Westacre* (n 43).
⁵⁰ Waller LJ went on to say: 'it seems to us important to emphasise that we are dealing with a case where it is apparent from the face of the award that (i) the arbitrator rejected the plaintiff's case that he had exported carpets purchased by himself which had then been sold by [the defendant] on his behalf; and (ii) the arbitrator was dealing with what he termed an illicit enterprise under which it was the joint intention that carpets would be smuggled out of Iran illegally', ibid 794F.
⁵¹ ibid 800F.
⁵² See *Westacre* (n 43) 315.
⁵³ ibid 302E.

> Some heads of public policy are based on universal principles of morality... Where a contract infringes such a rule of public policy the English court will not enforce it, whatever the proper law of the contract and wherever the place of performance.[54]

32.39 Third, if the underlying contract does not violate such fundamental principles of morality, but it implicates an activity which is prohibited or illegal, such as a contract for purchase of influence, the decision on whether the award is enforceable under English law will be taken on the basis of a private international law (conflict-of-laws) analysis, which necessitates the performance of a balancing exercise by English courts. In this balancing exercise, moral considerations wane and a number of other considerations come into play, notably the policy of English law to enforce arbitral awards, especially awards that fall under the scope of the New York Convention.

32.40 In *Soinco SACI v Novokuznetsk Aluminium Plant*,[55] NKAP, a state enterprise in the former Soviet Union, entered into long-term contracts with the claimants for the delivery of aluminium. As part of the agreements between the claimants and NKAP, the latter purchased a shareholding both in the claimants and their subsidiaries. Subsequently, NKAP was privatized and ceased all deliveries to the claimants, which commenced arbitration in Zurich.

32.41 In the arbitration, NKAP contended that the contracts with the claimants were invalid, because the contractual obligations to purchase a shareholding were in contravention of Russian exchange control regulations. The arbitral tribunal decided that, even if Russian exchange control regulations were breached, this had no effect upon the main obligation of NKAP to supply aluminium to the claimants. When the claimants sought enforcement of the award in England, NKAP argued that the enforcement would be contrary to English public policy because the underlying contract was illegal. NKAP further argued that enforcement would force NKAP to pay the award and effectively break the law of Russia.

32.42 The Court of Appeal rejected the public policy defence and allowed enforcement of the award. Waller LJ stated:

> I am unpersuaded that it is arguable that under English law enforcement of this award would be contrary to English public policy. The reasons are separate and distinct. First, it is the award with which the English court is concerned and not the underlying contract. The question of illegality having been raised and dealt with by the arbitrators, and there being no requirement as a result to perform some act which English law would regard as illegal under English law or contrary to the recognised morals of this country, the public policy is if anything in favour of abiding by the terms of the [New York Convention] and enforcing the award. Second, in any event if an offence will be committed by NKAP in Russia as a party to the award in paying the same, that is the result of their own failure to obtain the requisite consents, and English public policy would in my view be offended if that relieved that party from its obligation to meet the award.[56]

32.43 Under English law, thus, the private international law rule favouring the enforcement of a foreign award is in itself a rule of public policy.[57] This does not suggest that all foreign awards should be enforced in England. However, English courts will normally be willing

---

[54] *Lemenda* (n 45) (Phillips J) 459A–C.
[55] See n 44.
[56] ibid 735.
[57] See also Mills (n 39) 206.

to give effect to the public policy rule favouring the enforcement of foreign awards, unless exceptional factual circumstances and a number of contravening policies combine to tilt the balance against enforcement. This was clearly the case in *Soleimany v Soleimany*, where it was apparent from the face of the award that the arbitrator was dealing with an enterprise that was illegal under both the place of the performance of the contract and English law, notwithstanding that the contract was found legal under its governing law.

32.44 But the private international law rule of public policy favouring the enforcement of foreign awards under English law will not be easily overturned. In this regard, the well-known case of *Westacre Investments Inc v Jugoimport-SDPR Holding Co Ltd*[58] created a lot of noise and generated a heated debate about the limits of the public policy rule under English law in favour of the enforcement of foreign arbitral awards.

32.45 However, the factual circumstances in *Westacre* were more nuanced than is often stated and, according to the English Court of Appeal they did not warrant the non-enforcement of the foreign award. Westacre and Jugoimport entered into a contract, whereby Westacre would provide consultancy services to Jugoimport for the procurement of contracts for the sale of military equipment to Kuwait. The contract was governed by Swiss law, and provided for settlement of disputes under the ICC Arbitration Rules. Westacre claimed the fee under the contract, and the dispute was referred to arbitration in Geneva.

32.46 At the arbitration, the respondents contended that the contract with Westacre was against public policy because Westacre had bribed persons in Kuwait for the purpose of persuading those persons to exercise their influence in favour of the conclusion of the contract for the sale of military equipment to Kuwait. It was not suggested before the tribunal that the agreement was entered into with the intention that Westacre would or could bribe persons in Kuwait or that Westacre was a vehicle for receiving a bribe. The case of the respondents was simply that the consultancy agreement was actually performed in a way that was corrupt. The tribunal did not find that the bribery allegations had been established and found in favour of the claimants. The respondents sought to set the award aside on the ground that it was contrary to public policy.

32.47 Before the Swiss Federal Tribunal, the defendants this time sought to suggest not only that Westacre had performed the contract by bribing, but that in fact Westacre was a vehicle of a member of the Kuwaiti Government, who through Westacre was claiming a bribe for his role in the procurement of the military equipment by Kuwait. The Swiss Federal Tribunal heard evidence by the arbitrators that the respondents in the arbitration never relied on the role of the member of the Kuwaiti Government. The Swiss Federal Tribunal admitted that the new allegations, if proved, would make the agreement void under Swiss law, as against public policy, but on the basis of what was pleaded before the arbitral tribunal the award did not contravene Swiss public policy.

32.48 Unlike a contract to bribe, a contract to lobby is not contrary to public policy in Switzerland. Westacre then sought to enforce the award in England, but Jugoimport applied to set aside the leave to enforce on the ground that enforcement of the award would be contrary to English public policy. Before English courts, the defendants contented that the enforcement of the award would violate English public policy on the grounds that the contract

---

[58] See n 43.

with Westacre was effectively an agreement to pay the member of the Kuwaiti Government a bribe. To that effect, the defendants adduced new evidence in the form of an affidavit.

32.49 While the main question before the English courts turned out to be whether a party in enforcement proceedings is entitled to prove the question of illegality of the main contract by relying on new evidence,[59] the Court of Appeal looked into English rules on public policy too, stating that whether an award that enforces a contract for bribe is unenforceable under English law depends not only on English law, but also on the attitude of the law of the place of performance towards that contract. In this regard, the Court of Appeal distinguished the facts in *Westacre* from the facts in *Soleimany*, in that in the latter it was plain on the face of the award that the award was enforcing a contract that was unlawful at the place of performance.

32.50 By contrast, in *Westacre*, there was nothing in the award to suggest that a contract for the purchase of personal influence short of bribery would be contrary to the public policy of the place of performance, namely Kuwait. Furthermore, and this was a new element in the English public policy rules for enforcement of foreign awards, the Court of Appeal took account of the attitude of not only the place of performance of the contract, but also the place of the arbitration, in this case Switzerland, observing that the contract was neither illegal nor against public policy under Swiss law.

32.51 Waller LJ concluded that 'there is nothing which offends English public policy if an arbitral tribunal enforces a contract which does not offend the domestic public policy under either the proper law of the contract or its curial law, even if English domestic public policy might have taken a different view'.[60]

D. Evidence of Violation of Public Policy in English Arbitration Law

32.52 The pro-arbitration policies underpinning English rules on public policy become clearer from the kinds of evidence which English courts are willing to admit when deciding on the enforceability of an arbitral award, as opposed to the evidence they admit when deciding on the enforceability of a foreign judgment.

32.53 Under English common law, a person against whom a foreign judgment has been given is allowed to resist enforcement simply on the basis that the foreign judgment was obtained by corrupt evidence, such as perjury, notwithstanding that the truth of that evidence was an issue before the foreign court.[61] English courts typically treat allegations of fraud in the foreign proceedings as a matter of great significance, allowing a party to rely on evidence of fraud which was examined but rejected by the foreign court or which was not relied upon at the foreign proceedings, albeit available at the time.

32.54 This clearly distinguishes the treatment of domestic from foreign judgments. As Dicey and Morris note, an attempt to resist a domestic judgment on the basis that it was obtained by fraud will be summarily dismissed, unless the plaintiff:

> can produce evidence newly discovered since the trial, which evidence could not have been produced at the trial with reasonable diligence, and which is so material that its production

---

[59] See Part D, below.
[60] *Westacre* (n 43) 305C–D.
[61] *Aboulojf v Oppenheimer & Co* (1882) 10 QBD 295.

at the trial would probably have affected the result, and (when the fraud consists of perjury) so strong that it would reasonably be expected to be decisive at the rehearing and if unanswered must have that result.[62]

32.55 The justification for the different treatment between domestic and foreign judgments is that an English court will naturally refrain from questioning the decision of another English court which has examined and rejected, on the evidence before it, allegations of fraud. An English court will accept to review allegations of fraud only if new decisive evidence has been discovered in the meantime. The same applies for judgments coming from a member state of the European Union.[63]

32.56 The Brussels Convention and subsequent Regulations have created a harmonized legal framework based on the fundamental principle of mutual trust which warrants the facilitation of enforcement of EU judgments. Within Europe, a judgment coming from a Member State is not a foreign judgment; rather, it is a European judgment, which is accorded similar treatment to domestic judgments. Accordingly, English courts will not reopen allegations of fraud when deciding whether a 'European judgment' is enforceable, unless there is new evidence of corruption.[64]

32.57 However, English courts will not be willing to show the same level of deference and trust in the decision of a foreign court, other than a court of a European Member State, and they will routinely reopen the issue of fraud, even on the basis of evidence that was examined and rejected by the foreign court.

32.58 It is thus very interesting to observe that foreign arbitral awards, under English law, are accorded the same deferential treatment as a domestic English or a European judgment. While a foreign judgment can be attacked on grounds of fraud without any requirement that the evidence be newly discovered and material to the outcome of the rehearing, a foreign arbitral award cannot. The Court of Appeal decision in *Westacre*[65] illustrates the point.

32.59 In *Westacre*, there was new evidence in the form of an affidavit supporting the defendants' allegation that the contract was in fact a contract to bribe rather than just a contract to lobby. More importantly, the defendants sought to rely on the fraud defence, namely that the award was obtained by fraud, because some witness testimonies were perjured. The defendants alleged that Westacre dishonestly put forward the case at the arbitration that the agreement was a genuine consultancy agreement, although according to the defendants the agreement was a vehicle for bribery and corruption. However, English courts refused to admit new evidence of fraud and revisit the issue of illegality. The Court of Appeal concluded:

> If it is open to a party to seek to get an enforcing court to retry issues of fact which the arbitrators had before them, and which they had to and did determine, it would appear to present an

---

[62] Lord Collins of Mapesbury and others (eds), *Dicey, Morris and Collins on the Conflicts of Laws* (12th edn, Sweet & Maxwell 1993).

[63] In *Interdesco SA v Nullifire Ltd* [1992] 1 Lloyd's Rep 180, Phillips J noted that, for Brussels Convention judgments, the rule in the *Aboulof* case had no application because English courts are generally not entitled to review the findings of another Member State court where the same points had been in issue before it.

[64] See Brussels I Regulation Recast, Recital 26, which provides: 'Mutual trust in the administration of justice in the Union justifies the principle that judgments given in a Member State should be recognised in all Member States without the need for any special procedure.'

[65] See n 43.

open invitation to disappointed litigants to relitigate their disputes by alleging perjury, and a major inroad would be made into the finality of Convention awards.[66]

The justification for this rule lies with the clear policy of English law, embodied in the English Arbitration Act 1996, favouring the enforcement of foreign awards, especially awards under the New York Convention. Waller LJ observed:

32.60

> It is difficult to think that if under section 68(2)(g) [of the Arbitration Act 1996] it were suggested an award had been obtained by fraud and that relief under Section 68(3) [of the Act] should be granted, the court would not insist on the same condition, ie, unavailability of the evidence produced as at the time of the arbitration, and that such evidence would have had an important influence on the result.[67]

This pro-enforcement policy of the English Arbitration Act 1996 is thus elevated in a rule of English public policy, so that a person is not allowed to resist the enforcement of an arbitral award on the basis of fraud, unless he can rely on newly discovered evidence.

32.61

E. Conclusion

As already mentioned, the above analysis on public policy rules in English law and English arbitration law in particular can enable broader observations about the function of public policy in law and about the suitability of the concept of transnational public policy in international arbitration.

32.62

Transnational public policy was conceptualized by arbitration scholars as a legal construct in order to support the aspired concept of a truly transnational arbitration, namely the concept of a legally autonomous arbitration that is subject to no national legal system.[68] The project of transnational (autonomous) arbitration was the brainchild of liberal—mainly continental—arbitration lawyers, such as Fouchard, Goldman, and, of course, Lalive.

32.63

Having lived, studied, and worked in a number of different countries, these international arbitration lawyers naturally developed a strong international outlook and a unique appreciation of different legal cultures and traditions. Having developed a strong belief in the reformist power of international law, they conceptualized a body of substantive and procedural norms which are shared universally and which therefore comprise transnational public policy.

32.64

According to Lalive, the arbitration theorist and practitioner who widely introduced the concept of transnational public policy in the 1980s, 'the international arbitrator does have, and is bound by, a private international law, but ... such private international law can only be a "transnational" one, constituted as it is by a number of general principles, either common to all the parties (including States) concerned by a given case, or universal'. More recently, Gaillard with his treatise on the 'Legal Theory of International Arbitration'[69] and

32.65

---

[66] ibid 306.
[67] ibid 307.
[68] See also Mills (n 39) 215.
[69] Emmanuel Gaillard, *Legal Theory of International Arbitration* (Martinus Nijhoff 2010), who notes that the content of truly international public policy is to be determined on the basis of a 'comparative law

Paulsson with his monograph on 'The Idea of Arbitration'[70] have further developed the concept of substantive transnational public policy, whereas Lew has theorized on transnational procedural public policy.[71]

32.66 For transnational arbitration scholars, transnational public policy (or *ordre public international*) was meant as a constitutional framework of moral and legal norms which would lend support to the concept of autonomous transnational arbitration and enhance its integrity. Relying on transnational public policy, international tribunals would always be able to refuse to enforce repugnant contracts, irrespective of the law chosen by the parties. More importantly, if international tribunals had a duty to observe transnational public policy, national courts would have fewer reasons to scrutinize international arbitral awards.

32.67 Despite its intellectual appeal, the concept of transnational public policy in arbitration raises a number of questions. First, it is doubtful whether it can effectively preserve the integrity of international arbitration. *Ordre public international* is a slender version of international public policy which comprises the lowest common denominator of the very fundamental state policies.[72] Such a narrow concept of international public policy naturally fails to cover anything more than the very obvious, blatant, and really uncommon cases of violation of international law, such as 'drug or human organ trafficking', 'violation of embargo or boycott laws', 'assembling mercenary army to support an insurrection against a legitimate government', 'agreements to transport children intended for slavery or under age labour', 'supplying armaments to a terrorist organisation and the supply of illicit drafts', 'bribery and corruption of public officials', and 'smuggling of goods of individuals into another country'.[73] Although public policy was always seen as a dynamic concept, *ordre public international* in effect operates as the counterpart of *ius cogens* in public international law.[74] Therefore, *ordre public international* is a rather static concept that fails to take into account the developments of the evolving civilization of arbitration, and it hardly corresponds to the increasing complexity and nuance of contemporary transnational commerce.[75]

32.68 Second, as discussed in the previous parts of this chapter, public policy at least at a national level does not operate as an amorphous, abstract notion of fairness and morality, and it should be clearly distinguished from the legal concept and function of equity.[76] While many of the

---

approach and on the existence of international instruments adopted with respect to specific matters and which reflect a broad consensus among the community of states'.

[70] Jan Paulsson, *The Idea of Arbitration* (OUP 2013).
[71] Julian D M Lew, 'Achieving the Dream: Autonomous Arbitration' (2006) 22 Arb Int'l 179.
[72] Pierre Lalive, 'Transnational (or Truly International) Public Policy and International Arbitration' in Pieter Sanders (ed), *Comparative Arbitration Practice and Public Policy in Arbitration* (ICCA Congress Series No 3, Kluwer Law International 1987) 257, 300.
[73] See for these examples Lew (n 2) paras 17.36ff; Gaillard (n 69) 126, 131; and ibid 290.
[74] Gaillard calls it the counterpart of *ius cogens* in international law. See Gaillard (n 69) 130.
[75] Christopher Gibson, 'Arbitration, Civilization and Public Policy: Seeking Counterpoise between Arbitral Autonomy and the Public Policy Defense in View of Foreign Mandatory Public Law' in Thomas E Carbonneau and Angelica M Sinopole (eds), *Building the Civilization of Arbitration* (Wildy, Simmonds and Hill Publishing 2009) 66: 'public policy informs the developments of the civilization of arbitration, even as concepts of both public policy and civilization continue to evolve ... public policy may play an increasingly significant role within arbitral proceedings themselves, and thus contribute to the aspiration of a common vision and coherent legal system. The public policy defence also serves as an interface for the exchange between arbitral civilization and other external communities, where state interest and sovereignty (reflecting the values of a particular country) are given weight.'
[76] Michael Akehurst, 'Equity and General Principles of Law' (1976) 25 ICLQ 801; Vaughan Lowe, 'The Role of Equity in International Law' (1988–89) 12 Aust YIL 54.

underpinning justifications and tests of public policy are broad, public policy operates in the form of structured legal rules. This contrasts with the very fluid concept of transnational public policy which, as Gaillard has observed, is to be determined on the basis of a 'comparative law approach and on the existence of international instruments adopted with respect to specific matters and which reflect a broad consensus among the community of states'.

32.69 Whether such a 'broad consensus' on international legal norms actually exists and how these legal norms translate into legal rules is open to question. What is important here is not whether there is broad consensus among the 'community of states' about whether, for instance, the principle of a fair hearing is a fundamental norm of transnational public policy. The vast majority of national legal systems would indeed accept such a broad norm as a fundamental one. Rather, the question is how this general norm is distilled in precise legal rules, and how different national courts actually apply such a broad principle. Here, the answer would probably vary considerably in different national legal systems.

32.70 Public policy at such a high level of general legal norms and abstract principles exists only as a matter of legal aspiration. When transnational arbitration scholars talk about principles of transnational public policy that are broadly shared 'among the community of states', they probably mean principles of transnational public policy that ought to be universally shared, according to their own legal and moral considerations. However, public policy does not operate as an ideal.[77] Public policy decisions are not taken on the basis of 'opinions of men of the world as distinguished from opinions based on legal learning'.[78] As discussed in the previous sections, the doctrine of public policy at least in English law evolved from a vague concept akin to reason and natural law into a shaped concept, comprising rules that, despite their wide scope, have clear normative content and are confined to certain areas of law, such as illegality of contracts. Although such a question would go beyond the scope of this study, one would imagine that the concept of public policy in other national laws must have undergone a similar process of delimitation and concretization.

32.71 However, it is doubtful whether such a process of transformation of public policy from abstract norms to legal rules can occur, or at least has occurred in international arbitration. This is for a number of practical as well as theoretical reasons, including, for example, the lack of legal precedent in international arbitration, the dearth of international awards, at least publicized awards, dealing with public policy, and the philosophical stance of many arbitrators who see themselves as service providers rather than arbiters of a transnational arbitration system.

32.72 This leads us to a final observation which is also our central thesis not only for this chapter, but also for our forthcoming book on public policy:[79] that public policy in law, and certainly in international arbitration law, operates as a structured set of rules, the primary purpose of which is to give effect to state public interest.

---

[77] William Holder, 'Public Policy and National Preferences: The Exclusion of Foreign Law in English Private International Law' (1968) ICLQ 951, referring to the statement of Lord Parker relating to domestic public policy in *Daimler Co Ltd v Continental Tyre and Rubber Co Ltd* [1916] 2 AC 307, 344.
[78] See *Rodriguez v Speyer Bros* (n 38) (Lord Haldane).
[79] Audley Sheppard and Stavros Brekoulakis, *Public Policy and Mandatory Laws in International Arbitration: A Common Law Perspective* (OUP 2016).

33

THE ROLE OF ABUSE OF PROCESS IN PROTECTING THE INTEGRITY OF ARBITRATION AWARDS

David J Sandy

A. Introduction

33.01 Parties readily agree that arbitration awards should be final and binding. Quite often they agree to comply with any award immediately and without delay. But once an award is issued, the losing party often takes a rather different view of those obligations. That party might commence a second set of proceedings on slightly different grounds from the first (so that strict principles of *res iudicata* are not applicable) in an attempt to raise doubt over the status and enforceability of the first award and/or to delay enforcement.

33.02 In England, the doctrine of abuse of process has been utilized to prevent a second action being pursued, the purpose of which is to relitigate issues previously decided or issues which should have been raised in prior proceedings, but where the strict technical requirements of *res iudicata* are not satisfied. The English courts have developed the principle so as to prevent collateral attacks on prior judgments and, now, arbitral awards, and by so doing, ensure the finality of judgments and awards.

33.03 The purpose of this chapter is to outline the reasoning behind these decisions and to ask whether there is a basis upon which such powers should be available in arbitration more generally, whatever the seat, rules, procedural or governing law. Should the principle of abuse of process, in so far as it prevents a collateral attack on a prior arbitration award, be a power which is generally available to tribunals? If so, what is the source of that power and how should it be exercised? Will arbitration benefit from the recognition of this principle?

33.04 This chapter will suggest that the source of the principle of abuse of process (and indeed *res iudicata*) can in most cases be more readily found in the private agreement of the parties rather than having to be located in the public policy of any system of law which might be applicable.

B. The Development of the Principle of Abuse of Process

(a) An English development

33.05 The principle of abuse of process was developed in English law to prevent the relitigation of disputes in circumstances where the strict principles of *res iudicata* (cause of action and issue estoppel) were not available, eg because there was no identity of parties or because the facts or issues raised in the second proceedings were different from those in the first.¹ The leading case in England which defined abuse of process is *Johnson v Gore Wood & Co*.² Johnson was a case where neither cause of action nor issue estoppel were in play as there was no identity of the parties between the two sets of proceedings. In those circumstances, could the plaintiff in the second set of proceedings bring claims similar to those brought by his company in previous proceedings and which had been compromised?

33.06 In that case, Lord Bingham defined abuse of process as follows:

> But *Henderson v Henderson* abuse of process as now understood, although separate and distinct from cause of action estoppel and issue estoppel, has much in common with them. The underlying public interest is the same; that there should be finality in litigation and that a party should not be twice vexed in the same matter. This public interest is reinforced by the current emphasis on efficiency and economy in the conduct of litigation, in the interests of the parties and the public as a whole. *The bringing of a claim or the raising of a defence in later proceedings may, without more, amount to abuse if the court is satisfied (the onus being on the party alleging abuse) that the claim or defence should have been raised in the earlier proceedings if it was to be raised at all.* I would not accept that it is necessary, before abuse may be found, to identify any additional element such as *a collateral attack on a previous decision or some dishonesty, but where those elements are present the later proceedings will be much more obviously abusive*, and there will rarely be a finding of abuse unless the later proceedings involve what the court regards as unjust harassment of a party. It is, however, wrong to hold that because a matter could have been raised in earlier proceedings it should have been, so as to render the raising of it in later proceedings necessarily abuse. This is to adopt too dogmatic an approach to what should in my opinion be a broad, merits-based judgement which takes account of the public and private interests involved and also takes account of all the facts of the case, focusing attention on the crucial question whether, in all the circumstances, a party is misusing or abusing the process of the court by seeking to raise before it the issue which could have been raised before.³

33.07 Abuse of process is thus a more flexible weapon than cause of action or issue estoppel and can operate so as to prevent relitigation of issues which could and should have been brought in prior proceedings, even between different parties.

(b) Abuse of process and collateral attacks on previous judgments

33.08 As Lord Bingham noted above, a collateral attack on a previous decision by raising in subsequent proceedings issues which could and should have been raised in the prior proceedings 'will be much more obviously abusive'.

33.09 This aspect of the application of the abuse of process doctrine was developed in the 2003 case of *Secretary of State for Trade & Industry v Bairstow*.⁴ The Court of Appeal said:

> A collateral attack on an earlier decision of a court of competent jurisdiction may be but is not necessarily an abuse of the process of the courts … If the earlier decision is that of a court

---

¹ But note that conventional *res iudicata* can extend to prevent attempts by privies to relitigate issues which could and should have been raised in earlier proceedings; for a recent case which applies this principle, see the decision of Cooke J in *Deutsche Bank AG v Sebastian Holdings Incorporated and Alexander Vik* [2014] EWHC 2073 (Comm) in which it was held that a third party who was the 100 per cent owner and controller of the defendant company was estopped per *rem iudicatem* from seeking to raise in separate proceedings issues which could and should have been raised in the main proceedings. There is no reason why that principle should not also be applicable in arbitration, at least where English law is applicable.
² [2002] 2 AC 1.
³ Emphasis added.
⁴ [2003] EWCA Civ 321, [2004] Ch 1.

exercising a civil jurisdiction then it is binding on the parties to that action and their privies in any later civil proceedings. If the parties to the later civil proceedings were not parties to or privies of those who were parties to the earlier proceedings then it will only be an abuse of the process of the court to challenge the factual findings and the conclusions of the judge or jury in the earlier action if (i) *it would be manifestly unjust to a party to the later proceedings that the same issues should be re-litigated* or (ii) to permit such re-litigation would bring the administration of justice into disrepute.[5]

(c) Abuse of process and collateral attacks on previous awards

33.10 In the *Bairstow* case, what was in issue was the effect of a prior judgment of the court on subsequent proceedings. What was not decided in that case was whether this type of abuse of process would also be applicable if a party made a collateral attack on a previous decision of an arbitral tribunal.

33.11 That was the issue squarely considered in the English case of *Michael Wilson and Partners v Sinclair*,[6] a decision of Teare J. The claimant brought proceedings against the defendant asserting allegations of wrongdoing that had previously been dismissed in an earlier arbitration between the same claimant and a different respondent. Although the defendant to the litigation, Mr Sinclair, had not himself been a party to the previous arbitration in name, he had financed the defence of that arbitration and was a director of one of the respondents. However, because there was no identity of parties between the respondents to the previous arbitration and Mr Sinclair in the court proceedings, conventional *res iudicata* was not applicable. Further, the claims made in the litigation were not precisely identical to the claims alleged in the arbitration.

33.12 Notwithstanding the lack of identity between the parties and the claims in the two proceedings, Teare J struck out the court proceedings as an abuse of process holding that they constituted a collateral attack on the previous award, basing his decision firmly on the principles set out in the *Bairstow* case. His reasoning was that, in substance, Mr Sinclair had been centrally involved in the previous arbitration as was demonstrated by the fact that he had financed it and was a director of one of the principal respondents. Furthermore, the claims being brought in the court case were, in substance, claims which had been considered and dismissed in the previous arbitration.

33.13 In these circumstances, the judge held that it would be an abuse of process to permit the claimant to continue the litigation and he struck the case out on the basis that it constituted a 'collateral attack on an earlier decision of a court of competent jurisdiction' and that a decision of an arbitral tribunal was equivalent to a decision of a court of competent jurisdiction.

33.14 In the later case of *OMV Petrom SA v Glencore International AG*,[7] Blair J reached the same conclusion as Teare J that the doctrine of abuse of process could arise where there had been a previous arbitration award. In that case, the claimant alleged that it was an abuse

---

[5] ibid (Morritt VC, Potter and Hale LJJ concurring). Emphasis added.
[6] [2012] EWHC 2560 (Comm); see also the judgment of Hamblen J in *Arts and Antiques v Richards* [2013] EWHC 3361 (Comm), in which the judge cited *Sinclair* as authority for the proposition that abuse of process may be relied on where the earlier decision is that of an arbitral tribunal.
[7] [2014] EWHC 242 (Comm), [2014] All ER (D) 78.

of process for the defendant to seek to litigate an issue previously decided against it by an arbitration award in which the defendant had been the respondent, albeit the claimant in the arbitration proceedings was a different but related party to that in the subsequent litigation. The judge expressly cited the decision of Teare J in *Michael Wilson and Partners v Sinclair* in holding that it could be 'an abuse of the process of the court to seek to re-litigate in court proceeding issues which have been the subject of prior proceedings before an arbitral tribunal'.

Blair J went further in holding that it could 'be an abuse of process for a party which was successful overall in earlier proceedings to seek to re-litigate an issue on which it was unsuccessful'. Where abuse of process was under consideration, the judge held that the focus was on 'the undesirability of having the same matter adjudicated upon again where it would be manifestly unfair to do so, or would bring the administration of justice into disrepute'. Having decided that the abuse of process argument was available where the issue had been decided in prior arbitration proceedings, the judge held on the facts that there was no abuse of process in the present case. **33.15**

In further confirmation of this development, Flaux J in *Injazat Technology Capital Ltd v Dr Hamid Najafi*[8] held that the bringing of a second arbitration by a party was an attempt to reopen matters decided in a first arbitration and was an abuse of process. It necessarily follows that the judge formed the view that the process being abused was the arbitral process of the second arbitration rather than any court proceedings. **33.16**

As a matter of English law, there is now little doubt that an argument of abuse of process can be based on a prior arbitral award notwithstanding the fact that there may not be an identity of parties between the two sets of proceedings. **33.17**

(d) Abuse of process as a power available to a tribunal sitting in arbitration in England

In the 2003 Court of Appeal decision in *Hussmann v Pharaon*, Rix LJ held that an arbitral tribunal could itself apply the doctrine of abuse of process: **33.18**

> The trouble with this submission, however, as with the more homespun argument that Mr Pharaon was trying to have 'two bites at the cherry', is that properly analysed, it constitutes a submission that Mr Pharaon had irrevocably elected to have his rights in the arbitration determined solely on the basis that the Respondent was a Company; or that he had waived the right to an award in the name of himself or the Establishment; or that the attempt to seek a second award in the name of himself or the Establishment would amount to an abuse of process (see *Henderson v Henderson* [1843] 3 Hare 100, *Johnson v Gore Wood & Co* [2002] 2 AC 1). We are far from saying that such a submission could not succeed: but it goes either to matters of substantive law (election, waiver) which are for the arbitrators to decide, or to matters of procedure which are equally for the arbitrator. The rule in *Henderson v Henderson* used to be regarded as a branch of the law of res iudicata or issue estoppel; *now it is recognised as being a broader merit-based rule designed to prevent abuse of process (Johnson v Gore Wood): in either event, and however it should be categorised, it is a rule, like any rule of res iudicata or abuse of process, which is for the Tribunal itself to determine* and does not go to the tribunal's substantive jurisdiction but to its willingness to act...[9]

---

[8] [2012] EWHC 4171 (Comm).
[9] [2003] EWCA Civ 266, [2003] 1 All ER (Comm) 879, [85]. Emphasis added.

33.19 In *Nomihold Securities Inc v Mobile TeleSystems Finance SA (No 2)*,[10] Smith J considered whether the defendant, Mobile TeleSystems Finance, could raise in a new arbitration matters which the claimant, Nomihold, asserted it could and should have raised in the first arbitration. The judge said this:

> ... if the new arbitrations proceed, the arbitrators in them would be entitled to determine Nomihold's contention based upon estoppel per rem iudicatam, issue estoppel and what it calls the principle of *Henderson v Henderson* (and might more exactly be called the doctrine of *Smith v Johnson* (15 East 213). *I cannot see, and it was not suggested, that there is any relevant difference between the ambit of the powers available to tribunals in the new arbitrations to dispose of claims and the power that a court would have to dispose of the complaints on the basis of arguments such as Nomihold's re-arbitration complaints, including the principle in Henderson v Henderson.*[11]

C. The Tribunal's Power to Dismiss Proceedings for Abuse of Process

33.20 The position in England, therefore, is that an arbitral tribunal has the same ability as a court to deal with abusive claims in circumstances where one party seeks to bring a second arbitration as a collateral attack on the award in the first. There seems no valid point of distinction between court and arbitration proceedings. Why should only a court be in a position to prevent a collateral attack on a previous arbitration award?

33.21 Since the *Nomihold* and *Injazat* judgments, there has been at least one decision of an arbitral tribunal in an English seat in which a claim has been dismissed for abuse of process as distinct from *res iudicata*. The context in which this arbitration arose is interesting in demonstrating the limitations of strict cause of action or issue estoppel. There had been a previous arbitration in which the tribunal had dismissed claims of misrepresentation in upholding the validity of the contracts in dispute. Allegations of money laundering had been raised but not pleaded or pursued by the losing party to the first arbitration.

33.22 The losing party then commenced a second arbitration against the victorious party under the same contracts that had been the subject of the first arbitration, asserting that they were invalid as a consequence of money laundering allegations raised but not pursued in the first arbitration.

33.23 The respondent in the second arbitration (the successful claimant in the first arbitration) made an application to the tribunal to dismiss the claim on the basis, *inter alia*, of *res iudicata* and/or abuse of process. The experienced tribunal decided that the claims based on money laundering were not precluded by the traditional *res iudicata* doctrine of issue estoppel (it was not asserted that the claim was precluded by cause of action estoppel).

33.24 The tribunal then considered whether the claim in the second arbitration should be dismissed by reference to the doctrine of abuse of process. The tribunal accepted that the concept of abuse of process, as developed in English law, was applicable to an arbitration with an English seat as a matter of procedural law. It rejected the argument by the claimant

---

[10] [2012] EWHC 130 (Comm).
[11] Emphasis added.

that the abuse of process doctrine was only applicable to proceedings in court where there was a public interest to protect (the same conclusion to which the English court had come in the *Sinclair, OMV Petrom*, and *Arts & Antiques* cases). The tribunal considered that the rationale of abuse of process included consideration of private interests; and in any case, there was a public interest in ensuring that arbitrations were conducted properly or, at least, not abusively.

33.25 In light of the authorities considered by the tribunal, the necessary implications drawn from the agreement of the parties in the 1998 LCIA Rules, the tribunal concluded that the doctrine of abuse of process could be applied in appropriate circumstances by a tribunal sitting in England under the LCIA Rules and held that the claims based on money laundering advanced in the second arbitration could and should have been pursued in the first arbitration. Furthermore, the tribunal considered that the bringing of the claims in the second arbitration constituted in effect a collateral attack on the award in the first arbitration as it was the avowed intent of the claimant to the second arbitration to use any award in its favour in that arbitration to prevent enforcement of the first award.

33.26 The tribunal concluded that the motivation behind the bringing of the second arbitration was to raise an unwarranted and indefensible obstacle to the enforcement of the first award and had no doubt that the respondent in the second arbitration was being harassed by the pursuit of that arbitration. Accordingly, the tribunal dismissed the claims made in the second arbitration on the basis of abuse of process without any requirement for a full (and expensive) merits hearing. The principle of abuse of process was utilized to reinforce the final and binding nature of the first award in circumstances where the strict requirements of *res iudicata* were not met.

D. Wider Applicability of the Principle

33.27 As the foregoing makes evident, in the English jurisdiction both courts and arbitral tribunals can and have dismissed claims which constitute collateral attacks on previous awards or judgments. But is there any reason why that power should be confined to tribunals in an English seat or applying English law?

33.28 The source of the doctrine of abuse of process (and in particular that preventing a collateral attack on a previous judgment or award) may suggest an answer. As Lord Bingham observed in *Johnson v Gore Wood*, the public interest underlying abuse of process is the same as that underlying cause of action and issue estoppel, namely that there should be finality in litigation and a party should not be proceeded against twice in the same matter. In the *Bairstow* case, the Court of Appeal focused on the unfairness of the respondent having to relitigate what were in essence the same issues.

33.29 There will, of course, be jurisdictions in which the principle of abuse of process is unknown in the domestic court system and it might be thought anomalous that a tribunal should have the power to dismiss a claim which constitutes a collateral attack on an award in circumstances where the court in that jurisdiction does not have a similar power. However, the distinction may lie in the fact that judgments in many jurisdictions (particularly civil law) do not contain the kind of full reasoning characteristics of common law judgments (where the abuse of process doctrine has been developed). By contrast, most arbitral awards are reasoned in the common law style, and it is therefore much easier to review the reasons set out in the award in order to determine whether the subsequent arbitration represents a collateral attack on that award.[12]

33.30 Support for the wider applicability of the principle of abuse of process can also be found in the 'International Law Association Recommendations on *Lis Pendens* and *Res Judicata* and Arbitration'. Recommendation II.5 states:

> *An arbitral award has preclusive effects in the further arbitral proceedings as to a claim, cause of action or issue of fact or law, which could have been raised, but was not*, in the proceedings resulting in that award, provided that the raising of any such new claim, cause of action or new issue of fact or law amounts to procedural unfairness or abuse…[13]

33.31 It will be seen that this Recommendation was based on extensive discussion among the ILA Committee.[14]

33.32 But the availability of the principle can also be justified by reference to what the parties intended and agreed, as demonstrated by the applicable rules or laws governing the arbitration. Indeed, in most circumstances it is perhaps unnecessary to look to public policy justifications for applying the principles of *res iudicata* or abuse of process. All developed judicial systems recognize some form of *res iudicata*, even if there is no consensus as to the precise content of that principle. Applicability of that principle is, however, complicated by the necessity to identify the system of law which might be applicable to the issue in dispute; is it the substantive governing law, the law of the seat, the law of the enforcing jurisdiction, or some other law? However, if the source of the principle can be found in the agreement of the parties, then this makes it much easier to identify the scope and content of the principle and obviates the need to identify the law which might be applicable to this issue.

E. Arbitration Rules

33.33 Almost all arbitration rules provide that an award will be final and binding. See, by way of example, Article 34.2 of the UNCITRAL Rules ('awards … shall be final and binding on the parties'); Article 34.6 of the ICC Arbitration Rules ('Every award should be binding on the parties'); Article 26.8 of the LCIA Rules ('Every award (including reasons for such award) shall be final and binding on the parties'); Rule 28.9 of the SIAC Rules ('an award should be final and binding on the parties from the date it is made'); Article 24.2 of the HKIAC Rules ('Awards … shall be final and binding on the parties and any person claiming through or under any of the parties'); Article 30.1 of the ICDR Rules ('Awards … shall be final and binding on the parties').

33.34 Curiously, the CIArb Arbitration Rules (2000 edition) had no express provision that an award should be final and binding. However, this has been remedied by Article 34(2) of the 2015 edition of the Rules.

---

[12] Note that the 2014 LCIA Rules state expressly that the 'award (including the reasons for an award) shall be final and binding'.
[13] Emphasis added.
[14] See ILA, 'Interim Report on Res Judicata and Arbitration' (Berlin Conference, 2004) and ILA, 'Final Report on Res Judicata and Arbitration' (Toronto Conference, 2006).

33.35 Most rules also provide that the parties should carry out any award immediately or without delay. See, eg, Article 34.2 of the UNCITRAL Rules ('The parties shall carry out all awards without delay'); Article 34.6 of the ICC Arbitration Rules ('the parties undertake to carry out any award without delay'); Article 26.8 of the LCIA Rules ('the parties undertake to carry out any award immediately and without any delay'); Rule 28.9 of the SIAC Rules ('the parties undertake to carry out the award immediately and without delay'); Article 34.3 of the HKIAC Rules ('The parties undertake to comply without delay with any award'); and Article 30.1 of the ICDR Rules ('The parties shall carry out any such award without delay').

33.36 Again, the CIArb Arbitration Rules (2000 edition) were silent on the obligation of the parties to carry out awards made under those Rules. This has again been remedied by Article 34(2) of the 2015 edition of the Rules.

33.37 Most recognized arbitration laws also provide that awards shall be final and binding; see, by way of example, section 58(1) of the English Arbitration Act 1996, which provides that an award 'is final and binding both on the parties and the persons claiming through or under them'. Article 190.1 of the Swiss PIL also provides that awards shall be final. Interestingly, the new French law on arbitration provides at Article 1484 that an award shall be *res iudicata* with regard to the claims adjudicated in that award. The German ZPO similarly provides that an arbitral award shall have the same effect between the parties as a final and binding court judgment. Article 35(1) of the UNCITRAL Model Law provides that an award shall be 'recognized as binding'.

33.38 Accordingly, through a combination of the relevant rules and law, almost invariably the parties to an arbitration will be taken to have agreed that any award made will be final and binding and that they will carry out any award immediately or without delay. This is supportive of a doctrine of abuse of process in so far as that protects the finality of awards.

F. The New York Convention

33.39 A further and authoritative source of the principle of finality can be found in Article III of the New York Convention, which states:

> Each Contracting State shall recognise arbitral awards as binding and enforce them in accordance with the rules of procedure of the territory where the award is relied upon, upon the conditions laid down in the following article...

33.40 A collateral attack on an award in the second set of proceedings is plainly an attack on the binding nature of such an award and, as such, contrary to the terms of the New York Convention, which sets out in Article V the limited grounds upon which recognition and enforcement of an award may be refused.

G. Is There a Public or Private Interest in Bringing an End to Arbitration?

33.41 It might be argued that there is a public interest in bringing an end to litigation but not a private interest; the resources of the state judicial system should not be abused by relitigation, but the same principle does not apply to private arbitration where the parties pay for the process.

33.42 The cases in England make it clear that the private interests of the parties are just as important as the public interest in bringing an end to abusive proceedings. Thus, in the leading case on collateral attack of *Bairstow*, Vice-Chancellor Morritt held that it would be an abuse of the process of the court to challenge the factual findings and conclusions of the judge or jury in the earlier action in subsequent proceedings involving a different party if 'it would be manifestly unfair to a party to the later proceedings that the same issue should be relitigated'.

33.43 It is clear that the English court took the position that it was the unfairness to a party of the relitigation which was of itself sufficient reason to have proceedings struck out on the basis of abuse of process. In the *Michael Wilson* case, Teare J was strongly influenced by the unfairness which would have been caused to the defendants in the second set of proceedings if those had been allowed to proceed and therefore struck out the proceedings on the basis of abuse of process, notwithstanding the fact that there was no strict identity of parties in the two proceedings.

33.44 The lack of any obvious public interest is therefore not a good reason for not recognizing the principle of abuse of process in arbitration; the private interest of the party is sufficient. Having said that, there is arguably a public interest in ensuring the finality of arbitration as well as litigation. The public resources of the state are utilized to enforce arbitration awards both through domestic procedures and the New York Convention, so there is, to that extent, a public interest in protecting the state process of enforcement of awards from being abused by attempts by private parties to obtain duplicative awards or awards which would have the purpose of undermining previous awards.

H. Conclusion

33.45 The above suggests that there is a sound juridical basis for tribunals to utilize the principle of abuse of process to prevent a second arbitration being brought which has the purpose of undermining the final and binding nature of a previous award (or, indeed, judgment). That power arises from the agreement of the parties; but there is also a public policy interest in preventing abusive arbitration. This is not to suggest that tribunals should have some form of wide-ranging power to punish or prevent any abuse of the arbitral process; the suggestion in this chapter reflects the recommendations of the ILA in arguing that tribunals have a power to prevent parties to a subsequent arbitration raising issues of fact or law which could and should have been raised in prior proceedings if to do so would be unfair to the respondent. This is focused and limited power.

33.46 The English courts have recognized that tribunals sitting in England have this power and, as noted above, such a tribunal has indeed dismissed a second arbitration for abuse of process on the basis that the claims raised in that arbitration could and should have been raised in the prior arbitration. The wider recognition and utilization by tribunals of such a power will have the effect of preserving the integrity of arbitration awards and discouraging abusive challenges to such awards. This surely must be good for the health of arbitration.

Part XII

INTERNATIONAL ARBITRATION
Myths and Perspectives

34

ARBITRATION IN THE UAE
Demystifying the Myths

Gordon Blanke

A. Introduction

There is a general perception in the international arbitration community that arbitration in the Middle East is an untested science and a risky, unpredictable business. Practitioners uninitiated to the practice of arbitration in the Middle East are therefore often misguided into advocating the submission of Middle Eastern disputes to arbitration abroad at—what in their view are—better-suited and more experienced places of arbitration with a more arbitration-friendly judiciary under—what they think are—superior rules of institutional arbitration. This view is one-sided and fails to give credit to the long-standing history of arbitration and ADR more generally in the Middle East. Arbitration in particular has played a determinative role in the formation of the dispute resolution landscape of prominent Middle Eastern jurisdictions since pre-Islamic times[1] and has left an indelible mark in the civil procedure codes of most of these jurisdictions,[2] bar their adoption of the UNCITRAL Model Law in a drive of modernization.[3]

34.01

The UAE in particular has led by example in establishing a modern arbitration jurisdiction that, by and large, meets international standards and best practice. This chapter endeavours to demystify the practice and procedure of arbitration as they prevail in the UAE and show that—contrary to common belief—arbitration the way it is practised there is modern and at times even genuinely *avant-garde*.[4] In other words, especially taking account of its young history, the UAE compares well with other leading, yet longer-established

34.02

---

[1] For a detailed historical overview, see Kaashif Basit, 'United Arab Emirates' in James H Carter (ed), *The International Arbitration Review* (4th edn, Law Business Research 2013) 526–36; and Patrick Bourke, Bilal Ambikapathy, and Andrew Cooke, 'Arbitration in the Gulf: An Overview' in Christian Klausegger and others (eds), *Austrian Arbitration Yearbook* (Manz'sche Verlags- und Universitätsbuchhandlung 2009) 329–42.

[2] See, eg, the provisions on public policy and their in-built notion of the Islamic Shari'ah (cf Art 3 of the UAE Civil Transactions Code).

[3] eg Egypt, which adopted the UNCITRAL Model Law with minor amendments in 1994.

[4] Note that this chapter will primarily focus on the application of the UAE Arbitration Chapter and, to a lesser degree, discuss the ins and outs of the DIFC Arbitration Law, whose provisions—based on the UNCITRAL Model Law—are generally intelligible to international arbitration practitioners and contain few (if any) surprises. For further details on arbitration in the DIFC, see Gordon Blanke, 'Arbitration in the DIFC: Some Initial Insights' in Beata Gessel-Kalinowska vel Kalisz (ed), *The Challenges and the Future of Commercial and Investment Arbitration: Liber Amicorum Professor Jerzy Rajski* (Wolters Kluwer 2015) 587–605.

arbitration jurisdictions in the world and no doubt has grown into a prominent leader—setting standards of arbitral practice and procedure across the Middle East. It serves as a role model for how arbitration in the Middle East has been developing into the preferred dispute resolution mechanism of international commercial disputes in the region and sets the pace for other Middle Eastern jurisdictions to follow suit.

B. The Jurisdictional Landscape of Arbitration in the UAE: Civil v Common

34.03 As is commonly known, the UAE is a civil law jurisdiction, which is divided into a total of seven Emirates: Dubai, Abu Dhabi, Ajman, Sharjah, Ras Al Khaimah, Fujairah, and Umm Al Quwain. Despite its civil law origin,[5] arbitration in the UAE offers a jurisdictional choice that is largely unique worldwide by being seated in the DIFC, a six-acre offshore free zone carved out of the heart of the Emirate of Dubai.[6] The DIFC constitutes a stand-alone offshore common law jurisdiction that is equipped with its own courts and is governed by its own laws, including a self-contained arbitration law, which is based on the UNCITRAL Model Law, the DIFC Arbitration Law.[7]

34.04 As such, the DIFC may be chosen as a legal seat of arbitration, which in turn triggers the application of the DIFC Arbitration Law as the curial law of the arbitration and the competence of the DIFC courts as the curial courts. By contrast, seating an arbitration in mainland Dubai or elsewhere in the UAE, eg in Abu Dhabi, will provoke the application of the arbitration-specific provisions, ie Articles 203 through to 218, and 235, 236 and 238, of the UAE Civil Procedures Code, also known as the UAE Arbitration Chapter.[8] This unique situation, whereby the offshore DIFC offers a common law alternative to the existing civil law framework of the wider onshore UAE, has earned the DIFC a reputation as a 'common law island in a civil law ocean'.[9]

34.05 It is worth noting that both the UAE and DIFC judiciaries are comparatively arbitration-friendly. Presided over by Chief Justice Michael Hwang SC, the DIFC judges in their majority come from a common law background and were often trained in jurisdictions that have an intimate understanding of the importance of and the role played by arbitration in modern legal systems.[10] The UAE judiciary, in turn, even though sometimes regarded with

---

[5] This being said, it is interesting to note that the UAE is, of course, not entirely unfamiliar with common law. In actual fact, before the formation of the Emirates, the then truncal states, which formed an integral part of the British Commonwealth, were largely governed and hence their legal thinking influenced by English law. The re-orientation to a civil law system only materialized after consummation of the Union, taking the Egyptian Civil Code for a blueprint.

[6] On the unique positioning of Dubai on the arbitral dispute resolution landscape of the UAE, including extensive discussions of the role played by the DIFC, see Gordon Blanke and Celine Abi Habib Kanakri, 'Arbitration in Dubai: A Basic Primer' in Christian Klausegger and others (eds), *Austrian Yearbook of International Arbitration* (Manz'sche Verlags- und Universitätsbuchhandlung 2011) 217–55. For an initial insight into the DIFC as a seat of arbitration, see also Gordon Blanke, 'The DIFC: A Brave New World of Arbitration' (2009) 75(3) Arbitration 422.

[7] DIFC Arbitration Law No 1 of 2008 as amended.

[8] For a full article-by-article commentary, see Gordon Blanke, *Annotated Guide to Arbitration in the UAE*, vol I: *The UAE Arbitration Chapter* (Thomson Reuters 2014), electronically available on Westlaw Gulf.

[9] As per the DIFC Courts' Michael Hwang CJ during his address to the Lawasia Conference, Kuala Lumpur, 1 November 2011.

[10] On this question, see also Blanke and Abi Habib Kanakri (n 6) 225–7.

some scepticism by outsiders, have been largely supportive of arbitration. This is in particular borne out by the UAE courts' consistent practice in finding in favour of party autonomy, *kompetenz-kompetenz*, the doctrine of separability,[11] the prohibition of a supervisory court review on the merits,[12] and the partial enforcement of awards in the event of procedural irregularity,[13] on the one hand, and their limited intervention as curial courts in ongoing arbitral proceedings on the other. In this context, it is also worthwhile mentioning that over the past few years the DIFC and UAE courts have established close links of cooperation.[14] This, no doubt, will assist in promoting the cross-fertilization of best practice and standards in years to come. The DIFC courts, it may be noted, have also reached further afield.[15]

C. The Institutional Choice of Arbitration in the UAE: No Limits

The UAE also hosts a wide range of institutional arbitration bodies that may assist in the administration of arbitral proceedings. Almost every Emirate boasts its own arbitration institution with its own set of procedural rules. First and foremost among these are the DIAC with its seat in Dubai and which administers arbitrations under the DIAC Rules of Arbitration[16] and the ADCCAC, which is headquartered in Abu Dhabi and administers arbitration proceedings under the so-called ADCCAC Regulations.[17] The ADCCAC has only recently revised its Regulations, successfully upgrading them to a more modern international standard.[18] The wording of the DIAC Rules of Arbitration largely reminds one of the ICC Arbitration Rules and the DIAC itself has drawn administrative staff from the ICC International Court of Arbitration in Paris to ensure highest standards in administering proceedings under the DIAC Rules. In addition, the DIAC Panel of Arbitrators is truly international and offers a wide range of highly qualified arbitrators with all sorts of specialist backgrounds from all over the world.[19]

34.06

---

[11] See the extensive comments on the application of UAE Arbitration Chapter, Art 203(1) in Blanke (n 8).
[12] See UAE Arbitration Chapter, Art 217 and Case No 176/Judicial Year 17, Ruling of the Federal Supreme Court (Abu Dhabi) (21 November 1995).
[13] See, eg, Case No 282/2012, Real Estate Cassation, Dubai Court of Cassation (3 February 2013), in which the court only nullified the cost award (for further details on which, see Part F, below).
[14] See, eg, Protocol of Enforcement between Dubai Courts and DIFC Courts 2009 <http://difccourts.ae/wp-content/uploads/2015/08/Protocol-of-Enforcement-betwen-the-DIFC-Courts-and-Dubai-Courts-23-April-2009.pdf> accessed 25 September 2015, which provides for the mutual enforcement of DIFC and Dubai Court Orders in the two jurisdictions resectively.
[15] See in particular Memorandum of Guidance as to Enforcement between the DIFC Courts and the Commercial Court, Queen's Bench Division, England and Wales (23 January 2013) <http://www.judiciary.gov.uk> accessed 25 September 2015 and <http://difccourts.ae/wp-content/uploads/2015/08/Protocol-of-Enforcement-betwen-the-DIFC-Courts-and-Dubai-Courts-23-April-2009.pdf> and Memorandum of Guidance between the DIFC Courts and the Supreme Court of New South Wales (9 December 2013) <http://www.difccourts.ae> accessed 25 September 2015.
[16] For a full electronic copy of the DIAC Rules of Arbitration 2007, see the official website of the DIAC at <http://www.diac.ae/idias/rules> accessed 25 September 2015.
[17] For further details, see the official website of the ADCCAC at <http://www.abudhabichamber.ae/English> accessed 21 October 2015. The revised ADCCAC Regulations are not yet accessible electronically on the official website of the ADCCAC.
[18] For contemporaneous commentary, see Gordon Blanke, 'The New ADCCAC Arbitration Rules: The Game Is On … Is It?' (2014) 80(3) Arbitration 37–47.
[19] It is worth noting in this context that the ADCCAC list of arbitrators is much more selective and hence does not offer as wide a choice of arbitrators as would be the case under the DIAC Rules. This is particularly so given that registration as arbitrator with the ADCCAC is subject to payment of regular membership fees.

34.07 The DIFC hosts the DIFC-LCIA, a sister organization of the LCIA, which administers arbitration proceedings under the DIFC-LCIA Arbitration Rules.[20] These are closely modelled on the LCIA Arbitration Rules[21] and import into the UAE a set of rules that is readily accessible to any international practitioner familiar with the application of and practice under the LCIA Arbitration Rules. In fact, DIFC-LCIA arbitrations are administered by the LCIA Secretariat in London and provide access to the LCIA Panel of Arbitrators in London. For the sake of completeness, the DIFC-LCIA also administers *ad hoc* proceedings under the UNCITRAL Arbitration Rules.[22]

34.08 Further, the choice of any of the above arbitration rules may be combined with the selection of any seat within the UAE (or indeed elsewhere in the world). So there are no inherent restrictions on the use of the local arbitration rules in an international arbitration context. In addition, the UAE courts have also recognized the choice of foreign arbitration rules, such as those of the ICC, in combination with a UAE seat.[23]

34.09 Apart from arbitration institutions, there are a number of Western arbitration organizations that have taken root in the UAE to promote international practices, professional ethics, and procedures of arbitration. From among these, the CIArb with its branch in Dubai[24] and the ICC through the ICC UAE National Committee have established a viable presence. It is also worth noting the recent establishment of the DIFC Arbitration Institute, which aims to promote arbitration within the DIFC more specifically.[25]

D. The Local Infrastructure for Arbitration in the UAE: Truly International

34.10 The UAE's local infrastructure is extremely arbitration-friendly—its international airports allow international mobility through international aerial connectivity, which makes Dubai and Abu Dhabi easily accessible for witnesses, arbitrators, and other arbitration professionals as venues of arbitration in the Middle East. Hotels as well as arbitration institutions, such as the DIAC, offer state-of-the-art hearing facilities and are used to accommodating and servicing the needs of arbitrating parties from around the world.

34.11 In addition, as has been seen previously, the UAE offers access to a sizeable pool of international arbitrators with varying legal traditions and national backgrounds, including both Middle Eastern and Western jurisdictions of both common and civil law origin. Equally,

---

[20] For further details and a full electronic copy of the 2008 DIFC-LCIA Arbitration Rules, see the official website of the DIFC-LCIA at <http://www.difc-lcia.org/arbitration.aspx> accessed 25 September 2015.

[21] Note, however, the recent revision of the LCIA Arbitration Rules, which is (not yet) reflected in the DIFC-LCIA Rules. For now, these remain modelled on the previous 1998 version of the LCIA Arbitration Rules.

[22] 2010 UNCITRAL Arbitration Rules, accessible electronically in their last amended 2013 version at <http://www.uncitral.org> accessed 25 September 2015.

[23] See, eg, Case No 304/Judicial Year 23, Ruling of the Federal Supreme Court (Abu Dhabi) (25 March 2003).

[24] The UAE branch of the CIArb is particularly active in the promotion of arbitration in the UAE and the Middle East more generally. It offers regular membership courses as well as seminars and workshops that aim at teaching the particulars of arbitration in the UAE, including award-writing, etc. For that purpose, it frequently cooperates with leading arbitration institutions on the ground, including the DIAC. The author is a tutor of the Institute in the region.

[25] For further details, see Gordon Blanke, 'DIFC introduces Arbitration Institute' (*Kluwer Arbitration Blog*, 4 June 2014) <http://www.kluwerarbitrationblog.com> accessed 25 September 2015.

competent international arbitration professionals with a specialism in Middle Eastern arbitration are easily accessible. Ancillary service providers, such as engineers, quantity surveyors, claims consultants, and maritime experts, are available for assistance in construction and shipping disputes, among others. Finally, there is ready accessibility to translation services in the event that there is a need for translating arbitration-relevant documents from or into Arabic.

E. Arbitrability: Scale and Scope

34.12 Most matters are arbitrable under UAE law. This includes both matters of contract and tort.[26] As a general rule, all matters that can be conciliated, ie resolved by settlement between the parties, may also be arbitrated. In other words, matters that cannot be settled or are irreconcilable are excluded from arbitration. Irreconcilable matters are mainly those that raise concerns of the Islamic Shari'ah, including matters such as *riba al-nasi* (usurious interest in consideration of a deferred debt payment) and an advance charged at a premium.[27] In addition, any matters relating to public policy are non-arbitrable. Even though the true scope of public policy remains debatable under UAE law, it most certainly includes criminal matters and matters that are reserved for resolution by a competent public authority, such as matters relating to the registration of real estate.[28]

34.13 Finally, there are a number of laws that contain express restrictions on arbitrability and reserve exclusive jurisdiction for the courts, including in particular: (i) Article 6, UAE Federal Law No 18 of 1981 on Commercial Agencies (as amended by Law No 14 of 1988), which prohibits the arbitration of registered commercial agency disputes, and (ii) Articles 6 and 7 of UAE Federal Law No 8 of 1980 on Labour (as amended). This being said, competition matters, in particular follow-on damages actions, within the meaning of the new UAE Federal Competition Law[29] have been argued to be arbitrable.[30] In addition, the competence of special committees or tribunals[31] has been confirmed to leave intact the proper jurisdiction of arbitral tribunals.[32]

---

[26] This being said, as a golden rule, it should be borne in mind that there is a general preference under UAE law that in the presence of a contractual relationship between disputing parties, disputes should be articulated in contractual (rather than tortious) terms, except where the underlying dispute is unambiguously tortious in nature.

[27] Note in this context in particular the wording of Art 733 of the UAE Civil Transactions Code, which essentially confines matters of irreconcilability to the Islamic Shari'ah.

[28] Which in the Emirate of Dubai are to be dealt with by the Dubai RERA, see Dubai Law No 13 of 2008 (in relation to the interim registration of off-plan real estate properties in the Emirate of Dubai) and Appeal No 282/2012 (n 13), which allows arbitrators to draw the civil law consequences from issues of non-registration of off-plan properties in the Emirate of Dubai. See also the discussion in Essam Al Tamimi, 'Arbitrators dealing with real estate property disputes—is it a matter of public policy?', *Al Tamimi Law Update* (June 2014).

[29] UAE Federal Law No 4 of 2012 Concerning Regulating Competition, which entered into force on 13 February 2013.

[30] See Gordon Blanke, 'The new UAE Competition Law: Is it arbitrable or is it not arbitrable?—That is the question …' (*Kluwer Arbitration Blog*, 19 February 2013) <http://www.kluwerarbitrationblog.com> accessed 25 September 2015.

[31] As established by Dubai Government Decree No 57 of 2009, establishing a tribunal to decide the disputes related to the settlement of the financial position of Dubai World and its subsidiaries, dated 14 December 2009; Dubai Government Decree No 61 of 2009, forming a special judicial committee to settle the disputes related to Amlak Finance PJSC and Tamweel PJSC, dated 27 December 2009; and Dubai Government Decree establishing a special judicial committee to settle disputes related to Zabeel Investments LLC, dated 9 February 2011.

[32] For further details, see Blanke and Abi Habib Kanakri (n 6) 229–31; Practice Direction No 1 of 2010 issued by the Dubai World Special Tribunal, dated 30 March 2010; and Practice Direction No 61 of 2009 Concerning Formation of Special Judicial Committee to decide in the Disputes Relating to Amlak Finance PJSC and Tamweel PJSC issued by the Dubai Government, dated 27 January 2010.

34.14 Taken in the round, apart from matters that raise issues of the Islamic Shari'ah, the scale and scope of arbitrability under UAE law are not unusual and find parallels under the arbitration laws of other leading arbitration jurisdictions in the world. Added to this is the overall limited role played by the Islamic Shari'ah in arbitration in the UAE, as further outlined below, which in turn confirms the by and large secular nature of arbitration there.

34.15 Furthermore, any limits placed on arbitrability by the concept of public policy under UAE law apply *mutatis mutandis* to arbitrations seated in the DIFC.[33]

F. The Conduct of Arbitration in the UAE: Procedural Dos and Don'ts

34.16 The procedure of arbitration in the UAE is quite formalistic compared to Western arbitration jurisdictions.[34] In order to ensure the enforceability of a resultant award, it is crucial to ensure full compliance of the arbitration process with the procedural niceties required under UAE law. Essentially, this means that care has to be taken that the arbitration process remains in compliance with overarching principles of due process and does not violate public policy as understood in the UAE within the meaning of Article 216 of the UAE Arbitration Chapter. More specifically, Article 216 empowers the UAE courts to nullify an award on the basis of a limited list of procedural grounds, including, in particular: (i) an arbitrator's failure to rule without a proper mandate or outside the terms of his mandate; (ii) deficiencies in the issuance of the award; and (iii) any irregularities in the arbitration procedure.[35] This latter ground opens up Article 216 to a number of procedural challenges despite its seemingly limited scope and the restrictive interpretation given to it by the local courts.[36]

34.17 The following will give a flavour of the procedural formalism that informs arbitration under UAE law, failure to comply with which may result in procedural challenges to a resultant award.

(a) The obligation to arbitrate

34.18 UAE law recognizes the liberty or autonomy of contracting parties to conclude arbitration agreements and hence to contract into an obligation to arbitrate.[37] The UAE courts enforce obligations to arbitrate provided a contracting party raises the arbitration defence, ie the existence of the arbitration agreement, in the first hearing before them. In the event that a contracting party fails to do so, it will be considered to have waived the right to resort to

---

[33] Public policy is of a federal nature and as such impacts offshore arbitration in the DIFC in the same way as it impacts onshore arbitration elsewhere in the UAE. For further explanation, see Part I, below.

[34] See Blanke (n 8).

[35] Note that the public policy ground was added by relevant UAE court case law: see Case No 449/Judicial Year 21, Ruling of the Federal Supreme Court (Abu Dhabi) (11 April 2001); and Case No 146/2008, Ruling of the Dubai Court of Cassation (9 November 2008).

[36] See, eg, Case No 834/2010, Ruling of the Abu Dhabi Court of Cassation (30 December 2010); and Case No 32/2009, Ruling of the Dubai Court of Cassation (29 March 2009) (always subject to the public policy addition, on which see the preceding footnote).

[37] See UAE Arbitration Chapter, Art 203(1), and confirmatory case precedent. See, eg, Case No 170/Judicial Year 4, Ruling of the Abu Dhabi Court of Cassation (28 April 2010); and Case No 795/Judicial Year 4, Ruling of the Abu Dhabi Court of Cassation (9 December 2010).

arbitration and the arbitration agreement will be regarded as null and void.[38] As a result, the UAE courts will consider themselves competent to hear the underlying dispute.[39]

(b) Formation of valid arbitration agreements

In the terms of the constant jurisprudence of the UAE courts, the right to resort to court for the resolution of disputes is regarded as fundamental.[40] Only the right holder himself may contract out of the right to resort to court, bar the provision of a special power of attorney.[41] In this sense, recourse to arbitration (as an alternative to recourse to the courts) is considered exceptional within the terms of the prevailing case law.[42] As a consequence, in order to ensure their enforceability, arbitration agreements must be concluded by persons specifically authorized to submit (read: commit) a disputing party to arbitration.

34.19

A further safeguard is the requirement for arbitration agreements to be in writing in the terms of the UAE Arbitration Chapter.[43] This requirement, however, has received a comparatively expansive interpretation by the competent courts, including the valid submission to arbitration by exchange of (electronic) correspondence between authorized signatories[44] or through *ex post facto* ratification by an authorized signatory.[45] Arbitration agreements may also be incorporated by reference under certain circumstances.[46] Managing directors of limited liability companies are presumed to have authority to bind to arbitration.[47] Public and private joint stock companies, however, can only be bound by express empowerment to bind to arbitration through general assembly or a board resolution in terms expressly authorized in the articles of association.[48] Lastly, arbitration obligations under an insurance contract have to be contained in an agreement separate from the insurance policy.[49]

34.20

(c) Valid representation

Valid representation in arbitration equally requires a special power of attorney.[50] Failure to provide a special power of attorney will hence result in the invalidation of the arbitration

34.21

---

[38] See, eg, Case No 1283/2010, Ruling of the Abu Dhabi Court of Cassation (11 October 2011); and Case No 38/2009, Ruling of the Dubai Court of Cassation (4 April 2010).
[39] See, eg, Case No 491/Judicial Year 24, Ruling of the Federal Supreme Court (Abu Dhabi) (28 November 2004); and Case No 38/2009 (n 38).
[40] See, eg, Case No 22/Judicial Year 22, Ruling of the Abu Dhabi Court of Cassation (3 March 2002); Case No 92/Judicial Year 25, Ruling of the Federal Supreme Court (Abu Dhabi) (8 June 2003); and Case No 148/2008, Ruling of the Dubai Court of Cassation (16 September 2008).
[41] Within the meaning of UAE Arbitration Chapter, Art 58(2).
[42] See again the case law referenced at n 40 above.
[43] UAE Arbitration Chapter, Art 203(2).
[44] See, eg, Case No 64/2005, Ruling of the Dubai Court of Cassation (18 April 2005); and Case No 174/2005, Ruling of the Dubai Court of Cassation (19 December 2005).
[45] See, eg, in Case No 204/2008, Ruling of the Dubai Court of Cassation (12 October 2008) (agent–principal relationship).
[46] See, eg, Case No 100/2004, Ruling of the Dubai Court of Cassation (9 January 2005) (a reference to the FIDIC standard form conditions).
[47] See Art 237 of the UAE Federal Law No 8 Concerning Commercial Companies 1984 and Case No 955/Judicial Year 4, Ruling of the Abu Dhabi Court of Cassation (29 December 2010); and Case No 164/2008, Ruling of the Dubai Court of Cassation (10 October 2008).
[48] See Arts 103 and 216 of the UAE Commercial Companies Law, corresponding to Arts 154 and 265 of the new UAE Commercial Companies Law respectively.
[49] See Art 1028(d) of the UAE Civil Transactions Code.
[50] Again within the meaning of UAE Arbitration Chapter, Art 58(2) and Case No 321/Judicial Year 19, Ruling of the Abu Dhabi Court of Cassation (25 April 1999); and Case No 191/2009, Ruling of the Dubai Court of Cassation (13 September 2009).

process, bar the *ex post facto* ratification of the arbitration process through the rights holder himself or an authorized signatory.[51]

(d) Terms of reference and the tribunal's mandate

34.22 Even though terms of reference are not compulsory under UAE law,[52] they are considered best practice under some local arbitration rules.[53] This being said, the UAE Arbitration Chapter recognizes the concept of submission agreements (*compromis*) and accepts terms of reference as a valid source of the arbitrator's proper mandate (especially in the absence of a valid arbitration agreement).[54] Under UAE law, invalid or pathological arbitration agreements can therefore be amended or replaced by terms of reference to ensure the proper validation of the arbitrator's mandate and the parties' proper submission to arbitration.

34.23 Irrespective of the foregoing, the tribunal must not step outside the boundaries of its mandate and rule *extra petita*. Such a ruling will be challengeable as unenforceable.[55]

(e) Constitution of the tribunal

34.24 The constitution of the tribunal is essentially left to the parties in compliance with the prevailing doctrine of party autonomy. The parties are at liberty to choose the method of appointment of the tribunal and the criteria with which individual members must comply. This being said, the number of the members of the tribunal has to be uneven to avoid challenges of due process. This is a matter of public policy raised by the UAE courts *ex officio*: non-compliance will constitute a ground for invalidation of the arbitration process and the nullification of a resultant award.[56]

(f) Conditions precedent

34.25 Prior to resorting to arbitration, disputing parties are required to comply with any contractual conditions precedent. These commonly include notice requirements[57] and pre-arbitral references to amicable settlement or decision-making processes involving, for instance, an engineer within the context of construction disputes.[58] In addition, arbitration against a governmental entity or the sovereign requires the exhaustion of a number of pre-arbitral requirements.[59]

(g) Defaulting parties

34.26 UAE law has put in place a number of safeguards to prevent defaulting parties from frustrating the arbitration process. Most importantly, failure to sign terms of reference will not

---

[51] See again the case law cited at n 50 above.
[52] See Case No 924/Judicial Year 3, Ruling of the Federal Court of Cassation (17 December 2009); and Case No 67/2009, Ruling of the Dubai Court of Cassation (24 May 2009).
[53] cf practice under the DIAC Rules of Arbitration.
[54] See UAE Arbitration Chapter, Art 203(1) and the comments made in Blanke (n 8).
[55] See UAE Arbitration Chapter, Art 216(1)(a) and, eg, Case Nos 267 and 297/Judicial Year 20, Ruling of the Federal Supreme Court (14 May 2000).
[56] See Case No 186/Judicial Year 2, Ruling of the Abu Dhabi Court of Cassation (8 June 2008).
[57] Always provided there is the parties' express agreement, see, eg, Case No 84/Judicial Year 22, Ruling of the Federal Supreme Court (Abu Dhabi) (22 January 2002); and Case No 64/2005 (n 44).
[58] See, eg, Case No 140/2007, Ruling of the Dubai Court of Cassation (7 October 2007); and Case No 204/2008 (n 45).
[59] eg Dubai Law No 6 of 1997, Art 36, read together with Dubai Instruction Order of 6 February 1998; Arts 8 and 9 of Dubai Law No 32 of 2008; and Council of Ministers Decision No 406/2 of 2003.

result in the invalidation of the arbitration process.[60] Further, a party's failure to make a required submission—whether it be a statement of defence or a reply to counterclaim—does not prevent a tribunal from continuing with the arbitration and from proceeding to render a final award.[61] Nor does a party's failure to appear at a hearing without good cause prevent a tribunal from going ahead with the hearing and proceeding with the completion of the arbitration process.[62] A party's failure to pay an advance on costs will ultimately result in its claims (or counterclaims) being considered withdrawn.[63] Overall, a party's failure to participate in the arbitration process, whether by complete absence from the outset or occasional silence, does not prevent a tribunal from proceeding to complete the arbitration process and from rendering a final award.

(h) **Hearings**

Hearings are optional in UAE arbitration. The disputing parties may agree to conduct the arbitration on the basis of documents only.[64] This being said, any fact and expert[65] witness evidence has to be presented under oath.[66] Failure to do so will prevent a tribunal from relying on the evidence in its deliberations at the risk of the potential nullification of the resultant award.[67] The oath-taking requirement has been found not to apply within the context of international arbitral awards.[68] Finally, in the event that a hearing does take place, a tribunal is well advised to keep a record of it in the form of a transcript in order to comply with the minute-taking requirement under Article 208(3) of the UAE Arbitration Chapter.[69]   **34.27**

This being said, the UAE Arbitration Chapter imposes an obligation on the tribunal to schedule a time and venue for a preliminary meeting with the parties within 30 days from acceptance/inception of its mandate.[70] During the preliminary meeting, the tribunal and the parties will typically agree the provisional procedural timetable, which sets out the procedural milestones going forward in the arbitration.   **34.28**

---

[60] Signature of terms of reference not being compulsory in UAE arbitration. See again n 52 above.
[61] See UAE Arbitration Chapter, Art 208(2).
[62] See DIAC Arbitration Rules, Art 28.5.
[63] See Appendix on Costs of the DIAC Arbitration Rules, Art 2.9.
[64] As is frequent practice in smaller real estate disputes that are referred to arbitration.
[65] In this author's understanding, expert evidence is only subject to the oath requirement in the event that the appointed expert is not sourced from the list of UAE court experts. UAE court experts give a permanent oath to serve as experts, which is also binding upon them in the context of their service as experts in arbitrations. Other experts that are not UAE court-listed will have to take an oath in order for their evidence to be admissible to a UAE tribunal's deliberations.
[66] See UAE Arbitration Chapter, Art 211, and Case No 503/2003, Ruling of the Dubai Court of Cassation (15 May 2005); and Case No 322/2004, Ruling of the Dubai Court of Cassation (11 April 2005). For further discussion on oaths, see Audley Sheppard, 'Oaths and Perjury' in Julio César Betancourt (ed), *Defining Issues in International Arbitration: Celebrating 100 Years of the Chartered Institute of Arbitrators* (OUP 2016) ch 20.
[67] See the infamous *Bechtel* case, which generated a lot of publicity internationally: *Int'l Bechtel v Dep't of Civil Aviation of the Gov't of Dubai*, Case No 503/2003, Dubai Court of Cassation (15 May 2005). Proposed formula in accordance with Art 41(2) of the UAE Law of Evidence: 'I swear by Almighty God that I shall tell the whole truth and nothing but the truth.'
[68] See *Airmec Dubai, LLC v Maxtel International, LLC*, Appeal for Cassation No 132/2012 Commercial, ruling of the Dubai Court of Cassation of 18 October 2012, in which the Dubai Court of Cassation accepted enforcement under the New York Convention despite the award debtor's allegation that witness evidence had not been submitted under oath.
[69] Although minutes, in the literal sense of that term, are not compulsory. See, eg, Case No 32/2009 (n 36).
[70] See UAE Arbitration Chapter, Art 208(1). This may vary to 30 days from receipt by the tribunal of the file in the arbitration (see Art 22 of the DIAC Arbitration Rules).

(i) Rules of evidence

34.29 Importantly, a tribunal is not bound by the UAE Law of Evidence, bar the application of mandatory provisions of that law,[71] in particular the prohibition of a party testifying in its own cause.[72] This being said, parties will typically opt into adoption of the IBA Rules on the Taking of Evidence in order to facilitate the admissibility of testimony of party officers.[73]

(j) Formalistic requirements of the award

34.30 To ensure their enforceability, arbitral awards must comply with a number of formalities under UAE law. These include the following form and content requirements more specifically:

(1) the award must be produced 'in writing';[74] electronic publication (in the terms permitted, for example, under the UNCITRAL Model Law) is not permissible;[75]
(2) the award must be signed by a majority of arbitrators;[76] proper execution of the award requires the initialling of each page of the award by each signing arbitrator, with a full signature on the final page of the award; where the reasoning and the dispositive part of the award overlap, it is sufficient to initial the overlapping page with a full signature on the final page of the award;[77]
(3) the award must make reference to any dissenting opinion;[78]
(4) the award must contain a summary of the arbitration agreement.[79] There is no need for terms of reference, but some arbitration institutions consider it best practice to append a full set provided one is available;[80]
(5) the award must set out a summary of each party's case (including all relevant evidence presented by each party), the tribunal's reasoning (unless the award is a consent award), and a dispositive/operational part;[81] and
(6) the award must set out the date and place of issuance.[82]

34.31 On a further note, if expressly authorized by the disputing parties to do so, the tribunal may rule as *amiable compositeur*, ie on the basis of equity and fairness outside the strict boundaries of the law.[83] A tribunal may also render a consent award provided it is agreed by the parties.[84]

---

[71] See UAE Arbitration Chapter, Art 212(1).
[72] See Art 41 of the UAE Law of Evidence.
[73] In the terms of Art 4.2 of the IBA Rules on the Taking of Evidence.
[74] See UAE Arbitration Chapter, Art 212(5).
[75] Note in this context also that in accordance with UAE court practice, for ratification and enforcement purposes, it is imperative to serve an original copy of the award.
[76] See UAE Arbitration Chapter, Art 212(5).
[77] See, eg, Case No 16/Judicial Year 23, Ruling of the Federal Supreme Court (Abu Dhabi) (29 April 2003); Case No 233/2007, Ruling of the Dubai Court of Cassation (13 January 2008); and Case No 156/2009, Ruling of the Dubai Court of Cassation (27 October 2009).
[78] See UAE Arbitration Chapter, Art 212(5).
[79] ibid, read together with Case No 225/2005, Ruling of the Dubai Court of Cassation (12 December 2005); and Case No 67/2009, Ruling of the Dubai Court of Cassation (24 May 2009) (there being no need for a full copy of the arbitration agreement or a verbatim inclusion of the wording of the arbitration agreement).
[80] cf practice under the DIAC Rules.
[81] See UAE Arbitration Chapter, Art 212(5).
[82] ibid.
[83] See UAE Arbitration Chapter, Art 205 and the constant jurisprudence of the UAE courts, eg, Case No 294/1994, Ruling of the Dubai Court of Cassation (26 November 1994); Case No 186/1996, Ruling of the Dubai Court of Cassation (5 January 1997); Case No 207/2009, Ruling of the Dubai Court of Cassation (19 April 2010). Subject to considerations of public policy, as confirmed by UAE Arbitration Chapter, Art 212(2), and Case No 118/Judicial Year 23, Ruling of the Federal Supreme Court (Abu Dhabi) (21 January 2004).
[84] See, eg, Art 39 of the DIAC Rules of Arbitration.

(k) Tribunal's power to award costs

The UAE Arbitration Chapter empowers a tribunal to award and allocate the costs of arbitration, including in particular the tribunal's own fees and expenses.[85] The extent to which this power may be extended to include an award of counsel fees and other party expenses depends on a proper reading of the underlying arbitration rules[86] or the parties' express agreement in the original arbitration agreement or the underlying terms of reference, as the case may be.[87] The allocation of costs may be based on the principle of 'costs that follow the event' or on the basis of relative success, as appropriate.

34.32

(l) Issuance of the award

Under UAE law, an award must be issued within six months from the date of the preliminary meeting, unless otherwise agreed by the disputing parties.[88] An agreement otherwise may be by election of a set of arbitration rules that contain express provisions on the proper extension of the statutory time limit for rendering an award.[89] More recent case law of the UAE courts has confirmed the enforceability of mechanisms for extension contained in local arbitration rules.[90] Importantly, for an extension to be valid, it must be contiguous with the date of expiry of the previous time limit.[91] A prospective award creditor is therefore well advised to ensure the timely extension of the time limit, failing which a resultant award may prove unenforceable.[92]

34.33

Further, pursuant to the UAE Arbitration Chapter, an award has to be communicated to the parties within five days from the date of issuance.[93] Timely communication will be ensured by the local arbitration institution under whose auspices an arbitration is being conducted.[94]

34.34

---

[85] See UAE Arbitration Chapter, Art 218.
[86] See Case No 282/2012 (n 13), where the Dubai Court of Cassation found that the notion of 'costs of arbitration' within the meaning of Art 2.1 of the Appendix on Costs of the DIAC Rules of Arbitration was not sufficiently wide to encompass counsel fees and other party costs. For criticism, see Gordon Blanke, 'Dubai Court of Cassation finds against recoverability of counsel fees in DIAC arbitration' (*Kluwer Arbitration Blog*, 23 June 2013) <http://www.kluwerarbitrationblog.com> accessed 25 September 2015.
[87] ibid.
[88] See UAE Arbitration Chapter, Art 210(1), read together with Case No 447/Judicial Year 4, Ruling of the Abu Dhabi Court of Cassation (30 September 2010); and Case No 141/2006, Ruling of the Dubai Court of Cassation (10 October 2006).
[89] See, eg, the DIAC Rules of Arbitration, Art 36, pursuant to which a DIAC tribunal may extend the initial time limit by a further six months of its own motion and any further extensions are to be approved by the DIAC Executive Committee.
[90] See *Middle East Foundations LLC v Meydan Group LLC (formerly Meydan LLC)*, Case No 249 of 2013, Commercial Appeal, Ruling of the Dubai Court of Appeal (15 January 2014), deciding on the extension mechanism contained in the DIAC Arbitration Rules in particular. For contemporaneous commentary, see Gordon Blanke, 'Dubai Court of Appeal confirms time extension provisions under the DIAC Rules and other pro-arbitration dicta' (*Kluwer Arbitration Blog*, 28 April 2014) <http://www.kluwerarbitrationblog.com> accessed 25 September 2015.
[91] See, eg, Case No 178/1996, Ruling of the Dubai Court of Cassation (25 January 1997); Case No 141/2006 (n 88); and Case No 156/2009 (n 77).
[92] See, eg, Case No 640/Judicial Year 22, Ruling of the Federal Supreme Court (19 November 2002) and Case No 157/2009, Ruling of the Dubai Court of Cassation (27 September 2009).
[93] See UAE Arbitration Chapter, Art 213(3).
[94] cf DIAC practice to the required effect.

G. Court Support in Arbitration in the UAE: International Standards

34.35 Both the UAE and the DIFC courts are empowered to lend support to arbitrations seated in mainland UAE and in the offshore DIFC respectively. Forms of interim relief obtainable from the local courts typically include preservation and freezing orders[95] and as such compare well with the types of interim relief available in other leading arbitration jurisdictions worldwide. No attachments can be made over assets or property owned by the government or the ruler in a number of Emirates.[96] The UAE courts also provide assistance in the taking of evidence from third parties.[97] Most recently, the UAE courts have confirmed the availability of attachment orders in support of domestic enforcement actions.[98] This goes a long way towards providing award creditors a form of security in the prolonged ratification process prevailing under UAE law.[99]

34.36 Apart from the availability of interim relief of the kind described above, the UAE courts are also available for default appointment of arbitrators in *ad hoc* arbitration.[100] For the avoidance of doubt, there is little (if any) court intervention unless expressly requested by the arbitrating parties or to the extent provoked by violations of public policy, which turns the UAE into a comparatively arbitration-friendly jurisdiction.

H. Enforcement of Arbitral Awards in the UAE: Promises and Prospects

34.37 Contrary to common expectation—and following a slow start[101]—the UAE courts have faithfully complied with their enforcement obligations under the New York Convention since 2010.[102] Since then, the UAE courts have routinely enforced around five New York

---

[95] For an exhaustive discussion, see Gordon Blanke and Khalil Mechantaf, 'United Arab Emirates' in Lawrence W Newman and Colin Ong (eds), *Interim Measures in International Arbitration* (Juris 2014) 795–847. In the alternative, see Gordon Blanke, 'Court-Ordered Interim Relief in the United Arab Emirates' in Diora Ziyaeva and others (eds), *Interim and Emergency Relief in International Arbitration* (Juris 2015) 121–44.

[96] See, eg, Law No 10 of 2005 Amending Certain Provisions of Government Lawsuit Law No 3 of 1996, Art 3(1) (no attachments over assets owned by the government, including public institutions and corporations, or the Ruler of Dubai).

[97] See in particular UAE Arbitration Chapter, Art 209(2)(b).

[98] See Appeal No 519/2013, ruling of the Abu Dhabi Court of Cassation of 2 October 2013. For commentary, see Gordon Blanke, 'Attachment orders in support of enforcement actions of arbitration awards: An Abu Dhabi Court of Cassation invention' (*Kluwer Arbitration Blog*, 5 January 2014) <http://www.kluwerarbitrationblog.com> accessed 25 September 2015. Importantly, there is no reason to believe that the Abu Dhabi court's findings would not also apply within the context of enforcement actions in relation to foreign arbitral awards.

[99] For further details on which, see Part H below.

[100] See UAE Arbitration Chapter, Art 204(1). For detailed explanation, see Blanke (n 8).

[101] The UAE joined the New York Convention in 2006.

[102] Bar one setback in Case No 156/2013, ruling of the Dubai Court of Cassation of 18 August 2013 (more widely known as the *Canal de Jonglei* case), which—it is arguable—was politically motivated given the involvement of the Sudanese Government as award debtor. For contemporaneous commentary, see Gordon Blanke, 'Recent ruling of Dubai Court of Cassation on enforcement of foreign arbitral awards: Back to square one it is …' (*Kluwer Arbitration Blog*, 21 October 2013) <http://www.kluwerarbitrationblog.com> accessed 25 September 2015. For a full review of relevant case law, see Gordon Blanke and Soraya Corm-Bakhos, 'Enforcement of New York Convention Awards: Are the UAE Courts Coming of Age?' (2012) 78(4)

Convention awards[103] solely in reliance on the terms of the New York Convention itself.[104] In doing so, the UAE courts have adopted the following enforcement mantra, which accords with the spirit of the New York Convention:

> it is ... established pursuant to Article 238 of the UAE Civil Procedures Code that international conventions that come into full force and effect in the United Arab Emirates by ratification shall be construed as internal law applicable in the State and as such, the judge shall be required to apply the provisions thereof to the disputes brought before him concerning the execution of judgments made by foreign courts and foreign arbitral awards. As it is established in Federal Decree No 43 of 2006 ... that the [UAE] approve to accede to the New York Convention ... its provisions shall be applicable to the [present reference].[105]

34.38 Interestingly, given that the UAE has not entered into any reservations on joining the New York Convention, it is technically bound by extremely wide enforcement obligations under the Convention, including in relation to foreign awards issued in non-Convention countries.[106] This being said, the UAE is also member of other bilateral[107] and multilateral[108] enforcement instruments, which to date have remained little tested[109] and

---

Arbitration 359; and Gordon Blanke, 'Enforcement of New York Convention Awards in the UAE: The Story Re-told' (2013) 5(3) IJAA 19–36. For a full discussion, see Gordon Blanke, 'Recognition and Enforcement of Domestic and Foreign Awards in the UAE: Practice and Procedure' in Gerold Zeiler and others (eds), *Austrian Yearbook of International Arbitration* (Manz'sche Verlags- und Universitätsbuchhandlung 2015) 395–436.

[103] The main references being: Case No 35/2010, Ruling of the Fujairah Federal Court of First Instance (27 April 2010) (LMAA award rendered by a sole arbitrator in London), which was subsequently not appealed; Case No 679/2010, Ruling of the Abu Dhabi Court of Cassation (16 June 2011); Case No 531/2011, Ruling of the Dubai Court of Appeal (6 October 2011) (SIAC award rendered in Singapore); Case No 132/2012 (n 68) (DIFC-LCIA award rendered by a sole arbitrator in London); and Case No 1/2013, Ruling of the Dubai Court of Appeal (9 July 2013) (ICC award rendered by a sole arbitrator in Stuttgart), recently affirmed by the Dubai Court of Cassation in Case No 434/2014, *Al Reyami Group LLC v BTI Befestigungstechnik GmbH & Co KG*, with comments by Gordon Blanke, 'Dubai Court of Cassation further consolidates pro-NYC enforcement practice' (*Kluwer Arbitration Blog*, 14 April 2015) <http://www.kluwerarbitrationblog.com> accessed 17 October 2015.

[104] For detailed case summaries, see Gordon Blanke and Soraya Corm-Bakhos, 'Recognition and Enforcement of Foreign Arbitral Awards in the UAE: Practice and Procedure' (2014) 1(1) BCDR Int'l Arb Rev 3.

[105] See, eg, Case No 132/2012 (n 68) (translated by the author).

[106] For a confirmation of this proposition, see also Essam Al Tamimi, 'United Arab Emirates' in 23 ICC Int'l Ct Arb Bull, 2012 Special Supplement, *ICC Guide to National Procedures for Recognition and Enforcement of Awards under the New York Convention* 377.

[107] These include: Treaty on Judicial Cooperation in Criminal Matters, Extradition of Offenders, Cooperation in Civil, Commercial and Personal Matters with Morocco (2006); Treaty on Mutual Legal Assistance in Criminal Matters, Extradition of Offenders, Cooperation in Civil, Commercial and Personal Matters, Service of Judicial and Extra-Judicial Documents, Obtaining Evidence, Commissions and the Recognition and Enforcement of Foreign Judgments and Arbitral Awards with Sudan (2005); Agreement on Legal and Judicial Cooperation with Syria (2002); Agreement on Legal and Judicial Cooperation with Egypt (2000); Agreement on Legal and Judicial Cooperation with Jordan (1999); Treaty on Judicial Cooperation, Recognition and Enforcement of Judgments in Civil and Commercial Matters with France (1992); Agreement on Legal and Judicial Cooperation with Somalia (1972); and Agreement on Legal and Judicial Cooperation with Libya (1999).

[108] These include: the Riyadh Convention on Judicial Cooperation between States of the Arab League (opened for signature 1983, entered into force 1999); the GCC Convention for the Execution of Judgments, Delegations and Judicial Notifications (opened for signature 1987, entered into force 1995); and the ICSID Convention, which the UAE joined in 1982.

[109] See Case No 764/Judicial Year 24, Ruling of the Federal Supreme Court (Abu Dhabi) (7 June 2005) as the only presently published case of enforcement under a bilateral enforcement instrument, the Convention on Judicial Cooperation and the Recognition and Enforcement of Judgments in Civil and Commercial Matters between the UAE and the Republic of France. For further commentary, see Blanke, 'Enforcement of New York Convention Awards' (n 102).

are in any event subject to diminishing significance given the ubiquitous importance and wide applicability of the New York Convention in the pre-stated terms.[110] For the avoidance of doubt, in their enforcement practice, the DIFC courts are bound by the same enforcement instruments as the UAE courts given that for the purposes of the UAE's obligations under international conventions, the DIFC is considered to form an integral part of the UAE, the DIFC courts in turn qualifying as a UAE court.[111]

34.39 The enforcement of domestic arbitration awards is somewhat more challenging and requires a comparatively extensive ratification process before the UAE courts,[112] bar the voluntary compliance by an award debtor with the terms of the award; however, this is exceedingly rare in the UAE. This ratification process is based on a procedural review of the award and the arbitration process only[113] and as such excludes a review on the merits.[114]

34.40 This being said, violations of UAE public policy will result in a refusal to enforce and a full review of the underlying dispute on the merits.[115] For these purposes, the UAE courts will raise public policy issues *ex officio*.[116]

34.41 Last but not least, there are a number of instruments in place that facilitate the enforcement of domestic awards throughout the UAE. To start, the 1973 Law on Judicial Relationships between the Emirates[117] promotes the free movement of arbitration awards and enforcement orders between the jurisdictions of the various Emirates. Article 7 of the Judicial Authority Law of 2008 as amended[118] in turn promotes the mutual recognition of enforcement orders of arbitral awards between the Dubai/UAE and the DIFC courts. It is also worth noting in this context that, more recently, the DIFC courts have confirmed their willingness to serve as a host jurisdiction for the enforcement of both domestic and international awards rendered outside the DIFC.[119]

---

[110] For further details, see Blanke and Corm-Bakhos, 'Recognition and Enforcement of Foreign Arbitral Awards' (n 104).

[111] See Art 42(1) of the DIFC Arbitration Law, which provides that 'where the UAE has entered into an applicable treaty for the mutual enforcement of judgments, orders or awards the DIFC Court shall comply with the terms of such treaty'.

[112] Which takes the form of a full court proceeding, often going through two stages of appeal, ie the Court of Appeal and the Court of Cassation. A typical ratification process would usually take between six months to around one year.

[113] Taking into account and testing the formalities outlined at Part F above.

[114] See UAE Arbitration Chapter, Art 217 and Case No 176/Judicial Year 17, Ruling of the Federal Supreme Court (Abu Dhabi) (21 November 1995); Case No 263/Judicial Year 18, Ruling of the Federal Supreme Court (Abu Dhabi) (8 December 1996); Case No 449/Judicial Year 21 (n 35); Case No 32/Judicial Year 23, Ruling of the Federal Supreme Court (Abu Dhabi) (8 June 2003); Case No 118/Judicial Year 23 (n 83); Case No 403/2003, Ruling of the Dubai Court of Cassation (13 March 2004); Case No 56/Judicial Year 27, Ruling of the Federal Supreme Court (Abu Dhabi) (21 May 2006); Case No 273/2006, Ruling of the Dubai Court of Cassation (4 February 2007); and Case No 72/2007, Ruling of the Dubai Court of Cassation (10 June 2007).

[115] See Case No 449/Judicial Year 21 (n 35); Case No 225/2005 (n 79); Case No 72/2007 (n 114).

[116] ibid.

[117] Federal Law No 11 of 1973 on Judicial Relationships Amongst Emirates.

[118] ie Dubai Law No 12 of 2004 as amended by Dubai Law No 16 of 2011.

[119] See *X1, X2 v Y1, Y2*, Case No ARB 002/2013, DIFC Court of First Instance (2014); and *Banyan Tree Corporate PTE Ltd v Meydan Group LLC*, Case No ARB 003/2013, DIFC Court of First Instance (27 May 2014). For contemporaneous commentary, see Gordon Blanke, 'DIFC Court of First Instance confirms its status as host jurisdiction for recognition of both domestic and foreign awards' (*Kluwer Arbitration Blog*, 7 June 2014) <http://www.kluwerarbitrationblog.com> accessed 25 September 2015. For earlier thinking on the subject matter, see also Gordon Blanke, 'Enforcement of New York Convention Awards in the UAE (Part II): The DIFC

I. Public Policy in the UAE: Between Secularism and the Islamic Shari'ah

The development of the concept of public policy[120] within the UAE arbitration context has been a story of unruly Trojan horses and equally unruly Arabian camels along the shorelines of the Emirate of Dubai.[121] The core of the concept of public policy in the terms in which it prevails in the UAE is contained in Article 3 of the UAE Civil Transactions Code, which provides verbatim as follows: 34.42

> Public policy includes matters relating to private status such as marriage, inheritance, and lineage, as well as provisions relating to sovereignty, free trade, distribution of wealth, rules of private ownership and the other rules and foundations upon which society is based, in such a manner as not to conflict with the definitive provisions and fundamental principles of Islamic Shari'ah.

Despite some occasional digression from the core of this provision,[122] the UAE courts have largely interpreted the scope of public policy by reference to the limitation to the Islamic Shari'ah built into the wording of Article 3. Essentially, this means that anything that affects the Islamic Shari'ah will be considered public policy under UAE law. As has been intimated previously in this chapter, the UAE is a comparatively secular jurisdiction and as such gives a fairly restrictive meaning to the concept of the Islamic Shari'ah. It has hence little significance in daily arbitration practice. By way of example, interest—whether simple or compound[123]—is readily recoverable under UAE law. Equally, loss of profit and/or opportunity are readily awardable both before courts and tribunals, provided they have been foreseeable since the moment of contracting and are quantifiable with a measure of certainty.[124] 34.43

UAE law does not distinguish between concepts of domestic and international public policy.[125] With this in mind, it has been argued that the domestic definition of public policy will also likely find application under the public policy exception within the meaning of Article V of the New York Convention.[126] Finally, it is important to bear in mind that the 34.44

---

as 'host' jurisdiction?' (*Kluwer Arbitration Blog*, 4 September 2012) <http://www.kluwerarbitrationblog.com> accessed 25 September 2015. For latest developments on the subject matter, see Gordon Blanke, 'United Arab Emirates' in Gordon Blanke (ed), *Arbitration in the MENA* (Juris, forthcoming 2016).

[120] Or 'public order' as commonly put under UAE law. Importantly, UAE law does not draw any distinction between 'public order' or 'public policy' as more sophisticated arbitration jurisdictions may do.

[121] On this wording, see Gordon Blanke, 'Public policy in the UAE: has the unruly horse turned into a camel?' (*Kluwer Arbitration Blog*, 14 October 2012) <http://www.kluwerarbitrationblog.com> accessed 25 September 2015; and contemporaneous commentary by Gordon Blanke, 'Public Policy in the UAE: The Story about the Unruly Horse that Turned into a Camel' (2013) 79(1) Arbitration 98.

[122] See, in particular, the UAE courts' erratic approach to the public policy concept within the real estate sector, which, however, has since been rectified. See Case No 181/2011, Dubai Court of Cassation (12 February 2012); *Baiti Real Estate Development v Dynasty Zarooni Inc*, Case No 14/2012, Dubai Court of Cassation (16 September 2012); and Blanke, 'Public policy in the UAE' (n 121).

[123] The latter only, however, if expressly agreed by the disputing parties.

[124] eg UAE courts' case law on the recoverability of loss of profit and opportunity cost.

[125] See Gordon Blanke, 'On Recent Developments of "Public Policy" and Their Potential Implications for the Enforcement of New York Convention Awards in the UAE: Is It a 'Camel' or a 'Trojan Horse'?' (2013) 18(1) IBA Newsletter 46.

[126] ibid, for this proposition.

UAE notion of public policy also plays a role in DIFC arbitration given that the DIFC forms an integral part of the federation for public policy considerations.[127]

J. Conclusion

34.45 By way of conclusion, there can be little doubt that the UAE has been growing into a modern arbitration jurisdiction with international appeal. Provided the requisite level of familiarity with the procedural niceties of arbitration in the UAE is satisfied, there is little to fear. This being said, even these niceties are likely to be further eroded in the near future pending the UAE's intention to adopt a stand-alone federal arbitration law, which may ultimately implement the UNCITRAL Model Law for both domestic and international arbitrations seated in mainland UAE.[128]

34.46 On a further note, the DIFC courts have more recently confirmed their creativity and sense of innovation by initiating a consultation exercise on the potential conversion of DIFC court judgments into arbitral awards[129] in order to ensure their enforcement internationally under the New York Convention and other multilateral enforcement instruments.[130] These more recent developments can hardly leave any doubt that the UAE is committed to evolving into an ever-more-modern arbitration jurisdiction with a distinctly competitive edge.[131]

---

[127] On the basis of the explanations given in n 33 above.

[128] A number of draft federal arbitration laws have been circulated within professional circles over the past five years. It is presently not certain when it is that one of the draft texts will finally be adopted.

[129] For further guidance, see <http://www.allenovery.com/publications/en-gb/lrrfs/middleeastandafrica/Pages/DIFC-Courts-introduce-unique-mechanism-to-convert-DIFC-money-judgments-into-arbitral-awards-n.aspx> accessed 25 September 2015 and Practice Direction No X of 2014 amending Practice Direction No 2 of 2012 DIFC Courts' Jurisdiction, electronically accessible on the official website of the DIFC Courts at <http://www.difccourts.ae> accessed 25 September 2015.

[130] For contemporaneous commentary, see Gordon Blanke, 'The DIFC and arbitration: Raising the stakes?' (*Kluwer Arbitration Blog*, 20 July 2014) <http://www.kluwerarbitrationblog.com> accessed 25 September 2015.

[131] Since initial drafting of this chapter and the proofing stage, DIFC Court Practice Direction No 2 of 2015 has now been adopted. For further reporting, see Gordon Blanke, 'DIFC Courts Practice Direction No 2 of 2015: Adopted at last!' (*Kluwer Arbitration Blog*, 31 March 2015) <http://www.kluwerarbitrationblog.com> accessed 16 January 2016. For further details, see also Blanke, 'United Arab Emirates' (n 119).

Part XIII

DISPUTE RESOLUTION IN THE CONSTRUCTION INDUSTRY

35

MANAGING CONSTRUCTION CONFLICT
Unfinished Revolution, Continuing Evolution

Thomas J Stipanowich *

A. Introduction

Two decades ago, many believed we were experiencing a revolution in the way conflict was managed.[1] Although observed changes were affecting virtually every aspect of human interaction, nowhere was the upheaval more momentous than in the construction sector. Frustration with the costs, delays, risks, and limitations of lawyer-driven adjudication prompted growing attention to informal methods aimed at early resolution of disputes, with those who 'owned' the dispute back in the driver's seat.

35.01

Contractors, architects and engineers, insurers, agencies and other owners, and, yes, construction attorneys were suddenly talking about collaboration, team-building, early settlement, and interest-based bargaining. It suddenly appeared as though the world might turn upside down, with 'advocate-controlled, adversarial, formalised, rights-based, lengthy, and costly' giving way in large measure to 'client-controlled, cooperative, relational, informal, interest-based, flexible, early, expeditious, and efficient'.

35.02

A smorgasbord of options for preventing, managing, and resolving conflict was suddenly on the table. There were strategies aimed at the very roots of conflict, including contractual terms aimed at promoting collaboration and reducing the chance of serious conflict,[2] and partnering, aimed at establishing a 'collaborative ethic and working "partnership"' on a construction project.[3] There were mechanisms for 'real time' dispute resolution on the jobsite by a project neutral, or by a group of construction experts sitting as a Dispute Review board (DRB).[4]

35.03

---

* The author thanks Tiffani Willis, Pepperdine School of Law Research Librarian; Hao Wu, Pepperdine School of Law LLM in International Commercial Arbitration, 2014, and Mark Lemke, LLM candidate, for their invaluable research support. Special thanks to Zach Ulrich, Straus Research Fellow, for his assistance with the CCA and IAM Surveys. This chapter was originally published in a special issue of *The Construction Lawyer*, which has given permission for its re-publication in this *liber amicorum*.

[1] See generally CPR Construction Disputes Committee, *Preventing and Resolving Construction Disputes* (CPR 1991) (excellent compendium developed under the leadership of Jim Groton and Jim Wilson, with assistance from Peter Kaskell); Thomas J Stipanowich, 'Beyond Arbitration: Innovation and Evolution in the United States Construction Industry' (1996) 31 Wake Forest L Rev 65 (discussing results of industry-wide survey on conflict management and dispute resolution processes).

[2] ibid, *Preventing and Resolving Construction Disputes*, chs 2, 3.

[3] ibid, ch 5.

[4] ibid, ch 6.

35.04 Dispute Resolution Advisors (DRAs) offered a more refined, project-centric means of managing conflict.[5] Phased or tiered dispute resolution might include early negotiation and, if necessary, negotiation with the assistance of a mediator;[6] mediation promised to be a particularly flexible tool for facilitating resolution of individual disputes and promoting improved communications and relationships on projects.[7] There were even proposed new twists on binding arbitration, the long-standing traditional alternative to litigation of construction disputes.[8] Part B briefly explores this 'Quiet Revolution'[9] in construction conflict management.

35.05 Twenty years on, the 'Quiet Revolution' has borne considerable fruit. Partnering remains a critical element of construction for some agencies, and broader contract-based platforms incentivizing collaboration and reduced conflict are available as Integrated Project Delivery (IPD) systems. Dispute boards are an established feature of many US and international infrastructure projects. Tiered 'filtering systems' for resolving construction conflicts are ubiquitous elements of construction contracts, and mediation has become a dominant intervention strategy for dispute resolution in the United States and other common law countries and is gaining considerable steam elsewhere. Arbitration is the focus of unprecedented international discussion and debate.

35.06 On the other hand, things have not turned out quite the way many of us expected. Among other things, we underestimated the grip and staying power of the litigation-oriented legal culture, and the 'gravitational pull' it exerts on everything it touches, especially mediation and arbitration. The legal profession inhabits and dominates these vast swathes of the commercial conflict management landscape and is the primary determinant of its contours. Within these realms, lawyers largely control the shape and timing of dispute resolution processes, who gets in, and who runs or facilitates the process (typically, lawyers); the shadow of litigation and the litigation model hangs heavy over the scene. In some ways, it is as if, 20 years after 1776, the British Crown was not only still in control of the American colonies, but had actually taken charge of the revolution! The yin and the yang of today's construction management spectrum are the focus of Part C.

35.07 Nevertheless, if we have learned one thing from experience, it is that human operations constantly evolve and change. That has never been more true than today, as we are confronted with rapid developments on multiple fronts. Looking to the future, Part D considers pertinent trends in the rapidly morphing realm of information technology; the increasing globalization of society; the surprising new insights made possible by behavioural science and the mining of 'big data'; the impact of longer productive lives and 'active retirement'; and the never-ceasing drumbeat for new forms of professional education and credentialling. Indeed, it may be that the real revolution is ahead of us.

---

[5] ibid 387–8.
[6] *Preventing and Resolving Construction Disputes* (n 1) 4.1–4.3.
[7] Thomas J Stipanowich, 'The Multi-Door Contract and Other Possibilities' (1998) 13 Ohio St J on Disp Resol 303, 364–78.
[8] *Preventing and Resolving Construction Disputes* (n 1) ch 8.
[9] See Thomas J Stipanowich, 'The Quiet Revolution Comes to Kentucky' (1992–93) 81 Ky LJ 855, 859–61 (discussing recent wave of initiatives focused on managing and resolving conflict).

B. Harbingers of a 'Quiet Revolution' in the Construction Industry

By the last decade of the twentieth century the US construction industry was sick, concluded the CII; the malady was the growth of litigation. The Business Roundtable found the construction industry to be one of America's least efficient sectors, largely because of the ' "adversarial dance" between parties to the construction project, [creating] a constant state of confrontation'.[10]

35.08

In earlier times, construction claims and controversies tended to be resolved informally and early through jobsite negotiation, decisions by design professionals, or, if necessary, informal binding arbitration without much lawyer involvement. But things had changed due to the growing size and complexity of the industry, inflationary pressures on contractors, tighter owner budgets and time frames for construction, and risk-shifting by owners. More emphasis was placed on lawyered adversarial processes, with many disputes being postponed and eventually consolidated in massive arbitration or litigation proceedings. The economic, business, and relational costs were huge.[11]

35.09

Suddenly, it seemed everyone was exploring and proposing solutions to the construction industry's crisis.[12] These included initiatives focused on tackling the roots of construction conflict and promoting jobsite collaboration, including partnering and contract terms to more thoughtfully allocate risk and incentivize collaboration. There were new 'real time' analogues to the old short and informal arbitration proceedings such as DRBs and adjudication. Finally, there were proposals for phased handling of disputes through successive 'sieves'—unassisted negotiation, followed (if necessary) by mediation and, finally, binding arbitration. Early perspectives on and experiences with these approaches were explored in a series of surveys developed through the cooperation of the ABA Forum on the Construction Industry, the AGC, the DPIC, and the AAA.[13]

35.10

(a) Partnering

A concept borrowed from the manufacturing and distribution sectors and pioneered by the US Army Corps of Engineers, partnering was designed to encourage collaboration and teamwork by deliberate early efforts to create an atmosphere of trust and cooperation on projects.[14] Facilitated partnering workshops were commonly conducted shortly after contract signing and attended by owner representatives and key members of the design and construction team. The aim was stronger individual bonds, better understanding of each other's objectives and expectations, and non-adversarial approaches for resolving problems on the job.[15] Surveyed contractors saw partnering as a superior means of reducing

35.11

---

[10] *Preventing and Resolving Construction Disputes* (n 1) 1.1.
[11] ibid 1.2.
[12] See generally *Preventing and Resolving Construction Disputes* (n 1).
[13] The author helped organize and implement these efforts and analysed the results. See generally Stipanowich, 'Beyond Arbitration' (n 1); Thomas J Stipanowich and Leslie King O'Neal, 'Charting the Course: The 1994 Construction Industry Survey on Dispute Avoidance and Resolution—Part I' (November 1995) 15 Constr Law 5; Thomas J Stipanowich and Leslie King O'Neal, 'Charting the Course: The 1994 Construction Industry Survey on Dispute Avoidance and Resolution—Part II' (April 1996) 16 Constr Law 8.
[14] ibid 5.1; Adam K Bult and others, *Delivering Dispute Free Construction Projects: Part III—Alternative Dispute Resolution* (Navigant Construction Forum, June 2014) 7–10.
[15] ibid, Bult.

dispute-related time and cost, enhancing understanding, opening channels of communication, and preserving job relationships;[16] the large majority of contractors expected its usage to grow.[17]

(b) Relational contracting

35.12 New attention to the causes of conflict on construction projects also centred on contract terms, including provisions for more equitable and efficient allocation of risks on construction projects.[18] Other efforts focused on contractual incentives aimed at aligning contractors' goals with those of owners, thereby promoting collaboration.[19]

(c) DRBs (adjudication)

35.13 Reclaiming some of the territory once served by informal arbitration as an efficient mechanism for resolving jobsite disputes, the DRB evolved as a short, sharp method for independent expert evaluation of disputes on infrastructure projects and large engineered jobs.[20] The concept involved the establishment of a standing panel of construction and engineering experts to periodically convene on site to review, and render summary non-binding opinions on, disputes regarding subsurface conditions and other issues. The idea was that the standing and expertise of the decision-makers would stimulate a quick settlement of the dispute, avoid prolonged conflict, and obviate traditional binding arbitration or litigation.

35.14 The DRB's British analogue was 'statutory adjudication'.[21] The procedure, which was established as a required method for resolving various project payment disputes by the Housing Grants, Construction and Regeneration Act 1996 (HGCRA),[22] consisted of a very short review and decision-making process. Given the temporal limitations, adjudication was necessarily 'rough' justice; one English QC suggested that the result might be 'little more than a gut reaction' to the dispute.[23] Under the law, the adjudicator's determination was only preliminarily binding, and the dispute could later be taken to binding arbitration or litigation.

(d) Dynamic conflict management: the DRA

35.15 In 1991, a custom-designed system for the renovation of a Hong Kong hospital incorporated many different elements in a programme that represented a quantum leap in the evolution of jobsite dispute resolution and 'project neutrals'. Because the contract called for demolition and construction to be performed while keeping the hospital and operating theatres operational, the public owner required a system that would identify and resolve disputes in the shortest possible time and prior to completion of the project. The result was a programme with tight time frames for jobsite decision-making and handling of claims, and a flexible, dynamic dispute resolution system centred upon the figure of a

---

[16] Stipanowich, 'Beyond Arbitration' (n 1) 147, tbl DD.4.
[17] ibid 156, tbl EE.4. See also Erik Larson, 'Project Partnering: Results of Study of 280 Construction Projects' (1995) 11(2) J Manage Eng 17.
[18] *Preventing and Resolving Construction Disputes* (n 1) ch 2.
[19] ibid, ch 3.
[20] Stipanowich, 'The Multi-Door Contract' (n 7) 360–4.
[21] ibid 363–4; Robert Gaitskell, *Trends in Construction Dispute Resolution* (SCL Papers No 129, 2005).
[22] s 108.
[23] John Tackaberry, *Flexing the Knotted Oak: English Arbitration's Task and Opportunity in the First Decade of the New Century* (SCL Papers 3, May 2002).

DRA, a construction expert with dispute resolution skills who would remain throughout the project.[24]

35.16 The DRA first met with job participants to explain and build support for a cooperative approach to problem-solving. Thereafter, the DRA made monthly visits to the site to monitor the status of the job and facilitate discussions regarding emerging issues. In the event of a formal challenge to a project decision, certificate, or evaluation, the parties were given time to resolve the matter through negotiation, failing which the DRA could make arrangements for mediation, mini-trial, or expert fact-finding. If assisted site-level negotiations failed, the DRA was to prepare a report identifying the key issues in dispute, the positions of the parties, and perceived barriers to settlement and make either a recommendation for settlement or a non-binding evaluation of the dispute.

35.17 The report would be used by senior off-site representatives of the parties in further negotiations, perhaps assisted by the DRA. Should matters not be resolved within 14 days of the issuance of the DRA's report, the DRA would set into motion a short-form arbitration procedure or other mutually acceptable means recommended by the DRA. The DRA procedure worked well. Despite the usual problems and several hundred owner-ordered changes, no disputes reached the stage of non-binding evaluation.[25]

(e) Mediation

35.18 Ultimately, the most significant development in American dispute resolution during the final decades of the last century was the widespread use of mediation. Construction lawyers came to know mediation through court referrals or agency programmes, word of mouth, and, ultimately, the incorporation of mediation in the dispute resolution provisions of contracts. What Texas mediator Eric Galton has referred to as the 'childhood cycle' of mediation was a period of attitudinal change for most of a generation of lawyers, including many once-sceptical litigators, some of whom embraced mediation with the fervour of religious converts.[26]

35.19 In a 1991 Forum Survey, construction attorneys registered generally positive attitudes towards mediation and saw it as appropriate for the maintenance of business relationships, promoting privacy and confidentiality, resolving disputes quickly and economically, providing an objective perspective on a case, overcoming impasses, and dealing with strong emotions.[27] Presaging future developments, a slight majority thought it would be appropriate for standardized construction contracts to provide for mediation prior to arbitration or litigation of disputes involving large sums of money.[28]

(f) Arbitration

35.20 Meanwhile, binding arbitration, the time-honoured mechanism for informal adjudication of construction disputes, was increasingly being viewed as a surrogate for litigation and

---

[24] Colin J Wall, 'The Dispute Resolution Adviser in the Construction Industry' in Peter Fenn and Rod Gameson (eds), *Construction Conflict Management and Resolution* (Routledge 1992) 328.
[25] Stipanowich, 'The Multi-Door Contract' (n 7) 387–9.
[26] Eric Galton, 'The Preventable Death of Mediation' (2002) 8(4) Disp Resol Mag 23, 23.
[27] Stipanowich, 'Beyond Arbitration' (n 1) 94–6.
[28] ibid 96–7.

being evaluated by that benchmark.²⁹ A mid-1980s Forum Survey of arbitration under the AAA Construction Industry Arbitration Rules indicated that construction lawyers generally compared arbitrators favourably with judges and juries when it came to fairness in decision-making; most viewed arbitration as a speedier and somewhat less costly procedure than bench or jury trial, especially in cases under US$250,000.³⁰

35.21 However, concerns regarding the quality of arbitrators fed into support for broader judicial review of awards, for reasoned awards, and generalized dissatisfaction with all aspects of arbitration. Attorneys also expressed concerns regarding the differing needs of small and large cases and tended to support procedural reform such as the use of preliminary hearings to arrange for discovery, for the narrowing of issues, and or establishing a schedule; mechanisms for joinder of parties or consolidation of hearings; and arbitrator supervision of document discovery.³¹

35.22 Responding to such concerns in the mid 1990s, the AAA's National Construction Dispute Resolution Committee modified the Construction Industry Rules to create 'tiers' of arbitration procedures for construction disputes of varying size and complexity, including expedited procedures formulated for low-dollar-value cases and a more extensive process for so-called 'large, complex' cases. The AAA also pared down its national rosters of neutrals and established stricter experiential and training requirements for arbitrators.³²

C. The Unfinished Revolution

35.23 Today, the spirit of the envisioned 'Quiet Revolution' is still evidenced in programmes anchored in 'real time' and on the jobsite. Some create a platform for collaboration among members of the construction team to constructively avoid conflict and manage the claims that are inevitable by-products of performance; others use on-call expert intervention before positions harden and thereby increase the cost, complexity, and potential disruptive impact of conflict. In the 'lawyered' domains of mediation and arbitration, however, the irresistible force of the revolution in conflict resolution collided with the immovable object of the legal culture and its litigation orientation; present trends and practices reflect the push and pull of these forces.

(a) Tackling the roots of conflict: collaborative contracting

(1) Partnering

35.24 Despite the early expectations of many in the industry, partnering never came into general usage and is typically a feature of public construction programmes, notably state departments of transportation. Some studies have indicated that the use of partnering has resulted in more projects being completed on or ahead of schedule, in improved contract administration, reduced claims and disputes, reduced owner engineering and

---

²⁹ See Stipanowich, 'The Multi-Door Contract' (n 7) 336–57. For a good summary of the historical background of construction arbitration, see Philip L Bruner and Patrick J O'Connor, *Bruner & O'Connor on Construction Law* (West Group 2002) paras 20.1–20.2.
³⁰ Thomas J Stipanowich, 'Rethinking American Arbitration' (1988) 63 Ind LJ 425, 458–61.
³¹ Stipanowich, 'The Multi-Door Contract' (n 7) 339–41.
³² ibid 343–7.

administrative expenses, and more value engineering.[33] The California Department of Transportation employs project partnering alongside DRBs (for projects over US$10 million) and DRAs.[34]

(2) IPD

Elements of partnering and relational, collaboration-oriented contracts are melded into the concept of IPD,[35] a relative newcomer to the US marketplace of delivery systems that has thus far been utilized on only a few domestic projects.[36] IPD models are founded on a multi-party agreement between primary stakeholders in design and construction, a commitment to collaboration built on trust, and defining success mutually in terms of project outcomes rather than individual goals.[37] IPDs enable design decisions to be enhanced by the involvement of all team members and the free flow of technical and budgetary information. **35.25**

Successful IPDs, therefore, require effective, open communication, and for this reason considerable effort must be given to establishing protocols for the use and management of information, including Building Information Modelling (BIM).[38] The many non-traditional aspects of IPD place new challenges upon participants (such as the criteria for selecting co-venturers,[39] the precise contractual form of collaboration, and protocols respecting the measurement of performance of specific goals, including achievement of project milestones, health and safety requirements, life-cycle costs, sustainability, etc).[40] However, proponents point out that traditional project methodologies and accompanying adversarialism have contributed to significant continuing inefficiencies in the construction industry.[41] **35.26**

(b) 'Real-time' jobsite resolution

(1) DRBs (adjudication)

According to early statistics developed by the Dispute Review Board Foundation, the leading advocacy group for the process, DRBs achieved an extraordinary level of success, both in terms of the number of claims apparently settled after a DRB hearing and the prophylactic effect on disputes of the very presence in place of a DRB.[42] Although there is little **35.27**

---

[33] Bult (n 14) 9.
[34] James G Zack, 'Delivering Dispute Free Construction Projects: Part II—Construction & Claim Management' (Navigant Construction Forum, March 2014) 4–5.
[35] See generally AIA National/AIA California Counsel, 'Integrated Project Delivery: A Guide' (2007 version 1) (hereinafter, 'Integrated Project Delivery'); CMAA, An Owner's Guide to Project Delivery Methods, 1, 28–30 (hereinafter, CMAA, 'Owner's Guide').
[36] ibid, CMAA, 'Owner's Guide' 28. Examples of foreign applications of IPD included project alliancing approaches in the United Kingdom and Australia. See ACCL Princeton Symposium, 'Building the Future', ACCL J 147–54 (Special Edition, May 2007) (comments of Michael Wilke, COO Americas, Parsons Brinkerhoff).
[37] 'Integrated Project Delivery' (n 35) 5.
[38] ibid 10.
[39] CMAA, 'Owner's Guide' (n 35) 29.
[40] ibid 11.
[41] 'Integrated Project Delivery' (n 35) 3.
[42] See Carol C Menassa and Feniosky Peña Mora, 'Analysis of Dispute Review Boards Application in US Construction Projects from 1975 to 2007' (2010) 26(2) J Manage Eng 65 (more than 90 per cent of cases heard by DRB panels settled in the wake of panel recommendation; effectiveness of DRB as a prevention technique observed on 50 per cent of projects where no disputes were ever heard by a DRB panel).

quantitative evidence actually linking DRBs to lower project costs and fewer delays and disruptions,[43] industry perceptions of the DRBs tend to be very positive;[44] a number of public contracting authorities are convinced of their value and committed to their use.[45] DRBs were even utilized on the nation's largest construction project, the Boston Central Artery/Tunnel Project, for which standing panels were established for all contracts over US$20 million.[46] The 'Big Dig' offers a cautionary tale, however: due to the sheer volume and complexity of disputes and claims, disputes over entitlement were not concluded in 'real time', but were left to be resolved at the end of each contract; ultimately, the backlog of claims had to be resolved through a 'retrofitted' programme of negotiation and mediation.[47]

35.28 The potential impact of an abbreviated, preliminary expert decision-making process on the landscape of conflict resolution is also revealed in the extraordinary growth of 'statutory adjudication' in Britain,[48] where the 'vast majority' of adjudication decisions are accepted by the losing parties.[49] One authority reports that 'well over 80% of the adjudication decisions are simply accepted, with the losing party content that it has had a fair chance to put its case to an independent tribunal'.[50] Explains one judge: 'The clear message appears to be that in broad terms the industry is content with adjudication.'[51]

35.29 As of 2006, DRBs had been employed on more than 1,300 projects, including many major infrastructure projects, and were credited with directly resolving almost 1,600 disputes.[52] Dispute Boards are being used on major projects around the globe; and international financial institutions are now mandating the process use on large infrastructure projects.[53] Dispute Adjudication Boards (DABs), which render decisions that are binding unless and until they are reversed by arbitration or litigation, are provided for in FIDIC Conditions.[54] The ICC recently published its own Dispute Board documents.[55]

(2) Project mediation (standing mediator)

35.30 Although for some reason project mediation appears not to have seen extensive use, the appointment of a 'standing' dispute resolution professional to mediate issues as they arise

---

[43] However, a recent study of 3,000 projects over a ten-year period indicates that projects that used DRBs 'faced reduced costs and schedule growth' when compared to non-DRB projects. See Duzgun Agdas and Ralph D Ellis, 'Analysis of Construction Dispute Review Boards' (August 2013) 5(3) J Legal Affairs & Disp Res in Eng'g and Constr 122.
[44] See generally Kathleen Harmon, 'Effectiveness of Dispute Review Boards' (2003) 129(6) J Constr Eng'g & Mngmt 674.
[45] See, eg, 2009 Caltrans DRB-DRA Amended 2006 Specifications. Caltrans' specifications call for a DRB in contracts over US$10 million and individual DRAs in other projects.
[46] Kurt L Dettman, Martin Harty, and Joel Lewin, 'Resolving Megaproject Claims: Lessons from Boston's Big Dig' (Summer 2010) 30(2) Constr Law 5.
[47] ibid 10.
[48] Gaitskell, *Trends in Construction Dispute Resolution* (n 21) 1–5, 10, 13.
[49] ibid 11 ('Figures given anecdotally show that there have been about 15,000 adjudications thus far ... Of this enormous number only about 300 have reached the courts, and of these about 200 reported decisions have resulted').
[50] ibid.
[51] Frances Kirkham, *The Future of Adjudication* (SCL Papers No 51, September 2004) 1–2.
[52] Data published by the DRBF. See <http://www.drb.org> accessed 25 September 2015.
[53] See, eg, 'EIC Contractor's Guide to the MDB [Multilateral Development Bank] Harmonised Edition (June 2010) of the FIDIC Conditions of Contract for Construction' (April 2011) 28 Int'l Constr L Rev 439.
[54] Axel-Volkmar Jaeger and Götz-Sebastian Hök, *FIDIC—A Guide for Practitioners* (Springer Verlag 2010) 396–7.
[55] See generally Nicholas Gould, *Establishing Dispute Boards—Selecting, Nominating and Appointing Board Members* (SCL Papers No 135, December 2006).

during the course of a construction project can be of value in keeping the job on track and helping to limit the number of claims that must be subjected to more formal and expensive dispute resolution procedures.[56] DRAs have seen limited use, although the highly customized and dynamic approach used in Hong Kong may not have been replicated in other venues.

(c) Mediation: multi-dimensional instrument, whistle-stop on the litigation line

35.31 In the United States, mediation has become the dominant template for third-party intervention in conflict, including construction disputes, and it appears to be in a growth mode throughout the world. Since construction mediation came onto the scene in the United States late in the twentieth century, mediation has become a standard feature of contractual stepped procedures for resolving construction disputes,[57] and in most parts of the country it is almost unimaginable that a case would proceed through litigation without at least one 'stop' along the way for mediation. As a lawyer in one of my recent arbitrations put it, 'by this time in a case [late in discovery] we have usually had at least one mediation, and sometimes two!' Mediation has also come to the fore in other leading common law countries such as the United Kingdom, Canada, Australia, and New Zealand, and user demand is taking root in other parts of the world.

35.32 But in the United States, where modern mediation first took root, mediation processes, like arbitration, have evolved along lines very different from those imagined by early proponents. Some originally envisioned mediation as a revolutionary mechanism capable of encouraging disputants to assume a primary role in resolving their own conflict, repairing broken relationships, promoting interest-based solutions, and even opening up the justice system by engaging people from different disciplines and community sectors as mediators. But while mediation is capable of achieving all of these things and to some extent has done so, some believe it has fallen short of its promise.

35.33 Peter Adler, a consultant with deep roots in the modern history of US mediation, recently conducted an informal survey of mediators he knew personally or by reputation and found that although their stories were an interweaving of the good and the bad, there was a group sense that mediation had largely devolved into a game of numbers, or positional bargaining.[58] Lawyers had gradually established 'hegemony, a takeover of the mediation work and a slow but steady disenfranchisement of non-lawyers'. Although there are many positive aspects to the continuing, evolving relationship between lawyers and mediation, there is concern about the potential for lawyers to frame and dominate the process, game the system, limit the mediator's role, and control communications[59]—at worst, turning mediation into a mere whistle-stop on the litigation line.[60]

---

[56] See Nicholas Gould and others, *Mediating Construction Disputes: An Evaluation of Existing Practice* (King's College London, Centre of Construction Law and Dispute Resolution 2010) 17 (discussing project mediation in the United Kingdom and CEDR's Project Mediation package).
[57] See Thomas J Stipanowich, 'Arbitration: The "New Litigation"' (2010) Ill L Rev 1, 29–30.
[58] Peter S Adler, 'Expectation and Regret: A Look Back at How Mediation Has Fared in the US' (7th National Conference, CMC, London, 2 May 2013) 5.
[59] ibid 6–7.
[60] I am indebted to litigator-turned-mediator John Van Winkle for the highly appropriate 'litigation train' metaphor. See John R Van Winkle, *Mediation: A Path Back for the Lost Lawyer* (ABA 2001) 1.

(1) Evolution of construction mediation as a lawyered process

35.34 Given the inherent flexibility of mediation and the critical importance of maintaining clear lines of communication and good relationships between project team members during the course of a project, it seemed natural that mediators might be able to step in early for the purpose of helping nip conflict in the bud, fostering better job communications and strengthening relational ties. Sometimes this happens.[61] From early days, however, the mediation of construction disputes tended not to focus on those things, but rather on settling cases along the road to trial or arbitration. From the beginning, mediation usually came about after—often long after—the parties had 'lawyered up'; it was rarely embraced as a strategy of 'real time' intervention on a job, while the conflict was fresh and positions not yet hardened. Instead, it was usually prompted by a court or by attorneys.[62] The mediator was nearly always a lawyer, and sometimes a retired judge.[63] And sooner or later the process nearly always got down to the hard slogging: the back-and-forth of distributive bargaining resulting in a monetary settlement.[64]

(2) Experienced lawyers in mediation

35.35 As mediation of construction disputes has become settled practice, a trend reinforced by the inclusion of mediation as an element in stepped contractual dispute resolution provisions, the early patterns have continued. The difference is that most litigators now have garnered extensive experience with mediation and with a wide variety of mediators. They may use these insights in a variety of ways. They may work strategically with the mediator by, for example, providing helpful information about the dynamics of the dispute and the personalities of the participants, and by ensuring that the negotiation 'dance' proceeds in a way that best protects their client's interest while exploring trade-offs, and, occasionally, options for value creation.[65] While it is expected that some degree of manipulation will occur as attorneys withhold information or mask intentions from the mediator (just as mediators manipulate the process and parties in various ways, consciously or unconsciously), mediators believe the process generally works. More than three-quarters (76.7 per cent) of respondents to a 2014 Straus Institute Survey of experienced mediators in the membership of the IAM viewed the increasing familiarity of counsel with the mediation process as a positive development.[66]

---

[61] See, eg, Zack (n 34) 32 (noting that mediation is always an option in resolving job claims and disputes); Stipanowich, 'The Multi-Door Contract' (n 7) 368–9 (discussing successful example of use of standing mediator on public project).

[62] See Stipanowich, 'Beyond Arbitration' (n 1) 111, tbl J (65 per cent of reported cases involved mediation by post-dispute agreement of the parties; about 29 per cent were mediated pursuant to a court order or court rules).

[63] ibid 116, tbl O (64.5 per cent of mediators in reported cases were attorneys; 21.1 per cent were retired judges).

[64] See ibid 120, tbl R (the vast majority of settlements (298 out of 315 cases) involved money; a much smaller percentage resulted in an agreement to perform certain work (32 out of 315); only a handful of cases produced other outcomes from settlement).

[65] An excellent discussion of advocacy during mediation may be found in Dwight Golann, ch 12, 'Advocacy at Specific Stages' in Dwight Golann, *Mediating Legal Disputes: Effective Strategies for Neutrals and Advocates* (ABA 2009) 255.

[66] The IAM-Straus Institute Survey on Mediator Practices and Perceptions was sent to 153 individuals, all IAM Fellows, and 85.0 per cent (130 individuals) participated in the survey; 78.4 per cent (120 individuals) completed the entire survey. The respondent pool included individuals who stated they 'regularly practised' in: Africa; Asia, including the Middle East; Australia and New Zealand; Canada; Europe (both Western and Eastern, with a majority from the United Kingdom); Latin America; and the United States. These and other data from the IAM/Straus Institute Survey will be published in Thomas J Stipanowich and Zachary P Ulrich, 'The IAM-Straus Survey on Mediator Practices and Perceptions' (forthcoming).

On the other hand, attorneys may contribute to mediation dysfunction by actively misleading the mediator regarding the prospects for settlement and ensuring that the day of resolution is postponed in order for the litigation train to proceed through full discovery.[67] The vast majority (84.2 per cent) of respondents to the IAM/Straus Institute Survey of experienced mediators indicated that attorneys sometimes use mediation as a means of continuing the litigation process with no intent to settle.[68] While counsel may not be faulted for wanting to have material information in hand before concluding a settlement, this does not mean that full discovery is necessary; indeed, a skilful mediator may be able to help the parties identify and target priorities for information exchange.

35.36

Counsel sometimes employ mediation for the sole purpose of obtaining information regarding the opposition's case. Moreover, according to Peter Adler, mediators are expressing growing concern about lawyers taking control of the mediation process, limiting joint sessions, and insisting that all communications go directly through them.[69]

35.37

Thus, the increasing sophistication of attorneys has many positive and some negative implications for successful mediation. It must also be said that their experience has undoubtedly equipped many attorneys with the skills and understanding to more successfully engage in direct negotiations with their counterparts, thus easing the need for mediators.

35.38

(3) Mediation as professional practice

Today, mediation is a professional livelihood for a growing number. Nearly half (47.7 per cent) of those responding to the 2014 IAM/Straus Institute Survey indicated that mediation practice occupies 90 per cent or more of their work time. Almost 80 per cent of the respondents devote more than half their time to mediation practice. Nearly three-quarters (73.8 per cent) of respondents had mediated 1,000 or more cases.[70]

35.39

(4) Mediators: styles v strategies

Since the earliest days of 'modern mediation' there has been discussion and debate about the techniques mediators use. Thousands of mediators received training based on the principle that mediators should respect party autonomy by avoiding any expressions of opinion regarding the issues in dispute or the prospects for recovery in court (a reality that is still pervasive in mediation training in other parts of the world), but it soon became clear that many mediators were engaging in some form of evaluation at some stage of mediation, and that parties often sought out such input.[71] 80 per cent of the mediators responding to the IAM/Straus Institute Survey indicated that their reputation as a mediator who can offer useful assessments of parties' cases is a factor of some importance in attracting and maintaining clients.[72] Indeed, in the 1991 Forum Survey of specific mediation experiences of construction attorneys, there was actually a statistically significant correlation between evaluation and settlement. Of course, approaches to conveying evaluations vary considerably.

35.40

Hoping to chart the evolving territory of mediation practice, Professor Len Riskin's famous 'grid' identified a spectrum of mediator approaches differentiating 'facilitative' from

35.41

---

[67] Susan N Exon, *Advanced Guide for Mediators* (LexisNexis 2014) 71–2.
[68] See n 66 above.
[69] Adler (n 58) 7.
[70] See n 66 above.
[71] Stipanowich, 'The Multi-Door Contract' (n 7) 367.
[72] ibid.

'evaluative' techniques, and another spectrum distinguishing 'narrow' emphases (focusing on the issues in dispute, party positions, the likely disposition of the dispute in the absence of a negotiated settlement) and 'broad' emphases (embracing concerns about underlying party interests, needs, and other factors).[73] Our growing self-awareness of and continuing discussion about what mediators do and why they do it led Riskin to tinker with his grid, reflecting more nuanced insights.

35.42 For present purposes, several points are particularly important. First of all, we know that it is common for mediators to tailor their approaches to the circumstances, and 'move around the grid' during the course of a single mediation.[74] Second, there is appreciation of the fact that mediators' activities are directed not only at substantive discussions, but at process management; both are critical elements of the recipe for resolution, and mediators' approaches to both these elements will vary depending on mediator styles or strategies. Finally, we understand that some mediators' approaches are purely reflexive—that is, a matter of their individual style or character traits—and that some successful construction mediators are sought out precisely because they always handle cases in a particular way. That said, most mediators will best serve the parties and process by using approaches reflectively and strategically—that is, as a deliberate response to specific circumstances.[75]

(5) Convening 'upfront' work

35.43 Just as experienced arbitrators are coming to grips with the need to set the stage for the arbitration process through carefully planned pre-hearing conferences, today's mediators tend to place great emphasis on preliminary preparation before the actual mediation session(s).[76] In addition to developing a picture of the issues in dispute, they may familiarize themselves with the history of negotiation, the 'temperature' of the parties, and key personalities at play. They may work with counsel to lay the groundwork for an appropriate mediation process, including the agenda for initial joint sessions and the tentative timing and even the planned duration of caucuses. Extensive forward planning is critical for the mediation of complex construction cases involving many parties.

(6) Mediators' varying approaches to the process

35.44 Data from the IAM/Straus Institute Survey also confirm the notion that mediators employ various approaches to different elements of the process, exemplified by their use of joint sessions and caucuses.[77] Some mediators (52.4 per cent) always or usually begin mediation with all parties in a joint session; others (39.7 per cent) always or usually begin the mediation with all parties in caucus. Some (24.6 per cent) always or usually keep parties in caucus during the entire mediation; others (29.4 per cent) never do so. Some tend to tell parties that all information shared during caucus will be confidential unless they instruct the mediator to share it; others tend to tell parties that they will share any information learned during caucus with the other party as they see appropriate, unless instructed not to share it. A large minority (42.8 per cent) say they 'sometimes reveal information to parties in caucus that

---

[73] ibid.
[74] As one successful construction mediator vividly remarked: 'I am facilitative in the morning and evaluative in the afternoon.'
[75] See, eg, Marjorie Aaron and Dwight Golann, 'Merits Barriers: Evaluation and Decision Analysis' in Golann (n 65) 145–62 (discussing if, when, and how mediators might offer evaluations).
[76] ibid 35–50.
[77] See n 66 above.

may be construed as sharing more information than I have been given direct permission to share'.

(7) Stepped processes (mediation and arbitration)

35.45 Today, mediation of construction disputes is likely to occur pursuant to a provision in a multi-phased dispute resolution procedure that begins with some form of job-based initial procedure and culminates in some kind of adjudication (arbitration, litigation, or hearings before an administrative tribunal).[78] Stepped dispute resolution provisions are a straightforward response to the reality that most construction disputes are amenable to a negotiated resolution, and that there are multiple benefits associated with early, informal resolution.[79] Stepped approaches are intended to function as a series of sieves or filters to cull all of the issues and controversies that may be resolved short of binding adjudication. Where direct negotiation between representatives of the parties is unavailing, the intervention of a mediator may help break the logjam and craft a workable resolution.[80]

35.46 But the linear arrangement of elements in multi-stage dispute resolution templates does not take account of the reality that dispute resolution is very often 'non-linear'. It is frequently not viewed as possible or practicable to settle a case before the filing of an arbitration demand. This may be because of differing (and often, unrealistic) expectations on the part of counsel or parties regarding the likely disposition of issues should the case go to trial or arbitration or the settlement value of a case;[81] the perceived need for more information;[82] law firm economics; or other factors.

35.47 Recent empirical research indicates that legal advocates' judgments and choices regarding settlement may be clouded by, and settlement delayed by, lawyers' excessive reliance on intuition; the desire to avoid perceived loss; the tendency to seek confirmation of the biases they bring to litigation; the notion that it is always better to have more information; and concerns about justifying previously spent dollars in litigating a case.[83] When settlement does not occur during the preliminary stages of dispute resolution, the arbitration proceeding becomes the backdrop against which negotiated settlement discussions will occur. In many such cases, mediation is postponed until a relatively late stage in the pre-hearing process when discovery is completed or well advanced.[84]

---

[78] This section is adapted from Thomas J Stipanowich and Zachary P Ulrich, 'Commercial Arbitration and Settlement: Empirical Insights into the Roles Arbitrators Play' (2014) 6 Penn St YB Arb & Mediation 1, 8–10.
[79] See Thomas J Stipanowich and Peter H Kaskell (eds), *Commercial Arbitration at its Best: Successful Strategies for Business Users* (CPR 2001) ch 1 (discussing importance of multi-tiered approaches for management of conflict and avoiding stand-alone arbitration provisions). See also 'CEDR Commission Report on Settlement in International Arbitration' (Final Report, November 2009) 4, 4.2.1 (hereinafter, 'CEDR Commission Report') (discussing benefits of multi-tier dispute resolution clauses).
[80] ibid, CEDR Commission Report, 11–14.
[81] Andrew J Wistrich and Jeffrey J Rachlinski, 'How Lawyers' Intuitions Prolong Litigation' (2013) 86 S Cal L Rev 571, 576; Paul M Lurie, 'Using the Guided Choice Process to Reduce the Cost of Resolving Construction Disputes' (2014) 9 CLInt'l 18, 21.
[82] ibid, Lurie.
[83] See generally ibid, Lurie. See also Randall Kiser, *Beyond Right and Wrong: The Power of Effective Decision Making for Attorney and Clients* (Springer 2010) 89–195 (discussing 'decision errors' by attorneys and related psychological and institutional factors).
[84] See Lurie (n 81) 19 (noting that 'mediation is frequently seen as a tool to be used close to trial or an arbitration hearing as a hedge against an unfavorable judgment or award').

35.48 Over the years, there have been efforts to 'think outside the box' of the linear framework of stepped dispute resolution by exploiting its potentialities in different ways. For example, it has been suggested that mediators be equipped with a wider variety of tools to break impasse at early stages of conflict (such as a more nuanced appreciation of cognitive factors affecting negotiations).[85] They may also facilitate the parties' focus on key factual issues and related, limited information exchange[86] or targeted binding or non-binding decisions by judges or arbitrators that could lay the groundwork for resolution of conflict.[87] Even where substantive issues cannot be resolved in mediation, mediators may nevertheless focus on facilitating agreements regarding dispute resolution process elements and helping parties to set the stage for arbitration proceedings with features that are effectively tailored to the issues at hand.[88]

35.49 Finally, some have promoted or participated in forms of 'med-arb', by which we mean a proceeding in which a single third party serves, or agrees to serve, as both the mediator and arbitrator.[89] Sometimes, arrangements are made between disputing parties and a third party 'neutral' prior to the commencement of any services that the latter will mediate the dispute and, failing a complete resolution of the dispute, will arbitrate all outstanding matters.[90]

35.50 A variant of this kind of arrangement is 'MEDALOA'—mediation followed by last-offer (or final offer) arbitration.[91] Sometimes, third parties who are engaged in mediating a dispute are asked to shift to an arbitral role and adjudicate the dispute;[92] in other cases arbitrators are invited to assume the role of mediators.[93] These kinds of dual-role arrangements raise a variety of legal, practical, and ethical issues that have led many US practitioners and neutrals to avoid them,[94] although dual roles tend to be more readily embraced in some other parts of the world in some formats such as conciliation within arbitration.[95] There are indications, however, that many US dispute resolution professionals do engage in such activities, albeit relatively infrequently.[96]

---

[85] ibid 19–20.
[86] Stipanowich and Kaskell (n 79) 19.
[87] Lurie (n 81) 20–1. cf Wistrich and Rachlinski (n 81) 624–6.
[88] ibid 19–20. Paul Lurie's Guided Choice concept actually centres on the notion of using mediation to 'diagnose' a dispute and assist parties in structuring an appropriate dispute resolution process, possibly including an appropriately tailored form of arbitration.
[89] See Stipanowich and Kaskell (n 79) 20–4. For a discussion on med-arb, see Jeffrey Waincymer, 'Optimising the Use of Mediation in International Arbitration: A Cost–Benefit Analysis of "Two Hat" Versus "Two People" Models' in Julio César Betancourt (ed), *Defining Issues in International Arbitration: Celebrating 100 Years of the Chartered Institute of Arbitrators* (OUP 2016) ch 28.
[90] ibid, Stipanowich and Kaskell.
[91] ibid 25–6.
[92] ibid 22–4 (setting forth suggested guidelines for handling such arrangements).
[93] ibid 29–30 (setting forth suggested guidelines for handling such arrangements).
[94] ibid 20–2 (discussing attitudes of leading arbitrators and practitioners on CPR Commission and concerns regarding med-arb); Thomas Stipanowich, 'Contract and Conflict Management' (2001) Wis L Rev 831, 853–5 <http://www.ssrn.com/abstract=1377917> accessed 25 September 2015. See also 'CEDR Commission Report' (n 79) 3, 11–12 (November 2009) <http://www.cedr.com> accessed 25 September 2015 (reporting results of a commission sponsored by CEDR, the London-based mediation and mediation training organization).
[95] For an excellent tabular summary of different national laws and their posture regarding arbitrators' promotion of and involvement in settlement efforts and related issues, see 'CEDR Commission Report' (n 79) App 4, 18ff. See also 'Reflections on Med-Arb and Arb-Med: Around the World' (Spring 2009) 2 NY Disp Res L 71–119 (collection of articles highlighting use of med-arb and variants).
[96] See Stipanowich (n 94) 853–4.

(8) International trends

Beside the United States, 'modern' mediation is most fully developed in the United Kingdom, Canada, Australia, and New Zealand, but it is developing at various rates in many other countries. The IAM, a leading body of experienced mediators, includes members from the United States, Canada, the United Kingdom and other countries in the European Union, Australia and New Zealand, Latin America, the Middle East, other parts of Asia, and Africa. Following up on its Directive on mediation, the European Union has provided various forms of support for the development of mediation in member countries. All of this will help to promote greater use of mediation in international disputes.   35.51

(d) **Arbitration: coming to grips with 'new litigation'**[97]

(1) Decline in domestic construction arbitration

As long as any of us can remember, binding arbitration has been a dominant feature in the landscape of construction conflict. But in recent years, arbitration has faced increasing challenges. The AAA's important construction caseload dropped off dramatically in recent years, as shown in Table 35.1. Significant reductions in the number of mediations and arbitrations reflect the impact of the Great Recession, the worst economic downturn since the Great Depression, on activity in the construction sector.[98] However, while the number of mediations decreased by about one-third between 2008 and 2013, the arbitration caseload dropped by an even greater proportion (around 43 per cent).   35.52

Table 35.1 AAA Construction Caseload (2008–13)[99]

Construction	2008	2009	2010	2011	2012	2013
Arbitration	3,075	2,805	2,322	1,817	1,733	1,767
Mediation	994	940	807	743	707	666
Total	4,069	3,745	3,129	2,560	2,440	2,433

One reason for the disparity may be the very fact that increased use of mediation has lessened the demand for arbitration by producing more early settlements. Or perhaps some attorneys believe that many of the benefits traditionally sought from arbitration, including efficiency, expedition, privacy, and business-oriented results, are more effectively achieved in mediation. But neither of these explanations fully explains why, a mere decade after the debut of a mediation stage in the AIA documents, the drafters elected to remove arbitration as the default process for binding adjudication.[100]   35.53

Moreover, when results from a 2011 survey of corporate counsel in major corporations are compared with data from a similar survey in 1997, there is a decided decline in the number   35.54

---

[97] Portions of this section are adapted from Thomas J Stipanowich, 'Reflections on the State and Future of Commercial Arbitration: Challenges, Opportunities, Proposals' (2014) 25 Am Rev Int'l Arb 297.
[98] Deltek Clarity 35th Annual Architecture and Engineering Industry Study (2014) 4.
[99] Emails from Ryan Boyle, Vice President—Statistics and In-House Research, AAA, to author (6 September 2013; 16 June 2014).
[100] For a discussion of the recent evolution of dispute resolution provisions in standard construction contracts, see Stipanowich (n 57) 30.

of companies currently using arbitration for commercial disputes;[101] also, fewer corporate counsel are expecting their companies to use arbitration for commercial disputes in the future.[102] The question is, why would arbitration, which for so long was synonymous with dispute resolution in the construction industry, be perceived as inferior, and not superior, to litigation as a means of adjudication?

(2) Users' contrasting perspectives on arbitration

35.55 All indications are that business users and counsel seem to be divided in their views of arbitration as a substitute for litigation in court. Lawyers who choose litigation over arbitration may do so because of the perceived need for process control—that is, the sort of control that comes with the stages of litigation as framed by federal and state court procedures, including broad discovery, rules governing the admission of evidence, adherence to legal standards, and appeal on the merits.[103]

35.56 Outside counsel, the advocates who typically handle adjudication, are likely to be even more biased in favour of litigation. One long-time, well-regarded consultant to the construction industry shared with me that the outside attorneys he deals with, retains, or represents generally prefer litigation to arbitration. While he believed that this preference among outside counsel is in some respects a matter of familiarity and comfort with evidentiary and procedural rules in court, the main reason was economic.

35.57 Once the litigation train begins to roll, full-blown discovery permits law firms to 'milk the juice out of a case' by deploying armies of associates (billing long hours at high rates) and paralegals; as discovery winds down and the law firm has made the bulk of its potential fees, the case often settles. Even cases taken on a contingency may incentivize such conduct since contingencies are often mixed with an adjusted but still substantial hourly rate. Leaving the larger ethical and moral questions aside, it is significant that a white paper jointly produced by the American College of Trial Lawyers strongly disparaged the 'one-size-fits-all' character of modern US discovery and called for the facilitation of appropriate choices to fit specific circumstances.[104]

35.58 Of course, many attorneys understand that arbitration is an 'engine of choice'.[105] Choice-making in arbitration should depend on the goals and priorities of users. For some, this could mean a procedure tailored to 'getting it right' in a litigation sense, with full-blown court-like due process. If the parties so desire, arbitration can be tailored to provide virtually all of the key elements of litigation (but in a decidedly more private setting, subject to rules or agreements promoting confidentiality).[106] Appellate arbitration rules even permit a surrogate form of appeal on the merits.[107] But for other businesses, the greater part of justice may be getting

---

[101] See Thomas J Stipanowich and Ryan J Lamare, 'Living with ADR: Evolving Perceptions and Use of Mediation, Arbitration and Conflict Management in Fortune 1,000 Corporations' (2014) 19 Harv Negot L Rev 1, 46–8 <http://www.ssrn.com/abstract=2221471> accessed 25 September 2015.
[102] ibid 49–50.
[103] ibid 63.
[104] IAALS, 'Final Report on the Joint Project of the ACTL Task Force on Discovery and the IAALS' (11 March 2009) 3.
[105] See generally Thomas J Stipanowich, 'Arbitration and Choice: Taking Charge of the "New Litigation" (Symposium Keynote Presentation)' (2009) 7 DePaul Bus & Comm LJ 383, 388 (discussing how business users and counsel may make more effective use of arbitration through the exercise of choice).
[106] Stipanowich (n 57) 64–6.
[107] Stipanowich (n 105) 429–30. The AAA published new appellate arbitration procedures in 2013. AAA Optional Appellate Rules (1 November 2013).

the dispute over with and getting on with business, or having a clear and final decision as a foundation for forward planning;[108] in other words, justice is about how a fundamentally fair result can be achieved with speed, economy, and finality. Arbitration can accommodate and facilitate these and other goals by permitting parties to make choices regarding:

(i) decision-maker(s) (permitting the selection of persons with specific substantive knowledge or experience, professional qualifications, or process management skills, or a tribunal melding these attributes);
(ii) process, from federal-court-like procedures to streamlined/expedited approaches;
(iii) the standards by which decisions are made (legal, trade, technical, or, perhaps, 'equitable');
(iv) the degree of privacy of the hearing room, and the confidentiality of arbitration-related information;
(v) venue;
(vi) the law governing the arbitration process; and
(vii) the level of supporting administration services.

(3) 'Drift' towards a litigation model

35.59 Over the last two decades, however, arbitrations have tended to drift in the direction of a more formalized, lawyer-dominated model with many of the trappings of litigation in federal or state court.[109] In the words of one industry expert with whom I spoke, many attorneys 'want to make arbitration as much like litigation as they can'. This means, among other things, a much stronger emphasis on the pre-hearing process, including sometimes-extensive discovery and motion practice. These realities have presented new challenges for arbitrators.

(4) Responses to concerns about increasing cost and delay

35.60 Not so long ago, cost-effectiveness and speed were among the primary reasons for choosing arbitration over litigation.[110] However, as arbitration processes take on more of the characteristics of litigation in court, cycle time and costs inevitably increase, reducing the relative benefit of the arbitration alternative in some eyes.[111] These developments recently inspired a number of US and international initiatives, such as the 'College of Commercial Arbitrators Protocols for Expeditious, Cost-Effective Commercial Arbitration',[112] premised on the notion that increased cost and delay are a shared problem of business users and counsel, outside counsel, arbitrators, and arbitration provider institutions. The protocols offer pertinent guidelines and proposed action steps for all four sets of stakeholders.

35.61 Importantly, the AAA and other leading provider organizations have recently placed greater emphasis on giving arbitrators tools to more effectively manage the pre-hearing process.[113]

---

[108] Stipanowich (n 105) 388.
[109] Bult (n 14) 21; Stipanowich (n 57) 8–24 (discussing evolution of arbitration as the 'new litigation').
[110] See Stipanowich (n 57) 64–5.
[111] In the 2011 Fortune 1,000 Survey, more companies viewed the costs of arbitration as a barrier to its use than in the 1997 Survey.
[112] Thomas J Stipanowich and others (eds), *Protocols for Expeditious, Cost-Effective Commercial Arbitration: Key Action Steps for Business Users, Counsel, Arbitrators & Arbitration Provider Institutions* (CCA 2010) (hereinafter, 'CCA Protocols').
[113] See, eg, AAA Commercial Arbitration Rules, r 9 (integrating mediation into process for larger cases); r 21 (preliminary hearing); r 22 (pre-hearing exchange and production of information); r 23 (enforcement power of arbitrator); r 33 (handling of dispositive motions); r 38 (emergency measures of protection); r 58 (sanctions by arbitrators); 'CCA Protocols' (n 112) 78–80 (listing JAMS, CPR, ICC, and other procedures).

Some providers also now offer a variety of 'accelerated', 'expedited', 'streamlined', or 'fast track' rules;[114] it remains to be seen whether clients and counsel will embrace these procedures for cases involving more than relatively small amounts in dispute. In order to encourage resort to such alternatives, it is up to providers or other proponents of arbitration to collect data on the performance of arbitrations conducted pursuant to such rules and publish resulting statistics along with pertinent success stories or cautionary tales.[115]

35.62 It appears that many arbitrators are now embracing the concept of proactive case management at all stages of arbitration. Responses to the recent survey of many of the most experienced US arbitrators by Pepperdine's Straus Institute for Dispute Resolution in cooperation with the CCA indicates that seasoned arbitrators are tending to recognize the importance of their role in actively managing the arbitration process from the outset, beginning with thorough preliminary hearings or pre-hearing conferences.[116] Two key priorities are managing discovery and motion practice—both primary sources of cost and delay. Veteran arbitrators are also employing a wide array of techniques for managing hearings, including (with consent of counsel) 'chess-clocks' to enforce definitive bounds on time allocation and 'hot-tubbing', the practice of putting expert witnesses on the stand at the same time for the purpose of promoting real mutual engagement on key points in controversy.

(5) Demise of the multi-disciplinary tribunal

35.63 Another aspect of arbitration 'drift' towards a litigation model is the increased emphasis on appointing arbitrators with legal backgrounds and a commensurate de-emphasis on the use of multi-disciplinary panels. The pervasiveness of lawyer-arbitrators was reflected in responses to the recent CCA-Straus Institute Survey: all of those who responded to the survey claimed backgrounds in the law and legal practice; 9.4 per cent were retired judges. Many of these respondents arbitrate construction cases.[117] Today, some national and regional provider organizations are wholly built on the notion that people want dispute resolution professionals of legal or judicial background. But is this always the best solution for construction disputes?

35.64 It is understandable that parties to construction disputes would want attorneys on their arbitration tribunal. In addition to being particularly well attuned to addressing legal issues, they tend to bring special skills and insights into the management of processes for the handling of claims. But is it really necessary or appropriate for all three members of an

---

[114] See 'CCA Protocols' (n 112) 79–80.
[115] ibid 43–4.
[116] The CCA-Straus Institute for Dispute Resolution Survey on Arbitration Practice (Fall 2013) (hereinafter, the 'CCA-Straus Institute Survey') was conducted under the umbrella of the Straus Institute's Theory-to-Practice Research Project in connection with a report on the future of arbitration which Professor Stipanowich was invited to present to the CCA during the fall of 2013. The survey consisted of 65 multiple-choice and short-answer questions on respondents' arbitration experiences and opinions on arbitration practices and the future of the arbitration field-at-large. The survey asked questions pertaining to both 'domestic' (defined in the survey as 'in the US between US parties') and 'international' (all other) arbitrations. The survey was sent electronically to 212 individuals, all CCA Fellows, of whom 134 individuals (63.2 per cent of the subject pool) completed the survey instrument. The survey and associated data are available from the author upon request. These and other data from the survey are presented in full in Thomas J Stipanowich and Zachary P Ulrich, 'Arbitration in Evolution: Current Practices and Perceptions of Experienced Arbitrators' (2014) 25 Am Rev Int'l Arb 395 and discussed in Stipanowich (n 97). Portions of this section are drawn from the latter.
[117] Slightly less than half (45.7 per cent) of respondents claimed experience with construction cases. See the 'CCA-Straus Institute Survey' (n 116).

arbitration tribunal to be attorneys? We should stop to consider what we are giving up by eschewing a panel that includes not just lawyers, but professionals of other disciplines.

For, while attorneys may have the edge when it comes to applying principles of law, matters such as evaluating conflicting expert testimony on, for example, professional standards of care, testing procedures, or assessing damages for lost productivity may be most effectively handled by one who has skills not in the typical lawyer's wheelhouse. As an arbitrator alongside two other lawyers, I occasionally feel like I am in a boat with all the oars on a single side: in some respects, our collective expertise is redundant, and in other respects insufficient. I welcome the wisdom and expertise of an experienced, respected engineer or contractor as a touchstone on some key issues relating to design and construction practice. **35.65**

Furthermore, if parties are determined to use only lawyer-arbitrators, do they really need three? The conventional wisdom is that three minds may be better than one, and tend to limit the likelihood of an unsound award. (There may be other reasons, as noted below.) On the other hand, a multi-member tribunal entails relatively high transaction costs, including increased cycle time. The CCA-Straus Survey reveals that many arbitrators have experience as the sole decision-maker in cases involving high stakes,[118] and more consideration should be given to 'one in lieu of three'. **35.66**

Much more could be said regarding the general lack of diversity in the ranks of dispute resolution professionals, and the subject should be of concern in the arena of construction disputes. Among the experienced arbitrators who provided gender information for the CCA-Straus Institute Survey, only 19 of 123 (15.4 per cent) identified themselves as female.[119] This disparity, which probably reflects the long-time under-representation of women in the senior ranks of law firms (most notably in construction), will hopefully be rectified with time. **35.67**

(6) Application of the law and other standards in decision-making

Do arbitrators follow the law? Adherence to legal standards appears to be a primary concern of many users of arbitration, along with the old saw that arbitrators tend to engage in inappropriate compromise.[120] **35.68**

Although these concerns linger, one wonders to what extent they are relics of past decades, when construction arbitration was much less 'legalized' and, most importantly, arbitrators often rendered decisions without an accompanying statement of reasons and perhaps without a claim-by-claim breakdown. In the absence of such information, aggrieved parties might imagine arbitrators were engaging in all sorts of inappropriate behaviour in decision-making. **35.69**

Today, the environment of arbitral decision-making is much changed, and the recent responses of experienced arbitrators tend to underline the attention given to legal authority in arbitration. Not surprisingly given their legal background and orientation, an overwhelming majority of experienced arbitrators in the CCA-Straus Survey said they do pay close attention to legal arguments. Nearly all arbitrators (97.7 per cent) asserted that they **35.70**

---

[118] ibid.
[119] ibid.
[120] See Stipanowich and Lamare (n 101) 53, tbl P; see also Thomas Schultz and Robert Kovacs, 'The Law Is What the Arbitrator Had for Breakfast: How Income, Reputation, Justice, and Reprimand Act as Determinants of Arbitrator Behaviour' in Julio César Betancourt (ed), *Defining Issues in International Arbitration: Celebrating 100 Years of the Chartered Institute of Arbitrators* (OUP 2016) ch 23.

always 'carefully read and reflect upon legal arguments and briefs presented by counsel', while the rest usually do so. The great majority (86.7 per cent) indicated that they always 'do [their] best to ascertain and follow applicable law in rendering an award' in the absence of a contrary agreement between the parties; most of the rest (11.7 per cent) usually do so. It is also quite common for arbitrators to invite counsel to brief legal issues in the case (with 54.7 per cent always extending an invitation and another 35.2 per cent usually doing so).[121]

35.71 All of that said, the responses also offer a puzzling caveat: more than a quarter of respondents (33 out of 128) stated that at least sometimes they '[felt] free to follow [their] own sense of equity and fairness in rendering an award even if the result would be contrary to applicable law'.[122] For present purposes, it is sufficient to note that depending on which arbitration procedures control and how those procedures are to be interpreted, arbitrators may or may not find themselves wrestling with the interplay between rules of law and their own concepts of equity or fairness. Where facing such issues, arbitrators are well advised to reflect upon and seek to understand the relevant expectations of the arbitrating parties. Of course, the best solution is for arbitrating parties to make sure that the arbitration procedures they adopt clearly reflect their joint expectations regarding applicable standards.

35.72 In cases where the parties' agreement and incorporated procedures do not make clear their intent regarding applicable norms, arbitrators may always seek guidance at the outset from the parties. However, compelling hints may often be gleaned from surrounding circumstances. In today's law- and lawyer-dominated environment, parties (or at least, their legal representatives) seem to be sending messages that legal doctrine and the normal run of judicial remedies should control, and my own experience of recent years is that arbitrators do their best to understand and follow applicable law. Legal issues are briefed and argued, and, often, blueprints for final awards put forward. Moreover, most arbitrators probably adhere to the view that a reputation for applying personal justice in lieu of the law is unlikely to enhance one's résumé as an arbitrator since it might be perceived as promoting unpredictability and risk in arbitration and, moreover, being inconsistent with the goals of the parties.

35.73 At the end of the day, there may still be circumstances where arbitrators believe that in the name of fairness they have no alternative but to refuse to follow the law. But for the very reason that arbitrators' awards are almost entirely immune to vacatur on substantive grounds, arbitrators bear a particular ethical responsibility to ensure that they are acting in accordance with the expectations of the arbitrating parties. In other words, far from being a sanction for ignoring the law in favour of one's own brand of personal justice, the broad leeway given by courts to arbitral awards should be balanced by an enhanced ethical obligation of the arbitrator to wield authority with care and dutiful attention to the understanding of the parties.

35.74 For those parties who need further assurance against the risk of an errant award, there are alternatives such as final-offer (baseball) arbitration, bracketed arbitration, and appellate arbitration procedures.[123]

---

[121] See Stipanowich and Ulrich (n 116).
[122] ibid.
[123] Jay Folberg and others, *Resolving Disputes: Theory, Practice and Law* (2nd edn, Aspen Publishers 2010) 598–9, 601.

(7) Arbitration and settlement

It should come as no surprise that arbitrators are reporting that a higher percentage of arbitrated cases are being settled prior to award or even prior to hearing.[124] This development parallels the reduced incidence of trials in US litigation, although our current information indicates that a much higher percentage of arbitrated cases apparently still go to hearing.

These realities prompt a number of questions. Why, for example, are some arbitrators reporting much higher rates of settlement in their cases than others? What role, if any, might arbitrators appropriately play in setting the stage for settlement? While most US arbitrators appear to be wary of switching hats midstream and becoming mediators in a case, their pre-hearing management of dispositive motions and of discovery may offer some avenues for 'teeing up' settlement discussions.

(8) Party-appointed arbitrators: independent, partisan, or 'predisposed'?

Many construction cases are heard by tripartite panels that include wing arbitrators appointed unilaterally by the parties. This approach, which is also the prevailing approach for resolution of international commercial disputes, may result in a panel that works well and produces reasonably satisfactory awards. However, there are perceptions that some party-appointed arbitrators are predisposed to the parties that appointed them and may lean towards their appointing party's position in rendering awards even when applicable procedures call for them to be independent and impartial.[125] In a given case, participants may have very different understandings of what the party-arbitrators are actually doing, and this is not a healthy state of affairs. Both in the United States and internationally, these perspectives underpin a continuing debate about the role of party-appointed arbitrators and the expectations of participants in this regard. There are some who support the notion of 'predisposed initially but able to be fair', while others find that concept problematic. If the debate is ever resolved in some fashion, it may be with the help of new studies regarding brain science and the origins of bias in decision-making.

(9) The professional crunch

As the first and second generations of construction lawyers continue into and through active retirement, retirees' forward plans often include service as an arbitrator and mediator.[126] Although these attorneys well remember the days when service as a construction arbitrator was almost invariably carried on as an occasional activity with a strong public service component, retirees now expect to enter the burgeoning ranks of a *corps professionnel*, commanding fees commensurate with their age, experience, and accustomed rates. Some will succeed.

However, recent research reinforces the conclusion that many lawyers-turned-dispute-resolution professionals may not be welcomed with an over-abundance of appointments.[127] In the construction arena, the hard reality of too many would-be arbitrators chasing too few cases is exacerbated by the devastating impact of the recent economic downturn on construction. The construction arbitrator oversupply appears to have been exaggerated by the fact that in recent years some construction attorneys, lacking legal

---

[124] For an in-depth discussion, see Stipanowich and Ulrich (n 78).
[125] See Stipanowich and Ulrich (n 116).
[126] For this reason, the identities of the ACCL and the CCA are becoming increasingly conflated in my mind.
[127] See Stipanowich and Ulrich (n 116).

business, have reportedly turned to 'neutral work' in the hopes of supplementing their revenues. The new phenomenon of decades-long active retirement, and how to channel active retirees' considerable time, energy, and desire to engage is one of the great challenges for our future.

(10) International arbitration

35.80 Today, construction arbitration is more and more frequently concerned with international disputes.[128] Given the particular advantages arbitration offers companies doing business across borders,[129] including an alternative to national court systems, confidentiality, worldwide enforceability of awards, and flexibility of procedure,[130] corporations rely heavily on arbitration to resolve international disputes[131] and tend to be satisfied with the process.[132]

35.81 The AAA's international caseload through the ICDR, including both arbitration and mediation, has grown dramatically over the past decade, from 646 cases in 2003 to 1,091 cases in 2013.[133] US-based parties, counsel, and arbitrators are increasingly interacting with counterparts from many different countries and legal systems in variegated processes that have been likened to Frankenstein's monster—'a legal entity comprised of body parts originating from different jurisdictions and imbued by life only after its creation'.[134] In this procedural amalgam, US arbitration practice has influenced international practice and been influenced in turn.

D. The Continuing Evolution: Five Transformative Trends

35.82 Our world is evolving and changing at an unprecedented pace, and it is perhaps foolhardy to hazard a guess at where we may be two or three decades on.[135] It is therefore appropriate to briefly highlight five trends that are likely to have a growing impact on our lives, on law practice, and on the management of conflict.

---

[128] For an excellent treatment of international construction arbitration, see John W Hinchey and Troy L Harris, *International Construction Arbitration Handbook* (Thomson West 2008).
[129] Nigel Blackaby and others, *Redfern and Hunter on International Arbitration* (5th edn, OUP 2009) 31–4.
[130] ibid 8.
[131] 2008 QMUL Survey, 'Corporate Attitudes and Practices: Recognition and Enforcement of Foreign Awards' 5 <http://www.arbitration.qmul.ac.uk/research/index.html> accessed 25 September 2015 (44 per cent of respondents said they used international arbitration to resolve international disputes more than litigation, mediation, or other ADR mechanisms). See, eg, Camille A Laturno, 'International Arbitration of the Creative: A Look at the World Intellectual Property' (Spring 1996) 9 Transnat'l Law 357, 371 n 92 ('Arbitration is increasingly the preferred forum for dispute resolution in international commercial transactions of all kinds'); Leon E Trakman, ' "Legal Traditions" and International Commercial Arbitration' (2006) 17 Am Rev Int'l Arb 1, 29; California Bar Association, *Current Trends in International Arbitration* <http://international.calbar.ca.gov/Portals/18/documents/2013-09-06_international-arbitration.pdf> accessed 25 September 2015 ('international arbitration continu[es] to grow rapidly as a preferred method for resolving cross-border commercial disputes').
[132] 2008 QMUL Survey (n 131) 5 (86 per cent of respondents said they are satisfied with international arbitration).
[133] Email from Ryan Boyle, Vice President–Statistics and In-House Research, AAA, to Tiffani Willis, 27 August 2013.
[134] Veijo Heiskanen and Emmanuel Gaillard, 'Aspects philosophiques du droit de l'arbitrage international' (2009) 20 EJIL 942, 946.
[135] Portions of this part of the chapter are adapted from Stipanowich (n 97).

(a) Technology

35.83 In every aspect of our lives, documentation and communication is increasingly digital and virtual, and the implications for managing and resolving conflict are immense. In an age when clients demand greater value for money, and rapid results, technology offers many opportunities for achieving efficiency and economy and, hopefully, providing fair and satisfactory experiences and results. It also presents many new challenges.

35.84 As a primary means of communication across distances and even within homes and offices, email has become an indispensable element in conflict and its resolution. Electronic interchange is the backbone of modern business transactions; therefore, students in my negotiations class regularly bargain online with students across the country, learning by experience the benefits, limitations, and protocols of negotiation through electronic media.[136] Email is also a prime ancillary tool for dispute resolution professionals in mediation and arbitration,[137] as well as a major element in the vast and expanding mass of electronic data that represents the greatest emerging challenge for parties and arbitrators seeking to actively manage discovery in the interests of efficiency and economy.[138]

35.85 Arbitration hearings in complex construction cases are often high-tech events, with arbitrators and counsel utilizing digital displays on two or three monitors at once. Lawyers and arbitrators are deriving important benefits from services such as LiveNote, which permits the viewing, highlighting, and annotating of testimony in real time,[139] and may feature streaming video feeds permitting testifying witnesses to be observed long-distance.[140] Electronic transcripts available via cloud offsite storage enable practitioners to search the content of transcripts from anywhere in the world with Internet access.[141] Moreover, transcripts in electronic formats are easily searchable, helping counsel locate and direct a witness's or arbitrator's attention to key portions of the transcript,[142] and saving arbitrator time during award preparation.[143]

35.86 Providers are moving to paperless secure online systems such as AAA Webfile® for the filing of cases and subsequent documentation.[144] However, despite the growing embrace of various forms of technology in arbitration, we have yet to see significant transplantation of mediation or arbitration hearings from in-person settings to online.[145] In this pioneering era

---

[136] See Jay Folberg and Dwight Golann, *Lawyer Negotiation: Theory, Practice and Law* (2nd edn, Aspen Publishers 2011) 165–80 (discussing pros and cons of online negotiations).

[137] See Thomas Schultz, *Information Technology and Arbitration: A Practitioner's Guide* (Kluwer Law International 2006) 153–67.

[138] It has been estimated that '90% of all business information is electronically stored'. Richard Posell, 'E-Discovery in Arbitration' (May 2010) <http://www.mediate.com> accessed 25 September 2015. If parties have not already set parameters for preservation of data, the best practice is for counsel and the arbitrator to resolve early on issues such as the preservation of such information, and the scope and manner of its production. This proactive approach may avoid intractable disputes down the line. See, eg, 'CCA Protocols' (n 112) 53–4.

[139] Thomson Reuters, LiveNote Stream <http://www.legalsolutions.thomsonreuters.com> accessed 25 September 2015).

[140] ibid.

[141] ibid.

[142] AgileLaw <http://www.agilelaw.com> accessed 25 September 2015.

[143] Thomson Reuters, Case Notebook <http://www.legalsolutions.thomsonreuters.com> accessed 25 September 2015.

[144] Filing a case with the AAA <http://www.adr.org> accessed 25 September 2015.

[145] See Julio César Betancourt and Elina Zlatanska, 'Online Dispute Resolution (ODR): What Is It, and Is It the Way Forward?' (2013) 79(3) Arbitration 256, 262–3.

of online dispute resolution (ODR), existing systems tend to be rather limited in scope and flexibility, suitable for simple cases with the most basic fact patterns as opposed to the broad run of commercial disputes.[146] At present, the real benefit of online mediation and arbitration is in high-volume, low-value disputes between parties separated by great distance; in such cases e-mediation or e-arbitration offers a methodical approach to cost-effective, efficient dispute resolution.

35.87 But there are indications that change is afoot. Today, for example, many routine court appearances take place telephonically via CourtCall. Despite some judges' complaints, telephonic appearances are now commonplace; the next, and growing iteration is Internet-based video appearances. CourtCall recently introduced video conferencing services in some court rooms,[147] 'allowing judges to simulate a typical day in court'.[148] The video conference may be one- or two-way, meaning that judges retain the option of whether to appear themselves on video, or merely via audio feed.[149]

35.88 Not surprisingly, arbitration providers are beginning to offer similar services. JAMS recommends the use of their 'Virtual Conference Room' service;[150] another provider offers binding 'Virtual Arbitration',[151] in which the entire arbitration is conducted via the web.[152] Then there is eQuibbly, which assures users that '[a] former official court [j]udge will resolve your dispute online in a matter of weeks'.[153]

35.89 The benefits of online appearances are multiplied in international arbitrations, where travel costs are exponentially greater. Moreover, video appearances may assist in preserving the continuity of arbitral proceedings, obviating the need to suspend proceedings until minor parties or witnesses are available, or where unavoidable delays in international travel arise. One would expect that even if participants are resistant to conducting hearings on the merits online, the method could be utilized for some preliminary conferences and arbitrator deliberations. The '2007 ICC Commission Report: Controlling Time and Costs in Arbitration'[154] urged arbitrators to consider the need for physical meetings, and to identify instances where information technology could be utilized for greater efficiency and cost savings.[155] The report recommended the use of video conferencing for procedural hearings, and allowing witnesses the opportunity to appear via video at evidentiary hearings.[156]

35.90 Another fascinating opportunity afforded by digital media, coupled with a large and expanding pool of self-described 'neutrals', is the concept of an online 'community court'

---

[146] ibid.
[147] CourtCall Video Conferencing <http://www.courtcall.com> accessed 25 September 2015.
[148] ibid.
[149] ibid.
[150] JAMS Virtual Conference Room <http://www.jamsadr.com> accessed 25 September 2015.
[151] The Virtual Arbitrator <http://www.thevirtualarbitrator.com> accessed 25 September 2015; see also Virtual Courthouse.com <http://www.virtualcourthouse.com> (another completely online ADR and arbitration venue) accessed 25 September 2015.
[152] ibid.
[153] eQuibbly <http://www.equibbly.com> accessed 25 September 2015.
[154] See ICC, 'Commission Report: Controlling Time and Costs in Arbitration' (2007) <http://www.gjpi.org> accessed 25 September 2015.
[155] ibid 11 (recommendation 28) and 12–13 (recommendation 39).
[156] ibid 17 (recommendation 74).

that offers advisory or binding evaluations of legal or factual issues.[157] Tapping the market for early independent evaluation and case assessment,[158] providers of dispute resolution services may now make it possible to submit summaries of issues in dispute with supporting arguments (and, perhaps even streaming video of select witness testimony) for evaluation by not just one 'neutral', but five, ten, or fifty. The input of the evaluators might include responses to specific questions and comments on the strengths or weaknesses of a position. Such approaches might become an important factor in early settlement of complex construction disputes.

Will computers ever replace humans as mediators and adjudicators? Even without getting into the debate between legal positivists and their detractors,[159] such concepts raise many concerns. As Richard Susskind observed some years ago: 35.91

> computers cannot yet (if ever) satisfactorily recognize speech, understand natural language, nor perceive images ... Computers have not yet been programmed to exhibit moral, religious, social, sexual and political preferences akin to those actually held by human beings. Nor have they been programmed to display the creativity, craftsmanship, individuality, innovation, inspiration, intuition, commonsense and general interest in our world that we, as human beings, expect of one another as citizens but also of judges acting in their official role.[160]

Time will tell. 35.92

Of course, the most significant technological opportunity facing the construction industry is BIM, which is the set of information and work collaboration tools, including shared database, 3D models, and related tools to simulate a building, its performance, and its construction that creates a perfect setting for integrated project delivery.[161] As Howard Ashcraft explains: 'Building information models are platforms for collaboration.'[162] Interestingly, a recent experimental study in which architecture and construction students completed projects using traditional design and construction approaches as well as multidisciplinary BIM teams indicated that teams using BIM are more likely to engage in integrative or issue-based, constructive conflict, and less likely to engage in competitive conflict or avoidance.[163] 35.93

(b) Globalization

As society becomes increasingly global, US parties and counsel are likely to be drawn into conflict with international partners, thus entering territory that is unfamiliar in many 35.94

---

[157] See Colin Rule and Chittu Nagarajan, 'Leveraging the Wisdom of Crowds: The eBay Community Court and the Future of Online Dispute Resolution' (2010) 4 ACResolution <http://www.law.northwestern.edu> accessed 25 September 2015.
[158] See Stipanowich and Lamare (n 101) 43–4.
[159] See Richard Susskind, 'The Computer Judge: Early Thoughts' in Richard Susskind, *Transforming the Law: Essays on Technology, Justice and the Legal Marketplace* (OUP 2000) 275–92.
[160] ibid 286–7.
[161] 'Improved Building Industry Results through Integrated Project Delivery and Building Information Modeling' <http://www.images.autodesk.com> accessed 25 September 2015.
[162] Howard W Ashcraft, 'Building Information Modeling: A Framework for Collaboration' (2008) 28(3) Constr Law 5, 5.
[163] See Tamera L McCuen, 'The Effect of Building Information Modeling on Conflict and Conflict Management in Interdisciplinary Teams' <http://www.ascpro0.ascweb.org/archives/2009/CERT173002009.pdf> accessed 25 September 2015.

respects from American domestic practice.¹⁶⁴ For example, although the US 'modern mediation' model has been highly influential, there are places where the very concept of retaining an independent professional mediator for the express purpose of resolving commercial disputes has not been meaningfully embraced. In China, for example, mediation is normally conducted by individuals who operate from a position of authority relative to the parties. Chinese judges often act as conciliators prior to adjudicating a case, and the rules of leading Chinese institutions sponsoring private arbitration likewise provide that arbitrators may try to informally resolve the dispute prior to rendering a decision on the merits.¹⁶⁵ However, these approaches tend to be far different from modern mediation as practiced in the US.¹⁶⁶ Although institutions such as the BAC partnered with Western parties to develop and promote stand-alone Western-style mediation procedures,¹⁶⁷ it remains to be seen whether the latter will take hold in China.¹⁶⁸

35.95 Other countries have established a national framework for mediation, but have yet to generate significant demand due to lack of understanding of the nature and value of mediation and resistance by the legal profession. Greece now has laws promoting and regulating mediation, including extensive guidelines for mediator training and accreditation, pursuant to which a thousand mediators have been credentialled. Greece lacks only one thing: parties and attorneys willing to mediate litigated cases!¹⁶⁹

35.96 Finally, although American commercial mediators tend to be accustomed to engaging in evaluation, mediators from many other countries view such activities as beyond the scope of their role and incompatible in some respects with the concept of mediation as a 'facilitated' process.¹⁷⁰ Conversely, dispute resolution professionals from other jurisdictions may be more comfortable than US counterparts with arbitrators rendering non-binding evaluations of parties' cases in their role as 'conciliators'.¹⁷¹

35.97 Legal practitioners and mediators are thus being drawn into a global conversation—face-to-face and online—regarding virtually every aspect of mediation theory, doctrine, procedure, and practice. The same is equally true of arbitration. On occasion, this dialogue (when systematically conducted by reputable organizations) has produced procedural solutions that help to bridge differences among systems and modes of practice, such as the IBA's widely embraced Rules on the Taking of Evidence and other evolving 'soft law' guidelines.¹⁷²

35.98 A broader effect of the continuing interchange may be to encourage and help people to be more thoughtful and deliberate about the way they practice, whether internationally or domestically. Construction lawyers and arbitrators are now considering the pros and cons

---

¹⁶⁴ See generally Michael McIlwrath and John Savage, *International Arbitration and Mediation: A Practice Guide* (Kluwer Law International 2010); Jean-Claude Goldsmith and others, *ADR in Business: Practice and Issues across Countries and Cultures*, vol 1 (Kluwer Law International 2006).
¹⁶⁵ See generally Thomas J Stipanowich and others, 'East Meets West: An International Dialogue on Mediation and Med-Arb in the United States and China' (2009) 9 Pepp Disp Resol LJ 279.
¹⁶⁶ ibid 385–8.
¹⁶⁷ ibid 379–80.
¹⁶⁸ ibid 385–6.
¹⁶⁹ Interview with Dimitra P Gavril and Theodora Syriou (8 August 2014) (notes on file with author).
¹⁷⁰ See, eg, Gould and others (n 56) 5–6 (discussing distinctions made in the United Kingdom between mediation and conciliation).
¹⁷¹ ibid. See also CEDR, 'Commission Report' (n 79).
¹⁷² See generally Lawrence W Newman and Michael J Radine (eds), *Soft Law in International Arbitration* (Juris 2014).

of extensive witness statements as a substitute for direct examination, various international procedures for the handling of multiparty disputes, the filing of joint reports by expert witnesses detailing points of agreement and disagreement, and other elements from other systems.

(c) Insights through behavioural science and 'big data'

35.99 Concepts from the realm of cognitive psychology, such as risk aversion, anchoring, attribution error, and reactive devaluation, have recently become a part of the lexicon of negotiation and conflict management.[173] As our sights are broadened by interaction on a global scale, experiments with cognition and the mining of 'big data' have opened yet another frontier for exploration. We are being given new opportunities to reflect on the impact of our perceptions on lawyering and resolving conflict and to glean new insights into group behaviours by analyzing masses of information.[174]

35.100 Thanks to the work of behavioural economists and others, we are coming to understand that far from being engines of rationality, human beings operate subject to the dictates of mental processes that skew our perceptions and steer us onto unpredictable paths.[175] In one way or another many of these insights are relevant to managing and resolving conflict. Russell Korobkin and Chris Guthrie, among others, advanced our awareness of dynamics at the bargaining table.[176] Studies by Guthrie, Jeffrey Rachlinski, Judge Andrew Wistrich, and others are deepening our appreciation of the psychological factors affecting judicial decision-making.[177]

35.101 These insights are reinforced by the parsing and rigorous assessment of available data. Susan Franck's assessments of data relating to international investment arbitration are offering a more nuanced understanding of those procedures.[178] Randall Kiser has used datasets from VerdictSearch California to offer in-depth analysis of decision-making by lawyers during settlement negotiations.[179] Employing 'neural networks, predictive modeling, and genetic algorithms', Donald Philbin isolated trends across groups of similar negotiations and within particular negotiations, and created Now Picture It Settled®, web-based software that allows negotiators to 'optimize their concession strategies and predict where a round will end'.[180]

35.102 A decade ago, lawyers and dispute resolution professionals had very little awareness of these dynamics. Going forward, they can ill afford to ignore them.

---

[173] See Exon (n 67) 62–72.
[174] See generally Jennifer K Robbenholt and Jean R Sternlight, *Psychology for Lawyers: Understanding the Human Factors in Negotiation, Litigation and Decision Making* (ABA 2013).
[175] See Dan Ariely, *Predictably Irrational: The Hidden Forces That Shape Our Decisions* (HarperCollins 2008).
[176] See, eg, Russell B Korobkin and Chris Guthrie, 'Heuristics and Biases at the Bargaining Table' (2004) 87 Marquette L Rev 795; Chris Guthrie and Dan Orr, 'Anchoring, Information, Expertise and Negotiation: New Insights from Meta-Analysis' (2006) 21 Ohio St J Disp Resol 597.
[177] See, eg, Chris Guthrie, Jeffrey J Rachlinski, and Andrew J Wistrich, 'Blinking on the Bench: How Judges Decide Cases' (2007) 93 Cornell L Rev 1; Chris Guthrie, Jeffrey J Rachlinski, and Andrew Wistrich, 'Inside the Judicial Mind' (2001) 86 Cornell L Rev 777.
[178] See, eg, Susan Franck, 'Empirically Evaluating Claims About Investment Treaty Arbitration' (2007) 86 NCL Rev 1.
[179] See generally Kiser (n 83).
[180] <http://www.csoftx.com> accessed 25 September 2015.

(d) Longer productive lives (active retirement)

35.103 As discussed above, the progress of the first generations of ADR-acclimatized attorneys into and through decades of active retirement presents challenges as well as opportunities. Lawyers-turned-dispute-resolution professionals in their 60s, 70s, and 80s are vigorously seeking employment as mediators and arbitrators alongside younger colleagues, many of whom are still in law practice. While all will not be equally successful in promoting a dispute resolution practice, their abundant time and energy may be productively channelled in a variety of ways. These include helping develop guidelines for managing conflict, producing blogs, participating in continuous online discussion and debate regarding developments in related law and practice, teaching as adjunct instructors, and even offering their services for online evaluations as described above.

E. Professional Practice, Education, and Credentialling

35.104 Although the legal sector has been particularly resistant to innovation, the consumers of legal services are putting pressure on law firms—especially large firms—to improve services and shorten dispute resolution cycle times while reducing cost.[181] Driven by the changing legal job market and ABA Standard 302(a)(4), adopted in 2004, law schools (which are themselves increasingly driven by market pressures) are expanding all kinds of skills instruction, including clinics, externships, and role-playing simulations.[182]

35.105 Prominent among these offerings are courses aimed at counselling and advocacy in negotiation, mediation, and arbitration;[183] the Pepperdine's Straus Institute is among programmes offering LLM and other master's degrees, as well as a concentration on dispute resolution for law students. Graduates will therefore be increasingly prepared for a world in which a brace of tools for effective conflict management is central to practice, and more attuned to embrace emerging practice models like collaborative law[184] (which has yet to become a significant practice alternative in the construction or commercial arenas).

F. Conclusion

35.106 As discussed earlier, many current and former litigators and transactional lawyers are marketing themselves as dispute resolution professionals. Even with training, however, not every lawyer (or non-lawyer) possesses the skill set and instincts to function effectively as a mediator or arbitrator, and concerns about informed choice and transparency have driven a growing international dialogue regarding professional credentialling.[185] As noted above,

---

[181] See J Stephen Poor, 'Re-Engineering the Business of Law', *NY Times* (New York, 7 May 2012) (Op-Ed by chairman of Seyfarth Shaw).
[182] ABA Section of Legal Education and Admissions to the Bar, 'A Survey of Law School Curricula: 2002–2010', 15.
[183] Julie Macfarlane, 'What Does the Changing Culture of Legal Practice Mean for Legal Education?' (2001) 20 Windsor YB Access Just 191.
[184] Jim Hilbert, 'Collaborative Lawyering: A Process for Interest-Based Negotiation' (Summer 2010) 38 Hofstra L Rev 1083.
[185] See, eg, Doug Jones, 'Comments on the Speech of the Singapore Attorney General in International Arbitration: The Coming of a New Age?' in Albert Jan van den Berg (ed), *International Arbitration: The Coming of a New Age?* (ICCA Congress Series No 17, Kluwer Law International 2013) 29 (discussing certification

even some countries that lack substantial demand for mediation have already established a regulatory framework for the process, including professional certification.[186]

Moreover, the very presence of a raft of regional, national, and international organizations seeking to engage the attention of the field and the energies of participants adds momentum to such efforts. Nevertheless, many questions remain about how credentialling should be done and, equally importantly, who should do it. Ultimately, one must ask: what organization, or group of organizations, is most likely to be responsive to the needs of users in specific sectors or settings (including, for our present purposes, construction owners and those engaged in design and construction) and is broad enough to embrace the full range of potential dispute resolution professionals, including non-lawyers? **35.107**

---

of arbitrators and mediators through the CIArb); Irena Vanenkova, 'The Unique Value of Becoming IMI Certified' <http://www.mediate.com> accessed 25 September 2015 (touting the IMI's worldwide credentialling system for mediators).

[186] See above text accompanying note 169.

36

SHIFTING THE BURDEN OF PROOF
Revisiting Adjudication Decisions

Andrew Tweeddale and Keren Tweeddale

A. Introduction

36.01 It was an honour to be asked to write a short chapter for this *liber amicorum* in recognition that the CIArb has been established for 100 years. The CIArb received its Royal Charter in 1979 and the object of the Institute 'is to promote and facilitate worldwide the determination of disputes by arbitration and alternative means of private dispute resolution other than resolution by the court (collectively called "private dispute resolution")'.[1] With over 14,000 members around the world and ADR becoming increasingly popular, the CIArb seems well placed to go forward for another century.

36.02 We have decided to write a short chapter on a core subject that affects all forms of adjudicative dispute resolution. The concept of the burden of the proof is a fundamental part of any adjudicative procedure—whether it be court proceedings, arbitration, or adjudication. Stepped dispute resolution clauses are now the norm in construction contracts and we wanted to look at how these clauses affect the burden of proof.

36.03 Construction contracts are different from many other forms of commercial contracts. The works can take months, if not years, to complete and, therefore, to ensure the smooth functioning of the contract, a third person (eg an architect, an engineer, or a project manager) is appointed to deal with the certification of payments and claims. Adjudication clauses are now found in many forms of international construction contracts, such as FIDIC, and are a statutory requirement for English construction contracts. The adjudicator has the power to open up, review, and revise the decisions of the architect, engineer, or project manager and correct a decision. This allows for disputes to be settled while the contract proceeds and the decision of the adjudicator binds the parties on an interim basis.

36.04 It is fundamental for the parties, the adjudicator, or the arbitral tribunal to know where the burden of proof lies. The introduction of stepped dispute resolution provisions into construction contracts has added a new level of complexity. The arbitral tribunal when considering the dispute must decide who has the burden of proof. Where an adjudicator has made a decision in relation to a payment or awarded an extension of time, the arbitral

---

[1] CIArb Royal Charter, Art 4(1) <http://www.ciarb.org> accessed 25 September 2015.

tribunal must ask whether that decision has any effect on the burden of proof or whether the slate is wiped clean and the party claiming payment or time is obliged to prove its entitlement again.

The following example is typical of the problem.[2] A contractor applies for an extension of time of one year for delays caused by the employer. The engineer reviews the claim and awards the contractor a six-month extension of time. The contractor refers the matter to an adjudicator, who reviews the claim. The adjudicator decides that the contractor's claim is valid and awards a full year's extension of time. The employer is dissatisfied and refers the dispute to arbitration. In the above scenario, the employer is the claimant in the arbitration. However, who has the burden of proof? Does it rest with the contractor who has claimed that it has been delayed or with the employer who is challenging the decision of the adjudicator? Under English law, there is no conclusive authority on point.

B. The Burden of Proof

It is an unequivocal principle of English law that it is the party which makes an assertion that has the burden of proving it and not the party that denies it (*ei qui affirmat non ei qui negat incumbit probatio*). Who has the burden of proof depends on the circumstances under which the claim arises.[3] As Viscount Maugham stated in *Joseph Constantine Steamship Line Ltd v Imperial Smelting Corp Ltd*: 'It is an ancient rule founded on considerations of good sense and it should not be departed from without strong reasons.'[4] The principle that '[e]ach party must prove to the satisfaction of the tribunal the factual veracity of its allegations' has been described 'as a general principle of law; admitted as such in international jurisprudence'.[5] Klaus Peter Berger succinctly stated, 'every party bears the burden of proof for the facts supporting its claim'.[6] This principle can be dated back to Roman law[7] and is now so deeply rooted in all laws that it forms one of the key principles of the *lex mercatoria*,[8] of international law,[9] and arbitration.[10]

Most arbitration laws do not address the issue of burden of proof in relation to making or defending claims, although it is addressed in some arbitration rules.[11] There can be various kinds of burdens of proof, such as the evidential burden, the burden of persuasion, the burden of production, and the tactical burden. These burdens may be linked to presumptions,

---

[2] This is the same example used by Peter Coulson, *Coulson on Construction Adjudication* (2nd edn, OUP 2011).
[3] *Joseph Constantine Steamship Line Ltd v Imperial Smelting Corp Ltd* [1942] AC 154.
[4] ibid 172.
[5] Georgios Petrochilos, *Procedural Law in International Arbitration* (OUP 2004) 219.
[6] Klaus Peter Berger, *Private Dispute Resolution in International Business: Negotiation, Mediation, Arbitration* (2nd edn, Kluwer Law International 2009) 536.
[7] Paulus, 'On the Edict' Book LXIX: 'Proof is incumbent upon the party who affirms a fact, not upon him who denies it'.
[8] See Trans-Lex website, Principle No XII.1—Distribution of Burden of Proof <http://www.trans-lex.org> accessed 25 September 2015.
[9] John L Simpson and Hazel Fox, *International Arbitration: Law and Practice* (Steven & Sons 1959) 194.
[10] Petrochilos (n 5) 214.
[11] See, eg, Art 27 of the 2010 UNCITRAL Arbitration Rules and Art 19 of the 2009 ICDR Arbitration Rules.

standards of proof, and shifts and distributions of burdens of proof.[12] There may be situations where one party has to overcome an initial burden.

36.08 In ICC Award No 10982, the arbitral tribunal addressed a situation where this occurred.[13] The respondent alleged that there had been fraud in the procurement of a deed, which formed the basis of the claimant's claim. The arbitration was under the UNCITRAL Arbitration Rules. The arbitral tribunal stated that the party who based its claim upon the deed had first to produce a document which inspired a minimally sufficient degree of confidence in its authenticity. The burden then moved to the party alleging fraud to show that it had been produced by fraud.[14]

36.09 English law provides that in cases where the burden of proof is not clear—because the parties' cases are equally weighted—the burden of proof lies on the party who would be unsuccessful if it did not produce any evidence.[15] Also, it does not matter if a party is making an affirmative or negative assertion, the burden of proof still lies with that party.[16]

C. The Orthodox View—the Burden of Proof Does Not Move

36.10 Sir Peter Coulson, in the leading textbook on adjudication,[17] and a number of English and Scottish cases, discussed below, suggest that the burden of proof remains with the party making the initial claim and the adjudicator's decision, once challenged, is of no effect whatsoever. Coulson states:

> Once the decision has been formally challenged by the issue of subsequent litigation or arbitration, the contractor in the example noted above is not entitled to rely on the existing decision as having any status whatsoever, let alone one that changes or displaces the ordinary burden of proof.[18]

36.11 However, in *Walker Construction (UK) Ltd v Quayside Homes Ltd*,[19] Gloster LJ cast doubt on this view. For the reasons set out below we consider that Gloster LJ's obiter dicta statements on this point are correct and that the burden of proof is shifted by an adjudicator's decision.

36.12 The issue of whether an adjudicator's decision shifts the burden of proof was first addressed by the courts in the Scottish case of *City Inn Ltd v Shepherd Construction Ltd*.[20] The contract was a JCT Standard Form with Quantities and provided explicitly for adjudication. Clause 41A.8.1 stipulated that:

> The decision of the Adjudicator shall be binding on the Parties until the dispute or difference is finally determined by arbitration or by court proceedings or by an agreement in writing between the parties made after the decision of the Adjudicator has been given.

---

[12] Hendrik Kaptein, Henry Prakken, and Bart Verheij, *Legal Evidence and Proof: Statistics, Stories, Logic* (Ashgate Publishing 2009) 223.
[13] Yves Derains, Note to ICC Case No 10982, Award (2001) 2005 JDI 1256, 1263.
[14] ibid 1265.
[15] *Amos v Hughes* (1835) 174 ER 160, 1 Mood & R 464.
[16] *Abrath v North Eastern Railway Co* (1886) 11 App Cas 247.
[17] Coulson (n 2).
[18] ibid [14.48].
[19] [2014] EWCA Civ 93.
[20] [2002] SLT 781.

36.13 In the *City Inn* case, a dispute was referred to adjudication and the adjudicator held that, in addition to the extension of time awarded by the architect, the defenders were entitled to a further extension of time of five weeks. Lord MacFadyen then addressed the question of whether this decision had any effect on the onus of proof. City Inn submitted that it did not and argued that the burden of proof remained with Shepherd Construction Ltd to justify the extension of time which they sought. Reference was made to the marginal note beside clause 41A.8.1 which stated:

> The arbitration or court proceedings are not an appeal against the decision of the Adjudicator but are a consideration of the dispute or difference as if no decision had been made by the Adjudicator.

36.14 City Inn submitted that the note correctly stated the law. Shepherd Construction, on the other hand, stated that the effect of the adjudicator's decision was to throw onto City Inn the burden of showing that the extension of time which the adjudicator awarded was not justified. It argued that the binding quality of the adjudicator's decision continued, not merely until the dispute was made the subject of litigation, but until the court proceedings were finally determined. That, said Shepherd Construction, meant that during the proceedings, the adjudicator's decision remained binding and had to be rebutted by the party arguing for a different result.

36.15 Lord MacFadyen stated:

> In my opinion, [City Inn's] submission is correct. As has been observed in a number of cases, the function of adjudication, as contemplated in the 1996 Act, is to provide a speedy means of reaching a binding interim determination of disputes arising under construction contracts. It goes no further than that. I agree with [City Inn] that the side note to clause 41A.8.1 correctly states the law. It is, in my view, no part of the function of an adjudicator's decision to reverse the onus of proof in any arbitration or litigation to which the parties require to resort to obtain a final determination of the dispute between them. It is reading too much into the reference in clause 41A.8.1 (and Section 108(3)) to the adjudicator's decision being binding 'until the dispute or difference is finally determined' to construe it as affecting the burden of proof in the arbitration or court proceedings... The burden of proof in any such action lies where the law places it, and is unaffected by the terms of the adjudicator's decision.[21]

36.16 Lord MacFadyen therefore concluded that the words in section 108(3) of the HGCRA that the adjudicator's decision is binding 'until the dispute or difference is finally determined' should not be read as having an effect on the burden of proof in an arbitration or litigation.

36.17 A number of cases that have followed *City Inn* have accepted that the burden of proof remained unaffected by the adjudicator's decision.[22] In the recent cases of *Aspect Contracts (Asbestos) Ltd v Higgins Construction Plc*[23] and *Bellway Homes Ltd v Seymour (Civil Engineering Contractors) Ltd*,[24] the party challenging the adjudicator's decision had pleaded its case on this basis and, despite being the claimant in the litigation, it did not bear the onus of proof. However, in neither of these cases did the court address the question of who actually had the burden of proof.

---

[21] ibid [58].
[22] See, eg, *CFW Architects (A Firm) v Cowlin Construction Ltd* [2006] EWHC 6 (TCC).
[23] [2015] UKSC 38; [2013] EWCA Civ 1541; [2013] EWHC 1322 (TCC).
[24] [2013] EWHC 1890 (TCC), [2013] All ER (D) 82 (Jul).

D. *De Novo* Hearing—a Rationale for the Orthodox View

36.18 A court or arbitral tribunal, when being asked to reconsider a decision of an adjudicator, undertakes a *de novo* review of the dispute. The fact that the hearing is to be *de novo* is sometimes used as a basis for arguing that the adjudicator's decision has no status.[25] In *The Construction Centre Group Ltd v The Highland Council*, Lord MacFadyen considered the words 'open up, review and revised' and stated that: 'I do not consider that the use of the word "revised" in Clause 66(4) and (6)(iv) compels the conclusion that the arbiter's task is not to approach the resolution of the dispute *de novo* but to review the adjudicator's decision'.[26]

36.19 However, the fact that there is a *de novo* hearing does not mean that the adjudicator's decision has no status or that the burden of proof goes back to the original party making the claim. For example, where an arbitrator revises a decision of an engineer or architect there is a *de novo* hearing; however, in such cases the engineer's or architect's decision does not necessarily lose its status. In the case of *Beaufort Developments (NI) Ltd v Gilbert-Ash (NI) Ltd*,[27] Lord Hope stated that in determining the rights of the parties the court was entitled to look at all the facts and so could take account of the architect's certificate and either agree with it or not as it was not conclusive.

36.20 In the United States, there are state-administered compulsory arbitration schemes dealing with consumer disputes. One of these relates to the purchase of vehicles which are said to be 'lemons'.[28] On a trial *de novo* before the circuit court the party challenging the decision of the arbitral tribunal has the burden of proof to show that the decision of the arbitral tribunal is wrong, despite the trial being a *de novo* hearing.[29] In *Mason v Porsche Cars of North America*,[30] the court held that any benefit of compulsory arbitration would be lost if simply by filing a challenge to the decision, the burden of proof was placed back on the successful party. Equally, it may be argued that the benefits of statutory or contractual adjudication would be lost if a party simply needed to issue a notice of dissatisfaction so that the burden of proof reverted to the person initially making the claim.

E. Shifting the Burden—the Approach in *Walker v Quayside*

36.21 The issue of who has the burden of proof when challenging an adjudicator's decision came squarely before the English courts in the case of *Walker Construction (UK) Ltd v Quayside Homes Ltd*.[31] The facts of the case were that Walker Construction undertook to carry out drainage and highway works for Quayside. The contract was under an NEC form. A dispute arose, which was referred to adjudication, and the adjudicator awarded Walker Construction the sums that it claimed were due, which included £8,941.16. Quayside paid Walker Construction. Quayside then raised a counterclaim that there were defects in the

---

[25] Coulson (n 2) [14.48].
[26] [2002] ScotCS CSOH 354.
[27] [1999] 1 AC 266, 292.
[28] Florida's Lemon Law—see Chapter 88-95, Laws of Florida.
[29] 621 So 2d 719 (Fla 5th DCA 1993); and *Aguiar v Ford Motor Co* 683 So 1158 (Fla Dist Ct App 1996).
[30] ibid.
[31] See n 19.

works and claimed in the county court repayment of sums paid to Walker Construction plus further damages. His Honour Judge Bailey in the county court awarded Quayside £10,035.91 for the defects, but rejected the claim for repayment of the sum of £8,941.16 awarded by the adjudicator.

36.22 Quayside argued that on bringing the claim in the county court the adjudicator's decision became effectively null and void and that Walker Construction had the burden of proving its entitlement to be paid before the court. Quayside framed its claim on the basis of restitution. His Honour Judge Bailey summarized Quayside's case as follows:

> the adjudicator's decision has no status or value whatsoever in subsequent legal proceedings. The determination, the reasons and the evaluation of parties' case in adjudication are to be ignored by the court. The slate is wiped clean. The burden of proof lies where the law placed it. The adjudicator's decision does not affect this burden. In other words, submits Quayside, the court, when considering claims which have been the subject of an adjudication must turn the clock back to the position prior to the adjudication.[32]

36.23 His Honour Judge Bailey accepted that he did not have to take account of the adjudicator's decision in forming his judgment. His Honour agreed with Lord MacFadyen in *City Inn v Shepherd*[33] and with the comments by Sir Peter Coulson. However, he dismissed Quayside's claim because he could not discern a cause of action. The judge concluded that Quayside may have had a right in contract to claim repayment of the monies paid, but had failed to plead any breach of contract, or even assert that there was a breach of contract. The learned judge then considered whether there was a claim in restitution, but decided that there was no basis for this in law.[34] Quayside therefore lost this part of the case based on the fact that: (1) no cause of action had been pleaded for the breach of contract argument; and (2) there was no basis in law for a claim for restitution.

36.24 Quayside appealed this part of the decision to the Court of Appeal. In the appeal, neither party adduced any evidence. Walker Construction had already been paid so it took the view that it was unnecessary. Quayside relied on the orthodox view that the burden of proof remained with Walker Construction. Quayside based its case on Walker Construction's failure to discharge its burden to adduce evidence of its entitlement to the £8,941.16. It also argued that because this sum had not been certified, it was not contractually due.

36.25 Gloster LJ, giving the leading judgment at the Court of Appeal, rejected Quayside's submission and held that Quayside's claim should be dismissed. However, Gloster LJ's reasoning was different from that of His Honour Judge Bailey. Her Ladyship held that Quayside had failed to adduce evidence in support of its assertion that it was entitled to be paid back this sum. Her Ladyship held that the burden of proof in the court action was on Quayside because its counterclaim was in essence a claim to set off damages in respect of allegedly defective works. The burden of proof did not rest on Walker Construction because it had already been paid and was not claiming any further payment. Gloster LJ agreed with Walker Construction that it was irrelevant that the sum of £8,941.16 in question had not been certified by the engineer.

---

[32] ibid [111]
[33] See *City Inn* (n 20).
[34] In *Aspect Contracts (Asbestos) Ltd v Higgins Construction Plc* [2015] UKSC 38 [24], Lord Mance held that an independent restitutionary obligation did exist to claim an overpayment. It follows that the reasoning of His Honour Judge Bailey on this point must now be considered as being incorrect.

36.26 Gloster LJ then considered *City Inn Ltd v Shepherd Construction Ltd*[35] and the burden of proof issue. Her Ladyship found difficulties with the MacFadyen/Coulson view that the adjudicator's award could never have an impact in a subsequent proceeding. Her Ladyship suggested that as the award exists until it is overturned or affirmed, the burden of proving that it was wrong should shift to the party who referred the matter to arbitration or litigation and not to the party that was not seeking to contest the adjudicator's decision. Referring to the *City Inn* case, her Ladyship stated:

> In those circumstances, why should the defendant contractor, for example, on the facts of *City Inn Limited v Shepherd Construction Limited* not be entitled to contend that, until the contrary was proved to the court's satisfaction, the adjudicator's decision that the contractor was entitled to an extension of time remained binding, and that therefore the onus of proof was on the claimant employer (the losing party in the adjudication) to adduce evidence, and prove on that evidence, that no such extension was justified and it was entitled to its money back?[36]

36.27 Gloster LJ stated that if the burden was reversed so that it shifted to the party who was not making any claim in the litigation or arbitration then the result would be a legal fiction. Her Ladyship argued that placing the burden of proof on the party who was not claiming would be an incorrect hypothesis.[37] This approach, we suggest, is correct. The orthodox approach places the burden on a party who is not seeking to challenge an adjudicator's decision and is contrary to the established principle that where the burden of proof is not clear because the parties' cases are equally weighted, the court considers that it is the party who would be unsuccessful if it did not produce any evidence that has the burden of proof.[38] Moreover, the orthodox approach could lead to a proliferation of negative declarations and, as stated by Longmore LJ in *Aspect Contracts*,[39] it would be counterintuitive to expect a person who says he is not liable to have to take the initiative and himself start legal proceedings.

F. The Difficulties Arising from the Orthodox View

(a) Recovering monies which have been overpaid

36.28 The question of how to claim back monies overpaid under an adjudicator's decision has been the subject of much recent judicial scrutiny. The issue was recently addressed by the Supreme Court in *Aspect Contracts*.[40] Lord Mance held that a paying party had 'a directly enforceable right to recover any overpayment to which the adjudicator's decision can be shown to have led, once there has been a final determination of the dispute'. His Lordship then stated that the right arose 'either by contractual implication [an implied term] or, if not, then by virtue of an independent restitutionary obligation'.

36.29 The right to recover in restitution had previously been doubted in a number of cases. In the Scottish case of *Castle Inns (Stirling) Ltd v Clark Contracts Ltd*,[41] Lord Drummond Young held that 'the use of an implied term of the contract is a more natural mechanism than a

---

[35] See n 20.
[36] *Walker Construction* (n 19) [51].
[37] ibid.
[38] *Amos* (n 15).
[39] [2013] EWCA Civ 1541.
[40] [2015] UKSC 38 [23]–[24] (Lord Mance).
[41] [2005] ScotCS CSOH 178.

restitutionary obligation based on unjustified enrichment, which is necessarily an extra-contractual obligation'.[42] Lord Drummond Young's reasoning was derived from the case of *Dollar Land (Cumbernauld) Ltd v CIN Properties Ltd*,[43] where Lord Hope of Craighead held that:

> An obligation in unjustified enrichment is owed where the enrichment cannot be justified on some legal basis arising from the circumstances in which the defender was enriched. There can be no better justification for an enrichment than that it was obtained and is being retained in the exercise of a contractual right against the party who seeks to invoke the remedy.[44]

36.30 Criticisms had also been made with regard to implying a term in order to recover overpaid monies. At first instance in *Aspect Contracts*[45] Akenhead J had doubted whether there was an implied term. The test for implying a term into a contract is not easily met. In *BP Refinery (Westernport) Pty Ltd v Shire of Hastings*,[46] Lord Simon of Glaisdale identified the following tests for the implication of a term: (1) it must be reasonable and equitable; (2) it must be necessary to give business efficacy to the contract, so that no term will be implied if the contract is effective without it; (3) it must be so obvious that 'it goes without saying'; (4) it must be capable of clear expression; and (5) it must not contradict any express term of the contract. Lord Hoffmann in *AG of Belize v Belize Telecom Ltd*[47] added some further embellishments to the test. His Lordship stated that:

> The question of implication arises when the instrument does not expressly provide for what is to happen when some event occurs ... The most usual inference in such a case is that nothing is to happen. If the parties had intended something to happen, the instrument would have said so.[48]

36.31 Gloster LJ, in *Walker Construction (UK) Ltd v Quayside Homes Ltd*,[49] followed Akenhead J's view that there was no need to imply a term and the test for implication of a term had not been met. Her Ladyship took the view that the relevant cause of action in court proceedings to reclaim money, following an adjudication's decision, flowed from the underlying construction contract itself. Her Ladyship held:

> I agree that, for limitation purposes, no new cause of action arises either as a result of an implied contractual term, or on the basis of a restitutionary claim, and that, when an unsuccessful party to the adjudication subsequently brings court proceedings, it is doing so on the basis of its original rights under the construction contract to claim payment under the contract, damages for breach of contract or a negative declaration that it is not in breach.[50]

36.32 Although Lord Mance, in *Aspect Contracts*,[51] expressly overruled these obiter observations of Gloster LJ, the question remains whether a court would imply a right to repayment in all circumstances. For example, where the construction contract contained an entire

---

[42] ibid [14].
[43] 1998 SC (HL) 90.
[44] ibid [94E]–[F].
[45] See n 23.
[46] (1978) 52 ALJR 20.
[47] [2009] UKPC 10.
[48] ibid [17].
[49] See n 19.
[50] ibid [63].
[51] See n 23.

(b) Recovery under the contract and the concept of temporary finality

36.33 In many construction contracts, before the introduction of adjudication, the engineer or architect would make a decision which would have interim binding effect on the parties until overturned by arbitration. In the case of *Royal Brompton Hospital NHS Trust v Hammond (No 3)*,[52] the House of Lords had to consider an arbitration clause which provided the arbitrator(s) with the power to 'open up, review and revise any certificate, opinion, decision [of the architect] and to determine all matters in dispute … as if no such certificate, opinion, decision … had been given'. The facts of the case were that the architect overcertified an extension of time to the contractor. The employer brought a claim against the architect for negligently overcertifying. Lord Steyn, referring to the employer's case, stated: 'In such a case the Employer must go to arbitration in order to restore his position. He has the burden of proof in the arbitration and has to face the uncertain prospect of succeeding in what may perhaps be a complex arbitration'.[53] The case was remitted back to the High Court and it was subsequently held that the architects had been negligent in overcertifying an extension of time and that the employer had suffered a loss, as it no longer had an entitlement to claim liquidated damages.[54] The employer now had the burden of proof of opening up, reviewing, and revising the architect's extension of time award and proving that the extension of time should be less than that awarded.

36.34 Adjudication has now added a further layer in the dispute resolution process. Adjudicators under the scheme or under contractual provisions have the power to decide a dispute and have the power to open up, review, and revise any decision taken or certificate given unless it has become final and conclusive. The power to open up, review, and revise is seen as an important power because it involves modifying the agreement of the parties.[55] This permits the adjudicator or the subsequently appointed arbitrator to challenge a decision of a certifier, which is binding on the parties until it is revised.

36.35 In *Northern Regional Health Authority v Derek Crouch Construction Co Ltd*,[56] the question of whether the courts had the same powers to open up, review, and revise the decision or certificate of an architect/engineer was considered. The Court of Appeal held that while it had the power to deal with breaches of contract by a certifier, it did not have the power to modify the agreement of the parties and impose its own views.[57] A court could therefore not open up, review, and revise a decision. The Court of Appeal made a distinction between the powers of an arbitrator and the powers of a court. Sir John Donaldson MR stated that an arbitrator had 'to declare the rights of the parties on the basis of the situation produced by his own revising activity'.[58] This was not a power the court possessed because there was no cause of action. The Crouch decision was subsequently distinguished in *Partington & Son*

---

[52] [2002] 1 WLR 1397; [2002] App LR 04/25.
[53] ibid [23].
[54] *Royal Brompton Hospital NHS Trust v Hammond and Others* [2002] EWHC 2037, [258]–[259].
[55] *Northern Regional Health Authority v Derek Crouch Construction Co Ltd* [1984] QB 644, [1984] 2 WLR 676, [1984] 2 All ER 175 (CA).
[56] ibid.
[57] ibid [48] (Wilkinson LJ).
[58] ibid [67].

v *Thameside*⁵⁹ and expressly overruled in *Beaufort Developments (NI) Ltd v Gilbert-Ash (NI) Ltd*.⁶⁰ In *Beaufort Developments*, the House of Lords held that it had the same powers as an arbitrator to open up, review, and revise.

Many construction contract disputes arise from a challenge to an architect/engineer's certificate or determination.⁶¹ An adjudicator must therefore first determine the status of the certificate or determination and who has the burden of proof. In *Royal Brompton Hospital NHS Trust v Hammond (No 3)*,⁶² the House of Lords indicated that the burden of proof had moved when an architect/engineer issues a certificate or makes a decision. The party challenging the decision or certificate has the burden of proof of showing that the decision or certificate was wrong. **36.36**

Recently, in the Scottish case of *SGL Carbon Fibres Ltd v RBG Ltd*,⁶³ Lord Glennie arrived at the same conclusion as Lord Steyn in the *Royal Brompton Hospital* case.⁶⁴ Lord Glennie held that when an arbitrator (or adjudicator) looks at the decision of a certifier the decision of the certifier stands until the certificate or decision is corrected: **36.37**

> The onus must be on the party seeking to persuade the arbitrator to depart from the assessment … made by the Project Manager. In so far as the Contractor (RBG) seeks further payment, the burden is on him. In so far as the Employer (SGL) seeks to argue that the Project Manager's assessment is too high, it must shoulder the burden.⁶⁵

Lord Hoffmann in *Beaufort Developments*⁶⁶ similarly described an architect/engineer's certificate as having 'provisional validity', meaning that it was enforceable until it was challenged. There seems to be no rationale for not taking this one step further. Where an adjudicator reviews and revises the certificate or determination of the architect/engineer, then that determination should replace the previous decision of the architect/engineer.⁶⁷ The party challenging that decision should then have the burden of proof of showing that the adjudicator's decision is wrong. **36.38**

If an architect/engineer's decision or certificate has the effect of shifting the burden of proof, then why not an adjudicator's decision? There appears to be no logical rationale for treating an adjudicator's decision as having less value than that of an architect/engineer. The adjudicator is appointed to act fairly and impartially. The adjudicator's role is to correct the errors made by the architect/engineer and to determine the rights and losses of the parties. In other jurisdictions, the courts have held that an adjudicator's decision has a binding effect which 'endures, at least, until it has been so revised. It is clear from the wording of clause 20.4 [FIDIC Red Book] that the intention was that a decision is binding on the parties and only loses its binding effect if and when it is revised'.⁶⁸ **36.39**

---

⁵⁹ (1985) 33 BLR 150.
⁶⁰ [1999] 1 AC 266, [1998] 2 All ER 778, [1998] 2 WLR 860.
⁶¹ In most construction contracts a claim is first referred to the architect, engineer, or project manager, and then, if a party is dissatisfied with the decision, to adjudication.
⁶² See n 52.
⁶³ [2012] CSOH 19.
⁶⁴ See n 52.
⁶⁵ ibid [26].
⁶⁶ See n 27.
⁶⁷ In contrast, see *The Construction Centre Group Ltd v The Highland Council* [2002] ScotCS CSOH 354.
⁶⁸ *Tubular Holdings (Pty) Ltd v DBY Technologies (Pty) Ltd* (2013) Case No 06757/13 (South Gauteng High Court, South Africa).

36.40 The term 'cause of action' is, however, at variance with what the court or arbitral tribunal is required to do if it is asked to 'open up, review and revise' an adjudicator's decision. Courts, when they consider a cause of action, look for legal rights which arise from breaches of contract, from negligence or from nuisance. It is therefore not surprising that lawyers and judges have struggled when looking for a cause of action in order to overturn an adjudicator's decision. The problem is that there is no cause of action in the traditional sense because the court is not being asked to determine the legal rights of the parties. This point was made by Lord Nolan in *Beaufort Developments* when considering the phrase 'open up, review and revise any certificate, opinion, decision':

> The language used is not that of the Supreme Court Practice. It seems to suggest an informal and constructive approach to the resolution of problems occurring in the course of the building work, an approach appropriate to the work of an arbitrator who is chosen because he is an architect rather than a judge.[69]

36.41 There is a consensus that an adjudicator's decision has a temporary binding effect.[70] However, the courts appear to have struggled to agree on when that temporary binding effect comes to an end. Section 108(3) of the HGCRA provides that '[t]he contract shall provide [in writing] that the decision of the adjudicator is binding until the dispute is finally determined by legal proceedings, by arbitration (if the contract provides for arbitration or the parties otherwise agree to arbitration) or by agreement'.[71] Wording to the same effect is found in the JCT, FIDIC, and NEC forms of contract, among others.

36.42 The concept of 'temporary finality' aims to provide 'a quick and interim, but enforceable, award to be made in advance of the final resolution of what are likely to be complex and expensive disputes'.[72] One of the purposes of adjudication was to improve cash flow, which prior to the enactment of the HGCRA was a problem in construction contracts and resulted in the insolvency of many sub-contractors. The debates in the House of Lords, as reported in Hansard, reveal that initially there was a drive to make an adjudicator's decision final and binding, but the construction industry advocated against this as being arbitration by the back door. The industry desired a quick temporarily binding dispute resolution method which could be revisited through arbitration or litigation. However, no one appears to have addressed the question of who has the burden of proof when seeking to challenge an adjudicator's decision.

G. Conclusion

36.43 It is surprising that the issue of who has the burden of proof has not come directly before the courts earlier. It is perhaps more surprising that for over a decade parties and their lawyers have unquestioningly assumed that the burden of proof does not shift when an adjudicator makes a decision. We suggest that the Sir Peter Coulson/MacFadyen approach is open

---

[69] See n 67.
[70] The concept of temporary finality is found at s 108(3) of the HGCRA 1996 and s 23(2) of the Scheme for Construction Contracts.
[71] Similar wording is used in s 23(2) of the Scheme which provides that '[a]n adjudicator's decision is binding on the parties, and they shall comply with it until the dispute is finally determined by legal proceedings or arbitration'.
[72] *Bouygues UK Ltd v Dahl-Jensen UK Ltd* [2000] EWCA Civ 507, [2001] 1 All ER (Comm) 1041 [2] (Buxton LJ).

to question and that the approach adopted by Gloster LJ is to be preferred.[73] There seems no logical reason why an architect/engineer's decision or certificate should be treated any differently from a decision by an adjudicator. In fact, logic would seem to dictate that the decision of an adjudicator should have greater standing than the decision or certificate of an architect/engineer. The reason for this is that the adjudicator is independent, whereas the architect/engineer is appointed by one of the parties.

In *Tubular Holdings (Pty) Ltd v DBT Technologies (Pty) Ltd*,[74] the court considered enforcement of an adjudicator's decision under a FIDIC contract. The court held that the adjudicator's decision is binding and only loses its binding effect if and when it is revised. The court concluded by stating that the giving of notices of dissatisfaction 'merely allow a possible revision of these decisions without affecting their interim binding nature'. The indication from the South Gauteng High Court in Johannesburg was that while the court had the power to open up, review, and revise a decision, it did follow that it had to exercise that power and replace the adjudicator's decision with its own decision. There may therefore be a distinction between contractual adjudications and statutory adjudications. The orthodox view, if it is correct, may be limited only to statutory adjudications, whereas the logic for wiping the slate clean does not necessarily apply to contractual adjudications because the parties have expressly agreed for an independent person to determine their rights. **36.44**

---

[73] See paras 36.26 and 36.27 earlier in this chapter.
[74] An unreported decision of South Gauteng High Court, South Africa.

Part XIV

FINAL REFLECTIONS AND LOOKING AHEAD

37

RECOLLECTIONS OF PAST EVENTS AND REFLECTIONS ON FUTURE TRENDS

*Martin Hunter**

A. Introduction

37.01 I do not ordinarily write for publication using the 'first person singular'. However, for this *liber amicorum*, which marks the CIArb's special anniversary, I was invited by the editor to include recollections of my personal experiences involving the Institute and, more generally, the world of arbitration. When I started to prepare this commentary I tried to write in the usual 'third person', but the text soon became extraordinarily ponderous and I therefore abandoned the attempt.

37.02 I do not recall precisely when I became a member of the Institute, but it would have been approximately 50 years ago, in the mid 1960s, soon after I qualified as a solicitor in 1964 and joined the corporate department of the firm in which I was working. One afternoon, the senior partner called me and requested me to come to his office. When I got there, Alan Redfern, who was the first (and only) litigation partner in the firm at the time, was with him. The senior partner, Sir Charles Whishaw, explained that the firm had recently been instructed in two major international arbitrations involving foreign governments (Sudan and Kuwait)—one as claimant and the other as respondent.

37.03 Sir Charles said that Alan's primary duty was to manage the firm's (quite new) litigation department and, while Alan would be working on the cases himself, he would need a recently qualified assistant to help gather the evidence, etc, on a temporary 'secondment' basis until the cases were completed. I was the most recently qualified solicitor in the firm, and my desk was relatively clear. Would I be willing to be assigned to the task? My reply was, naturally, 'Of course, Sir Charles, I will be happy to do whatever the firm would like me to do'. He thanked me courteously, and indicated that Alan would brief me on the details of the assignment later.

37.04 As I was leaving the room, I stopped, turned back to face Sir Charles, and asked him how long my secondment to Alan's department was expected to last. He replied, 'I am afraid I don't know, I will have to ask Alan to answer that question'. Alan said, 'I don't know either, but my guess is that it will be not less than six months, and not more than one year'.

---

* © Martin Hunter 2016. The author acknowledges with thanks the valuable contribution of his current research assistant, Valerio Salgado from Sao Paulo, Brazil, who at the time of writing was an LLM candidate at King's College London.

I recounted this story 30 years later, in 1994, in the remarks I made during my 'retirement speech' to the Litigation Department—by which time I had worked at the firm for 33 years; been a litigation partner for 27 years; and had become the founder and first head of the International Arbitration Group within the department, while Alan continued to be its leader (and managing partner) within the firm's overall governance structure.

37.05 I do not now recall, but I think I joined the Institute soon after my 'secondment' to what is now called 'DR' (an abbreviation for 'Dispute Resolution'). Soon after I became a partner, in 1967, I suggested to Alan that we should generate contacts with the Institute. He agreed, and we invited the then Chairman of the Institute, as well as its Secretary-General, Bertie Vigrass, to lunch in our offices, and this event initiated a long and fruitful relationship. For the next 20 years or so, I took an active interest in the 'technical' (arbitration) side of the Institute's activities, albeit (while I admired the commitment of those who did) not in the 'governance' or 'political' aspects of its affairs.

37.06 During this period I became a member of various committees of the Institute, including the 'Arbitration Committee' which was, *inter alia*, responsible for assessing current, and possible future, practices in connection with the conduct of arbitrations by tribunals composed of sole arbitrators or three members, qualified in accordance with the Institute's criteria, and pursuant to its training courses. I also became a Fellow of the Institute, and—later, when the classification was introduced—a Chartered Arbitrator.

B. Taking Evidence

37.07 One particular aspect of the conduct of arbitrations that was (and still is) of particular interest to me is the taking of evidence by arbitral tribunals. I have always regarded this as a matter of supreme importance, because (in my experience) most commercial disputes are decided by arbitral tribunals on the basis of the material facts, rather than on an erudite analysis of the transaction agreement, or a microscopic evaluation of the provisions of the applicable national law.

(a) Common law jurisdictions

37.08 Historically, the reception of evidence by courts and arbitrators in most of the common law countries (with the exception of India) has for centuries been influenced by the existence of jury trials. In the US courts, disputed facts are determined by juries in criminal and in civil cases; in England the material facts are determined by juries only in criminal cases (as well as in some defamation lawsuits); in India (by far the most populous nation among the common law jurisdictions) in no cases—civil or criminal—are the disputed facts determined by juries. Thus, there is no general procedural practice in the leading common law countries. It is unrealistic to expect jurors who are not trained in the law to ignore evidence that they have read, or heard, but should not take into account when assessing the evidentiary value of materials put before them.

37.09 This scenario has led to the development of a substantial body of law on the admissibility of evidence. Those who have watched television coverage of US trials, whether 'real-life' or fictional, may have been struck by the frequent use of the intervention, 'Objection, your honour'. This can lead to long, and expensive, hearings. In civil law countries, if my understanding is correct, juries are never used in the civil courts, and only rarely in criminal cases. The judge

(b) National and international arbitrations

37.10 Where does this leave us in national and/or international arbitration? In England and Wales (in the context, Scotland and Northern Ireland are different jurisdictions), the position has evolved over the last 20 years or so. The first edition of the most authoritative published work of the era stated that:

> It is widely believed that an arbitrator, merely because he is an arbitrator, is empowered to act on evidence which would not be strictly admissible in a Court of Law. This is not so. Arbitrators are bound by the law of England, and the rules of admissibility are part of that law.[1]

37.11 Identical wording was adopted in their second edition, published in 1989.[2] Meanwhile, in 1985, UNCITRAL had published its Model Law on International Commercial Arbitration. This led the UK Government—through the Department of Trade and Industry (as it was then named)—to establish a committee to undertake a comprehensive review of English arbitration law. This very thorough exercise took three years to complete, and in early 1996 a new English Arbitration Act 1996 was passed into law. The new Act introduced a number of innovations, mainly directed at increasing 'party autonomy' in arbitration. In the context of the present commentary on the taking of evidence (or 'fact-finding', as it is sometimes called), section 34 implements a major change of direction from the previous position as described above in Mustill and Boyd:

Procedural and evidential matters
(1) It shall be for the tribunal to decide all procedural and evidential matters, subject to the right of the parties to agree any matter.
(2) Procedural and evidential matters include—
   (a) when and where any part of the proceedings is to be held;
   (b) the language or languages to be used in the proceedings and whether translations of any relevant documents are to be supplied;
   (c) whether any and if so what form of written statements of claim and defence are to be used, when these should be supplied and the extent to which such statements can be later amended;
   (d) whether any and if so which documents or classes of documents should be disclosed between and produced by the parties and at what stage;
   (e) whether any and if so what questions should be put to and answered by the respective parties and when and in what form this should be done;
   (f) whether to apply strict rules of evidence (or any other rules) as to the admissibility, relevance or weight of any material (oral, written or other) sought to be tendered on any matters of fact or opinion, and the time, manner and form in which such material should be exchanged and presented;
   (g) whether and to what extent the tribunal should itself take the initiative in ascertaining the facts and the law;
   (h) whether and to what extent there should be oral or written evidence or submissions.
(3) The tribunal may fix the time within which any directions given by it are to be complied with, and may if it thinks fit extend the time so fixed (whether or not it has expired).

---

[1] Michael J Mustill and Stewart C Boyd, *The Law and Practice of Commercial Arbitration* (1st edn, Butterworths 1982) 310–12.
[2] ibid (2nd edn, 1989) 352–4.

37.12 Thus, the position in England appears to have evolved significantly between the time that Sir Michael Mustill and Stewart Boyd QC wrote the two editions of their seminal work in the 1980s and the time of the passage through Parliament of the English Arbitration Act 1996, particularly in relation to the application of 'strict rules of evidence' in section 34(2)(f).

37.13 In its role as the leading teaching organization of practical skills for arbitrators,[3] based in London, the CIArb has within its grasp the opportunity (some might say the duty) to emphasize the flexibility under English law for arbitrators to assist arbitration in fulfilling its design objective of creating a private, fair, reasonably speedy, and cost-effective system for resolving civil disputes between corporate entities and 'consenting adults' (under English law, minors are not capable of entering into enforceable arbitration agreements).

37.14 Another significant element in the evolution of evidence-gathering procedures in arbitration has been the work carried out by the IBA, which has—since 1983—formulated three successive editions of its IBA Rules on the Taking of Evidence, the most recent being the 2010 version. These Rules are specifically designed to be used in the cross-cultural ambience of international arbitrations, in which up to five different legal systems may be applicable.[4] They are comprehensive in covering document production, fact witness evidence, expert evidence (both party and tribunal-appointed), and inspection of the subject matter of the dispute.

37.15 The IBA Rules on the Taking of Evidence are generally acknowledged to be the internationally accepted standard in the context of the search for an efficient fact-finding system. They take an informed path between the civil law approach (in which the parties produce nothing more than the evidentiary materials they consider necessary to fulfil their respective burdens of proof) and the common law system (in which old-fashioned and unsustainable twentieth century 'discovery' procedures provide for the compulsory production of all material that is 'relevant' to the issues in dispute). To this end, the drafters of the Rules designed a two-stage system for producing both documents and witness testimony, aimed at the target of providing the decision-maker(s) with sufficient materials within reasonable time and cost parameters.

37.16 Concerning document production, the two stages are (1) the parties produce the documents on which they rely and (2) they may serve on each other 'Requests to Produce' additional documents, which must be for documents that are not only 'relevant', but also 'material to the outcome' of the case.[5] This permits the tribunal to deny requests that it considers to be 'fishing expeditions'.[6]

---

[3] Julio César Betancourt, 'The Chartered Institute of Arbitrators (1915–2015): The First 100 Years' (2015) 81(4) Arbitration 375–80.

[4] The five different legal systems which may be applicable are: (a) the law applicable to the arbitration agreement; (b) the law governing the arbitration itself, and its procedure; (c) the substantive law applicable to the transaction agreement (and the merits of the dispute); (d) the law(s) applicable to the parties (eg as to capacity to arbitrate); and (e) the law(s) applicable to the tribunal, and the individual arbitrators.

[5] On the IBA Rules on the Taking of Evidence, see Mark McNeill and Margaret Clare Ryan, 'Meeting the Requirements of Article 3(3) of the IBA Rules: Recommendations for Successful Requests for Document Production' in Julio César Betancourt (ed), *Defining Issues in International Arbitration: Celebrating 100 Years of the Chartered Institute of Arbitrators* (OUP 2016) ch 17.

[6] I recall arbitrations in the twentieth century in which witnesses were subjected, literally, to several days of cross-examination, which hardly ever enlightened the arbitral tribunal in making its decision on contested facts. In the twenty-first century it is rare for any witness to be cross-examined for more than a couple of hours in an international arbitration. For a discussion, see Lawrence W Newman, 'Cross-Examination of Fact Witness Statements in International Arbitration' in Julio César Betancourt (ed), *Defining Issues in International Arbitration: Celebrating 100 Years of the Chartered Institute of Arbitrators* (OUP 2016) ch 18.

Concerning fact witness testimony, the first stage is for the parties to produce signed written witness statements, which are normally treated as their 'evidence-in-chief' (or 'direct testimony'). The second stage is for the witnesses to appear for oral examination, by the tribunal and the parties' counsel, in order that their written testimony may be tested. 37.17

Both of these practices are now widely adopted in international arbitrations. They are considered by many practitioners—both counsel and arbitrators—to work well at the level of cost-efficiency, and effectiveness in assisting international arbitrators to determine the facts that are 'relevant and material' to the outcome of the case. 37.18

With some adjustment to take account of the differences between international and national (sometimes referred to as 'domestic') arbitrations, the IBA Rules on the Taking of Evidence may be viewed as valuable guidance in teaching the enhancement of efficiency and cost-effectiveness to arbitrators and prospective arbitrators in both types of arbitrations. 37.19

Of course, there will always be some high value commercial disputes which the parties wish to resolve by arbitration, for confidentiality or other reasons, but also wish to treat as if they were in effect High Court lawsuits, but behind closed doors. Under the English Arbitration Act 1996 they are entitled to do this, if they so agree. They may instruct the most expensive lawyers and arbitrators, and leave no stone unturned in the quest for a favourable result. There is nothing repugnant, or immoral, about this in principle, as long as it is done lawfully and in good faith. Valid questions may arise in the occasional cases in which undue influence (such as bribes or other forms of unlawful pressure) are deployed. However, the vigilance of arbitral institutions, professional bodies, and responsible commentators (as opposed to uninformed media-type 'gossip') are generally sufficient to keep such abuses under reasonable control. 37.20

C. Conclusion

Unfortunately, I believe that some arbitrations are allowed to escalate into extravagant events that become unduly expensive. Whether or not this is the fault of the opposing lawyers, or the result of other factors, is a matter of speculation—and most likely it varies from case to case. However, it is, or should be, the function of the arbitral tribunal (whether it is composed of a sole arbitrator or three members) to do its best to ensure that the costs incurred by the parties are reasonable. 37.21

I believe the Institute has, or should have, a duty to educate its members and students—during their certification process—as to the importance of cost control, and to use their discretionary powers to allocate the costs of legal representation (and other costs) in their awards in a manner that will discourage excessive expenditure by the eventual winning party. Almost all modern sets of institutional international arbitration rules (as well as the UNCITRAL Arbitration Rules) confer powers on the arbitral tribunal designed to give effect to this philosophy. What is needed now is a body of dedicated educationalists to 'spread the word'. 37.22

In closing, I wish to congratulate the CIArb and its leaders, past and present, on reaching this important milestone in its history in good shape, and to offer my best wishes for the future. 37.23

INDEX

AAA Webfile 35.86
abuse of process doctrine
  arbitration, in
    applicability 33.03, 33.18–33.19
    powers to dismiss
      proceedings 33.20–33.26, 33.45
    public interest, and 33.24
  benefits 33.07
  civil law jurisdictions, in 33.29
  collateral attacks on previous awards 33.10–33.17
  collateral attacks on previous
    judgments 33.08–33.09
  generally 33.01–33.04, 33.45–33.46
  historical development 33.05–33.07
  jurisdiction, applicability 33.27–33.32
  lack of identity, and 33.11–33.12, 33.17
  principle of finality, and 33.33–33.40
  public vs private interests, and 33.41–33.44
  purpose 33.05–33.06
  sources of 33.04, 33.28–33.40
ad hoc arbitration
  vs institutional arbitration 2.04–2.08
admissibility
  arbitral award enforcement 7.51
  evidence 37.09
  procedural arbitrability 7.06–7.10, 7.07–7.10, 7.19–7.24, 7.29, 7.51
after-the-event insurance 26.25, 27.36, 27.39
aggressive tactics *see* behaviour in tribunals
American Arbitration Association
  arbitration caseload 35.81
  code of ethics 13.04
  National Construction Dispute Resolution
    Committee 35.22
annulled awards
  arbitrator reprimands for 23.83–23.88
  foreign decisions, enforceability of 31.29–31.30
  ICSID Rules 2.13
  jurisdictional challenges 1.22–1.27
  seat of arbitration, at 1.22–1.27
Appeal Chamber for the Special Tribunal for
  Lebanon 13.11
appeals *see also* judicial review
  grounds for 1.14–1.17
  problems with 1.20–1.21
  procedural fairness model 1.18–1.21
applicable language
  choice of
    bilingual cases 10.29–10.30
    changes 10.35
    conflict, practical solutions to 10.35–10.36
    convenience of parties 10.34, 10.36
    English, benefits and disadvantages 10.07, 10.09
    implications 10.06–10.07, 10.13–10.17
    practical consequences 10.07–10.08
    silence regarding 10.02, 10.14–10.17
    substantive consequences 10.09–10.12
    underlying contract, and 10.11–10.12
  definition 10.04–10.05
  identification 10.06–10.12, 10.37–10.38
    contract, applicable law 10.21–10.24
    contract, language of 10.19–10.20
    equal treatment principle, and 10.31–10.34, 10.38
    evidence, language of 10.26–10.27
    priorities and presumptions 10.19–10.20
    seat, language of 10.25
    witnesses, language of 10.28–10.30
  translations 10.06–10.07, 10.10
applicable law
  award enforcement 8.42
  choice of law clauses 8.17, 8.43–8.46, 9.01–9.02
  enquiry into, need for 9.05–9.14
  generally 1.34–1.37, 8.10–8.13
  group of countries doctrine 8.17–8.18
  implied choice 9.22–9.23, 9.27–9.28
  importance of 8.14–8.23, 9.39–9.40
  interpretation conflicts 8.17–8.23
    Born's approach 8.12, 8.40–8.47
    cumulative approach 8.12, 8.40–8.47
    law governing arbitration agreement 9.05–9.09
    law governing proceedings *(lex arbitri)* 9.05, 9.07, 9.26
    law governing substance of dispute *(lex causae)* 9.05–9.08, 9.15–9.23
    law of seat, of 9.19–9.20, 9.24–9.29
    main contract approach 9.15–9.23
    Mustill's approach 8.28–8.35
    Spigelman's approach 8.36–8.39
    SulAmérica test 8.24–8.27, 9.16–9.21, 9.25–9.27, 9.36, 9.40
    transnational approach 8.31–8.35, 8.37
  pre-arbitration requirements 8.23
  separability principle 8.42–8.43, 9.09–9.10
  validation principle 9.37
arbitrability 7.52
  burden of proof 7.47, 7.50
  choice of law clauses, validity 7.33, 7.35
  definition 7.03–7.06
  formal validity 7.45–7.46
  interpretation
    award enforcement stage of dispute, in 7.04, 7.16, 7.22–7.24, 7.26, 7.31, 7.37–7.51
    French approach 7.25–7.29
    preliminary stage of dispute, in 7.04, 7.11–7.29, 7.26–7.27
    tribunal stage of dispute, in 7.04, 7.26, 7.30–7.36
    US approach 7.19–7.24
    validity-preferring approach 7.34–7.35
  judicial inconsistencies 7.31
  judicial review 7.16

Index

arbitrability (cont.):
   kompetenz-kompetenz negative effect 7.16–7.29
   non-arbitrable subject matter 7.44
   non-existence of agreement 7.49
   party autonomy, and 7.32–7.33, 7.35
   scope, issues of 7.50
   seat of arbitration, applicable law 7.36
   separability 7.12–7.15
   setting aside awards 7.37–7.43, 7.48
   substantive validity 7.47–7.48
   substantive vs procedural arbitrability 7.07–7.10, 7.19–7.29, 7.51

arbitral institutions, generally *see also* **institutional arbitration; international arbitration; individual institutions by name**
   efficiency 2.29
   fees 26.08–26.10
   flexibility 2.30
   informal interactions 2.31
   institutional vs ad hoc arbitration 2.04–2.08
   party involvement 2.32
   personal interactions 2.33–2.34
   purpose 6.10–6.11
   roles of 2.09–2.17

arbitration agreements
   applicable law 8.10–8.23
      Mustill's approach 8.28–8.35
      SulAmérica test 8.24–8.27, 9.16–9.21, 9.25–9.27, 9.36, 9.40
   arbitrability, definition 7.03–7.06
   autonomy of 7.12–7.15, 9.09–9.10
   choice of law clauses, validity 7.33
   conflicts of law, convention rules 9.12–9.13
   contract clauses 6.06
   drafting
      appointing sole arbitrator 12.16–12.22
      default provisions 12.16, 12.19
      documents only arbitration 12.38
      expedited arbitration 12.23–12.33
      over-engineering, and 12.14
      summary dismissal 12.34–12.45
   submission agreements 6.07–6.09
   validity, challenging 7.01–7.02

arbitration awards, generally *see also* **annulled awards; enforcement of arbitral awards**
   binding nature of 33.33–33.38
   foreign judgments, differences from 31.28
   independence 31.23–31.24
   legal status 31.23–31.24
   non-state law choice, and 31.17–31.19
   perjury, and 20.31

arbitration conventions, generally *see also* **New York Convention; UNCITRAL Model Law**
   failings of 8.41–8.42

arbitration, generally
   absence of law, and 1.04
   appeal grounds 1.14–1.17
   attitudes towards 23.60–23.67
   benefits of 4.24–4.31, 11.12, 12.09
   challenge criteria 1.14–1.17
   challenges for 1.39–1.40, 1.45
   choice of, influences on 12.09–12.14
   choice of law, and 31.10–31.16
   client-centred processes 4.11–4.16
   conflicts 1.14–1.17, 1.21
   contract law, and 1.06, 1.08–1.09
   duration of cases, trends 12.03–12.04
   essential steps 1.33
   flexibility 2.30, 4.26–4.31
   hard vs soft law 1.10–1.13
   historical development 6.24–6.25, 29.02–29.15
   informality, benefits of 1.42–1.43
   judicial specialization 30.10–30.14
   jurisdiction 1.08, 1.29–1.33
   legal principles, differences from 1.34–1.37
   limitations 1.13
   litigation, differences from 11.10–11.12
   motivation 1.01–1.03
   preference for, trends 12.02
   procedural fairness model 1.18–1.21
   purpose 1.01, 1.03, 1.08, 1.41–1.42, 11.20
   questions of law or fact 1.14–1.17
   sanctions 1.05, 1.12
   scope of cases 1.39–1.40, 1.42
   types, comparison of 21.14–21.15
   in writing requirement 1.09, 6.17, 9.11

arbitrators, generally *see also* **behaviour in tribunals; emergency arbitrators**
   active retirement trends 35.78–35.79, 35.103
   alienating 11.03
   behavioural determinants 23.10–23.15
   bias, waiver of 1.28
   characteristics 11.23
   choice of language, and 10.07–10.09
   conduct guidelines 3.12, 3.37–3.44
   disciplinary procedures 13.28–13.29
   education 30.03–30.08
      arbitral institution approaches 30.18–30.22
      conferences and seminars 30.15–30.17
      governmental and NGO approaches 30.23–30.25
      outreach initiatives 30.18–30.27
      private promotion programmes 30.26–30.27
      trends 35.104–35.105
   fame and prestige 23.48–23.59
   incentives and constraints 23.06–23.09
   influences on 23.01–23.02
   initiatives 22.84
      arbitrator experience, and 22.59–22.62
      ascertain and apply law, to 22.41–22.48
      clarify party requests, to 22.83
      default proceedings 22.77–22.79
      discretionary exercise of 22.49–22.83
      establish facts, to 22.06–22.40
      institutional rules basis 22.21–22.40
      nature of arbitration, and 22.58
      parties' background and experience 22.56–22.57, 22.63–22.65
      parties' expectations, and 22.55
      powers to take 22.06–22.83
      procedural agreements on 22.54
      procedural efficiency, and 22.66–22.69
      procedural fairness, and 22.70–22.72
      public policy or interest, and 22.72–22.77

Index

standards, facts vs law issues 22.80–22.82
statutory basis 22.07, 22.09–22.20
justice, as aim of 23.68–23.82
market value 23.18–23.24
morality 23.03–23.05
orientation 22.01
perceptions of 23.60–23.67
powers
  agreement-based 21.01–21.03
  anti-misconduct 13.11–13.14
  discretionary 21.09, 21.11
  dismiss abusive proceedings,
    to 33.20–33.26, 33.45
  disqualify counsel, to 21.30–21.33
  fulfil adjudicatory function,
    to 21.24–21.25, 21.41
  implied 21.07–21.08, 21.11–21.13, 21.15–21.22
  impose sanctions, to 21.26–21.29
  inherent 21.10, 21.12–21.15, 21.23–21.37
  investigate fraud or corruption, to 21.29
  kompetenz-kompetenz doctrine 21.16–21.17
  restrictions on 21.15, 21.21–21.22, 21.34–21.37
  scope and limitations 21.04–21.05, 21.39–21.42
  take initiative, to 22.06–22.83
remuneration 2.15, 23.16–23.44
social capital 23.25–23.28
sole arbitrators, use trends 12.17
specialization 23.29–23.31
Australia
expert conferencing 19.07
judicial specialization 30.10
Australian Centre for International Commercial Arbitration
costs allocation 25.23
emergency arbitration 14.06–14.07, 14.15–14.20, 14.32

BATNA analysis 28.32–28.33
before-the-event insurance 26.25
behaviour in tribunals
arbitrators, of
  avoiding reprimand for annulled/challenged
    awards, and 23.83–23.88
  behavioural determinants 23.10–23.15
  conduct guidelines 3.12, 3.37–3.44
  fame and prestige 23.48–23.59
  incentives and constraints 23.06–23.09
  income, and 23.16–23.44
  influences on 23.01–23.02, 23.89–23.94
  justice, and 23.68–23.82
  market value, and 23.18–23.24
  misunderstandings 22.01–22.03
  morality, and 23.03–23.05
  reputation, and 23.42, 23.45–23.47
  social capital, and 23.25–23.28
  specialization 23.29–23.31
cognitive psychology insights 35.99–35.102
confrontation or aggression from parties
  11.01–11.02, 11.10–11.12
  arbitrator reluctance, and 11.17–11.19
  causes 11.13–11.19
  client wishes, and 11.13–11.14
  cultural expectations 11.16

  implications 11.20–11.24
  lawyers' obligations 11.13–11.14
  practitioner unfamiliarity 11.15
  prevention approaches 11.30–11.32
consensus 11.04–11.09
  non-signatory involvement, and 11.08
costs allocation, influences on 25.28–25.35, 25.48
counterproductive advocacy 11.25
  aggravating tribunal 11.28
  poor presentation 11.29
  reluctance to agree 11.27
  unmeritorious tactics 11.26
management of
  document presentation rules 11.34
  formality and authority 11.31–11.32
  oral advocacy 11.33
misconduct 11.22
  arbitrators' conduct guidelines 3.12, 3.37–3.44
  party representation guidelines 3.39,
    13.03–13.04, 13.15–13.19, 13.20–13.23
  trends 13.01–13.02, 13.05, 13.30
misunderstanding between counsel and arbitrator
  avoidance mechanisms 22.03
  causes 22.01–22.02
Belgium
oaths in arbitration 20.40
best alternative analysis 28.32–28.33
best practices 12.07–12.08
bias
arbitrators, freedom from 23.24
waiver of 1.28
bifurcation 12.34, 12.37
breach of good faith 7.43
bribery
enforcement of arbitral awards 32.35
public policy and interest, and 32.44–32.51
Building Information Modelling (BIM) 35.93
burden of proof
arbitrability 7.47, 7.50
arbitration, role in 36.07–36.08
award enforcement 7.47, 7.50
discovery in foreign proceedings conflicts 16.12
establishment, importance of 36.04
interim measures 15.14
principle 36.06, 36.09
relevance of documents requested 17.19
shifting 36.43–36.44
  adjudicators' decisions 36.33–36.42, 36.44
  arbitrator's decision impact on 36.08–36.42
  de novo hearings 36.18–36.20
  difficulties with 36.28–36.42
  judicial powers to open up, review and
    revise 36.33–36.42
  orthodox interpretation 36.10–36.17, 36.27
  recovery of overpayments 36.28–36.32
  temporary finality, and 36.33–36.42

Cairo Regional Centre for International Commercial Arbitration
interim measures 15.08
case management conferences 4.21–4.23
caucusing 28.34–28.37, 28.41

Index

Chartered Institute of Arbitrators
  binding nature of awards 33.33–33.34, 33.36
  costs recovery rules 27.31
  disciplinary procedures 13.28–13.29
  history 36.01, 37.02, 37.05–37.06
  interim relief powers 15.06
  role of 36.01
China
  ethical conduct 13.07
  mediation trends 35.94
China International Economic and Trade Arbitration Commission
  arbitrators' initiatives 22.36
  costs allocation 25.23
  expedited arbitration 12.28–12.31
choice of law
  legal pluralism, and 31.32–31.33
  limitations 31.08
  non-state law
    arbitration, and 31.10–31.16
    arbitration awards, independence of 31.23–31.24
    arbitration awards, judicial enforcement 31.17–31.19, 31.28–31.31
    benefits of 31.07
    dispute resolution, and 31.23–31.31
    inconsistencies 31.18–31.22, 31.28–31.31
    litigation, and 31.05–31.09
  party autonomy, and 31.05, 31.16
  party intention, and 31.06
Christianity
  arbitration rulings 1.05
  oaths and affirmations 20.05, 20.08–20.09
client-centred processes
  case management conferences 4.21–4.23
  challenges 4.40–4.66
  client expectations, care of 5.01–5.11
  compromise 4.32–4.39
  early identification of issues 4.47
  flexibility 4.26–4.31
  need for 4.11–4.16
  preliminary issues 4.33–4.34, 4.36–4.39, 4.42–4.44, 4.48–4.66
  reducing time and costs 4.19–4.39
  risk in court proceedings 4.46–4.47
  summary judgment procedures 4.37–4.41
codes of conduct
  CCBE Rules 3.37, 3.39
  IBA Guidelines on Party Representation 3.39, 13.03–13.04, 13.15–13.19
  LCIA General Guidelines for the Parties' Legal Representatives 13.03, 13.20–13.23
  LCIA Rules 3.37–3.44
  sanctions for misconduct 3.38–3.40, 3.43
  self-regulation 3.40–3.41
communication
  technology influences on 35.83–35.93
community court 35.90
conditional fee arrangements 26.21–26.22, 27.37, 27.39
confidentiality
  mediation 28.43–28.47
  third-party funding 26.36

consensus 11.04–11.09
conservatory measures *see* interim measures
construction contracts
  arbitration clauses 36.03
  burden of proof, and
    adjudicators' decisions 36.33–36.42, 36.44
    de novo hearings 36.18–36.20
    establishment, importance of 36.04
    judicial powers to open up, review and revise 36.33–36.42
    recovery of overpayments 36.28–36.32
    shifting, difficulties with 36.28–36.42
    shifting, judicial interpretation of 36.08–36.42
    temporary finality, and 36.33–36.42
  features of 36.03
  implied terms 36.28–36.32
  stepped dispute resolution clauses 36.02, 36.04–36.05
construction disputes
  adjudication 35.13–35.14, 35.27–35.29
  arbitration 35.20–35.22
    arbitrators, active retirement 35.78–35.79, 35.103
    arbitrators, diversity of 35.63–35.67
    arbitrators, independence of 35.77
    case management, and 35.62
    costs and delays 35.60–35.62
    domestic trends 35.52–35.54
    fast-track processes 35.61
    flexibility in 35.58
    international trends 35.80–35.81
    legal standards role in 35.68–35.74
    litigation, compared with 35.56–35.59
    multi-disciplinary tribunals 35.63–35.67
    perspectives on 35.55–35.58
    settlement, and 35.75–35.76
    stepped approaches 35.45–35.50
  collaborative contracting 35.24–35.26
  dispute resolution advisors 35.15–35.17
  dispute resolution trends 35.01–35.07, 35.10
  dispute review boards 35.03, 35.13–35.14, 35.27–35.29
  dynamic conflict management 35.15–35.17
  filtering systems 35.05
  Integrated Project Delivery (IPD) 35.05, 35.25–35.26
  litigation culture, and 35.06, 35.08–35.09
  mediation 35.18–35.19
    caucasing 35.44
    development 35.32–35.33
    lawyers, role in 35.34–35.38
    MEDALOA approach 35.50
    methods and styles 35.40–35.44
    preliminary preparations 35.43
    professional role, as 35.39
    project mediation 35.30
    stepped approaches 35.45–35.50
    trends 35.31, 35.51
  partnering 35.04–35.05, 35.11, 35.24
  'Quiet Revolution' 35.04–35.05, 35.23
  'real time' jobsite resolution 35.27–35.30
  relational contracting 35.12
  stepped resolution approaches 35.45–35.50

Index

contingency fee arrangements 26.21–26.22, 27.37, 27.39
corruption
  arbitrators' power to investigate 21.29
  public policy and interest, and 32.35, 32.38, 32.44–32.51
costs *see also* funding
  agreement protocols 25.44, 25.48
  allocation of liability for 25.06
  anticipated 25.02
  awards, time limits for 25.48
  breakdown of 2.16
  central costs 25.10, 25.12
  classification of 25.10–25.12
  common practices 25.19
  conduct in proceedings, and 25.28–25.35, 25.48
  counsel's fees 26.11–26.12, 27.12, 27.14
  discretion, principles of 25.14–25.39
  expert witnesses 26.13–26.18
  features of 25.13
  incentives, as 25.07–25.08
  institutional charges 26.06–26.07
  institutional rules 25.23, 25.32–25.33, 25.38–25.39, 25.46–25.47
  legal representation, for 25.21–25.22
  limitations on arbitrators' powers 21.35–21.36
  management, importance of 26.01–26.04, 26.38
  miscellaneous 26.19
  offers of settlement 25.41–25.42, 25.48
  party costs 25.10
  perceptions of 25.03–25.05
  recovery 27.55–27.56
    administrative and procedural costs 27.12–27.13
    allocation difficulties 25.40–25.45, 25.48
    allocation trends 25.24–25.27, 25.36–25.39
    categories eligible for 27.09–27.14
    contested costs 27.15–27.50
    contingency fee arrangements 27.37, 27.39
    cost shifting 25.06, 25.39
    criteria 27.04–27.08
    genuine and demonstrable 27.06
    in-house costs 27.02–27.03, 27.17–27.26, 27.52
    legal costs 27.14, 27.45
    management and staff costs 27.27–27.33, 27.53
    purposes of arbitration, for 27.07
    reasonable and necessary 25.07, 27.08
    success basis 25.20–25.27, 25.46
    third-party funding 27.02–27.03, 27.34–27.50, 27.54
  security for 25.43
  tribunal fees and expenses 26.08–26.10
Council of Bars and Law Societies of Europe
  code of conduct 3.37, 3.39
counsel *see also* behaviour in tribunals
  arbitrators' powers to disqualify 21.30–21.33
  fees 26.11–26.12, 27.12, 27.14
  in-house, costs recovery 27.02–27.03, 27.17–27.26, 27.52
  orientation 22.01
CourtCall 35.87
courts, generally
  interpretation role 1.01–1.06

cross-examination 18.13–18.18
  approaches 18.09–18.10, 18.13–18.18, 18.23–18.24
  benefits 18.22–18.23
  disadvantages 18.10–18.11, 18.13, 18.21
  preparation 18.25–18.26
  rules 11.33
  time limits 18.15

damages-based agreements 26.21, 26.23
de novo hearings 36.18–36.20
DIS *see* German Institution of Arbitration
discovery *see also* requests to produce
  broad vs narrow interpretation 16.01–16.03
  foreign proceedings conflicts
    burden of proof 16.12
    discretionary factors 16.08–16.12
    flexible approach 16.06–16.07
    lack of receptivity 16.11
    resolution difficulties 16.09–16.11
    strict approach 16.04–16.05
  US Federal Rules 16.01–16.03, 16.13
dispute resolution, generally *see also* construction disputes; mediation
  development, influences on 35.82
    active retirement trends 35.78–35.79, 35.103
    behavioural science 35.99–35.102
    big data 35.99–35.102
    credentialling 35.104–35.107
    globalization 35.94–35.98
    legal education trends 35.104–35.105
    technology 35.83–35.93
document presentation *see also* evidence
  guidance on 11.34
documents only arbitration 12.38
drug trafficking 32.38

efficiency *see* procedural efficiency
electronic transcripts 35.85
email 35.83
emergency arbitrators
  ACICA Rules 14.06–14.07, 14.15–14.20, 14.32
  application, key features 14.07
  benefits 14.14–14.32, 14.33–14.34, 14.37
  disadvantages 14.35–14.36
  emergency, definition 14.15–14.21
  enforceability 14.27–14.32
  ICC Rules 3.26–3.28, 14.06–14.08, 14.18–14.20, 14.32, 15.23, 15.26
  interim relief powers 15.05, 15.10
  jurisdiction 14.03
  LCIA Rules 3.08, 3.12, 3.19–3.28, 14.06–14.07
  market need for 14.22–14.26
  purpose 14.02
  SCC Rules 3.26–3.27
  SIAC Rules 3.26–3.27, 14.06–14.07, 14.29, 14.32
  trends 14.03, 14.23–14.25
  vs court-ordered interim measures 14.02, 14.10–14.13
'encounter common ley' 32.07
enforcement of arbitral awards
  admissibility 7.51
  applicable law 8.42

enforcement of arbitral awards (*cont.*):
  arbitrability 7.04, 7.16, 7.22–7.24, 7.26, 7.31, 7.37–7.51
  bribery, and 32.35
  burden of proof 7.47, 7.50
  convention rules 7.44–7.48, 8.42, 21.29
  formal validity 7.45–7.46
  illegal acts or contracts, and 32.20, 32.26–32.27, 32.35–32.42
  mediation, and 28.48–28.50
  non-arbitrable subject matter 7.44
  non-existence of agreement 7.49
  non-state choice of law, and 31.17–31.22, 31.28–31.31
  public policy or interest, and 32.20, 32.26–32.27, 32.33–32.42
  scope issues 7.50
  setting aside 7.37–7.43, 7.48
  substantive validity 7.47–7.48
  unenforceable awards 21.29
English law
  choice of
    arbitration, and 31.10–31.16
    arbitration awards, independence of 31.23–31.24
    arbitration awards, judicial enforcement of 31.17–31.19, 31.28–31.31
    dispute resolution, and 31.23–31.31
    inconsistencies and limitations 31.03–31.04, 31.18–31.22, 31.28–31.31
    international arbitration, and 31.01–31.02
    legal pluralism, and 31.32–31.33
    litigation, and 31.05–31.09
    recognition and enforcement of judgments rules 31.28–31.31
    reputation, and 31.01–31.02
  precedents, role of 32.11
  principles of morality 32.10–32.12, 32.38–32.40
  public policy or interest
    arbitration law, and 32.32–32.61
    conflicts of law 32.26–32.30
    foreign judgments, enforcement 32.26–32.30, 32.43–32.51
    historical development 32.05–32.24
    illegal acts or contracts 32.20, 32.26–32.27, 32.35–32.42
    legal challenges 32.14–32.23
    limitations of doctrine 32.21–32.23
    private international law, and 32.25–32.31, 32.39–32.51
    reasonableness test 32.19
    restraint of trade 32.19
eQuibbly 35.88
ethics *see also* **misconduct**
  arbitrators, morality of 23.03–23.05
  behaviour trends 13.01–13.02, 13.05, 13.30
  institutional guidelines
    arbitrators' conduct 3.12, 3.37–3.44
    party representation 3.39, 13.03–13.04, 13.15–13.19, 13.20–13.23
  justice, and 23.72–23.76
  principles of morality 32.10–32.12, 32.38–32.40
  third-party funding 26.34

evidence *see also* **discovery**
  admissibility of 37.09
  document presentation rules 11.34
  perjury, proof of 20.16–20.19
  requests to produce 37.16
    burden of proof 17.19
    discovery, difference from 17.05
    good faith, and 17.33
    identification requirement 17.08
    materiality requirement 17.18–17.25
    narrow and specific requirement 17.04–17.05, 17.07, 17.09–17.17
    possession, custody, or control 17.26–17.34
    scope of production 17.05–17.06
    timing 17.21
    unreasonable burden 17.34
  taking, processes
    civil law jurisdictions, in 37.09
    common law jurisdictions, in 37.08–37.09
    importance 37.07
    national and international arbitrations, in 37.10–37.20
  taking, rules for 13.08
    arbitrators' initiatives 22.37
    good faith 25.29–25.30, 37.20
    IBA Rules 6.23, 17.01–17.02, 17.05–17.34, 20.36, 22.37, 25.29–25.30, 37.14–37.16
    oaths and affirmations 20.36
    purpose 17.01–17.02, 37.19
    requests to produce 17.05–17.34, 37.16
    witness testimony 20.36, 37.17
expedited arbitration
  benefits 12.31
  common features 12.29
  deadlines 12.26, 12.30
  disadvantages 12.31
  drafting clauses for 12.23–12.33
  LCIA Rules 3.13, 3.19–3.23
  reasons for 12.24
  SCC Rules 12.27–12.31
  SIAC Rules 12.27–12.28, 12.30–12.32
  time extensions 12.26
  UNCITRAL Model Law 3.21
  use trends 12.32
expert witnesses *see also* **cross-examination**
  appointment, reasons for 19.02–19.03, 19.06
  challenging 19.12–19.16
  costs of 19.01, 26.13–26.18
  ethics 19.10
  expert conferencing 19.07
  expert teams and stars 19.17–19.20
  independence 19.11
  oaths and affirmations 20.13
  purpose 19.02–19.05, 19.08–19.13, 19.22
  vs consultants 19.09

fame 23.48–23.52
fast track arbitration *see* **expedited arbitration**
fees
  counsel's fees 26.11–26.12, 27.12, 27.14
  determination of 2.27

expert witness fees 26.13–26.18
tribunal fees and expenses 26.08–26.10
finality, principle of 33.33–33.40
Finland
costs allocation, success basis 25.21
foreign judgments
arbitration awards, differences from 31.28
enforcement, under English law
domestic treatment, differences from 32.53–32.55, 32.58
EU judgments 32.55–32.56
fraud 32.53–32.59
public policy, and 32.26–32.30, 32.43–32.51
recognition, and 31.28–31.31, 32.43–32.51
France
applicable law, transnational approach 9.31–9.32
arbitrability 7.25–7.29, 7.38, 7.40, 7.51
arbitration awards
annulment 1.23
binding nature 33.37
setting aside 7.38, 7.40
arbitrators' initiatives 22.10–22.11, 22.46
costs allocation trends 25.36–25.37
kompetenz-kompetenz negative effect, approach to 7.25–7.29
fraud 32.38
arbitration awards obtained by way of 20.31
arbitrators' powers to investigate 21.29
foreign judgments, enforceability 32.53–32.59
free trade agreements
jurisdiction conflicts 1.31
frustration
judicial review 29.31–29.43
functus officio **principle** *see also* **termination of proceedings**
definition 24.01–24.02, 24.45
historical development 24.01
funding 26.20, 26.40
attorney-led methods 26.21–26.23
conditional fee arrangements 26.21–26.22, 27.37, 27.39
damages-based agreements 26.21, 26.23
insurance 26.24–26.25, 27.36, 27.39
third-party funding 26.26–26.30
benefits 26.31–26.32
costs recovery 27.02–27.03, 27.34–27.50, 27.54
disadvantages and criticisms 26.33–26.37, 27.44
types 26.21–26.28

German Institution of Arbitration (DIS) 2.25–2.27
arbitrators' initiatives 22.33–22.35
expedited arbitration 12.29–12.30
Germany
arbitrability 7.42, 7.49, 7.51
arbitration awards
binding nature 33.37
setting aside 7.42
arbitrators' initiatives 22.12–22.15, 22.25–22.27
costs allocation, success basis 25.21
oaths in arbitration 20.41
globalization 35.94–35.98

good faith
breach of 7.43
conduct in proceedings 25.29–25.30
requests to produce 17.33
Greece
mediation framework 35.95
group of countries doctrine 8.17–8.18, 9.33
guerrilla tactics *see* **behaviour in tribunals**

harm and urgency
interim measures 15.13–15.23
Heilbron Guidelines, document presentation 11.34
Hinduism
oaths and affirmations 20.10
Hong Kong International Arbitration Centre
arbitration awards, binding nature 33.33, 33.35
choice of language rules 10.16
emergency arbitration 14.06–14.07, 14.32
model clause 8.08–8.09

International Court of Justice
interim measures 15.18, 15.21–15.22, 15.27
illegal acts or contracts
public policy or interest, and 32.20, 32.26–32.27, 32.35–32.42
violation, in arbitration law 32.52–32.61
India
judicial specialization 30.10
institutional arbitration
efficiency of 2.09–2.17
vs ad hoc arbitration 2.04–2.08
insurance
arbitration funding, for 26.24–26.25, 27.36, 27.39
interim measures 15.29 *see also* **emergency arbitrators**
arbitral institution rules 15.05–15.07
burden of proof 15.14
CIArb Rules 15.06
definition 14.01
emergency arbitrators, and 14.02, 14.10–14.13, 15.10
enforceability 14.28, 15.11–15.12
harm requirement 15.13–15.20
ICC Rules 15.17, 15.23, 15.26
jurisdiction 15.27–15.28
LCIA Rules 15.06
lex arbitri 15.07–15.12
likelihood of success, and 15.24–15.26
national courts role 15.02–15.03
purpose 14.01, 15.01, 15.18
UNCITRAL Model Law 15.07–15.08, 15.20
urgency requirement 15.21–15.23
international arbitration, generally
applicable law, Mustill's approach 8.28–8.35
arbitration agreements 6.06–6.09
attractions of 31.10–31.13
benefits 6.01, 6.29
contract clauses 6.06
disadvantages 6.18–6.23
institutional vs ad hoc arbitration 2.04–2.08
lex arbitri 6.13
limitations 6.27
purpose 6.01
role of law 6.14–6.17

Index

international arbitration, generally (cont.):
  seat of arbitration 6.13, 6.15
  submission agreements 6.07–6.09
  transnational approach 8.31–8.35, 8.37, 9.30–9.39
International Bar Association
  conduct of arbitration guidelines 6.23
  evidence taking rules 6.23
    arbitrators' initiatives 22.37
    development 37.14–37.15
    good faith 25.29–25.30
    oaths and affirmations 20.36
    purpose 17.01–17.02, 37.19
    requests to produce 17.05–17.34, 37.16
    witness testimony 20.36, 37.17
  party representation guidelines 3.39, 13.03–13.04, 13.15–13.19, 13.31
  requests to produce
    burden of proof 17.19
    discovery, difference from 17.05
    good faith, and 17.33
    identification requirement 17.08
    materiality requirement 17.18–17.25
    narrow and specific requirement 17.04–17.05, 17.07, 17.09–17.17
    possession, custody, or control 17.26–17.34
    scope of production 17.05–17.06
    timing 17.21
    unreasonable burden 17.34
International Centre for Dispute Resolution Rules
  arbitration awards, binding nature 33.33, 33.35
  termination of proceedings 24.13–24.16
  witness testimony 20.33
International Centre for Settlement of Investment Disputes
  anti-misconduct powers 13.11, 13.14
  arbitration awards, annulment 2.13
  costs allocation trends 25.27
  interim measures 15.25, 15.27
  oaths and affirmations 20.35
  Secretariat role 2.13
  summary dismissal 12.41, 12.43
  summary judgment procedures 4.37–4.39
  third-party costs recovery 27.41
  witness testimony 20.35
International Chamber of Commerce Arbitration Rules
  arbitration awards
    appeals 29.41
    binding nature 33.33, 33.35
  arbitrators' initiatives 22.23–22.31
  case management 4.21, 12.07
  choice of language rules 10.14–10.15
  costs recovery 25.16, 25.32, 27.13, 27.24
  efficiency requirement 12.06
  emergency arbitrators 3.26–3.28, 14.06–14.08, 14.18–14.20, 14.32, 15.23, 15.26
  fairness and impartiality 4.34
  group of countries doctrine 9.33
  interim measures 15.17, 15.23, 15.26
  model clause 8.03
  seat of arbitration conflicts 3.29
  Secretariat role 2.12
  summary dismissal 12.39
  witness testimony 20.34
International Law Association
  abuse of process rules 33.30–33.31
international law, generally
  choice of law principles 31.05–31.08
  public policy, and 32.32, 32.62–32.63, 32.66–32.69
  treaties and agreements, choice of arbitration style 2.04–2.08
interpreters
  oaths and affirmations 20.13, 20.29
investigations
  fraud or corruption, powers of 21.29
investment arbitration
  justice, and 23.73–23.74
  perceptions of 23.60–23.67
investment treaties
  disclosure, possession or control 17.32
  jurisdiction conflicts 1.31
Iran-United States Claims Tribunal 2.18–2.21, 13.11
Islam
  arbitration in UAE 34.12, 34.14
  arbitration rulings 1.05
  oaths and affirmations 20.05, 20.10
  public policy in UAE 34.43
  Shari'ah law 34.12, 34.14, 34.43
'Italian Torpedoes' 3.12, 3.48–3.50
iura novit curia 22.41–22.46, 22.54

Japan Commercial Arbitration Association
  emergency arbitration 14.06–14.08, 14.32
Judaism
  arbitration rulings 1.05
  oaths and affirmations 20.05, 20.08–20.09
judicial performance
  difficulties with 30.01–30.03, 30.06, 30.28
  judicial specialization, and 30.10–30.14
  jurisdictional differences, and 30.04–30.05, 30.08–30.09
  practitioner education, and 30.03–30.08
    arbitral institution approaches 30.18–30.22
    conferences and seminars 30.15–30.17
    governmental and NGO approaches 30.23–30.25
    outreach initiatives 30.18–30.27
    private promotion programmes 30.26–30.27
judicial review
  nineteenth century law 29.05–29.09
  Arbitration Act 1979 29.16–29.30
  Arbitration Act 1996 29.44–29.52
  case trends 29.48–29.52
  frustration 29.31–29.43
  historical development 29.01–29.15
  judicial inconsistencies 29.16–29.17
  kompetenz-kompetenz approach 7.16
  law of damages, and 29.50
  medieval law 29.02–29.03
  public interest in arbitration 29.10–29.15, 29.46
  right to
    contracting out 29.44–29.45
    entrenchment 29.24–29.29

error or question of law 29.16, 29.18–29.21, 29.27–29.28, 29.37, 29.53
excess of power, and 29.53
exclusions 29.24–29.29, 29.31–29.43
law reform 29.16–29.30, 29.44–29.52
limitations 29.44–29.52
special case procedure 29.10–29.23, 29.38
supranational agreements 29.22, 29.25
jurisdiction *see also* **choice of law**
abuse of process doctrine 33.27–33.32
annulled awards 1.22–1.27
applicable law 1.34–1.37
arbitrability, and 7.34–7.35
conflicts 1.29–1.33
court selection clauses 1.08
interim measures 15.27–15.28
mediation by dual-role neutrals 28.27–28.28
seat of arbitration, applicable law 7.36
substantive arbitrability 7.06–7.10, 7.19–7.29
justice
arbitration approaches to 23.77–23.82
arbitrator's aim, as 23.68–23.82
best possible outcome 23.78
changing the world 23.69–23.71
community stakes in 23.72–23.76
cultural influences on 23.75
precedents, creating and following 23.79, 23.82
rule of law, and 23.79
societal values, and 23.780
third-party funding, and 26.31
Justinian's Digest 24.01

kompetenz-kompetenz
arbitrators' powers 21.16–21.17
negative effect 7.16–7.29
French approach 7.25–7.29
US approach 7.19–7.24
Kuala Lumpur Regional Centre for Arbitration
interim measures 15.08

language *see also* **applicable language**
choice of
arbitral institutions rules 10.14–10.16
English, benefits and disadvantages 10.07, 10.09
implications 10.06–10.10
social and cultural influences 10.10
translations 10.06–10.07, 10.10
definition 10.04–10.05
importance in law 10.01
legal education 30.03–30.08
arbitral institution approaches 30.18–30.22
conferences and seminars 30.15–30.17
governmental and NGO approaches 30.23–30.25
outreach initiatives 30.18–30.27
private promotion programmes 30.26–30.27
trends 35.104–35.105
legal pluralism 31.32–31.33
legitimate expectations, breach of
client presentation of case, inadequate 5.03–5.04
common problems 5.02–5.11
de novo review, lack of 5.10–5.11
dislike of counsel, and 5.07

formalistic approach 5.08–5.09
rushing through pleadings 5.05–5.06
time for proceedings, inadequate 5.02
lex mercatoria 8.33, 29.02, 29.57, 31.14–31.16, 31.18–31.19
loi vs *droit* 1.10
London Court of International Arbitration
history 3.01
model clause 8.04
proceedings
commencement 3.13–3.18
default procedures 3.52
electronic communication/filing 3.12, 3.14–3.16
emergency arbitrators 3.08, 3.12, 3.19–3.28, 14.06–14.08
expedited formation of tribunal 3.13, 3.19–3.23
length of case 3.17–3.18
role and functions 2.14, 2.22–2.24, 3.04
Rules, generally
abuse of process doctrine 33.25
arbitration awards, appeals 29.41–29.42
arbitration awards, binding nature 33.33, 33.35
changing composition of tribunal 21.33
choice of language 10.15–10.16
costs recovery 25.23, 25.33, 25.46–25.47, 27.14, 27.24
efficiency requirement 12.06
emphasis 3.03
expert witness fees 26.15
historical development 3.02–3.05
interim relief powers 15.06
oaths and affirmations 20.32
party representation guidelines 13.03, 13.20–13.23, 13.31, 26.15
purpose 3.52
witness testimony rules 20.32
Rules, of 2014
arbitral seat 3.12, 3.29–3.30
arbitrators, conduct guidelines 3.12, 3.37–3.44
arbitrators, nationality of 3.12, 3.45–3.47
benefits 3.52–3.53
delays and expenses, avoiding unnecessary 3.12, 3.51
disputes relating to land 3.10
drafting 3.06–3.08
electronic communication/filing 3.12, 3.14–3.16
emergency arbitrators 3.08, 3.12, 3.19–3.28, 14.06–14.08
influences on 3.07
Jivraj problem solutions 3.12, 3.45–3.47
multi-party disputes 3.12, 3.31–3.33
nationality, interpretation 3.11
party representation 3.12, 3.34–3.36, 13.03, 13.20–13.23, 13.31, 26.15
revisions 3.09–3.12
sanctions for misconduct 3.38–3.40, 3.43, 13.20
Slovenia problem solutions 3.12, 3.34–3.36
specific performance of promise to arbitrate 3.12, 3.48–3.50
West Tankers problem solutions 3.12, 3.48–3.50
summary dismissal 12.37–12.39

Index

market value
  arbitrators, of 23.18–23.24
mediation
  arbitration, relationship with 28.02–28.05
  benefits, generally 28.01
  construction disputes, in 35.18–35.19
    caucasing 35.44
    development 35.32–35.33
    lawyers role in 35.34–35.38
    MEDALOA approach 35.50
    methods and styles 35.40–35.44
    preliminary preparations 35.43
    professional role, as 35.39
    project mediation 35.30
    stepped approaches 35.45–35.50
    trends 35.31, 35.51
  dual-role neutrals, by
    attitudes to 28.05–28.07
    benefits and disadvantages 28.12–28.50, 28.53–28.54
    caucusing 28.34–28.37, 28.41
    confidentiality 28.43–28.47
    conflicting powers or duties 28.29–28.30
    coordination 28.17–28.18
    cost-saving 28.51
    criticism of 28.11
    enforcement 28.48–28.50
    functions 28.09
    immunity 28.31
    improper conduct, and 28.25–28.26, 28.35
    jurisdictional challenges 28.27–28.28
    negative party incentives, and 28.23–28.24
    reality testing 28.32–28.33, 28.41
    settlement approach 28.15–28.16
    timing 28.19–28.22
  globalization, and 35.94–35.97
  legal basis for 28.08
  methods
    evaluative 28.10–28.11, 28.38–28.42
    facilitative 28.10–28.11, 28.38
    optimal design 28.02–28.03, 28.05–28.06
    preliminary indication of views 28.40–28.41
  perceptions, national variations 35.94–35.96
  principles 28.01
  unsuccessful, implications 28.02
  waiver, applicability 28.46, 28.49
Mexico
  costs allocation, success basis 25.22
  kompetenz-kompetenz negative approach 7.28
midnight clauses 8.06–8.07
misconduct
  arbitrators, by 13.24–13.29
    CIArb disciplinary procedures 13.28–13.29
    cultural interpretations 13.07
    guerrilla tactics 13.05–13.07, 13.30
    IBA Guidelines on Party Representation 3.39, 13.03–13.04, 13.15–13.19, 13.31
    LCIA General Guidelines for the Parties' Legal Representatives 13.03, 13.20–13.23, 13.31
  parties, by 13.05–13.23
    procedural powers regarding 13.11–13.14
  reduction mechanisms 13.08–13.10
  sanctions for 3.38–3.40, 3.43, 13.17, 13.20
  trends 13.01–13.02, 13.05, 13.30
model clauses
  disadvantages 8.06–8.07, 8.38
  HKIAC 8.08–8.09
  ICC 8.03
  LCIA 8.04
  SIAC 8.05

nationality
  arbitrators, of
    LCIA Rules 3.12, 3.45–3.47
negative effect *see kompetenz-kompetenz*
Netherlands
  arbitration awards, annulment 1.26
  non-consensual powers 3.32
neutrality 12.09–12.10
New York Convention
  arbitration awards
    appeals 29.42
    binding nature 33.39–33.40
    enforcement 7.44–7.48, 8.42
    formal validity 7.45
    substantive validity 7.47–7.48
    unenforceable 21.29
  benefits 6.02–6.04, 11.12
  choice of law clauses, validity 7.33
  conflicts of law rules 9.12–9.14, 9.28
  consensus rules 11.04–11.05
  emergency arbitrators 3.27, 14.28, 14.31
  extraterritorial jurisdiction 8.32
  'Italian Torpedoes' 3.49–3.50
  judicial education 30.22
  limitations 8.42
  most favourable right provision 7.46
  non-arbitrable subject matter 7.44
  non-existence of agreement 7.49
  public policy interpretation 32.01–32.02
  seat of law, applicability 9.28
  separability principle 8.42–8.43
  in writing requirement 9.11
NGOs
  judicial education initiatives 30.25
non-arbitrable subject matter 7.44

oaths and affirmations
  arbitration, use in 20.28–20.31, 20.44
    different jurisdictional approaches 20.39–20.43
    law of the seat, and 20.37
    procedural rules 20.32–20.38
    prohibition 20.40
  definitions 20.04
  expert witnesses 20.13
  interpreters 20.13
  justice, historical role in 20.05–20.07
  lawfulness test 20.12
  perjury, and 20.07, 20.15–20.27, 20.29–20.31
  persons who may administer 20.13
  prescribed wording 20.08–20.11, 20.13

Index

religious use of 20.05, 20.08–20.10
solemn affirmations 20.11
use trends 20.03
witness testimony, and 20.14, 20.32
online dispute resolution 35.86–35.90
oral hearings
  interim relief, and 15.07
  rules for 11.33

Paris Arbitration Rules
  costs recovery 27.28
parties *see* **legitimate expectations; third-party**
party autonomy
  arbitrability, and 7.32–7.33, 7.35
  arbitration agreements, and 7.12–7.15, 9.09–9.10
  choice of law, and 31.05, 31.16
  summary dismissal, and 12.43
perjury
  arbitration proceedings, in 20.29–20.31
  conviction, proof required for 20.16–20.19
  prevention by oath 20.07
  prosecution
    judicial powers 20.20
    trends 20.22–20.23, 20.27
  sanctions and sentencing 20.15, 20.24–20.26
  seriousness, judicial views on 20.21
Permanent Court of Arbitration
  role of 2.07, 2.14
predictability 12.09–12.10, 12.14
preliminary issues 4.33–4.34, 4.36–4.39, 4.42–4.44, 4.48–4.66
prestige 23.53–23.59
private international law
  public policy or interest in English law 32.25–32.31, 32.39–32.51
procedural arbitrability 7.07–7.10, 7.19–7.24, 7.29, 7.51
procedural efficiency
  attitudes to 12.01–12.02
  benefits of arbitration, and 12.09–12.14
  best practices 12.07–12.08
  duration of cases, compared with litigation 12.03–12.04
  flexibility benefits 12.01, 12.05
  institutional requirements 12.06
  'least worst' alternative, as 12.05–12.06
procedural fairness model 1.18–1.21
public policy or interest
  arbitration, and
    abuse of process 33.24
    initiatives 22.72–22.77
  English law, in
    arbitration law, and 32.31–32.61
    conflicts of law 32.26–32.30
    foreign judgments, enforcement 32.26–32.30, 32.43–32.51
    historical development 32.05–32.23
    illegal acts or contracts 32.20, 32.26–32.27, 32.35–32.42
    legal challenges 32.14–32.23
    limitations of doctrine 32.21–32.23

  private international law, and 32.24–32.30, 32.39–32.51
  reasonableness test 32.19
  restraint of trade 32.19
  importance 32.01
  interpretation 32.01–32.03, 32.68–32.72
  judicial review, and 29.10–29.15, 29.46
  justifications 32.10–32.12, 32.38–32.39
  legal norms, and 32.68–32.71
  national influences on 32.03
  nature, complexity and dynamics 32.01–32.02
  transnationalism, and 32.32, 32.62–32.63, 32.66–32.70
  UAE, in
    arbitration award enforcement 34.40
    interpretation 34.43
    Islamic Shari'ah law, and 34.43
    principles of 34.42–34.44

recovery of costs *see under* **costs**
remand of proceedings 24.19–24.28
  institutional rules 24.20, 24.21
  reconstitution without remand 24.29–24.34
  time limits 24.25–24.28
remedies
  recovery of overpayments 36.28–36.32
  specific performance of promise to arbitrate 3.12, 3.48–3.50
remittal of proceedings *see* **remand**
remuneration
  arbitrators 23.16–23.44
  judicial 23.16–23.17
  market value, and 23.18–23.24
  maximising 23.32–23.44
  social capital, and 23.25–23.28
  specialization, and 23.29–23.31
reputation 23.42, 23.45–23.47
  fame, and 23.48–23.52
  prestige, and 23.53–23.59
requests to produce 37.16
  burden of proof 17.19
  discovery, difference from 17.05
  good faith, and 17.33
  identification requirement 17.08
  materiality requirement 17.18–17.25
  narrow and specific requirement 17.04–17.05, 17.07, 17.09–17.17
  possession, custody, or control 17.26–17.34
  scope of production 17.05–17.06
  timing 17.21
  unreasonable burden 17.34
resuscitation of duty 24.17–24.19

sanctions
  arbitrators' powers to impose 21.26–21.29
  misconduct, for 3.38–3.40, 3.43, 13.17, 13.20
  perjury, for 20.24–20.26, 2015
  witness intimidation, for 21.27–21.28
seat of arbitration
  annulled awards at 1.22–1.27
  applicable law 9.19–9.20, 9.24–9.29

seat of arbitration (*cont.*):
  arbitrability 7.36
  definition 6.15
  ICC rules on conflicts 3.29
  international arbitration, in 6.13, 6.15
  language of 10.25
  oaths rules 20.37
separability principle 1.08, 7.12–7.15, 8.42–8.43, 9.09–9.10
setting aside
  arbitrability 7.37–7.43, 7.48
  remand of proceedings 24.20–24.21
  UNCITRAL Rules 7.40, 24.20, 24.24
Sikhism
  oaths and affirmations 20.10
Singapore International Arbitration Centre
  arbitration awards, binding nature 33.33, 33.35
  choice of language rules 10.16
  emergency arbitrators 3.26–3.27, 14.06–14.07, 14.29, 14.32
  expedited arbitration 12.27–12.28, 12.30–12.32
  model clause 8.05
  summary dismissal 12.40
social capital 23.25–23.28
soft law vs hard law 1.10–1.13
Spain
  arbitrability 7.49
  expert witnesses 19.05
specialization 23.29–23.31
specific performance
  promise to arbitrate 3.12, 3.48–3.50
Stockholm Chamber of Commerce Arbitration Institute
  choice of language rules 10.15
  costs allocation 25.23
  emergency arbitrators 3.26–3.27
  expedited arbitration 12.27–12.31
  summary dismissal 12.37
strike-outs 4.33–4.35, 4.38–4.41
submission agreements 6.07–6.09
substantive arbitrability 7.07–7.10, 7.19–7.28
substantive validity, award enforcement 7.47–7.48
SulAmérica **test** 8.24–8.27, 9.16–9.21, 9.25–9.27, 9.36, 9.40
summary dismissal
  abusive motions, restrictions on 12.45
  benefits 12.36, 12.46
  bifurcation, and 12.34, 12.37
  cost-shifting rule 12.45
  disadvantages 12.42–12.44
  documents only arbitration 12.38
  drafting clauses for 12.34–12.45
  efficiency, and 12.43–12.44, 12.46
  enforcement 12.46
  ICC Rules 12.39
  ICSID Rules 12.41, 12.43
  LCIA Rules 12.37–12.39
  party autonomy, and 12.43
  SCC Rules 12.37
  SIAC Rules 12.40
  summary judgment, distinction from 12.34–12.35
  UNCITRAL Rules 12.37

summary judgment
  procedures 4.37–4.41
  summary dismissal, distinction from 12.34–12.35
Sunday hearings 1.28
Sweden
  arbitrators' initiatives 22.20, 22.32
  oaths in arbitration 20.40
Switzerland
  arbitration awards
    binding nature 33.37
    setting aside 7.40
  arbitrators' initiatives 22.16–22.18, 22.43, 22.46
  costs allocation 25.23, 25.36–25.37
  emergency arbitrators 3.26–3.27
  kompetenz-kompetenz negative approach 7.28
  oaths in arbitration 20.41
  transnational approach, applicable law 9.37

technology
  big data 35.99–35.102
  Building Information Modelling (BIM) 35.93
  dispute resolution trends, and 35.83–35.93
  electronic transcripts 35.85
  online dispute resolution services 35.86–35.90
  video streaming/conferencing 35.85–35.90
temporary measures of protection *see* **interim measures**
termination of proceedings
  applicable law variations 24.06
  certainty, need for 24.07
  continuing mandates 24.24, 24.43–24.44
  exceptions 24.13–24.16, 24.41–24.42
  finality, and 24.05–24.16
  functus officio, definition 24.01–24.02, 24.45
  practical issues 24.03–24.04
  public and private interests in 33.41–33.44
  reconstitution without remand 24.29–24.34
  remand 24.19–24.28
  res iudicata doctrine, and 24.06
  resuscitation of duty 24.17–24.19
  settlement agreements, and 24.35–24.40
  statutory and institutional rules on 24.08
  time limits for 24.25–24.28
  UNCITRAL Rules 24.08–24.10
terrorism 32.38
Tokyo Maritime Arbitration Commission
  costs allocation 25.23
translations 10.06–10.07, 10.10
transnationalism
  applicable law approaches 8.31–8.35, 8.37, 9.30–9.39
  costs allocation principles 25.38–25.39
  development, influences on 9.35–9.38
  limitations and problems 9.33–9.34
  public policy, and 32.32, 32.62–32.63, 32.66–32.70

UNCITRAL Model Law 2.27
  arbitration awards
    appeals 29.42
    binding nature 33.33, 33.35, 33.37
    setting aside 7.40, 24.20, 24.21

Index

arbitrators' initiatives 22.32
benefits 6.04–6.05
choice of arbitration style 2.07
choice of language rules 10.16
conflicts of law rules 9.12–9.13, 9.28
consensus rules 11.04–11.05
costs allocation, success basis 25.23
emergency/expedited arbitration 3.21
emergency arbitrators 14.29
fairness and impartiality 4.34
interim measures 15.07–15.08, 15.20
judicial education 30.22
most favourable right provision 7.46
nationality of arbitrators 3.47
remand of proceedings 24.20, 24.21
revisions (2010) 3.07
role of 6.16–6.17
seat of law, applicability 9.28
summary dismissal 12.37
termination of proceedings 24.08–24.10
witness testimony 20.34
in writing requirement 6.17
UNIDROIT Principles of Transnational Civil Procedure
costs allocation 25.38–25.39
United Arab Emirates
arbitration in
  arbitrability 34.12–34.15
  arbitration agreement formation 34.19–34.20
  awards, enforcement 34.37–34.41
  awards, formalities 34.30–34.31
  awards, insurance 34.33–34.34
  conditions precedent 34.25
  costs rules 34.32
  court support for 34.35–34.36
  defaulting parties 34.26
  development 34.45–34.46
  DIFC, role of 34.03–34.05, 34.07, 34.41, 34.46
  evidence rules 34.29
  hearings 34.27–34.28
  institutional bodies 34.06–34.09
  interim relief 34.35–34.36
  Islamic Shari-ah law 34.12, 34.14
  jurisdictions for 34.03–34.05
  legal representation 34.21
  limitations 34.12, 34.14–34.15
  local infrastructure 34.10–34.11
  oaths and affirmations 20.42–20.43
  obligation to arbitrate 34.18
  procedures 34.16–34.34
  role of 34.01–34.02
  terms of reference 34.22
  tribunal constitution 34.24
  tribunal mandate 34.22–34.23
  views on 34.01, 34.05
composition 34.03
  common vs civil law jurisdictions 34.03–34.05
public policy
  award enforcement, and 34.40
  interpretation 34.43
  Islamic Shari'ah law, and 34.43
  principles of 34.42–34.44
United Kingdom *see also* **English law**
arbitration awards
  annulment 1.26
  appeals 29.44–29.52
  binding nature 33.37
  foreign judgments, differences from 31.28
  independence 31.23–31.24
  judicial enforcement 31.17–31.19, 31.28–31.31
  setting aside 24.21–24.22
  strike outs 4.41
arbitration funding arrangements 26.22–26.23
arbitration law, historical development 29.02–29.15
arbitrators
  initiatives 22.07, 22.09, 22.11, 22.22, 22.46
  nationality of 3.12, 3.45–3.47
  sanctions for misconduct 3.39
costs recovery rules 25.22, 25.37, 27.10, 27.39, 27.41
disclosure rules 17.29–17.30
English law, choice of (*see* English law)
expert witnesses 19.04, 19.06
foreign judgments
  arbitration awards, differences from 31.28
  fraud, and 32.53–32.55
  recognition and enforcement 31.28–31.31, 32.26–32.30, 32.43–32.51
group of countries doctrine 8.17–8.18
public policy or interest (*see* English law)
remand of proceedings 24.21–24.22
statutory adjudication 35.14
summary judgments 4.41
termination of proceedings rules 24.11
tiered clauses, interpretation 8.19–8.21
transnational approach, applicability of law 9.33–9.34
United States
arbitrability 7.19–7.24, 7.41, 7.51
arbitration awards
  annulment 1.25, 1.27
  setting aside 7.41
burden of proof, shifting 36.20
discovery rules 16.01–16.03
interim measures 15.11–15.12
judicial education initiatives 30.19–30.21
jurisdiction conflicts 1.29–1.31
kompetenz-kompetenz negative effect, approach to 7.19–7.24
mediation, modern method 35.94
strike outs and summary judgments 4.41
Supreme Court, guide to conduct in 4.02–4.10
termination of proceedings 24.13–24.16
third-party funding recovery 27.40
transnational approach, applicability of law 9.35–9.36
unjust enrichment 36.28–36.32

video streaming/conferencing 35.85–35.90
Virtual Arbitration 35.88
Virtual Conference Rooms 35.88

witnesses *see also* **expert witnesses**
  cross-examination 18.13–18.18
    approaches 18.09–18.10, 18.13–18.18, 18.23–18.24
    benefits 18.22–18.23
    disadvantages 18.10–18.11, 18.13, 18.21
    preparation 18.25–18.26
    rules 11.33
    time limits 18.15
  fact witnesses 18.02–18.18, 37.17
  harm from, assessing 18.06–18.12
  hostility 18.09
  intimidation, sanctions for 21.27–21.28
  language used by 10.28–10.30
  limitations 18.19–18.20
  oaths and affirmations 20.14, 20.32
  preparation 18.19, 18.25–18.26
  statements 18.02–18.05, 20.14
  testimony
    evidence taking rules 37.17
    reinforcement of 18.11
    untruthful 18.20
    video streaming 35.85, 35.90
World Intellectual Property Organization Arbitration Rules
  costs allocation 25.23
  witness testimony 20.33
World Trade Organization Appellate Body 13.11
worst alternative analysis 28.32–28.33

Printed and bound by CPI Group (UK) Ltd, Croydon, CR0 4YY